The Dominion's Dilemma:

The United States of British America

James F. Devine III

ISBN-13: 978-1481150354
ISBN-10: 1481150359
LCCN: 2013903431

To my beloved grandfather, **James F. Devine I**, who instilled in me his love of history, and, hopefully, a bit of his enormous writing talent.

ACKNOWLEDGMENTS

This novel originated from dinner party table talk some years ago: an acquaintance and his wife were discussing the American Revolution with friends. "What would have happened," she asked, "if we had lost the Revolution?" In the gym the next morning, he posed the same question to me. "It would have been bloody, vicious and barbaric. A better question, though, is: 'what would have happened if there had *not* been an American Revolution?'"

This book offers and explores one possibility as an attempt at serious alternate history.

The project has extended more than six years. Encouragement and enablers have come...and gone. The late Barry Connell of Haworth, NJ, was vital in the early going, along with his wife, Eileen. Anita Boyle of Northvale, NJ produced much-needed research on the careers of some early 19th century statesmen, both American and British. Newton Scherl, MD of Tenafly, NJ and Clifford Gold, P.E. of Fort Lee, NJ offered insightful commentary and critique. John Giorgio of Demarest, NJ knows his assistance was vital. As was that of my sister and her husband, Mary Beth and Gerry Quirk of Bergenfield, NJ.

Wendy Lawrence of Dumont, NJ noted contradictions, confusions and historical/cultural impossibilities as she patiently waded through each chapter as it emerged from the computer.

Having banged my head repeatedly against the Catch-22 of first-time authors---to interest publishers you must have an agent; but to interest agents you must be published---I thank Bart Zoltan of Old Tappan, NJ for encouraging me to step into the quagmire of self-publishing. Bart again came to the rescue when it appeared this project would flounder in the self-publishing minutia: formatting; legal arrangements and dealings with the printer/distributor.

Likewise, Cathy Ann Fasano, also of Old Tappan, appeared in the nick of time when the original illustrator suddenly withdrew.

My thanks to Mary Riskind, director of the Bergenfield Public Library, and her staff, especially head research librarian John Capps. With the sole exception of an 1836 Washington, DC map obtained from the New York Public Library, all other important research and maps were found under their direction and supervision in Bergenfield.

All battlefield descriptions are based on the U.S. Military Academy's *West Point Atlas of American Wars* project, Volume I. The complete series is available for reference at the Bergenfield Library and, naturally, at The Point. The photographs of the historical figures are also courtesy of the USMA Museum, West Point, NY.

The America of 1833 was a country whose stock was primarily of English, Scotch-Irish and Dutch decent, with a sprinkling of French and Germans. The major ethnic immigration waves of the 19th and early 20th centuries---Irish, Italians, Germans, Eastern Europeans and Armenians---were yet to arrive. Therefore, the fictional characters had to bear names so corresponding. Those of a certain age who grew up in Bergenfield may recognize certain Anglo-Saxon-ish names. I have taken the liberty of borrowing those names, of old friends and teammates. For better or worse, there were few Bowlins, Hurleys, Giordanos, DiMaggios, Germakians, Oceaks or Greenbergs. Or even Pepitones... I trust those old friends whose names I have borrowed will be pleased with the portrayals of their fictional counterparts.

Finally, without the unwavering support of my love, Lucille, and her mother, Mrs. Angelina Pepitone, this book would still be resting quietly in the documents section of my computer.

.

AUTHOR'S NOTE

The alternate history genre comes in two brands: serious and science fiction/fantasy. This book is an attempt to tell a story---what might have happened in the year 1833 (when the British Empire abolished slavery) in an America that had settled in as a prosperous dominion of that Empire---in a serious but readable, adult manner.

That is to say: there are no time travelers; alien invaders; vampires; climatological cataclysms or offended gods in this tale.

Instead, the reader is offered a glimpse of a Jacksonian America in many ways identical with the one familiar in most history books. The major difference is that the question of final allegiance is not to the Stars and Stripes...but to the Union Jack. For this imagined world is populated by the same leadership---Clay, Calhoun, Webster, Van Buren, General Scott---as actually was in office at that time. Joined by a---hopefully---colorful cast of fictional characters, both male and female. All citizens of the United States of British America and all therefore owing, presumably, final allegiance to the Union Jack...and the Crown.

Both historical characters and fictional characters are offered participating in the constructed drama as human beings actually would participate: the historical characters acting much as they did in real life; the fictional ones as ordinary people of the time, both groups caught in an extraordinary situation.

There are no superheroes in this tale (though some might consider a certain plantation mistress as such). The actions of the historical characters are based on exploits and episodes of their actual careers. For instance, a senior military figure of the time is offered as surrendering a major military post to rebels in exchange for a general's commission in the insurgent forces. That same individual did in fact surrender the U.S. Military District of Texas in exchange for a full general's commission in the Confederates States Army.

Likewise, there actually was a full-blown European crisis in 1833 brought on by the Ottoman Sultan's invitation to the Czar to land an army in Syria to turn back an invasion of the Anatolian heartland by a rebellious Egyptian pasha. British fury at the possible implications for their Indian trade route and desired Suez canal---Czarist, Communist or modernist, Russia never relinquishes occupied land without a fight---almost started a major European war.

The fortuitous advent of that totally unexpected crisis, coming in the same year as Parliament debated the abolition of slavery throughout the British Empire, makes plausible the series of imagined events in North America: Britain's comparatively small standing army, on alert to deal with a possible Near Eastern war versus a major European power, could not have simultaneously been available to put down a potential insurrection in the USBA.

CHAPTER ONE

Lexington, Virginia
October 20, 1870

This *pagentry*, Thomas Wilder thought, would have embarrassed Robert. *In fact, if anything could penetrate that marble façade of his, an elaborate funeral ceremony*---his funeral ceremony---*would do the trick.* Tom momentarily brightened at the thought of his old West Point roommate, Robert E. Lee, looking down from the great parade ground in the sky.

'Course, ol' Scott must be loving it. Tom grinned. *Betcha he's busting Robert, too*:

"Well, Mr. Lee. A fine ceremony. If somewhat smaller, you'll agree, than the one they threw for me at The Point four years ago." *Those blue eyes, which could drill through you like they were penetrating butter, would be twinkling at Robert's obvious discomfort.*

Thomas, who had risen to colonel in the Dominion forces under Winfield Scott which had defeated the Confederate States of America in the British American Civil War some 36 years prior, was standing outside the spacious President's House on the Washington College campus. The trustees had built it after Robert had returned from conquering Mexico to become the college's president.

Nearby stood Maj. Gen. (ret.) Thomas J. Jackson, as cold and rigid as he had been when he won his famous nickname at Santa Cruz in '62. Jackson insisted that *Stonewall* was really meant to describe the brigade he led in the second Mexican conflict. That was Jackson's conceit; everyone knew General Bee had uttered the famous "look at Jackson: standing like a stone wall" during that stunning British American victory, just before a Frenchman ran his cavalry sword through poor Bee's neck.

Stonewall was standing, erect and expressionless, a few feet away from Colonel Wilder at the bottom of the Lee home's steps, along with the rest of the honorary pallbearers. Who included Wilder's other West Point friend, Maj. Gen. Joseph Johnston (ret.); former Governor-General Jefferson Davis and another hero of both Mexican conflicts, Pete Longstreet.

Tom Wilder didn't know Brig. Gen. James Longstreet well. In fact, they had only met a few times at formal events in Georgetown and Richmond. But now Longstreet grinned at Tom.

"Good morning, Colonel Wilder. Hope you slept well last night? The Lee boys think we're too old to actually carry the General's casket over to the chapel. But take a look at Johnston and Davis. They look ready to pound each other right now."

They both laughed. Pete was Class of '42, 14 years after Johnston, Robert and Tom had graduated West Point. Thanks, in Tom's case, in large part to Lee, as Wilder's aversion to engineering principles nearly ended his military career on the banks of the Hudson. But Lee had drilled him like an NCO. *And I barely survived to graduate. Only time I ever saw Robert lose his temper, though they tell me he gave that young pup Jeb Stuart the dressing down of a lifetime after Stuart took his cavalry joyriding round the French army before Second Cerro Gordo back in '63...*

A generation younger or not, Pete, like every other West Pointer, knew the enduring legend:

Cadet Johnston had challenged Cadet Davis, whose sense of self-importance and righteousness was already fully developed at age 22, to step outside Bennie Haven's tavern one cold night in Highland Falls in the winter of '26-'27. Davis was a year ahead, but since Bennie Haven's was off-limits to all West Point cadets, rank didn't matter, in or out of the big circle they drew outside:

Johnston chopped Davis down like a big skinny sapling. Then, Joe went back inside to enjoy the fruits of his victory: the undivided attention of Dora, Bennie's buxom daughter...

The whole Regular Army---and most of Georgetown---could recite the tale by heart.

The Lee boys, Rooney and the rest, were coming down the steps now. With them came their wild cousin, Fitzhugh Lee, who had been with Stuart when a Frog bullet ended the Last Cavalier's life near the outskirts of Mexico City. Staff aides said Robert had cried silent tears when they brought him the news; Stuart had been his favorite since Lee's stint as Point Superintendent after the original Mexican War.

As Governor-General, Jeff Davis had almost single-handedly talked Her Majesty's Government into that second Mexican adventure. Basically by assuring London that the Royal Army, still reeling from the Indian Mutiny and already caught up in the Second Opium War in China, wouldn't be needed to throw the French and their puppet emperor, Maximilan of Austria, out of Mexico.

The hardcore anti-war Whigs had accused Davis of being "disingenuous, hypocritical and cynical" by arguing that the Dominion had experience fighting wars without the RA's help. *Considering that Davis fought on the losing side in that bloody, futile gamble by old Calhoun, Polk, Taylor and some others to make the South an independent Dominion...or maybe an independent country,* thought Colonel Wilder, *I could see some validity in the Whig argument. Since the whole point of the damn rebellion had been to hold on to the South's "peculiar institution." Slavery, to be more precise.*

Of course, Davis hadn't been alone: Lee and Johnston had also served the so-called "Confederate States of America." And they might have gotten away with it, if not for "Old Fuss and Feathers": Winfield Scott, the greatest general in Dominion history.

Of course, time heals all wounds...that and prosperity. The dawning of the mechanized age had made the South, or at least the white South, prosperous again by 1845. The former slaves, however, were a different story: their condition continued to be the Dominion's gravest problem...as well as its biggest embarrassment...

The Southerners had gradually worked their way back to positions of authority, due, chiefly, to the First Mexican War. And to General Scott. Wilder's old boss had argued successfuly for the inclusion of former Rebel officers in the USBA forces organizing to battle Santa Anna. Their successes, including Lee's as chief engineer of Scott's own campaign to capture Mexico City, had led to their regaining influence in Dominion military and political affairs. Colonel Lee, for instance, went from Mexico City to The Point as superintendent, before going west to fight Comachees. Eventually, in 1862, he had been promoted to lead the USBA Army's second conquest of Mexico.

Now former Rebs were spread out throught the Army and the government. Davis' victory in the '60 election had seemed, to many, the symbolic, formal reuniting of the Dominion.

The "honorary" pallbearers formed up now and followed the Lees across campus to the chapel. Mary Lee---*after all these years she still hasn't forgiven me; blames me personally for the loss of Arlington House back then*---riding behind in a carriage. Open, despite the cold, nasty late October western Virginia weather, with her daughters, Mary, Mildred and Agnes. The procession quickly picked up other mourners along the way, so that the line snaked back virtually to the Lee home by the time the coffin finally reached the chapel.

There was a pause before entering and the Lee boys gratefully lowered the casket. Which, to Tom's relief at least, was covered solely by the Stars and Stripes of the United States of British America. *Not that the old Rebel Stars and Bars aren't visible damn near everyplace else...*

Word came down that the cause of the delay was Sam Grant---Ulysses Simpson Grant himself---17th Governor-General of the USBA. The G-G's train had finally arrived at Lexington Station. He would be appearing any minute. That Grant, who 10 years prior was clerking in his father's Galena, Ill. dry goods store, was G-G was something most people still found difficult to believe.

But Sam had been asked to organize and command a regiment of Illinois volunteers to fight the French-backed Royalists in Mexico, based on his service in the First Mexican War. *And off he went, like one of those rockets whose red glare Francis Scott Key described so poetically in the Dominion anthem. The ones that illuminated Fort McHenry when a Frog fleet bombarded it back during the Napoleonic wars.*

Grant moved quickly up the chain of command in the northern theatre along the Rio Grande. And there won everlasting fame for defeating a significantly larger Franco-Royalist army at Ciudad Aquna, across from the dusty Texas town of Del Rio. This, while Lee was simultaneously replicating Scott's march to Mexico City.

The Whigs, who had restored their party's original name, "Republican," in the patriotic hoopla that followed the new war's outbreak, nominated William Seward of New York to run against Davis in '64, while the war still raged. The mendacious Davis' insistence on personally overseeing all aspects of government, including the war, had left him the most reviled man in Georgetown---and the Dominion---by election day. Looking to balance the ticket with a Westerner, who also happened to be a war hero, the Republicans plucked Grant from the Army to run for Vice G-G.

No one, of course, thought Seward would have the bad manners to die late in his term, leaving Sam in charge...

Official mouners and the public alike began shivering as the wind grew stronger, the clouds darkened and the wait lengthened. Grumbling at the delay, Maj. Gen. William T. Sherman, Grant's No. 2 in Mexico and now commander of the USBA Army, marched over to Wilder.

"Colonel Wilder, sir!" *I haven't put on a uniform since shortly after the end of the Rebellion. But people insist on using my military title. Hell, if it makes them happy…*

"Quite a turnout, right Colonel? Looks like the whole South is here." Sherman looked at Tom shrewdly. "But you, Sam and I seem to make up the majority of the Northern contingent. Once Sam gets here, of course…" The laugh came from deep down Sherman's throat and the red head shook with the effort.

"Good to see you, Cump." Wilder had known Sherman forever, or at least since the General's step-father, former G-G Ewing, brought Cump and his brother John to Georgetown in the late '30s. Before Cump, too, disappeared into The Long Gray Line…

"How's things on the Plains?" Cump's major duty was protecting the settlers, miners, ranchers, trappers and various persons of lesser repute from the increasingly angry Indians. *Who have the audacity to think a treaty with the USBA is worth more than the scrap of paper they had made their mark on…*

"Damn tough, Colonel." Sherman took off his uniform hat and wiped his brow, which, despite the chilly weather, looked remarkably moist. "The Plains Indians are the best light cavalry in the world. We have our hands full. And these damn miners and wagon masters! They sneak on or across Indian land. Some make it, some don't. But it's the Army's fault if we don't protect them all!" The high cheek-boned face was now almost as red as the hair. *Or those fearsome Sioux the newspapers keep screaming about.*

"Well General, we've had problems with the Indians, particularly the Sioux, ever since my day. In fact, the Rebellion might have been over a lot sooner if General Scott hadn't been forced to detail so many troops out west…"

"Didn't know you'd been out that way, Colonel…"

"Wasn't, really. Did spend time in Arkansas Territory. But then I came back East as General Scott's so-called 'intelligence aide.' Saw the whole damn Rebellion unfold."

Tom looked up at the dreary sky. Rain, or maybe sleet, was beginning to fall.

"Right from the day the General found out that the Royal Navy had turned the Atlantic Squadron's most powerful fighting ship into a mail packet…"

Philadelphia, Pennsylvania
June 17, 1776:

"I don't care what agreements Franklin has worked out with Burke, Pitt or any of the King's other puppets." John Adams was roaring, his words rattling off the ceiling of Carpenter's Hall and bouncing back into the open galley housing the daily session of the Continental Congress. "We've come too far to back down one inch. To do so now would convince London that we're not united, not serious about self-government and not capable of implementing our words with deeds.

"To accept this compromise would place ourselves forever at the mercy of the King, the Prime Minister and Parliament. We've gone beyond that. They're 3000 miles away. It is time for these united colonies to become united states!"

Edward Rutledge of South Carolina looked around at his fellow delegates from 13 diverse colonies: from Samuel Chase of Virginia to John Jay of New York to Pennsylvania's John Dickinson. Some were Southerners to whom maintaining their own 'peculiar institution' was as important as possible independence. Some were radicals like the Adams cousins. Others were moderates like Maryland's Charles Carroll. Still others were as conservative as Dickinson.

As he finished counting heads, Rutledge shook his own. "You don't have the votes, my Massachusetts friends. This Congress wants self-government, free trade and a say in the imposition of taxation. A few skirmishes don't make a war. Who's to say Washington can defeat entire British armies...to say nothing of their overwhelming naval support? No, this compromise proposal Franklin has received from London is a Godsend. Let's approve this 'Colonial Compact' and end this turmoil and divisiveness before more blood is needlessly shed!"

There was a general murmur of agreement in the well of the Congress. Hearing and accepting it, John Adams knew that his final plea for a declaration of independence from the British Empire had failed. "Though I am firm in my belief that the King and his government think of us as little more than ignorant colonials...The Almighty's---and this Congress'---wills be done.

"I pray future correspondence and communication with London will bring the peace, stability and justice this correspondence promises. Though I doubt such a thing is…"

Rutledge smiled. "Now John, don't take it all back."

But for 56 years, much to the amazement of Adams, his contemporaries and later Americans, the Colonial Compact had provided precisely the peace and stability British America craved.

Then…

London, England
January 4, 1833:

The icy rain which had been pelting central London when Harry Bratton's carriage left the Colonial Office had changed to snow by the time he arrived at the remote dock chosen by the Admiralty to receive *HMS Irresistible* at the conclusion of its record-setting 19-plus day run from Baltimore.

You'd think the bloody Royal Navy would schedule these things for a more civilized hour, Bratton thought as he stepped from the carriage. *Two o'clock in the morning is no time to be waiting for a damn ship to show up from British America, no matter how important the dispatches it is carrying. And why did His Lordship insist that I come down here in the middle of this miserable January night to take possession? Surely the Colonial Office could wait until 8 a.m. to see if Andrew Jackson has won the plebiscite for a second term as British America's Governor-General! Or if this chap Clay has unseated him in the non-binding popular vote.* (Not that any plebiscite winner had ever been denied appointment by the King under the system hammered out by Edmund Burke and Franklin fifty years before.)

No, thought Bratton as he pulled his cloak tightly around his neck, *Earl Goderich not only wants the results immediately, but has convened some sort of meeting for 5 a.m.--five o'clock in the bloody morning!--to review them.* Bratton shook his head, as much in wonderment as to dislodge the snow that was now blowing horizontally and sticking to his face below the protection available from his hat's brim. As he peered down the dock towards the River, he began to make out a lamp and the vague outline of a figure holding it. Captain James Akkridge of the Admiralty, no doubt. *I wonder how long he's been standing out there in this atrocious weather? Well, that's the Royal Navy for you. Chaps don't know when to come in out of the rain…or in this case, snow.*

Apparently hearing the approaching footsteps, Captain Akkridge turned suddenly toward him. "Ah, Harry, good of you to come. Can't make out the *Irresistible* yet, but she's bound to be close. Shouldn't be much longer."

"Careful how quickly you move about there, James, or they'll be fishing your frozen corpse out of the Thames at first light. This dock is getting somewhat slippery." As Bratton got closer, he could see that Akkridge was holding a large lantern in his gloved right hand. "Is that to guide the *Irresistible* in, James? I'd think they'd have some better navigational aids on the Thames than that."

"Heavens no, old chap. Simply to provide us some light. So what is this all about, eh, Harry? My orders were simply to meet you here, see you were handed over a dispatch from the colonies and then conduct *HMS Irresistible's* captain immediately to the Admiralty. Strange bit of work, don't you think?"

Bratton smiled into his cloak as he fought off a shiver. "Don't know myself what's in the dispatch box, Captain Akkridge," he blandly lied. "I'm only the postman, you see. And I'd be careful how you refer to the semi-autonomous, self-governing dominion formally named the United States of British America, if I were you. Quincy Adams and the rest of the British American delegates to Parliament will have you assigned to a very different sort of colony---Australia, perhaps---if they hear you refer to their native shore like that!"

Akkridge snorted as the outline of the frigate, one of the first of the new screw-designs, began to emerge through the snow and fog. "Yes and isn't that the damnedest thing? Half of Britain had no real representation in Parliament until last year and here these damn colonials have, what, 23 or 24 delegates now? No wonder the resentment and calls for Parliamentary reform kept growing. Harry, without reform there would have been blood in the streets within months!"

James Akkridge has to be the most liberal Royal Naval officer I've ever met, Bratton thought. He could now see the bulk of the *Irresistible* as it closed the dock. "I'll leave reform to the politicians...and public safety to the Home Office. I've got enough to handle at the Colonial Office as it is."

"There, you've proven my point," Akkridge said with a laugh. "If British America isn't a colony, why is its administration overseen from the War & Colonial Office? Come, old chap, tell me how I'm wrong."

"Technically, Captain Akkridge, as you well know," Bratton began in a formal tone before breaking into a grin, "I am employed by the American Office..."

"Which itself is simply a desk in the Colonial Office. Though, for the sake of the USBA delegates to Parliament and others who revere the fine print in the Colonial Compact, it is called a Cabinet-level office. How can that be when the 'American' Secretary is also the Colonial Secretary? Simply a ruse to keep the simple-minded Americans happy, lest they rise in revolt once again."

"The Compact, Captain, saved the Empire from a bloody and costly war, which we could very possibly have lost."

Akkridge snorted again. "Why, just because Washington and that rabble he called an army managed to drag enough artillery onto the hills overlooking Boston that Lord Howe decided to evacuate the town? His Lordship was massing his forces in Nova Scotia for an invasion of New York when word of the Compact came down. He'd have gone through the colonies like a hot knife through butter. The rebellion would have been crushed in a matter of months."

"I'm not so certain of that, and remember: I'm the one who graduated from Sandhurst. Even before Washington arrived, 'that rabble' bloodied our collective noses at Lexington, Concord and Breed's Hill. When you allow the Americans to fight in their own manner, that is to say, as light infantry, Indian-style, they are very effective. Certainly they demonstrated that in their conquest of the Louisiana Territory and over here in the Boney wars. To say nothing of the way their General Scott put down the French Canadian insurrection 20 years ago. Anyway, it appears *Irresistible* has finished laying its gangplank. Shall we proceed aboard?"

Captain Akkridge nodded and began to walk briskly toward and up the gangplank, shifting the lantern to his left hand as he accepted and returned salutes from half-frozen sailors now on the dock. The Colonial Office man moved more gingerly. *This whole damn dock is turning into one bloody sheet of ice. I'll be lucky if they don't have to fish me out of the Thames at dawn...*

The snow was falling harder than before but the Royal Navy proprieties had to be observed. After being properly piped aboard, Captain Akkridge saluted another officer who had materialized on the main deck. "Welcome back to Blighty, Sir Stephen. Made it in record time. No mid-Winter North Atlantic storms, I gather?"

Sir Stephen---Captain Sir Stephen Richards, master of HMS

Irresistible---returned the salute. "Hardly, Captain Akkridge. The North Atlantic was its usual nasty self. The gales pushed us along nicely, however. So did stripping the ship to its essentials. Did make for a bit of a rocky crossing at times, though." Sir Stephen glanced at the tall civilian and back at his fellow RN colleague.

"Forgot my manners, Sir Stephen. This is Harry Bratton of the Colonial, excuse me, 'American' Office. He's here to collect that diplomatic pouch you brought with you from Baltimore." Turning to Bratton, he added: "Harry, Sir Stephen Richards, commander of the fastest warship in the King's Navy, as *Irresistible* has demonstrated on this crossing."

Bratton nodded. "My pleasure, Sir Stephen. What news have you brought us from the USBA? Any tidbits I can feed Lord Goderich?"

Sir Stephen smiled. "Our American cousins are busy in their usual pursuits: making money, fighting Indians and arguing colonial, or should I say, dominion politics. On the fringes, both the Creoles and the French Canadians seem resigned to the fact that Napoleon isn't rising from his grave, or from that tomb the Frogs are building for him in Paris...

"But if you're the man I'm to give this pouch that I risked my men and ship to bring across the North Atlantic in dead of winter, I'd better retrieve it for you now." Sir Stephen nodded to a waiting aide, who hurried off into a cabin with keys the Captain handed him.

"Any news of the Governor-General plebiscite," Bratton asked nonchalantly, "before you pulled anchor?"

The warship's captain nodded. "Yes, unofficial, of course, but it seems old Jackson is again the electorate's choice. He seems to have defeated his opponent, ..."

"Clay. Henry Clay of Kentucky."

"Ah, yes, that's the fellow. Seems to have beaten him rather conclusively. Not that it will do Jackson much good. From the looks of him at a dinner I attended in Georgetown last month, he may not last long enough to accept His Majesty's reappointment. Poor old man looked ghastly."

Akkridge chuckled. "So this Clay chap may get the prize after all, what? All good things come to he who waits, eh?"

Bratton shook his head. "No, James. If Governor-General Jackson dies or is incapacitated---assuming King William reappoints him for another four-year term---his new Vice Governor-General would step in." Knowing the answer full well, he asked Sir Stephen, anyway: "Which would be who? I seem to have forgotten."

"I don't recall the chap's name, but he has served regularly in their government. A Dutch name, Van something..."

"Oh yes that's right. Van Buren. Martin Van Buren, formerly a Senator from New York and their Secretary of the Interior."

Shaking his head, Captain Akkridge asked the Colonial Office man how he remembered "all these colonial politicians? I suppose it is your job and all, but...."

Having obtained with causal banter the information he knew was contained in the dispatch pouch, Bratton was now anxious to speed the news to the Secretary before the damn 5 a.m. meeting. He noted with relief the approaching return of the subaltern and changed the subject.

"Did I hear you mention, Sir Stephen, that you crossed the North Atlantic with only limited ammunition? Rather sporting of you, wasn't it?"

The two Naval men glanced at each other and managed, with simple facial twinges, to look quite amused. Eyes twinkling, Sir Stephen drawled: "So who would we have likely met in a North Atlantic battle, Mr. Bratton? A Viking ship, perhaps? The Frog Navy is limiting its voyages to Algiers these days and I'm quite certain the Hapsburgs haven't found their way out of the Mediterranean yet. China perhaps? And Czar Nicholas' Navy is mostly iced-in this time of year. Yes, I guess we can consider ourselves fortunate to have escaped the wrath of a latter day Eric the Red!"

The three men laughed and Bratton turned to glance at the gangplank. "Can I offer you gentlemen a ride? We go close by the Admiralty on the way to the Office."

"Thank you, Harry, but I have a carriage waiting. Sir Stephen doesn't know it yet, but he's to accompany me back. Seems the First Lord is anxious to wish him a belated Merry Christmas! Be careful on that dock. Wouldn't want that dispatch *Irresistible* brought so far so quickly to end up water-logged..."

CHAPTER TWO

Georgetown, D.C.
December 17, 1832:

Lt. Thomas Wilder had a love-hate relationship with his assgnment. Both parts of it. He loved the access to power that being an aide to the Governor-General provided. He also loved the access to information that aided him in his other role as an aide to the commanding general of the USBA Army. His ear for languages---he spoke French and Spanish fluently and knew enough German, Russian and Dutch to understand and be understood---made him invaluable at those Residency social situations involving the diplomatic corps.

Wilder hated, however, his function of formally introducing at such receptions foreign diplomats who undoubtedly knew each other better than he knew any of them. M. Jean-Claude, the French counsel-general, for example, had probably served with his Prussian counterpart, Von Benes, at one or another European court. And the chances were good they might have run across each other on some European battlefield, too.

Mending the social fences damaged by the increasingly-cantankerous Governor-General could also be a difficult chore. Although the G-G could demonstrate, when the mood struck him, social skills that any London hostess might approve, he seldom displayed them. 'Old Hickory' treated the diplomatic corps generally as if it was a regiment of raw Tennessee recruits. The atmosphere was somewhat better when the G-G's niece was in Georgetown, but Emily Jackson Donelson had returned to The Hermitage, Jackson's plantation outside Nashville, last summer. So far, there was no word of her return. That meant that Sunday's Christmas reception for the capital's elite would probably be short...if not sweet.

The Residency post provided a good cover for Wilder's real job, gathering and analyzing information for the commander of the USBA Army. While the Lieutenant loved fitting together seemingly unrelated pieces of information to help develop a theory or to make clearer the bigger picture, he did not always relish presenting his analysis to the commanding general. Winfield Scott dominated any room he entered with a physical presence even more commanding than Jackson's. At 6-foot-7 and at least 275 pounds, Scott towered over virtually everyone. His piercing blue eyed-stare seemed to drill a hole completely through anyone he fixed it upon and was, actually, more effective than any of Jackson's profanity-laced outbursts.

The Lieutenant was equally grateful to and intimidated by Scott: grateful that the General had rescued him from service with the Dragoons in Arkansas and intimidated by this legendary soldier whose record dated back to frontier firefights against the French and their Indian allies at the turn of the century. Scott had in fact conquered more of the Louisiana Territory than Jackson had, though there was no major city in the Northwest to provide the lasting fame that Jackson's capture of New Orleans had brought. Along with Jackson, Scott had served in the Peninsula Campaign in Spain under the Duke of Wellington but had hurriedly returned to the USBA to command the forces that put down the French Canadian insurrection of 1811. While Jackson had entered politics after the conclusion of the Napoleonic Wars, serving as Tennessee governor and later USBA Senator---along with a brief, unfortunate stint as the state's delegate to Parliament---Scott had remained in the Army, rising to become its commanding officer.

In that capacity, the General personally approved the commissioning of each West Point cadet as an officer in the USBA Army. Wilder had graduated precisely in the middle of his class of 46, due to a lack of aptitude for math and engineering equally as obvious as his ear for languages. In fact, if not for the intervention and late night tutoring of his friend and classmate Robert Lee, Wilder might not have graduated at all. His deficiencies in the two subjects that formed the core of the Point's curriculum had ruled him out of the choice post-graduation assignments to the Engineers or the Artillery. Scott had approved his assignment to the Dragoons mostly because he was considered the Point's best horseman...at least among cadets from states above the Mason-Dixon Line. Three years later, however, the General had called him to Georgetown and offered the dual posts at The Residency and the War Department.

Wilder was now on his way across Pennsylvania Avenue to see Scott, although what the summons was about he had no real idea.

Thinking it might have to do with the upcoming Christmas reception, he carried with him the list of military and naval invitees, both Royal and USBA. The combined list was slight, as, subtracting the Royal liaisons to the USBAA and the Coastal Guard, there were few senior Royal military and naval officers in-and-around the Georgetown area. Most senior USBAA and CG officers were also assigned elsewhere. Scott ran a tight ship and he wanted his officers---for the CG was also under his nominal command---out where the action was, not holed up in the capital. *Well, whatever is on the Old Man's mind, I'll soon know*, thought Wilder as he climbed the War Department steps. Despite the raw, wet weather---Georgetown was equatorial in summer and damp and dismal in winter---the Lieutenant paused to clean the Pennsylvania Avenue mud off his boots and straighten his uniform. *They don't call the General 'Old Fuss and Feathers' for nothing. He's a spit-and-polish tyrant who would chew a soldier out if he came in out of a blizzard with a button missing. But the old-timers say his men would follow him to hell in battle…*

Wilder opened the main doors and walked briskly down the hall to the Commanding General's office, pausing only to exchange greetings with the few clerks and other officers situated outside. The General's secretary, Lieutenant Beaufort, looked up from papers spread out on his desk, rose and saluted. "I'll let the General know you're here Lieutenant." But Scott himself was now filling the doorway. "Come in Lieutenant." Turning to his secretary, Scott ordered: "No interruptions." The General eased his bulk back behind his desk after indicating Wilder to a chair in front of him. "So Lieutenant, is the Governor-General set for his annual Christmas reception this Sunday?" The blue eyes began to twinkle. "I know how much he enjoys entertaining."

"Well sir, I think he'd be happier if the guest list was limited to Tennesseans, but he's resigned to hosting the Congress, the Cabinet, the Court, the diplomatic corps and the other guests. At least, those members of Congress and the Court who are still in town. Though I doubt he'll be wishing M. Jean-Claude a particularly Merry Christmas…"

"No the Governor-General does not care much for the French, that's true enough." Scott's heavy eyebrows rose with amusement. As a teenage prisoner, Jackson had suffered a merciless beating from a French officer for refusing to clean the man's boots. The beating had left him with scars on his head and left hand. He and his brother,

Robert, also taken prisoner in the endless, faceless skirmishing of the 1780s, both contracted small pox. Robert died soon after their release. The incident left the G-G with a lifelong hatred for the French.

"As for the guest list, you should have been here when he was inaugurated. The Tennesseans were all over The Residency. Wrecked everything. Good thing Mr. Adams left town immediately after the swearing-in. He would have been outraged..."

John Quincy Adams, the previous G-G, had been mortified when "that frontier barbarian," as he invariably referred to Jackson, trounced him in the 1828 plebiscite. He had had to be persuaded from leaving Georgetown even before the inauguration.

Wilder began to wonder whether he had been summoned simply to help the General pass a few unscheduled minutes. Scott, however, began shuffling papers on his desk and his tone became more businesslike.

"As you are no doubt aware, Mr. Wilder, the results of the recent plebiscite were officially tallied and published two days ago. The previous night, however, a Royal Navy frigate," he glanced down at the paper in front of him, "the *Irresistible,* left Baltimore unannounced and unscheduled. I am told she had been stripped of her weaponry and other equipment unneeded for a quick crossing of the North Atlantic and was headed for London. Does that strike you as unusual, Mr. Wilder?"

"Sir, I must admit I am only vaguely aware of Royal Navy procedures..."

"Mid-winter North Atlantic crossings are not normal Royal Navy procedure, Lieutenant, nor is stripping down one of the Royal Navy's most powerful warships and risking it on such a crossing. Why do you think the Admiralty would sanction such a risky journey?" Scott's eyes were now focused directly on the Lieutenant, who could feel the drill grinding through him.

"I would venture that the Admiralty---or someone in Lord Grey's government---wanted someone or something pretty badly, Sir. Though what or who it is, I have no idea."

Scott drummed his thick figures impatiently on the polished desktop. "Lieutenant, what have I been trying, apparently unsuccessfully, to train you to do this past year? Analyze odd, disjointed pieces of information to determine if they fit together. In the intelligence business, there is always a 'who,' a 'what,' a 'when,' a 'where,' a 'how,' and a 'why.' The first five can usually be identified rather quickly. Correctly identifying the sixth is what I'm attempting to train you to do."

Wilder's face was flushing and he squirmed anxiously in his seat. "Sir, we have a 'when,' the 15th of December, two nights ago. And a 'what,' the departure of a Royal Navy warship stripped to its essentials for a peacetime North Atlantic crossing..."

"Let me stop you there, Lieutenant. The voyage is the 'how.' The 'who' or the 'what' is the person or information London wants. And wants in a hell of a hurry, by all indications. If we know which it is, we can move forward to the all-important 'why.' Any ideas?" The fingers resumed their drumming.

Wilder was silent as he thought back over the beginnings of the conversation. "Sir, we know the warship."

"*Irresistible.*"

"Yes sir, *HMS Irresistible* left Baltimore the night before the plebiscite results were publicly announced and is reported to be on her way to London. London has traditionally stayed out of plebiscite campaigns. How quickly have the results been reported to England after previous plebiscites?"

"With the first departing merchantman, Lieutenant. Even in '28, when London was clearly concerned that General Jackson might get hold of the Residency, there was no RN vessel standing by to speed the results to England."

"But General, it doesn't make much sense. It was pretty much a foregone conclusion that the Governor-General would win again. London must have known that."

Scott nodded. "Yes, all indications were that Andrew Jackson would win again. And I'm certain our friends over at the Liaison Office have been informing London of that fact since early summer. So that still leaves us with the 'why,' Lieutenant. Why is London so impatient to get the news?

"I want you to go back over all the correspondence we have on file from and to the various military ministries in London. Do the same across the street. Analyze anything that appears the least bit odd, or different. Somewhere, there may be a request or order that will tie in to this puzzle. I want you to find it and bring it to me post-haste. Is that understood?" Scott looked directly at the younger officer, who nodded his head vigorously.

"Yes, General. I'll begin reviewing all correspondence, both here and at The Residency. If there's anything there, it will come out." He stood, saluted, turned and headed out. Scott smiled to himself. *That boy has the makings of a fine officer. Even if I doubt he'll ever figure out how to properly sight a cannon…*

THE COLONIAL COMPACT OF 1776

Washington's stunning victory at Boston in early 1776 astounded the British populace and led to the immediate fall of Lord North's government. The Earl of Chatham, William Pitt the Elder, who had led the call for reconciliation with the Colonies, was the obvious choice to reoccupy #10 Downing Street. King George III, not yet fully in the throes of the mental illnesses that would eventually destroy him, reluctantly sent for Pitt. The Earl had been in regular contact with Benjamin Franklin, who until the previous year had been in London as the agent (later generations would have described him as the "lobbyist") for Massachusetts, Pennsylvania and a number of other rebellious American colonies. Franklin had finally thrown up his hands in disgust at the autocratic attitude of the North government and returned to North America, where he had taken his seat in the Continental Congress.

Pitt had immediately rushed Edmund Burke, the outspoken orator and colonial proponent, to Philadelphia by fastest naval transportation, with a stunning secret compromise proposal for Franklin. The ship docked on June 3, 1776.

Burke and Franklin hammered out, over a period of several days' intensive negotiation, the document that became known as the Colonial Compact. Burke had arrived in Philadelphia as the Continental Congress struggled with the truly unthinkable concept of separation from the Mother Country and---always lurking in the background---the question of slavery. With a collective sigh of relief, the majority of the delegates---John and Samuel Adams of Massachusetts not among them---grasped eagerly at the Compact, when Franklin presented it in secret session, as a way out of the dilemma. They quickly agreed to the armistice offered by the Pitt government. By the fall of '76, Washington's army, which had marched south to New York in anticipation of a British invasion, had been demobilized.

In March 1777, a constitutional convention called by the Congress had met in Philadelphia. Under Washington's guidance---Franklin had returned to London with Burke as intermediary to Pitt's government---a tentative constitution for the new "United States of British America" slowly evolved. Washington himself, along with the principal authors, Thomas Jefferson and James Madison of Virginia and the youthful prodigy from New York, Alexander Hamilton, sailed for London in the spring of '78 to present the document for ratification by Parliament and the signature of the King.

It was the proposition that the British American states would have direct representation in Parliament that was to be the chief obstacle to ratification, of course. The diehard Tories in both Houses could not conceive of 'colonials' on their benches. But the logic in Pitt's argument that the Empire had very nearly lost its crown jewel over 'taxation without representation' in the end won the day. The "colonials" would be permitted one delegate from each 'state' to the House of Commons. The new USBA would have limited self-government, in that London would continue to set foreign policy and have oversight of the elected USBA government.

The Crown, in turn, would accept the principle that only native born British Americans could serve as candidates for the Governor-Generalship and the various state governorships. The USBA would maintain an organized defense force in view of the threat from then-Spanish Louisiana and the increasingly difficult Indians, as well as a small naval force to help patrol the coasts. The appropriate military ministries in London would oversee both forces. Tariffs and other taxes on various products would fund the Dominion---for that was the newly-coined term for the USBA's status in the Empire---and state governments. An initial plebiscite for the Governor-Generalship and the two houses of the first USBA Congress was scheduled for the fall of 1780. The King would then officially approve the plebiscite's winner as G-G for a term of four years, with the potential for succeeding terms. (The principle of the King's final veto power over the Governorship was a key element in the final agreement designed by Burke and Franklin.)

Franklin returned home once again to a tumultuous welcome and near-unanimous approval for the Governor-Generalship. Washington was the overwhelming choice for Vice Governor-General and was in fact actually responsible for much of the evolution of the new Dominion government during a period later affectionately labeled the 'Era of Reconciliation.'

It was during the Washington Administration that began in 1789 that the 'factions' in Dominion political life---agrarian/weak central government versus manufacturing/strong central government---began to evolve into the two-party political system that continued through the plebiscite of 1832, which the Democratic candidate, Andrew Jackson, won convincingly over his Dominion-Republican rival, Henry Clay, garnering some 765,000 of the approximately 1,325,000 votes cast. Two minor candidates had no effect on the outcome. It was

25

CHAPTER THREE

Georgetown, D.C.
December 20, 1832:

Tom Wilder glanced at his pocket watch and shook his head. Twelve noon. He had spent the better parts of three mornings shifting through all the correspondence between The Residency and London dating back six months. Mention of the plebiscite, when discussed at all, was prima forma: the Dominion's plans for organizing and securing the vote in the various states; dates of the voting in each state, plans for the official tallying and subsequent announcement. The on-going controversy over the increase in tariffs---the issue which had caused the bitter "nullification" split between Jackson and his first Vice G-G, John C. Calhoun of South Carolina---dominated the correspondence, along with the usual traffic concerning Indians and the sullen French Canadians in Quebec. The fight over the Bank of the USBA, which bored Wilder as much it bored the great majority of the Dominion's citizens, seemed of major interest to London, however.

From the perspective of this correspondence, London's interest in our affairs is more financial than political, Wilder thought as he wearily rubbed his eyes. *As long as we contribute our fair share to the Empire's profitability, it doesn't seem like Buckingham Palace, Parliament or Downing Street really cares who runs what over here. Maybe the Treasury Department has come up with a new tariff proposal. Looks like our masters across the water would be very interested in that...but enough to strip down a frigate for a mid-Winter run? I doubt it.*

Well, there's nothing more here. I'd better get over to the War Department and finish checking those files. Though I'm fairly certain the Royal Army is more interested in the winding down of the Black Hawk War out in Illinois.

Wilder was still envious that his friend and classmate, Joe Johnston, had seen action in that campaign with the 4th Artillery. He, meanwhile, had languished on the Arkansas frontier until rescued by General Scott upon the General's return from leading the successful campaign.

As Wilder walked down The Residency steps, he saw a familiar figure emerge through the front gates and begin walking toward the building. David Harper was a career Interior Department official, a born bureaucrat, but nevertheless a hit with the ladies that Wilder ruefully conceded he himself was not. Tom had seen Harps in action in both polite society and in some of the District's less reputable back alleys. Slight but handsome, with wavy brown hair and a quick wit, Harper charmed all kinds of women effortlessly.

I wish some of that charm would rub off on me, especially when Lucille Latoure is around…as she will be at the G-G's reception two evenings from now.

Harper saw Wilder coming and grinned. "Well, Thomas, thought I'd find you here when you weren't across the street." The Interior and War departments were housed in the same makeshift 'temporary' Georgetown building. "I'm dropping some documents off here with the G-G's secretary. Won't take a minute. How about joining me at the Golden Eagle?" The Eagle was a prominent gathering place for the younger Executive Department officials. It had recently been purchased by a former barmaid, Joanne Casgrave, who was rumored to have funded the purchase through profits from services of a more private sort. Services now apparently readily available on an upper floor…

Wilder hesitated only briefly. "All right, Harps. I was on my way back to the Department, but I could use a bowl of soup and a beer. Didn't take time for breakfast this morning."

Ten minutes later they were comfortably seated at a back table near the Inn's roaring fire. "God, that feels good," Harper said. "This damn Georgetown weather goes right through you." The Lieutenant nodded his agreement as a barmaid arrived to take their orders.

Winter in Georgetown was unlike the exhilarating cold of Wilder's Brooklyn childhood, or even the more bitter bite of West Point's under-heated barracks and classrooms. Here, the damp chill invaded the chest, sinuses and bones in November and took up residence till spring arrived in early March. Two months later, of course, the blast-furnace heat and oppressive humidity made any normal---Northern---person long for January. Harper, being from Northern New Jersey, had much the same opinion of the capital's climate.

"Tom, your eyes are blood-shot. Have you been lighting the social candle at both ends without me? Or does 'Old Hickory' have you burning the midnight oil at The Residency?"

Wilder smiled wearily. "Neither, Dave. General Scott has me looking for some elusive information which may or may not exist. I was on my way over to continue the search at the War Department when we bumped into each other. But tell me, how do the plebiscite results affect your Department?"

"Hell, hardly at all, Lieutenant. Both Jackson and Clay were in favor of 'internal improvements' to the Dominion, so it really didn't matter who won as far as the day-to-day workings of the Department were concerned. Clay might have put one of his own people into the top position, but my job was pretty secure, either way. Since Mr. Van Buren was Jackson's running mate, we were certain to get a new boss, whoever won. Rumor has it old Livingston will keep the job, or maybe Louis McLane will move in. I doubt it will make much difference. They're both close allies of Matty Van. How about you?"

"Same with me. And I doubt General Scott was too concerned. Henry Clay wasn't about to dismiss him. Let me ask you, though: Does your Department have much communication with London? Or do they leave you pretty much alone?"

Harper nearly choked on his newly-arrived chicken vegetable soup. "Much communication? Hardly. We hear from the American Office every so often, but it's all routine. We send in reports regularly; whether they're even read over there is anyone's guess. Mine is that there aren't enough people in that so-called 'Office' to study half of what we send them. Then again, the more they leave us alone, the better it is for us." Harper paused and looked thoughtful. "Did have a rather unusual communication last spring, but it didn't come from the American Office. The Chancellor of the Exchequer, if you can believe it."

"Exchequer?" asked Wilder, the surprise apparent in his voice. "That's a new one on me. Don't think I've ever seen anything at either The Residency or the Department from them. I imagine the Treasury Department does correspond regularly, though. What did they want?"

"A breakdown on slavery, of all things. How many slave states, how many free? Percentage of slaves in the overall population of each state, that sort of information."

"How did you respond?"

"Oh, we used the census. Spent several days copying it all out, but it seemed to satisfy them. Haven't heard a word since."

An idea was forming in Wilder's brain, but he pressed ahead as if still baffled by the response. "The census? I didn't realize the census results had been finalized, yet alone published."

"Approved last May. That Tennessee protégé of the G-G's, Polk, pushed it through the House. They've ordered up 10,000 copies, though that sluggardly printing house the State Department uses hasn't gotten around to publishing them all yet. The census is pretty impressive, or alarming, depending on your point of view. Did you know there are just over 2,000,000 slaves, mostly in the 10 states and two territories south of the Mason-Dixon Line? They constitute less than 15% of the USBA's overall population, but anywhere from 20% to more than 50% in the Southern states. No wonder Nat Turner had the planters in such an uproar."

On August 21, 1831 a slave named Nat Turner had instigated an uprising of some 30 fellow-slaves in Southampton County, Va. In a single night of indiscriminate slaughter, some 70 white men, women and children, mostly small farming families, died before Turner and his band fled into the forests. The Virginia state government had hunted the rebels down ruthlessly; Turner himself was caught alive and subsequently hanged on November 11, 1831. The aftershocks were still being felt throughout the South: in Richmond the House of Burgesses in midyear had come stunningly close---seven votes---to abolishing the institution altogether. (Incongruously, it had then reversed itself and tightened the terms of bondage outright.)

"Well, Harps, this is all very interesting, but if I don't soon come up with the information General Scott wants, I may be back in Arkansas with the Dragoons. I better get back to the Department." He drained his beer. "Coming?"

Harper, too, rose from the table. "Hate going back out in this weather, but I suppose I'm due back, too. By the way, tell me about the guest list for the G-G's reception. I've copped an invitation."

––––––––––––

As expected, Lieutenant Wilder found nothing in his review of recent War Department correspondence with their London superiors that would explain the *Irresistible's* mysterious departure. Harper's offhand remark about Exchequer's unexpected request was the only 'odd or different' information Wilder had been able to unearth in more than three full days of searching.

Now he was seated outside the General's office, awaiting Scott's arrival. Although Lewis Cass of Michigan, as Secretary of War, was Scott's nominal boss, there was little doubt who really ran the Department. Cass was a politician, one of the G-G's closest advisors. It was the morning of December 21st and Georgetown was blanketed by the first real snow of the season as the General's carriage pulled up to the Department. 'Old Fuss and Feathers' wore a long blue and tan military great cloak as he stomped down the hall towards his office. "Come in Lieutenant. What have you got for me this God-awful morning?"

Well, thought Wilder, here goes. *He better like this, or I could be headed south by New Year's.* "General, my review of The Residency's correspondence with London failed to reveal anything 'odd or different.' Likewise, this Department's correspondence with both the Royal Army and the Admiralty failed to produce anything significant. Nor did a review of recent requests both here and at The Residency from the Liaison Office turn up anything unusual.

"A personnel review also determined that no Royal officer or key Liaison staff has recently been ordered back to London. And Baltimore reports that *Irresistible* sailed immediately upon receiving a dispatch sent directly from the Liaison Office."

The Lieutenant could feel the drill starting up as the stone-cold blue eyes stared directly at him.

"I did discover one thread that winds through almost all our communication with London, however, Sir."

"Yes Lieutenant?"

"Finances, Sir. In one way or another, virtually all the communication between London and Georgetown centers on money: whether its taxes, tariffs or fighting the Indians, finance is the key. How much revenue will be generated; how much revenue will be spent. That's the constant."

The fingers began drumming their tattoo on the desktop. "That's all, Lieutenant? You think the *Irresistible* stripped down and upped anchor to let London know who Jackson's new Treasury Secretary will be?"

In spite of himself, Wilder smiled at the sarcasm. "Not exactly, Sir. You see, I did come across one piece of information that seems out-of-the-ordinary. But it came from the Interior Department. Last May, the Chancellor of the Exchequer's Office in London requested a breakdown on slavery in the USBA. Total number of slaves; their percentage of the overall population; the states where slavery is a major economic factor; that sort of thing."

The drill dug deeper. "Go on, Lieutenant. How does this fit into your stunning discovery of the Empire's abiding economic interest in this Dominion? And, more importantly, how does it fit into the *Irresistible* mystery?"

"Sir, am I correct in thinking that any and all taxation legislation set before the British Parliament by the Prime Minister initially is drafted by the Chancellor of the Exchequer? In the manner that the Treasury Department here has initiated taxation proposals in this and previous Administrations?"

The drill began to slow down. "That's pretty much correct, Lieutenant. So what's your conclusion?"

Wilder took a deep breath. "Sir, I believe the Crown is about to seek a tax on all slaves held in this Dominion. There's no other reason for the Exchequer's interest in the slave numbers. And I believe that proposed tax will be significant. So significant that the Crown believes it will have a major impact on the USBA during the next Administration."

A slight smile played at the corners of Scott's mouth. "And why might that be, Lieutenant?"

"Because, Sir, while both---all four, including Wirt and Floyd---of the plebiscite candidates own slaves, the winner is a planter. Who may be considered unlikely to support or enforce a significant tax on his own property, now that he has been declared the electorate's choice for another term. Mr. Clay, on the other hand, does own a handful of slaves, but is also a leader in the movement to gradually free all the slaves and send them to Liberia. Governor Floyd wants a quick end to slavery, while old Wirt is, well, old...if I may be so bold, Sir."

"No Lieutenant, Andrew Jackson is not likely to support or gather a tax on himself and his fellow planters even if it comes with a companion tax on Northern manufactories." Scott paused, drumming his fingers while looking toward the ceiling.

"A Governor-General who won't support or implement Crown policies...

"That could be why London wants the results as quickly as possible. They presuppose Jackson's opposition." The General leaned back in his oversized chair and appeared to again contemplate the ceiling. Several minutes---they seemed unending to the Lieutenant---passed in silence. Then:

"The question is: how far are they willing to go in dealing with it? If you're right, Lieutenant Wilder---and its one theory that makes sense---we are in for a constitutional crisis the likes of which this Dominion---and this Empire---hasn't seen since 1775.

"It may not make for such a Happy New Year!"

Georgetown, D.C.
December 23, 1833:

Lieutenant Wilder gazed at his image in the full-length mirror late that following Sunday afternoon in something close to disgust. No matter how becoming his dark blue full dress uniform with the bold gold stripe down each leg, he simply didn't do it justice. *Harps could carry this off*, he thought; *not as well as my polished classmate, Joe Johnston, and certainly not as well as Bobby Lee. But Robert is down on the Virginia Peninsula single-handedly, if you believe General Scott, turning Fortress Monroe into the 'Gibraltar of Chesapeake Bay.'*

Lee, Tom knew, was expected back across the Potomac at Arlington for the holidays, though not until late tomorrow.

Mary was kind enough to invite me over to Arlington House for Christmas Eve and Christmas dinner, even though she hasn't seen Robert since the baby's christening last fall. Johnston and Harper, though, are here in Georgetown and will be at The Residency tonight...as will Lucille Latoure.

Wilder had long ago conceded that 'Black Irish' he was not. No, he was a typical 'Mick'---short, stocky and blond-haired---with freckles to boot! Even if his grandfather had left Cork back in the '60s and had made his fortune as a shipping magnate in the fledgling port of New York. No matter; Wilder knew he still looked as if he was just off the boat.

Lucille Latoure wasn't beautiful in any classical sense; but men forgot that when she favored them with that singular smile which made them feel like world conquerors. Unfortunately, she was also an incurable flirt, a classic "belle" who possessed---and flaunted---a remarkable body. The total package had ninety-percent of the eligible (and many seemingly ineligible) males in the District of Columbia in a state of perpetual excitement whenever she appeared in town.

Wilder had become fatally infatuated---there was no other operative phrase---with Miss Latoure, the elder daughter of a

33

deceased planter and merchant from nearby Alexandria, at his first Residency reception the previous January. He had come upon her talking with a CG officer and made a bold misogynistic remark. She had shot him a look that electrified him---feigned outrage that camouflaged enjoyment---that had addicted him immediately and permanently.

Satisfied with her conquest, Lucille had proceeded to make his life miserable on those occasions when they were together. Planters, other officers, senior government officials: she encouraged them all. And left Lieutenant Wilder wondering why he banged his head against this stonewall of feminine arrogance.

Well, if Lucille is in the mood to run roughshod over me again tonight---or simply doesn't make an appearance---there is always Candice Samples.

Mrs. Samples, the big, blond and brassy widow of one of Maryland's most successful planters, was the proud processor of the most spectacular chest in Georgetown. Wilder had met her at a dinner-party hosted by Mrs. Scott the previous summer. They had left together in the Widow Samples' carriage; by the time an exhausted Thomas had stumbled from her townhouse late the next morning he had absorbed intensive instruction in techniques new and thrilling.

The ample Mrs. Samples was ever-eager, and ever-available, but the Lieutenant, who estimated her age to be at least 15 years older than his somewhat-worldly 26, simply had no interest in Candice once the initial animalistic struggling was finished.

She's a nice person, ungodly rich and insatiable in the bedroom, but I'm not looking to nurse some old lady into the grave. At least, not while Lucille is available! Still, the Samples' townhouse is a lot more appealing than my room at the Indian Queen Hotel. Why is it that Candice Samples won't let me alone; yet Lucille Latoure doesn't seem to care less? I'd like to see 'Old Fuss and Feathers' explain that one...

CHAPTER FOUR

London, England
January 4, 1833:

Visibility had dropped to near zero in central London as Harry Bratton's carriage made its way back from the Thames docks. As the carriage groped slowly through the near white-out, Bratton was deep in thought. *The Liaison Office in Georgetown has been predicting a Jackson victory for months, so it's not only the idea that he'll be in The Residency for four more years that has His Lordship concerned. Even though I know the entire Grey cabinet would have preferred Clay or one of the other candidates. Jackson's behavior when he was here in Parliament offended almost all proper London society, I'm told.* After a while, even the Duke had apparently had enough...

Still, there has to be more to this than social contempt. I know Lord Grey wasn't happy last year with Jackson's speech hinting that taking Texas from the Mexicans should be a primary goal of the Empire.

Lord Palmerston himself had fired off a sharp note reminding 'Old Hickory' that foreign policy for the Empire, including the USBA, is determined only in London!

I doubt Their Lordships understood the real rationale for Jackson's hint, however. Their concern is keeping the Western Hemisphere off limits to the other European powers, especially France and Russia. Jackson's motive is more provincial: the balance of power in the USBA Congress between the free and slave states. Simply put, the slave owners are running out of room for expansion. As the rest of the Louisiana Territory is populated and organized, and eventually, the vast Canadian West, too, the new states will come from areas where slavery is economically-unfeasible. Unless they can get their hands on all that territory from Texas to California, the slave states---and their representatives in Congress---face becoming a permanent minority. There are 26 states right now, including Ontario and Quebec. Just 10 are slave states, with the Florida and Arkansas territories likely to join them before the decade is out. As things now stand, that will be it: a block of 12 slave states plus Quebec against 15 or more free states.

Freeing the slaves is not the issue, he continued. *No one's considering that, certainly! The two blocks simply have differing goals for the Dominion. And the Southerners aren't willing to relinquish the power they've wielded in Georgetown these many years. That's where Jackson was headed with his Texas hint. Not that anyone of influence in His Majesty's Government knows enough about USBA politics to figure it out…or allow me explain it to them.*

Captain Harry Bratton, of His Majesty's Coldstream Guards, (on half pay as a civilian official) came from an old Salisbury Plain family whose roots, if traceable, would have led back past Roman times. Brattons had fought, not always on the winning side, in virtually all of England's wars: civil as well as overseas. Bratton's great-great-grandfather had distinguished himself on Marlborough's staff and his grandfather had fought beside Wolfe at Quebec. Bratton's father had survived the worst of the Napoleonic Wars, only to die in the mopping-up operations after Waterloo.

Harry, then 15 and the second eldest of five children, had always been pointed toward a military career. He had graduated from Sandhurst in 1819. His polish and quick intelligence, as well as his reputation as a crack shot and good horseman, had been noted both there and with the Guards. He was identified as a 'diplomatic' and sent to India in 1823. Three years later, he joined the Liaison Office in Georgetown. There, he was credited with quietly attending to some 'under the rose' business in Montreal, as well as the dispatching of a French agent in New Orleans in 1828.

Dapper, an even six foot tall, he was an accomplished ladies man. Even though, much to his disgust, the traditional early-30s Bratton hairline retreat had commenced even before he had joined the Colonial Office's American desk. Still single at 34, he was considered a good catch by London society matrons despite his lack of a noble title. (Knighthood had usually been as far as Brattons rose; though Marlborough's aide had been made a Viscount.) He enjoyed the company of cultured women, and was certainly heterosexual in his tastes, but had never found the correct circumstances for a long-term relationship. For Harry, danger was the great aphrodisiac: his only truly-memorable relationships had been with a minor Indian princess and the wife of an American politician. Yet, he could be equally happy with the occasional visit to St. John's Wood. And there had been that Georgetown barmaid, Joanne, with the sad story of her Army officer husband, cut down by cancer, who had left her destitute.

As Bratton's carriage pulled up at the War & Colonial Office, he was stunned to make out through the whirling snow the identifying markings on some of the other broughams parked outside the building. *My God,* he thought, *that's the Duke's carriage! And who got Pammy out of bed at this hour (or did he come straight from his usual nocturnal pursuits)?*

As Bratton made his way into the dark old building, he came across Frederick John Robinson, 1st Viscount Goderich himself. "Good morning, Sir," Bratton said, shaking off the last of the snow that had clung to his cloak. "Just back from the Thames. Have the pouch you wanted...."

The Colonial Secretary quickly stuck out his hand. "Yes, Harry, hand it over. The documents inside will determine whether or not this meeting will go as planned. Bye-the-bye, don't go far. I 'spect we'll have need of your counsel soon enough."

"Yes, Sir," Bratton managed to get out in amazement. "I'll be right..."

"To hell with that, Bratton. Tell me: did that uncouth old man win another term? Or, as I've prayed these many months, did Mr. Clay oust him?"

"Sir, I've certainly not broken the seal on this pouch," Bratton said, helping the Secretary open the leather-bound briefcase. "However, I'm reliably told by the ship's captain that General Jackson was the clear-cut winner, outpolling Mr. Clay by more than a half-million votes."

"Damned colonials deserve what they get," Robinson muttered, just loud enough for Bratton to realize he was intended to hear the minister's disgust. "I don't suppose William Wirt or the Virginia governor made a difference?" Virginia's legal legend and that state's maverick governor, John Floyd, had also run in the plebiscite. (Together they had received a combined popular vote of less than a quarter-million. Jackson, by contrast, had received over 750,000 votes.)

"No, Sir. It was strictly a Jackson landslide, as the Americans would say."

The Viscount cast a quick sideways look at his aide. "Caught many of their sayings and mannerisms, did you, Mr. Bratton, during your years across the water? How long have you been back home?"

"Minister, I served as an Army liaison officer in Georgetown from 1826-29. After I came home and went on half-pay, I joined the

THE DOMINION'S DILEMMA: THE UNITED STATES OF BRITISH AMERICA

Office. I've been working the 'American' desk ever since."

"Then you know a damn sight more about the Americans than most anyone else who'll be here this morning. Sit tight. Have a cup of tea; you look frozen. We'll be calling for you soon enough." Robinson disappeared into the conference room as a dazed Bratton found a peg for his cloak in the outer office and walked over to the fireplace.

It's going to take more than one cup of good hot English tea to get the chill out of my bones, he thought, as he rubbed his hands over the fire. *And more than one to help clear my head. The Secretary, Lord Palmerston, the Duke, and God knows who else in there, want* my *counsel? Well, Harry old chap, this should be interesting…*

––––––––––––

The historic meeting ordered by Prime Minister Grey and chaired by Lord Palmerston, the Foreign Minister, began secretly at the War & Colonial Office at 5 a.m. on January 4, 1833. In addition to Viscount Goderich, Henry Brougham, Lord Chancellor; and Lord Durham represented the Government. Home Secretary Lord Melbourne, the consensus choice among the Whigs to replace Lord Grey whenever that ailing old man resigned, was also in attendance. Sir Arthur Wellesley, the Duke of Wellington, though the leader of the opposition Tories---for the Whigs had regained power in the 1830 election---had been asked to attend for several vital reasons. Not least among them was his relationship with the USBA Governor-General. Though Bratton was still unaware of the fact, another figure had arrived at the Colonial Office in the snowy pre-dawn: John Quincy Adams, the previous USBA G-G and present Massachusetts delegate to the House of Commons. This blue-ribbon committee had been selected by the Prime Minister months earlier to develop and implement a policy that would leave Bratton speechless when he realized its scope and possible consequence some hours later.

"Well, Frederick, what news from the Dominion? Did the electorate make our job a bit easier by refuting Jackson in favor of Mr. Clay?"

The Colonial Secretary looked up from reviewing the report and shook his head in disgust. "No, Mr. Chairman, these results indicate that General Jackson was a runaway winner in the plebiscite, trouncing Mr. Clay by more than half-a-million votes. The other two candidates were non-factors."

The Duke of Wellington turned amused eyes and hook nose on the lone Committee member eligible to vote in the plebiscite. "Well, Mr. Adams. Your people seem to have permanently lost their taste in selecting leaders, wouldn't you say?"

Quincy Adams' long slope of a forehead reddened, but his reply was dryly precise: "As the British electorate, Your Grace, apparently did two years ago?"

The others, including Wellington himself, laughed. The Duke's controversial term as P.M. had ended when the Reform-minded Whigs swept his party out of Parliamentary power in 1830. "Yes, there is no helping the taste of the electorate. Especially when you widen eligibility to the extent we now have on both sides of the Atlantic. We'll just have to hope, Mr. Adams, that both electorates regain their senses in due course."

"Now then, gentlemen," Lord Palmerston said in a formal, commanding tone. "With the USBA plebiscite results in, we can get down to it. We are all quite aware of the magnitude of the question before us, and its potential implications for the Empire. I've asked the Chancellor of the Exchequer to sit in this morning as his Office has determined the financial cost of the plan we have agreed must be implemented. As we look at the question in the King's various provinces…and Dominion," he quickly added, glancing at Mr. Adams, "Earl Spencer will chime in with the appropriate fiscal calculations. Let's begin with the West Indies, shall we?"

Viscount Goderich shuffled papers set on the table in front of him. "There may be as many as 1,700,000 slaves scattered throughout our West Indies possessions. It is difficult to obtain an accurate count. But certainly, in number they dwarf the white population. If not for the Army and the Royal Marines, we would have had a Haitian situation on our hands a generation ago."

Emboldened by the war in Europe, and the subsequent drawdown in French troops, Tousaint L'Ouverture had sparked a slave revolt that resulted in Napoleon eventually abandoning France's portion of Hispaniola in the century's first decade. The independent Haiti had tottered on the brink of anarchy ever since, but no serious effort had been made by any European power to regain control. This was attributed by some to the stunning valor demonstrated by the blacks the amazing L'Ouverture had trained and led. By others, to the malarial conditions that had so weakened the large army of Dutch, Swiss and Germans Bonaparte had sent to put down the revolt that they had proved no match for the Haitians.

"The slaveholders have no real choice. Either they accept the phased-in compensation plan His Majesty's government will offer, or we can militarily enforce the emancipation of the Negroes without compensation. The resulting chaos would ruin them financially, of course, so, as I say, they will have no choice other than to accept a buyout."

"Are we agreed on the terms we're proposing?" Lord Brougham broke in. Brougham, who among other things had designed the carriage type parked outside the Office, was a leading abolitionist.

Palmerston nodded at Goderich. "Well, Mr. Secretary?"

"A phased-in emancipation over seven years, with the former slaves indentured to their former owners three days per week. During the other four, they are free to toil any land they can obtain for themselves; be paid to work for their former owners or anyone else, or not work. In return, they will be clothed, housed and fed by their former owners until the completion of the seven-year period. Any freemen of course remain free and any child born once the emancipation process begins is also free.

"In return, His Majesty's government agrees to a phased compensation to the owners of…how much, Chancellor?"

"Twenty million pounds. Paid out over the seven-year period."

Palmerston looked at the grave faces around the table. "Any other comment, before we move on to The Cape Colony?"

Adams looked both awed---for him---and somber. "Almost two million slaves on those few small islands alone! And the slave trade abolished a generation ago. Thank God for William Wilberforce. Think how many more poor devils would have been dragged across the Ocean if he hadn't been so committed!"

"And think how much richer those West African chieftains who sold their fellow blacks into slavery would be if not for Wilberforce's determination…and the vigilance of the British Navy." Wellington was dry.

William Wilberforce, an early British abolitionist, had campaigned for almost 20 years before Parliament, in 1807, had outlawed the slave trade in the Empire, and therefore, in the Western World. The Royal Navy had enforced the policy ever since. Consequently, virtually all the slaves in the Western Hemisphere were at least second generation, though many, of course, were descended from African tribesmen and women kidnapped or captured during the previous 150 or more years. They had then been sold to multinational slave traders and ferried across the Atlantic in nightmarish conditions.

"A pity Wilberforce didn't complete the job," Lord Durham said with a sigh. 'Radical Jack,' as he was widely known, was also a longtime abolitionist.

"Just doing what he did took two decades and ruined his health," Lord Melbourne observed. "Besides, His Majesty's Government wasn't in any financial position in those days to compensate anyone. The Empire damn near went bankrupt putting Napoleon on St. Helena. Though, if Pitt the Younger had lived, the thing might have been accomplished 15 years ago."

The brilliant and precocious second son of the Prime Minister who had saved North America for the Empire---P.M. at 24---had supported his lifelong friend, Wilberforce, in his crusade. Pitt, however, was chiefly concerned during his two terms as P.M. with the containment and/or defeat of Bonaparte. Called a 'genius of evil' by the French Emperor, Pitt's policy of financing coalitions against the French was a major financial drain on the Empire. Despite poor health, and against the advice of doctors and family, Pitt had helped forge the Third Coalition against Napoleon when he returned to office in 1805. The glorious British naval victory at Trafalgar that year notwithstanding, the subsequent Coalition land defeats at Ulm and Austerlitz had shattered the exhausted Pitt. He had died even before the slave trade abolition bill passed Parliament. Stripped of his key political connection, Wilberforce had been unable to follow up in convincing Parliament to ban slavery itself. He had remained in Parliament until 1824, when his own declining health forced him into retirement. He was still alive, writing and calling for abolition, at his small estate north of London, in Mill Hill.

"Well, enough ancient history," said Lord Palmerston gruffly. A silence that lasted almost a minute had descended over the table as the Committee members contemplated the enormity of their mission. "It's the history we're gathered here to make now and in the immediate future that we need concentrate on. What about the Cape, Frederick?"

"Well, Mr. Chairman, there's nowhere near the number of slaves in South Africa that there are in the West Indies. We can't even approximate as no reliable census has been conducted. However, our Governor-General in Cape Town, Sir Galbraith Lowery-Cole, estimates about 100,000. Those are split between large planters, mainly British, and the small farmers, overwhelmingly Boer. That's how the descendents of the original Dutch colonizers of Cape Colony style themselves.

"Governor-General Lowery-Cole feels the British plantation owners, who also utilize slaves in the gold, silver and diamond mines, will reluctantly accept emancipation, as long as they are duly financially compensated. His estimate is approximately a half-million pounds. Remember now, these slaves do more than work in the fields and mansions. They carve out precious metals, too."

"What about the Dutch, Frederick? How will they accept our decision?" Lord Brougham.

"Not well, Henry, according to Sir Galbraith. But that may be a plus for us, nevertheless. You see, the Boers have been threatening to pull up stakes and migrate north---out of British authority---almost since the day we took control of the Cape. If this planned emancipation forces their hand, so much the better for us. We won't have to pay them and, if they survive further into Africa, why, we send an armed force to take over their new colony whenever it suits us."

The ensuing laughter around the table wasn't shared by the British American, who, nonetheless, determined to keep his dismay to himself. Instead, Adams asked the rhetorical question: "Are we doing this for our conscience alone...or to help these poor people? Surely we care as much about the blacks caught in slavery by the Boers as we do about those in the West Indies...or in the British American South!"

It was Wellington who answered, expressing the prevailing view of most of his colleagues and countrymen: "Don't bombard us with your self-righteousness, Mr. Adams. Your New England got religion after it got economics. Your predecessors decided slavery was a great evil after they realized it was too costly in your climate. You simply couldn't afford to house, clothe and feed slaves 12 months a year when you could only have them in the fields for half that time... If Massachusetts had the growing season and could produce the tobacco and cotton that comes out of Virginia and the Carolinas, with slaves working 11 or 12 months per year, at least some of your people would be employing overseers to this day."

Wellington paused momentarily and looked around at the nodding faces of the other committee members. "I'm glad we're agreed here to proceed in this most Christian---and overdue---endeavor, but don't tell this Committee that this great crusade is something your region and state have been committed to long before the rest of us."

Adams, his head now entirely scarlet, stared at the Duke. "Your Grace, we in Massachusetts have traditionally favored freeing the Negroes…going back to 1775!"

Wellington nodded condescendingly. "Yes, Mr. Adams, because your previous generation read its Adam Smith on those dark, snowy nights when it wasn't plotting treason…"

Lord Palmerston's facial features had not yet turned the cartoonists' delight that they would in coming years. Yet his nose and cheeks had become a bright pink. "Gentlemen, we are, hopefully, all on God's side here. We must demonstrate a unified front in Parliament. No matter our particular partisan position, we must demonstrate that all parties are settled on this course of action.

"I believe a short break may be in order. Then, if we can get back to the business of considering the issue in the British American South…"

Harry Bratton had begun wondering whether he should return to the American Desk. Whatever direction the secret meeting in the conference room had taken, it seemed his *counsel* wouldn't be necessary after all. Then the door opened suddenly and Earl Goderich emerged. "We've broken for a few moments, Harry. You'll be called in shortly. Meanwhile, concentrate your thoughts on the sectional issues in the Dominion: political, economic and military. What will likely be the new Congress' makeup; how deep is Jackson's support in the North; those sort of things… You'll be in directly."

Goderich marched back into the conference room and shut the door as Bratton stared incredulously at his retreating figure. *What in hell? Am I to be asked to give a bloody seminar on the Dominion within the next 45 minutes or so? After I've been waiting outside all this time when I could have done some preparation? And 'economic sectionalism?' What the devil is going on in there? I'd better get back to my desk and get my hands on a few documents….*

Lord Durham had taken a visibly upset Quincy Adams aside as the Colonial Secretary reentered the room. The entire Committee, in fact, had broken into small groups of two and three as they quietly sipped tea and munched breakfast biscuits.

"I'm sure there is nothing personal in the Duke's remarks, Mr. Adams," 'Radical Jack' said in a soothing low voice. "He's just a blunt old soldier…but…he is committed to our cause. Emancipation, you'll remember, was first seriously discussed while he was still in Downing Street! And, as we've discussed before, his influence over this man Jackson may be key to our success in the USBA."

Adams nodded slowly. "I'm well aware of those facts, Lord Durham. But to question the sincerity of my people when we have been opposing this barbarity for so long is outrageous…"

The Lord Privy Seal smiled softly. "In the end Mr. Adams, it is unimportant how we all arrived at this juncture. It is only important that we have."

Lord Palmerston had resumed his place at the head of the conference table. "Now, gentlemen, let's take up the issue in British America. If you would continue, Lord Goderich…

"Yes, Mr. Chairman. At this time I would like to call in the Office's resident expert on the USBA. Mr. Harry Bratton has been following events in the Dominion for over four years, immediately preceding which he served as a military liaison officer in Georgetown. So, with the exception of our esteemed friend from Massachusetts," he nodded at Adams, "he is considerably more learned in USBA affairs than any of the rest of us. He's waiting outside."

Bratton was on his feet and moving toward the conference room even before the door fully opened. Only with considerable effort was he able to maintain a stiff upper lip as he recognized the assemblage of distinguished figures at the table. *My God, the Chancellor of the Exchequer and…Quincy Adams of Massachusetts? What the bloody hell is going on here?*

"Mr. Bratton, if you'll take a seat behind the Colonial Secretary. I don't need to remind you that everything that you see and hear this morning remains within the confines of this room for present. Is that understood?"

Palmerston flashed a commanding stare at the younger man, who nodded his head vigorously. "Certainly, My Lord…"

"Now, if you would, Lord Goderich…"

Goderich had risen and was now walking toward a draped easel that had been set up at the far corner of the table. He pulled off the cover to reveal a detailed map of the USBA with the various states marked by different shades of coloring. Picking up a pointer, he addressed the Committee. "These shadings indicate the intensity of the slave population in the USBA, with the shadings growing darker as that population intensifies.

"According to the latest census, published last May, the USBA has a total population, including Quebec and Ontario, of just over 13,500,000. There are 2,009,058 slaves in the USBA, including," he continued in a flat professorial drone but with eyes bright, "four in the state of Massachusetts. All there, apparently, female…"

A sudden epidemic of coughing seemed to break out simultaneously around the table, though one distinct cackle was discerned coming from the vicinity of the Duke of Wellington. Adams' face burned scarlet once more.

"However, while Vermont was the only state reporting no slaves at all---though a total of 881 free colored reside there---the great majority are held in the 10 states, the District of Columbia and the two territories below the Mason-Dixon Line. In fact, there are just 6875 slaves in the combined 15 states and the Territory of Michigan that lay above the Line. Do you have anything to add to that, Mr. Bratton?"

"Very little, Sir," said an astonished Bratton, who was beginning to wonder the actual direction of this briefing. "While the slaves make up less than 15% of the USBA's overall population, they constitute anywhere from 20% to over 50% in the Southern states. In South Carolina, there are actually about 50,000 more slaves than whites and free blacks combined. The slaves outnumber the free population by a few thousand in Louisiana, also. I would be remiss not to add, however, that some 2200 slaves are currently held in New Jersey."

Adams interrupted. "If you extend Mason and Dixon's line due east, it would cross Southern New Jersey. I'm sure the great majority of those slaves are therefore, technically as well as physically, in the South."

Bratton, grateful for the chance to have grabbed every note he could gather from his desk, hesitated, but then determined to push on. *Well, they did ask me in here for my 'counsel.'* "Not exactly, Mr. Adams. I've traveled through that beautiful state many times coming and going to and from New York and New England. Bergen County, as I'm sure you are aware, is somewhat northwest of New York City and more than 100 miles north of the theoretical Line. Yet the census lists it as having 584 slaves, the most in the state."

Lord Goderich broke back into the discussion. "The location of and reasons for New Jersey's slave population are of little concern to this Committee. Suffice to say, slaves do not constitute a significant portion of that state's population. Our concern is the states where they do. The question is: can we apply the same formula to the USBA that we are utilizing to bring about emancipation in the rest of the Empire? Phased-in compensation under terms to be overseen by the Army and the Royal Marines?"

An excited chatter broke out across the table, while behind it, a flabbergasted Bratton wondered if he had correctly heard the Colonial Secretary's question. *Emancipation of the slaves? Dear Mother of God, it that what this is all about? No wonder they wanted Jackson defeated. He's a planter. They don't trust him to carry out the emancipation! But surely they don't intend to send in the Army and the Royal Marines?*

It will be 1775 all over again!

Lord Brougham seemed to be echoing Bratton's thoughts. "Let's be clear that we are not advocating a military solution here," he said. "The USBA is not the West Indies! The first question is: how much must we sweeten the pot in order to convince the slaveholders to agree to emancipation? And, secondly, how much can this Government afford to sweeten said pot? Those are the issues on the table."

"Well put, Henry," said Lord Palmerston. "I'd like to hear Mr. Adams' thoughts next, before we hear a financial report from the Chancellor of the Exchequer."

"Personally, as you all well know, I'd be inclined not to pay the slaveholders another shilling," said Adams. "They've made far too much money off the sweat of others as it is. But, I realize the catastrophic impact on the USBA economy of such a draconian approach. And, I'm ashamed to add, the majority of my fellow British Americans who live in the so-called free states---and who aren't as opposed to slavery as they should be---would unfortunately sympathize with the slaveholders. As quickly as the movement is growing in the North, there are still too many who do not see the emancipation issue as their fight.

"I do not wish to be considered overly-pessimistic, but, as I've stated at previous meeting of this distinguished Committee, I am not at all certain that the slaveholders will be willing to relinquish their...'peculiar institution'...at any price. It may all depend on the attitude of that frontier barbarian who now occupies The Residency.

As a planter himself, he will be the lightening rod, so to speak, on this issue. If Jackson agrees to accept the proclamation of emancipation by His Majesty's government, he may be able to stare down the more radical elements. Just as he so ably, it pains me to admit, did in the 'nullification' crisis of '31."

Adams paused before adding: "After all, he does claim to swear allegiance to the union of our states..." The former G-G looked around the table at the somber faces staring back at him. "Gentlemen, we are about to test that allegiance to the fullest."

The Chancellor of the Exchequer broke the ensuing silence. "For the record, gentlemen, based on the twenty million pounds we have earmarked for the West Indies, and the fact that Sir Galbreath in Pretoria believes emancipation in the Cape Colony can be had for less than another million pounds, His Majesty's Government expects to allocate another 23 millions for the project in the USBA. That is, of course, with the understanding that the Empire remains in a state of peace for the next seven years. A major European war could not be financed while this project is underway."

"Ah yes, Frederick, that would be a problem," said Lord Palmerston. "However, foreign affairs are on my watch and I see little likelihood of a major conflict. I must admit we are monitoring this situation within the Ottoman Empire. Seems this Egyptian vassal of the Sultan, Pasha Mehemet Ali, is flexing his muscles against Constantinople. He's sent a force north through the Gaza and into Palestine. Unless the Bear decides to interfere, we shall probably allow them to settle that dispute internally. In any case, I do not see major war clouds threatening on the horizon."

Lord Melbourne had been relatively quiet all morning. But then, the Home Secretary was famous for keeping his own counsel. Now he addressed the Chair. "We've heard Mr. Adams today repeat what he's told us in prior meetings: much depends on Governor-General Jackson. I'd be interested in hearing now from our professional in the American Office. Mr. Bratton, you've heard enough now to understand our deep concerns that this most worthy plan to abolish slavery throughout the Empire might trigger a crisis in the USBA. Based on the plebiscite returns and other information at your disposal, what do you feel will happen over there when word of emancipation reaches the USBA?"

A shaken Bratton rose rather unsteadily to his feet as all eyes focused on him. *Should I tell them I think this is ludicrous and could trigger a full-scale rebellion by the South? Let the damn planters keep their slaves for now. The bloody institution is bound to die out in the next few generations anyway, as strides in machinery make it obsolete.*

"My Lords, and members of Parliament," he bowed his head to Adams, the only fellow commoner in the room. "I have of course been made privy to this information only within the last hour and haven't thought it all out." He paused briefly. "My initial reaction to this breathtaking proposal is that, yes, the Governor-General is the key. Jackson commands wide support in the West and in the South, despite the fallout from that nullification battle Mr. Adams alluded to previously.

"However, I am not as certain as Mr. Adams of the absoluteness of Jackson's allegiance to the union. In his speech to the Mississippi Legislature last Spring, in which he raised the possibility of the Empire acquiring Texas…"

More than one chuckle was heard and several amused faces turned to the Foreign Secretary, who shook his head with disgust.

"…in that speech, General Jackson was subtly raising an issue that has become of paramount concern among the Southern upper classes: the gradual erosion of their political power in Georgetown. Look again at this map, if you would, gentlemen." He walked over to the easel and picked up the pointer the Colonial Secretary had put down.

Pointing to the southeast corner of the map, he continued: "Here the slave power thrives in a tightly-held area of 10 physically-connected states and two territories, Florida and Arkansas, soon to become states. As the Dominion expands north and west," he pushed the pointer past the center of the map, "we run out of territory where slavery is economically feasible. The weather in the still-to-be organized portions of the Louisiana Territory simply rules out slavery, for the most part. And that's without knowing what crops are most suited for the soil there. As we go further northwest into the vast uncharted lands we call the Canadian West, slavery is completely out-of-the-question.

"Yet these areas will also eventually be organized and will send representatives to Georgetown. Unless the slaveholders can similarly expand, they will become a permanent minority in Georgetown, with or without their current alliance with Quebec. And, they have come to realize that with the abolitionist movement steadily gaining strength in the Northeast and, more slowly, in the West, as a permanent minority, they may not be able to hold on to their 'peculiar institution.'"

Bratton paused again and glanced briefly at the Colonial Secretary, who smiled slightly and nodded for him to continue.

"So Jackson's suggestion that the Empire acquire Texas was not simply interference in foreign policy. It was the opening salvo in the Southerners' drive to expand into areas where slavery makes sense: the lands stretching from Louisiana's current border with Mexican Texas all the way to California." The pointer pushed west from the Gulf of Mexico across to the Pacific. "Lands that can be carved up into new slave states.

"And add Cuba to the equation, which is the reason the Southern newspapers and orators have lately begun decrying Spanish 'oppression' of the native population."

There was complete silence in the room as the Committee members stared at the American Office official in shock and dismay. Silence, that is, until John Quincy Adams, of the Massachusetts' Adamses, broke it with a loud clapping of his hands and a louder "Bravo."

While the other members of the Committee sat stunned as they tried to grasp the full implications of Bratton's analysis, the British American took command of the meeting.

"Gentlemen, I have been aware of General Jackson's intentions even before his Mississippi speech. Unfortunately, due to my well-known personal apathy for the man, as well as my reputation as an abolitionist, to have raised the issues presented with such clarity just now by Mr. Bratton would have been counterproductive.

"Now, having proven himself extremely knowledgeable in the political affairs of the USBA, I would like the young man's opinion on the question originally posed him: what will happen when word of the emancipation bill reaches the USBA?"

Bratton put on a face as grave as that of Adams himself. "I believe the Governor-General and the South will fight any emancipation of their slaves, with compensation or otherwise...to the fullest extent of their abilities and resources."

"Militarily, as well as politically?" Lord Durham probed.

"To the fullest extent, including armed resistance," Bratton reluctantly replied.

Adams, who had been sitting erect, his hands clutching the

conference table tightly, fell back in his chair, a look of victorious satisfaction on his face. "I fully concur."

This time the silence did exceed 60 seconds. In fact, almost two full minutes passed before Lord Melbourne spoke.

"So gentlemen, the dreadful possibility we had previously hoped would be negated by the USBA electorate suddenly must be faced. The tool we will use to eradicate this blot on humanity in other parts of the Empire may not be effective in the USBA. The culture of slavery may be too embedded among too large a portion of the population to simply be bribed out of existence. In the USBA, as we have come to realize, slavery is a political, as well as an economic, issue. Therefore it must be addressed politically as well as economically. Fortunately, we have also planned for this contingency. I suggest we put our plan into operation as soon as possible."

"Is that the consensus of this Committee?" asked Lord Palmerston. "That, as discussed, we send the Duke to Georgetown as soon as the Royal Navy ship which brought us this plebiscite dispatch can be readied for a return run? And that he briefs as soon as he sees fit the current Governor-General to ascertain his acceptance of His Majesty's Government's emancipation plans? With full authority from the King under the terms of the USBA constitution to remove the incumbent if he refuses to enforce said emancipation?"

Bratton's jaw had dropped, but the concept was apparently a contingency fully discussed at previous meetings. Slowly, each Committee member voiced his approval…some more reluctantly than others.

Lord Palmerston began replacing his papers in his pouch. "I will go immediately to see the P.M. Thence, I expect, to Buckingham Palace. Meanwhile, Sir Arthur, I suggest you begin packing for an unpleasant journey. The North Atlantic is bound to be brutal, but we must resolve this crisis before it can escalate into bloodshed. God willing, we are underestimating Andrew Jackson's commitment to the Colonial Compact and all it represents. That will be up to you to ascertain…and to take whatever measures are deemed appropriate."

As the meeting broke up, the Duke motioned the Colonial Secretary and Bratton to the side. "Frederick, I believe it is mandatory that the American Office become mobile. Don't you agree?"

"I certainly do, Sir Arthur. Harry, pack your own luggage. You'll be going back to your old duty station with the Duke of Wellington."

CHAPTER FIVE

Georgetown, D.C.
December 23, 1832:

The Residency had not regained the puritan fastidiousness of the Quincy Adams' tenure after its near demolition by celebrating Westerners the night of Jackson's inauguration. Despite the best efforts of the G-G's niece---his wife Rachel had died soon after the 1828 plebiscite---the old house had neither quite regained the look of the fine Southern mansion that Dolly Madison had rebuilt after a devastating fire early in her husband's second Administration.

No, thought Lieutenant Wilder. *I've been to 'real' Southern mansions; including a huge one in Westminster, Maryland.* He grinned to himself. *The Residency simply doesn't compare.* He looked around the oval room where the formal reception would be held before everyone moved into the main dining room for a buffet-style supper and dancing. *Now this room, at least, offers a great view of the Potomac River and the blue/green Virginia hills of Arlington.* Including, he thought somewhat enviously, the Custis plantation, which Robert Lee stands to inherit, now that he's finally married Mary. *This house, though, reminds me of the Nashville Inn, where I stayed last Spring when General Jackson stopped off at his plantation on the way back from his tour of the Deep South.*

Wilder had arrived at 5 p.m., 90 minutes before the official Governor-General's Christmas reception was to begin. Most of the guests would begin arriving early---*what else is there to do in this miserable excuse for a capitol city*---but some would be fashionably late, in order to make the grand entrance. *It's a toss-up who'll show up later, Lucille Latoure or Candice Samples, but the daughter of the new Russian Counsel-General, Countess Caroline Renkowiitz, is a good bet to upstage them both. Well, we'll see what unfolds. Now its time to play social aide to 'Old Hickory,' though that's an oxymoron if I've ever heard one...*

The official carriages were rolling up to the Main Portico as Wilder hurried into the spacious vestibule dominated by the wide staircase leading to the G-G's private quarters. The guests---the handful of members of Congress and their wives still in Georgetown, members of the Dominion Supreme Court, the diplomatic corps and favored government appointees and special guests, as well as a few senior military officers and their wives---were now pouring into the building, handing off their cloaks to various Negro ushers and drifting into the oval room. Wilder greeted Jacques Jean-Claude, King Louis Philippe's representative, entering with his beautiful wife, Jacqueline, as well as, surprisingly on schedule, towering Count Karl Renkowiitz, the Russian C-G, with daughter Caroline in tow. (Renkowiitz's wife had taken one look at Georgetown when the Count had first arrived and fled immediately back to St. Petersburg.)

"Well, Mr. Wilder. Enjoying yourself yet?" The Lieutenant spun around at the gruff growl of General Scott. The General's dark-haired wife, Maria, seemed doll-like clinging to his arm. Yet Mrs. Scott was no more than an inch shorter than Wilder himself. "Well, Sir, on occasions such as this, if the diplomatic corps leaves without a declaration of war being threatened, I've been told to consider it a successful evening."

"Why, Thomas," drawled Mrs. Scott, like her husband a Virginia native, but unlike the General, the proud possessor of a Southern accent, "surely the Governor-General is fond of all his guests. Why, he told Sarah Polk just last week how much he was looking forward to tonight."

Yes, to it being over, I'm sure, Wilder thought to himself. From the slight smile on General Scott's face, it was obvious his other boss had once again read his mind. *Damn, 'Old Fuss and Feathers' doesn't miss anything.* "Well Mrs. Scott, General Jackson is always more comfortable at these affairs if his niece is around. He's come to rely on her more and more."

The tall, gaunt figure of the G-G was now making his way down the staircase, with the aid of a cane, assisted by a lean, muscular hard-faced man of early middle age. "My dear," gasped Mrs. Scott, clutching the General's arm more tightly, "that can't be who I think it is…can it?"

Even General Scott seemed taken back, though he recovered his aplomb quickly. "I believe you're right, Maria. Unless I'm mistaken, that's the former Governor of Tennessee." Turning to a bewildered Wilder, he asked: "Were you aware Sam Houston was in town? When did he arrive?"

Wilder shook his head slowly. "He's not on the official guest list,

Sir. And when I left here at noon to return to the Department, there was no word or sign of him. Though I would not have known who he was until you identified him."

A more expected guest now made his way out of a circle of Congressmen and their ladies and toward the Scotts. The elegant little figure—no more than 5-foot-5 and 130 pounds, with short dark hair circling his bald head like a wreath--was the newly-chosen Vice Governor-General, Martin Van Buren. A consummate politician, he was famously nicknamed 'The Little Magician.'

"Congratulations and Merry Christmas, Mr. Van Buren," said Scott, reaching out a huge paw that engulfed Van Buren's dainty right hand. Wilder winced in sympathy as a look of real pain shot briefly across 'The Little Magician's' face. *I truly believe the General has no conception of his own strength.*

"Thank you and a Merry Christmas to you and the ever-lovely Mrs. Scott," Van Buren softly---he never spoke much above a whisper---replied, extricating his now-reddened extremity from Scott's powerful grasp. Turning to Wilder, he added: "And to you too, Lieutenant…?"

"Lt. Thomas Wilder is an aide to the Governor-General, as well as at the War Department. He's from your state, as well." General Scott smoothly followed up Van Buren's inferred question. "Tonight, his job is to see that the diplomatic corps finds something in common with the Congress, besides the food and drink. Isn't that so, Lieutenant?"

Wilder had worked under Scott long enough to know an order, even when it was not enunciated. With a smile, he made his excuses to the powerful and backed away. In doing so, he backed directly into David Harper, who managed to keep his glass of champagne from spilling onto Wilder's formal uniform. "Well, Thomas, mingling with the powers-that-be. Looking to change the shape of your insignia?"

"Hello Harps. No, I was simply doing my job, working to keep this wonderful assemblage happy, when I ran into the General and his wife. The new Vice G-G came over to say hello to the Scotts, so I made my retreat. Right into you. Enjoying yourself?"

"I'd enjoy it a lot more if you could introduce me to that cute little blonde over there. Though I suppose she's the property of the Count, if that's the Russian C-G, as I think it is."

"That's his daughter, David, not his mistress." Wilder was dry. "How should I introduce you? As the incoming Secretary of the

Interior?"

"A 'high Interior Department official' will do. I'll take it from there."

Wilder snorted but was saved from immediate international matchmaking by a signal from General Scott. "You're on your own. The General beckons. Maybe later, during the dancing. Just don't cause a diplomatic incident, okay? I've got enough problems this week."

The General was now standing apart from the crowd, near the window overlooking the Potomac. His wife had disappeared, while the new Vice G-G was now gingerly shaking his swollen hand with the just-arrived Chief Justice of the Dominion Court, the elderly John Marshall. Wilder made his apologies as he moved through the throng surrounding the G-G and his special guest and approached Scott.

"I've given your thesis more thought, Lieutenant. And I double-checked: only a pouch, not a passenger, went aboard the *Irresistible* before she sailed. So it is information they want in London and the plebiscite results are the only information of importance to have originated here in some time. Your thesis is as close to a rational reason as any I can come up with. When the government reopens on December 26th, I want you to determine when that ship will dock in England. Also, how long it would take to resupply and get back to Baltimore. We may be anticipating the news she'll be carrying...or we could be dead wrong. In either case, let's determine the timeframe for when we might expect to hear something.

"Also, use your Residency position to find out why Houston is here. The last time I heard about him, he was communing with the Cherokee." *I have my suspicions*, thought Scott, *and I hope to the Almighty I'm wrong about them.* "Now then, where did Mrs. Scott get off to?"

"Yes, Sir," said Wilder in a low tone that fell off even further as he glanced past Scott to the other side of the now emptying oval room. Led by the G-G, with Mrs. Polk on his arm, the guests were filing into the main dining room. That gave Wilder a full view of Lucille Latoure as she strolled into the mansion on the arm of Lt. Joseph Johnston. At virtually the same time, Mrs. Scott called from across the room. Standing with her, décolletage most prominently in view, was Maria's good friend, Candice Samples.

Dead heat, thought Tom.

"Come, Lieutenant, let's join the ladies, shall we?" General Scott, trying unsuccessfully to keep the amusement from his voice. "Unless you'd rather say Merry Christmas to ol' Joe Johnston over there instead?" Scott was having trouble keeping his huge shoulders from shaking with laughter.

Jaysus, Mary and Joseph, does he know about this, too? "Yes sir, let's join the ladies. I believe the lady with Mrs. Scott was at your dinner party last summer, was she not?" *Two can play this game, General...*

The General look down at his aide with merriment in his eyes. "Yes, Mr. Wilder. I believe she arrived---and left---in her carriage."

Candice Samples had glimpsed the Lieutenant while his back was turned, talking with General Scott. *I'll have him under my Christmas tree,* she thought. *Either here or at Twin Peaks.* The Samples plantation in Westminster, Md., was set in rolling countryside that afforded views of the Blue Ridge to the west and the flat Pennsylvania countryside to the north. From either of its two hills, the Potomac was visible on a clear day. Mrs. Samples' late husband, Charles, had led the 3rd Maryland Infantry under Jackson in the Lower Louisiana Territory campaign and came home to marry a teen-aged Candice in 1810.

After a career as a planter and Maryland legislator, including one term as the state's governor, he had vigorously supported his old commander during Jackson's first, unsuccessful, try for the Governor-Generalship in '24. That was the campaign in which the hypocritical---in Candice's view---Henry Clay---a Southern gentleman who owned slaves himself but yet favored abolition!---had thrown his support to the insufferable---in Candice's view---John Quincy Adams. *That unspeakable pretentious Puritan!* Candice's husband was chosen by Jackson four years later to be his Secretary of War. But Charles, an indefatigable fox hunter, had fallen from his horse during a hunt soon after the campaign. He was dead by the time the other members of the hunting party had gotten him back to Twin Peaks, leaving Candice a very wealthy widow.

And a merry one. Colonel Samples had been 38 when he married the 18-year old Candice and thus had been 56 at his death. He had been more interested in hunting and politics than the bedroom, or, perhaps, Candice had simply exhausted him. At any rate, he had looked the other way while she engaged in a series of discreet encounters during the second decade of their marriage, including influential members of the government and, briefly, a Liaison Office official.

Although Candice could and did have her pick of the eligible bachelors her own age in and around the District, Lieutenant Wilder had caught her eye the previous summer at a party at the Scotts. His flashing blue eyes, blond hair and quick wit had aroused her interest, as had the promise a of hard young Army body under the blue-grey summer uniform. She had offered a ride home, upon hearing him tell another guest that he had walked from his hotel. They had barely made it back to her townhouse…for her driver knew without being told where to go…with their clothes intact. Once indoors, that had immediately changed. *Thomas may have graduated from West Point, but his real education began that night,* she thought now with satisfaction and excitement as the Lieutenant accompanied his boss across the room.

Maria Scot knew the look in her friend's eye and feigned shock. "Candice, you're not…still…?" She giggled softly. "He's just a boy…the General thinks he has promise…"

"Winfield isn't the only one who feels that way, Maria. Then, the General has his hopes and uses for Thomas…and I have mine.

"Merry Christmas, Winfield. And you, too, Lieutenant."

The General, beaming broadly at the two ladies, took Candice's hand and kissed it softly. "Merry Christmas to you, Candice. You remember my aide, Lieutenant Wilder?"

Turning to Thomas, who hoped his cheeks were not as red as he feared, Scott was equally sarcastically formal. "Mrs. Candice Samples. You may recall Mrs. Samples from Mrs. Scott's dinner party last summer…"

"Certainly I do, General. It's good to see you again Cand…Mrs. Samples. And Merry Christmas." Thomas wondered how long this charade might go on.

Scott, however, had other ideas. Turning to his wife, he said: "Maria, I don't want the G-G to think we're boycotting his party. And there are some people here tonight that I've yet to greet. Lieutenant, if you'll escort Mrs. Samples in, before you get back to your other duties assisting General Jackson…"

Candice took the Lieutenant's arm as they crossed into the main room, where the guests were helping themselves to the lavish buffet set up along one long wall. Wilder could see the G-G now talking with an elderly man dressed in the antiquated eighteenth century style, with Houston and the Polks close by. He could also see Lucille Latoure making her way around the room on the arm of his West Point classmate, that damn Joe Johnston.

"We haven't seen enough of each other this fall, Thomas. It's my fault, as I've been staying home at Twin Peaks too much of the time."

I can see plenty of you now, Thomas thought. *I swear, those things look bigger every time I see them.* "Candice, as the General says, duty calls. I'll deposit you with the Scotts. When the party's over, however, I'm free 'till day after Christmas..."

"Not any more you're not. We can decide tomorrow whether to stay here in Georgetown or go back to Twin Peaks. I'll make my rounds. I do want to wish Andy a Merry Christmas; he does look poorly.

"But we'll leave together. I have my carriage..."

M. Jean-Claude, or, rather, his beautiful wife, Jacqueline, was at the center of an international circle that included Sir John Burrell of the Liaison Office and the Russian CG. Count Renkowiitz's daughter was not in sight. "I am so glad you gentlemen have agreed to put politics aside and come to our townhouse for Christmas," she was saying in a sonorous, upper-class French. "Even in frontier outposts, we must try to bring some culture and civilization. Though in this place..."

Wilder bit his lip to keep from smiling as he walked past the diplomats on his way to General Jackson. *You'd be amazed, my dear Jacqueline, to discover how many British Americans would agree with you...*

The G-G was still talking to the tall, sloop-shouldered old man outfitted in the style at least 20 years out-of-date. At first glance, the ancient looked like someone dressed up to impersonate George Washington. But then Thomas overheard Congressman Polk's comment to the man identified by the Scotts as Sam Houston.

"Those old Virginians stuck together politically of course. That's why they ruled us for more than a quarter century," Polk was saying. "That doesn't mean they particularly liked each other, however. Take Monroe, here. Madison told me last year that Washington detested him personally. And that the feeling was mutual. Now look at him. He's Washington's spitting image!"

Thus did Wilder discover that the old man was former Governor-General James Monroe.

THE DOMINION'S DILEMMA: THE UNITED STATES OF BRITISH AMERICA

Wilder always thought of Jackson as a volcano minutes away from eruption.

Tonight, Vesuvius seems calm. With enough Tennesseans around him, he usually is. Between the Polks and this man Houston---must find out why General Scott's eyes and ears pricked up at the recognition of him---the G-G's a good bet to weather the reception without adding any fodder for the various diplomatic pouches. Unless he signals me, I'll let him be.

Trying to keep from making eye contact with Lucille, who was now dazzling "The Little Magician" with her singular smile while holding tightly to that SOB Joe's arm, the Lieutenant was suddenly and uncomfortably aware that he hadn't seen Harps in sometime. Nor was the Russian girl visible in the milling groups that continued to eat, drink and dance as if Lent, rather than Christmas, was just hours away. Not that many of the British Americans assembled in The Residency tonight were Catholic...*though Lucille is or was one*...but Wilder was still surprised at how many of the ancient traditions of his religion were still practiced in varying forms by the numerous Protestant sects which dominated the USBA.

Harper and the Renkowiitz girl had apparently made contact after all. Thomas could now see them on the dance floor over by the bar in the far corner of the room. *I guess the girl is fluent in English, because I know Harps doesn't know any Russian*, he thought, grinning. *I do recall him bragging that he knew enough French, though, "to make things exciting."* Things *could* get exciting, damn it all, if Harps holds her any tighter and the Count sees them. *I'd better get over there...before a squad of Cossacks shows up to drag him away.*

But the music was ending and Harper was reluctantly unhanding the Countess while the Lieutenant made his way across the room. If Maria Scott looked doll-like next to her imposing husband, Caroline Renkowiitz looked doll-like next to any man. Even with her bright blond hair made up and in a formal gown and jewels---*how wealthy is the Count?* Thomas thought curiously---the girl was so slender as to have virtually no curves at all. *Yet David has the look of a man who has struck gold...*

"Well, Lieutenant Wilder, have you met the Countess Caroline Renkowiitz yet? Countess, the Lieutenant is the real brains of the War Department—when he's not on duty here advising our

59

Governor-General."

Wilder shook his head in disgust. "Don't believe anything this 'gentleman' tells you, Countess. I'm just an errand boy for the two Generals."

The Countess smiled but it was another young---American---female voice that answered him.

"Now Lieutenant, don't mislead our visitor. We don't want the diplomatic corps to think General Jackson invites just any old poor white trash to The Residency, now do we?"

Thomas didn't need to turn around to know Lucille had joined the group, Joe Johnston firmly in tow. A grinning Joe, impeccable in his finely-cut uniform, stuck out his hand. "Merry Christmas, Tom. You remember Lucille Latoure, don't you?" In a low cut gown that matched her auburn hair, Lucille looked the most desirable...and frustrating...woman on earth to the War Department aide.

Tom gritted his teeth. "Of course I do, Joe. Good evening, Lucille. A pleasure to see you again. It's been a while, since..."

"Why since the Lee baby's Baptism, I believe. Darlin' little Custis. Lieutenant Johnston was at Arlington House that day, too. But enough of that! Forgive Tom's manners, for not introducing us," she said brightly, turning to Caroline. "I'm Lucille Latoure of Cranford Plantation and this is Lt. Joe Johnston of the 4th Artillery. You must be Countess Caroline, of the Russian Consulate. And, Joe, this is Mr. Harper, of the...what Department was that again?"

"Interior," said Thomas grimly. "David is a high Interior Department official," he added, looking at the Countess.

"Glad to meet you, Lieutenant," said Harps, warily reaching out his hand to Johnston, who shook it enthusiastically.

"The pleasure is mine, Mr. Harper. I believe I've seen you in the building the few times I've been there." Johnston was stationed at the 4th's headquarters just outside Georgetown. "It is also a pleasure to meet you, Countess Caroline."

That the Countess could follow the banter is impressive enough, thought Thomas, *but she actually seems to have picked up on the undercurrents. There may be more here than it first looks. Ol' Harps may have his hands full...*

"Well, Thomas, will we see you tomorrow evening at Arlington House? Robert is due home in the afternoon and Mary has invited us for a late Christmas Eve supper." Lucille smiled sweetly and innocently.

That does it, thought Thomas. *Candice Samples it is for the holiday. I'm not going to ruin my Christmas watching Lucille prance around with my 'old friend' Joe.*

"Unfortunately not, Lucille, though I was looking forward to it. General Scott has other plans for me." *Well, 'Old Fuss and Feathers' did push Candice on me tonight.* "I hope to see Robert before he goes back to Fortress Monroe, though."

"Oh my, that's too bad, Tom. I was so looking forward to us all being together."

Yeah, right, Wilder thought. *The two-and-one-half happy couples. You know something, Lucille? I was born at night. Only, not last night....*

"Well, I'd love to spend the remainder of the evening with the four of you, but duty once again calls. Have a Merry Christmas, everyone." He stared quickly at Lucille and moved back into the crowd. Her usual amused smirk was back in place.

Candice Samples had a smirk of a different sort on her face as she watched her prey work the room in what she considered his 'official' capacity. Secure in her own sexual allure, she was unaware of Thomas' infatuation with and frustration over the Latoure girl; who, anyway, seemed quite content with her own Lieutenant. *I'll bet yours gets more sleep than mine will tonight, sweetie...In fact, your Lieutenant will get more sleep tonight than Thomas will get right through Christmas...*

I wish I could order up my carriage right now....

CHAPTER SIX

St. Petersburg, Russia
December 23, 1832:

Nicholas I, Czar of All the Russias, looked out the window of the opulent Winter Palace conference room. Last night's snow was blindingly bright as the sun's rays bounced off to light up the huge square in front of the Palace. The onion turrents of the nearby churches and cathedrals also shone brilliantly in the clear, cold morning's light. *I wonder what the long-dead Czar Peter would say if he could see how his city has grown*, he thought idly: the wide, splendid boulevards, the mansions, the museums.

I believe I do know what he'd say: 'Now build an empire to match its capital!' Well, that's what we are sworn to do. Day by day, year by year until Mother Russia is invincible and unchallengeable! The decisions made at this conference, once carried out, are simply more small steps down the road toward that inevitable day.

Nicholas was still deep in thought as his Foreign Minister, Count Karl Nesselrode, hurried into the room, carrying the agenda for the third and final day of the planning conference. Like the high-level meeting scheduled for early next month in London, this conference had been months in the planning. Unlike the London meeting, this conference was an annual affair.

"Well my dear Count, what is left on the agenda? I am tired of conferences. I don't wish to spend a third full day in this room." Already such major issues as the proposed meetings with the Emperor Francis II of Austria and his First Minister Prince Metternich in April at Munschengratz and with the Prussians later in the year at Berlin to formalize the three-nation autocratic alliance against the democratic monarchies of the West had been reviewed. Plans to end the irritating insurgency by the bandit Shamil in the Caucasus had been finalized. What new concessions could be squeezed out of the Persians to follow up on the recent annexation of that kingdom's former provinces of Nakhickevan and Erivan had also been discussed during the previous two days.

"Majesty, the major agenda item is the request by the Sultan for assistance against the forces of Pasha Mehemet Ali in Palestine. The Egyptians are moving on Syria and Constantinople seems helpless to stop them. This is a golden opportunity. Especially as none of the other Powers can object, as the Turks have actually invited us in."

"Yes, the Sultan's request is a wonderful Christmas gift. We'll discuss this 'golden opportunity' with my other ministers. Is that all that remains?"

"No, Your Majesty. Prince Lieven has received a letter from the Princess in London. He has urged that the information it offers be added to the agenda."

The Czar smiled slightly. "If it was not from Princess Dorothea, I would not consider it. But as my late brother often said, 'It is a pity the Princess wears skirts. She would have made an excellent diplomat.' " Czar Alexander I had in fact entrusted the Princess with a secret overture to the British government in 1825 that bypassed her husband, the longtime Czarist ambassador to the Court of St. James. Since that time, she had played astonishing diplomatic roles in the rebirth of Greece and the creation of Belgium.

"Well, if the Princess has some information for us, perhaps we will consider it. Has Prince Lieven discussed it with you?"

"Princess Dorothea has learned that the British may be considering the abolition of slavery throughout their Empire."

The Czar smiled. "I fail to see how such a possible edict belongs on the agenda of this conference, Count Karl. Unless you are implying that I should follow their apparent example…"

"Surely not, Your Majesty. It appears Lord Grey's government is concerned about possible reaction in the British American province. Count Nicholas Ignatieff has also picked up similar rumblings from his English sources." Ignatieff, a childhood friend of the Czar's, was a chief in Russia's informal secret intelligence services. A broad-shouldered yet wiry, strikingly handsome black-haired man in his mid 30s, he was renowned for the half blue/half brown coloring of his right eye, a trait that went back several generations in his family. It was one he had also passed on to his newly-born son.

"Well, since Count Nicholas will undoubtedly bring it up anyway, put it on the agenda." The Czar sighed. "But the Ottoman opportunity has priority. Obtaining a warm weather port is vital to Russia's long-term goals. The Persian war gave us naval access to the

THE DOMINION'S DILEMMA: THE UNITED STATES OF BRITISH AMERICA

Caspian Sea. Perhaps this Egyptian uprising against the Ottomans will give us access through the Bosporus Straits!"

At the Czar's signal, the veteran Foreign Minister—he had been in office since 1814—moved to admit the other ministers and high-ranking generals to the room.

———————————

Count Nicholas Ignatieff knew what his department's role in response to the Sultan's request would be. Even before Russian troops were landed in Syria to block the Egyptian advance on the Anatolian Peninsula, his agents would be on the ground, both in Syria and in Palestine. This in addition to the agents he normally maintained in and around Constantinople.

That he would do so before a decision was finalized was indicative of the man: headstrong, confident to the point---some would argue far past that point---of arrogance...and deadly. The Count was a crack shot with both pistol and rifle and excelled with the saber; he had ended duels with at least two unfortunate Russian noblemen with well-aimed pistol shots and another with an overmatched Polish noble with the saber. All three, of course, had been over women; two wives and one sister. How many others he had terminated in the line of duty was debated within the Russian secret services; most observers credited him with seven-to-eight 'official' killings over the past decade.

The intelligence coming from London had Ignatieff concerned...as well as fascinated. For that reason, he was only half listening as the Czar and his advisors agreed to land 10,000 troops---sent through the Bosporus, for the first time ever to be opened to the Russian Navy---on the Syrian coast. The force would move inland to confront the Egyptian army under Ibrahim Pasha and force him, preferably without a battle, to retreat to Egypt.

That the Turks were so weak that they needed assistance to put down the revolt did not surprise Ignatieff. The Count was well aware of Constantinople's helplessness. He and the Czar had thoroughly discussed the possibility of an invasion, but had reluctantly discarded the idea. The other Powers would simply not sit still while Russia got its paws on Constantinople and the Straits. *But that the Sultan would actually request us to intervene militarily is almost too amazing. Meanwhile, I already have my Ottoman operation in motion.*

He was still turning the news from London, both Princess Dorothea's letter and his own intelligence reports, over in his head. The long-range goal of Romanov foreign policy had always been to supersede the British in India. A later Russian autocrat, Lenin, would call India the 'depot of the world.' It was one of the few times the two Nicholases, Czar and Count, would have agreed with him. The British had pushed aside the Portuguese and Dutch and were merrily looting the subcontinent. With the riches of India flowing to St. Petersburg instead of London, Russia would supplant Great Britain as the world's foremost Power.

But how to accomplish such a gigantic feat?

Even by the most optimistic estimates, it will take our forces another 10-to-15 years to arrive at India's borders utilizing the overland route through Central Asia. Waging the successful Persian War in 1827 and annexing those two provinces was a start, but all those khanates in the wild Central Asian plain still block the way, even before the specter of Afghanistan can be confronted. But what if the British were to be distracted elsewhere? Perhaps by a rebellion in North America? A rebellion that Lord Grey's government in London apparently considers more than a remote possibility?

If the British were tied up in a long-term war in North America, would they have the strength to resist a Russian Army sent through Persia, bypassing the khanates and Afghanistan? Surely the Persian War has shown that Teheran can not stop such an Army. Perhaps the Shah could be bribed into allowing our forces free transit, especially if we agreed to look the other way while he moved into the Valley of the Euphrates toward Baghdad. The dream in Teheran, after all, is to reassemble the ancient Persian Empire. Why not allow them mastery of all that sand and dust?

This must be brought to His Majesty's attention immediately...

The Count's musings were suddenly interrupted by a savage pounding that literally rocked the conference table. The red-faced Czar had risen from his seat and was barely able to choke back his anger as he glared at Prince Alexander Chernyshyov.

"Don't ever again suggest, even in jest, that I consider selling or trading off so much as a square inch of the realm," he said, slowly and icily.

"My Alaska province is our foothold in North America. We have already begun to expand down the eastern Pacific Coast. Our settlement of Fort Ross has put both the British and Mexicans on notice: I will not acknowledge any God-given right of the British to hold North America. And the Mexicans must realize that they can not stop us from advancing further into their California province! We expand, not retreat! Is that perfectly clear? I will require a plan from you within 30 days as to how we can build up our North American presence. Never again let me hear any of you speak of relinquishing Russian territory…"

The shaken War Minister was vigorously shaking his head in agreement. Apparently, Ignatieff realized, the Prince had suggested that the seemingly-worthless Alaskan tundra---just an extension of Siberia, in Ignatieff's view---be sold or otherwise offered to the British in exchange for a hands-off policy as things developed in the Turkish adventure.

"…Well gentlemen, if my policy is now completely clear to each of you, is there anything left on the agenda?"

Count Nesselrode, anxious to change the subject, brought up the Princess Lieven's news from London.

Turning to his ambassador, the Czar said: "Yes Prince Khristofor, as I understand it, your lovely wife is reporting some interesting developments within the British Empire. Expand on the news, please."

"Your Majesty, my wife has written me that Lord Grey's government has secretly continued with the plans first apparently discussed under the previous Tory government to abolish slavery throughout the British Empire."

"At what level of the British government did this secret emerge, my dear Prince?" asked the Czar. "How common is the knowledge of this proposed action?"

"My wife informs me that it comes from the very highest levels of the government and is a tightly-held secret, or was when she dispatched her letter."

"Begging Your Majesty's pardon," broke in Count Sergey Uvarov. Officially the newly-appointed Education Minister, Count Uvarov was one of the pillars of Nicholas' reactionary regime. As such, he was one of the very few who could successfully survive interrupting an Imperial conversation. "I fail to see how this, err, rumor meets the criteria as a discussion point on today's agenda."

"I'm not certain either, Sergey. But I am certain the Prince…and others…will explain. Proceed, Prince Lieven."

"Yes, Majesty. The British, you may be vaguely aware, abolished the African slave trade over 25 years ago. However, slavery has continued to flourish in substantial portions of their Empire, notably, the West Indies and the Southern portion of British America. The plan seems to be one of financial compensation to the slaveholders, paid out over a period of years."

"To reiterate Count Uvarov's question, why would this be of interest to Russia?" asked the Czar, a strange smile on his face.

The Foreign Minister broke in. "If I may, your Majesty. I believe Count Ignatieff has an interesting explanation."

"Well Nicholas. You've been quiet all morning. Have you been considering this issue, too?"

"Yes, Your Majesty, I have." Ignatieff leaned forward in his chair. "I, too, have received information from London, though not from the level at which the Princess so ably operates." He nodded formally to Prince Lieven, though the malice was evident in his eyes.

The Prince flushed at the obvious implication of Ignatieff's remark. Though formerly a general who had fought successfully against Napoleon, he was now 57 years old and soft from years of diplomatic work. He would be no match for the younger, stronger and steadier Count in a duel. *But I will find a way to strike back, Ignatieff. You are not as invulnerable as you think, you malicious bastard.*

"My information confirms," Ignatieff was saying, "that a proposal to abolish slavery will be presented to their Parliament this spring. The concern seems to center on the reaction in British America." The Count then proceeded with a briefing that, while not as detailed or as lucid as the one Bratton was to give in London two weeks later, nonetheless educated the Russian leadership to the potential explosiveness of the abolition issue.

"So, it appears the Lion may be in for some internal strife," said the Czar, the smile playing at his lips, at the conclusion of Ignatieff's report. "I don't suppose you have any thoughts on what our position should be if this most unfortunate strife should come to pass?"

"Your Majesty, I have given this matter serious consideration. I have some ideas on how advantage can be taken, if and when the situation ignites."

Before a hard-faced group whose glares gradually softened as the potential for Imperial gains became more enticing, Count Ignatieff painted a picture of Russian advancement to the very gates of India.

"Now all of this, of course, is mere daydreaming if the potential crisis is settled peacefully. But there may be an opportunity here, if British America erupts in violence. If we can edge that crisis toward violence, I consider it our holy duty to do so."

"'Holy' duty, I question, Nicholas," said the Czar, smiling now broadly. "'Imperial duty,' definitely. How do you suggest my government should proceed?"

"Your Majesty, I propose that I travel to London at once, in order to ascertain on the spot if abolition will be ordered; and how the Grey government thinks the issue will be received in British America. If abolition has been submitted to Parliament, and if the government is still worried about the reaction, I shall then proceed to British America, to make contact with any leaders of a rebellion, or potential one. In order to offer them your Majesty's friendship and assistance, financially and perhaps otherwise."

The Czar of All the Russias was on his feet. "Count Ignatieff, you are ordered to proceed to London immediately, there to determine what course of action is in the best interests of my country. You will work closely with Princess Lieven, of course, as well as with the Prince, once he returns to England."

Ignatieff nodded with satisfaction at the Czar's order. *Yes, I've always had a craving to 'work closely' with the Princess...*

"Gentlemen," said the Czar with evident relief and a hint of warning, "unless there is further comment or other issues left to be discussed, I declare this conference closed."

CHAPTER SEVEN

London, England
January 18, 1833:

It had taken the better part of two weeks of hard-driving, winter travel but Ignatieff had arrived in London two nights ago. He had spent yesterday and most of today in discussions with his own agents, reviewing reports, mostly fragmentary, from their sources within the British government. Information sometimes purchased; sometimes obtained by blackmail or the threat of force. The conclusion: the emancipation bill would be introduced into Parliament shortly; certainly before Easter.

Ignatieff was a hard man and was hardly ever taken back, but the cost staggered him: the British were willing to spend up to 50-million pounds sterling over seven years to underwrite the plan. *For that price, we could bribe every khan in Central Asia into selling us his kingdom! We could be overlooking India from the Afghan passes in two years...*

More importantly, he had also ascertained that the Grey government sensed possible trouble in the British American South as a result of the bill, which apparently would face no great opposition in Parliament. What the government planned to do to alleviate such trouble was more difficult to pin down, but a high-level meeting had been held earlier in the month, apparently concerning British American reaction to the emancipation issue. His agents were still unclear as to what decisions, if any, had been made; in fact, they were still attempting to find out exactly who had attended.

Ignatieff hated to proceed into any meeting without holding the upper intelligence hand. Physical toughness, skill with weaponry and cold bloodedness: he prided himself on possessing all three. So, however, did many others, including those he had, literally, stepped on and over during his rise in the secret intelligence apparatus. It was the ability to obtain and marshal information that set him apart, as well as the will to ruthlessly act on the conclusions the intelligence suggested. That's what troubled him about tonight's private dinner meeting with the Princess Lieven: *does she know more than my sources can tell me about what happened at that high level meeting? And what actions, if any, emanated from it?*

Still a breathtaking beauty, though in her late 40s, Princess Dorothea had utilized her position as wife of the longtime Russian ambassador to become a leader of London society. She had, in turn, utilized her society position to gather political information that established her as a political and diplomatic force in her own right.

Ignatieff had met the Princess during previous visits to London, but had never shared more than a few meaningless words with her. Now he was on fire to be alone with the legendary Dorothea, but unexpectedly unsure as to how to proceed, at least on a professional plane. (On the personal level, the Count was quite sure of himself. Thoroughly misogynistic to an extent astounding even for a Russian nobleman, he had no doubt that the evening would end in her bedroom. He considered the Princess to be little more sexually exclusive than the servant girl he had ravaged the preceding night.) Never before had he scheduled a meeting with a female on a professional level. And a meeting at which, remarkably, she might have the upper hand when it came to information.

———

Somewhere in the MidAtlantic Ocean
January 18, 1833:

HMS *Irresistible* had fought its way through a second blizzard and had emerged into bright, if freezing, morning sunshine when Harry Bratton cautiously made his way out of his cabin and onto the main deck. *There is a reason Brattons have always avoided the Senior Service: we can get bloody well seasick in the middle of a pond.*

The Captain---the Duke of Wellington had informed Harry upon sailing that he was back on full pay for the duration of this crisis--- had begun suffering before England was out of eyesight. He had remained seasick through most of the nine days they had been at sea. The Duke, whose previous long-distance seagoing had been limited to an Indiaman's lumbering three-month voyages to and from the subcontinent, hugging the European, African and Asian coastlines, had also been seasick, though more sporadically. *Captain Sir Stephen Richards, on the other hand, must have a cast iron stomach,* Bratton thought.

The fellow acts like this hellish punishment—up-and-down, back-and-forth, winds howling and snow coming down interminably—is a bloody Sunday afternoon pleasure cruise down the Thames. Well, Sir Stephen estimates 13 more days till we see Baltimore harbor. Dear God, give us a few days of calm weather...

"Well Captain, you look like you may, perhaps, survive. I've had my doubts..." The Duke was also up-and-about, his distinctive hook nose eagerly breathing in the rich sea air. "If you feel up to it, I wish to go over certain points I am somewhat unclear on." Captain Bratton shook his head affirmatively, if gingerly. "Certainly, Your Grace. Perhaps if we go below so I can refer to my notes..."

"Unnecessary, Captain. Just brief me on the backgrounds of these gentlemen we'll be meeting in Georgetown. You know them, or of them, eh?"

Bratton nodded again. "Yes Your Grace. I am familiar with almost all the British American leaders, by reputation if not personally."

"Good. Now then: Jackson, of course, I am familiar with. Stubborn, high strung. What the Americans call Scotch-Irish. Which, in my private opinion, is about the worst epitaph any man could be labeled, but nonetheless... Jackson is a fighter; when he forms an opinion, he won't change it, no matter what evidence to the contrary. There'll be one question when I meet with the General: which is greater, his allegiance to the Colonial Compact or his allegiance to the institution of slavery? If it is the former, our task in British America, though still crucial, will be easier. If it is the latter, well, in that case our problems have just begun...

"Now, what do you know about this man Van Buren, with whom I may have to replace Jackson?"

Bratton was still amazed at the casualness with which the Duke and the Committee members referred to the most controversial---though never as yet utilized---defined power of the Colonial Compact. He paused to gather his thoughts before beginning:

"Martin Van Buren is a master of the American political craft; in fact, his nickname is 'The Little Magician' for the ease by which he gets things done. Van Buren is from New York State and became involved in that state's political affairs after joining a prestigious New York City law firm right after the turn of the century. He rose through the state legislature and was elected to the USBA Senate about 12 or 13 years ago. By the '28 plebiscite, he was a key Jackson supporter and manager and is credited with winning the vote for Jackson by brilliant organization of what the Americans call the 'grassroots,' meaning the local level. He himself was elected governor of New York that year and resigned from the Senate. After Jackson's inauguration, he was appointed Secretary of the Interior, the most influential department in the Cabinet. When Jackson broke with his Vice Governor-General, a man named Calhoun, over the question of 'nullification,' that is, a state's right to nullify a Dominion law, Van Buren was the obvious candidate to succeed Calhoun."

"Sounds altogether a slippery eel," the Duke observed with obvious distaste. "We've too many of his sort in Parliament."

"Well, Sir, the 'Little Magician' does seem to always pick the winning side, though I believe he has a bit to do with making it the winner. However, there is something else you should know that may or may not come in handy: Van Buren is rumored to be the illegitimate son of one Aaron Burr. Does that name ring a bell with Your Grace?"

The Duke frowned. "No, I'm not sure it does. Now why should it?"

"Well, Sir, Aaron Burr was once Vice G-G himself. He served under Jefferson. Late in his term, I believe in '04, the Vice G-G became engaged in an affair of honor with Alexander Hamilton..."

"Yes, that's why the name registered, if vaguely. Hamilton was a sort of financial genius who served under Franklin and Washington, I believe."

"Yes Sir. Hamilton is credited with devising the USBA financial system. A brilliant financier but a truly terrible politician. His fight with Mr. Quincy Adams' father, the third G-G, allowed the Jefferson-Burr ticket to win the 1800 plebiscite. In any case, Burr killed Hamilton in a duel, after which Jefferson dropped Burr. Burr had also somehow allowed his own political base in New York to erode during his term as Vice G-G.

"So he went west, presumably to start over again as a representative from Kentucky or Tennessee. Jefferson, however, had him arrested on treason charges. Claimed he was attempting to set up his own country in the West. This, at the time the battle over the Louisiana Territory with the French was heating up. Burr was eventually acquitted in a trial, but his political career was ruined."

"An interesting story, Captain, but of what relevance to our mission?"

"Well Sir, Burr is still alive, practicing law in New York City, at last report..."

"So?"

"Sir Arthur, though Burr was the only one brought to trial, there were charges at the time that a certain militia general in Tennessee was his chief supporter. One Andrew Jackson..."

Wellington shot the Captain a look of impressed surprise.

"Also, Sir, among Burr's defense lawyers was a young man named Henry Clay..."

"Captain, you will ascertain the whereabouts of this Mr. Burr as soon as we land. I see where he might be useful...

"Now, what do you know about this Calhoun chap? He sounds like a real fire-eater...but wait till we go below. It's nearing noon. I've my appetite back. How about you? You appear to have lost at least a stone..."

Thus did the trip pass for Captain Bratton, alternating between discussions with the Duke and bouts of paralyzing sea sickness.

Cranford Plantation, Virginia
January 18, 1833:

If there is anything a woman, especially a proud beauty like Lucille Latoure, can not stand, it is to be ignored. Which is precisely what Lieutenant Wilder, by accident of circumstance more than by design--for he did not have a good enough understanding of the female psyche to have hatched so effective a strategy---had managed. His ignoring of Miss Latoure was not studied, but a combination of overwork and ignorance.

Lucille had been surprised when the Lieutenant, at the conclusion of the G-G's Christmas reception, had simply strode by as she and Joe said their good nights to the Scotts atop the Main Portico. Thomas saluted the General and continued purposefully down the steps toward a waiting carriage. The Scotts had exchanged strange mirthful looks but had not commented as the carriage rolled away the moment Thomas disappeared inside.

A colored Residency usher had meanwhile hurried outside and spoken to the head doorman. "The Governor-General is too late, I'm afraid," the doorman replied, pointing to the departing carriage. "I believe Mrs. Samples' carriage has already left."

The exchange, overheard by all on the Portico, including Lucille, Joe and the Scotts, had rendered her speechless and mortified. A mortification that was not alleviated---quite the contrary---by words the General spoke to her in a quiet voice only she and Mrs. Scott could hear while Joe went down the steps to see about their own carriage. "Miss Latoure, we have an old saying in the Army: 'The battle is most often won by he who gets there firstest with the mostest.' I commend that adege to you... Now, I see our carriage has finally appeared. Good night, my dear."

Lucille's mortification had deepened the following evening when Lieutenant Johnston escorted her to Arlington House. There she discovered that Thomas, true to his word, would not be joining them. He had already come and gone.

"Poor Tom looks exhausted," Mary Lee said, accepting a glass of Madeira from a house servant. "He could only stay an hour. Said he had to get right back to Georgetown. The poor dear, working so hard, even on Christmas Eve! And he said he won't be able to leave Georgetown to come to Christmas dinner tomorrow, either. Trying to serve two masters like General Scott and the Governor-General is wearing him out."

Joe nearly spit his mouthful of Port across the room. Even the 'Marble Monument,' as Robert Lee had been nicknamed by his classmates, allowed himself a somewhat embarrassed smile.

"Yes, my dear, Thomas did mention that General Scott has had him searching for some information which may or may not exist. Perhaps all that research is the culprit." He flashed a warning glance at his old friend Joe, who looked ready to keel over in laughter.

"Yes," said Joe. "That must be it. It's all that nighttime research he's been doing."

Lucille's mortification turned to outrage. How dare he! And with that...that...over-aged floozy!

Lucille Latoure was used to having her cake...and eating it, too. In this case, she had wanted Tom to come to the Custis mansion at Arlington for Christmas Eve, even though she had also invited Joe. But Lieutenant Johnston was to be away on official duty and thus unavailable for the New Year's Eve ball she and her younger sister,

Jaine, were planning for Cranford Plantation. All the leaders of Northern Virginia society, including the Lees, were coming. Lucille had expected Thomas dutifully---and gratefully---to be her escort.

She had not gotten around to so informing Tom of his good fortune until the afternoon of December 28th, however, when she dispatched a servant to Georgetown. The servant, Sebastian, freed momentarily from direction, had dallied on the way and had not arrived at the Latoure townhouse until after dark, too late to deliver Lucille's note that evening. The next morning, he had been unable to locate Lieutenant Wilder at either the War Department or The Residency. General Scott's secretary had sent back a private note informing Lucille that the Lieutenant had left on leave that noon and would not return until after the first of the year.

Lucille, now faced without an escort for her own ball, had rushed the several miles to Arlington House to prevail on Robert to locate Tom. Robert had uncomplainingly ridden into Georgetown on the 30th and returned to pen Lucille a short note she received late that evening. Thomas, Robert had blandly noted, was required to notify the War Department of his anticipated whereabouts even when on leave. From December 29th through January 1st, he was scheduled to be visiting a plantation in Carroll County, Md., returning to Georgetown late on New Year's Day.

There weren't many plantations the size of Cranford in the Virginia and Maryland countryside that surrounded the District of Columbia. The Custis plantation, Arlington House, was one. The only one of such dimensions in all of Western Maryland, including Carroll County, Lucille knew, was Twin Peaks, home of that over-aged blond bitch, Candice Samples. How dare Thomas do this to her! She'd never speak to him again!

Now, almost three weeks later, it appeared her vow had validity. Thomas had made no attempt to contact her. And Joe had gone off somewhere with the 4th!

Lucille had been invited by Mrs. Scott to dine with her and other Georgetown ladies on the 24th. She resolved to drive in to the family townhouse in Georgetown the day before and let Thomas know she would not tolerate such incivility and insensitivity…Candice Samples! How dare he!

Sebastian hadn't, in fact, dawdled on the way to deliver Lucille's New Year's Eve invitation to Tom. Being the butler and major domo at as large a plantation as Cranford called for a degree of intelligence higher than most Southerners would acknowledge in any slave...or other African.

The 40-ish Sebastian had been around a long time and had kept his eyes and ears open while keeping his mouth shut. At least around the Latoures. He had surreptitiously learned to read and write; elementary but enough to make a difference. And he had made himself invaluable in the years since the Massa, Mr. Latoure, had died.

Cranford ran remarkably well. Mrs. Latoure, with help from a now-elderly overseer, Clement Labine, who had trained under, and had been a drinking companion of, her husband, followed the operational system Mr. Latoure had devised. That; the fact that the plantation lay so close to Georgetown and the knowledge among the slaves that the family-owned Alexandria Import-Export business---with its full complement of white male workers---was nearby tended to keep things peaceful. As did Labine's---and Mrs. Latoure's--- record of considerate care of the "people."

And, of course, the example of what had happened to Nat Turner and his followers.

So Cranford was ripe for the selective exploitation Sebastian had been practicing for some years: the smuggling of occasional escaped slaves from Southern Virginia and the Carolinas, utilizing the plantation's slave quarters as a safe house.

Those in the know called the system "Exodus". Even *those* didn't know much: Sebastian only knew that the refugee---sometimes plural, though it was considered almost suicidal to attempt to move multiples---would show up with only a day or two's notice. He would hide the escapees, usually younger men, women and an occasional child between eight and 12, until "Moses" could be contacted. Then, as quickly as they had appeared, the refugees would be on their way.

The Latoure "people" of course were aware of what was going on. More than one Cranford malcontent had disappeared, with Sebastian's blessing, into the system, but most were content to hide and feed the escapees until their departure. Cranford people knew there were always three meals and a place to sleep, among their own. Who knew exactly what the outside world was like? Sebastian was positive Old Man Labine had no idea what was happening behind his back. Nor did, he believed, the Latoure girls. The Mistress, though, was a different matter: there had been times when he had been sure she was well aware, even on the occasions when one of her own slaves vanished...

So Sebastian had taken advantage of his relative "freedom" to detour that day to the "Church of Jesus Christ, Liberator," where "Moses" presided as minister, Georgetown Exodus station chief and unofficial but acknowledged leader of the capitol's small population of black freemen and women.

"So, the head house nigger makes an appearance. Whaz a matta: the white folk too cold to party tonight?" Moses grinned down from his towering 6-foot-7 height. Sebastian shrugged off the insult. He and Moses had that kind of relationship: taunting each other was simply a sign of mutual respect. Certainly, few in Georgetown's freemen's community would ever have dared his rebuttal: "Shut up, you big dumb ape, or I'll see to it you're sold to a rice planter from Charleston...or, better yet, a merchant ship captain..."

Moses' laugh rumbled from deep in his enormous chest. "Charleston? No thanks, old man. Ben dere. Ain't planning on goin' back..."

The minister's expression grew quickly somber. "I hope this is a social visit. Don't want to risk all we've built up, just 'cause some Carolina nigger decided to escape during the dead of winter..."

Sebastian smiled. "Just come socializin'. Wanna to wish the biggest, dumbest freeman in Georgetown a Happy New Year. Speaking of which, you got brandy? It's damn cold and damp out there."

Moses smiled and turned toward a cabinet. A moment later a bottle and two glasses had all appeared in his ham-like hand. "Sure do, old friend. Let's us toast the New Year. And another successful year for Exodus..."

London, England
Evening of January 9, 1833:

Despite her love of all things English, Princess Dorothea remained a Russian patriot. As such, she was always mindful of the need for intelligence that could be valuable to the Czar. She had first begun picking up rumblings of a major British social initiative early in the fall, even before her husband had departed for St. Petersburg. It was the P.M. himself who let slip during a private moment that abolition was being considered. She thus knew about the scheduled secret meeting to review the plebiscite returns in time to write to her husband in early December. By January 5, she had known that the Duke of Wellington would soon depart for Georgetown to inform the Dominion government that emancipation was coming. And she knew that the Grey Government feared armed defiance from the slave power in the southeast.

All this she kept in mind as she awaited Count Ignatieff in the ornate main dinning room of the Embassy. A long, low table dominated the room, with a massive chandelier containing hundreds of candles, less than half now lit, hanging directly over the center of the table. The Princess stood by a roaring fireplace to the left of the room, which featured priceless paintings and tapestries, many brought from St. Petersburg over the years, but others of English design.

The Princess wore an off-the-shoulders brown gown which, complimented by an elaborate necklace, emphasized the creaminess of her flawless skin.

She had not so dressed for Ignatieff's benefit. Dorothea despised him as nothing more than a sanctioned assassin with high level connections whose intelligence credentials were based on torture rather than deduction. In fact, if not for the tragic death of Alexander, which had lifted his brother Nicholas to the throne, Ignatieff, by chance a childhood playmate of the new Czar, might never have risen so far in the intelligence hierarchy.

No, a quick, quiet dinner, attended by multiple servants, to share political information…and she would be off---alone---into the London society she helped rule.

CHAPTER EIGHT

London, England
Evening of January 9, 1833:

The Count was announced into the room and strode over to her, immaculate in a bemedaled white tunic over jet black pants stuffed into brilliantly-shined high black military boots. Although no weapons were visible, the Princess knew a derringer and a knife were somewhere hidden in his uniform.

And, at close inspection, it was actually true: under his mane of rich black hair, he had one brilliant blue eye—and one half blue/half brown. He looked altogether, she thought with an involuntary shiver of fear, like a wolf.

The Count caught the shiver but mistook it for one of anticipated pleasure as he took her hand and kissed it lightly. *She is as beautiful as ever*, he thought, *and tonight she will be mine.* "It is a pleasure to be with you again, my dear Princess Dorothea," he said, continuing to hold her hand in his. "And in a setting less…formal shall we say…than the receptions of the past."

"The pleasure is mine, I'm sure, Count. So, I understand the meetings in St. Petersburg went well?" *Let's get right to business before this wolf gets any ideas.* "The note I received from the Ambassador simply stated that you have been ordered here as the initial step of a possible diplomatic mission of great potential to our motherland." *And the note from Count Nesselrode said to brief you on the emancipation issue and to assist you in any way possible in determining whether you'll go on to the USBA as quickly and quietly as can be arranged.* "Shall we have dinner?"

Ignatieff's smile faded as the Princess withdrew her hand from his and walked over to the table, sitting down at the head in a chair pulled back by a waiting servant. *Well, if its business first, so be it*, he thought. *I'll melt the ice right off you yet, Princess, but that can wait.*

The Princess seemed to have assembled a cast of servants more suited for a state banquet than a private dinner. Ignatieff became increasingly privately agitated as the servants continued to hover as the courses were duly served. He drank more than he normally allowed himself under such circumstances as he and the Princess calmly--and passionlessly--discussed how to turn the emancipation issue to Russia's advantage. Course followed course, fish, foul and beef, which she partook of sparingly, while wine and vodka glasses were emptied and refilled immediately. Yet the Princess kept the conversation strictly--and importantly--professional.

"So, my dear Count," Dorothea said as dessert was served, "you now are aware of all the ramifications of the situation.

"I suggest you book passage to British America as soon as possible. Under an alias, of course. Undoubtedly the British 'diplomatics,' as they style themselves, are aware by now that you are in London. You must vanish before they can ascertain the reason for your visit. And before they can learn where you're headed next."

She suddenly rose from her chair. "Speaking of soon, I am due at Buckingham Palace in less than an hour for a long-anticipated reception. Send me word of the details of your voyage," she added, turning to the door.

With the outer haughtiness that only an Empress' lady-in-waiting could project, while inwardly trembling with fear that the wolf would pounce, the Princess walked quickly out without another word, uttering an audible sigh of relief only when a servant closed the door behind her. *The Foreign Minister was correct to warn me of him. I'd rather be alone with a drunken Cossack!*

It took the Count another hour of solitary vodka drinking at the long table to work into the condition that would haunt the Embassy for years to come. *How dare that icy bitch walk out on me, leaving all those servants to laugh behind their hands at Count Nicholas Ignatieff!*

He finally stumbled from the dining room, yet another vodka bottle in hand, and staggered toward the luxurious bedroom he had been assigned. His previous desire for the Princess had now morphed into an alcohol-fueled rage of lust and hatred. The snickers he had previously imagined emanating from the servants were now howls of laughter ringing through his addled brain, becoming louder and more dismissive as he bounced off corridor walls and into terrified servants and the guards who attempted to gently ease him to his room. Loudest were the peals of laughing contempt he could hear in the pearly, arched tones of the Princess herself. *So she has not left the*

Embassy after all. I'll yet turn that laughter into screaming pleas for more pleasure. Now he could see Dorothea standing in the doorway of his room, though she had changed from her gown of brown into the uniform of a maid. Her dark hair also had brightened dramatically and now hung down her neck.

"My Lord, don't you think it is time for you to sleep? We don't have to replay last evening just yet. There is always tomorrow…"

He pushed her into the room and slammed the door. She was beginning to look at him with the mixture of fear and desire that always acted as a tonic on him. Holding the neck of the vodka bottle in one hand, he ripped at the front of her dress before pushing her to the floor. *No soft bed for you tonight, Princess. I'm going to take you right on the floor.* He swigged from the bottle with his left hand while ripping open his pants with his right. Now he was descending on her with a force that splintered the glass as the bottle hit the floor. She screamed as he lifted the back of her head into an almost upright position with his right hand, and then quickly pulled it away to fondle a firm young breast, allowing the head and neck to drop backwards with a crash.

The back of the servant girl's neck was impaled on the raggedly broken neck of the vodka bottle. Shivers of glass penetrated into the back of her brain. Almost instantly, her bright blond hair turned a deep, almost blackish red. Already brain-dead, she quickly bled to death even as the drunken Count continued to ravage her beautiful young body.

Count Ignatieff had passed out on top of the still-bleeding body when guards, alerted by servants seeing a blackish red mixture of blood and vodka flowing out into the hallway, broke down the door.

The Count had never even learned her name…

CHAPTER NINE

Somewhere in the MidAtlantic
January 19, 1833:

The Duke might be casual in regard to the powers inherent in the Colonial Compact, thought Captain Bratton, *but he is anything but causal in his approach to the impending crisis that may arise from any application of those powers.*

At dinner the preceding day (the first full meal Bratton had been able to keep down since the *Irresistible* pulled anchor 10 days before), Sir Arthur had requested a thorough briefing on John C. Calhoun, the fallen Vice G-G, who (as yet unbeknownst to either Bratton or Wellington) had been elected to the USBA Senate from South Carolina.

Apparently, Quincy Adams had advised the Duke before *Irresistible* sailed that, of all the fire-eaters in the South, Calhoun was the most dangerous. Not that such men as Troup and Gilmour of Georgia (Troup was known as the 'Hercules of States Rights') and fellow South Carolinians like Robert Hayne and George McDuffie weren't vigorous, outspoken proponents of slavery. Calhoun, however, displayed that intangible combination of intelligence, eloquence, leadership and forcefulness that set him apart

"He broke with Jackson over the 'nullification' issue last year and lost," the Duke had noted. "A man like that is not used to losing and will learn from it. Even if Jackson agrees to enforce emancipation, Calhoun will be its foremost opponent. And if a defense of slavery causes their reconciliation, Calhoun may emerge as the real leader of a rebellious South if only due to Jackson's age and health."

Today, another (*thank God*, thought Bratton) sunny-though-freezing, clear, relatively calm day, Wellington's mind had shifted from the political to the military. As they stood on the main deck, enjoying the fresh air, the Duke wished to review the military leadership in the USBA, with an eye toward identifying those who potentially could lead rival forces in the field.

"Scott I am of course familiar with," Wellington was saying as the ship for once was pushed along by the strong breeze, instead of fighting through it. "General Scott was born in Virginia, but unless he's changed dramatically---and Scott is not a man to tilt with the political winds---he is a staunch adherent of the USBA. If, God forbid, fighting does break out, I expect Scott to be in command of the USBA forces. I plan to meet with him immediately once we're in Georgetown. I haven't kept up on the other USBAA leaders, however. What can you tell me?"

By now Bratton was used to the Duke's modus operandi and thus had prepared notes on the USBA Army's senior officers.

"Well Sir, there are six senior officers behind Scott who have fought the French and the various Indian wars for 25 years or more. Three are Northerners, Wool, Thayer and Worth. Col. John E. Wool is from Newburgh, N.Y. and is the Army's Inspector General. He's traveled extensively in Europe, observing military organizations and operations..."

"Yes, I recall Wool's role in the French Canadian insurrection campaign under Scott. He should be an asset, though more confrontational than cunning."

Bratton glanced down at his notes. Dark clouds began to become visible in the distance, heralding an end to the outdoor conferencing that Wellington apparently preferred. "William Worth is also from New York and has commanded men ever since the French wars. Another Northerner of distinction is Col. Sylvanus Thayer. Originally from Massachusetts, Thayer is more an engineer than a fighter, chiefly known for developing the USBA Military Academy at West Point, where he is superintendent."

"From what I understand, West Point has become a first-rate engineering and officer training institution," Wellington said. "Not Sandhurst, mind you, but well on its way to distinguishing itself. There are three Southerners, you say. What about them?" The Duke was also eyeing the approaching storm with a bit of apprehension, pulling his cloak more tightly around him.

"Brig. Gen. Edmund P. Gaines is a Virginian whose rise in the USBAA is rather mysterious. He fought the French and the Indians in the northern Louisiana campaign and somehow was credited with a key victory at Fort Erie, though the French assault had been contained by another general whose wounding left Gaines in command. A few days later, he was seriously wounded himself by

French artillery fire which effectively ended his participation in that war. His post-war career seems to have been aided by political influence. He is, however, second-in-command to Scott. It is reported that they can not stand each other. On a side note, Gaines, as a young officer, commanded the troops that arrested Aaron Burr in the Mississippi Territory on Jefferson's apparently trumped up treason charge.

"Charles Gratiot was born in Missouri and is the USBAA's chief engineer. If he chose, in the event, to join a Southern uprising, he'd play the key role in organizing their defenses."

The wind had shifted and was now coming at the *Irresistible* from a northwest slant. The ship began its ominous bucking. Officers and sailors ran about, while Sir Stephen Richard grinned down at Bratton from the quarterdeck. "Might be a good time for you gentlemen to go below. Might get a bit bouncy. Not enough weight with the guns gone."

The Duke took one look at his aide's greening face and nodded. "Yes, let's finish this in my cabin. It appears our reprieve is over."

Minutes later, in the Duke's cabin (normally the quarters of Sir Stephen), Bratton hoped he could finish the briefing before the dreaded pressure-packed feeling took command of his body.

"The final Southerner is Col. Zachary Taylor, Sir. Still another Virginian by birth, though he grew up in Kentucky. Colonel Taylor is known as 'Old Rough and Ready.' He has headed campaigns against the Seminoles in Florida; last year fought in the Black Hawk campaign and, of course, originally distinguished himself against the French and their Indian allies. In fact, he once held off a vastly superior number of Frogs and Indians under the famous chief Tecumseh. He is noted for his distaste of military uniforms and protocol. Sir, he actually favors riding side-saddle during a fight! He's also been known to go into battle wearing a planter's hat and an open-necked shirt..."

"Traits which have no doubt endeared him to Winfield Scott." Wellington was dry. "Still, he sounds more formidable than the others. If the Southerners do raise a force to resist the emancipation, he seems the logical Regular Army officer to lead it. I'll be sure to have a word with 'Old Fuss and Feathers' about this 'Old Rough and Ready.' Isn't it astounding the names these colonials have for their leaders?"

So rhetorically observed the man universally known as the 'Iron Duke.'

London England
January 10, 1833:

Count Nicholas Ignatieff, of the Imperial Russian secret intelligence services, suddenly snapped awake. He tried to raise his head, but the sudden pain in his temples and behind his eyes was matched by pains across his chest and knees, as well as in his wrists and ankles. He attempted to rise from the cot again, more slowly this time, but realized he was tightly tied down by heavy, rough roping. A bright light thrust into his face nearly blinded him until the candle was pulled back.

"Well, Major, the rapist seems to have come to at last," a harsh, though familiar, voice sounded in sneering tones Ignatieff was more used to issuing than hearing. "What do you suggest we do with him?" Ignatieff realized with amazement that the man looking down at him with such contempt was none other than Colonel Igor Terravenissian, his own subordinate and station chief for intelligence in England. The previous day, Ignatieff had roughly grilled Terravenissian for information on the Palmerston committee's meeting and had mocked him for his incomplete knowledge. Whoever the 'Major' was, Ignatieff could not yet ascertain.

"Untie me at once, Terravenissian, before I have your balls nailed to the wall," Ignatieff croaked, his mouth bone-dry. "And get me some water, now!"

The Colonel looked down and spit in the Count's face. "Water, the Count commands, my dear Valery. Shall we oblige him?"

The other man laughed grimly. "Of course, Colonel. May I?" The man approached the cot as Colonel Terravenissian stepped back. A sudden torrent of icy cold water slammed into Ignatieff's face and for an instant, the Count actually though he might drown. But the bucket was finally emptied and the man stepped aside.

"Pardon my bad manners, my dear Count. I should have introduced your waiter. This is Major Valery Brummel, chief of security here at the Embassy... Oh yes, you're still here in London, at our Embassy, although your accommodations have changed somewhat. Neither the Major nor I could guarantee your safety in your former quarters, now that word has passed through the staff as to your despicable, inhuman actions last night. Though, if it were up to me, I'd give the servants five minutes alone with you…"

"What, what the hell are you talking about?" Ignatieff croaked hoarsely, in a tone more wondering that demanding, as his pounding brain attempted to clear the fog of his last remembered hours. *Dinner alone with Dorothea; she disappears; what else?*

"Look Major, he is confused. Our country's most feared intelligence chief can not recall his actions of last night. Well," Terravenissian added, his voice changing from a mocking wonderment to a snare, "perhaps another drink of water will refresh his memory, as well as his taste buds." Again a huge tidal wave of icy water came crashing down on Ignatieff, who this time at least managed to close his eyes before the tuasimi hit.

"Do you begin to remember, my dear Count?" Colonel Terravenissian moved in close, a long pick-like knife dangling from his right hand. "Do you remember the Princess leaving you alone in the main dining room? Do you recall guzzling half the vodka in London? Then staggering to your room, where you were met by a beautiful young servant girl?" Terravenissian's voice was rising ominously.

"Whose clothing you ripped off before you pushed her to the floor and raped her? And whose slender neck you impaled on the broken neck of still another vodka bottle you brought from the dining room? Continuing to utilize her body even as she slowly bled to death?" The Colonel's voice had lowered to a dangerous icy whisper as he waved the knife closer and closer to Ignatieff's throat.

Out of the fog, sudden flashes of remembrance began to appear before the Count's bloodshot eyes. Suddenly, he knew it was true. And simultaneously knew the danger he had brought on himself.

With a sudden oath, Brummel sprung on him, wrapping thick calloused fingers around his throat, swearing as he banged Ignatieff's head back repeatedly onto the cot. It took all of Colonel Terravenissian's strength---at an even six foot and 200 pounds, he had two inches and some 20-plus pounds on the security chief---to pull him off. With a final yank, he thrust the sobbing Brummel back across the room.

"That, my dear Count, is simply an indication of what everyone here at the Embassy would like to do to you. Including myself…

"However, you are, at Princess Dorothea's personal direction, to be given a brief reprieve. You will be kept tied up in this room until tomorrow evening when, disguised in an English workman's clothes, you will be taken to the Thames docks, there to board a British American passenger vessel…in steerage class…for the crossing to New York City. You will then have seven days to make your way to the British American capitol at Georgetown, using money supplied by an agent whose name and address in New York will be given you upon departing.

"I'm sorry you will have to find your own way from New York to Georgetown, but the *Pride of the Hudson* is the only passenger vessel scheduled to cross the Atlantic for several weeks. I'm sure you'll enjoy the trip…"

The Colonel smiled menacingly down at his former tormentor. "If you fail to appear at the Consulate in Georgetown within those seven days, you will be declared a traitor and subject to arrest if you ever again set foot on Russian soil.

"Likewise, if you fail in the mission the Princess has discussed with you, you will also be declared a traitor. Succeed and you will be allowed to return in triumph, with this most unfortunate and ugly incident forgotten in the name of the greater glory of our motherland.

"Fail and I suggest you lose yourself in the American West."

Terravenissian gave the Count a long last look of withering contempt. "By the way, your victim came from the same village as Major Brummel. For that reason, my people will guard you tonight.

"And, if you have any decency at all, you'll remember forever her name: Katrina."

Georgetown, D.C.
January 23, 1833:

Winfield Scott was not in a good mood, which meant no one on his staff, including Lieutenant Wilder, was particularly cheerful, either.

Scott had felt in his bones for days that the Lieutenant's thesis concerning the sudden sprint by *HMS Irresistible* to England was not entirely correct. Not wrong…incomplete. The problem was that he simply could not come up with a better rationale. And the damn Georgetown weather, after a splendidly cold and snowy holiday season, had turned dismal once again: an early January thaw had turned the snow-covered streets to mush and then frozen mud when the temperature dropped to hover consistently in the low 30s.

We'll be lucky not to all catch pneumonia at this rate. Then, come May, we'll be frying again. Damn Hamilton for agreeing to the old Virginians' proposal to move the capitol here from Philadelphia in exchange for their support of his Dominion fiscal reform plan. And damn those wily old Virginians, yes, including Washington, who made a collective financial killing selling this godforsaken swamp to the Dominion...

And I still can't find out why Sam Houston was here...or where he's vanished to since. Wilder tells me he was a house guest of Jackson's right up until the Lieutenant left on leave a few days before New Year's. When Wilder went back to The Residency on January 2nd, Houston was gone, as mysteriously as he had suddenly appeared.

Why do I think this has something to do with Texas? Because Houston burned his bridges, by all accounts, in Tennessee, after resigning the Governorship and leaving his new bride to head off into the wilderness with the Cherokee. Then he came back here last April and got into a disgraceful brawl with Congressman Stanbery of Ohio. What was more disgraceful was that Congress put him on trial for whacking Stanbery with a hickory cane; but didn't censure Stanbery for firing a pistol at Houston. A pistol that fortunately---for Houston---misfired. Then he left Georgetown and wasn't heard from till the reception.

But if he's reconciled with Jackson---the G-G was aghast when Houston resigned the Governorship---I have a bad feeling that something is afoot. And, dammit, that something has to do with Texas. I can read between the lines of a political speech as well as anyone. And I know Jackson. The G-G wouldn't have gone out on a limb suggesting the Empire acquire Texas unless he had specific goals in mind. While I may not be a politician, I can count heads. And the count in Congress suggests the slave power is in trouble. Jackson may have reconciled with Houston in order to begin the process of bringing Texas and the rest of the Southwest into the USBA. As slave states.

I have Zach Taylor in command at New Orleans. Zach is rather informal, but he's a good soldier. I think I'll alert him to be on the lookout for Houston along the Texas-Louisiana border. We can't stop him from entering Texas, but we can make some contingency plans in case he does.

Reaching a huge paw out to grab his coffee mug, Scott called for his secretary, feeling better by the minute. But then he remembered that damned *Irresistible*. Well, he thought, *Wilder says the earliest she could return to Baltimore is the end of the month. We'll just have to wait to see if anything develops.* He slammed the mug back down angrily.

Taxing the slaveholders! Do those people in London realize how that would heat the pot past the boiling point? Not only will the slaveholders be furious, but the damn abolitionists will object, too, once they get over their initial euphoria concerning the financial hit the slave power stands to take. It won't be long before they realize that once London gets accustomed to that annual revenue stream, the Imperial Government won't want to give it up... Far from leading to the abolition of slavery, a tax would in effect legitimize it!

Scott shook his huge head in disgust. *Surely I'm not the only one who can see that? Taxing the slaveholders...London certainly knows how to stir things up!*

Jurgurtha Numidia, aka "Moses", had answered to many names in his life. Today being a mid-week workday, "blacksmith" was the main one. Jurgurtha didn't mind that; "hey blacksmith" usually meant work...and wages. More wages than he could hope to receive as Minister of the Church of Jesus Christ, Liberator.

And more money than he received from the New England Abolitionist Society as Georgetown station chief. *Hell, even if I didn't have to use that purse for supplies and cash to speed the refugees on, it still wouldn't equal what I make as a smithy,* he thought with a disgusted grunt while hammering on a wheel shaft in his damp stable.

Jurgurtha had started life as "Little Jack," son of the biggest slave on a South Carolina lowlands rice plantation. When Big Jack took fatal offense to one too many undeserved lashes from the overseer, an embittered minor French aristocrat bankrupt and exiled before the Revolution, the plantation Massa sent dogs to find and devour him in the swamps. Satisfied that Big Jack was dead, but furious that such a valuable asset had had to be destroyed, the Massa put Big Jack's family on the auction block. A British American sea captain, in port to pick up a hold of rice for delivery to Boston, had purchased young Jack.

Though still technically a slave, Little Jack had the run of the merchant ship and grew successively taller, broader and stronger over the course of several years and voyages up and down the Atlantic Coast and into the West Indies. The ship's master, Captain Van Dyke, took a liking to the strapping young man who, absorbing the lesson of his father, never showed his anger or bitterness in the Captain's presense. During the long, often dull voyages, Captain Van Dyke in fact ignored protocol by privately educating the boy in the "three r's".

This fairly happy time ended on a bright, hot July morning in 1795, when the French warship *Vergennes* stopped the merchant ship off the coast of Georgia and impressed nine able-bodied seamen...and Jack. Life on the *Vergennes* was hard on the entire crew, but especially on a 13-year old former cabin boy now thrown down into the riff-raff of the ship's crew. It took just one fight---and one death---before the ship's company learned not to tamper with Jack, however. A drunken crewman went overboard with a splash that signalled that Jack was no man's plaything...

It took five years, however, for Jack to find the right time to escape: when the *Vergennes* anchored in Port-a-Prince harbor during a lull in the on-again, off-again rebellion raised nine years earlier by Tousaint L'Overture, a former house servant turned rebel general. Though Tousaint would be remembered by succeeding generations as the "George Washington" of the Haitian revolution against Napoleon, he had actually been captured and sent in chains to France, where he died ignomously in a prison in the Jura region.

Fortunately for Jack, he had made his way to another rebel army, led by Jean-Jacques Dessaline, who was at best an unreliable ally of Tousaint. It was Dessaline who outlasted Napoleon, when Bonaparte's interest in Haiti faded after the conquest of his Louisiana lands by Scott and Jackson. By the end of 1804, Jack had become an officer under Dessaline, leading a regiment of hard-eyed and skilled guerrillas. Jack had long since adopted the name Jurgurtha Numidia, after learning of the Numidian king who had fought with and against the Romans a generation before Caesar. As Jurgurtha, he planned to live out his life as an officer in the Haitian Army, enjoying all the prerequisites that such a position entailed.

Unfortunately for Jurgurtha---and Haiti---the new nation, having won its independence, had no idea what to do with it: the country spun into a seemingly-bottomless well of chaos. Finally throwing up his hands in disgust in 1811, he booked passage to Boston, made contact with the Abolitionist Society and eventually was sent to Georgetown. Whether Jurgurtha would have done so if he had heard the terrifying news from New Orleans, or if such news actually spurred him back to British America, was not known, even to his handlers and associates.

What was known was that Jurgurtha at some point learned that, in that same year of 1811, a 500-man slave rebellion in and around New Orleans, under the leadership of Charles Deslondesa and his partner Quamana, had been put down by Dominion troops and Louisiana planters with such fury that Deslondesa's and Quamana's heads had been among the 100 fastened to pikes on the gates of New Orleans streets.

A Tousaint-style rebellion in British America, Jurgurtha Numidia could see, stood no chance. Peaceful, if surreptitious, means would have to be employed to set his black brethren free...

So, at age 50, Jurgurtha Numidia, aka Moses, now preached to his flock on weekends, tended to his smithy business...and ran escaped slaves past the Virginia, Maryland and Georgetown authorities. *All in all,* he thought, *a fairly contented life,* especially when his wife Melissa was in town. *Except for young Tousaint...*

Tousaint L'Overture Numidia was the son of Jurgurtha's Haitian wife, Brigette, a tawny mullatto beauty who had died in childbirth in 1809 in Port-a-Prince (whether *that* had influenced Jurgurtha's decision to flee Haiti was also not known to his friends. He never mentioned her name.). Born free and educated at Williams College, a struggling Massachusetts backwoods facility always on the verge of closing, Tousaint was hotheaded, outspoken and fearless in his denouncation of slavery. All attributes, his father thought, that were fine in Georgetown's freeman's community...but not in the outside world. Tousaint was now working as a clerk in Daniel Webster's Congressional office...to the outrage of the entire Southern delegation, to say nothing of most Northern Congressmen.

Webster was a hard boss, who made him burn the midnight candle, Tousaint had repeatedly told his father when scolded for never being home. Jurgurtha doubted that; Webster was brilliant, but a man-about-town. His speeches were clearly of his own creation. *Unless Tousaint is drafting the Congressman's social calander,* Jurgurtha thought, *the boy is either partying himself...or planning mischef with the small group of followers he has cultivated.*

Knowing his son, Jurgurtha hoped for the former...but believed the latter... And hoped for the best...while anticipating the worst.

"Well Lieutenant, now that I've got things straightened out at the Department, how about joining me at the Golden Eagle? It's past noon, you know."

Lieutenant Wilder looked up from behind the desk in his tiny Residency office and smiled. "Harps! Where have you been? At first I was afraid the Cossacks might have come for you while I was on leave. But I heard you left Georgetown around New Year's yourself."

"Went home to New Jersey, Tom. A family emergency. Tell you about it at the Eagle. By the way, have you run into that sweet young Countess on your diplomatic rounds?"

Discussion of Countess Renkowiitz---and how David could get in touch with her---occupied the conversation on the way down Grant Street to the Eagle, where they were seated by the proprietress herself. Mrs. Casgrave, a short, black-haired woman in her late 30s or early 40s, resembled Countess Caroline in build, except for a very definable pair of hard breasts and an equally defined rear. Her dark eyes flashed as she recognized David but she gave the Lieutenant no more than a cursory glance.

"David, where have you been...and when did you get back? The girls and I have missed you!"

"I returned last night from New Jersey, Joanne. So this is the first chance I've had to drop by." Harper didn't even blush as the woman planted a sensuous kiss on his mouth. "However, I plan to have supper here tonight."

The woman looked down with what, even to Wilder's unprofessional eye, was a practiced polished projection of false girlish modesty. "I look forward to it." She led them across the room, holding Harper's arm tightly. "This should be a nice, quiet booth. I'll send over something special."

Wilder grinned as Mrs. Casgrave sashayed away. "Her, too? Damn Dave, do you have them stashed all over Georgetown?"

Harper returned the grin contentedly. "Joanne likes younger men. I'm younger. What can I say? So how was your holiday season, Lieutenant? Any progress on the Cranford front?"

Wilder shook his head in disgust. "Nothing doing there, I'm afraid. Looks like Lucille Latoure prefers the Artillery to whatever the hell you'd call what I do."

"But you were away for New Year's. I know, I looked for you that week before I knew I was leaving but they said you'd be gone till January 1st. So where did you go off to, if not Cranford Plantation?"

Harper looked across the booth in amusement. "Or should I ask how things are at Twin Peaks? And you rib me about 'older women'!"

Wilder reddened but slightly. "Well Dave, as they taught us at the Point: 'A man has to do what a man has to do.' Anyway, so what took you back to Jersey? I hope it all turned out all right..."

Harper looked up as a waitress appeared with steins of beer, a basket of fresh hot bread and a steaming plate of hot chicken. "Compliments of the Golden Eagle," she said with a smile. "Joanne said there's plenty more if you're still hungry..."

Harper grinned as he broke open the bread and prepared to spear a quarter of chicken: "See Tom, it never hurts to be in good with the owner of your favorite tavern... But seriously, as you know, my family has owned and operated a hotel and tavern in a little town called Schraalenburgh since my grandparents' time. Someone made a substantial offer for The Midway---that's the name of our place---and we had a family conference to consider the offer."

"So what was the outcome?"

"We're turning it down. My brother will run the place, now that my parents are slowing down. We have a good location. Bergen County is mostly farms, but the area is growing. Schraalenburgh is midway on a main north-south road and our hotel is almost directly in the middle of the town, right on the main road. That's why we call it 'The Midway.' I expect my family to operate it for years to come..."

Lieutenant Wilder usually spent mornings at The Residency and afternoons at the War Department. He and Harper walked up 17th Street to the grandiosely-named 'Pennsylvania Avenue'---at this time of year a rut-filled expanse of frozen mud---and the 'temporary' building, erected late in the last century, which housed both War and Interior. It was at the bottom of the building's steps that the pair, once again discussing David's chances of arranging a meeting with Countess Caroline, literally bumped into Sebastian, the Latoure family servant.

"'Cuse me, suh, you be Lieutenant Wilder, am I correct?"

Tom looked at the well-put-together coffee-colored man of about 40 in surprise. "Yes I am. And you'd be Sebastian, one of the Latoure people, if I'm not mistaken."

"Yes suh, Ah am. Ah got a note here from Miz Lucille that Ah'm to hand you direct." He reached into an inner pocket and produced a light green envelope addressed to 'Lt. Thomas Wilder,

War Department, Georgetown.'

Taken back, Tom took the envelope with the familiar faint scent and put it into his uniform. "When did Miss Lucille give you this note, Sebastian?"

"Less than an hour ago, Ah 'spect. Tol' me give it to you an' only you. Ah was on mah way over there." He indicated The Residency at the other end of the wide park-like grounds. "Seein' as you wasn't here. But now Ah has the privilege of returning to the townhouse and tell Miz Lucille you accepted her note."

"You mean Miss Lucille is here in Georgetown? How long has she been here?"

"Why, Ah done drove her in maself this morning, suh. Yep, left Cranford at the crack a' dawn. Got here 'bout hour ago. Come straight on. Better luck this time than the last. Miz Lucille was real mad Ah couldn't find you to give you her note 'fore New Year's."

Harps laughed at the look of astonishment on Tom's face. "Well Lieutenant, looks like you evacuated to Twin Peaks a little too soon. But then, 'a man's got to do what a man's got to do'..."

Tom looked at his friend with annoyance: "Harps, will you shut the hell up?" Turning to the servant, he added: "Thank you Sebastian. I appreciate all the effort to find me."

"Suh, Miz Lucille 'pects me to wait for an answer..."

With an embarrassed shake of his head, Wilder reached into his pocket and pulled out the note. "You're really enjoying this, aren't you Harps?"

"Thomas, the only thing that's missing is a Twin Peaks person coming across Pennsylvania Avenue. That'd really make my day..."

Wilder glanced briefly at the note and looked up at Sebastian. "Tell Miss Lucille I will be there at approximately 6:30."

"Yes suh, Ah'll go tell her right 'way," Sebastian said with a grin.

Wilder stuck the note back in his pocket. It read:

Thomas:
Mrs. Scott has invited me to dine with her and some other
Georgetown ladies tomorrow, so I came into town earlier
today. Please join me at our townhouse for supper this
evening at 6 p.m.
Lucille

Harper turned to his friend with a straight face as they ascended the stairs. "Well Tom, I guess you won't be joining me at the Golden Eagle tonight. Joanne will be so disappointed..."

Wilder looked grim. "Harps, with my luck, Lucille just wants me to be the first to know that she and the 'hero of the Black Hawk War' are not only married, but are expecting twins..." He turned and walked down the hall towards General Scott's office as Harper laughed softly and headed to Interior's section of the building.

———

The afternoon passed interminably for Tom, who, nonetheless, was dreading his scheduled 6:30 p.m. rendezvous. Even though he really didn't believe Lucille and Joe were engaged, much less married, there was bound to be a scene tonight. If Lucille had really been upset that he was unavailable when Sebastian came to town in late December, it meant there had been something more in that note than New Year's wishes.

And his bravado performance at the conclusion of the G-G's holiday reception was beginning to haunt him. He should have arranged to meet Candice's carriage at a side entrance to The Residency. But he was, of course, Irish. And so his response to Lucille's teasing about Christmas Eve at Arlington had naturally involved throwing the taunt right back in her face by boarding the Samples carriage in full view of the entire exiting crowd on the Main Portico. No doubt she had learned---from her new friend Mrs. Scott, perhaps?---where he had gone for the New Year's holiday. A 'holiday' he had barely since recovered from, he thought, cheering up somewhat. *That Candice is insatiable...it wouldn't surprise me if her husband took that header off his horse out of pure exhaustion...*

Thomas' amorous reveries were permanently interrupted by the sudden appearance of General Scott in the doorway of the closet that passed for his War Department office. "Lieutenant, I'm wanted at The Residency. As are you. Get your cloak on. Have any idea what this might be about?" The General's grim demeanor startled Thomas back into reality.

"No sir. When I left there at noon, all was quiet. The Governor-General was scheduled this afternoon with Major Layne and Sir John Burrell, but it was just the routine monthly briefing session. Nothing out of the ordinary. Other than that, the main topic there is still the

Bank."

"Well, something's got the G-G's attention. Maybe Houston is back, or another of those crackpot Tennesseans. God help us if Davy Crockett's come to town to tell us he's started another war with the Creeks while the Congress was home campaigning... Let's get over there."

At five-foot-six, there was no way Thomas' stubby legs could keep up with his long-limbed six-foot-seven boss, especially when the General went down the steps and across Pennsylvania Avenue in a purposeful stride. The aide had to break into a virtual trot to keep pace. That and the cold rain that had begun in mid-afternoon put a damper on further conversation until they were in The Residency itself. "The Governor-General is awaiting you gentlemen in his office," the head usher said, after taking their wet cloaks, indicating the way as if Scott, who had been attending business and social events at the mansion since the Madison Administration, and Wilder, who maintained another miniscule office in the building, were first-time visitors. The hallway grandfather's clock was chiming four-thirty.

The gaunt Governor-General had his back to the door, leaning on a cane, and was looking out a window toward the Parade Ground and the Long Bridge when Scott and Wilder entered his office. At six-foot-one, Jackson towered over Wilder, but gave away five inches and over 125 pounds to his Army chief. Now, turning slowly while still leaning on the ever-present cane, he eyed them with a fiery stare, not inviting them to sit in the comfortable chairs facing his desk. The Secretary of War, Lewis Cass, already sat in one of them.

"General, my monthly briefing today with those two Liaison Office types, Layne and Burrell, centered, as usual, on those damn French Canadians up there in Quebec. Layne thinks they're arming themselves again for another go at independence. Why haven't you informed me, or the Secretary of War, about this? Or are the Liaison Office's sources better than yours, eh?"

Scott stared back at Jackson and Wilder could begin to sense the drill warming up. "Mr. Governor, the Liaison Office's intelligence agents justify their livelihoods dreaming up French-sponsored plots from Quebec City to the Florida Keys. The French Quebecois are sullen, as usual, but not mutinous. I had a report from Colonel Worth, who's in command up there, at year's end to that effect. Worth's a good officer. I believe him. I'll forward you the report.

Lieutenant, see to it first thing tomorrow morning."

"Huh," snorted Jackson. "Now then," he glanced down at notes on the desk in front of him. "Have either of you gentlemen heard, by chance, of HMS *Irresistible*? Well?"

Wilder knew better than to glance over at General Scott, who he knew was maintaining icy eye contact with the heated-up G-G.

"Of course, Mr. Governor. HMS *Irresistible* is one of the newest Royal Navy frigates. What they call the 'screw design' type. One of the fastest and most powerful ships in the Fleet. She was sent over here on a three-year mission of slave ship and smuggling patrol back in '31…"

"A mission, General Scott, which was apparently interrupted last month. What do you know about that…and why wasn't I informed, damn it?" The G-G slammed his cane down on the desk, almost losing his balance in the process. "Layne had the unmitigated gall to tell me that the ship was temporarily detached from patrol duty for a 'classified' mission! The arrogant bastard! Too highly classified for the Governor-General of the USBA to know? That's an insult not just to me, but to this office and all of our citizens!"

Well, at least we know this doesn't involve Davy Crockett, thought Wilder. *I know how the General detests him. I can't wait to hear this explaination, though…*

The drill was still aimed at the G-G who apparently was beginning to feel some of its sting, for Jackson dropped into a chair and indicated the two military men to do the same. *You know something, Mr. Governor,* Scott thought, *one of these days these ridiculous temper tantrums are going to put you in the ground. Then we'll see how Van Buren deals with taxing the slaveholders, or whatever it is London's up to.*

"Mr. Governor, I was informed the day after the ship sailed that HMS *Irresistible* had pulled anchor in Baltimore harbor with England as its apparent destination. In case Major Layne failed to mention the fact, *Irresistible* left most of its armaments harbor side, under Royal Marine guard, where they remain at this minute. Neither the Royal Navy nor the Liaison Office informed the Coastal Guard of the ship's departure or the rather unusual stripping of most of its guns."

Jackson's seething glare had faded to a cold, calculating expression as Scott paused for a second.

"Our own forces at Fort McHenry observed the entire operation and alerted me. Subsequently, I had Lieutenant Wilder attempt to ascertain a rationale for what amounts to a covert action, since our own people in Baltimore reported that *Irresistible* had been ready to pull anchor for three or four days. Ultimately, we discovered they'd been waiting for a pouch that was delivered on the evening of December 15th. I was subsequently informed that the pouch contained the plebiscite returns, which were not officially announced until the next day."

"So why wasn't I informed, General? Damn it all! And what about Mr. Cass here?" The famed Jacksonian temper was rising but seemed to have no visible effect on the USBAA commander.

"Inform you of what, Mr. Governor? That the Royal Navy has turned one of its premier war vessels into a mail ship? Until we can discover why *Irresistible* stripped down for a fast and potentially dangerous midwinter North Atlantic crossing, any conjecture would be useless and fruitless guessing." *Even though I've been doing just that for a month.* "For all we know, King William and Lord Palmerston had a bet on the plebiscite."

A crafty, mirthless smile began to break out at the corners of Jackson's mouth. "That's a very convincing sugar-coating, General Scott. But *I* didn't get to The Residency and *you* didn't get to run the Army by being naive... Now tell me what you and this young man think London is up to. Straight and unvarnished."

Wilder was startled as the office clock banged out the half hour in the sudden silence. *Five-thirty already. And I promised Lucille I'd be at the Latoure townhouse in an hour! This could go on all night, once they start analyzing the possibilities. I'm stuck here and Lucille will think I purposefully broke our supper engagement. Of all the damn nights for the G-G to find out about* Irresistible!

"Well, General, cat got your tongue?" The Secretary of War had been sitting in the right chair in front of Jackson's desk. He now moved it so that he was facing both the G-G and the two officers. Scott, who had resumed his staring contest with Jackson during the enforced verbal silence brought on by the clock's noise, barely glanced at his politically-appointed boss. As young commanders, they had clashed bitterly over tactics during the Upper Louisiana Territory campaign years before. Scott resented the fact that Cass had turned his less-than-glorious service in that war into an extended---18-year---governorship of the Michigan Territory. Jackson, for strictly political reasons, had put him in charge of the War Department 18 months before. The relationship between Secretary and Army commander was tenuous, at best.

"No, Mr. Secretary, I'm trying to frame a confusing and perhaps unexplainable situation in an understandable 'straight and unvarnished' way.

"Mr. Governor, neither the Lieutenant nor I know for certain why London apparently wanted the plebiscite results so quickly that they ordered the stripping down of one of the Royal Navy's newest and fastest warships. Even in '28, the results were sent by the first available merchantman. Since the situation here is not in turmoil, which even your biggest detractors in London would acknowledge…"

"Huh," the G-G less-than-successfully tried to cover a laugh with a snort.

"…then it stands that the rationale for being so rapidly informed as to the results must stem from something emanating, or about to emanate, over there. I had Lieutenant Wilder here intensively review all correspondence between the War Department and the various military ministries in London dating back six months. While he was at it, he also reviewed Residency correspondence with #10 Downing Street."

Cass leaned forward in his seat and broke in: "You had this Lieutenant reviewing high-level Dominion correspondence with London? I consider that a startling breach…"

"That's his job, Lewis," the G-G said dryly. "Continue, General Scott. What did this 'intensive review' uncover?"

"Nothing that justified the sudden departure of *Irresistible*, Mr. Governor. However, the Lieutenant did discover an unusual information request from the Chancellor of the Exchequer's Office to Interior. Lieutenant, tell the gentlemen what Exchequer wanted."

Thomas had remained silent for the almost 90 minutes the meeting had thus far lasted and had not expected to participate in the conversation to any meaningful degree. Fortunately, he had worked closely enough with both Jackson and Scott that he was less nervous than resigned that his supper engagement---and any hope of a future---with Lucille had probably just taken a devastating body-blow.

"Mr. Governor-General," (Thomas always used the complete title when addressing Jackson) "last Spring the Chancellery asked Interior for a detailed, state-by-state breakdown of the slave population in the Dominion, including total number and percentage of each state's population…"

He could see Jackson wince visibly at the first mention of slavery. Cass, on the other hand, remained impassive, though perhaps on the defensive after the G-G's brush-off of his earlier tirade.

"And Interior gathered this information and sent it to London, I assume? How did they gather it?" Jackson was again becoming angry. "I saw no correspondence on this," he added, glaring from Scott to Cass. Scott nodded for Thomas to continue.

"Apparently they sat on the request, knowing the census report was being finalized. Then they simply extracted the necessary information, copied it and sent it on to the Exchequer. As I understand it, there has been no follow-up correspondence." He looked at the General, wondering whether to proceed. Scott, however, broke back in.

"Mr. Governor, Exchequer's interest in the numbers of slaves in the various states indicates to us that some sort of tax or tariff on slaves, and/or their sale here, is possibly being considered by the Whig government in London…"

"I fail to see the connection to the plebiscite, General Scott," Secretary Cass interrupted. "One does not…"

"I see the connection, Mr. Cass." The G-G's voice had lowered, thought Thomas, to the hiss of a rattlesnake. "General Scott has skillfully danced around it, but his conclusion is obvious, Lewis: The General is saying London may be about to propose a tax on slaves…and, just maybe, they don't trust me to enforce it. They wanted the results in a hurry on the possibility that I might have been defeated. That would have helped grease the skids in Parliament for an easier passage…as well as easier enforcement."

The silence in the room was deafening. Cass sat with his jaw ajar, unable to speak. Jackson and Scott were again staring at one another, but this time in mutual recognition of the potential crisis Thomas' supposition presented. It was Scott who spoke first:

"I see no other rationale that in any way connects the questions raised by both *Irresistible's* voyage and the preceding Exchequer information request. However, we may be entirely wrong and the two issues are not connected. Maybe Exchequer was cooking up a study on slavery throughout the Empire: the total value of the slave population, Empire-wide, perhaps. And, again, perhaps there was a high level wager on the plebiscite. Or perhaps Quincy Adams and the rest of the USBA delegation asked the Admiralty to expedite the news. I will say this Mr. Governor: I do believe Mr. Wilder is on to something here. Yet I am not entirely certain we have drawn the correct conclusion…"

Thomas' was not the only head that jerked up at Scott's words.

"I am certain, however, of one thing: It is useless conjecture to sit here guessing what this is all about. There is nothing we can do until London decides to inform us of their plans, if any. According to Mr. Wilder's calculations, the earliest *Irresistible* could get back here is month's end. From a military standpoint, the issue is on hold until then. From a political standpoint, well, that is another matter. Mr. Jackson, I do not believe it is proper for me to participate in any such discussions. I ask permission to withdraw."

"You're correct, General Scott. The military forces of the USBA have no role to play unless and until a political crisis does develop; and then it will be a limited one just as occurred last year when I was forced to send the Coastal Guard to Charleston Harbor over the 'Nullification' issue. Just have the Coastal Guard keep an eye out for any Royal Navy vessels coming into Baltimore in the next few weeks. You are otherwise excused." Scott rose, glanced at the Lieutenant with an odd gleam in his eye and left the room.

The G-G turned to Thomas. "Mr. Wilder, have the chief usher find you my secretary. Wake him up, if necessary. Then you can go. Tomorrow, you will assist Mr. Donelson in making the arrangements for an emergency Cabinet meeting. When did you say that ship might be back?"

"The earliest is about February 1st, Sir. That's given that it reached London safely by the 5th or 6th, then 72 hours-to-96 hours for refitting. More realistically, about the 5th of February."

"Tomorrow's January 20th. Lewis, we'll meet formally on the 27th. One more thing, Lieutenant. On your way out, also have the chief usher send servants to find Mr. Van Buren and across the way to Frank Blair's house. I want to see both of them tonight."

Jackson tuned to the Secretary of War: "Mr. Cass, the four of us have a lot to discuss. I'm determined to shut down this damn Bank of the USBA. I thought that had priority. But now this, too. It will be a long night."

———

It was almost 9 p.m. when Thomas finally left The Residency. Andrew Jackson Donelson, the G-G's secretary, had left the mansion to supper with friends and had to be tracked down. Francis P. Blair, a prominent member of the 'kitchen cabinet,' had been at home, but the Vice G-G to-be had also been dining, with a delegation of fellow New York Democrats.

The Lieutenant sighed as he glanced at his pocket watch. *I don't think it would be a good idea to show up on 10th Street at this hour,* he thought, ruefully. *That's if she hasn't already torn the townhouse down...I'll wait and send her a note tomorrow, after she's had a chance to cool down. Meanwhile, I might as well join Harps at the Golden Eagle after all. That is, if he and that 'older woman' of his aren't dining privately...*

I don't like or trust that Joanne, but she does run a nice establishment (at least, on the ground floor). And I do need a few beers and maybe some stew while I try to sort out today's turns-of-events. All of them...

CHAPTER TEN

Georgetown, D.C.
January 31, 1833:

Like most British Americans, Winfield Scott had long since become bored with the ceaseless arguing over the Second Bank of the USBA. Like most, he didn't see it as the threat to individual liberty that it's most vehement critics, led by Jackson, charged that it was. (Scott's attitude about the USBA Bank---and all other banks--- could be expressed in one sentence: 'The only time banks will loan you money is when you no longer need it.') And how the Bank exposed the Dominion to control by 'foreign interests,' as the G-G had claimed in his message to Congress vetoing its re-charter last year, Scott, like most others, was at a loss to understand.

And now the G-G has called a special session of Congress for early March to deal with the Bank issue! Thought we'd have them out of our hair until next December... That's when the Constitution calls for the new Congress to convene. Now Jackson wants them back here just months after the last Congress adjourned. I just don't understand the need for it!

What he did understand, however, was that while Jackson recognized the potential crisis looming if a bill to put some sort of tax on the USBA's slave population passed Parliament, the G-G was still undecided as whether to support or oppose it. 'Oppose', the General thought grimly, as in 'refusal to enforce.' The Cabinet had met throughout the 27th and 28th, and Jackson had been locked in The Residency with his other advisors---the so-called 'kitchen cabinet'---almost constantly since the morning after Scott's own meeting with the G-G. How much time was being devoted to the separate issues, he could not tell. (Wilder, of course, had no entry into that circle, while he and Cass were barely on speaking terms.)

Speaking of Wilder, he had sent the young man to Baltimore yesterday to await the possible return of *Irresistible*. A short change of scenery was something the Lieutenant seemed to require; he had been depressed for days. At first, Scott had assumed it had to do with

103

the potential upcoming crisis; only in casually remarking on his aide's low spirits to Maria a few nights ago had he learned another reason: apparently their grueling session at The Residency after the G-G first learned of *Irresistible's* voyage had forced Wilder to miss a previously-scheduled private supper with Miss Latoure. That high-spirited young lady, in Georgetown to attend Mrs. Scott's monthly ladies-only dinner party the next afternoon, had not taken Tom's unintended and unavoidable snub lightly; she had refused to accept his increasingly-desperate explanatory notes before heading back to her plantation in a huff a day or so later. At least, that was how Maria understood the situation.

The fact that Candice Samples, who had an open invitation to the monthly get-togethers, had unexpectedly made an appearance had simply added wood to the Latoure bonfire.

His aide's romantic misadventures provided some much-needed comic relief for the General, whose intuition told him that more than Imperial revenue enhancement was at the bottom of the *Irresistible* mystery.

Even a sales tax of two USBA dollars per head annually--the average selling price of a slave was less than $800--would generate only a few thousand pounds sterling, gross, if that. An annual tax of two dollars per slave would also amount to about four million pounds, if collectable. After the collection overhead was deducted, was the net high enough to justify the effort? Or the controversy? After all, hadn't 'taxation without representation' been at the heart of the troubles back in the '70s?

And there was still no word out of The Residency about Houston. Sam had simply vanished.

If he went back to Tennessee, I would have gotten word by now. He looked during that Residency Christmas reception as if his Cherokee phase is finally over, so I'm betting he's on his way to Texas. Zach Taylor won't get my message for a few days yet; if Houston slipped out of Georgetown to head straight to Texas, he'll have too big a head start for Zach's people to catch up to him. Damn Jackson! First the nullification nonsense, now the Bank battle and, possibly, something to do with slavery. This is no time to go Empire-building on your own. Just remember the last time you went near that golden apple!

Only this time, it won't be Aaron Burr who'll be up on charges: it will be you!

Scott had been at the Burr trial in Richmond those many years ago...

I was still undecided between the Army and the law, he thought with a grin. *Some fool of a lawyer I'd have made… But the array of legal talent on both sides was awesome. The Chief Justice, John Marshall himself, presided. The case collapsed because Jefferson never presented any real proof of Burr's wrong-doing.*

But I still wonder what Burr---and Jackson---was up to… I'll bet Matty Van knows. But he'd just smile and act as if he never heard the question if I ever asked him. Interesting, Jackson's Vice G-G is assumed by many people to be Burr's bastard son…

Ft. McHenry
Baltimore, Maryland
February 1, 1833:

Lieutenant Wilder was awakened by a brisk knocking on the door of a chilly visiting officer's cubicle. At first, he couldn't comprehend what he was doing in the small, cell-like room, but his head quickly cleared. "Yes, coming…" He looked at his pocket watch. It was 5:42 a.m.

He opened the door to the salute of a young private. "Sorry to wake you at this hour, Lieutenant, but Captain Judge thinks you should get up to the seawall as soon as possible. Looks like an incoming Royal Navy ship."

"Tell the Captain I'll be right there. And thanks for waking me." The private saluted again and left. Thomas saluted back, thinking what a damn-fool thing to be doing, dressed only in a pair of USBAA pants. *Well, that's the Army for you.* The Lieutenant quickly threw water over his face, pulled on boots and a uniform top and made his way across the Fort's main yard to the wall facing out into Chesapeake Bay. The ship, whatever kind it was, was still too far away to see with the naked eye, but Captain Brian Judge, second-in-command of the Fort, held a telescope in his hand as he conferred with a grizzled sergeant. He looked over as Thomas inexpertly pulled himself up the ladder to the deck that ran around the inside of the Fort.

"Can't tell for sure, Lieutenant," he said, ignoring the formality of a salute (to the disgust of the veteran non-com). "Sergeant Potts here spotted something out there about 20 minutes ago. Looks like it's riding too high for a merchantman or a fully-armed warship. Big enough, though, that's why there's a chance it could be *Irresistible*."

105

Wilder and Judge had supped the previous night at one of Baltimore's famous harbor seafood houses and Thomas had learned, to his amazement, that the Captain hailed from Schraalenburgh, the same sleepy North Jersey town as David Harper. Judge, a six-foot-five, lanky man whom later generations would have described as a 'tall drink of water,' remembered a "skinny little kid whose folks owned The Midway," but the Captain, who had finally been promoted to that grade just last year after 17 grueling years as a junior officer, hadn't been back to Bergen County in over a decade. He and his wife, Susan, also from Schraalenburgh, maintained a home on Long Beach Island, on the Southern New Jersey coast. "And I'll be retiring there 29 months from tomorrow," he had said over last night's grilled shrimp and crab cakes. Despite the age difference, he and Wilder had hit it off. Both were West Pointers who liked to have a good time and didn't consider the USBAA regulations to be a replacement Bible.

"How long before we'll know for sure?" Wilder asked. Judge turned to Potts. "She's coming on strong, but it'll be about 6:30 before she can be definitely identified, Sir," Potts said, taking the telescope from Captain Judge for another look.

Wilder and Judge exchanged looks. "I think we should signal harbor side for a rider to stand by, Captain. Do you agree?"

The Captain nodded and turned to call for an aide in the yard.

General Scott's orders were to send a messenger to Georgetown the moment *Irresistible* was identified. Another messenger was to leave as soon as the ship docked and Wilder could ascertain if any important news or papers had been carried across the Ocean. Even if the Royal Navy, which tended to look down its collective nose at the 'colonial' Army, refused to disclose what was in the news or papers, Scott still wanted to know as soon as possible that something of importance was on its way to the Liaison Office. Wilder borrowed the telescope from Potts for a moment and walked quickly around the deck until he was facing the inner harbor.

He searched the entire dock area, including the still-closed inns. No sign of any Liaison-like figures: just a few dockworkers and stevedores yawning and sipping from flasks. He heard Judge coming up behind him. "Doesn't look like the Liaison Office is expecting anything this morning, Captain," he said, handing the telescope back to Judge, who took a quick visual tour.

"No, Lieutenant, it doesn't. And, as you're quite aware, once you know what to look for, those Liaison people stand out like a sore thumb." The two 'colonial' officers grinned at each other. "Sergeant Potts has the best eyes on the Fort. Let's get back and see if he's identified her yet."

The Sergeant was squinting out to the Bay and nodding to himself as the two officers made their way back to his post. He took the offered telescope again, looked quickly and grunted. "That's her, Captain. That's *Irresistible*. I thought so, the way she cut through the water. I've been watchin' her come and go for more than 18 months now and she just moves more smoothly than the other ships…"

"I need a visual, Captain, before I send a messenger towards Georgetown. General Scott likes facts, not hunches."

Potts turned and gave the Lieutenant the peculiar puckered-lip look that veteran NCOs have been utilizing to voicelessly express their frustrations with young junior officers since the Pharaohs first sent armies north to battle the Assyrians. "Got that too, Lieutenant. Right up by the bow in big letters. See for yourself," he said, handing Thomas the telescope and adding, helpfully, "the bow's the front end of the ship, Sir."

The Captain seemed suddenly to have something caught in his throat but said nothing as a red-faced Thomas pulled the telescope out of Potts' oversized hand and looked out into the Bay.

Thomas put down the telescope and looked at Judge. "I'm convinced. That's her. Let's get that message off to General Scott…"

Less than three minutes later, they could see a USBAA rider mount his horse and begin making his way from the harbor area. He carried a note transcribing Thomas' flashed message:

'Ship identified as *HMS Irresistible* sighted off harbor at 6 a.m. Anchorage anticipated by 8 a.m.'

Captain Judge looked down at the Lieutenant. "Well, Mr. Wilder, as it seems Major Porter is under the weather again this morning, I suggest you and I make ourselves presentable and then row over to the dock area. Looks like we'll be the only greeting party." Judge had inferred the previous night that the Fort's commanding officer had a drinking problem. His non-appearance now seemed to confirm it. As did the 'frog' that suddenly caused Sergeant Potts to loudly clear his own throat…

Ninety minutes later, the duo, attired in formal dress uniforms, was standing on the east side of the inner harbor, watching as *Irresistible* tied up and prepared to drop her gangway. Although they could see an RN officer Captain Judge identified as Sir Stephen Richards, captain of *Irresistible*, talking with two other men on the quarterdeck, neither USBAA officer had any idea of their identities.

Not even General Scott had expected *Irresistible* to bring the Duke of Wellington into Baltimore Harbor.

Despite the last four days of cold but calm weather that had restored his appetite and color, Captain Harry Bratton could not wait to get his feet back on dry land. He had vowed, hundreds of times, during the crossing that even if the Duke's political mission---they had agreed it would be billed publicly as a 'tour of the Dominion'--- ended before summer, he, Harry Bratton, was not making another Atlantic crossing until June, or preferably July, or maybe, never. He had lost at least 1 1/2 stone and knew he would not be himself for close to a week. *Bloody nonsense, crossing this damn Ocean in January...*

The Duke, on the other hand, had gradually adapted to the *Irresistible* and had hardly seemed to notice the conditions during the second half of the crossing. *He's eager to get started and actually seems to be relishing the idea of a crisis over here,* Bratton thought. Sir Stephen escorted them down off the ship and, barely glancing at the two USBAA officers, quickly looked around the inner harbor. "It appears word of our crossing is as yet unknown on this side of the Atlantic, Your Grace. There is no Liaison Office here in Baltimore, but I'll send someone to speed the arrival of the Station commandant, whom we signaled on the way in. Our Naval Station is a few hundred yards to the east. You may have noticed it as we entered the harbor."

"I did, Sir Stephen. And wondered why we were not docking there," said the Duke.

"The Station returned signal, Your Grace. Their anchorage is filled up. Happens, this time of year. No one really relishes those North Atlantic gales, eh Captain Bratton?"

Now that he was on dry land, the Colonial Office man could, and did, vigorously shake his head in disgust without again feeling sick.

Perhaps it was because he was, in fact, becoming a trained intelligence officer, or, perhaps, because portraits of the Duke hung in various places at the Point and the Department, as well as in The Residency. Then again, there was only one hook nose in the world like the one visible on the older gentleman's face. For whatever reason, Lt. Thomas Wilder, USBAA, suddenly and firmly realized that he was staring at the world's foremost soldier.

Jaysus, Mary and Joseph, he breathed to himself. *Wait till Scott and the G-G find out about this!*

Captain Judge was gazing at the visitors with a distinct lack of love when he heard Thomas' mutterings. He turned and looked down on the Lieutenant's excited face. "You look like you've seen a ghost, Mr. Wilder, or else George Washington. Which is it?"

Thomas looked up at the Captain. "Captain Judge, set yourself. After I finish, I suggest you turn slowly and casually. The older gentleman speaking with the Royal Naval officer is, I am positive, the Duke of Wellington. We wondered what *Irresistible* was bringing from London! Little did we realize..."

Judge stared down and then slowly turned. "I'll be damned, Lieutenant, you could be right." He could also see the younger of the two gentlemen with the naval officer, both in civilian dress, look him and Wilder over. The man, over six-foot and well-built, with a rapidly receding hairline, said a word to the hook-nosed older man and walked toward them.

"Excuse me, gentlemen, but I recognize the uniform. Are you the official Fort McHenry welcoming committee, or is there another reason for you to be waiting here at the dock?"

As the ranking officer, Captain Judge looked Bratton over. *Careful, Brian, this one's polished, but a hard man at the core.* "I'm Captain Judge, second-in-command of Fort McHenry. This is Lieutenant Wilder from Georgetown. And you Sir?" It was a deliberately ambiguous though honest answer. *What are we doing at this dock? This is our country, you arrogant SOB...*

"I am Harry Bratton, of the Colonial, err American, Office in London. I ask again, are you the official welcoming committee? If not, what are you doing here?"

The tension between the two was thickening, so Lieutenant Wilder decided to defuse the situation somewhat. "Mr. Bratton, I work for both the Governor-General and the USBAA commander, General Scott. I was assigned to meet the *Irresistible* if and when she landed, and ascertain how I could be of assistance. In the absence of the post commander, who is ill, Captain Judge commands at the Fort.

So it is also his duty and responsibility to be here to meet *Irresistible*.

"Now then, how best can we assist you and the Duke?" Tom was matter-of-fact, though his pulse had climbed rapidly. He had purposely saved the announcement of his identification of the older man as Wellington for last.

Bratton was a professional and thus managed to keep his surprise covered, except for the look in his eyes. "Very good, Lieutenant. Not every USBAA junior officer, on seeing a somewhat elderly gentleman wrapped tightly in his winter cloak, would recognize the Duke himself at first glance. If you gentlemen will follow me, you will discover what, if anything, His Grace, the Duke of Wellington might have in mind for you."

As they walked, the two USBAA officers exchanged looks of disgust. Upon getting to know one another the previous evening, they found themselves in agreement in their contempt for the English nobility's titles and airs. The Captain's people had left Cornwall in the late 1600s because of their refusal to kowtow to the local aristocracy, while Wilder, of course, was Irish Catholic...

Another Royal Naval officer was riding toward Wellington and Sir Stephen from the direction of the RNS as Bratton escorted the USBAA officers to the gangway. Bratton's group arrived first.

"Your Grace, these USBAA officers are Captain Judge, in command this morning at Fort McHenry, and Lieutenant Wilder, a representatives of the powers-that-be in Georgetown. They were assigned to meet *Irresistible* if and when she arrived and provide any wanted or needed assistance. Lieutenant Wilder, by the way, recognized you as we came down the plank."

Wellington looked them over as Wilder supposed he might a pair of carriage horses he was considering purchasing. Peering down his long nose he suddenly snapped: "How is it that Georgetown knew *Irresistible* was landing today...or coming at all? Or does the USBAA have such an abundance of junior officers that it can assign one to this harbor on the off chance a British man-of-war might sail in? Eh? And how did the Governor-General, or General Scott, know I would be aboard?"

So the Duke possesses a drill about as sharp as General Scott, Wilder thought. *Let's hope he's as honest and straightforward.* "Your...Grace..." *Let them think I'm nervous. It's probably better than them knowing how distasteful that is to spit out.*

"...no one in Georgetown had any idea you might be aboard. However, the Governor-General and General Scott, recognizing the, err, 'singularity' of *Irresistible's* mission to London last December, anticipated an early return. The Coastal Guard projected a possible arrival period of between yesterday and about February 5th.

"I arrived day before yesterday to take up the watch. One of Captain Judge's lookouts spotted a ship at approximately 5:35 this morning. By 6:30, we had the ship identified."

"Well Captain, I commend your command on its eyesight." The Duke was dry. Turning back to Thomas, he demanded: "And why did Jackson and Scott send you in particular? What did Captain Bratton say your title was?"

Well, so this hard case from the Colonial Office has a military title, too. "I am an aide at the War Department and at The Residency, Sir. I gather, review and analyze information in both positions, though my official Residency title is that of social aide."

"A social aide to Andy, eh? Does that mean you keep him from dueling...or do you fight his duels for him? Never mind, I withdraw the question. Come to think on it, I don't envy you that portion of your job!"

The second RN officer had dismounted, saluted and carried on a brief side conversation with Sir Stephen while the Duke grilled Lieutenant Wilder. Sir Stephen now turned and addressed the Duke: "Your Grace, this is Commodore Jeffrey Fischer, commandant of RNS Baltimore." The Commodore saluted sharply. "An unexpected honor, Your Grace. However, we are prepared to offer accommodations, transportation or anything else your party requires."

"That's a fine animal, Commodore. Do you have two more like him? That and some provisions and we'll be on our way."

"Certainly, Your Grace. The Royal Marines keep a fine stable. Ah, provisions for how long, Sir?"

The Duke turned to Lieutenant Wilder. "Well, Lieutenant? How far to Georgetown? You'll escort Captain Bratton and me. How many nights' provisions?"

Wilder swallowed both his astonishment and a smile. "If we leave by 10 a.m., Your Grace, we can make Georgetown tomorrow afternoon. As for provisions, well, there are satisfactory inns on the way. Provisions can be limited to something to eat while we rest the horses this afternoon."

"A good plan, Lieutenant. Commodore, arrange for satisfactory mounts and some light provisions. Sir Stephen, see that our trunks are unloaded and given to a Royal Marine detail that should follow us later today. I'll expect them at the Liaison Office in Georgetown tomorrow night, Commodore Fischer. Now, Lieutenant, see to your transportation. We will depart this harbor for Georgetown in exactly..." the Duke glanced at his pocket watch, "...86 minutes."

Thomas and Captain Judge saluted and walked towards the rowboat which would return the Captain to the Fort. Thomas spoke in a quiet voice: "Two things, Captain, if you would. While I get my horse from the stable, if you could send the crew for my things. More importantly, we need to alert the General. Better get a rider out of here before we leave. If the War Department is closed by the time he makes Georgetown, he should have secondary orders that can direct him to General Scott's home."

"Not a problem, Mr. Wilder. Our distinguished visitors will never know what's going on. The message will be brief: 'Lt. Wilder escorting Duke of Wellington and staff aide to Georgetown, departing 10 a.m. Stopover expected undetermined inn Georgetown-Baltimore Road. Arrive 2/2/33 late morning.' I'll see to this immediately. What's this all about? Do you have a clue?"

Thomas squinted up into the sun's glare, which made the Captain's face unrecognizable. "I'm not sure, Captain Judge. If worst comes to worst, you may retire a Major, though." He saluted and turned to walk to the stable situated on a side street.

CHAPTER ELEVEN

Georgetown-Baltimore Road
February 1, 1833:

They had actually gotten started by 9:45 a.m. The Royal Marines indeed kept a fine stable and provided Wellington and Bratton with their two finest mounts. Wilder had been waiting with Bay Ridge, the beautiful blue-black stallion his parents had given him as a West Point graduation gift which had seen him through his Dragoon days in Arkansas, when the two British officials reemerged from *Irresistible*. They had climbed aboard their horses immediately and, with little fanfare, followed Thomas through the narrow streets and out of Baltimore.

If they had seen him confer a last time with Captain Judge, no mention was made of it. The Captain indicated that, as planned, the second USBAA rider had left for Georgetown at 8:50 with the message for General Scott. Their commander would have the astonishing news by early evening, if all went according to plan. *The G-G doesn't know it yet, but he and his kitchen cabinet will be burning the midnight oil again tonight. Only this time, they won't be discussing that damn Bank. I wish I could be there to see the look on Jackson's face when Scott gives him the news. Hell, I'd give a month's pay to see the look on the* General's *face when he reads Judge's note!*

They rode at a brisk pace, but one moderated by Thomas to allow the USBAA messenger to outdistance them. (On his way to Baltimore, Thomas had alerted farmers along the route holding Army replacement mount contracts to be ready; this was not the first time express service between the capital and its major port would be required. The two veteran Fort McHenry riders selected by Captain Judge were well-acquainted with the remount stops.) The Englishmen seemed to accept Tom's pace, while the wind and cold kept conversation to a minimum until they stopped in early afternoon to rest and water their horses at still another roadside farm.

As they stood eating the cold RNS provisions, and enjoying some hot tea provided by the farmer's wife, Wellington, after a brief inquiry into Wilder's background and qualifications for the information-gathering positions, probed for comments on the political climate in the capital and the country. Bratton said little, but seemed to study the Lieutenant intently.

"From your two vantage points you must have a good view of the political situation, Lieutenant," the Duke said. "Did the plebiscite returns surprise you? Or the electorate as a whole?"

General Scott had repeatedly warned the Lieutenant to shy away from political discussions, especially with high-ranking officials. Few came any higher than the Duke of Wellington, but a direct question required a direct answer. "Well, Your Grace," he began, thinking how much it galled him to be forced to repeatedly use that damn title, "the plebiscite was generally quiet and its outcome more or less expected. Much more so than in '28, as I recall. Mr. Clay's candidacy never seemed to catch fire, if you'll understand the expression. General Jackson even picked up some significant support in the Northeast, where he was routed the last time."

"Why do you think that was, Lieutenant? Jackson picking up support in the Northeast, I mean," Wellington asked.

"Well Sir." *To hell with the damn 'Your Grace' every other sentence!* "New England appreciated his strong stand on nullification, as many people up there think South Carolina was testing the waters. Also, the Vice G-G elect, Mr. Van Buren, is considered the politician of the age. I know General Scott admired the way he organized General Jackson's campaign. Said it was a model of sound strategy and tactics; compared it to a military campaign."

The Duke turned and, sipping his tea, looked briefly at Bratton. "Yes, I've heard of Van Buren's mastery of politics. Has a nickname, does he not? 'The Little Magician,' I believe. But I'm interested in this 'testing the waters' business. What's that about, eh? Not familiar with the phrase. Are you, Captain Bratton?"

"I believe, Your Grace, that 'testing the waters' is an American colloquialism that we might better understand as a 'test case.' Am I right, Lieutenant?"

"That's a good comparison, Captain," Tom began before the Duke interrupted:

"A 'test case?' A test case for what, Mr.Wilder?"

"Sir, the abolition movement is gaining strength in New England. Its proponents see the nullification battle over tariffs as a, err, 'test case,' if you will, for the day when they will introduce emancipation legislation in the Congress. You see, Your Grace," *(Thomas didn't mind using the term when he doing the lecturing)* "if a state has the right to nullify one Dominion law it dislikes, how could it be stopped from nullifying any other? In other words, if nullification was to become an accepted legislative practice, what use would a Dominion emancipation bill be? If the states at which it was aimed---those where slavery now flourishes---could simply 'nullify' the law and continue on their merry ways?

"That, at any rate, Sir, is the abolitionist argument. And, to bring this full circle, why General Jackson gained increased Northeastern support."

The Duke and Captain Bratton were staring at one another. "Hmm, very interesting, Lieutenant, and well done. I begin to see why General Scott has you at the War Department. We'll continue this discussion tonight at whatever inn we stay. Meanwhile, gentlemen, we've still a long way to go, wouldn't you say, Mr. Wilder?"

They remounted and continued southwest to Georgetown: the two Britons with a slightly different perspective on the sophistication of the USBA's political process, and Thomas, cheerful for the first time in a week, basking in the Duke's offhanded praise.

Georgetown, D.C.
February 1, 1833:

Winfield Scott sat at his huge desk, rubbing his eyes and flexing his tree-trunk neck. *It's the damn paperwork that'll send me into retirement some day*, he thought with disgust. *That damn Gaines is a born paper-pusher. He eats this stuff up. Me, I need to get into the field more. Going out to Illinois for the Black Hawk War was a tonic. Not the fighting and dying, of course, just being in the field...*

The General rose from his chair and walked around the room, letting the blood circulate in his massive legs. *Almost 5 p.m. Think I'll call it a day. Wonder what damn fool event Maria has us scheduled for tonight?*

If it was up to my wife, we'd never stay home…well, she deserves her fun where she can find it. Georgetown isn't exactly London or Paris---or even New York--- when it comes to excitement.

The General was reaching for his cloak when his secretary, Lt. Luke Beaufort, appeared in the doorway. "Excuse me, sir. Rider just in from Fort McHenry." The secretary handed Scott Lieutenant Wilder's message: 'Ship identified as *Irresistible* sighted off harbor at 6 a.m. Anchorage anticipated by 8 a.m.' Scott folded the message and handed it back.

"Get this over to the Governor-General, Lieutenant. His hand only, you understand? Tell General Jackson I will hand deliver the follow-up message when received, no matter the hour." Scott tossed his huge head, indicating to the secretary to leave. He leaned back against the front of the desktop as he watched his aide depart. *Well, she got back in a hurry, didn't she ever! Let's see: December 16th to February 1st. Forty-seven days. That's got to be record time. Which means something's up. If it's not a slave-based tax, it's something of comparable importance. I wonder what, if anything, Wilder has found out…*

Georgetown-Baltimore Road
February 1, 1833:

Darkness comes early to southern Maryland in midwinter but Wellington and his party pushed on till the lights of Brady's Fox Hunt Inn began to become visible after 5 p.m.

"I suggest we stop here, Sir," Wilder said as the three horsemen slowed their pace several hundred yards north of the Inn. "We're still about 30 miles from Georgetown and there isn't a better inn within 10 miles. The food is good here and it doesn't look too crowded. Shouldn't have trouble getting rooms."

Wellington had nodded at the suggestion to stop and laughed at the reference to rooms. Bratton, however, seemed to bristle. "Are you suggesting that the Duke of Wellington would be turned away at the inn, Lieutenant? Bloody little chance of that, I would expect…"

Wilder looked at the Englishman as they dismounted and handed their reins to the stable boy. *You pompous jackass! You come over here and treat us like second class citizens in our own country. This isn't Ireland. Here, we push back*: "I'm sure there's room for the Duke, Captain Bratton. I was referring to the chances of *you* bedding down in the stable…

"However, that does raise a serious question, Sir," he added, turning to the still chuckling Duke. "We've not discussed whether this is a public visit to the USBA. Am I to announce you to Mr. Brady, who is, as the sign says, the innkeeper, or simply to refer to Your Grace as a distinguished visitor from Great Britain?"

Even in the half darkness of the lantern-lit yard, Wellington's eyes sparkled as Scott's sometimes did when Wilder said something sharp. "Very good, Lieutenant. I am here on a tour of the Dominion, but one that has yet to be announced publicly. I believe it will be easier all around if I remain incognito until we reach Georgetown and I can pay my respects at The Residency. You will introduce me as 'Colonel Wellesley, British Army, ret.' And the Captain as 'Captain Bratton of the Coldstream Guards.' Now, let's go in, shall we?"

An hour later, their gear stashed in their rooms (to Thomas' disgust, he was forced to share his space with Bratton) and the dirt of a hard day's riding washed from their hands and faces, Wilder and the two Englishmen were seated at a back booth near a roaring Inn fireplace.

A waitress, one of the owner's daughters, Erin, had already served a round of drinks: hot rum for the 'Colonel'; Port for Captain Bratton and a mug of beer for the Lieutenant.

"Even in the dead of winter, Mr. Wilder?" Bratton said, pointing to the stein. "And you Americans still drink it chilled, too, I see."

"I'm not one for spirits, Captain Bratton," Thomas said without, he hoped, a trace of a blush. "I do enjoy fine wines in the appropriate settings, and an occasional glass of Port. However, I acquired my taste for beer naturally. And I refined it at the Point. That's all we could get, at Benny Haven's…"

Wellington, who seemed to enjoy the biting give-and-take between the Colonial Office man and this surprisingly feisty young USBAA officer, broke in: "What's that? 'Acquired your taste naturally?' Eh? And what was this about 'the Point?'"

Well, it was bound to come out sooner or later. Thomas looked the Duke in the eye. "I'm a third generation British American of Irish Catholic descent, 'Colonel Wellesley.' So I naturally like my beer. I also graduated from West Point, the USBA Military Academy, back in '29. Benny Haven's is a rather disreputable tavern outside the Main Gate. Like every West Pointer, I remember it fondly…"

There was a short silence at the table, which the Duke broke with a snort that seemed to denote acceptance rather than disdain. "Well, Lieutenant, we Englishmen enjoy an occasional pint ourselves, eh Bratton? But not on a cold winter's night. Have that waitress bring over another round and tell us what's on tonight's menu…"

Over their meals---'the Colonel' and Captain Bratton chose two of the Inn's specialties: prime rib and a steak served sizzling hot, respectively, while Tom ate a hearty beef stew---'the Colonel' steered talk back to the political situation.

"Captain Bratton, Lieutenant, served in the Liaison Office at Georgetown back in the late '20s. He has emphasized to me the political importance of the slavery issue in the USBA. So your observations this afternoon about emancipation and nullification made an impression. Tell me, have you any indication that the abolitionists are planning to introduce an emancipation bill in the upcoming Congress, which for some reason doesn't convene until next December, if I'm not mistaken?"

Taken back by the news that Bratton had first-hand knowledge of the USBA--*did the Captain realize he had deliberately slowed their progress to Georgetown?*--the Lieutenant paused before focusing his thoughts on the 'Colonel's' question.

"An emancipation bill is the abolitionists' long-term goal, 'Colonel.' At least ten years down the road, from all I've heard and read. Perhaps I overemphasized their strength in the North at present. It's growing solidly in New England, where it's begun to have an affect on local political races. In New York and Pennsylvania, the movement doesn't yet have the political clout it now does in New England, but is drawing more attention than ever. In the West, people are more concerned with developing the land than arguing social issues that have no direct impact on their lives. Even out West, however, there seems to be growing conviction that slavery is a moral blot on our society. Yet everyone realizes that, even if the abolitionists managed to get a bill introduced and passed---which is remote at best---they'd never muster the two-thirds majority necessary to see it into law."

Captain Bratton leaned forward across the remnants of his sizzling steak. "And why do you say that, Mr. Wilder? Why a two-thirds majority?" The 'Colonel,' too, looked puzzled.

"Because, gentlemen, according to our constitution, it takes a two-thirds majority to overturn a gubernatorial-general veto. That's a veto

118

which is automatic, at least for the next four years, as long as the G-G's health holds up.

"After all, if there is anything as sure as death and the British Empire, it is that Andrew Jackson would veto any emancipation bill placed before him. That, 'Colonel,' I don't believe any British American citizen, including the most rapid abolitionist, would argue."

The political talk seemed to die off shortly thereafter, and the 'Colonel' soon excused himself and went to bed. The two younger officers remained in the tavern, where Bratton quizzed the Lieutenant on the Georgetown social scene, both high level and low. He seemed particularly impressed that Joanne Casgrave had taken over ownership of the Golden Eagle.

Georgetown, D.C.
Evening, February 1, 1833:

Winfield Scott was relieved that his wife had not made plans for the evening. He needed to stay home to await the arrival of the second Fort McHenry rider.

With a complete trust in Maria's ability to keep official secrets, a trust earned in the almost two decades of their marriage, the General had long before discussed the *Irresistible* mystery with her. She of course knew that Thomas had been sent to Baltimore and was aware that messages were expected if-and-when the ship was sighted. Only the timing surprised her. Winfield hadn't expected *Irresistible* for a few more days, at the earliest.

After relaxing over glasses of Port, the couple was preparing to sit down to supper when a servant went to answer a sudden knock at the front door. "General, a soldier who identifies himself as from Fort McHenry is in the vestibule. He requests to speak with you."

Scott glanced at the clock and shared a look with his wife. It was 7:12 p.m. He strode out without a word. Saluting the obviously tired but still awestruck corporal, he took the message from the man's hand before speaking. "Thank you, Corporal. When did you leave?"

"About 8:50 this morning, Sir. Been in the saddle all day, except for remounting."

"It will be noted on your record, son. Good work. I assume you know the drill as far as food, lodging and care for your horse?"

"Yes, Sir, I've ridden this route before." The Corporal saluted and left.

Scott was tearing open the message and reading it even before the door closed behind the non-com. He could count on one hand the times he'd truly been taken back during his years in the service, but this message left him dumbfounded. His old commander from the Peninsula campaign, General Sir Arthur Wellesley, now formally the Duke of Wellington, had come across the Atlantic on *Irresistible!* And was within 40 or so miles of Georgetown, escorted by Scott's own aide. The General read the message a second time. '...Stop expected undetermined inn Georgetown-Baltimore Road. Arrive 2/2/33...'

Tom's giving us overnight to prepare...good boy. Should I send an escort troop up the road tonight? No, wait till morning. Let's not look too concerned...even though this is one delicate situation.

Maria had taken the message from his hand and gasped as she read it. "Win, Wellington himself here? Why do you think...?"

Scott's face settled into a puzzled frown. "I'm not sure, but something tells me all hell is about to break loose, my dear. The Duke didn't take to the North Atlantic in January for fun. London's planning something so big that they've sent the most prestigious name they could to inform us. I'd better get over to see Jackson. Don't wait up." He kissed her softly on the forehead and, pulling on his heavy military great coat, called for the carriage he had ordered to stand by as soon as he had arrived home.

CHAPTER TWELVE

Georgetown, D.C.
February 2, 1833:

After consultation with a---for once---stunned-into-silence Jackson, Scott had decided against sending a troop to meet Wellington and escort him down to Georgetown. The strategy he and the G-G had devised in their late night meeting with Blair, Van Buren and others of the kitchen cabinet called for cloaking their preparations with apparent surprise.

Scott now knew that Jackson had initially been violently against any Imperial-imposed tax on slaves and/or their resale but was now reconsidering, having realized its potential for countering the abolitionist movement. Blair, for one, had grasped that a tax---with or without a companion bill on Northern industrial growth---would indeed have the unforeseen effect of legitimizing slavery by making its existence directly financially beneficial to the Empire. He favored a public voicing of opposition but a tacit silent agreement of support. Van Buren apparently---it was never crystal clear with the 'Little Magician'---favored sending a special delegation to lobby Parliament to drop the proposal. (That the USBA already had a Parliamentary delegation didn't seem to affect Matty Van's thinking; he apparently wanted to talk the bill to death...or to so appear.)

Scott hadn't left The Residency until well after midnight but was back in his War Department office by 8 a.m. No matter what the purpose, a visit by as distinguished a dignitary as London could possibly send---a former commander-in-chief as well as former Prime Minister---called for formal welcoming ceremonies. His office was already working on the details and would coordinate with The Residency as soon as Lieutenant Wilder arrived. Meanwhile, at Jackson's orders, Donelson was overseeing a hurried freshening up of the old house itself.

Having given orders that the 4th Artillery and the other ceremonial units standby, Scott returned to the real issue: why was

Wellington here? *What has London decided to spring on us? And why, in God's name, now?*

Georgetown-Baltimore Road
February 2, 1833:

They had risen before dawn and, after a quick breakfast of tea and biscuits that Tom had arranged with the innkeeper the night before, they were ready to ride. As they were reining their horses toward the road, the proprietor came out into the yard. A barrel-chested man in his early 50s with the map of Ireland imprinted on his face, Ed Brady had fought in the Napoleonic Wars before emigrating to the USBA.

"I hope the food and accommodations were acceptable, gentlemen?" he asked. Informed that they were, Brady added, looking up to the 'Colonel': "And will Your Grace be leading the commemorative services at Waterloo for the 20th anniversary? Some of the lads from Third R.I. Fusiliers have written me that something may be planned…"

Thomas was unable to swallow a chuckle, though Bratton's snort was clearly one of disgust. But the Duke smiled and thrust out his hand. "Third Royal Irish, eh? A good regiment, though a bit lax on discipline. You should have identified yourself last night, sir. It's always a pleasure to meet one of my old boys. Yes, the Waterloo anniversary is coming up. I've heard something is in the works, but haven't kept up on the details. Well, we both have time yet. Meanwhile, thank you for your hospitality, ah…"

"Former Sergeant Brady, Sir. The honor was mine."

The trio of riders was silent as they headed down the road, though the Duke could be heard softly whistling 'Rule Britannia.'

Georgetown, D.C.
February 2, 1833:

The ugly brown dome of the Capitol Building was visible on its hill as they rode into the outskirts of Georgetown. Bratton observed that the 'city' hadn't grown much, if at all, since his departure four years before. Wilder's mood was a mixture of relief that the journey was concluding without incident, mixed with disappointment that the adventure was over. The Duke, of course, exhibited his usual serene air of confidence.

"Well, Sir, this is the metropolis," Wilder said, as they reined up their horses at Silver Spring. "Do you wish to go straight on to The Residency, or stop off at the Liaison Office?"

The Duke looked around carefully, one hand cupping his saddle's horn. *Reminds me of hamlets I marched through in Portugal. Fifty something years and this is the best they can do? They tell me Philadelphia is a real city. Well, I'm sure there's some reason they moved their capital here…and I'm sure it smacks of a sordid political deal. Doesn't everything over here?*

"You'll escort me to The Residency, Lieutenant, which I would guess is that lonely-looking building over towards the river, with all the parkland around it." Wellington pointed out towards the southwest, where a large white mansion of sorts stood out rather forelornly. "Captain Bratton will be announcing our presence at the Liaison Office. Which I'm sure you can find without any help, eh Captain?"

"Yes, Your Grace. Georgetown seems unchanged since I left in '29. I'll inform Sir John and Major Layne of your arrival. Should I await you at the Office, or go on to The Residency myself?"

"Consult with Sir John. I'll either send for you or come over myself. A surprise visit like this is highly irregular. No protocol, you understand. We'll have to play it by ear at first. Well, let's get on with it, shall we?"

They proceeded into Georgetown, riding on, and passing across, streets with grand names like 'Vermont Avenue' and others as simple as 'Tenth Street.' Some were wider than others, but all were pockmarked by ridges of frozen mud and dirty ice. Bratton saluted and turned off short of the park grounds, heading west on Pennsylvania Avenue, while Wilder led Wellington across Pennsylvania (which cut through) and onto The Residency grounds. They rode up the driveway to the Main Portico (reminding Tom for the first time in several days of Lucille and his unfortunate bravado performance the night of the Christmas reception) as Andrew Jackson Donelson made his way down the steps. It was now almost 11 a.m.

Donelson was one of the select few who knew Wellington's arrival was imminent. (General Scott in fact had notified The

Residency an hour earlier that the trio of riders had been sighted on the Silver Spring Road.) Both Residency and War Department were geared up for the arrival. Now Donelson, selected by Jackson to play the key opening role of baffled Residency representative, came down the steps as if to leave the grounds on official business. Thomas, who had seen the civilian-dressed USBAA lookout get off a signal to Georgetown as they had come down the Silver Spring road, knew the G-G's nephew well enough to realize the man never left the building during office hours. Something was afoot...

"Good morning, Mr. Donelson," Tom said as he brought Bay Ridge to a halt in front of the Portico. "Is the Governor-General well disposed? I need to present this gentleman to him immediately."

"Why yes, Lieutenant, the G-G is in his office. He is in conference with Mr. Blair, but if this is urgent, I'll break in. I was off to the Interior Department, but I'll postpone that trip to later, if necessary..." Donelson indicated the pouch under his arm and put on a quizzical face as he stared up at the riders. "Who should I say your guest is, Lieutenant?"

Thomas looked over at the Duke, who smiled somewhat mischievously. "Mr. Donelson is Governor-General Jackson's private secretary, as well as nephew, Sir."

The Duke looked condescendingly at the young Tennessean: "If you will tell General Jackson, Mr. Donelson, that an old comrade from the Iberian Peninsula days has come to visit. Minus his army."

Managing to look both startled and mystified, Donelson headed back up the steps as the riders threw their reins to waiting grooms and walked up the steps themselves. *You ought to consider the stage, Mr. Donelson,* Wilder thought. *You even have me half convinced you don't know what's going on.*

Donelson had disappeared into the G-G's office by the time Lieutenant Wilder escorted the Duke into the main foyer. The chief usher was still taking their cloaks when Jackson came hobbling out on his cane. Frank Blair trailed behind him.

"By the Eternal, what's all this about the 'Iberian Peninsula' now? Where's Lieutenant Wil..." Jackson suddenly broke off as he eyed his old chief. "By God, it *is* you, General: the Duke of Wellington himself! By the Eternal, General, what brings you to the USBA? And in the dead of winter, no less!" Jackson gave a good account of a flabbergasted Governor-General. "Never expected to meet up with *you* again on this earth, General. Don't tell me you too finally had enough of *London society*!" The G-G spit out the last two words with an anger that made Wilder, Blair and Donelson each wince.

The Duke, however, seemed to take Jackson's vehemence in stride. "Yes, Andrew, London still reveres you, too. Why, when my tour of the USBA was publicly announced, I can't tell you how many leaders of society asked to be remembered to you…"

The two men stared at each other for a short moment and broke out laughing before embracing.

"'Old Hickory.' Just as belligerent and cantankerous as ever…"

"And you, General, or should I say: 'Your Grace, the Duke.' Just as sleek and high flaluten' as ever.

"Well, I sent the Lieutenant here up to Baltimore a few days ago to see what news the *Irresistible* might be carrying across the Atlantic to our 'poor colonial shores.' Never thinkin' he'd ride back into Georgetown with you in tow…

"Come into my office, General. You look a mite chilled. Some fine Tennessee whisky will warm you right up. By the way, this is Frank Blair, my most trusted advisor…" The door shut behind them, leaving Wilder and Donelson in the hall.

"Well, Mr. Donelson, would you like me to drop off that pouch at the Interior Department? I must report immediately to General Scott."

"Nonsense, Tom. You knew that was a ruse the moment you saw me. General Scott brought the message from Fort McHenry that you were escorting the Duke here about 8:00 last night. Things have been in an uproar ever since. Let's hope the Duke was taken in, though. The G-G instructed everyone to act amazed…" Donelson smiled broadly. "So, Lieutenant, what's the word? Why *is* he here?"

Wilder shrugged his shoulders. "Honestly, Andy, I haven't figured it out. You heard him: he's *touring* the USBA. All I know is…he peppered me with questions about politics, the abolitionists, Army preparedness and so forth whenever we stopped and even on horseback, when the wind died down. I haven't answered that many questions since my last finals at the Point…or since General Scott wanted some information." He paused thoughtfully. "They seem a lot alike, Scott and the Duke: blunt, honest and miles ahead of me. Can't tell where Wellington was going with his questions. One thing I do know: like General Scott, his questions are all for a purpose.

"Speaking of which, I'd better get over to the War Department. Before 'Old Fuss and Feathers' orders my arrest for dereliction of duty."

Winfield Scott was pacing his office when he noticed his aide giving his horse's reins to an enlisted man at the entrance to the building. *That's one beautiful animal he has there,* the General noted. *I wonder where Tom found him? More importantly, what has the Lieutenant found out?*

Scott waited impatiently for Wilder to make his way through the building and appear at his office doorway. When the Lieutenant did appear, it was obvious he had taken the time to brush much of the dirt of the morning's ride from his uniform and boots. "Come in Lieutenant," he boomed, "and close the door.

"So, Mr. Wilder, the Duke of Wellington's come to town. Did he say why?" The General's tone bordered on frivolity, but the Lieutenant knew his boss well enough to know he had been ordered to make a complete and thorough report.

"Sir, the Duke states his trip is a *private tour* of the Dominion. He is accompanied by a single aide. That aide, however, Captain Bratton, was at the Liaison Office here in the late '20s and since has apparently served in a civilian capacity in the American Office in London. Beneath the polished ven…"

"I know Bratton…Beneath the polished veneer, a hard man. That is your assessment, is it not?"

"Yes Sir. A hard man. Not quite your average tour guide…"

"So, Lieutenant?" The drill was starting up as the icy stare fixed on Thomas.

"General, for the entire trip, at every stop and whenever the wind died down enough for horseback conversation, the Duke peppered me with questions, mostly of a political nature: was the plebiscite's outcome generally expected? About the abolitionists and the nullification crisis; even about the new Vice G-G, about whom he seemed to know a remarkable bit. That's in addition to the more-expected questions about the Army and conditions on the frontiers."

"What's your conclusion, Lieutenant? Did the Duke really come here on a midwinter sightseeing trip? And what about your celebrated theory on a slave tax?"

Thomas reddened slightly at mention of his much-maligned theory, but quickly moved to answer Scott's questions. "Sir, this is no *sightseeing* trip. From spending the better part of a day-and-a-half with the Duke, answering questions that followed up answers to questions I was asked earlier, I'd say this is a fact-finding mission disguised as a pleasure trip.

"And General, based on the direction the questions always seemed to take, I think the subject has to do with slavery."

"Continue Mr. Wilder." The drill was slowing as the General's eyes now indicated a more thoughtful mood was in ascendance.

"Yesterday afternoon, while we rested the horses, Sir, the Duke began asking about the plebiscite. And why General Jackson did so much better in New England this time. That led to a discussion of the long-term implications of the nullification battle, at least from the abolitionists' perspective."

The General continued to look thoughtful and Tom hurried on. "That if the nullification principle was upheld, any state could nullify any Dominion law, thus making any attempt in Congress to abolish slavery worthless from a legal standpoint." Tom paused again, but Scott nodded for him to continue. "Then last night, over supper, he returned to the issue of an emancipation bill. Wanted to know if I felt one would be introduced in the new Congress. *That* led to a discussion of the G-G's veto powers, of which neither he nor Bratton seemed previously aware. That was after I explained that emancipation was the abolitionists' long-term, not short-term, goal.

"Also, he stated categorically that Captain Bratton 'emphasized the political importance of the slavery issue' to him, apparently during the crossing."

"Did he bring up the new Congress or did you?"

"The Duke did, Sir. Knew it is not scheduled to convene until December. One other thing, General.

"After I pointed out that even the most extreme abolitionist is not so politically naive to expect Andrew Jackson to sign an emancipation bill, conversation sort of drifted away from politics…"

Scott rose from his desk and walked over to the window. He gazed out towards The Residency and the Potomac River, his huge hands folded behind him. Finally, he turned to Thomas, who had been standing at parade rest since beginning the report.

"Quite a report, Mr. Wilder. The Duke certainly kept you on

your toes. Well done, particularly in extending the trip overnight. Not only did you obtain some interesting information, but it gave us here time to prepare. Now freshen up and be back here in an hour. We've pulled the plans for welcoming a Prime Minister from the files. You'll coordinate them with Donelson, who has done the same over there. I imagine there'll be a formal ceremony tomorrow, sometime. Get at it.

"One more thing. The G-G is already, reluctantly, planning a Residency dinner for the Duke. You'll be in attendance in both your official social and intelligence capacities, so I'll expect you to be at your sharpest. Therefore I've arranged to fine comb the guest list so that you'll have no distractions. General Jackson agrees with me that the, uh, timing of this dinner is such that only Congressional leaders as well as ranking military and government and consular officers and their ladies will be invited. Remind Mr. Donelson that all outlying planters, their wives, widows and daughters are to be excluded...Understood?"

The boy's face is about the color of that exotic new fruit Maria helped introduce into Georgetown society last Summer, thought the General. *What did they call it? A tomato, I believe.* "You are dismissed, Mr. Wilder," the General barked, turning back to the window before the Lieutenant could see the smile that was uncontrollably breaking out on his face. He remained facing the window until Thomas could be seen walking down the steps.

We had better get him fixed up with the Latoure girl, he thought with a chuckle. *Otherwise, that Candice is going to be the ruination of a potentially fine Army career...*

Wellington and the two British Americans saluted each other with glasses of Tennessee whisky served neat by Blair. "Congratulations on your resounding victory, Andrew, and all the best in your second term." The Duke was at his most cordial. "Incidently, among those in London most moved by your reelection was the Parliamentary member from Massachusetts..."

Blair nearly spit his whiskey across the room, while Jackson's hand moved to tightly grip his cane, Wellington observed, much as a younger Jackson might have gone for his knife.

"Yes, I'm sure that Puritan bastard was *moved*, as you say, Duke. By the Eternal, if I ever get my hands..."

"Now Mr. Governor-General," Blair was formal. "Certainly Adams and Clay conspired to steal the '24 plebiscite from you. But, in the end, you're the one standing. You beat Adams four years later and now have trounced Clay." He glanced at Wellington, whose eyes were sparkling in enjoyment, either of Jackson's reaction or of the Tennessee whiskey. Or, perhaps, a combination thereof.

Jackson's fit of anger was over. He looked directly at the Duke. "Now then Your Grace," he began in a formal manner that indicated his seriousness, "what does bring you to the Dominion at this time of year? We've precious little for you to see just now but mud and snow. For the former, you could have stayed in London and for the latter, gone with King Billy to Balmoral..."

"Actually, Andrew, I thought I'd visit the South and perhaps New Orleans this month, before returning here for your inauguration. Then, as the weather improves, tour the Middle States and the West. I'm anxious to see all this land you and Winfield took from the French at the point of your cannon. From there, Ontario and, I suppose, Quebec, too, before wrapping up my tour in New England."

"Are we to understand, then, that you've retired from politics, Duke? Surely such a long time away from Parliament for the leader of the opposition is, *unusual*, to say the least?" Jackson cast a shrew eye at his guest, his face plainly indicating his reluctance to accept the Duke's blandly proposed plans.

Wellington, however, refused to be baited: "Unfortunately, Andrew, the Whigs are firmly in the saddle right now. Even if Lord Grey's health forces his resignation---a very possible thing---the King will ask Lord Melbourne to form a new government. To simply take over the existing one, actually, with little change. So, a good time to fulfill my long-time dream to visit these splendid shores!"

Blair sat watching the verbal chess match tensely, slowly sipping his own whiskey. *Andy's not fooled and Wellington knows he's not, but the Duke won't give Andy the satisfaction of acknowledging that fact. Something real big is brewing here, but Wellington isn't ready to spill the beans about it yet. Maybe Scott was right about a slave tax... Let's hope Andrew doesn't lose his temper. This isn't Layne or Jean Claude he's dealing with here!*

Blair decided to try to lighten the mood by pretending to accept the Duke's pronouncement of the *tour*. He framed his question in a way that would allow the first reference to Wellington's traveling companion to come from the Duke himself.

THE DOMINION'S DILEMMA: THE UNITED STATES OF BRITISH AMERICA

"Well, Your Grace, we can put together an itinerary for you quick enough, but concerning a traveling party: do you prefer civilian or military aides?" The lines around Jackson's eyes showed that the G-G understood and approved the thinking behind the question.

"No need for a *traveling party*, as you put it, Mr. Blair. As I said, this is strictly a private tour. And I've brought my own *traveling party* with me. The Colonial Secretary was good enough to assign one of his men, Harry Bratton, who served here in the '20s, as a sort of tour guide. We'll travel fast, loose and light. Speaking of which, I dropped Harry off at the Liaison Office on the way in. I don't suppose you'll have room to put him up here for a few days, while we attend to details of the trip?"

"Now Sir Arthur, of course, we'll put your aide up here," Jackson was cordially hearty. "There are plenty of extra bedrooms. God knows, that damn Quincy Adams carved the whole of the second floor up into them. Man had more children than Abraham...We'll see to getting you settled in and we'll dine at 3 p.m. Frank, here, will join us and I'll send for the incoming Vice G-G..."

"Ah, yes, the 'Little Magician' as I believe he is known. I'm looking forward to hearing about the plebiscite campaign from him. I understand he played a key role."

Jackson and Blair exchanged surprised looks as Wellington walked over to the fireplace to rub his hands. "Your Tennessee whiskey is medicinal, Andrew, but 23 days at sea and 1 1/2 on the road...I can't seem to shake the cold out of my bones."

There's a coldness in my bones, too, Blair thought. *Because you, Sir Arthur, are hiding something from us: the real reason you're here.* He looked again at the G-G. Jackson was staring at the Duke's back and shaking his head. *Good, he senses it, too. A good performance, Your Grace. But we're not the country bumpkins here you apparently think we are. Something's up. It's just a matter of time till we find out whether Scott's right and it's a slave tax...or something else. I'm going to keep a close eye on that* 'itinerary.'

Thomas had spent much of the afternoon reviewing the details of the Army's role in the formal welcoming ceremonies. The Residency had sent word the ceremonies would take place the next day, Sunday, at high noon, in front of the Capitol. Even though the Congress was not in session, Jackson wanted the Capitol steps, as he reportedly felt it ridiculous to welcome the Duke to The Residency, when the honored guest would have already spent a night there.

Now, a bit after 4 p.m., Tom was on his way on foot across the park to The Residency to meet with Donelson and coordinate the plans. He was, however, overtaken by Bratton, coming from the Liaison Office on horseback.

"Well, Lieutenant, just the man I need to see. I'm to meet a Mr. Donelson concerning some sort of ceremony tomorrow and also to be assigned a room in the Mansion. Must say, I've been here for social events and such, but never to board…"

Thomas looked up at Bratton in time to be hit with the first snowflakes in several weeks. The weather had been steadily worsening over the course of the day, with temperatures plummeting. *Just our luck, to have snow for this ceremony. Well, better than riding down from Baltimore in it…*

"I'm meeting with Donelson, myself, Captain, to coordinate plans for tomorrow. Come with me and we'll handle this, and then find you a bed. Won't have to worry about you sleeping in the stables here…"

"Very good, Lieutenant. Ah, incidentally, is the Golden Eagle still operating at the same location? Grant Street, I believe? "

Wilder grinned: *the fox is out in the open. Wonder what's between him and that damn Joanne? I better let Harps know he has competition.* "The Eagle's still right over there." He pointed through the sudden snow squall to a side street running off The Residency's grounds to the southwest. "There've been some *changes,* shall we say, recently but it's still in the same place. Shall we go find Mr. Donelson?"

———————

The planning meeting had lasted more than an hour, followed by a briefing session with the G-G and the Duke, who, despite the so-called 'private' nature of his trip, apparently had expected some sort of official greeting. Thomas left The Residency well after 6 p.m. and walked in blinding wet snow the several blocks to his room at the Indian Queen Hotel. Donelson, meanwhile, had assigned a Negro servant to take Captain Bratton to his small bedroom on the second floor living quarters. The Duke, of course, was to occupy the primary guest bedroom.

All in all, an interesting, if tiring, day, Tom thought as he crunched his way through the snow-covered streets. *It will also be interesting to hear what the General has to say tomorrow morning.* Tom knew the Scotts were probably now already on their way to The Residency for an informal get-together. "Just three broken-down old soldiers," Jackson had laughingly growled in telling the aides about it. *Maria Scott won't be too badly bored,* Tom smiled to himself; Emily Donelson, Andy's wife and the official Jackson hostess, had returned last week from Tennessee. *I just hope I won't be a primary topic as Mrs. Scott brings Emily up to speed on the latest Georgetown gossip... That must have been some dinner-party at the Scotts, once Lucille saw Candice.* He grimaced, then grinned: *Though knowing Candice, she was probably oblivious to it...*

Well, he thought as he entered the Queen and luxuriated in the warmth, *a quick change out of this uniform, a few beers in the taproom and something to eat. Then it's bed for this boy. Tomorrow's going to be another long day...*

Like Thomas, Harry Bratton had been up since predawn, but he had plans for the evening anyway. He was dining at the Liaison Office at 7 p.m. with Major Layne. Then, perhaps, a stop at the Golden Eagle would be in order...

Bratton had the luxury of a White House carriage, graciously arranged by Andrew Donelson. So he declined Major Layne's offer of a room at the Liaison Office compound and headed out into the still-falling snow a few hours later. Officially, as he told the Major, he couldn't chance not being available in case the Duke wanted to discuss something late tonight or in the early morning hours. The Major, who had unsuccessfully pumped Harry for an explanation for the Duke's unexpected visit---the Office had been thrown into a panic when Bratton had causally appeared at the front gate that afternoon---was openly skeptical of the 'tour' concept. Though, to be frank, he had admitted, after three years in Georgetown, he'd give anything for some "real excitement."

Watch out, Major, Harry thought, keeping a stiff upper lip. *You just may get what you wished for...and more.*

The Residency carriage had now deposited Harry at the door of the Golden Eagle, which in the snow looked unchanged from his last visit some 40 months ago. He pushed open the door and entered the half-empty tavern, stomping wet snow from his boots.

The bartender, a tall, emaciated man whom the waitresses called Richard, poured him a glass of Port. A group of card players were intently studying their hands near one fireplace. Meanwhile, a mixed group of young men---Wilder had told him the Eagle was still the main gathering place for junior government officials---and women--- from the looks of them, off-duty waitresses---were carrying on more boisterously in an alcove. At other tables in separate parts of the room, two pairs of gentlemen were finishing up their meals. *Lobbyists and their prey,* he thought wryly. *Some things in Georgetown never change...*

As he had come across the room, he had seen all four men give him a quick inspection. Once they recognized the military uniform, they had immediately lost interest.

He addressed the bartender, Richard, as the man refilled his glass. "I understand Mrs. Casgrave is the proprietress now," he said.

The hollow-checked man snickered. "Proprietress, you say? I've heard Joanne called a lot of things, but that's a new one on me, now, soldier. What's it mean?"

"It means, you unschooled fellow, that she is now the owner-operator of this establishment."

Richard snickered again. "Yeah, she's the boss, alright. And I think she's doing some operatin' right now, by damn. Ain't that right Kathy?"

'Kathy' proved to be the waitress, a tall buxom blond with dirty blond hair and rouge covering up some telltale facial marks. *Smallpox,* Bratton thought. *At least she survived. Most don't, either here or in London.*

Kathy looked the Captain up-and-down. "Haven't seen you here before, darlin'. New to the Liaison Office or just passin' through?"

Maybe this was what Wilder meant by 'changes,' thought Bratton. "I mentioned to your colleague that I understood Joanne Casgrave now owns and operates this establishment. He seemed to find that somewhat amusing."

"He called her the 'propra-something, Kathy...'"

"Proprietress." She turned to Bratton. "Yes, you could say that. Madame Joanne is the proprietress, the boss, whatever: she owns the place."

"This man says she is 'operating.' Does that mean she's here but unavailable at the moment?"

Kathy looked Harry up-and-down once again. In the back of her mind, she began to recall stories of Joanne and an English officer. She smiled, but there was no mirth in her eyes. "Madame Joanne has an appointment this evening. In fact, it began about an hour ago. I believe she'll be busy through closing time. However, perhaps someone else can entertain you? There's still room at the inn, don't you know?"

So that's how she got the money to buy this place. Bloody hell. Should have gone directly back to The Residency. "No, thanks. Just inform her in the morning, if you would, that an old acquaintance stopped by." He finished his Port, pushed some coins toward the bartender and turned to leave. Kathy put her meaty hand on his arm.

"And who should I say came to call? Sir Galahad himself?"

Bratton pulled his arm away and tossed his cloak over his back. "No, just Henry the Eighth." It was an old joke between them. He walked out and climbed into the carriage.

CHAPTER THIRTEEN

Georgetown. D.C.
February 4, 1833:

With an assist by some nonparticipating members of the 4th Artillery, the Capitol workmen had pushed the almost 18 inches of heavy, wet snow off the building's steps in time for the ceremony to begin just an hour late, at 1 p.m. yesterday. There had followed a welcoming reception at the Liaison Office compound that had continued on into Sunday evening. Every Counsel-General in the city had of course attended, along with members of the Dominion Supreme Court and the Cabinet. The few members of Congress who had already returned to town, or had never left, were also in attendance. It was during the reception that the Duke arranged to call on General Scott in his War Department office at 1 p.m. today.

From his window, the General could now see Lieutenant Wilder escorting the Duke across the park. Bratton, the Colonial Office man, had been present throughout the Liaison reception yesterday but was not with them. *He and that damn Layne may be cooking something up. Better make a note to keep an eye on him. Perceptive of young Wilder: under the polished veneer, a hard man, this Bratton. And none too happy to be here, judging from his attitude yesterday. Seemed formally, Britishly, depressed…*

The entire Department came to attention as the Duke entered the building. Scott moved out across the room to greet his guest. He stepped outside and spoke in formal tones. "Welcome to the War Department, Your Grace, headquarters of the Army of the USBA and also our Coastal Guard. Please come in."

The Duke returned the greeting and walked into the inner office. He was taking off and hanging up his cloak as Scott signaled to his secretary, Lieutenant Beaufort, for a fresh pot of tea. "Well, Winfield, in all your glory. I say, that's a remarkable view of The Residency and the Potomac." They settled in as the secretary poured coffee for Scott and tea for his guest before leaving.

"By the way, Winfield, your aide, young Wilder. A rather feisty pup."

Scott smiled: "Feisty? In what way, General?"

"Well, he gives as much as he takes, I've observed. Certainly, he hasn't allowed my man Bratton to intimidate him. Holds his tongue till he's asked a question, then expresses his firm opinion, for better or worse. Actually looked me in the eye and boasted of his heritage: 'Third generation British American of Irish Catholic descent.' Just like that. Imagine!"

Scott nodded his huge head and smiled again. "You'll find things a little more, shall we say, *relaxed*, here, Sir Arthur. In British America, you'll find the social barriers you are used to down, simply because they were never put up. Here, a man is judged by what he does, not by who his connections and family tree may be. The Lieutenant's family are rather well-off ship-builders in the port of Brooklyn, near the Royal Naval Station in New York harbor. Yet he fought to graduate from West Point, despite an unfortunate aversion to mathematics. He has an analytical mind and is an accomplished linguist. That's why he's here: he has the makings of a fine intelligence officer." *By God, I'm beginning to sound like a proud father. Mustn't ever let the young man hear me like this...*

"He reported to you, Winfield, I'm sure, on the dialogue we conducted during the course of our journey?"

Scott's face became graver and his tone more professional: "He did, General. Reported that the dialogue seemed always to return to the issue of slavery."

"Did this feisty young 'intelligence' pup offer a firm opinion on why that may have been?"

"No Sir Arthur. Though it seemed to confirm somewhat a theory we have been developing here since the *Irresistible* vanished."

It was the Duke now whose face turned graver and his tone more professional: "And what theory is that, Winfield...and who holds it?"

General Scott looked his old commander in the eye: "That, somehow, slavery was tied into London's desire to learn as quickly as possible whether Andrew Jackson would retain occupancy of that old house over there. As for who holds the theory: I do. Though the G-G and his key advisers are aware of it.

"Sir Arthur, the fact that you and I are sitting here today simply reinforces it. Yes, I understand that, officially, you are here on a private tour of the Dominion. Frankly, General, I don't buy it. You are here on a fact-finding mission. And the facts you are seeking to find concern slavery."

The Duke put his tea cup down on the front of Scott's desk and, continuing to lean forward, returned Scott's hard gaze. "Tell me, General Scott, what is your position on slavery? As a soldier, as a British American subject of the King and as a man?"

Scott leaned back in his chair and put his immense hands on the arm rests. "As a man, I detest it. As a British American subject of the King, I recognize that it is legal under our constitution, as well as British law. As a soldier, I am sworn to uphold that constitution. And I will, as long as I am physically able to do so."

The Duke was hard and fast: "And British law as well? Even if it, shall we say, 'nullifies' a part of your Dominion constitution?"

Scott felt a lightening-like jolt race down his spine. "The USBA constitution mandates compliance with overall Empire laws."

Wellington relaxed back into his own chair. "So you would not be in favor of non-compliance with a Parliamentary-passed bill signed by the King that would ban something now legally functioning in parts of the Dominion under the USBA constitution? "

The electric-like tingling had now extended through his arms and legs to Scott's hands and feet. *Great God, where the hell is this going?* "I would not, Sir, any more than I would now be, have been or ever will be in favor of one or more states nullifying legislation passed by our Congress and signed into USBA law by the Governor-General. Unless and until such legislation is declared unconstitutional by our Supreme Court, it is the legally-enforceable law of the land."

Wellington rose and poured himself another cup of tea. "Winfield, do you see where this conversation is headed? Is this the theory you and General Jackson and his advisors have discussed?"

Scott pulled himself from his chair and strode over to his own pot of coffee. "There is no one in the USBA outside this room, Sir Arthur, who has the slightest inkling of where this conversation appears to be headed. And that direction is not the theory I've discussed with the G-G and the kitchen cabinet. Quite frankly, Duke, my theory, developed in part by research Lieutenant Wilder did into official London-Georgetown correspondence of last year, pointed to an Imperial tax on slaves, or, perhaps, their sale and resale.

"If I am reading you correctly, taxing the slaveholders is not quite what London has in mind."

Wellington had returned to his chair as Scott spoke and now

took his time responding, instead stirring his tea vigorously. Finally, he raised his head and looked up at Scott, who had come around to lean against the front of his desk, coffee cup steaming in his right paw.

"Winfield, a bill will be introduced into Parliament by Easter---60 some days from now---which will seek the emancipation of all slaves held anywhere in the British Empire. I anticipate little serious opposition, as the bill has support on both sides of the floor. Among its sponsors will be at least one British American delegate. It will pass by late summer. The P.M. formed a blue ribbon committee to study the impact of such legislation well over a year ago. Although your South is not the only area where this reprehensible practice still flourishes, it is the only one the committee identified as a potential trouble spot." He paused and sipped his tea, then looked at Scott, inviting comment.

The General's cup was now on the desk next to him. He straightened up and took a deep breath before walking slowly back behind the desk. Gripping the back of the chair so tightly that Wellington had visions of splinters flying toward him like so much shrapnel, Scott twice opened and shut his mouth, as if unwilling to verbalize his thoughts. After a pause of more than 30 seconds, he began a third time:

"I said I am not in favor of slavery, General. But neither am I in favor of destroying the economy of half the Dominion in one fell swoop. Or in encouraging armed resistance by the white population of that section of the USBA!

"I believe your committee has been getting some bad advice. I see Quincy Adams' fine hand here. Has he gone mad? We've 2,000,000 slaves in the South. To suddenly let them roam free? Who's to feed and house them? Who's to toil the land and pick the crops that provide the prosperity the South now enjoys? London has bitten off a chunk here that could end up choking this Dominion! This land has peacefully prospered under the Colonial Compact, Sir Arthur, North and South both, yes, and Canada too, despite what those damn Frogs up there think. What you are proposing could set off the most serious crisis we've seen since 1775..."

Wellington was holding up his hand. "Calm down, Winfield. Do you not think this has been thought through? Do you think we'd arbitrarily drop this on you and then tell you to pick up the pieces? Heavens, no! Now hear me out."

The Duke outlined the Empire-wide phased-in seven-year emancipation plan, with its built-in 23,000,000-plus pound compensation to the Southern slaveholders. Scott's fearsome grip on the chair's back gradually eased, to the Duke's relief, as the terms were explained. He began nodding his head slowly, not in agreement, but in understanding as pieces of the *Irresistible* puzzle began to come together.

Wellington, however, paused, thinking Scott had accepted the plan. *It's always about the money with these Yanks! Inside their chests beats not a heart, but a big dollar sign…*

"Winfield, we've been led to believe by certain so-called 'experts' on the USBA---Quincy Adams and my man Bratton chief among them--that slavery here is a political, as well as an economic, issue. From your reaction, perhaps that political angle has been overemphasized?"

Scott's thoughts had turned to Jackson's response to all this. *By the Eternal! That'll be some explosion…*

Now he backtracked to digest Wellington's question.

"Pardon me, Your Grace, but you misinterpreted my reaction to your outlining of the emancipation plan. The compensation, especially, clears up the riddle as to why the Chancellor of the Exchequer requested our Interior Department to come up with facts and figures on the slave population last spring. That's what led to the theory of a tax. And my nodding…

"Your *experts* are dead-on concerning the importance of slavery as a political issue here. That can not possibly be overemphasized. It is at least as important a factor as the impact on the economy and the human issue of how best to handle the slaves once freed. From what you say, politics is not an issue in the Indies, or the Cape. It is a far, far different story here. Their mutual need to protect the institution of slavery has molded the Southern states into a voting block that has dominated our politics since the organization of the Dominion. The South has become accustomed to that political power. In fact, you could say that there has been a complete reversal: *while the South became a voting block to protect slavery, it is slavery that now protects the voting block*…and, by extension, the South's on-going political power in the Dominion."

Scott was now pacing the floor behind his desk. "Without slavery to bind them to the others, the northern-most slave states--- Maryland, Kentucky, Missouri---would have little reason to continue in alliance with the deep South; the same with states like New Jersey and Delaware, which are considered 'free' states but still harbor significant numbers of slaves and often vote with the Southern block."

The pacing stopped and Scott again fiercely gripped the back of his chair. "The South's power in the Dominion depends on slavery. I question whether any amount of money will convince them to accept its demise. And that's before we take into account the financial blow it will be to their economy."

Wellington remained silent, thinking: *This is one remarkable man. I am glad he is on my side.*

Scott broke the extended silence with a smile. "Well, Sir Arthur, I do begin to see one purpose of your 'tour.' You'll be sounding out the political leadership in the various sections of the country. And, you have several months to do so, as any news of the introduction of an emancipation bill won't reach here till early May."

The General glanced down at his desk and then stared at Wellington again, his face hardening once more. "May I ask if you have already broached this topic across the street? Because, if you have not, General, you have placed me in a very difficult and tricky position."

There was again silence in the office and Scott reached across his desk to retrieve his coffee. *Damn…cold.* He went back to the pot and poured himself another cup as he waited for Wellington's response.

The Duke looked out the window and across to The Residency, half camouflaged by the snow-covered park trees. He sighed and looked up at Scott. *My God, I'd half forgotten how big he is.* He sipped at his tea and sighed again.

"Winfield, your answers to my probing as to your personal and professional feelings on slavery, as well as your overall reaction to the news I've just sprung on you, are no more nor less than I anticipated from the moment I agreed to this mission. Your summation of the political situation here is masterful. It has been my intention from the beginning to alert you before anyone else, including the Governor-General. And then rely on your counsel thereafter. I realize you feel an allegiance, and rightfully so, to Jackson, in his role as commander-in-chief of the USBA defense forces."

The Englishman's voice suddenly hardened as he rapped out the next two sentences:

THE DOMINION'S DILEMMA: THE UNITED STATES OF BRITISH AMERICA

"However, your higher allegiance is to the King. As I am here as his representative, our conversations and subsequent actions take precedent."

Wellington gave Scott a hard, non-blinking look. "You do understand that, General Scott?"

Scott returned his own unblinking stare. "I do, Your Grace.

"However, you've still put me in one hellava spot!"

Wellington smiled, but there was no laughter in his voice or eyes. "Yes, Winfield, It is 'one hellava spot.' This legislation---criminally overdue however premature one may think it---puts us all in 'one hellava spot.'

"Now you know that man in The Residency well. You've served with him in war and in peacetime. Adams and Bratton tell me his reaction may well tip the scales towards acceptance—or rebellion. How will our 'frontier barbarian' react?"

Winfield Scott heard the Duke of Wellington's question and resisted the urge to give the obvious response: *Why, he'll explode, by the Eternal!*

Instead, Scott put on a frown and slowly turned and began to once more pace the office. *I'll wear out my boots and the rug if this keeps up much longer.*

Wellington watched calmly, knowing his old subordinate was reviewing the facts before issuing a measured, thoughtful answer. The minutes dragged on and the clock chimed 3 p.m. before Scott finally returned to his desk and sat heavily down. He stared across at the Duke and shook his head.

"The first response will be outrage, of course. He'll claim, as the Southerners always do in defense of their 'peculiar institution,' that the Colonial Compact and the USBA constitution both protect property rights. Since they consider the slaves to be mere chattel, just so much 'property,' neither Parliament nor the King has any right to tamper or intrude on their property."

Wellington nodded, and remained tensely quiet, allowing Scott's train-of-thought to proceed uninterrupted.

"Twenty-three million pounds translates to almost than 110,000,000 USBA dollars, if my hasty math is correct, at the going rate of one pound to $4.75. A great deal of money, to be sure, especially in the eyes of the Chancellor of the Exchequer. However, really just a token sum per slaveholder! Remember, we're talking about 2,000,000 slaves here.

"Great God, General, the compensation would be just a fraction of the price of a slave at auction! Take Jackson, for example. I've no idea how many slaves he holds at The Hermitage, but even if its 30, that would mean compensation of around $1650.00 or so. If he sold all 30, he would realize about $24,000! And while he'll receive their services by law four days a week for the next seven years, he'll have to feed, clothe and house them all seven days. So, economically, it only makes sense if the slaveholders are faced with no other choice: something or nothing!"

"Continue, if you please, Winfield." The Duke's voice was low and brief.

"So it becomes a matter of realism: will Jackson, after his initial explosion of outrage, recognize that there are no other viable options? Or will his pride and anger cause him to strike out by refusing to comply and by daring London to enforce its decree? Rallying the South around him, the Great Dominionist turned Ultimate Nullifier?"

Scott's head was down and his own voice was now barely a whisper: "This thing could very easily tear this Dominion apart, Sir Arthur...

"And I don't know with any certainty how Andy Jackson will eventually react."

He looked up at Wellington with a grim face. "You may have heard, Duke, of one of our earliest G-Gs, Thomas Jefferson of Virginia. I was not always his greatest supporter; in fact, even though---or perhaps because---he wrote much of the Constitution, I believe he ran roughshod over it as few other G-Gs have. I was at a gathering at The Residency about 10 years ago, however, a few months before Jefferson died. He said then that slavery was a "firebell in the night" that would inevitably cause chaos here unless ended."

Scott smiled ironically: "Of course, he never quite got around to freeing his own slaves...

"I've always remembered that warning, though. And now I can hear that firebell in the distance."

There was again sustained silence in the office, both men consumed with the specter of armed revolt breaking out in the South, fanned by the outrage of a staunch Dominionist's sense of betrayal.

It was the Englishman who spoke first. "Surely Jackson will weigh the risks and realize the South could not successfully rebel? Why, they're just a third of the Dominion. With you in command of the USBA Army---supported by a Royal Navy blockade of the coastline---they'd have no chance for independence!"

"Depends." Scott's tone was flat and neutral.

"Depends? Depends on what, by God? What exactly do you mean, General?"

Scott rose to his feet and walked around the desk again, settling against the front and staring down at the infuriated, sputtering Wellington. "Sir Arthur, you have not provided any rationale for the USBA Army---minus the portion of it which could conceivably form the core of any theoretical Southern resistance---to march South and fight their fellow soldiers. Or any rationale for volunteers from the North to rally round the Army, as volunteers in the South undoubtedly would the professionals who might choose to rebel.

"I believe my aide, Lieutenant Wilder, explained to you that the abolitionist movement is growing steadily in the North. It is, but I'm not sure the conviction that slavery is morally detestable is something they would consider worth dying for. General, as a whole, the British American people outside the South don't care that strongly about slavery---enough to die---one way or the other. It has no direct impact on their lives that they can see. On the contrary, a unilateral ban on slavery issued by London without any discussion of the matter over here may appear arbitrary and could possibly push Northern sentiment in the Southerners' favor."

Wellington now appeared more appalled than stunned, staring white-faced and open-mouthed at the American. A gargled, almost choking sound was forcing itself from his throat.

"One reason the Compact has worked all these years is that you have more or less left us alone. As an astute young officer observed to me some weeks ago, as long as we contribute our fair share towards the Empire's prosperity, it hasn't seemed that London much cares who is in charge over here, or what legislation is introduced, debated and voted on, or even what happens here. To suddenly force this emancipation down our throats may possibly cause widespread resentment, even among those who oppose or are ashamed of slavery. I'm not saying the rest of the Dominion would join in a revo…"

Now it was Scott whose face turned ashen as he stopped in mid-sentence and gaped, his own mouth open, at his visitor. "Dear God," he whispered. "It's in the Compact, isn't it? You referred earlier to the 'higher allegiance to the King,' and you being his 'representative' here.

"London is prepared---and has been for months---to invoke the article in the Compact which allows the King to remove a sitting Governor-General. That's why the *Irresistible* vanished as soon as the plebiscite results were official. Your 'blue ribbon committee' had been hoping Clay or one of the others would beat Jackson. Once the committee knew Jackson had won, they sent you over here to determine whether to invoke that article!"

Wellington rose so that he was closer to eye level with Scott. "Winfield, you stated several hours ago that your first loyalty is to the Crown. I don't believe you are alone in that loyalty. I believe most British Americans feel as you do. That is the essence, the beauty and the brilliance of the Colonial Compact. If this crisis tests that loyalty to the fullest, so be it. I believe Franklin and Burke recognized that there would be a litmus test, sooner or later. Perhaps that's what your Mr. Jefferson really meant by his 'firebell in the night.'

"You now know why I'm here and what steps I've been authorized to take to ensure that the wishes of Parliament and the King are carried out. I will require and will anticipate your all-out assistance. Is that perfectly clear, General?"

Wellington turned and marched toward the door, pausing to retrieve his cloak. "Winfield, you must help me resolve this dilemma, hopefully without bloodshed. We must convince Jackson and the South to accept this upcoming emancipation.

"Now, I am due at the Liaison Office for a private dinner with the staff. Strictly a morale booster, as we say. Bratton tells me Sir John, Layne and the staff are bored with Georgetown duty. Little do they know...

"I would very much enjoy accepting a supper invitation to your home tomorrow evening. We've spent so much time here today that another official meeting tomorrow might raise warning flags. Besides, I've been invited to sit in on tomorrow's Cabinet meeting. Doubtless, it will be a staged thing, but nevertheless...

"Then, I'm to dine with Mr. Van Buren. I'll let you know how that turns out. Bye the bye, General, your Mr. Jefferson. Is there any truth to the rumor that this chap Burr whom Jefferson forced from office is the new Vice G-G's natural father? I understand he may still be practicing law up in New York. Is it true that he and Jackson were once quite close? "

Scott was nonplussed: *Aaron Burr? Where the hell did that come from?*

The Duke smiled at Scott's look of amazement. "Well, I shall look forward to Mrs. Scott's formal invitation. Think on all we've discussed, Winfield. We have a grave storm approaching. A 'firestorm,' if you will. Good night."

Scott crossed the room in as close to a daze as he would permit himself and stood in the doorway. He heard the Duke address his aide:

"Oh, Lieutenant Wilder. Wasn't necessary for you to wait around. I can find my own way back to The Residency. You may want to check in with General Scott, however…Good evening, Lieutenant."

The front door of the War Department building shut behind him. It was 5:22 p.m.

CHAPTER FOURTEEN

Georgetown, D.C.
February 4, 1833:

Dave Harper had managed to see Count Renkowiitz's daughter at last and had promised to tell Thomas about it over supper at the Golden Eagle. As the General's meeting with the Duke of Wellington dragged on for so long, the Lieutenant wondered if he'd be able to keep the appointment. General Scott, however, had had little to say once Wellington left the War Department. He had simply instructed his aide to order up his carriage. So Tom had plenty of time to get back to his room and change into civilian clothes before meeting Harper at the Eagle at 7 p.m.

Since the subject was to be Caroline Renkowiitz, Tom was surprised to see Joanne Casgrave sitting with Harps in a back booth. Something about the woman gave off danger signals, but he chose to ignore them. *At least with her around, I know the food will be good. Nothing since breakfast again today, with all this Wellington business. And even that was just tea and a biscuit. Damn, I'm starved; thirsty, too.*

"Hello David. If is this a private conversation, I'll wait at the bar…"

"Nonsense, Tom, sit down. Joanne was thrilled to hear you were coming."

Tom was immediately on guard. *Thrilled, huh? Since when?* "Hello Joanne, good to see you."

"Hello Lieutenant." The petite woman flashed that patently false - modest smile that he had first detected when Harper returned from New Jersey. "As chilled as you look on this nasty night, I'm still betting you want a nice cold beer…and I have two steaks sitting in the kitchen with David's and your names on them."

Before Tom could even agree, Mrs. Casgrave had signaled the bartender, Richard, who responded by sending a tall, buxom blond waitress with a foaming mug for Tom, Port for Harper and a small glass of whiskey for herself.

Seeing the tall emaciated man's quick response, Harps asked Joanne: "How is it working out with Lawrence? Still resentful and moody?"

She smiled in a way that Tom didn't like. "I have him under control. He's really a lamb, unless he gets into the gin. So I make sure he doesn't... And I make sure he's taken care of when he's off duty. Sleeps in a little room downstairs, you know."

Harper laughed at Tom's look of bafflement. "The bartender, Richard. His last name is Lawrence. Gets into these spells where he thinks he's the King of England...or should be. Joanne says it's the gin, but I have to think he's a little off his rocker to begin with."

Joanne seemed to purr as she grabbed at Harper's arm, playfully. "David, really! Of course, you're right. He is a bit strange. Blames Andy Jackson for keeping him from the throne. Imagine! But when he's on the straight-and-narrow, which is where I keep him, he's not that bad. That's with the gin locked away, though." She purred again and Tom could begin to smell the perfume she was wearing, even with the combined smoke of a dozen cigars lit at tables across the taproom.

"Joanne has something she wants to ask you, Tom," Harps said, draining his Port. He smiled at the dark-haired woman cuddled up next to him and Thomas began to wonder if they would attack each other right at the booth. *At least Candice has the class to wait till we're alone,* he thought with a hidden grin.

Now the patented false-modest girlish look was again aimed his way. "Yes, Tom. I know you're involved at the highest levels at both The Residency and the War Department..."

Jaysus, Mary and Joseph. Here it comes. What does she want, an invitation to the Wellington state dinner? He put down his beer mug and waited.

"David says you escorted the Duke of Wellington from Baltimore the other day. He had an aide with him. Do you recall his name?" She smiled innocently.

It's a good thing I don't have any beer in my mouth. I'd either choke on it or spit it over the table, right towards both your faces. "Of course, Joanne. It's Captain Bratton, whom David has undoubtedly corresponded with at the American Office in London."

Harper was astonished. "Harry Bratton? What's he doing here?"

Tom smiled. "Like I said, Dave, it's 'Captain' Harry Bratton, late of the Coldstream Guards. Apparently, he's been on what they call 'half-pay' while at the American Office but was recalled to active duty for this trip. A friend of yours, Joanne?"

"I met him socially when he was here several years ago at the Liaison Office. A friend of my late husband's, actually. You didn't know my husband, Major Casgrave, by any chance, Lieutenant?" She smiled coyly.

"No, unfortunately, I did not, Joanne." *And neither did Harry Bratton, I'm willing to bet, unless 'Major' Casgrave was a procurement officer. In the Biblical sense...*

"What made you think Captain Bratton might have come with the Duke?"

"Oh, I received a cryptic message the other night. The kind of thing my dear husband said Captain Bratton was known for." She paused. "So he is here in Georgetown, then?"

I'll be damned, Tom realized. *Harps doesn't seem jealous in the least. That's a relief. Glad he's just having a good time...still, this is one devious woman. Don't trust her one damn bit.* "Well, haven't seen him since the welcoming ceremony yesterday afternoon, but my guess is he's still here. He's probably tied up tonight though. Wellington's dining with the Liaison Office staff. He may have some free time in the next few days. I understand the Duke may not start immediately on a tour of the South, as originally planned. Wants to rest up after his journey."

The steaks arrived and Joanne rose, after planting a kiss full on David's lips. "I'll leave you two alone to eat while I see how my other customers are doing." She smiled coquettishly at Thomas. "David and I will be having after-supper drinks, Tom. Perhaps you'll join us? Many of the girls have remarked on the handsome Lieutenant who comes here much too infrequently..."

I don't think so. I'm beginning to not like the atmosphere here. Well, there are other taverns in Georgetown. "Thanks, Joanne, but not tonight. In fact, not any night, at least till Wellington leaves. I'm basically on-call 24 hours a day until then. Thanks, anyway. I just about have time to enjoy my steak. Then I'll be off."

Joanne managed to look disappointed, with her same downcast eyes' little-girl smile. "Next time, then. And don't be a stranger." She turned and walked away, her compact behind swaying provocatively.

Thomas looked over at David, whose eyes were still fixed on the petite black-haired woman: "So Harps, and how is the beautiful young Countess Caroline?"

The Interior Department man grinned. "Looking very good, Lieutenant, at last night's Liaison Office affair. And where were you?

The Countess asked."

Tom looked surprised. "I wasn't invited, Dave. And how did you worm your way in?"

Harper was indignant. "I did no such thing. I was there officially, representing the Department!"

"Oh, of course: a 'high Interior Department official' such as yourself! How could I have forgotten?" The two friends grinned at each other.

"Actually Thomas, Mr. MacLane hasn't arrived in town yet and Van Buren was invited in his new role of Vice G-G. The invitation was just going to waste, so…"

Thomas snickered as he chewed his as-ordered medium rare steak. "So you seized the opportunity. I only hope you didn't 'seize' the Countess too closely. You know that without me there to hold you back, there's always the possibility of an international incident…"

Harps touched his cloth napkin to his lips primly. "I was the epitome of a gentleman. However, I was able to arrange to go riding with her Sunday, weather permitting."

Thomas flashed an impressed look, but couldn't resist: "That's if Joanne lets you out of her bed in time to keep your date."

David took the kidding in stride. "On Sundays, Joanne usually sleeps late. Then again, she doesn't get to sleep till near dawn…

"And how are things at Cranford Plantation, Lieutenant? Or should I instead inquire about the Maryland countryside?"

Tom looked down at his plate in disgust. "I wouldn't know how things are at Cranford, David. She still thinks I intentionally missed our supper engagement a few weeks ago…"

"Does she still think you were with the Mistress of Twin Peaks?" David could not resist laughing, even as an immediate scowl appeared on Tom's face.

"How would I know? Lucille won't communicate with me. She kept returning my notes till it got kind of silly to keep sending them. For all I know, this farce may have driven her permanently into the arms of the Artillery."

Tears of laughter were running down David's checks and he barely managed to get out the next question: "And the Widow Samples? Seeing much of her these days?"

"As a matter of fact, Mr. Harper, I was invited to spend the upcoming weekend at Twin Peaks. But those arrangements were made before the Duke showed up. I sent Candice a note late yesterday that I would be unable to travel outside Georgetown this weekend, but would be free, though on-call, here in town. I'm expecting an answer tomorrow or Wednesday. That townhouse is a major upgrade over my room at the Indian Queen…"

"And Candice Samples is a 'major upgrade' over any of Joanne's 'girls,' and…" Harper drained another glass of Port, "…a lot richer, too. Something for you to give serious thought to, Lieutenant. Ah, Joanne's beckoning me. Sure you won't stay? Variety's the spice, they say."

Tom rose and pulled on his cloak. "Yeah, and it'll be the death of you. Good night, Harps."

Somewhere in the MidAtlantic
January 29, 1833:

Count Nicholas Ignatieff, still dressed in the increasingly dirty and distasteful clothes of an English workingman, had already recovered from the shock of his ill-fated London visit. Behind a patch over his perfectly good but twin-colored eye that further disguised him, he had put his bitterness and anger at those in the London embassy aside---*they'll be dealt with in due time*, he thought, grimly---and quickly moved to the problems and opportunities ahead.

He had been given the name and address of a Russian merchant in New York, along with certain identifying papers. After a quick outfitting by the merchant, the Count intended to be in the saddle for Georgetown within hours of making port. He expected to reach the capitol in four-to-five days, as he vaguely recalled that New York was some 200 miles northeast of Georgetown.

Ignatieff intended to present himself at the Consulate as a private Russian of means, possibly borrowing the identity of the New York merchant. He would then reveal himself to Renkowiitz, whom he had never encountered. Renkowiitz, of course, would have no way of knowing about the unfortunate events in London (that bastard Terravenissian had said that this damnable old wreck, *The Pride of the Hudson*, was the only vessel crossing the Atlantic for weeks). He would act towards Renkowiitz as if nothing had happened. *By the time the Counsel-General receives any word from London or St. Petersburg* (and

Ignatieff doubted such news would be passed on to a mere C-G in such a backwater city), *I will have taken control of the Consulate under the emergency directive issued me by the Czar himself (of which that damn Dorothea obviously was unaware).*

Ignatieff planned a dual life once he reached Georgetown: inside the Consulate, he would mobilize whatever professional staff he would find to aid in the agitating of and comfort for whatever potential rebels he could identify in his outside role as an adventurous member of minor Eastern European nobility. (Doubtless these unsophisticated British Americans would be unable to distinguish between a Russian and other East Europeans, especially with Ignatieff's gift for language and accents).

The Count was well aware of the potential consequences of failure but dismissed them disdainfully. *If the British have sent their most distinguished public figure over here, they're clearly worried that this abolition issue is potentially explosive. All I need do is identify the most serious and strongest opponents—and then light the fuse.*

That's if and when this miserable excuse for a ship ever sights land...

Georgetown, D.C.
February 4, 1833:

Captain Bratton had escorted the Duke to and from the Liaison Office affair and had now given up hope of stopping in at the Golden Eagle. The Duke had actually seemed to enjoy himself with the staff. He had lingered until almost 10 p.m., some six hours after the reception-and-dinner had begun.

Now, back at The Residency at 10:40 p.m., Bratton debated whether to slip over to the Eagle, but decided against it, not relishing the chance that Joanne was again 'operating'--as that ignorant fool of a bartender had put it--with a 'customer.' *No*, he thought, *not worth it tonight, not when I leave for New York tomorrow morning.*

The Duke had reiterated his Ocean-crossing orders to locate this Aaron Burr and determine whether he was in both mental and physical condition to aid in the upcoming crisis. (Implicit in this, of course, was to determine Burr's own political views, if the old man still held any. And his feelings toward Jackson.) "This chap Burr may be our 'ace-in-the-hole,'" the Duke had said in the carriage returning from the Liaison Office. "I received the distinct impression from General Scott that while Burr may be a half-forgotten man, he still holds the keys to some impressive skeleton-infested closets in political circles over here. It's imperative we open a secret line of communication to him. Jackson is going to be, as my old British American troops on the Peninsula would say, 'a tough nut to crack.'

"Well, Burr may simply represent one more hammer. What time do you depart tomorrow morning?"

———

Fort Hill Plantation, S.C.
February 4, 1833

John C. Calhoun was in a hurry. Even though the new Congress would not convene for another two weeks, the newly-elected Senator from South Carolina wanted to be in Georgetown by the end of the week.

"There's much work to be done even before the Senate organizes for this special session," he told his wife Floride as their carriage carried them away from their beloved home and toward Charleston, where they would board a coastal steamer for the trip to the capitol. "I am determined to see this tariff issue settled to the South's satisfaction, whether that damnable traitor to our interests, Jackson, agrees or not. And we must be prepared for whatever other mischief the Yankees may have in mind! At least Jackson is on the right side of this Bank issue. That abomination must be destroyed before the Yankees can use it to finance all their damn internal improvement projects!"

Floride, whose lifework---despite the 10 children she had borne John--seemed to consist mainly of calming down her fiery spouse, smiled softly. "Now, Mr. Senator," she said gently as she inserted the needle, "weren't you once for tariffs, a national bank and internal improvements, as I recall?"

"Yes, damn it, and as you well know I repudiated those youthful mistakes in the Essay!"

Furious at his loss in last year's nullification battle, Calhoun had retreated to Fort Hill to pen the 'South Carolina Exposition and Protest,' a now-famous rejection of all the Dominionist philosophy he had once advocated. At the same time, he became the first man to resign the vice governor-generalship, instead electing to stand for the Senate. The South Carolina Legislature had overwhelming voted to send him back to Georgetown.

"You see, dear Floride, it is not simply the present battles we must fight. We must maintain the South's hold on government so that these despicable Abolitionists can not move against us. Despite my other disagreements with the G-G, I appaulded his speech to the Mississippi Legislature last spring. We must have room to expand into the southwestern lands of Texas and beyond. If we can not grow our Southern way of life in that area, adding Senators and Congressmen who will join our fight, then the Abolitionists will one day grow strong enough elsewhere to believe it their right to tamper in our internal affairs, damn them!

"Nullification is an issue that goes far beyond the question of tariffs, as odious as that one is. Why in God's name can't Jackson see that?"

Floride looked at her husband in concern. "John, you haven't articulated that particular position before. Do you think the Yankees mean to intrude into the private life of the South?"

Calhoun's look of red-faced fierceness softened as he turned to his wife. "Not any time in the immediate future, my dear. But I have followed the local elections in the Northeast closely these past few years. The Abolitionists are gaining strength. There will be a showdown, though I expect it's a decade or more off. I've corresponded with some of the others---Hayne, Troup, Gilmer---and they all agree. The Southern caucus will meet privately before Congress reconvenes. That's why we're going up there so early."

CHAPTER FIFTEEN

Georgetown, D.C.
February 8, 1833:

Winfield Scott was a Dominionist. But his allegiance to the union of the states and to the British Empire, in which, he was certain, the USBA was to play an ever-increasingly important role, did not stop him from closely watching political developments in his native Virginia.

So it was that Scott, over dinner at his home two nights before, had suggested that Wellington might like to sit down with John Floyd, the iconoclast governor of the 'Old Dominion.' Floyd, a long-time Congressman, had been elected governor in 1830 and had immediately embarked on a stunningly bold economic program (stunning at least for a Southern governor and state) that included a network of state-subsidized internal improvements designed to make Virginia, in his words, "a commercial empire." Although a staunch states rights man, he also opposed slavery as economically inefficient. Originally a Jackson supporter, he had felt betrayed when, after declining renomination for his secure House seat in 1827 in order to work for 'Old Hickory's' gubernatorial-general run, Jackson had failed to reward him with a cabinet post. The rift had continued throughout the G-G's first term.

All in all, Scott believed, a man the Duke should see.

(Scott, of course, did not know that Floyd had been London's secret hope in the recent G-G plebiscite. (Floyd had finished third, receiving only South Carolina's 11 electoral votes.) Palmerston's blue ribbon committee had put his name near the top of the short list of men Wellington needed to contact immediately on reaching the USBA.)

So, with time to kill before The Residency state dinner now planned for the following Wednesday, February 13, there was plenty of time for the Duke to ride down to Richmond. Wellington had of course agreed but had surprised Scott by mentioning that Major

154

Layne would accompany him. It seemed that Captain Bratton had already left town...

That was not the only surprise to come from the cozy little supper at which Maria Scott had fully participated. The Duke had also disclosed that he was considering, now that he understood the political ramifications of the slavery issue in the USBA, altering his original plans.

Instead of touring the Dominion and briefing the political and economic leadership in each state as to the Parliamentary emancipation bill, he now thought he might begin by addressing a joint session of Congress. He would announce the legislation at that time and meet with the various leadership groups later.

The idea of such an address had been raised at the Cabinet meeting Wellington had attended earlier Tuesday, before his afternoon dinner with the Vice G-G elect ("an even slipperier eel than I had been led to expect," the Duke had confided to Winfield and Maria). Van Buren had in fact brought up the idea of such a speech, apparently still focused on the 'slavery tax' concept.

"Of course he broached the joint session speech at Cabinet as a ceremonial one lacking in substance, but he told me privately, in that whispery voice, looking at me most earnestly, that if I had 'anything of importance to discuss with the British American people,' this was a proper forum.

"Ha!

"A political animal, through-and-through...not a Lion nor an Eagle...just a bloody eel. He'll need some growing into, as we say, if he's ever to live in that lonely old mansion.

"Speaking of which, I say: who's to blame for that place? Can't be Washington. I've always heard how beautiful his home is, to this day."

The Scotts smiled at Wellington's candor. "Well, Sir Arthur, when you suffer through as many changes-of-occupancy as that house has experienced in the past 30 years, you begin to look your age," the General said. "Jefferson was a born tinkerer, always building and tearing down. The Madisons rebuilt it after a fire some 20 years ago, but Quincy Adams tore the top floor apart to make bedrooms for his rather extensive family..."

"Oh, Win, tell the Duke the truth." Maria was laughing. "The fact is, Sir Arthur, the poor place still hasn't recovered from the night of Andy's first inauguration."

Scott, too, was laughing. "Well, Duke, the Vandals' sack of Rome was a tea party compared to what the Tennesseans did to The Residency that night. Good thing Adams had already left town. He'd have had apoplexy…"

Wellington joined in the laughter. "Pompous old Quincy! I must confess, I do enjoy bringing him down a peg. Winfield, Maria, you should have seen his face at the last meeting of the Palmerston committee before I sailed. He and I had just had a rather nasty exchange over the self-righteousness of the New Englanders toward abolition. Then the Colonial Secretary presented a breakdown on the number of slaves per state. 'And in Massachusetts, there are four… all, apparently, female!' Thought he'd keel over on the spot!"

As the laughter subsided, the Duke's face grew more serious. "So, Winfield. Tell me what you think of my idea to announce the emancipation bill before Congress. I've not discussed this with anyone, including Captain Bratton."

Scott rolled his wine glass between his gun barrel-sized fingers as he considered the proposal. "That's still almost a month away, Sir Arthur, which gives you plenty of time to get the lay of the political landscape here. I hadn't seen any need for this special session before your arrival, but perhaps its fortunate the G-G has called it after all. The fight over the Bank bores the few citizens it doesn't immediately put in a deep slumber. This issue should wake everyone up, by the Eternal!

"Yes, I think hearing this directly from you, as London's official voice, will have an impact. Even the most outspoken of the fire-eaters will have to concede that the bill is the result of much sober research, analysis and planning. Not that the concession will change their minds, but it will, perhaps, lift the debate to a more dignified level."

Scott glanced across at Maria, who was listening tensely, staring directly at her husband, before continuing.

"You'll have to inform Jackson before you address Congress, you do understand. That's one reason I'm suggesting you visit Richmond later this week. Governor Floyd will come at you from a unique direction. He wants an end to slavery, but not for humanitarian reasons. Simply thinks its staggeringly inefficient. Yet, he'll denounce the abolitionists for seeking a Dominion-wide legislative solution. Believes whole-heartedly in states rights.

"It is a different perspective than you've come across before. And it's important you hear it first-hand because, Sir Arthur, Virginia is the key."

The General glanced again at his wife. "Militarily, politically and economically: any way you wish to consider it. Without Virginia, there's no rebellion. Just a glorified riot. South Carolina, Georgia, Alabama and Mississippi. They wouldn't stand a chance. With Virginia would, in all likelihood, come North Carolina, Louisiana, perhaps Tennessee and those border states we spoke of yesterday. Then, we'd have a problem on our hands.

"So you need to sit down with Floyd and their two Senators, Tyler and Rives. Get their perspectives before you walk into The Residency and drop this on Andy. And before you start drafting your speech to Congress.

"And you also need to sit down with Calhoun. I expect he's on his way up here for the special session even now." Scott grinned. "I hear the G-G was livid when he found out old John C. has been returned to the Senate!"

Maria, smiling at the Duke, broke in. "I don't know why, Winfield. Everyone knew he would be back! Floride herself told me when they left last summer they'd see us again when the new Congress formed..."

Scott looked fondly at his wife. "Well, apparently someone forgot, or more probably, didn't have the nerve to inform Jackson. That reminds me, Duke. Of all the men around him, Frank Blair is the smartest and best. He should be there when you present the emancipation bill to the G-G."

Wellington was lighting another cigar but nodded in agreement. "Yes, Blair seems especially sharp. Don't think he bought my story of a private 'tour' at all. Now! What can you tell me about Calhoun and these South Carolina chaps? Nullifying any laws they don't like. Demanding new territories be opened to slavery. They sound collectively mad!"

Scott sipped his Port before answering. "We have a saying about South Carolina, Sir Arthur. Some think it's humorous:

"'South Carolina: too small to be a nation. Too large to be an insane asylum.'" There was no humor in the General's voice and the guffaw that was rising in Wellington's throat died there.

The talk had then shifted to the probable invitation list for the state dinner. Wellington had left soon thereafter.

Scott had been tied up on War Department business yesterday--an Indian tribe called the Sioux was raiding into the Minnesota territory, while there was a ridiculous catfight up in Portsmouth, N.H., where the Royal Navy and the Coastal Guard uneasily shared the Naval Station--and had not had time to concentrate on the emancipation problem.

Now he thought back over the long, enjoyable yet important supper with Wellington and reviewed the issues that had come up. For some reason, the disappearance of Captain Bratton kept running through his mind. Wellington had airily said that Bratton had "left town for a few days" but had failed to mention where the man had gone. Scott, who was one of the few British American officials who had known of Bratton's 'under the rose' work back in the '20s, doubted it was a pleasure trip...

The Duke has grasped the importance of Virginia in this whole situation. His decision to announce the abolition bill before a joint session, rather than in a series of private meetings, will indicate London's determination to see this thing through. And it is indicative of Wellington's own political acumen that he had already targeted the damn South Carolinians as the problem children, even as I was broaching the subject in my usual clumsy way...

The Residency had sent a rider down to Richmond Wednesday with the news that the Duke would be arriving late Friday for a two-day stay with the Governor. Apparently, Jackson, who was already showing signs that he wasn't comfortable with Wellington in town, had accepted the trip as the first in the 'tour' the Duke had announced. *What Frank Blair thinks is another matter.*

But then, The Residency, according to Lieutenant Wilder, was most concerned with this upcoming state dinner. *It was one thing*, Scott thought with a wry grin, *to get 'Old Hickory' to entertain his fellow citizens. Putting on a banquet to impress a man who regularly dines with Kings and Emperors--that's something else!*

Looking out his window toward The Residency, Scott could now see Wilder trudging through the slush that yesterday's thaw had made of the weekend's snowstorm. *This damn swamp can't make up its mind about the weather. A near blizzard on Saturday, then the high 40s three days later. I'd like to take Maria and get out of here for a few days, but that's out-of-the-question right now. Still, better get some leave before Wellington's speech. It'll be too late after that!*

Scott crossed his office in three long strides and stuck his head out the door. "Tell Lieutenant Wilder to come in here as soon as he's hung up his cloak," he ordered his secretary. *Trust Tom to have the latest from 1600 Pennsylvania Avenue...*

The General was moving back behind his desk when the realization hit him: Bratton and Candice! Hadn't there been rumors, back when Charles Samples was still alive, that Candice had added a young Liaison Office man to her list of 'admirers?' Yes, during the '28 campaign, while Charles was traveling extensively working for Jackson, he vaguely remembered Maria mentioning that Candice was spending an inordinate amount of time at the Samples' Georgetown townhouse. Especially considering the capitol's equatorial August weather. Then Charles returned and Candice was back at Twin Peaks...where she stayed, in seclusion, after the accident. And Bratton had been transferred back to England about the same time...

Great God, the General thought as Thomas came hurrying into the office, *you don't suppose that's where Bratton went? Twin Peaks? I must have a talk with Maria tonight. Both of these 'Romeos' are too essential to what's coming up to be diverted by a love triangle, damn it!*

From the fearsome glare on the General's face, Tom thought he was in for a royal dressing-down. Though for what, he had no idea, frantically backtracking mentally over events and orders of the past few days. Instead, the General motioned him to a chair. "Sit down, Lieutenant. How are things across the street?"

Thomas relaxed somewhat, watching as Scott's ever-present mug of coffee disappeared inside his huge right paw. *I swear, the General could palm a pumpkin with those hands.*

"Well, Sir, plans for the state dinner have been finalized, though there could be some last minute tinkering with the final guest list. General Jackson and Sir Arthur went over it Wednesday before the Duke left for Richmond..."

"Wellington is on his way, eh? Taken Major Layne with him?"

"Yes Sir. Apparently Captain Bratton left Georgetown early Monday morning on undisclosed business..."

"Any idea where he went, Lieutenant?"

"No Sir. But from the timing, it would appear premeditated. I mean, Sir," Tom was surprised at the quizzical look in his boss' eyes,

THE DOMINION'S DILEMMA: THE UNITED STATES OF BRITISH AMERICA

"that he arrived Saturday afternoon and departed less than 48 hours later. He's on an errand for the Duke that was planned before I finished escorting them here...possibly before they even landed."

To meet with someone who will not be here in Georgetown anytime soon, Scott thought. *Who has Wellington mentioned that would fit that category?* Scott nodded his huge head affirmatively and his aide was further surprised as the big, beefy face seemed to settle into lines of relief. "Well, see what you can find out. Most of these Liaison boys are so inept I don't bother about them. But Bratton is a different story. It won't hurt to determine what 'errand' he's running for the Duke...or how long he'll be gone. Speaking of Sir Arthur, he and Layne are definitely on the road to Richmond you say?"

"Well Sir, the Major appeared at The Residency around 8:30 yesterday. He and the Duke rode out less than 30 minutes later. That should put them around the North Anna River crossings about now. They should make Richmond by noon."

Scott got up and stretched, flexing his tree trunk-like neck. *Two days with Floyd and the Virginia 'nobles' and Wellington will have a new perspective on the situation here.* "What else is going on across the street? What's this about the guest list?"

The Lieutenant dug into a folder in his 'G-G' pouch. "They're following your suggestion to keep attendance to, uh, 'official Georgetown,'" he said, reddening slightly.

A smile began to play at the corners of the General's mouth just as a name popped suddenly into his brain. He remained silent, however, staring at the aide.

"The trouble is that the Congress has begun slipping back into town. There may be some late invitees based on arrival times."

"That's fine. Just no 'planter aristocracy' this time. What else?"

Thomas was glad to have the subject changed. "Well General, mostly the Bank." He paused. "If I may be so bold..."

"According to the Duke, you usually are unusually so, Lieutenant." Scott softened the shot with a smile. "But go on."

"Uh, yes Sir. General Jackson is a bit 'monomaniac' on this subject, if you will..."

"Actually, Lieutenant, I believe 'feisty' is the term Sir Arthur used to describe you. But you are correct. The G-G is obsessed with stopping the Bank. However, that issue is not on our agenda.

"Tell me, Lieutenant, what do you recall about a man named Aaron Burr?"

Thomas looked at the General with true surprise. "Aaron Burr, Sir? The old lawyer on Reade Street in Manhattan? Who was once Vice G-G and killed Hamilton? That Aaron Burr, Sir?"

Scott was laughing. "Well, it appears you know quite a lot, Lieutenant." Again he looked quizzical: "How's that?"

"My family has used the Burr law firm for as long as I can remember, General. Even though we live in Brooklyn, we do a lot of business in New York City. My father and his brother are members of Tammany, have been for years."

Scott looked puzzled, so Wilder started to explain. "Tammany is the Democratic political organization in New York..."

"I know that, Lieutenant, and I know that's where Matty Van got his start. But what does that have to do with Burr? And your family's ties to him?"

"Sir, Aaron Burr was one of the founders of Tammany, back in the '90s. My grandfather joined soon after for both political and business reasons. As far as I know, Shamrock Shipbuilding has retained the Burr firm ever since, even when the Colonel himself, ah, *traveled* in Europe 25 years ago..."

"You mean when he left the USBA after the treason trial."

Now it was Wilder's turn to be impressed. "Yes, Sir. And while that illegal murder charge still hung over his head."

Scott's bushy eyebrows went up. "*Illegal*, Lieutenant?"

Wilder was firm: "Sir, the 'interview' between Colonel Burr and General Hamilton took place at Weehawk, on the Jersey side of the Hudson. Charges in New Jersey were dismissed. The murder indictment in question was handed down by a New York County grand jury."

Scott smiled. "I see your point. Obviously, New York County did not have jurisdiction. Now then: do you, personally, know the old man?"

"No Sir. I was introduced to him once, when I was a kid. And I saw him on the Broad Way, when I was home on leave after you brought me back from Arkansas. As I said, my family retains him for the firm."

Scott was direct: "Then he's still sharp? Still have his wits about him?"

"As late as last year, yes. I can discreetly inquire, ask my father...if you so wish, General."

"Yes, Lieutenant, Write your father a 'discreet' note to that effect and send it off today."

"Yes General. Ah, one other thing, Sir?"

Scott had begun to shift through papers, a sure sign their meeting was over. He lifted his head and stared at his aide.

Wilder hesitated but, thinking that information was why the General had him on staff, decided to plunge forward: "Sir, this may seem to be gossip, and, actually is pure hearsay coming from me but..." He stopped in mid-sentence.

Another small smile began to break out on Scott's face as the familiar red crept onto the Lieutenant's cheeks. "You were about to add something, Lieutenant?"

To hell with it. "General, I have been told, in fact most of New York believes that...that Aaron Burr is the natural father of the new Vice Governor-General."

Scott nodded. "Yes, I've heard that rumor also, Lieutenant. Many times.

"And, having observed each of them at roughly the same time in their lives, I tend to give it credence. Now, send off that damn note!"

Slack-jawed and open-mouthed, Thomas rose, saluted and left. Unbeknownst to the Lieutenant, Scott was grinning as the door closed behind him.

CHAPTER SIXTEEN

New York City
February 8, 1833:

A clear, cold dawn was breaking as Count Nicholas Ignatieff stood with other early risers of the steerage section, watching what appeared to be church spirals become visible directly ahead as *The Pride of the Hudson* sailed past several small harbor islands and one rather large one to the left.

Even further left rose the cliffs of what Ignatieff would soon be told was New Jersey, while to the immediate east appeared more developed land. The Count could see what appeared to be a fort protruding out from this land mass, a massive pitchfork into the belly of the bay. Other ships and smaller boats cruised peacefully throughout the busy harbor area, moving in all directions. A huge British warship was visible where the north side of the pitchfork was separated from the bottom of the long, narrow church spiral-dominated port by a channel of no more than half a mile.

"No, no, that's not New York there," he heard a crewman impatiently explaining to a nearby group of dazzled passengers as he pointed toward the easternmost land mass. "That's Brooklyn there, behind Fort Hamilton and in from the Royal Naval Station. Behind Brooklyn is Long Island. The same landfall we sighted yesterday. There's New York," he added, pointing to the heavy cluster of buildings now becoming visible dead ahead. "And the big island we're passing is Staten Island, with Jersey right behind it. Those cliffs are called the Palisades. They run north for 50 or more miles."

The other passengers seemed impressed, even awed, by finally seeing their destination after some 29 interminable days at sea. Ignatieff, though, was furious, having realized that New York City was located on either a peninsula or an island. It didn't matter which; what mattered was that he'd have to get back across to the western side, this "Jersey," before he'd be able to start for Georgetown.

The Count knew his status as a steerage passenger ruled out

obtaining any expert directions to his contact's address. He decided to wait till he was ashore before asking questions. The contact, Vladislav Tretiak, lived or worked, according to the notes roughly pushed into his pockets by that damn Terravenessian, at 42 Christopher Street. Where in what appeared to be a quaint Dutch town minus only its dikes, Christopher Street was, he could only guess. *Another hour and I'll be off this damn wreck. I still intend to be in the saddle, if at all possible, later today.*

Ignatieff, when he reflected on it, had realized that the "seven-day" deadlines imposed by the Princess were meaningless. Who would know until well after the fact how long it had taken him to find Tretiak or then to get to the Consulate in Georgetown? *And, anyway, the final result is all that matters; not how long it takes to arrive!*

The Count waited impatiently until the upper class passengers had disembarked, then pushed roughly through the steerage crowd and, at long last, onto dry land. He strode off the dock to the adjoining thoroughfare, West Street, now almost devoid of the open and closed carriages that had jammed it when *The Pride* first docked. Now, only a few open wagons were left to cater to the remaining passengers, many of whom looked dazed or nervous over the prospect of what to do now that they were finally in New York.

Ignatieff grabbed a passerby and, in his ambiguous Eastern European accent, managed to learn, to his surprise and satisfaction, that Christopher Street met this West Street less than a mile north. Slinging his rough bundle of clothing and weapons over his shoulder---the Count intended to have Tretiak's servants burn the damn clothes as soon as he established contact---he began to move north, the combination of slick cobblestone and his own paper-thin boots slowing his pace somewhat.

Roughly 20 minutes later---10:50 a.m.---he finally stood in front of 42 Christopher. To his disgust, he had been forced to trek east on Christopher some blocks from West Street, but to his relief had passed several stables. If Tretiak didn't keep a stable of his own, several of the horses visible in and around the commercial stables looked healthy enough to at least start him on his way to Georgetown; as long as there was a way to ferry the beast across the damnable harbor!

The Count made his way up the steps of the old attached red brick house and banged impatiently on the door. After several more quick knocks, an old and obviously Irish servant woman answered and looked skeptically at the unshaven, dirty-haired apparition with the patch over one eye. He immediately pushed past her. In the vestibule, in clear, concise and upper class Russian, he demanded to know the whereabouts of her employer. At the blank look she returned, he switched to exasperated English: "Where is Mr. Tretiak? Is he here? Summon him at once, do you hear?"

Before the poor woman could react, the inner door to the vestibule opened and an elegant middle-aged man in a long brown robe of comfortable-looking fur stepped out.

"What is the problem here? What are you doing in my vestibule? Answer me!"

The Count's features lit up in the wolf's look that had startled and scared Princess Dorothea. Returning to Russian, he replied: "Nicholas Romanov sent me. He expects Vladislav Tretiak, born in the shadow of the Kremlin, to do his duty."

There was a momentary flash in the merchant's eyes. Then he stepped aside and, speaking in cultured Russian tones, invited the Count into his home.

———

The sun, which had risen behind Brooklyn and lit up New York Harbor to the arriving travelers from England, had awakened Captain Harry Bratton in the private residence off the Broad Way that the Liaison Office maintained for senior visiting officers in Manhattan.

Bratton had ferried over from Hoboken Thursday afternoon and had dispatched his card to the law firm of Craft & Burr on Reade Street after settling in. He had requested a "private meeting with Mr. Burr on behalf of a newly-arrived representative of His Majesty's government." The confirmation card, signed by Burr in an elegant small script, proposed an 11:30 a.m. meeting "as I will be in court first thing tomorrow."

With the evening to kill, Harry had amused himself with supper at the Shakespeare Tavern, a pleasant establishment with a literary bend he recalled from previous visits. Later, he had discovered that other, more private establishments of his recollection promised other charms, though to his disappointment at increased prices.

The Captain was still despondent that Joanne had been unavailable and that she had made a career of profiting from her uncommonly intense carnal desires. That would not stop him from sampling her delights after his return to Georgetown; but it seemed too bad that the 'romance' would probably not be there. Speaking of 'sampling,' he was at a loss as yet as to how to inquire after Candice Samples, if that was still her name. He had not been able, even at the Liaison reception for the Duke, to discreetly ask after her. Well, there'd be plenty of time for that. Perhaps he'd simply leave a card at her townhouse, if she still maintained the same one. Or, he'd send an innocuous message to Twin Peaks---that very aptly named plantation!

This morning he had walked the streets of the City, marveling that in contrast to Georgetown, New York was expanding at a faster rate than ever. Apparently, a recent fire had sparked a decision to cede lower Manhattan to commerce and industry, with the hotels, better restaurants and private homes moving gradually up the island. And the confidence of the burghers he had met last night! They foresaw development as far north as a line extending from Kip's Bay to the Hudson! *There's an excitement here unlike anything in that sleepy little hamlet on the Potomac. This is the real capital of the Dominion...not that unhealthy little swamp!*

He paused at the corner of Reade Street to compose his thoughts, then moved on toward the shingle proclaiming the 'Law Offices of Craft & Burr.'

The door opened smoothly and the Captain stepped down into a waiting room of sorts, illuminated chiefly by the large front windows. Behind a desk that centered what were obviously two private offices sat a plump tow-haired man in his mid 20s whose air of pompous self-satisfaction was negated by the unsure glaze of his eyes as he regarded this impressive, erect visitor.

Typical doorkeeper, thought Harry. *Wouldn't bet against him being a son-in-law of one of the principals.* "Good morning, or perhaps good afternoon. My name is Captain Harry Bratton, of His Majesty's Coldstream Guards. I have an 11:30 appointment with Mr. Burr."

The plump young man rose lethargically to his feet, his fat cheeks bulging. *My God, does this fellow dine exclusively on mashed potatoes and Madeira?*

"Ah yes, Captain. I'm Nelson Chase. Do take off your cloak. Colonel Burr has not yet returned from court, but I expect him at an..."

The door to the left side back office opened and a trim middle-aged man with a receding hairline and glasses shoved onto his forehead stepped out. "Bring Colonel Burr's visitor into his office, Nelson, and pour him some tea. It's not everyday we've a representative of the Crown..."

The man came around the outer desk and extended his hand. "I'm Mr. Craft, the Colonel's law partner. He should be back momentarily. Come into his office." They walked into a darker room dominated by a roaring fireplace. A large desk, strewn with newspapers, legal documents and what appeared to be letters, was pulled up closer to the fire than seemed safe. A writing table and several casually scattered old chairs completed the scene. A window off a sidewall provided the only other light until Chase lit a desk-top lamp.

"The Colonel lit the fire himself before he left for court," Craft explained. "The poor man is cold even in the August heat. Says he's been that way since the Battle of Quebec."

Craft laughed at the look of surprise on Bratton's face. "No, Captain. Not Wolfe's victory in 1763! And not the one in 1814 when General Scott finally put down the revolt, either.

"Colonel Burr, you see, was among those who marched into Canada in '75 in that ill-fated---ill-planned---excursion during the unpleasantness of that terrible year. Why, they say that General Mont..."

"...gomery died in my arms. An exaggeration, of course, though more dramatic than the truth. But, when it comes to me, never let it be said that the fact defeated the fiction."

A small, elegant figure stood in the doorway, resting easily on his cane, a fur hat pulled down over his ears and matching gloves on his small hands. Though age lines burst from the outside corners of his eyes like roads suddenly forking in several directions from single main highways, the eyes themselves retained their native shrewdness.

Taking off his cloak and hat and dropping them casually on his desk, Burr walked over to the fire and held his hands, still astonishingly gloved, over the fire. "General Montgomery was dead before he hit the ground. One of your sharpshooters atop the walls put a bullet between his eyes. Or perhaps it was a random, lucky shot. After all, it was snowing so hard I'm still not quite sure how close to the walls we were. At any rate, the General was dead when I picked him up and began the retreat. I've never shook the chill that invaded my bones on that awful pell-mell lurch back down to Lake

Champlain in all the years since."

The old man turned and grinned mischievously. "However, Captain, I doubt you're from the Imperial War Museum. Don't think you're here to record a survivor's account of that most unfortunate time. Sit down! Nelson, damn it, where's the Captain's tea? And bring me some fresh coffee, I'm still cold."

Craft chuckled as he withdrew. Chase poured as ordered before excusing himself as well. The old man settled in behind his desk and studied the British officer intently. "Now then, Captain, I was intrigued to receive your note. What's this all about?"

Bratton sipped his tea. *Hot enough, but I should have told him to skip the sugar. Wonder if this old man has a cushion on that chair, or if the seat is raised up. He's almost eye-to-eye, when I expected him to barely be able to see over the desktop.*

"Mr. Burr...err, forgive me for not using your military title, but I was unaware you had one until walking into this office..."

"Quite all right Sir. Every living veteran of those days---and the survivors who aren't veterans---claims to have been a senior officer in that bloody business. Unique experience, wouldn't you say? Only time a force composed entirely of generals and colonels took on the British Army and lived to tell about it..." They both laughed.

Bratton began again: "Colonel Burr, there is no reason to keep the identity of His Majesty's representative secret. The word will be all over New York in a matter of days. In fact, I'm somewhat surprised it hasn't already reached here. Then again, Georgetown was still digging out of a heavy snow when I left Monday morning."

Burr's eyes had brightened at the mention of the capital but he remained silent as Harry continued.

"I accompanied the Duke of Wellington from London. We arrived in Baltimore Saturday past and rode immediately to Georgetown. The Duke determined on the trip across that you may have a role to play during the mission he is embarking on. I was dispatched to ascertain your availability."

Burr laughed. "You mean to 'ascertain' whether I was still alive and alert, Captain."

Bratton nodded. "Yes, Colonel, that was the general idea."

The old man laughed again. "Well, Captain Bratton, and what will you report to the Duke concerning this doddering old rebel?"

"That you seem fit, mentally and physically, to play the role that the times may require." Bratton was blunt yet elusive.

"And what role may that be, Captain? Is the Duke here to officiate at Jackson's funeral? I know London has been secretly hoping for such a solemn event for these four years now. But I'm afraid I'm too old to be a pallbearer, even for my ancient friend, Andy." Burr's chuckle had a devilishly youthful sound.

"Hardly, Sir. The Governor-General appeared the picture of health at the formal welcoming ceremonies last Sunday..."

"Son," the devilish chuckle broke in, "I've known 'Old Hickory' 40 years. He's looked like death-warmed-over all that time. Means nothing, however. He'll outlive us all.

"Now then, what's this all about?"

Bratton rose and indicated the teapot. At Burr's nod, he poured himself another cup. "Colonel Burr, the Duke wishes you to be prepared to travel, incognito if possible, to Georgetown at a moment's notice within the next few weeks. I am not at liberty to give the reason; the Duke will brief you as necessary at the proper time. Suffice to say, Colonel, a crisis unlike any seen here since 1775 may be on the horizon. That's why the King has dispatched the Duke to the USBA."

Not a muscle in Burr's face had moved but the original brightness in the old man's eyes suddenly grew more luminous.

"The Duke feels your...influence...shall we say, not only with the Governor-General, but also with Mr. Van Buren, may be a decisive factor in the looming crisis."

Again, Burr remained stoic. *This must have been a hard man in his time*, Bratton thought. *I can see him having the rock-steady hand when he faced Hamilton.* "So Colonel, are you willing and physically able to undertake this mission, if called on?"

Burr's face lit with the look of an adolescent who has realized he can carry off a successful prank against the grown-ups.

"Indeed, Captain. I haven't been to Georgetown since I walked out of the Senate Chamber at the end of my term in '05. It will be worth the rigors of travel simply to know Jefferson will be turning over in his grave at the thought that I've returned to do more mischief...

"You may tell your Chief that I will be at his beck-and-call. By the Eternal! I can't wait to see the look on Andy's face when I enter his Residency!"

As Burr escorted him out the door some 15 minutes later after making arrangements to meet for supper, Bratton noted that the old man had never reacted to the reference to Martin Van Buren.

Georgetown, D.C.
Early Evening
February 8, 1833:

General and Mrs. Scott were in their carriage, enroute to supper at Chief Justice Marshall's home, when, while passing the Samples townhouse, Maria announced that Candice had arrived late in the afternoon. "She's invited me to a late breakfast at 11 a.m., Win. Seeing as we have no plans until tomorrow evening, I sent back an affirmative response."

The General smiled, relieved of the necessity of bringing up the subject himself. And also relieved that Bratton had obviously not gone to Twin Peaks. *I'll bet he's already tracked down old Burr. Wellington was a little too cute on this one...*

"Tell me, my dear," he began, purposefully looking out the carriage window, "do you recall the Duke mentioning the other night that his aide had 'left town for a few days'?"

Maria shook her head. "No, Winfield. Perhaps that went over my head. Or perhaps I was busy with the service at the time. I do recall seeing Captain Bratton at the Liaison reception last Sunday, however. Other than a longer forehead, he hasn't changed a bit."

"Hrrm, you mean he's getting bald, don't you my dear? He is, but that's not why I bring him up. Wasn't he rumored to be, ahem, among Candice's *admirers* back when?"

"Yes, darling. During the plebiscite campaign in '28, when Charles was off campaigning for Jackson. There was talk that Candice and the Captain had become 'acquainted'...

"Oh, dear! I see where you're headed. This could get sticky. Oh, dear!"

Scott looked directly at his wife. "Did Candice mention why she came down from Twin Peaks? Word hasn't gotten out already about the state dinner for Wellington, I hope! Which, by the way, is restricted to those holding political, diplomatic and military titles, and their ladies. I suggested that to Jackson myself."

Maria giggled. "Not in so many words, Winfield. But her note did mention that our get-together would give her a break from the 'wilder things' she has planned for the remainder of the weekend."

Scott grunted. "Yes, no doubt. The Lieutenant must have a late morning meeting at The Residency. I recall him mentioning that he'd be checking in at the War Department first thing tomorrow. Let's hope he doesn't come up the steps on his hands and knees!"

"Winfield!" Maria roughly poked her husband in his massive chest. "Do you really think that's *all* they do?"

Scott gently kissed his wife's check. "Certainly not, my dear. Mainly, I expect they read 'Caesar's War Commentaries.' Aloud. In the original Latin. Vini, vidi, vici!"

CHAPTER SEVENTEEN

New York City
February 9, 1833:

Neither Bratton---by plan---nor Ignatieff---by necessity--had left the City that Friday. The Captain accepted Burr's invitation to dine at 5 p.m. at a small restaurant on Water Street that featured, of all things, Italian food. The street sign proclaimed its name as "Luigi's." After an enjoyable meal with the fascinating old devil, he had stopped off at the Shakespeare Tavern for only a short time. His plans called for an early morning crossing back to Hoboken and the stable where he had left the horse belonging to the Royal Marines.

Ignatieff, on the other hand, restlessly spent Friday afternoon being fitted for several new outfits that Tretiak insisted he'd need for the journey south. The Count had anticipated leaving immediately after a bath and shave, propelled by funds the merchant had immediately arranged for and clothed by whatever Tretiak could quickly obtain. But by the time the new clothes were ready and Ignatieff's weapons cleaned and augmented by a sword and a small, two-shot revolver, it was too late to think of leaving till morning.

So Ignatieff reluctantly accepted Tretiak's invitation to dine with the merchant and his wife. The long, congenial Russian-style dinner, accompanied by almost a dozen different white and red wines and the inevitable bottles of vodka, had the desired effect on the Count, who finally relaxed and went to bed early. He had been mildly interested to learn that Tretiak's operations were not confined to New York, but included offices and warehouses in Providence, Baltimore and Richmond...wherever those exotic-sounding locales actually were! *Naturally*, he thought sourly, *the man has nothing that would be helpful in Georgetown...*

The two agents missed each other on the crossing, as the Captain took a 6 a.m. ferry to Hoboken, while Ignatieff, some 90 minutes later, boarded a small boat chartered by Tretiak which cut southwest across the harbor and landed the Russian in Sandy Hook. With that immediate early differential, the duo should never have come across each other on the journey. The Count, however, squandered part of his lead time in the search for an adequate horse. Ignatieff, who was used to commandeering any animal he wished at home, was infuriated by having to dicker with the insolent Jersey farmers. When he finally made a deal, it was late morning.

(He had discarded the idea of impersonating a minor nobleman of inconclusive national origin. After discussion with Tretiak---who knew only that he was on a special mission directly ordered by the Czar (the 'Nicholas Romanov' greeting had established his bona fides with the merchant St. Petersburg had quietly placed in New York years before)---Ignatieff had adopted the alias 'Andre Karlhamanov.' Karlhamanov was to be a dissident: a disillusioned Russian liberal and college professor whose wealthy family had worked out a deal to send him into exile in the USBA rather than to prison at home. Getting the necessary false documents had also taken time; in fact, Tretiak's people had labored most of the night to produce them.)

And so it was that Bratton, whose overland travel exceeded the Russian's by more than 20 miles, managed to arrive at the same Burlington County stop, Stegeman's Cock & Bull Inn, less than 45 minutes after Ignatieff's arrival. Nicholas, with the eye patch disguise (he had almost forgotten to pull it on before riding in), immediately sized up the British officer as potentially dangerous while he stood at the far end of the bar watching Bratton check in. For his part, the Captain paid little attention to the Russian agent as he hurried past the bar and made his way to his room.

Thanks to the loose mouth of the owner, a fat and 50-ish blond horror who seemed to bellow in a German accent her every word, the Count knew the British officer was assigned to the Liaison Office in Georgetown before Harry had had a chance to wipe the road's mud off his face. "Headed back from New York," she continued in booming tones to the short, skinny bartender who, it turned out, was her long-suffering husband. "Must have been a short stay. I remember him watering his horse here Wednesday afternoon..."

The bartender/husband glanced at Ignatieff and his other two customers, a local farmer and the village smithy, and shrugged his shoulders in a defeated, neutral way. "You hear all kinds of reports about these Liaison fellows. Some say they keep the Frenchie agents at bay. Other people think they're just here to remind us who's really in charge..."

The farmer shrugged his shoulders noncommittally, while the big smithy drained his beer and laughed. "As long as they help keep the doors open here and occasionally need to have their mounts reshod and their wagon and carriage wheels replaced, I say: 'who cares!' Let the soldier boys be."

Ignatieff had been careful to leave his pistols and sword hidden in his clothes-roll in his room and had come into the bar with only his ever-present boot dagger and the small two-shot derringer he concealed in the waist band under his jacket. He had identified himself on signing the Inn's lodging book as Karlhamanov, a visiting scholar seeking a look at this land of liberty and opportunity. That pose he maintained at the bar and, later, while eating alone at a fireside table.

He observed the big British agent come back into the bar, which began to fill up with others, obvious regulars whom the hen-pecked bartender greeted by name. Bratton got into a conversation with the smithy and another, better-dressed man, but between the constant barking of the proprietress and the rising level of bar noise, the Count was unable to follow Harry's conversation.

As he sat eating a very good sauerbraten dinner and drinking a passable local red wine, he was able to study the Captain. Harry remained at the bar, having moved from hot rum to a Port the bartender claimed was imported. *If this one's regularly assigned to Georgetown, our paths will cross again. I'll obtain his name tonight or tomorrow from the Inn's book and then have the Consulate staff investigate. He looks too sharp to be assigned to a dull post like this…unless he's being punished for some indiscretion.* Ignatieff grinned. *Then again, he could be in command of this 'Liaison Office,' whatever that is… No matter, I'll know all about this big Englishman within a week.*

Although he had no idea who the man was---and certainly wasn't on guard for signs of Russian espionage---Bratton had of course sized up the wiry yet broad shouldered, black-haired, athletic-looking man with the eye patch who kept to himself, uttering as few words as possible in an Eastern European accent as yet unidentifiable. *He's definitely a traveler*, Harry thought. *Question is: which way is he headed?* Bratton, who hated to eat at a table alone, had finally ordered at the bar. His steak medallions in a red wine sauce were surprisingly good for a country inn in the middle of nowhere. Then again, except for some hard bread and cheese washed down with lukewarm tea from his canteen, taken during a noontime break to feed and water his horse, he hadn't eaten since dining with Burr the previous evening.

That meal, or rather, the conversation, was more on the Captain's mind than was the identity of the one-eyed traveler. Burr had proven a fascinating dining companion, a gentleman of impeccable manners who was as good a listener as a conversationalist.

The old man had reminisced about first meeting Jackson back in the '90s, when Burr had been a Senator from New York and the future G-G came to Philadelphia as Tennessee's first delegate to Congress. He had been---or so it seemed---remarkably candid about the Western adventures that had landed him under arrest on the infamous treason charge. "'Old Hickory' was eager to testify but we didn't need him," Burr said. "It all boiled down to what legally and constitutionally constitutes treason, according to John Marshall, who presided in his role as chief judge of the Dominion circuit court that included Virginia. Jefferson simply had no proof that I planned, indicated or tried to separate our then-Southwestern lands from the Dominion to set up another country. One to also include lands then belonging to France!"

Burr was also willing to comment on more current events:

"...those idiots in South Carolina. Jackson was right to send in the Coastal Guard. Should have sent Scott down with a couple good regiments, too...

"I'm afraid of this Bank business; Andy has a blind spot when it comes to economics! You kill the Bank and I think all this prosperity we're enjoying now could dry up soon enough. All these 'little' banks he wants to replace it with! Isn't it easier and more sensible to regulate the actions of one Dominion Bank than try to keep hundreds of little ones on the straight and narrow?"

However, he danced deftly around the subject of the Vice G-G when Harry brought it up:

"I've known Matty Van since he came to Manhattan around the turn of the century. Was originally from Kinderhook, up by Albany, you know. I admire the quiet progression of his career; the way he gets things done so effortlessly!"

The old man grinned ruefully. "There seemed to be controversy in anything I tried to do. Jefferson, the Clinton family here in New York State, my old friend Hamilton… Matty simply has the 'touch,' if you will, that so many other would-be leaders so unfortunately lack. Myself included!"

But that was as close to the genesis of the Burr-Van Buren

relationship as the old man would go.

Having finished his steak, Bratton was lingering over a final glass of Port when the stranger in the eye patch rose from his table and made his way back to the bar. "I believe I heard earlier this evening that you, too, sir, are traveling to Georgetown?" the stranger asked in an accent that Bratton guessed might be Russian.

"Yes, as a matter of fact, I am," Harry replied with some surprise. "And may I ask how you discerned that from your table by the fire?"

"From the, shall we say, 'proclamation' of our hostess… I see that my knowledge does not please you. A thousand pardons, sir.

"I am sorry but I'm unfamiliar with military protocol, to say nothing of military insignia, here in your country." The Count, who was well aware that Bratton's uniform was British Army and his rank that of Captain, lied smoothly. "You see, I myself have only arrived in America in the past few days. I am on my way to Georgetown and thought perhaps we could ride together tomorrow. If that is against the custom here, I withdraw the suggestion."

Bratton sipped his Port and smiled. "Our hostess, eh! Yes, I can believe that!

"Well, sir, I will be on the road by 6 a.m. If you are an early riser, I have no objection to your accompanying me."

Yes you certainly are a British officer, Ignatieff thought. However, he swallowed any retort to the Englishman's condescension: "It would be an honor, ah…"

"Captain Harry Bratton of His Majesty's Coldstream Guards. Temporarily attached to the Liaison Office in Georgetown. And you, sir?"

"I am Andre Karlhamanov. I teach at the university in St. Petersburg. I am on sabbatical and hope to study the wonders of your country."

"Well, Mr. Karlhamanov, to do that you'd have to sail to England. This is not, technically, 'my country.' Or anyone else's, either… But the USBA is a vibrant part of the Empire. You are welcome to study the 'wonders' of this place. They do not include, however, that frightfully dull little village on the Potomac!"

For my purposes, they do, my dear Captain. However: "I must begin my tour by notifying our Consulate of my arrival, Captain. Only then am I free to move around the USBA."

"Well, Mr. Karlhamanov…"

"Please, call me Andre. Even for a Russian, my name is a

jawbreaker…"

"Well then, Andre, I, for one, need my sleep. I left New York at 6 a.m. and the same time tomorrow will come much too soon. I intend to pay my tab and go to bed."

"I, too, Captain, was up early. I will meet you outside at 6 a.m. Good evening."

Ignatieff left his unfinished drink on the bar and, bowing from the waist, turned and left. Despite his announced intention to leave, Bratton ordered one more as he thoughtfully reviewed their conversation. *A Russian intellectual touring the Dominion? Perhaps. Worth keeping an eye on, once we're in Georgetown. I'll have Major Layne's people investigate…*

Georgetown, D.C.
February 9, 1833:

There was nothing of urgency in the overnight reports a yawning Lieutenant Wilder shifted through shortly after 8 a.m. The latest from the Minnesota portion of the Michigan Territory indicated that the Sioux had vanished; apparently back to the distant Black Hills to go into winter quarters. There was no word yet from General Taylor in New Orleans on whether Sam Houston had been sighted. There was word, however, that some Comanche had been encountered in early December by the Dragoons along the Red River near the Arkansas border with Mexican Texas. That news snapped the Lieutenant, who had of course been awake most of the night, out of his Candice-induced lethargy. That was his old outfit. He hoped Captain Patterson and the boys had emerged unscathed. They were a good outfit that he remembered fondly…now that he was a thousand miles away!

General Scott's usual Saturday routine included dropping by the War Department about 11 a.m. after meeting politicians and/or senior government officials for an information-sharing early breakfast. By then the Lieutenant had normally gathered any late-breaking Residency information to augment whatever had arrived at the Department overnight. Knowing that his aide had intended to come in early before heading to The Residency for some sort of meeting, the General decided to make an early appearance himself.

Breakfast could wait...old Justice Marshall's cook had outdone herself last night.

A skeleton crew manned the War Department on Saturdays. Scott saw no need for his men to kill time at their desks if nothing of importance was popping. Cass, the civilian boss, had not taken the administrative reins and was never seen himself, at any rate, on weekends. Thomas was virtually alone except for the clerks who were sorting yesterday's late arriving mail.

So the Lieutenant was surprised by the sudden call to attention. Scott strode in, opening his military cloak as he walked and indicating with a nod of his huge head for Thomas to gather up his papers for an impromptu briefing. The Lieutenant was just heading into Scott's office when the General suddenly reappeared; no one had thought to make his coffee at this early hour. Grumbling, Scott settled for the remnants of the morning's first pot of tea.

"Well Lieutenant, you look fresh enough this morning. Early night?"

The gleam in the General's eyes told Tom all he needed to know: Scott was obviously aware of Candice's occupancy of her townhouse...and his own overnight stay. *How the devil does he do it? I didn't even tell Harps where I was going last night...*

"Well Sir, the G-G wants a final review of the state dinner menu and invitation list this morning before they go off to the printer, so I thought I'd better get here first. That meeting's set for 11 a.m. and there's no telling how long it will take, especially since I understand the Calhouns are back in town." *Maybe that'll shift the Old Man's attention away from last night...*

Scott's bushy---*'shrub-like' might be a better description,* thought Tom---eyebrows rose at the mention of the South's leading fire-eater. But the diversionary tactic still didn't work.

"Calhoun, eh? Well, that should liven up your meeting across the street! Good thing you got a good night's rest...

"So, what do we have this morning? And you can omit anything from Portsmouth, unless those idiots have started firing at one another. I'm in too good a mood to let the childishness up there ruin my weekend."

(In an economy move the previous year, the Royal Navy and Coastal Guard stations in the New Hampshire port had merged, with the old CG station sold to private fishing interests. The turf battles, which actually included---to Scott's disgust---reveille times and tunes, had been endless. Additionally, the on-going off-duty tensions had increased; two weeks prior, a squad of USBA Marines had invaded a favorite tavern of their Royal counterparts. At last report, more than a dozen combatants were still hospitalized.)

The Lieutenant gave a short rundown of the overnight mail, emphasizing the lack of information from Louisiana and the news from Arkansas. (There was nothing new from Portsmouth.) With an exasperated shake of his head at the news that still another Indian tribe apparently was looking for trouble, the General was blunt: "Looks like those Dragoons could be in for some action this Spring. The Comanche have not come across the Red River before but our new settlements up there might look like juicy targets. Can Captain Patterson handle things?"

Tom was nonplused at the General's question. But his boss apparently expected an answer.

"Come on Lieutenant, you served in that outfit," Scott said with a trace of annoyance. "Is Patterson capable of handling an incursion by these Comanche?"

"Yes Sir. Steve Patterson can handle things. And E Troop's a good unit. I don't know much about the Comanche, but E Troop'll hold them across the River."

"Good. Now, about Calhoun…" The conversation turned to the guest list and the need to make sure the new Senator from South Carolina was on it. Tom wasn't sure why, but Scott wanted Wellington to find out for himself as soon as possible what a zealot the Carolinian was. That made it mandatory that the Calhouns be present Wednesday afternoon. Yet the G-G must think the invitation his own idea.

"You do understand that, Lieutenant? The G-G's first inclination will be to ban the Calhouns. However long it takes, you and Donelson can not leave that meeting without Jackson's direction to invite them. I don't care if you're there till after nightfall… So, if you have other plans for the weekend, be quickly persuasive. Understood? Now, be on your way."

Thomas stood and saluted, then turned and walked across the room. As he reached for the doorknob, Scott stopped him.

"And Lieutenant! Enjoy your weekend." Tom could have sworn the General had winked…

CHAPTER EIGHTEEN

On the Road to Georgetown
February 10-12, 1833:

The Russian 'scholar' was dressed and tying his clothes-roll behind his horse's saddle when Harry Bratton walked out of the Inn in the predawn darkness. The Captain had passed a restless night; something about Karlhamanov bothered him, though he could not quite put a finger on it.

Nevertheless, the duo was soon on the road, with the Russian inquiring only how far Bratton expected them to make this day.

"As long as we connect with the Delaware Bay ferry at the precise time, we should manage to make northern Maryland by dusk, Andre. But if we have to wait for a ferry, we'll be forced to lodge tonight in southern Delaware. That will turn this ride into a full four-day jaunt."

Though the sky, once the feeble sun came up, stayed a dull gray, the weather held off and the riders made the South Jersey coast of the Bay before noon, leaving them time to feed and water their mounts before boarding the cross-Bay ferry for the short trip into Delaware. The ride through southern Jersey had given each man time to size the other up. Bratton, impressed with the Russian's horsemanship, wondered how a self-styled 'intellectual' had learned to ride so well. Ignatieff, for his part, had determined to play his role and not pepper the Englishman with questions that a Russian 'dissident' would never have known to ask.

"So what are your plans once you've checked in with your Consulate, Andre? I'd suggest you go South first, as winter is almost over in the Carolinas and Georgia." They were waiting for the ferry to dock on the Bay's southern Jersey shore.

"Yes Captain, a good point. I'll mention it at the Consulate. However, my direction will be dictated by whatever plans the Consulate officials draw up. You see, even when we travel outside Mother Russia, it is the government which determines when and where..." *That should sound passive enough to discredit me as any kind of man of action.*

Bratton's look of pitied disgust seemed confirmation. But then, the Count was unaware that his dagger had slid up his boot-top. The handle had become clearly visible when Harry had glanced down while feeding his Royal Marine horse its mid-day oats.

A man who carries a dagger in his boot---and God knows what other weapons concealed elsewhere---isn't about to let some Consulate paper-pushers determine his itinerary. I bloody well better keep a good eye on this one, especially after we get to Georgetown...

The two dined that evening near the Delaware-Maryland border at an inn with the remarkable name of 'Cormack's Roadhouse.' Despite the Irish-sounding name---Bratton was beginning to wonder if the bloody Micks had an exclusive franchise for running Mid-Atlantic inns---it was owned by, of all things, a Greek. "Cormack's has been here since the turn of the century," Bill Albanis explained in answer to Harry's question. "The original owner was an Irishman named Cormack Flood. I was his manager and bought the place about 15 years ago."

Despite his obvious distaste for the clientele, Andre was able to identify a porterhouse steak on the menu. Bratton, whose stomach tended to act up during extended rides, settled for shepherd's pie. Knowing that vodka was his Achilles Heel, the Count started with locally-brewed beer, then had Claret with the meal, while Bratton, who thought the American tradition of cold beer barbaric, had several Ports.

Continuing to build his identity as an *intellectual*, Ignatieff praised the British system of parliamentary government, while allowing, gradually, his 'opposition' to the Czar's autocratic reign to be noted. While sipping a final after-meal Claret, he finally 'admitted' that his 'tour' was not completely a voluntary one.

Bratton said little, taking the measure of his new acquaintance, while wondering simultaneously how much to believe and whether their meeting at the Burlington inn had been merely coincidental. The thought of a third straight day of 6 a.m. departure followed by 10 or more hours in the saddle had both Bratton and Ignatieff looking forward to sleep. They turned in fairly early.

The following day passed uneventfully, though Ignatieff began a gentle probing of Bratton's career and position in Georgetown over supper at Brady's Fox Hunt Inn. Harry, who remembered the Duke's satisfaction with the house prime rib, finally gave in and ordered a big meal, knowing they were less than a half-day's ride from the capitol. At his suggestion, Andre had the sizzling steak.

The Captain deflected most of the Russian 'intellectual's' seemingly innocuous questioning. He seized on Andre's confusion over the Liaison Office and its role at Georgetown to deliver a lengthy briefing on the USBA's political structure that lasted for most of the meal. The maneuver cut off the Russian's probing of a more personal nature and served as a test of his level of interest in the Dominion's political atmosphere. Andre's questions, Harry observed, showed a remarkable interest in Dominion affairs for someone so recently arrived.

At the close of the evening, Harry was still undecided: Karlhamanov was either an intellectual with a scholar's ability to grasp, digest, filter and store information; or he had been through a Czarist version of the training Bratton himself had absorbed in becoming a 'diplomatic.' And while he was now satisfied that their initial meeting had indeed been coincidental, he was beginning to suspect Andre was here on something more than a university 'sabbatical.'

They crossed the Silver Spring road late the next morning in a misting rain. Harry pulled up to enjoy the Russian's initial reaction to the Dominion capital. There was nothing contrived about 'Karlhamanov's' reaction: he was plainly, Europeanly, appalled. "My family, Captain, has a country estate in what was once Poland. The estate contains two or three separate villages that each resemble what I see in the distance.

"What in God's name have they been doing here all these years? At least New York is a real city, though too Dutch for my own taste, from what little I saw…"

Bratton laughed. "You'll find, Andre, that the Americans are rather, shall we say, 'different' from Europeans. They're not even much like Britons. In fact, I once had an upper class American lady, the wife of a well-to-do plantation owner, tell me that the British and the British Americans are 'two peoples separated by a common language.'"

They rode on into Georgetown and Bratton showed Andre the way to the Russian Consulate. For their own reasons, each wanted to keep in touch, so they agreed   tentatively to meet Thursday evening at 6 p.m. at the Golden Eagle.

As they departed, Karlhamanov still looked somewhat baffled. *Two peoples separated by a common language?* He shook his head as he reined his horse in the direction of the Consulate.

CHAPTER NINETEEN

Georgetown, D.C.
February 12, 1833:

Captain Bratton reported immediately to the Duke upon arriving back at The Residency. Wellington himself had reached Georgetown late the previous afternoon, after spending an enlightening weekend with the Virginia leadership: Governor Floyd and the two Senators, Tyler and Rives.

The entire party, in fact, left Richmond Sunday afternoon, as the Duke had invited the powerful trio to attend Wednesday's state dinner. As Scott had predicted, the Governor came at the slavery issue from a different perspective from the others. While all three were staunch states rights men who bristled at the idea of Dominion interference with the peculiar institution---no one as yet dreamed that London might intervene---Floyd alone wanted a quick end to slavery.

"It just makes no economic sense!" he had cried out Saturday evening during an elaborate dinner he had thrown in Wellington's honor. "There is no incentive for those who know they are being fed, housed and clothed to work any harder than the bare minimum demanded by the overseer. But make the same individuals aware that their welfare depends entirely on the fruits of their labors and we would see a massive increase in productivity."

Tyler had smiled at the Governor's tirade. "You'll have to forgive John," he had said to the Duke. "His interesting economic theories appear sound, appear progressive. Yet, simply allow the darkies to go their own way? The blacks need the discipline inherent in our system. If, in 50 years or so, the blacks of that age have demonstrated an ability to function under less direction, then perhaps it will be time for each state, individually, to reconsider the issue of their freedom. To free them now or in the near future---let them loose to work or not work at will---would cause both economic and social chaos in the South. No, Sir Arthur, the Governor is wrong. The South simply won't have it!"

Wellington was shaking his head as he described his conversations to Bratton. "And these are the more *progressive* Southerners, according to General Scott. God help us! What must Calhoun and the others be like?"

The Duke had been fascinated to hear that Aaron Burr was alert and eager to play a role, however as yet undefined, in the upcoming months. With the weather improving by the week, Burr had told Bratton, he would take a boat to Georgetown and could arrive within 48 hours of notification. "I took the liberty of telling him we'd provide transportation via the Royal Navy, Sir. The idea of, as he put it, "hopping off the King's sloop and onto Andy's dock," tickled him."

The Duke had roared, but quickly sobered when Harry related the reserved manner in which the old man had reacted to any mention of Van Buren. "He'll not do anything that might hurt Van Buren's chances of eventually occupying The Residency, that's clear," the Duke observed. "And why not? Every man wants his son to do better than he did. In this case, as a former Vice G-G, with a son who will be inaugurated in the same post next month, there's simply one more step to go.

"Some time in the next few days, I'm going to bring Burr's name up to Van Buren. His reaction should be interesting..."

Wellington looked at his pocket watch. "Well now Captain. You will accompany me to the Liaison Office. I've scheduled a meeting with Major Layne. I think its time we advised him of the real mission here. He's no political scientist; won't ever replace you in the, ahem, 'American Office,' but we can't afford to keep him in the dark any longer. Besides, I can't have you going off alone for days on private missions. He and his people will have to help bear the load."

"What about Sir John, Your Grace?"

"Briefed him already. Burrell's a sharper tack. Picked up the gist of it immediately."

It was on the short carriage ride to the Liaison Office that Bratton briefed the Duke on his new Russian acquaintance, Andre.

―――――――――

As the social aide to the Governor-General, it had fallen to Lieutenant Wilder to personally deliver the Calhouns' their last-minute invitation to the state dinner. He had done so the previous afternoon, telling the South Carolinian that The Residency had only learned over the weekend of his arrival in Georgetown. Now Tom was in Scott's office, describing the scene to the General.

"I never met Mr. Calhoun before, Sir. Sort of reminds me of one of those Old Testament prophets, always calling fire and brimstone down on the Israelites or their enemies…"

"It's that long hair, Lieutenant. Quite an affection, wouldn't you say?"

"Yes Sir. But he actually looked thunderstruck when I handed him the invitation. Didn't say anything, but I got the impression he hadn't anticipated walking up the Main Portico again any time soon."

"No Lieutenant," said Scott, "and it will be interesting to see the reactions when he and the G-G first meet face-to-face tomorrow night. However, I'm more interested in making sure Calhoun is properly introduced to Wellington. Damn Jackson for refusing to have a formal greeting line! If I'm not available for some reason when Calhoun arrives, you take him over to the Duke. Since you're the one who delivered the personal invitation, it won't seem out-of-the-ordinary. And, after all, you *are* The Residency social aide! Anything else to report from across the park?"

"Yes General. Captain Bratton rode in as I was leaving The Residency shortly after noon. Looked like he'd been in the saddle quite awhile. That's eight days he was gone."

Scott nodded but made no comment. To himself, however, he noted: eight days. Enough time to reach New York, find Burr and ride back. And it'll be a week or more before Wilder hears from his father. *Damn old Hook Nose. You're still ahead of me on this one…*

"Now Lieutenant Wilder, to the real reason the Dominion pays us so well. Get Lieutenant Beaufort in here with the Portsmouth file. We've got important matters to consider…"

Ignatieff had known his arrival would throw the Consulate into an uproar; he had counted on it. Upon arriving at the K Street gate, he had barked clear, crisp Russian, in military tones, demanding the Cossacks admit him. Acting on instinct born of their severe training, they had immediately done so. The Count was up the steps and through the front door before the guards could turn his horse toward the stables. An indignant aide to the Consul-General was silenced by a single look from the wolf-face, the right eye still patch-covered. "I wish to see the Consul-General immediately. Is he on the premises?"

The shaking aide nodded and gulped: "And who shall I say is calling?"

"A visitor from the Court of the Czar is all you need to know. Now bring me to him!"

The Consulate was simply two homes bridged by a ground-level addition of offices. Count Renkowiitz was leaving his private quarters in the 'western' building when the aide escorted Ignatieff down the corridor centering the offices and leading to the private quarters.

"Excellency, we have a visitor from St. Petersburg who wishes to see you." The white-faced aide indicated Nicholas, who pushed past him to step directly in Renkowiitz's path.

The towering C-G looked down at the intruder, his face reddening. "What is the meaning of this? Rossevich, call for the guards!"

Ignatieff caught the aide's arm in an iron grip of his left hand, looked up at Renkowiitz and again flashed the wolf's leer. "A thousand pardons, my dear Count," he said, bowing formally after pushing Rossevich against the wall as if the aide were a doll. "Did you not get the word from Nesselrode to expect me? I see that must be the case. Damn the slowness of the Imperial mail service. I see I will have to introduce myself."

He raised his face to look straight up at the C-G and, with a sudden lightening movement of his right hand and arm, removed the eye patch.

The aide's gasp of anticipated horror still echoed in the corridor as the C-G's angry red face turned pink on its way to whiteness.

"You see now, my dear Count Karl, why I presented no formal card or credential. You do know who I am?"

Count Renkowiitz stared at his visitor for another long moment as if assessing the implications of the appearance of this apparition. Even though they had never met, like everyone else in the Czar's diplomatic and secret services (which were, for all practical purposes, one-and-the-same) he knew of the legendary Count Nicholas Ignatieff whose right eye was half-blue and half-brown. He nodded his head affirmatively and turned slowly to the open-mouthed Rossevich.

"Escort our most distinguished visitor to the largest guest bedroom and assign servants to help him recover from his journey with a hot bath, massage, refreshments and anything else he requires." Turning back to Ignatieff, he bowed formally.

"Welcome to the Imperial Consulate, Count Nicholas. I place the staff, our resources and myself at your service."

The wolf's leer was replaced by a look of Imperial formality. "Thank you Count Karl. You are most gracious. I have been in the saddle for the better part of four days. I have looked forward to a bath and shave at journey's end. However, we have much to discuss. I wish to begin quickly."

Renkowiitz, whose immediate thought was to ply this unwanted visitor with whatever he required and to see him on his way as quickly as possible, bowed again. "Certainly my dear Count. I will have a special dinner prepared. Would 4 p.m. give you enough time to refresh and relax? If so, the servants will escort you to the formal dining room in two hours."

"That will be fine, Counsel-General. Restrict the place settings to two. I will divulge my rationale for being here, as well as my plans, to you alone.

"Now you," he commanded, flicking his head imperiously at Rossevich, "you will escort me to my quarters."

The meeting at the Liaison Office with Major Layne had taken little more than an hour. Layne, a tall, lanky man whose build brought to Bratton's mind the USBA Army captain who had met *Irresistible* at the Baltimore dock, had of course been stunned when the Duke outlined the true purpose of his visit. But Harry could see that the chance for action---and possible promotion---fired his enthusiasm.

At Wellington's direction, Bratton had also briefed Layne on his encounter with Karlhamanov. The Liaison man agreed that the Russian 'dissident' should be quietly followed to determine the validity of his identity. It was agreed that a Liaison agent would be at the Golden Eagle when the Captain and Andre met in two nights. An around-the-clock watch would be placed on the Consulate beginning this evening in case anyone resembling the 'dissident's' description entered or left.

Wellington was dining across Pennsylvania Avenue at Frank Blair's home this evening. Among the other guests were to be Joseph Kent, the newly-elected Senator from Maryland and Cabell Rives, the junior Senator from Virginia.

"So the menu will consist once again of tariffs, nullification, this damnable Bank business and who should pay for the 'internal improvements' these colonials all so incessantly demand or oppose," the Duke had sighed on the way back to The Residency. (Jackson was dining at Congressman Polk's home, as he apparently did at least once a week.)

"I begin to see, however, that the Southerners apparently have balled themselves into a fist on this issue of states rights. You and Quincy Adams may be correct. I question whether anything short of brute force will compel them to seriously consider emancipation now or anytime in the foreseeable future. They never mention the political consequences of emancipation in their screeches---just the economic---but its obvious: they are even more intent on retaining their power here in Georgetown than they are of retaining mastery of other human beings.

"They also apparently view the Compact in different terms than the Crown and the Northerners. They don't seem to consider it anything more than a bloody convenience, a road map, that they can follow or ignore at will." The Duke sighed once more. "Well, let us see if this Maryland chap, Kent, is any different. Though I would suppose, after what I've seen so far, that he too is a planter. By God, Bratton," he exploded, "Southern planters and Northern lawyers! Is that all their damn bloody government is composed of?"

With the Duke seen safely across Pennsylvania Avenue to the Blair house, Harry suddenly found himself free for the first time since his arrival night in Georgetown. And with his afternoon and evening cut out for him tomorrow due to the state dinner, he decided that tonight he would visit the Golden Eagle.

Cleaned up and attired in a freshly-laundered Coldstream Guards uniform, dress sword attached, he made his way the several blocks to the Eagle a bit past 6:30 p.m. Pausing at the door, he wondered how he would find Joanne after the passage of some four years: would she have missed him, or had too much time---and too many men---erased him from her mind?

He strode into the taproom and shook his head at the sight of the same tall, emaciated bartender. A boisterous crowd of what appeared to be young government officials had taken over the bar area and most of the room, while the obligatory lobbyists sat aloof with their clients nearer the fires and in the alcoves. Joanne was nowhere to be seen, but the tawdry buxom blond waitress he remembered as the heavy-handed Kathy spotted him as he shouldered his way through the crowd. He had already ordered Claret when Kathy put down her tray next to him. After yelling her order to the bartender, she turned to Harry and ventured a crooked-toothed smile.

"The proprietress is making her rounds in the back dining room, Sir Galahad. Shall I tell 'Mi Lady' you're here?"

Bratton shook his head and eased sideways. The woman's breathe, even at this early hour, smelled of cheap liquor and tobacco. "That will not be necessary. I plan on dining here tonight. I'm sure Mrs. Casgrave will be out at some point."

"Ah, you can be sure of that, Colonel. Especially when she hears there's a fine example of British nobility all alone here at the bar." Gathering up her orders, Kathy fought her way back through the crowd.

Even without a word from her waitress, it did not take Joanne long to emerge. Leaning against the bar and looking towards the back dining room, Harry caught sight of her as she pushed her way through the swinging doors. The petite, long-haired brunette---Harry could see that she hadn't gained an ounce in four years---looked out over the crowded taproom before glancing at the bar. Her black eyes began to glow and the charming little-girl smile he had loved---even after he had realized how fraudulent it could be---suddenly blossomed on her lean, dark face dominated by high, Indian-style cheekbones.

Joanne made her procession across the room, stopping at the occasional table and to listen to a whispered comment or two by standing patrons, but steadily working her way towards Harry.

"Well, Captain Bratton, a long time…"

"Hello, Joanne. Yes, 46 months and 43 days, to be precise."

The innkeeper's smile turned pouty. "I was referring, Captain, to the 11 days since you rode into Georgetown with the Duke of Wellington…"

"But my dear, I left town Monday a week ago and returned just this afternoon. I did call the night I arrived but you were, ah, otherwise occupied."

Joanne cast her eyes down and came up with her fabled look of innocence. "Hm, well, if that's the case, I forgive you. Now, I have to mingle with my customers, dear Harry, but you and I will share a late supper after the backroom clears out a bit." She paused and again cast her eyes demurely down before continuing. "Unless you have other plans?"

Well, this looks to be an evening to remember, he thought. "Not at all. I'll be right here when you're finished with your guests."

She reached up on her toes and kissed his check, her lips sliding over towards his right ear. "We'll make the extra 10 day wait worthwhile, won't we?" She then broke the embrace and turned back into the crowd of on-lookers, more than one of whom had realized his plans for the evening would not come to fruition.

As he had sworn he would, Lieutenant Wilder had found other places---notably the Indian Queen's own taproom---to relax and enjoy his late meals recently. Tonight, however, he had agreed to meet David Harper at the Eagle. With Wellington in town and the Congress shuffling back in for the special session, they had not been able to coordinate their schedules for any daytime meals...or nocturnal adventures.

Harps had managed to go riding with the Countess Caroline Sunday afternoon as planned. Tom was eager to hear about it; and relieved it had apparently produced no international repercussions after all. But as he walked in and saw the female innkeeper holding on to Captain Bratton, Tom immediately realized the evening held the promise of degenerating into a farce, in which he, for once, would be only a happy spectator.

Tom quickly saw that the Captain, whose embrace with the proprietress was just breaking up, had no way of seeing him in the crowd. The Lieutenant moved quietly to the end of the bar nearest the front doors and ordered a cold beer, then waited for the final actor in tonight's comedy to make his appearance.

Dave Harper strode in minutes later and, glancing around quickly, spotted Lieutenant Wilder. He fought his way next to him. "Well, Tom, I see you're still on your feet. What happened? Did the Mistress of Twin Peaks stay in the Maryland horse country all weekend? Or did General Scott keep you too busy to add a new chapter to your legend?"

Tom grinned contentedly and allowed himself another pass on

his beer mug before answering: "Not at all, Harps. Candice arrived Friday afternoon and we spent the majority of the weekend cozily camped out at her townhouse... Of course, I had to hit the pillow very early last evening to restore my strength. But it's your weekend that we're here to discuss." He gestured at the bartender, who was sullenly refilling order after order. "What will you have?"

Harps, surprisingly, ordered a beer and then turned to his friend. "Well, Lieutenant, aside from the fact that one of the damn Cossacks seemed to be in the saddle along with me and the other rode between us, my Sunday afternoon with the Countess went well. She's a fascinating person..."

Wilder nearly choked on his beer as his eyebrows went up in imitation of his commanding officer: "Of course. It's her inquisitive mind with its superior Russian education that attracts you..."

Harps was indignant: "Hell, Tom, she speaks four languages. That's damn near as many as you. And she does have an inquisitive mind. She has a fair grasp on the workings of our government and the political situation here." He grinned at his friend. "And, she wondered how you're making out with the, as she called her, 'formidable Miss Latoure.'"

"She didn't really call Lucille *formidable*?"

"Actually, she used a Russian adjective that I understand might best not be translated precisely in polite society." They both grinned.

"Well, I can't say I'm surprised. I got the feeling at the Christmas reception that Caroline had a pretty good idea of what was going on. So what's her background? And how come she's sticking it out here? They say her mother lasted less than a month. This must seem like an Indian village compared to St. Petersburg."

Dave was beginning to tell the Lieutenant that the Renkowiitzs were poor and very minor Russian nobility, despite Caroline's mother's pretensions, to whom any diplomatic post was a Godsend. But then he spotted the imposing British officer standing near the center of the bar in the now slowly-clearing taproom.

"That tall Brit over there, Tom. Have you seen him before?"

"Of course, Dave. Rode down from Baltimore with him last week. That's your American Office contact, Harry Bratton. Though this month he's obviously using his military title."

"Huh. So that's Bratton. Looks like he's waiting for someone. Couldn't guess who that might be, now..."

The two friends grinned at each other again. "What's the

matter, Harps? Aren't you going to do battle for your lady's hand?" Tom was pleased with himself for once being the one to insert the needle.

Harps was having none of it, however. "When and if I find a lady, I'll let you know, Lieutenant Wilder. If you're referring to Mrs. Casgrave, if I were willing to 'do battle' for that *lady's* hand, the dead would already be littering this taproom…"

The two laughed aloud. Tom was relieved that his suspicions concerning David's feelings for the brothel madam had proven correct.

"Well, I'm glad to hear that, Dave. I had a feeling you were none too serious. Glad to have that confirmed."

"Don't get me wrong, Tom. She's actually a lot of fun---if you don't cross her---and great in the sack; in fact, she's even taught me a few new tricks. But nothing to get emotional about." Harper drained his beer and signaled Richard for another round. "Course, if she owned a plantation that takes up half of Maryland, it might be a different story…"

Tom laughed as Dave's eyebrows, which had risen halfway up his forehead, retreated to their normal position. "Hey, it's your love life we're here to discuss tonight, Mr. Harper, not mine."

"True enough, Lieutenant, but just remember: being the squire of Twin Peaks isn't the worst way to go through life." It was the second time Harps had gently reminded his friend of his once-in-a-lifetime chance to court a millionairess…a sex-crazed one at that.

————————

Captain Bratton, in turning around to survey the remaining taproom crowd, had seen Lieutenant Wilder hoisting beers with another young British American. The two seemed to find the entire situation amusing. Harry finally got the younger officer's eye and the two nodded. As the room was now emptying rapidly---Georgetown early on had earned a reputation as an 'early-to-rise, early-to-bed' capital with a short, intense evening social life---he moved easily down the bar towards Tom and his friend.

"Ah, Lieutenant. Thought I might catch sight of you here. Establishment hasn't changed a bit. Just as I remembered it…"

Just wait till Joanne gets you upstairs. Then tell me if it's the same. "Well Captain, perhaps you have a slightly different perspective than mine.

"By the way, this is David Harper of the Interior Department. Dave tells me much of his correspondence to London is initially directed to you."

Bratton's eyes lit up. "I say, Mr. David Harper! Of course! Jolly good to meet you in person after all this time. Though I feel that in many ways we are already well acquainted after all the paperwork we've exchanged. Delighted to meet you. Was planning on getting over to the Interior Department within the next day or so. Should have done so sooner, but was called away on His Majesty's business right after the welcoming ceremonies..."

Harper shook the big Briton's hand warmly. "Glad to finally make your acquaintance in person, Mr. Bratton. Or should I say, Captain Bratton. Does resuming your military position mean you're no longer at the Office?"

"Certainly not, Mr. Harper. I'm simply back on full pay for the duration of His Grace's tour of the Dominion. By fall I expect to be back in my cubbyhole in foggy old London. I say, however, how about another round? Or are you, too, evacuating this fine establishment?"

Tom couldn't resist: "Another round would be much appreciated, Captain. And no, we're not evacuating. David and I plan to have a late supper here. We usually do two or three times a week, but the Duke's arrival has kept both of us on the run." He paused.

"Would you care to join us?"

Bratton, who kept peeking around toward the back room doors, shook his head. "Normally it would be my pleasure. However, I do have a late evening supper engagement of my own." Joanne at that moment emerged gliding through the doors. "Which I believe is imminent."

The proprietress was plainly not pleased to see two of her lovers sharing a round of drinks, joined by that damn young War Department aide. Joanne, who prided herself on her sexuality and ability to arouse any man, could not understand how the Lieutenant seemed somehow invulnerable to her wiles. Right now, however, she had more important things to worry about.

"Well Harry dear. I see you've identified the true powers behind our government. And they the true power behind the Empire..."

Taken unawares---for Lieutenant Wilder had mentioned her name sparingly in his references to the Eagle---Captain Bratton smiled uncertainly. "Ah, Joanne my dear. So the Lieutenant wasn't exaggerating. He and Mr. Harper actually are regulars. He's just told me they sup here two or more evenings per week."

The proprietress was icy: "Yes and how fortunate tonight is one of them. Hello David. I didn't expect you this evening. Nor your Army friend…"

Harps was splendidly neutral. "Well Joanne, as you said, Tom and I do have the affairs of the Dominion to determine. Instead of burning the government's candles, we thought tonight we'd take a break and utilize yours."

Stung by her offhand reference to him---and delighted to stroke a fire he could sense raging in the black-haired woman---Tom could not resist adding: "We've even asked the Captain to join us in order to bring a world perspective, but he seems to have a previous engagement." He offered his most innocent blue-eyed smile.

The look of rage that flashed across her face demonstrated that he had scored a direct hit. It also brought back Harper's earlier remark about not crossing her. *These two can have her. Am I glad I stopped coming here…*

Joanne had regained a measure of her self-control: "Captain, your table will be ready in 15 minutes. I'll send a waitress over to remind you." She turned and walked away, her compact behind frankly ogled by any number of men at the bar.

For all his British sophistication, Harry Bratton was taken aback by the turn in the conversation. "Well gentlemen! From the attitude of the proprietress, am I to deduce the pair of you absconded with the tavern silverware last week? Or were you overly rambunctious with some of the hired help, eh?"

Thomas laughed and pulled on his beer. "Sir, I am, by act of the USBA Congress, an officer and a gentleman. Certainly you don't think…"

"…that either of us would dally with the hired help in this establishment, Harry?" Dave completed in a tone of exaggerated injured shock. Harry joined in the general laughter as Harper continued:

"Anyway, the next round's on the Interior Department…." The trio lifted their glasses: "To the Interior Department." Shortly afterward, Bratton vanished into the backroom, while the two British Americans found an empty table by a fireplace. When they had finished their meals and paid the bill he had not yet returned…

CHAPTER TWENTY

London, England
February 13, 1833:

The dismal wet-and-dark afternoon matched the mood of Lord Palmerston as he emerged from his brougham in front of #10 Downing Street.

He carried in his pocket notes from a report just arrived from St. Petersburg that had the potential, in his view, to blow the elaborate emancipation program out-of-the-water even before the legislation was introduced in Parliament. *And that,* he thought, *is the least of its possible consequences.*

The Foreign Secretary passed quickly into the old house and was escorted directly to the Prime Minister's office by one of the secretaries. With the pained face of an old man who knows he has not long to serve, Lord Grey looked up from the papers spread across his desk: "Yes, Henry, what brings you up the stairs in such a rush? Surely Bonaparte hasn't returned to raise another Grande Armee?'"

Palmerston smiled as he shook his head but there was no mirth in his voice. "No Prime Minister. But the news is not good nevertheless. I've just received a visit from Baron Heytesbury, who's just home from St. Petersburg. The Sultan, it seems, has asked the Russians for assistance against the Egyptians. The damn fool has invited them to land a force in Syria to cut off the Egyptians' march on Constantinople!"

Lord Grey's spectacles slid down his many-veined nose. "And the Czar's response?"

"Why he's ordered an army to Damascus! The bloody Ottomans have agreed to open the straights to a Russian fleet, warships as well as transports. They're gathering at their Black Sea ports now. They'll sail within 30 days!"

The P.M.'s normally pale face had now gone gray. "Don't those idiots in the Porte realize that the Russians, once landed, won't leave until forced out? Why, the fools have virtually ceded Syria to the Bear!"

"And, Prime Minister, left the Bear within striking distance of our shortest potential route to India..." Palmerston shook his head. "Our dream of a canal across the Suez could turn into a nightmare." He balled his fists in frustration:

"How could the Turks be so incredibly stupid?"

Lord Grey had taken off his spectacles and dropped them on his stack of state papers. "Henry, this could upset the balance of power, not only in the Near East but in Europe itself..."

The Foreign Secretary was grim: "I agree Prime Minister. If the Russians should somehow gain unlimited access to the Mediterranean through the Bosporus Straits, they will soon bite off all the Balkans. That would make the eastern Mediterranean their private lake. Then they can gobble up the rest of the Ottomans' territory at their leisure: The Valley of the Euphrates, Palestine, Egypt. They'll push on through to Persia and..."

"And arrive at the gates of India fresh and ready to overpower us. Let St. Petersburg get its hands on India and the Romanovs will be invincible. We'd as well move His Majesty's seat of government to Georgetown!" Lord Grey held his head in his hands.

There was a tense silence in the room until Lord Palmerston cracked a smile. "Well Prime Minister, let us hope it does not come to *that*...

"Anyway, enough reason to call the Cabinet into session, wouldn't you say, My Lord?"

The P.M. nodded. "Yes Henry, this news puts policies domestic and international in a new perspective. By George, colonial, too! We'll meet tomorrow at 11 a.m. I assume all the members are in Town?"

Lord Palmerston nodded. "I would assume so. In any case, I will return to the Foreign Office. I already have some options being developed for presentation. I'll lay them before you and the Cabinet tomorrow. By the way, do you intend to notify Buckingham Palace?"

Lord Grey had risen and was looking out his window. "When we have agreed on a plan. No reason to alarm the King just yet..."

Palmerston nodded in agreement. "Yes...never alarm His Majesty unnecessarily..." They smiled and Palmerston turned to leave the room. Grey sighed heavily and returned to his desk. *Lord Melbourne, you are welcome to this old house. I've about had enough glory...*

Georgetown, D.C.
February 13, 1833:

John C. Calhoun took stock of the Southerners gathered in the Senate cloakroom for the noontime meeting. It was too soon, of course, for those from the southwest---Louisiana, Mississippi, Alabama and Tennessee---to have reached the capitol for the special session, but a good representation of the states closer to the District was in attendance. Unfortunately, he was disappointed in some of the faces, but felt the need to caucus before tonight's state dinner.

The fiery slavery advocate from Georgia, Senator George Troup, was here accompanied by the former governor of that state, newly-elected representative George Gilmour. Calhoun's staunchest ally, Representative George McDuffie of South Carolina, articulated the nullification argument, in Calhoun's view, better than he himself did and had traveled with him and Floride on the boat from Charleston. McDuffie was clearly not pleased that Georgia Representative John Forsyth was in the room; Forsyth was a loyal---"lapdog," in McDuffie's words---Jacksonian who opposed nullification and was, at best, lukewarm in his support of slavery.

The Virginians, Tyler and Rives, had come from Richmond with Wellington; Calhoun wanted their views on the significance of the Duke's visit. He knew where the two stood politically: Rives was a Jacksonian but a true Southerner in terms of states rights while Tyler's opposition to Dominionist legislation went back almost 20 years.

The two North Carolinians, Senators Willie Person Mangum and Bedford Brown, were moderates, but both had supported nullification. Calhoun felt he could count on them in any showdown. Also attending were Maryland's two Senators, Joseph Kent and Ezekiel Chambers. Calhoun had little faith in or respect for either, but thought Maryland deserved to participate in the caucus.

By the time the meeting broke up some 2 1/2 hours later, several things were clear: Maryland would stand with the South against the Bank but would not support any renewed nullification efforts; the group was united in its opposition to Dominion funding of intrastate internal improvement projects; more pressure must be brought on London during the session to annex, buy or seize Texas as the best way to offset growing abolitionist strength in the North; and Wellington's visit was disquieting. (The two Virginians had related the conversation at Governor Floyd's dinner party and subsequent follow-up conversations over the previous few days.)

"This visit is extraordinary and unprecedented," said Calhoun. "I'm baffled by Jackson's apparently cavalier response to it. And I don't accept for one moment that Wellington is here unofficially.

"There is something going on, gentlemen, which, while it may not be sinister, is definitely troubling. A former Prime Minister, who is now the leader of the Parliamentary opposition and who once defeated the greatest conqueror since Caesar, does not cross the Atlantic in midwinter simply to tour our Dominion.

"No, the Duke is here on the King's business. And, *whatever that business is*, it is *our business* to ascertain." Calhoun paused and glanced around the room at his confederates.

"Senator Tyler will introduce Troup and me to Wellington tonight and lead the conversation towards the slavery issue. As John has indicated, Sir Arthur has expressed a disquieting interest in it since arriving here. We must determine how strong that interest is.

"The rest of you should be sure to speak individually to the Governor-General concerning Texas. We want Jackson to know he has support on that issue for taking on the Foreign Office. I do not, of course, have any firm idea of his agenda for this special session, but we must not forego this opportunity to debate Texas on the floor of both Houses. So we need a strong statement from him in his speech to open the session."

With that, the group adjourned to prepare for the state dinner.

Count Nicholas Ignatieff was satisfied. Count Renkowiitz had taken one look at Ignatieff's directive from the Czar---*the one Terravenissian and the other fools in London failed to discover hidden in the handle of the long pistol returned to me when I boarded that damned Pride of the Hudson*---and ceded him control of the Consulate.

Ignatieff had predetermined to leave Renkowiitz (if found willing and able) in nominal charge of the Consulate's day-to-day activities, but answerable, of course, to him. For that reason, the Consul would be attending tonight's dinner at the residence of this colonial Governor-General, Jackson. The last thing Count Nicholas wanted was to draw attention to either the Consulate or himself while he familiarized himself with the situation and the players. He had ordered Renkowiitz to attend, taking with him the beautiful young Countess Caroline (perhaps there'd be time to attend to her at some point!), while he explored this drab little village in his 'Karlhamanov' guise.

Ignatieff had already learned that the capital had been stunned when Wellington had unexpectedly ridden in; this "state dinner" was in his honor. According to Renkowiitz, all the C-Gs in the city would attend, along with members of the Dominion government and what few ranking military figures there were. Renkowiitz had also mentioned that Jackson had called a special session of the provincial parliament for next week. Count Karl mentioned the issues, but emancipation of the slaves was not among them. Apparently, Wellington had not yet broken that news to Jackson or anyone else.

At Ignatieff's direction, the Consulate's political/intelligence staffer, Captain Alexei Drago, had been called in and ordered to prepare a briefing for Thursday morning on the overall political situation in the USBA. With that information and anything Renkowiitz came up with at the state dinner, he could then begin to develop a plan to identify any potential 'rebel' leaders.

Count Nicholas had also probed Drago about Captain Bratton, but neither he nor Count Karl knew anything about him. The Count did vaguely recall seeing an officer who matched Bratton's description at the Liaison Office's welcoming reception 10 days before, but he had been just another in a group of British Army officers who had stayed close to the Duke. Drago's assignment had thus been expanded to prepare a dossier on the Captain for the Thursday meeting.

Now, with Drago hard at work and Renkowiitz preparing for the affair at The Residency---a pretentious old building that seemed almost quarantined by its surrounding parkland from the rest of the *city*---he would assume his 'dissident' persona and do some personal exploring...

Lieutenant Wilder had been through a year's worth of planning for various White House social functions, but he had never yet seen anything like the tension and frenzy that marked the preparation for this evening's affair.

General Jackson was pulling out all the stops to impress his former commander, exhibiting a lack of concern for cost that matched a previously suppressed appreciation of and taste for sophistication.

Old Burr is supposed to be the gentleman of the age, according to my grandfather, but the G-G certainly seems to know how to throw a banquet. Once he's in the mood to do so....

Once again the oval room with its view of the Virginia hills (Arlington House sitting atop the nearest) was to serve as the initial reception room. This time, however, the formal dining room was dominated by a long centered table with elaborate candelabra placed in front of every fourth or fifth set of facing chairs. Other tables hugged each wall; the various courses would be deposited here in quantity so the servants could then present servings to the five or six guests each was assigned.

Tom was shocked at the number of courses to be served: an elaborate chowder was to be followed by game, to be followed by the main meats: hams, roasts of beef and various lamb and pork specialities. The side dishes were to include mashed and roasted potatoes, sweet meats, several green vegetables, rice, turnips, cauliflower, corn and roasted onions, as well as a creamed oyster dish that he had not encountered previously. All this to be washed down with nine separate wines (judging by the nine wine glasses arranged around each table setting). Deserts were listed on the menu to include iced creams, cakes, pies and French custard.

I'm glad all I have to do is meet and greet the guests. You couldn't pay me enough to assume the responsibility of preparing all these courses...and seeing that they are served at the appropriate temperatures!

It was now 3:30 p.m. and Tom was back at the Indian Queen, changing into his formal dark blue uniform with the gold stripe down each pant leg. The last time he had donned the uniform, Candice had ripped several of the gold buttons off in her haste to attack him while her carriage yet rolled---bumped---its way back to her townhouse, he remembered with a grin. No such luck tonight, though: he'd be on duty till the final guests were shown to their carriages and both the G-G and the Duke had retired to the upper floor. *Anyway, Candice is safely home at Twin Peaks and Lucille---*he still hadn't heard from her since the botched dinner engagement, he thought disheartenly---*won't be here either. At least, she's not on the guest list.*

No, tonight will be all work...which, come to think about it...will be a pleasure.

CHAPTER TWENTY-ONE

Georgetown, D.C.
Early Evening,
February 13, 1833:

Forty-five minutes later, Lieutenant Wilder, dress uniform freshly crisp and black boots shining (he had taken a for-hire hack from his hotel), stood inside the Main Portico awaiting the arrival of the first guests.

"Lieutenant! In your formal duds! Then again, I recall you did mention when first met that Residency social aide is one of your jobs!"

Captain Bratton was in his formal Coldstream Guards attire, bemedalled and glittering.

"Yes Captain. On the rare occasions such as this, my intelligence function is limited to joint introductions of people who probably know each other better than I know either party. As well as keeping single diplomats away from Congressional wives…and single Congressmen away from diplomatic *and* Congressional wives…"

Bratton laughed: "Lechery, lechery---still wars and lechery---nothing else holds fashion." At Tom's blank look, Harry shook his head. "Not a Shakespeare scholar, eh Lieutenant? Or hasn't the Bard yet arrived on these virgin shores?"

Tom reddened at the Englishman's condescension. "Shakespeare was not a part of the curriculum at the Point, Captain Bratton. Though I'm sure he's a favorite at Harvard and Columbia. I'm afraid my recall fades somewhere after 'Friends, Romans, countrymen…' Speaking of lechery: how did you enjoy the Golden Eagle?"

Now it was the British officer's turn to stiffen. "Most interesting, Lieutenant. You are correct, however: there have been some subtle changes. By the way, how late did you and Mr. Harper stay?"

"I left Dave at the bar at approximately 9:30, Captain. He was talking about a nightcap but I had an early day today, what with preparations for this dinner and all." *And how about yourself, Captain, did Joanne let you out of bed before dawn? Maybe I should inquire among the Residency ushers...*

Bratton was frowning. "A 'nightcap,' you say? Don't think I've heard that word before. To what does it refer?"

"Means a last drink before leaving, Captain. So I would say David was probably there till at least 10 p.m."

"Mr. Harper appears quite the night owl..."

"He doesn't seem to need much sleep, that's certain. It will be interesting to see if he is here tonight. The Interior Department's been invited, but the new Secretary, Mr. MacLane, hasn't arrived in town yet. David may exercise the invitation himself. There are certain people here he hopes to see..."

"That reminds me, Lieutenant. In reviewing the guest list with His Grace, it occurred to us that only, shall we say, *titled* personages and their ladies have been invited. Yet I recall the planter class and other *ordinary* citizens at these affairs in the past, even under the Adamses."

Tom smiled. "That's an astute observation, Captain. It was the G-G's decision to restrict this affair. I believe he feels the Duke should meet 'official' Georgetown first. As he tours the Dominion, he'll dine with more than enough planters and others, I believe the thinking is."

Harry's prodigious forehead was puckered. "Yes, I see. But the planters are still part of the capital's social life, you say?"

"On most any other occasion, yes. In fact, there were quite a few here for the last affair, the G-G's Christmas reception."

"And do you know them, Lieutenant? The individual planters, I mean?"

Tom's guard was suddenly up. *If this one's inquiring after Lucille, I'm going to be more than a little perturbed.* "Anyone in particular Captain Bratton?"

"Ah, yes. I had been introduced to a Maryland planter and his wife, Colonel and Mrs. Samples, some months before I returned to England. The Colonel was then involved, unfortunately, in a deadly riding accident, as I recall. Does his widow ever come to town? Or has she remarried?"

Tom's relief that Bratton's interest was not in Lucille was offset---to his amazement--by feelings of unexpected jealousy over

Candice. *So this is one of her old paramours. Man gets around better than Harper...Joanne and Candice. Well, let's steer him back to the Eagle...*

"Mrs. Samples has been here occasionally, Captain. She and the G-G are rather close. I've heard her say that the General helped her immensely after her loss. I believe she spends much of her time at her plantation, however."

Bratton was nodding his head. "I see. Yes, I do recall that Colonel Samples and General Jackson were old comrades from their Louisiana days. And the General lost his wife at about the same time..."

The first carriages were beginning to arrive. *Just in time,* thought Tom, *I've got to think this one through...*

"Well Captain, our evening begins. I believe that is Mr. Van Buren's carriage, with Mr. Webster coming up the grounds on foot. Time for us both to play social aide."

———————

Georgetown, D.C.
February 13, 1833, 7:30 p.m.:

Count Ignatieff had spent much of the day exploring Georgetown's various landmarks and other geographical points of interest. He always made a habit of studying the terrain; one could never tell when a vantage point or escape route might come in handy.

He had stopped at the unfinished Capitol and toured the quiet hallways. Groups of what he presumed to be legislators were meeting informally, while other sharp-eyed men waited to part the groups into ones and twos. He had also familiarized himself on the locations of the various consulates and the British Liaison Office. Later he had, of course, ridden down Pennsylvania Avenue to The Residency, studying the old mansion from the park.

The Count had assumed his Karlhamanov persona before leaving his own Consulate; the eye patch and expensive civilian clothing donned in his quarters before speaking with Renkowiitz, who was preparing for this so-called 'state dinner.' Drago was still inquiring into the background of Captain Bratton and thus had nothing new to report, though he expected some word from his source inside the Liaison Office before Ignatieff's planned meeting with the British official the following evening at the Golden Eagle. The Consul had departed for the formal dinner in late afternoon, taking his daughter with him. Countess Caroline, he had broadly hinted, was quickly assuming a position of popularity amongst the younger portion of Georgetown society.

Ignatieff was now on his way to the Eagle, unaware and unconcerned if the British had decided to trail him. He thought he might have detected someone following him early in the afternoon at the Capitol, but had decided it was simply a member of the building's staff. (As a Russian security chief, Ignatieff was accustomed to clouds of agents tracking foreigners in official---and non-official---St. Petersburg locations.)

As Count Nicholas paused outside the Eagle, he recalled that his last---successful---amorous adventure had come with the unfortunate London chambermaid. The low profile he had kept on the voyage over and while traveling in Bratton's company had excluded any physical contact. *Not that there was anyone in range on that damn ship who interested me,* Nicholas thought with a slight shudder. But Bratton had hinted that this tavern was a lively spot; perhaps he'd end his sexual fast with an American barmaid. *It will be interesting to see how bawdy these colonials are.* From his stopovers with the Captain, it seemed the Americans liked to have a good time. *Well, let's find out. I'm due for a good time myself.*

The Count was disappointed with his first impression of the Eagle's congregation. A tall, skinny, diseased-looking fellow presided at the mostly deserted main bar. Ignatieff, remembering the pitiful husband/bartender at the South Jersey inn, suddenly wondered if all American taverns posted their most innocuous, passive individuals behind the taps.

A fleshy blond well past her prime added to the distinct lack of luster, in the Count's eyes. *My God, is Bratton's taste this bad? This floozy looks like she's already taken on fully half the Ukrainian Cossacks...*

The blond, whose meaty hands matched her heavy breasts, carefully looked the stranger up and down before addressing the bartender as Ignatieff strode casually to the bar. "Another newcomer, Richard. Georgetown is brimming with them this month. And, pray tell, how did this gentleman hear of our lovely establishment?"

The sickly-looking man behind the bar, whose tall, shallow demeanor reminded Ignatieff of an over-ripe corn stork, grunted in return before addressing his new customer. "What'll it be? We've every beer known to man...and some you've likely never tried. Plus enough wine and more potent liquers to take the edge off your travels..."

Ignatieff tried to hide his distaste of both bartender and barmaid and wondered if he should simply about-face and find a more 'select' establishment. But Bratton's enthusiasm for the Eagle had led him to surmise that this place could be an intelligence gold mine. He decided to swallow the bile already rising in his throat and at least sample the tavern's wares.

"A bottle of your finest vodka, if you please. And be good enough to see that both bottle and glass are well-dusted."

"As his lordship insists." The sickly-looking bartender was sarcastic. "And would you like a second glass in the event the Duke of Wellington joins you?"

Ignatieff stifled the immediate reflex to throttle the impertinent servant. "No my good man, neither the Duke nor any one else will be joining me. I simply don't want to catch any of your diseases..."

The bartender snorted bitterly. "Hear that Kathy? This *gentleman* has concerns as to the healthfulness of our operation... What will the propratess herself think?"

Kathy, who had been observing Karlhamonov from several feet away, expanded on her earlier, unanswered, question: "And what brings so illustrious a gentleman to our humble establishment on such a quiet night, when all the rest of the bluebloods are kissing Andy's Scotch-Irish ass? As well as that of our most distinguished Limey visitor?"

Ignatieff was still formulating a reply designed to demonstrate his social superiority, while maintaining his anonymity, when the sudden silence was broken by a different female voice. While far from cultured, this one lacked the recognizable lower class bitterness inherent in Kathy's tone while also reflecting a practiced air of command:

"Perhaps our guest has had his fill of our local aristocracy. Or, perhaps, he is lately arrived in our burgeoning metropolis. At any rate, your jobs as servers are to fill his glass and to make him otherwise at ease. And to refrain from asking him impudent questions whose answers don't concern you..."

Ignatieff/Karlhamanov slowly spun around to eyeball the slight, black-haired woman standing in the doorway of the backroom. The woman's features included wide dark eyes and high cheekbones with the facial skin pulled gauntly across them. Less than 5-foot-2, she flaunted an impressive pair of firm breasts barely covered by her low-cut blouse. Her skirt emphasized her lower curves, and her lower legs were encompassed in dark stockings that ended in sandals laced provocatively up her shapely calves.

In the name of Holy Mother Russia, this is more like it. Nicholas' face broke out in its wolf's head grin. *This one will be mine tonight. Renkowiitz can have charge of the Consulate until at least noon tomorrow...*

For Joanne, the effect of the lopsided smile of unmitigated lust (when he was smiling, Ignatieff's eye patch unintentionally made him look more merry than menacing) was instantly intoxicating. Her resignation at the thought of, for once, sleeping alone vanished as she contemplated her newest potential partner. *He's not as big as Harry, nor as handsome as David, but he'll certainly do for tonight...*

She strutted across the room, never taking her eyes from the stranger's face. "Open my private stock," she commanded Richard, while ordering Kathy to "set a private table in the rear. Tell Joseph to prepare the finest meal available."

She knew instinctively that this man would see through her usual false-innocence routine and so made no attempt to hide her hunger. The well-built but wiry one-eyed stranger continued to focus his sea-blue left eye on her as he grabbed the new bottle pulled by Richard from behind the bar. Motioning for a corkscrew, he quickly popped it, continuing to stare at the dark-haired woman. Their glasses, quickly filled, clanked together and were equally quickly emptied. Only then did they address each other.

"My name is Andre. I'm newly arrived in your city and country. However, I begin to feel at home."

Joanne, despite imbibing only the one drink, felt her head spinning. "My name is Joanne. I am the owner of the Golden Eagle. Please consider this your new home."

Kathy, returning after arranging for the private dinner, shook her head in disgust. *The damn slut leads a charmed life. That big Brit, the young kid from the Interior Department, all these other Congressmen and government officials. How does the skinny little bitch do it? I just don't see it...though this one-eyed Don Juan certainly seems to find her irresistible.*

She watched in envy as the newly matched pair moved into the almost empty backroom.

Well, if that kid from Interior shows up tonight, I'll just head him off at the pass. Though the big Brit is more to my liking...

Monticello Tavern
9pm

Tousaint L'Overture Numidia was frustrated. Angry, rebellious, but, more than anything else, frustrated. Tousaint, at 23, had grown accustomed to the degree of freedoms---expression, thought, movement, opportunity---open even to the freeborn son of a former slave in rural Williamstown, MA.

Tousaint had joined the New England Abolitionist Society with the intention of moving up the ranks into a position of authority. Not the kind of authority exercised by an Exodus station chief, but the real authority of determining the Society's movement toward the ultimate goal.

But the Society was run in Tousaint's view by stiff-backed Puritan elders who might want the slaves freed...but did not consider blacks the white man's equal. They had, after training in Boston, sent the young Williams College graduate back to Georgetown and the arranged cover position with Senator Webster.

Such a cover, that of a low-key clerk, was, in Tousaint's view, behind and below him even if he had taken his degree from a small private college far from Harvard Yard. Georgetown, as Tousaint viewed it, was a despicable, unhealthy swamp populated by uneducated whites, bureaucrats and vulgar soldiers. When Congress was in session, it was even worse... And then there were the foreign missions, where minor European nobility and their staffs treated hired freeman and women exactly as plantation masters did, with the exception that they were forced to pay *their* blacks.

In other words, Tousaint was no different than most recent college graduates of or in any age, who invariably believe minimual exposure to information and knowledge makes them superior to those who have practiced their common vocation for any number of years, with or without formal education...

Tousaint, however, had another positive/negative which was an even bigger facor in his relationship with the world: he was a natural born leader. And, as such, he had gathered a small cadre of ultra-loyal followers, freeman sons of other Georgetown freemen and women, who looked up to him with awe because of his education.

So, because Tousaint believed the authorities in Georgetown, the USBA and the Empire itself---a concept most of his followers could not remotely grasp---were maliciously holding them back, these young freemen believed it, too. No mind that each of them had full-time employment---one with the Interior Department, one in the Spanish Consulate and one at a local hotel---that paid salaries many of the District's poor whites envied. Tousaint said they deserved better; it was difficult for them to disagree...

Tonight, as most nights, Tousaint and his group occupied a back table in a tavern unknown to white Georgetown. Unknown because it was located behind an unmarked door on a side street near Foggy Bottom. Run by a huge old woman who claimed to have been a concubine of former G-G Jefferson, the place, which regulars facitously called "Monticello," catered to the capital's young black freemen, black sailors off merchant ships and the occassional traveler from the West Indies.

Lawrence Eugene Doby, the big Interior Department clerk known to his friends as Ugene, was the last to arrive. The others greeted him sarcastically but with enough wit to demonstrate they were no different than any of the District's other residents when it came to news and gossip: "Aw, look at poor Ugene. Da Secretary musta kept 'im late, discussin' the Bank crises." (Although they were apparently unaware that Secretary McLane had yet to arrive in town.)

"Yeah, Ugene, if dat old bastard in The Residency really wanta store da gob'ment's gold elsewhere, tell da Secretary we be dee--lighted hold some for 'im..." Marion Motley, the Indian Queen Hotel worker, was the only one of the group Tousaint had not yet been able to cure of purposely mispronouncing the King's English regularly. But, with Motley a bruising 6-foot-4 and 230 pounds of rock hard muscle, Tousaint hadn't tried that diligently, either...

"Well, I wish we could get our hands on some of that gold." Tousaint knocked his glass against the table in frustration. "Could buy uhura for a lot of our maumba. Depending on the amount, maybe enough for all."

"Quit dreaming, Simba." Cris Donfield---Crispus Attucks Donfield to be precise---looked over his mug of cold beer at Tousaint. Though the foursome had no conceivable idea where in West Africa their ancestors had been snatched by rival tribesmen and sold to slavers generations ago, they like to sprinkle their conversation with a few Swahili words and phrases they had picked up from the seamen. No mind that they used the words and phrases indiscriminately and, usually, improperly...

Though "Simba" is properly defined as "lion" or "young lion", they misused it for "chief." "Uhura" means "freedom", while "maumba" translates as "brothers and sisters" or "brothers" or "sisters."

"There isn't enough gold in all the Treasury Department deposits to buy all our maumba uhura. Onliest way *they* get uhura is to run...and for us to help them whilst they're here in G-town." Doby was smug in the glory of his Interior clerkship.

"I'm not so sure." Tousaint looked around at the surprised faces and slowly sipped another hot rum toddy. "In theory, at least, all the Dominion's funds are really part of the British Empire treasury...what they call the Exchequer." Donfield and Motley hooted at the strange term, but Doby leaned forward over his own beer. "In theory, the Brits could claim all that gold...and do what they want with it..."

Even Doby had a smile on his face now, though it was a different kind than the smirk the others sported. "What makes you think, Simba, that London cares about our oppressed maumba down on the plantations? At least enough to do something about it?"

Tousaint put down his drink and ran his tongue over his lips before answering. "Can't say for certain they do, Ugene. But, did you know their Congress---what they call "Parliament"---outlawed the African slave trade over 20 years ago?"

A chuckle rippled up from deep in Motley's enormous chest. "Hell, Simba. Wez know about dat. All da people thought deliverence at hand. But like you say, dat was over 20 years ago...and slave ships still bring maumba to de wharves in Charleston and Savannah." The others nodded their agreement.

Simba's leadership was derived mainly from his superior education. But part was also his persistence. "Only now and then, when they slip through the blockade, Marion. I think London considers abolition long-term unfinished business." He looked directly at Ugene. "I happen to know the Interior Department sent a report over there last summer on the whole USBA slave population. And it was at the request of the Exchequer..."

"Probly don't mean nothin'." Motley was as stubborn as he was big. "An' how you know 'bout dis re-port?"

Tousaint looked at his companions and smiled. "Moses done tol'

CHAPTER TWENTY-TWO

London, England
February 14, 1833:

The incessant fog that gave London its slightly other-worldly feel was blanketing the city as Lord Palmerston's brougham pulled up at #10 Downing Street.

The damn fog isn't the only thing other-worldly this day, the annoyed Foreign Secretary thought as he entered the old house, carrying both Baron Heytesbury's written report on the Russian intrusion into the Turkish crisis and his own department's very thin list of options.

Options indeed, he thought angrily. *What options! The cork'll be out of the bottle before we can act! The bloody Bear has finally found a way through to the Mediterranean, with that fool of a Sultan holding the gate open for him at the Bosporus! How the devil do we turn his fleet around and stop this landing in Syria when those idiots in the Porte have invited the Russkis in? And that's if we can get word to the Mediterranean fleet in time!* Palmerston shook his head in disgust and headed into the second floor conference room that had already experienced so many crises. *And to think I so blithely told the emancipation committee just six weeks ago that we were inclined to let the Ottomans and the Egyptians battle this out amongst themselves!*

Two hours later, only the First Naval Lord had a light in his eye as the otherwise-grim faced Cabinet broke up. As the Senior Service, the Navy had taken only slightly less of a financial-pinching than the Army as Government after Government had tightened its financial belt to pay off the staggering costs of the Napoleonic Wars.

Now that this stunning development in the Near East threatens the all-important trade routes to India, thought Admiral Sir Thomas Hardy, *Lord Grey and the others are once again turning to the Navy to pull Britannia's chestnuts out of the fire. See if we don't get some rearmament funding out of this!*

Palmerston was anything but jubilant as he conferred with the Home Secretary in the meeting's aftermath. And that had Lord Melbourne worried. He knew that the mantle of leadership could fall onto his shoulders at any time: *Grey looks older, more exhausted and less interested by the day...the P.M. might go to Buckingham Palace with his resignation at any time. Then this mess will fall into my lap! And Pammy looks like he's run into one of 'Deaf' Burke's right hands!*

The Foreign Secretary did indeed look a bit punch-drunk. The Cabinet had been aghast at the news of the Russian gambit...and stunned to hear that the Foreign Office had no bold plan to checkmate the Bear. A discreet note to the Porte cautioning against allowing the Russians unlimited access through the Straits under the pretext of supplying their Syrian army was hardly countering St. Petersburg's boldness! Calling in the newly returned Prince Lieven would be equally futile and embarrassing: it would serve only to acknowledge the Russian diplomatic coup...and the Government's inability to do anything about it. Something the Prince and his charming wife obviously already realize!

Instead, Palmerston had recommended---and the Cabinet had, grudgingly, accepted----that the Government's stance must be to closely monitor the Russian build-up in Syria for the present and to work behind the scenes to ensure that the Bear did not conclude some sort of formal treaty with the Porte. Also, the Egyptian army's real capabilities must be determined. Would the Gypos come on against a legitimate European force? Or would they turn tail and flee back across the Sinai? The answer was important: it would determine if the Russians were in for a fight that could suck more troops, munitions and money into the Syrian adventure. Or would the Bear simply scare this Pasha Ali away, leaving the Czar to consolidate his position? A position that threatened current trade routes...and a possible Suez canal!

As dissatisfying as this passive stance was, it was all they could do...at least until the Russians landed and squared off against the Egyptians. That and get Admiral Hotham's fleet into the Eastern Med.

Nelson must be turning over in his grave....

The Residency
Georgetown, D.C.
February 14, 1833:

The Duke of Wellington wondered if the Governor-General would fulfill their breakfast engagement. In fact, The Iron Duke wondered if Old Hickory was in any coherent condition to have breakfast at all.

Last night's state dinner had begun successfully, with Jackson at his most dignified, though the lack of a formal greeting line both surprised and annoyed the Duke. Wellington was not happy with this democratic 'pell-mell' approach; for all the obvious ostentations of the formal greeting line (introductions to men and their ladies one has known for ages), it provides the occasional dramatic moment of meeting and immediately sizing up an important but previously unintroduced dignitary. That was how Wellington had expected to meet this South Carolina fire-eater, Calhoun.

Instead, the Virginian, Tyler, had simply brought Calhoun, his wife and another Southerner, Senator Troup, over and introduced them as if they were all trackside at Epson Derby!

While the Georgian Troup looked the part of the planter-aristocrat--blond hair, well-built, average height and affable--this Calhoun looked ever-ready to spit, as well as eat, fire. The man had approached wearing an angry glare that seemed, as the evening progressed, a permanent facial feature. Scott had described him as looking "as if he just swallowed a lemon whole." Thinking back on it now, Wellington wondered if Calhoun had emerged from the womb with lemon already inserted.

Calhoun had exhibited tact enough not to refer directly to the issues of the day in their brief conversation, saying only that he hoped to "expand upon the discussions you have had with Senator Tyler in Richmond." By then, the young pup Wilder was approaching with an impressive looking man who turned out to be the Massachusetts senator, Daniel Webster. Webster had merely grinned when Calhoun scowled at his arrival. He had greeted the Southerners lightly after offering Wellington his hand in greeting.

It's rather startling, Wellington thought: *socially, I feel more at home with the Southerners---even Calhoun---but politically, these uncomfortably-informal Yankees are more agreeable.*

The drama that had Wellington not entirely-facetiously concerned for Jackson's health had begun with the formal toasts over dinner. The Governor-General had risen and, looking pointedly around the room at the scattered Southern contingent, had said: "Our Federal Dominion…it must and will be preserved."

It was a sentiment that at face seemed designed to reassure the former Prime Minister of the USBA's loyalty to the Empire. And so it sat, its domestic implications simmering, until Calhoun had risen. Even the diplomats among the guests sensed the rising tension. The South Carolinian had waited till conversation had entirely ceased before speaking, looking slowly from Jackson to Wellington and back: "The Dominion; next to our liberty, most dear!"

An audible gasp rose from several sections of the long table, while Jackson seemed ready, in Wellington's view, to hurl his half-filled wine glass directly into Calhoun's face. The G-G's own face was suddenly a blackish-red, with the veins visible on his high forehead.

Frank Blair, however, sitting directly across from Jackson, had silently communicated with Emily Donelson, sitting at the G-G's right. Emily and Sara Polk, sitting at his left and next to Wellington, had managed to restrain Jackson from rising in retort. Jackson was almost incoherent with rage, however, until the new Vice-G-G rose splendidly to the occasion.

Though so short that guests far down the table had trouble seeing him, Van Buren, in a remarkably loud tone---for him---had offered a toast: "Our beloved monarch, King William! Our unity within his Empire has never been stronger!"

Wellington himself had then stepped into the breach, quickly rising to respond: "The United States of British America: jewel of His Majesty's Empire!"

The round of cheers, relief most audible, rocked the room as the tension slowly dissipated and the next course was passed. *At least Andy keeps a passable table*, Wellington thought with a grin. *Even the diplomats seem satisfied...*

The next spat of trouble came just minutes later. One of the other Southerners, McDuffie, he understood from this Mrs. Polk (*and what is her connection to our G-G?*), had risen to propose a toast: "Our Dominion: transcontinental its scope and glory!"

A hush fell over the gathering as the Mexican Counsel-General angrily rose and then, apparently deciding against a harsh response, stalked from the room.

Like the buzzing of swarms of angry bees, the noise again rose as shocked guests speculated on the consequences of the offended Mexican's actions. Jackson himself, having apparently regained his good humor since the clash with Calhoun, leaned across Mrs. Polk and spoke directly to the Duke. "I'm afraid Consul-General Valenzuela took that toast of McDuffie's a bit too literally, Sir Arthur. After all, the Empire's flag already flies over the Pacific in the far

Northwest...."

"Why, those Mexicans have a rather exalted opinion of themselves, I do believe." Sara Polk. "Just because they chased the Dons from Mexico City doesn't give them the right to claim the rest of North America. Sam Houston says they have less than a thousand troops and settlers in all of Texas. And even less in the lands to the west.

"Yet I have heard Senor Valenzuela say that our conquest of the Louisiana Territory is illegal under international law since Spain was coerced into handing it over to Napoleon. As the rightful descendants of the Dons, he says, all the West belongs to Mexico!"

It was the first time the tricky Texas situation had come up since Wellington had arrived. Though, he had intended to raise it with Jackson when they settled into serious discussions on the emancipation question in the next few weeks. He decided to defuse it, for the evening at least, with a joke:

"Well, my dear Mrs. Polk, since *I* threw the French out of Spain before the Dons were thrown out of Mexico, perhaps *I* have a pre-existing claim on Texas myself!"

Though Jackson's laugh had sounded hearty, the mirth had not seemed to originate in his chest. Across the table, Wellington met Frank Blair's troubled eyes. *So, this closest advisor is worried about the Texas issue getting out of hand, too. Must have a private chat with Blair at some point soon...*

The evening's third flashpoint---*do bad omens always come in threes,* the Duke idlely wondered---came as the men chatted in small groups over after-dinner cigars and brandy.

Webster, whom Wellington was learning was perhaps the most influential of the Northeastern Congressional contingent, was arguing the nullification question with Tyler and Troup on constitutional grounds: "My dear colleagues, you must admit that judicial acceptance of nullification as a state's right would hamstring the Dominion government. We would descend into a veritable Dante's Inferno of legislative madness if every bill were subject to the veto of a minority of as few as one state. How could the Dominion govern, knowing its mandate was invalid in some states, but the law of the land in others? Pure madness!"

Tyler was shaking his head vigorously. "The thirteen independently-governed colonies which automatically became states when the Colonial Compact was ratified joined the Dominion voluntarily, Mr. Webster. None forfeited its rights to self-government; the Dominion is simply a confederation that keeps the peace, encourages free trade and provides a uniform monetary system. Virginia did not come into the Dominion to forfeit the rights she previously enjoyed! And Virginia will not accept outsiders determining policies which directly affect her. No, Mr. Webster, the Governor-General is in error: neither South Carolina nor any other state must accept laws which are harmful to its self-interest!"

Bratton had approached the Duke with Jackson and Blair, but Wellington motioned for quiet as Webster began his counter-retort. "Let us call a spade a spade, Senator: it is not some damn fool tariff that has you upset. It is the danger to your 'peculiar institution!'"

The just-arrived G-G burst into the silence that accompanied the Massachusetts Senator's blunt assessment: "Mr. Webster, do not attempt to confuse the issues. The 'peculiar institution' was 150 years old when the Colonial Compact was signed. Tariff issues were not even dreamed of then. The Dominion must---*and will*---conduct economic policy that allows for the collection of tariffs and other taxes vital to the financing of the government! Whether it is to the benefit of all the member-states or simply a majority thereof. Laws passed by the Congress for the overall Dominion good *will be enforced!* Nullification is not an option in this regard.

"But an institution of such historic character---which does not impede the economic progress of states in which it is not currently implemented---must be left to evolve independently. The South does not tell New England how to operate its fishing industry nor New York or Pennsylvania its manufactories. Do not tell the South how to plant and harvest the crops necessary for its own survival! The institutions of the South must be allowed to evolve naturally. Nullification is not even an issue, much less an option, in this regard, as no Dominion legislation concerning slavery is now, or will ever be, constitutional in the first place. Sir!"

Wellington's gaze had been drawn past the immediate confrontation to a dark figure standing behind Senator Tyler. John C. Calhoun, for the first time all evening, had had the slightest of smiles on his formerly rigid face...

A knock on the bedroom door interrupted the Duke's review of the evening. The Governor-General was indisposed this morning, an usher reported. Might the Duke be instead free for a 5 p.m. meal?

Russian Consulate
Georgetown, D.C.
February 14, 1833:

While Count Renkowiitz had been only mildly surprised that Ignatieff had been reported off the grounds when he and his daughter, Caroline, had returned from The Residency late the previous evening, he had been shocked when Rossevich reported the unwanted visitor still missing this morning.

Renkowiitz had debated sending for his security chief, Captain Drago, but word came in after 9:30 a.m. that Ignatieff, still wearing his eye patch, had arrived back at the complex. Count Nicholas had called for a warm bath before sending Renkowiitz instructions to meet him for a noontime meal.

The danger that seemed to always radiate from Ignatieff---the sense of a wild animal ready to pounce---was somewhat lowered as the nominal head of the Russian legation joined the lounging Count Nicholas at table.

"So, my dear Karl, you survived your evening in this colonial society, I see. What happened that may be of interest to Mother Russia, eh? Relate everything. I'll make the judgment." Nicholas' eyes narrowed as if to emphasize his order.

Count Karl reddened slightly but acknowledged his recognition of the command.

"Despite the presence of the former British prime minister, my dear Count Nicholas, the tone of the dinner was about normal for this city: domestic politics dominated. These Americans are a quarrelsome, spoiled lot. Every issue that arises is looked at from a sectional perspective. I don't believe they've agreed collectively on anything since the day they signed their famous Colonial Compact."

Ignatieff leaned back and raised his head to contemplate the ceiling as his right hand's fingers began to tap impatiently on the tablecloth. "And what issues did they debate last evening, Count Renkowiitz, or were you too bored to pay attention?"

"Tariffs and Texas predominated, Count Ignatieff. There was also some sort of a confrontation late in the evening between a Virginia senator and one of the Yankees, but the Governor-General intervened to mediate the argument. Though Jackson himself appeared somewhat agitated by the Northerner."

"Is that all?"

"Well Count Nicholas, the Texas issue sent the Mexican Counsel-General away in a fury. I would enjoy reading the Liaison Office's report to London regarding that."

"What got the Mexican so incensed?"

Renkowiitz paused before answering. *How deeply did Ignatieff want to dive into the murkiness of these colonial issues that he himself could not always fathom?* "Someone proposed a toast to the "transcontinental glory" of the Dominion. Fernando Valenzuela immediately jumped up, but then stormed from the room without a word. The toast obviously angered him, but I heard later that even Governor-General Jackson was confused. As he reportedly said, the Dominion can be obviously be traced from here on the Atlantic Coast to some small settlements and forts on the Pacific well north of Mexican California."

"Perhaps, Count Karl, it is not the British presence in the Pacific Northwest that offends Senor Valenzuela's sensibilities?"

The permanent Russian representative in Georgetown slowly sipped his chilled white wine before responding. His daughter had raised the same point on the return carriage ride last night. *But should Caroline's opinion be brought to the attention of his superior? For a variety of professional as well as personal reasons?*

"Yes, Consul-General? I breathlessly await your considered opinion…"

"Count Ignatieff, as I have indicated, my daughter Caroline is taking her place among the younger set in what passes for society in this frontier village.

"Last night she offered the opinion, based on talk from within that set, that Texas is becoming a point of contention here between the slaveholding Southerners and those in the North known as 'abolitionists' for their desire to free the Southerners' slaves. The South is apparently looking to expand into Texas; the abolitionists are opposed and the Mexicans obviously have gotten wind of the controversy. Or so the talk goes."

Perhaps Countess Caroline should be the C-G instead of her big dumb oaf of a father, Ignatieff thought dryly.

"Shall we ask the young Countess to join us? I would be interested in her other impressions of last night…as well as any other insights into the political situation here which may have escaped her father's attention."

Fifteen minutes later, the Countess, pulled from an English language class she taught the Consulate's children thrice weekly, was seated at the table.

"Thank you for joining us Countess. Although this is our first official meeting, your father has impressed upon me your, shall we say, *familiarity*, with the British American political situation. Amassed, he proudly adds, by your successful admission into the highest ranks of the younger social set here in the capitol. My congratulations."

While impressed by Nicholas---*he was even handsomer than whispered in the Consulate's hallways*---she was not taken in. Caroline's slender physique camouflaged an iron will, while her youthful blond looks distracted most observers from a sharp intelligence. She had digested the rumors about this Count Ignatieff---lifelong friend of the Czar, ruthless man of action, sexual predator---and had been on guard since his arrival. She knew of her father's misapprehensions about having him here and so was determined to feed him any such information that might speed him on his way.

"While my dear father is of course most knowledgeable about the goings-on in this city, Count Nicholas, I too sometimes hear thing that can be helpful. What is it that I may perhaps expand upon?"

"As your father has so succinctly put it, Countess: tariffs and Texas. Also, I understand there was quite the little public spat involving the Governor-General and some of his guests late in last night's affair. Tell us about these events from your perspective."

Caroline paused only briefly before explaining the tension surrounding the toasts. Ignatieff's expression remained gravely neutral as she explained the nullification issue, but his eyes began to glow at her analysis of the background of the Texas toast.

A dawning look of excitement followed when she tied slavery into both issues.

"So, if I understand you correctly Countess, the Southerners intend to use this nullification theory to stop any government attempts to abolish slavery here in the USBA in the short term, while wanting to expand into Texas in order to increase the political power they now enjoy. Which in turn would help them maintain their 'peculiar institution' here? Am I correct?"

Caroline smiled. "Yes, Count Nicholas. In fact, the Southerners want to expand all the way into Mexican California, adding pro-slavery states as they proceed."

"And our poor little settlements around Fort Ross?"

"I doubt very much, Sir, that the Southerners are even aware of our presence in northern California."

Ignatieff nodded and called for a refill of wine for himself and Count Karl, while offering Renkowiitz's daughter a glass she demurely refused. He enjoyed her obvious discomfort with him but sated from his night with the remarkable Joanne---as wild a sexual partner as he had known---his mind this day was focused entirely on matters of state.

"There are several players here who interest me," he said, looking from Renkowiitz to the girl. "This Jackson seems equivocal; he is against nullification when it suits his purposes, yet seems passively in favor on other occasions. Am I right to assume he is a slaveholder?

"Then there is this man who gave the original nullification toast. As a Southerner, he is opposed to any attempt by the Dominion government to override local preferences, correct?"

Renkowiitz nodded. "Yes Count Nicholas, Calhoun is the leader of the Southerners, the ones they call the 'fire-eaters.' He champions this theory of 'states rights' and wants a weak central government. He was Jackson's vice governor-general until they broke on the tariff issue last year."

Ignatieff wolf's grin suddenly broke out: "But he and this Jackson are still in agreement on slavery, yes?"

The Countess looked at her father before replying. "It is assumed so, Count Nicholas. Especially in view of the Governor-General's reply to Senator Webster last night...."

"...but that is a non-issue, if you will, my dear Count." Her father interrupted. "Since slavery is not an issue at this time. Calhoun is thinking and planning down the years when his opponents may have gathered enough strength to make it an issue. Jackson thinks only of now."

Ignatieff abruptly stood up. "Thank you for your insights, both of you. I must consider all you have said. We will talk again." He bowed and walked briskly from the room, leaving the Renkowiitzs to stare at each other.

War Department
Georgetown, D.C.

February 14, 1833:

General Scott's grim demeanor this morning surprised Lieutenant Wilder, as well as the rest of the staff. They knew the General loved a party and thus had anticipated that last night's state dinner would put him in a good frame of mind for the remainder of the week.

Scott had stamped noisily and darkly through the hallway to his office shortly after 8 a.m., however, and had let the door slam behind him. The door stayed closed, except for one brief summons for Secretary Beaufort, until after 10:30. When Wilder heard himself summoned, he shrugged his shoulders at the silent questions from the other staffers as to the situation.

Thomas found the General standing over his desk, head-down studying maps, with other papers strewn across the desk. Scott's ever-present coffee mug was steaming; apparently the General had grabbed a refill after calling for him.

"Is that door shut tightly behind you, Lieutenant?" Scott asked without looking up. "If it is, sit down."

Scott kept turning his head from maps to papers, as if crossing off or matching up locales and information on the sheets. It was almost five minutes before he sighed, sat down and addressed Thomas:

"Tell me, Lieutenant, did you monitor that interesting little debate over the cigars and brandy between Senators Webster and Tyler last evening? Or were you occupied elsewhere?"

"Not first hand, Sir. I saw the Senators talking, but Mr. Cass was, ah, expressing his dismay over his seating arrangements to Andrew Donelson and me at that time."

Scott shook his head in disgust but made no comment before proceeding. "Well, Lieutenant, you missed out on an historic occasion. The first debate of the most serious crisis the Dominion has ever faced."

Wilder waited, but Scott only rose and walked over to the window facing The Residency and the Potomac. After a silence of several minutes, the General turned and, with a strange light in his eye, asked: "Well, Lieutenant, no comment? Where's that famous feistiness?"

"I'm sorry, Sir. I didn't realize you were asking for my opinion. Was our theory correct, then, that London is imposing some sort of a slavery tax?"

"No Lieutenant, I'm afraid not. In fact, if only that theory had panned out…

"You see, the distinguished gentleman from Massachusetts opened up Pandora's Box last night. And General Jackson, instead of slamming it closed, ripped the cover right off. As the Duke of Wellington watched."

Wilder could feel the drill of Scott's piercing stare cutting through him, but was confused by Scott's choice of metaphor. "I don't understand, General. If this is not about slavery, then what is this about?"

Scott was grim: "It's about slavery, son. But not about taxes. It's about abolition. Abolition now, not next decade, next generation or next century. Abolition now, mandated by the Crown."

Thomas sat speechless and open-mouthed. *He can't be serious. And if he is, why is he telling me?*

"Last night, Lieutenant Wilder, the Chief Magistrate of the Dominion declared the principle of human bondage to be immune from legislative or judicial tampering, based on its longevity in our society.

"In making that declaration, he spoke for a determined and united South. In the presence of the representative of King and Parliament sent here specifically to announce that emancipation is at hand."

Scott sipped his still hot coffee and looked bemusedly at the amazement apparent on his aide's face.

"There are about half-a-dozen people in Georgetown who are aware of the Duke's real mission here, Lieutenant, including you. I've let you in on it because I will require your help in developing a contingency plan for this Department in case the worst scenario should develop. This is, of course, a secret project of the highest degree. And since my secretary---as efficient as he is---was one of Mississippi's first graduates from the Point, you see why the burden falls on you.

"Lieutenant, you're going to help me see what kind of an army the Dominion can field. Without its Southern officers…"

British Liaison Office
Georgetown, D.C.
February 14, 1833:

Harry Bratton took one last look at the report and, shaking his head in frustration and dismay, locked it in the safe. He then crossed the tiny windowless room he was using as a temporary office and stood in front of the huge wall map of the USBA.

This Andre Karlhamanov was becoming something of a professional and personal annoyance. Taken at face value, everything he had said or done since meeting last Saturday evening had fitted with his story of a wealthy exiled Russian liberal: the trip from New York to Georgetown immediately upon landing in North America to check in with the Consulate; a day of rest followed by one of sightseeing around the capital; even a visit to a popular local inn the night before.

But exiled Russian liberals don't carry daggers in their boots, nor pistols under their waistbands; especially not exiled college professors. Nor do sightseers spend the time the Liaison Office's agent had observed Karlhamanov taking at various key locations and roads around Georgetown, as if perhaps committing them to memory. Nor should a professor be particularly interested in the locations of the consulates of the other leading powers. Or that of the Liaison Office mission.

And the visit to The Golden Eagle: he went in around 6 p.m. and emerged after 9 a.m. this morning. The Eagle did offer an assortment of ladies carefully stashed on the upper floors; maybe he had found one to his liking. *But Joanne is a tough and shrewd businesswoman: she charges her girls' time by the hour. Unless, of course, it was her bed he had shared all night!*

Well, it was nearly 5 p.m. Time enough for him to head back to The Residency to clean up before meeting Karlhamanov at the Eagle. He intended to discover the truth about this Russian 'professor' tonight, or at least begin to. He hadn't much time; the Duke was talking about a trip through the Middle Atlantic States after Jackson's speech to the Congress Monday about this unfathomable bank business. Then they'd come back to prepare Wellington's own address: the emancipation bombshell.

Let's start by finding out when Andre's own tour of the Dominion begins. And where he intends to go.

All the while, Bratton knew he should have his mind on the impending crisis: certainly Wellington was increasingly concerned that the USBA could fall apart over the emancipation issue. The Duke had voiced that concern during their noontime meal at the Liaison Office with Major Layne and his civilian counterpart, Sir John Burrell.

"I'm afraid we saw a preview of the immediate future over the cigars and brandy last evening," Wellington had glumly observed. "I recall that in London you warned Jackson might be more loyal to the South than to the Dominion, Captain Bratton. From his reply to that Yankee Senator, it would seem you may be correct."

"In theory at least, Your Grace. But Jackson was talking in the abstract. He has no idea that emancipation is anything more than wishful Abolitionist thinking. The true unveiling of his colors will come when you inform him of the Government's decision."

Major Layne had then demonstrated why he would never become an ambassador or high Army staff officer: "All this talk by the Southerners, Sir Arthur, is cheap. If they resist the will of the Government, we'd simply militarily enforce it, wouldn't we? A show of force and these planters will be working out labor contracts with their darkies, what?"

Bratton had actually felt sorry for the chap, as the Duke had silenced him with an icy glance.

"Major, though I have the power to replace you, by all indications you are doing an adequate job as chief military liaison to the Dominion government. However, you will refrain from any further political theorizing or commenting.

"Now then, Sir John. Do you realize why Major Layne's option is no option at all?"

Burrell had managed to look appalled, though he was secretly pleased that Layne's excursion into policy prognostication had so quickly blown up in his face. Although Layne seemed a competent officer, Burrell had encountered trouble before brought on by the Major's loose tongue.

"Well Sir. Apart from the fact that it would tie down most of the Army here for years, devastating the South and leaving us vulnerable in other parts of the world, it has always been my understanding that we are to allow the Americans, whenever humanly possible, to work out their own problems.

"Even when those problems are, as in this case, manufactured, shall we say, in London."

Wellington had looked relieved. "Quite so, Sir John. Quite so."

Harry was now waiting at the Golden Eagle bar for Karlhamanov to make his appearance. It was almost 6:30 p.m. and the Russian was nowhere to be seen. He had received a late, verbal report after coming down from his room at The Residency that Karlhamanov, for the first time all day, had departed the Russian Consulate around 4:40 p.m. *So the 'Professor,' or whatever he was, is indeed out-and-about.*

Ignatieff, eye patch firmly in place, chose that moment to make his appearance. Bratton, however, looking toward the Eagle's closed front door---darkness had brought a chill to what had been a spring-like day---failed to notice his presence until Nicholas/Andre was virtually next to him.

That was because the Russian emerged from the back dining room whence he had come from the rear staircase to the upper floors. He had left the inn/brothel-keeper drowsily satisfied in bed; Joanne had remarked that the Eagle staff and patrons would have to carry on without her for a few hours. Andre had promised to return after a previously scheduled meeting with a new acquaintance at the bar. At this point none of the trio was aware of any connection; though Joanne decided to send a 'girl' down to determine the possible identity of Andre's acquaintance.

So Harry was surprised to feel the slight tap on the shoulder and realize the Russian had gotten the jump on him. "Well Andre, and here I thought you might have forgotten our meeting. It appears that instead, I was tardy."

"Hardly, Captain, I arrived early to make some necessary housing arrangements. You are exactly on time."

Bratton couldn't control his eyebrows, which rose quizzically. "Housing arrangements, Andre? I thought you were anxious to begin your tour?" A sinking sensation began to affect the Captain's stomach.

"I am, my dear Captain. But since arriving I've become aware that this Congress of which I've heard so much is meeting in special session starting tomorrow. I thought this a great opportunity to study it before heading off into the wilderness."

Harry struggled to keep his tone light. "And the Congress is to meet here at the Eagle? I understood they've still not finished their Capitol building, but I was unaware it was uninhabitable this month."

Despite the British diplomatic's attempt at lightness, his Russian counterpart's sensitive antenna began to pick up the tension in his voice. *And why would he care where in Georgetown I lodge? He seems more interested in that than when I'm to leave. Could there be something personal in this? After all, it is even easier to keep a check on me here than at the Consulate...*

"Well Captain Bratton, the Consulate is rather full at this time and I am not exactly a guest of choice. Count Rentkowiitz has been good enough to put me up for a few days, but I'm about to overstay my welcome.

"At your suggestion, I visited here last evening and found the accommodations, ah, 'soothing.' The innkeeper, Mrs. Casgrave--- surely you are acquainted---was particularly kind. So I've just now made arrangement to lodge here for the next week or so. By then I imagine I will have seen this Congress fully in action and can begin my tour with a higher level of understanding of British American democracy."

Bratton was thankful the bar was comparatively dark. Although he was a skilled professional, there were some things he could not control. One was a tendency he shared with the American, Wilder, to redden when embarrassed or confused. In Harry's case, it was only his forehead that exhibited the rush of blood. Unfortunately, that forehead seemed to grow exponentially each day...

The Russian picked up on it nonetheless. Was this simply English prudity? Or had he stumbled across a chink in the Briton's armor? The difference was important. He decided his probe would be gentle and off-handed.

"So Captain, am I to assume you've been busy since we parted? I understand from Count Renkowiitz that some sort of social event involving those at the highest levels took place last evening. I take it you were there? Certainly I was informed that this place was unusually quiet due to the affair."

Glad to shift the conversation away from Karlhamanov's choice of lodgings, Bratton spoke in general terms of the state dinner while wondering when Joanne would make her appearance. The ever-present bartender, this chap Lawrence, had poured him a refill but had been corrected when offering the Russian a glass of vodka.

Instead, Andre had joined Harry in Claret.

"So Andre, what route has the Consulate picked out for you? Did you tell them of my suggestion that you head south first?"

Ignatieff's face lit up in a smile that made Bratton uneasy for as yet unfathomable reasons. "Yes Captain, the Consulate staff agrees that a tour of the South would be healthier at this time of year. In fact, I may circle the southern region, going west after reaching Georgia and then back north up the Mississippi. I am told it is the 'Queen of Rivers.'"

"I've seen it and it is a magnificent sight." *Well, whenever he leaves, he should be gone quite awhile. Maybe he is on a private tour. No political reason for a Russian to visit the southern states right now, is there?* "Nothing like it in England, I'll admit. Wouldn't know about your rivers, though, the Volga and such…"

Ignatieff had gotten a quick briefing from Drago this afternoon and thus now knew that Bratton was a feared British diplomatic agent who had served both here and in India. Drago had reported that Bratton was currently with the Colonial Office though detached for Wellington's visit. He fought off a tempting inclination to mention the Ganges.

"And your plans, Captain? You never did tell me: are you permanently assigned here? If so, my utmost condolences. This seems a big, beautiful country. With a small, ugly capital…"

Bratton smiled at the apparent candor and humor in Andre's observation. "In the British Army, no assignment is ever permanent, my dear Andre. I could receive orders tomorrow for Capetown or Australia. One never knows. However, while His Grace, the Duke of Wellington is visiting these shores, I believe my assignment here is rather temporarily permanent, yes."

A thorough professional, thought Ignatieff. *Won't even admit he's here as Wellington's aide.* "Yes, Count Renkowiitz let slip that the Hero of Waterloo is here in the USBA. In fact, I rather gather last night's celebration was in his honor, no?"

Bratton nodded as he sipped still another glass of Claret. "The local political establishment and the diplomatic corps turned out to dine with His Grace, yes. The dinner also coincided nicely with the opening of their Congress, in which you have so much interest."

Ignatieff glanced at his watch. Almost 7:30 p.m. *I will get nothing of importance from this one, no matter how much more Claret he drinks. And the delectable Joanne expects me back in her quarters. Let me reinforce my reputation as a civilian rake while at the same time watching this Englishman's response for any tell tail signs of jealousy.*

"Ah, Captain, you must excuse me. The delightful Mrs. Casgrave has arranged a private dinner. I must be on my way. Perhaps we'll meet again before I depart for the South."

Bratton glanced reflexively at the backroom when the woman's name was mentioned. Ignatieff also observed a slight reddening once again of the forehead. *Yes, Joanne has had her way with this one, no doubt. Perhaps he was expecting more himself, tonight? That knowledge may come in handy. I'll remember to probe her about the dashing Captain at some point this evening. Meanwhile…*

Ignatieff bowed formally and pivoted before leaving the bar as he had arrived: through the back dining room. Bratton, nonplused at the sudden termination of their meeting, stared at the Russian's retreating back before reaching for his glass. As he did, the bartender snickered.

"Well Captain, some unexpected competition for the propratress' hand, eh? The government kid ain't no match for a big, strong British officer such as yourself. But between the two of us, she's taken a likin' to this foreigner, you bet."

Harry sputtered as the Claret went down the wrong way. "I beg your pardon? What on earth are you speaking of? Answer me!"

Lawrence flashed his crooked toothed grin. "This fellow, whoever he is, she's partial to 'im. I can tell our Joanne's moods. Much more so than young Harper, who's also been to her 'private dinners' more than once. Like you was just the other night, eh Captain?"

Bratton fished in his pocket for a fistful of coins, threw them across the bar and walked out with as much dignity as he could muster. The bartender and some of his cronies were laughing as the door slammed shut.

CHAPTER TWENTY-THREE

War Department
Georgetown, D.C.
February 16, 1833:

Tom Wilder sat at his desk, sweating despite the relative coolness
of the open office. It was after 3:30 p.m. on Saturday afternoon and,
except for the guard detail, the building was empty. Thomas had put
in a long morning, between The Residency and the Department,
struggling on the one hand to come up with an adequate number of
tickets for the diplomatic corps and other dignitaries for the G-G's
Monday bank speech; on the other, trying to put together---and keep
secret---this study of an army with few or no Southerners.

Scott had checked in, as was his Saturday habit, after 11 a.m.;
apparently, a big breakfast with his Congressional friends had put
him in a better frame of mind than he had shown the previous two
days. The General had little comment about the latest---spotty---
news from across Pennsylvania Avenue and had grunted his approval
of Tom's work thus far on the officer study. The General and his
wife were on their way to Frank Blair's country home in Silver Spring
for the weekend; Wellington was also to be there.

"It will be a much needed get-away for all concerned," Scott had
said. "The Blairs are gracious hosts and, in the country, we can be
informal in a way that is seldom appropriate here in Georgetown. I
know Maria and I need a break, and Wellington probably does, too.
After all, how many Congressional hands can you shake before you're
a likely candidate for an insane asylum? To say nothing of diplomats.
No wonder Jackson prefers having all those Tennesseans around..."

Tom was now engaged in the umpteenth draft of a note to
Lucille. This one, however, didn't seek to explain the---tragic, in his
view---circumstances that had led to their botched dinner
engagement last month.

No, he simply had to get back into her good graces so that he
could begin to prepare the Latoures for the bombshell Wellington

231

would be exploding in the coming weeks. Tom didn't intend to inform Lucille and her mother that emancipation was apparently on the horizon; not just yet. He was under orders. But he had to regain her confidence so that he could gently break that astonishing news to them at the proper time.

He felt a duty to prepare them that he didn't feel concerning Candice. Yet the reason wasn't one, in his mind, of love over lust.

No, Cranford was a working tobacco and cotton plantation that relied on its slaves' labors, backbreaking as they may be. Twin Peaks was primarily a horse-raising plantation that contained a farm. Candice had slaves, yes, but Colonel Samples had employed skilled whites and free blacks to oversee his herds. Even the farm was operated by tenants; the Colonel had brought Germans down from Pennsylvania. Emancipation's impact on Twin Peaks would be felt most directly in the mansion. And Candice could certainly make the necessary adjustments!

Cranford Plantation posed multiple problems; emancipation was only the most obvious. Situated in northeastern-most Virginia, it could be along a main avenue of battle if it came to war. Cranford might be ruined for years, perhaps decades, if, as General Scott feared, Virginia joined in a theoretical Southern secession that the North chose to contest. (With its anti-nullification elected officials, Scott felt Maryland safe for the Dominion.) And the sheer number of slaves, "Latoure people," as Lucille always referred to them, could become a security threat to the family itself if war broke out.

The Latoure family had made its original fortune as merchants in the budding town of Alexandria during Lucille's great-grandfather's time. He had purchased the core of what had evolved into Cranford Plantation, though her father had made Cranford what it was today. What percentage of Latoure income came from the plantation and what came from Alexandria Import-Export Co. was a subject Tom had never raised with Lucille; he doubted she knew the figures herself. It was her sister, Jaine, who seemed to have a head for the business side of things, though Mrs. Latouree had always struck him as a wise woman.

Somehow, he had to get back into Lucille's good graces so he could help them if-and-when trouble broke out. But he was at a loss as to how to begin. Should he be forceful...or remorseful? Sternly business-like or caring? And would she read the damn note anyway? Or was she committed to that SOB Joe Johnston, his old friend from the Point who, thankfully, was back out West with the 4th Artillery guarding against a resumption of the Black Hawk troubles?

And what of Jaine? Who was that brilliant but independent young lady---she had actually attended a "Female Seminary" in Ipswich, Massachusetts---showing favor to these days? Had she resumed her off-and-on relationship with Lt. Luke Beaufort, General Scott's secretary? (Due to a scuffle at Bennie Haven's during their days at the Point, the relationship between Wilder and Beaufort was correct, but no more.) The answer was important, as the wrong word from the Mississippian or one of these Virginia cavaliers and the Latoures could end up on the rebel side of the struggle Scott was gloomily predicting might actually come...

Thomas had taken stock of his emotions since learning of Bratton's previous dalliance with Candice. He had spent a long Thursday evening debating with himself at the Indian Queen bar and had resumed the argument last night.

The result: while he still wanted a future with Lucille above all things---that singular smile and what lay behind still drove him to distraction and always would---he had come to the conclusion that Harps was right. Being the master of Twin Peaks was not a bad consolation prize. Candice had at least a decade left---if her insatiable sexual appetite didn't put *him* in the grave first---and the Samples fortune would grow even in a war. After all, the Army would need mounts; and everyone knew Twin Peaks produced the finest stock in Maryland! Yes, not a bad consolation prize indeed...

Yet, he had to try to make contact with Lucille. He owed it to her...and himself.

Lieutenant Wilder wasn't the only Georgetown bachelor whose mind was focused on problems and/or opportunities with the fair sex this weekend.

A disgusted Harry Bratton had reluctantly accompanied the Duke to Silver Spring after a disastrous interview with Joanne the previous evening. One look had told him that the inn/brothel-keeper was at least temporarily off the market; this Andre had definitely swept her off her feet. He had stormed out of the Eagle and had found a nondescript tavern several blocks away in which to drown his sorrows; the attentions of an earthly Portuguese-born waitress had helped. This morning he had dashed off a quick note to Candice's townhouse. She was not in residence, damn it all, it had been reported back. So he was off to the Maryland countryside to visit the Blairs. Perhaps he'd make an excuse and return to the Portuguese woman's tavern, The Wagon Wheel, later this evening.

The irrepressible Harper had taken his demotion in Mrs. Casgrave's affections in stride. The Interior Department official simply moved his base of operations to The Deerhead, another of Georgetown's numerous taverns, where he resided and was already well known. More importantly, David had another riding date scheduled for tomorrow with Countless Caroline; that would be the highlight of *his* weekend--and he hoped *her's* as well.

The Countess had been relieved that Count Ignatieff had made no further calls on her time since their Thursday conference. She, of course, did not know of his rendezvous' with the tavern-keeper; she knew only that he was frequently absent from the Consulate. And, she looked forward to her date with the handsome, witty young American...

Her father did know that Ignatieff had apparently found a mistress at the Golden Eagle. His relief overwhelmed his good judgment, however: Renkowiitz should have realized that a man did not rise to Ignatieff's position by falling victim to the charms of a colonial barmaid...

———

Count Ignatieff had already decided that the Golden Eagle might be an even better place to plan and implement his hoped-for havoc than the Consulate. Government officials came and went at all hours; he simply needed to observe and then mold his observations into a plan to assist any potential rebels once emancipation was announced.

When that would be Ignatieff was unsure; the political talk around the bar and dining rooms centered on Jackson's Monday speech on some monetary issue. But Wellington had already been here some weeks; surely he would begin to inform the Dominion officials of London's intent soon. Once that word was out, it would spread quickly. Ignatieff planned to quietly watch and listen before pouncing...

At the same time, he needed to begin talking to this man Calhoun. From all indications, he was the acknowledged leader of the pro-slavery forces. A dinner for the leading Southerners at the Consulate might be in order, therefore. He'd have Renkowiitz make the arrangements for early in the week; he himself would attend...whether as Count Ignatieff or as Karlhamanov would be decided later.

Joanne herself was a bonus he hadn't reckoned on: a tigress in bed, she was already his emotional slave out of it. And she ruled the Eagle with an iron fist; both the inn staff and the 'upstairs girls' were terrified of her. Nicholas could not quite understand the reasons why---physically she was dwarfed by most of them---but intended to capitalize on this oddity for his own benefit. Included among those under her thumb was this man Lawrence, the gangly bartender. The fellow was clearly not right in the head: 'King of England,' indeed! Yet, he might just come in handy...

The British agent, on the other hand, was clearly *not* under her thumb: the Captain had walked out on Friday evening after catching the two of them together at the bar. Joanne had already confessed that she and Bratton had been lovers years ago...and that the Brit had come to see her earlier in the week. Whatever the Captain's intentions had been, Ignatieff doubted whether he'd be seen inside the Eagle again any time soon!

All in all, an auspicious beginning. Now if only this damn Wellington would let slip about abolition! Then the game would really kick into play...

I wonder how the preparations for the Syrian landing are coming. I just hope the Czar has put someone competent in charge...opportunities like this come along just once in a lifetime!

CHAPTER TWENTY-FOUR

The Residency
Georgetown, D.C.
February 18, 1833:

Andrew Jackson was basking in the praise of his admirers in the aftermath of his apparently successful speech to the special joint session of Congress concerning the upcoming demise of the Second Bank of the USBA.

The G-G had made it clear that he would veto any legislation to extend the Bank's charter. And, he bluntly challenged its supporters, they did not have the votes to override. So the only reason for this special session's being, he had declared, was to come up with an acceptable alternative plan. As the Congress was set to permanently adjourn on March 3, they had less than two weeks to do so. Or else the new Congress---not scheduled to meet until December---would have to deal after-the-fact with remedies of his own choosing.

At the small reception that followed the speech back here at The Residency, Jackson's allies were overwhelmingly enthusiastic that he had finally put the hated Bank away for good.

Watching and observing, Wellington frankly could not understand what the hoopla was all about. It had always been his vague impression---economics were not his strong point--that the Bank of England was one of the pillars of the Empire. However, if these colonials didn't want a strong central banking system, he really didn't care.

What he did care about was Saturday, March 2. For that was the date he and Jackson had agreed upon for his own speech to the Congress, though the G-G was still unaware of the subject matter. Everyone expected Congress to have virtually wrapped up its business by then; his speech, it was generally perceived, would be a valedictory of Dominion-Empire loyalty and cooperation. *Little did they realize,* he thought with a grim smile...

The Duke had decided, after informal talks with Scott and Frank Blair at Silver Spring, he definitely needed a flavor of Northern thinking before delivering his address. (Blair was still under the impression that London was about to impose some sort of tax on slaves.) For that reason, the aides had this morning finalized the swing up to Harrisburg, the Pennsylvania state capitol, then moving east to Philadelphia and Trenton in New Jersey. He would cap his journey in Delaware and be back by the 26th or 27th, leaving two or three days to put his explosive speech together.

Jackson had been pleased to hear that Wellington was off to tour the MidAtlantic States. (The G-G was just happy that his old commander was getting out of Georgetown, if truth be told.) It was Jackson who had suggested that the Duke schedule his first stop at Harrisburg to see his close ally, Pennsylvania's Governor George Wolf. In fact, he had arranged a stopover at a western Maryland plantation owned by the widow of an old Louisiana campaign comrade, as the riders would not be able to make Harrisburg in one day. So Wellington and Bratton would be off to Westminster, Md. in the morning.

It was Bratton who, with a strange smile, had explained to the Duke the travel arrangements orchestrated by Donelson.

The Captain seems most eager to begin the swing; perhaps this miserable, boring little village is depressing him, Wellington thought. *Well, the pace will now start picking up...*

There is one last piece of business to set in motion before we leave on the trip, however. Major Layne will be sent by Royal Navy sloop to New York City later in the week. Once there, he will make contact with Aaron Burr, slip the old man the formal summons Bratton has prepared for my signature and accompany Burr back to Georgetown. Burrell, meanwhile, will make a discreet call on Martin Van Buren. It is essential that Burr be kept out-of-sight until I have informed Jackson about the Government's emancipation decision. I will take Burr and the Vice G-G into my confidence at some point before March 2. Until then, what better place to stash him, once the Navy deposits him in Georgetown, than at his own son's house.

Twin Peaks Plantation
Westminster, Maryland
February 19, 1833:

It took quite a bit to get Candice Samples flustered, but Jackson's note requesting that she host the "Duke of Wellington and his aide Tuesday evening to break up their journey to Harrisburg" had come close to doing the trick.

Candice was used to entertaining distinguished visitors---Charles had brought them home on many an occasion---but a world-renown soldier/statesman? One she had, of course, never met? She had flown into action, ordering an immediate, if unnecessary, freshening of the already-sparkling mansion. Candice also wondered about her own attire; there was no protocol, she thought amusedly, for such an occasion. *Well, it was her home. She would dress as she always did when receiving male visitors...*

Candice had known Wellington was in Georgetown and had been highly miffed that she had not been invited to last week's state dinner. A note from Maria Scott reminding her of Thursday's monthly luncheon had calmed her down somewhat, however; Maria had written that Jackson himself had limited the guest list to government, military and diplomatic figures and their wives. No other planters or locals had attended, Maria had emphasized. Even Frank Blair, she added, the laughter coming through the lines, had had to pull strings to make the list!

So Candice considered her home and herself ready when, in late afternoon, servants reported riders coming up the long driveway leading from the Taneytown Road. It was only when they drew close that she realized that the taller of the horsemen cut a vaguely familiar figure outlined against the blue-gray sky. Her gasp of recognition was echoed by the stifled giggle of her maid and confidante, Melissa. "Why Miss Candice, I do believe that be Captain Bratton! You mean he Duke Bratton now?"

Though stunned into momentary silence, Candice still had the presence of mind to shoot her lifelong friend a withering look. (Melissa and she were the same age and had played together as young girls at Annapolis, where Candice's family lived while her father, Commodore Mansfield, had run the Coastal Guard's main squadron in the '10s.) It was a look Melissa promptly countered with a second round of giggles.

Two waiting house servants quickly gathered up the horses' reins as the impressively uniformed British officers dismounted. In the best tradition of the stiff British upper lip, Captain Bratton formally introduced the Duke, though the laughter was evident in his eyes.

"Ah, Mrs. Samples, I presume? Good evening. May I assume that you have received the Governor-General's note concerning our arrival? If so, may I present to you His Grace, the Duke of Wellington..."

The Duke was at his most gracious: "It is an honor and a privilege to be here, Mrs. Samples. I trust we are not upsetting your plans for the evening, barging in, so to speak, on you like this?"

The Duke, Bratton could see even in the gathering darkness, had been taken back in astonishment by the sheer size of Candice's most prominently displayed attributes. *The only emancipation on the Old Man's mind tonight is those ridiculous rudders,* he thought, chuckling to himself. *Is it possible the bloody things have actually grown? How the devil does she remain upright?*

The usual satisfying feeling of sexual invincibility Candice experienced when men gaped at her overcame any initial nervousness as well as her shock at unexpectedly meeting an old lover presumed to be some 3000 miles away.

"Welcome to Twin Peaks, Your Grace," she said in a dignified, lady-like tone that gave the double entendre added emphasis. As she intended, the greeting left both Britons biting their tongues, while Melissa was fortunate to disguise an outright laugh as a sudden fit of coughing. "Why, it is an honor to have you both. It is not often that country folk such as ourselves have such distinguished visitors 'barge in,' even at Andy's request. Please do come in."

––––––––––

It was indeed fortunate, Candice thought, *that the second largest bedroom at Twin Peaks was situated on the far side of the second floor from her own private suite.* (Candice had remodeled after Charles' death, knocking down the wall that had given them adjoining bedrooms to create the apartment).

The Duke, of course, had been led immediately to that second bedroom, while his aide, sight-unseen, had been assigned a room off the connecting hallway. *Harry shouldn't have any trouble finding my apartment*, she thought archly; *after all, it's not like he's never been here before…*

She and the Captain had found time for a few private moments before the Duke came down for dinner. Harry had quickly explained the circumstances that had brought him back to America, as well as his frustration in being unable to contact her.

"I was very much afraid, dear Candice, that you might have married again. You can imagine my relief when a young Residency military aide informed me last week that you were still the Widow Samples…"

Candice was relieved her soon-to-be bed partner did not catch the sudden twitch when he mentioned "young…military aide." But the Captain had turned at the sound of the Duke's approach. *I wonder just what Thomas told him,* she thought with amusement. *I shall have to find out sometime later tonight. Yes, this is turning into a most enjoyable evening…*

Drumthwacket
Princeton, New Jersey
February 23, 1833:

The talks with Gov. Samuel Southard and the New Jersey political leadership had been as depressingly dull as those with Pennsylvania's Governor Wolf. Wellington's depression had been compounded by the like attitude of Philadelphia's elite.

To a man, the policy and influence-makers of the two states had declared continuance of the Dominion's current economic boom their major concern. Here in the MidAtlantic States, there was none of the righteous indignation over abolition that marked the views of both New Englanders like Webster and Adams and the Southern fire-eaters. Governor Southard, who, it turned out, was resigning his office in a few days after having been elected to the USBA Senate, had made the MidAtlantic States' position perfectly clear:

"Live and let live," Southard told Wellington during tonight's reception in his honor here at the Governor's mansion in this college town. "If the Southern economy requires slave labor to produce the crops, especially cotton, which we require in the North---and thus provide the capitol to purchase the manufactured goods we in turn produce---then the USBA will have to live with this damnable situation for the moment. Until such time as progress offers a more ah, 'modern,' labor system down there."

It was the Bank issue that had the leaders here worried, the Duke had been repeatedly told in terms he could at last grasp. A single, well-capitalized Dominion bank provided the credit necessary for business expansion. The MidAtlantic businessmen were worried that Jackson's cherished idea of hundreds of small---undoubtedly under-financed---banks might overextend credit and lead to an economic crash. And if they were worried, their bought-and-paid-for statesmen were thus equally concerned!

"Jackson won the support of the North primarily because of his tough stand on nullification," Governor Southard had pointed out, "not over this damn Bank issue. Obviously we'd have chaos if any state legislature could arbitrarily decide to ignore laws passed by the Congress and signed by the Dominion executive. That's why we voted for him.

"I understand Jackson has challenged Congress to come up with a plan by next week...or be forced to live with his strategy. That kind of aggressiveness may be good politics; but it is bad economic policy. And the chance to prosper under good economic conditions is all we ask of the Dominion government."

"Abolition is the last thing on these dollar-worshipping Yankees' minds," Wellington had sighed as he and Bratton had climbed the stairs to their respective bedrooms. "They obviously won't fight to enforce it. The question is: will they fight to save the Dominion if the Southerners use the emancipation bill as a pretext to secede?

"Or will they watch the Dominion break into regional pieces while they go about making money...and as the British Army alone imposes and enforces emancipation?"

French Consulate
Georgetown, D.C.
February 26, 1833:

On consideration, Nicholas, after talking with Count Karl, had decided his plan to meet the Southern fire-eaters for a private dinner at the Consulate would be ill-advised...as well as virtually impossible to arrange. Renkowiitz had no access to Calhoun and the others and, even if he had, the idea of discussing emancipation was premature, to say the least.

Instead, Nicholas, in his 'Karlhamanov' guise, had been added to the guest list for the big French Consulate supper this evening. While all the consulates were throwing parties during this Congressional special session, the French affair, due in large part to the glamorous touch of the acknowledged arbiter of the capitol's taste, Madame Jean-Claude, was the highlight. All the Congress' leaders, including Calhoun, were on the RSVP list.

Renkowiitz and his daughter, of course, had been invited; it took little arranging for the Consul-General to persuade his friend, Jacques Jean-Claude, to add the 'visiting professor from St. Petersburg.'

So the trio was now in a carriage enroute to the French Consulate on G Street.

Caroline had been looking forward to the affair and wondering chiefly if her indefatigable American admirer would find a way to make an appearance. Now she was uncomfortable. This Count Nicholas already gave her the chills! And tonight he not only was flaunting an eye patch, but he was, she had been instructed, to be introduced as a visitor from home on a private tour of the Dominion. *Andre Karlhamanov, Russian liberal university professor, serving out a gentile exile in the USBA! Something secret---and dangerous---is going on.* Just what, she as yet had no idea. But she intended to find out!

The line of carriages extended out the front driveway of the Consulate. The building had formerly been what passed for a mansion here, said to have been constructed for speculation in the early days of the town's reign as the Dominion's capitol by a consortium that included both Washington and Jefferson. An early Treasury Secretary, supposedly a financial wizard to rival Hamilton, had sold it---reportedly for a huge profit---when the Bourbons had been permitted to open a consulate a decade ago.

"Well, with any luck we'll be at the front door in time for dessert," Nicholas observed in disgust. "Am I to take it these provincial legislators have preference over representatives of the Great Powers at these affairs? Or is arrival dictated strictly on a democratic basis?"

"First come, first in, my dear Count, err, 'Andre,'" Count Renkowiitz said with a nervous laugh. "According to the unwritten social rules which govern this place, even the Governor-General must wait his turn. Not that he'll make an appearance, I'm certain."

"And why is that, Count Karl? Doesn't the ruler of this magnificent sub-Empire pay social calls?"

It was Caroline who answered with a nervous laugh of her own: "General Jackson hates the French...Andre. It goes back to the border wars before the turn of the century." She went on to explain the cause of the G-G's hostility before concluding: "I'm afraid we won't see the Duke, either. I'm told he's not expected back from his tour of the MidAtlantic States till tomorrow."

"You're told?" Nicholas/Andre looked at Caroline with renewed interest. *I had forgotten that she may indeed be the brains of this Consulate, despite her youth.* "Told by whom?"

"Ah, by the members of the younger ruling elite, 'Andre.'" Count Renkowiitz was looking at his daughter fondly. "As I have mentioned, Caroline is becoming a leading member of that set."

Ignatieff nodded. *The girl's contacts may be useful. Let her continue unabated...but watched. I'll have a private word with this Drago...*

———————

The festivities were in full swing by the time Wellington and his aide emerged from their carriage and climbed the steps of the Consulate. They had ridden in from Delaware ahead of schedule late this afternoon and the Duke---who never passed up a party---had quickly decided to attend.

Harry, however, had expected to deposit Wellington at The Residency. His plan had been to relax this evening. He had looked forward to some time with the Portuguese waitress at The Wagon Wheel---it had taken almost a week, but he had finally recovered from his bout with Candice---but he resignedly donned the formal Coldstream Guards uniform and accompanied Wellington to what he expected to be another dreary diplomatic evening.

Due to the size of the crowd, it was some time before he encountered Andre Karlhamanov.

CHAPTER TWENTY-FIVE

French Consulate
Georgetown, D.C.
February 26, 1833:

Jacqueline Jean-Claude loved to throw parties. And Georgetown society loved to attend them. The stunning wife of the French C-G, an olive-skinned, raven-haired beauty of interminable age, also delighted in opening her parties to the widest possible guest list.

So it was that Andre Karlhamanov had been invited, once the Russian C-G had a word with her husband. So too, had the Latoure ladies, Angeline, the matriarch, and Lucille, the auburn-haired, vivacious older sister. After all, they were descendants of the first French family to settle and prosper here (and she did so enjoy visiting their plantation!).

Lieutenant Wilder had been a grand help in several social situations over the past year---and had already secured for her extra seats for the Duke of Wellington's Saturday speech to Congress---so he had been invited. And the cute young Interior Department officer, M. Harper, was someone she had had her eye on for some time. *How was it possible he was not already spoken for? He was just what she needed to pass the time in this vulgar little outpost...*

Speaking of vulgarity, that haughty frontiersman in The Residency had again declined the Consulate's formal invitation. It had been Wilder who had brought word today that Jackson was "indisposed." Jacques and the Lieutenant had both played their roles in the little comedy perfectly. There was, of course, no disgrace in the Governor-General's absence; no one expected---or really wanted---him, anyway. And now that the Duke himself had unexpectedly made his appearance, the party was an unqualified success. Or would be, once she had a private word with young Harper...

While tensions sexual and otherwise played out, politics as usual regained supreme. Senator Calhoun had already congratulated Congressman Polk on their thus far successful strategy in limiting Bank debate by repeatedly interrupting to discuss supposed Mexican atrocities against British American settlers in east Texas. It was evident that Bank proponents had no cogent plan or coordinated effort to counter the G-G's plan to encourage local bank growth. By blowing some rumored---manufactured---minor incidents west of the Red River into a crisis, the Southerners were hastening the clock on the Bank's demise while giving supposed credence to their Texas demands.

"The G-G," Polk was telling Calhoun, "is pleased.

"Just refrain from bringing up nullification or the tariff and the session will go far toward healing internal Southern wounds." Calhoun had smiled a dark smile that Polk chose to regard as one of agreement.

Daniel Webster was a Dominionist. He detested slavery but held the growth of the USBA to be more important. It was simply his bluntness that had led him to make the comments he had at the state dinner. Now he stood with Sir John Burrell discussing the results of the session. And again was being blunt:

"Never let it be said, Sir John, that the South isn't solid." This, in response to the Briton's comment that the Southerners had put aside their rancor over the tariff to defeat the larger common enemy, the Bank.

"And the glue that holds them together is their damn 'peculiar institution.' The radicals, like Calhoun, are sensitive to any nuance that might affect their social order. The South Carolinians didn't like the tariff, but that was a more a handy drum to beat on to get everyone else's attention.

"And they're damn good at politics. They don't want the Bank because they don't think their agricultural economy needs it. The South does need room to expand, however, so they divert attention from the Bank to Texas." He smiled a whimsical but crafty smile at the Liaison Office's political chief: "Love to see your final report on this special session before you send it off to London, Sir John."

Burrell laughed politely. "Well, Daniel, I can tell you one person who won't love my report once he sees it: Lord Palmerston. He will be rather disappointed Texas has been resurrected as an issue. He was quite clear on that last year."

Webster laughed aloud. "Yes, Sir John. So I have heard…"

To say Thomas was surprised to see Lucille and her mother was an understatement. He knew she had been in Georgetown for Maria Scott's monthly luncheon last Thursday (the Old Man, damn it, had mentioned it before leaving the War Department that evening) but she hadn't responded to the note he had spent hours sweating over. Perhaps she hadn't received it before leaving Cranford Plantation. Or perhaps she had simply discarded it unread. At any rate, she was now standing across the room, in a group that included her mother and Van Buren.

At least Candice isn't here tonight, Tom thought with relief. The mistress of Twin Peaks had also attended the Scott luncheon and had remained at her townhouse for the weekend. So Tom had had little time to fret over the status of his Cranford note…he had literally staggered from her place Monday morning (*a hell of a way to start the work week*, he had realized!). Candice, meanwhile, had been on her way to Annapolis to deal with some Mansfield family business. Though she expected to be back for Wellington's speech. The Duke himself had invited her, she had trumpeted, describing the unexpected visit to Twin Peaks. An almost comatose Thomas had idly wondered if Captain Bratton had tied himself to the saddle for the next day's ride to Harrisburg…

Tom was wondering exactly how to approach Lucille and her mother when Dave Harper broke through the crowd. Tom grinned; he had become resigned to the fact that Harper had the unique ability to attach himself to any and every level of the capital's social stratosphere. So he was surprised at Harps' first words:

"Fancy meeting you here, Lieutenant. Did you get your invitation from the same fairy godmother who sent me mine?"

"What are you talking about David? Didn't you use your normal pretext of the open Interior invitation to slither in?"

Harps feigned insult: "I don't 'slither,' Lieutenant. Sometimes I come through the door sideways, but never 'slithering.' The new Secretary has finally arrived. He's here somewhere. I'm supposed to introduce him to the Congress. However, in this case, I also received a personal invitation yesterday. And you?"

Thomas put on an impressed face: "A personal invite, huh? I received mine for helping the lovely Jacqueline with seating arrangements for Wellington's speech. Surprised the hell out of me, too."

David nodded his head. "I was shocked, to tell the truth. Interior doesn't have much to do with the French Consulate, after all."

"No, only the Russian..."

Harps was imperturbable: "Now Lieutenant, as I recall, it was your doing that set *that* in motion."

"No David, it was my doing that kept the Cossacks from setting *you* in motion..." The two friends laughed and Thomas nodded toward a group in the corner of the room that included Countess Caroline, her father, a stranger with an eye patch and Congressman McDuffie of South Carolina.

"Well, Harps, looks like the love of your life is well protected tonight. You may have to simply admire her from afar..."

"At least for awhile. Meanwhile, I think I will express my gratitude to our hostess for inviting me. Speaking of 'life's loves,' though, didn't I see the, ahem, 'formidable' Lucille when I came in?"

Tom nodded. "Yes, she was over with Van Buren and some other New Yorkers. God knows who she's flirting with now. That older lady with her is her mother."

"Are you two on speaking terms yet? And where, pray tell, is the one-and-only Widow Samples?"

"In Annapolis, thank God. Especially since it's crucial that I speak to Lucille and her mother tonight."

Harps looked aghast.

"No David, it's not personal. But extremely important. Believe me."

The friends parted as Tom saw General Scott signal to him.

———————

The USBAA commander was standing by himself, observing the crowd's antics with a distinct lack of enthusiasm. Maria Scott was barely visible in a group that included Floride Calhoun, Sara Polk and Mrs. Latoure. Lucille, meanwhile, was nowhere to be seen, though Tom thought he could hear her flirtatious laugh in a separate group dominated by the senior Senator from Massachusetts. *Damn that Webster, he's just married a year or so...*

Scott was direct: "I've considered your request, Lieutenant. Can't see any harm in you briefing the Latoure ladies on the situation. You may do so Friday. Leave first thing in the morning. I'll arrange things with The Residency. I assume you've already been to their plantation? Cranford, isn't it?

"To be fair, however, I want you to stop at Arlington House first. I've ordered Mr. Lee here for the speech on Saturday, but I want you to brief Mary Friday morning on your way to Cranford. That way Lieutenant Lee will have some idea what to expect Saturday in case I don't have an opportunity for a word with him before the Duke's address. I expect he'll arrive at Arlington House late Friday evening."

Tom was surprised and grateful. He had not expected to be granted formal permission to brief the Latoures beforehand but felt it important enough to at least so request. Briefing Mary Lee, however, could be tricky; he was never quite sure how much Mary understood...or wanted to so let on.

"Thank you, General. I'll go over to Arlington House whether or not I go on to Cranford..."

"Not to worry, Lieutenant. I'm ordering you to Alexandria on War Department business. Mrs. Latoure already has the word to expect you. Meanwhile, see if you can rescue that charming young daughter of hers from that New England Lothario, Webster. That's an order."

George McDuffie hadn't taken much notice of the one-eyed Russian when their host, Consul-General Jean-Claude, had offered to introduce the fellow, who was standing alone with the towering Russian C-G and his lovely young daughter.

Jean-Claude, however, had mentioned that the gentleman---a college professor on holiday, the Frenchman had said--was about to embark on a tour of the South after spending the last week observing British American democracy in action.

"You'll be leaving at precisely the right moment, Sir." (McDuffie was not about to attempt the Russian's unpronounceable name, even if he could have remembered it.) "Spring comes earlier to our part of the South than here in northern Virginia."

Andre smiled innocently: "So I have been informed, Congressman. I also understand that with the special session over this weekend, most of you will be returning to your homes in time to enjoy the warmer weather. Perhaps I will have the opportunity to see you and Senator Calhoun when I visit South Carolina. I have so many questions to ask concerning your fascinating democracy..."

If McDuffie was taken back, he covered his surprise coolly: "Well, Sir, I can't speak for the Senator, but I will look forward to showing you some real South Carolina hospitality myself. And conversation with an educated gentleman such as yourself is always a pleasure to be anticipated."

McDuffie offered his hand and moved away.

"Well, 'Andre,' it appears you've made a favorable impression. The Congressman is a leader of the Southerners." Renkowiitz eyed the intelligence chief curiously.

"It's Calhoun I need to make arrangements to speak with, Renkowiitz, not some pompous Congressman. See if you can arrange an introduction. The Frenchman is the host. Have him bring me over."

Caroline had remained silent during the exchanges, projecting an air of restless boredom. Count Ignatieff's blunt proposal to visit the South Carolina leadership in their home state had startled her, however; why on earth would he wish to speak with Calhoun, who was obviously out-of-power? She had expected Ignatieff to insist on an introduction to the new Vice Governor-General. Yet the Count seemed disinterested in meeting Van Buren. It made little sense...

By the time Tom had located Lucille in the milling crowd, she had rejoined her mother and Maria Scott. "Lieutenant, there you are!" Maria called from across a short carpet-width away, waving him toward them. "Lucille here was just asking about you, weren't you dear?"

Lucille's smirk was as near to a sneer as Southern belles were permitted. "Actually, Mrs. Scott, I was simply wondering if there would be any upcoming openings on the General's staff which could bring Lieutenant Lee back to Georgetown. You know how lonely Mary is without him. And I'm sure he misses little Custis." She looked at and through Thomas.

So this is the way it's going to be, Tom thought. *Well, it's Mrs. Latoure I need to speak with, anyway.*

249

"Good evening, Mrs. Scott, Mrs. Latoure." He turned to Lucille: "I wouldn't know anything about that, Miss Latoure. The General doesn't share personnel decisions with junior officers. However, I do know there are no engineering projects scheduled at this time in and around Georgetown, so the odds are Robert will stay at Old Point Comfort until Fortress Monroe is completed." He smiled innocently.

Enough of this sniping back and forth, decided Mrs. Latoure. "I understand, Lieutenant, that General Scott has ordered you to Alexandria on Friday. I hope you intend to stop by Cranford? It's been so long since we've had the pleasure, hasn't it Lucille?"

Before her dumbfounded daughter could interject, Thomas was accepting the invitation. "I'd be delighted to, Mrs. Latoure. The General has scheduled several stops for me in your area that morning. I look forward to visiting Cranford again. With your permission, I will be there in early afternoon."

"My daughters and I will look forward to it, won't we, Lucille?"

The daughter's smirk was back in place. "With bated breath, Mother, I'm sure."

The Lieutenant politely nodded and moved away, leaving the older women to wink at each other as the fuming Lucille glared at her mother.

Lucille wasn't the only one in the increasingly boisterous crowd who was fuming. Captain Bratton was furious that those Liaison Office incompetents hadn't reported that Karlhamanov was here at the Consulate. (In actual fact, Major Layne had called off the tail on Andre several days earlier when it became evident that the Russian was spending most of his time at the Golden Eagle.)

Now Bratton---whose anger was strictly professional, as the thought of Joanne Casgrave at a diplomatic reception was inconceivable---could only stare as Andre was introduced to a circle of Southerners gathered around Calhoun.

The scene had also caught the eye of Frank Blair, who left a group that included the Prussian, Von Benes, and approached Harry. "The stranger with the eye patch, Captain Bratton. Do you know him? I don't believe I've ever laid eyes on him before. And official Georgetown is such an insular place such a thing hardly seems possible."

Bratton glanced at the American, whom he knew chiefly by reputation. *Better be cautious, now, Harry. Don't make a scene until you know more.* "Met him on the road from New York soon after I arrived, Mr. Blair. Answers to the name of Karlhamanov. Claims to be an exiled Russian liberal, a college professor. Haven't a clue what he's doing here tonight, though."

"A Russian liberal, eh? Well, it is possible. The French are in one of their own liberal phases at the moment. Perhaps he knew the Jean-Claudes in Europe." Both men could now see the French C-G move away after concluding the Russian's introduction to the circle of Southerners. Andre now remained with Calhoun and the others.

Perhaps he is setting up stopovers for his much-delayed tour of the South, Bratton thought. *I had dismissed him from my mind, thinking he'd already left. Then again, he may be having a difficult time tearing himself away from the arms of his paramour...*

A few minutes later, after bowing to the Southerners, Ignatieff looked around and saw the British officer and another, older, man watching. *So the good Captain has accompanied his superior to the party. Let me be most congenial.* He quickly walked toward the pair, his 'liberal face' fixed in place.

"My dear Captain. It is so good to see you again. And, of all places, on French soil, so to speak." He bowed formally and turned toward Blair. "I have not had the pleasure, Senator...?"

Bratton was direct: "Andre, this is Mr. Francis P. Blair, an advisor and confidant of the Governor-General. He was just inquiring about you. I was explaining that I thought you had left Georgetown to tour the South."

"A pleasure, Mr. Blair. I am Andre Karlhamanov, a dazzled visitor to your shores." He turned to Harry. "On the contrary, Captain, since there are two more important speeches to be given before this exciting session of the Congress adjourns, I postponed my trip. Fortunately, as it turns out, as several Southern members of the Congress have graciously extended me invitations to visit them in their home states. Apparently, this famous 'southern hospitality' is no myth."

And why would this 'liberal' be so interested in visiting with the most reactionary group of all the British American leaders?, Harry thought. A quick glance at Blair revealed that the American also seemed skeptical.

He decided to change the subject slightly. "Mr. Blair thought your presence here tonight might indicate a prior acquaintance with the Jean-Claudes, Andre. But I told him you had not mentioned it on our ride from New Jersey."

"On the contrary, Captain, Mr. Blair. I am here tonight on the coattails of Count Renkowiitz. He said this would be the most glittering night of the social season. I must agree. No one stages receptions like the French. I shall remember this while I am traveling the South. Though I doubt I will see the like till New Orleans. Even at Fort Hill Plantation."

Perhaps it was the unintentional reference to the site of his most dangerous assignment as a diplomatic. Or perhaps it was the Russian's arrogant hinting of an invitation to visit Calhoun. But Bratton would later remember this moment as when his instincts and training convinced him that Andre was no mere 'liberal Russian professor on tour.'

Blair too had been studying the Russian while elaborately lighting a cigar. "Well, sir. It is a pleasure to meet you. However, I believe we separately should circulate. I'm sure we all have people we have yet to meet and greet this night. I will look forward to seeing you again, Mr., ah…"

"Karlhamanov, Mr. Blair. I look forward to seeing you again, also." The Russian bowed in the European style. He then turned to Harry. "So Captain, how was your trip?"

"My trip, Andre?"

"Yes, I thought it common knowledge that you accompanied the Duke to some Northern states. Was it a successful tour?"

"Quite, from the Duke's perspective." He paused. *And how did he find out where we went? There's definitely more to this than meets the eye.* "I say, Andre. All this touring and exploring would make a fine travel book! Perhaps we could collaborate after our tours are completed." *Let's see his reaction to that.*

Andre looked startled, but recovered his aplomb quickly. "Why, what a brilliant idea, my good fellow. Perhaps we should met tomorrow and discuss it."

Bratton was direct. "Yes, Andre, that may be advisable. However, now I must attend to His Grace. We will talk again." *But not until I have determined your real identity, Russki. That will be tomorrow's first task…*

Ignatieff watched as the man he increasingly considered his nemesis worked his way through the crowd. *There may well be a book in this, my dear Captain. If so, however, it will not be by us, but* about *us…*

CHAPTER-TWENTY SIX

The Residency
Georgetown, D.C.
February 28, 1833:

Wellington had earlier today formally requested that Jackson clear his schedule for tomorrow afternoon so that he and the G-G could "review a number of matters regarding my presence here, including Saturday's speech to the Congress." Further, the Duke's note had mentioned, the meeting would take place at the Liaison Office.

Jackson, although privately grumbling that the session would adversely interfere with the writing of his inaugural address (scheduled for Monday), had of course agreed. His advisors had been surprised by the choice of locations. Jackson however recognized the request for what it was: a summons.

"Private tour or whatever the case, Wellington is the King's representative while in the USBA. And now His Majesty's designated alter ego wants a word with the chief colonial. So I am summoned to his presence. This would, of course, be well nigh impossible if we met in *my* office," he had sarcastically explained before exploding:

"Ah, the Court of St. James! By the Eternal, I do so despise their whole damnable system!

"Sometimes I think we'd have been better off if Franklin and Burke had been lost at sea, allowing Washington and Howe to fight it out."

He had slammed his desk in anger; then, slowly looking up, had smiled at Blair and the other advisors. "However, sometime after noon tomorrow I will board my official carriage and ride in state to the Liaison Office. We'll show these 'Royal gentlemen' that we simple Americans have a sense of protocol, too, by the Eternal!"

Pleased with the way the special session was winding down, the G-G planned to concentrate on his banking system revisions and a plan for stepped up Dominion-funded internal improvements in his second inaugural address, while also calling for further exploration and settlement of the West. He and the 'kitchen cabinet' had been concentrating on these key points ever since yesterday's Senate vote had demonstrated that, as expected, the opposition could not override his planned Bank charter veto.

Now he would have to put that work aside to sit with Wellington, who had, strangely, stated that the two would meet with a single designated aide apiece. The Duke would presumably be attended by Bratton. He had requested that Frank Blair sit in with Jackson. The G-G thought Blair could be more useful crafting the final drafts of his own address, but, sighing, had given Frank the word. Though thinking Andy Donelson would have been more appropriate.

British Liaison Office
Georgetown, D.C.
February 28, 1833:

Jackson had been right with regard to rank but wrong with regard to aides.

Wellington had of course chosen the Liaison Office for their meeting to underline the fact that, as the King's official representative, he outranked the G-G. It was a point that would be crucial when Jackson realized the implications of what he was being told, the Duke had explained to Sir John when informing the Liaison's political chief that he would sit-in on the meeting. And Blair, who struck him as a cool, cautious customer, would have a calming effect if the fiery G-G looked to be losing control.

That Burrell, not Bratton, would be Wellington's second might surprise Jackson, but the rationale was not appropriate for discussion with the colonial leader, the Duke continued. The information was still too sketchy and preliminary (and perhaps too delicate) to share with the Americans: while going through official correspondence from London that had arrived during their tour of the MidAtlantic States, Captain Bratton had come across a rather startling report.

Something extraordinary had occurred within the walls of the Russian Embassy in early January; something so dramatic and stunning that the Princess Von Lieven had cancelled all her social engagements for the better part of a week and had remained in seclusion. The Foreign Office was still sorting out the details, but it

THE DOMINION'S DILEMMA: THE UNITED STATES OF BRITISH AMERICA

appeared that a personal representative of the Czar had arrived secretly from St. Petersburg to much internal Embassy fanfare. Within days, however, he had vanished without a trace after some sort of shocking event.

Sources with ties to the Embassy staff---the Russians of course manned the place entirely with their own people, but still needed to do business with London merchants---said the Czar's man had been smuggled out of England under the tightest security. The Russians were apparently too terrified to add more, though one had described the operative as an average-sized man of obvious noble birth. The description was useless---it could have fit a thousand men---except for one added feature: the man's eyes were somehow distorted.

Harry had come across the report Wednesday afternoon, during a break in their preparations for the emancipation speech. That Karlhamanov fit the description was obvious, he had reported soberly to Wellington and Burrell, except it made no sense: why would the Czar send a top operative to British America? And via London?

Major Layne had been away on his Burr errand, so his assistant had been called in. When he admitted that the tail on the Russian had been arbitrarily dropped while Wellington and Bratton were up North, Burrell thought the Duke would erupt in rage. But Wellington had merely shook his head in disgust and ordered the mortified---and terrified---junior officer to reinstitute it at once.

"Harry, you will take charge of the surveillance," he had ordered. "I still need your help in preparing to brief Jackson, but make it your business to determine once and for all who and what this one-eyed Russian of your acquaintance really is. And why he's here. Meanwhile, Sir John, you will have to take a larger role in the overall preparations for this address. I trust your political instinct is better than your colleague's talent for espionage..."

British Liaison Office
Georgetown, D.C.
March 1, 1833, 12:30 p.m.:

Harry hated the idea of missing this historic face-to-face meeting with the temperamental Jackson, but his role would have been a passive one. Instead, having prepared His Grace as best he could---he had argued the G-G's part in practice sessions with the Duke---he now was meeting with the embarrassed Major Layne to review the Karlhamanov situation. Unfortunately, the Liaison Office had no sources within the Russian Consulate; there had been no reason, Layne was explaining: "We've always considered the French to be our major concern, Captain, as you well know from your own days here."

Still, there had to be a way to penetrate the Russian screen. Some way to discover the truth behind Andre's sudden immersion into Georgetown's social and political life!

The two men rose from their chairs at the sound of outside commotion: Jackson's carriage was rolling up the driveway towards the Royal Marine honor guard drawn up at the foot of the Office's steps. Harry watched as the officer commanding Jackson's own mounted guard leaped down from his horse; surprisingly, it was not Lieutenant Wilder. The officer was opening the carriage door when the thought struck Captain Bratton: *Wilder's friend, Harper of the Interior Department! Hadn't he seen that young swan dancing with the Russian C-G's daughter at the French Embassy several nights ago? And hadn't Wilder jokingly warned that he might require aid "if the Cossacks show up to haul Harps away"?*

Well now, a word with young Mr. Harper may be in order! I'll send a messenger to arrange a meeting for tonight...

Arlington House Plantation
Arlington, Virginia
March 1, 1833, 7 a.m.:

Tom had ridden out of Georgetown over the Long Bridge in the predawn darkness and had arrived at Arlington House well before breakfast. Mary Lee had been surprised but delighted to see him. She had received word from General Scott on Wednesday that her husband would be home this evening on a short unscheduled leave and was happily counting down the hours.

After breakfast, Tom had suggested a walk around the grounds; he wanted total privacy when he broke the emancipation news. Mary's demeanor had changed before he had finished his report. Her previous display of sisterly-like affection for one of her husband's closest friends was replaced by a nasty frostiness that bordered on outright hostility: the Yankee intruder come as predicted to destroy her wonderful way of life!

"You have to understand, Mary, that this is London's decision, not the North's. There are less than a dozen people in all the USBA, yourself included, who know what Wellington will say tomorrow!"

"Yes Thomas, but once the announcement reaches the North, church bells will be ringing in celebration! You Yankees have been planning this for years and now you've somehow gotten King and Parliament to do your bidding.

"And now you and your General Scott expect my Robert to join in ramming this down the South's throat, don't you? That's why he has been ordered here, so General Scott can convince him to side against his own family, against his own people, against the South!

"Well Sir, he won't do it. Arlington has been my family's home for four generations. It is his home. He will defend it, I know he will!" She turned heel and ran back to the mansion, leaving a stunned Thomas with two thoughts:

Was this a preview of what he faced at Cranford? And did Mary truly epitomize the South's reaction to what Wellington would be spelling out tomorrow?

Cranford Plantation
Alexandria, Virginia
March 1, 1833, 1 p.m.:

The General's other errands had been routine (an obvious excuse to get him to Cranford). Thomas rode up the hill toward the big, Iconic-columned house a few minutes before 1 p.m., wondering if he'd be stoned back down the rise within a few hours. He was still shocked by Mary's visceral hatred; he had often remarked on her apparent indifference to affairs beyond her immediate sphere. Now he realized that Arlington and her family were fiercely---entirely--the world as she knew and wished it.

Sebastian was waiting in front of the mansion with a wide, wise smile when Tom pulled up. "Good afternoon, Lieutenant Tom," he grinned. "Miz Angeline tol' me be on the lookout for you. Allow me to 'cort you in…"

The Latoure ladies were gathered in the main hall when Thomas came through the door. The smiling matriarch was flanked by her daughters, one of whom could barely contain the laughter evident in the features of her finely-carved face. While the other's eyes resembled daggers aimed directly at the USBA officer.

Damn, this is going to make this morning's little tragedy look like a picnic on the Brooklyn Heights, Tom thought.

Greetings exchanged--hissed, in one case--and Tom's Army cap taken by Sebastian, the Lieutenant countered Mrs. Latoure's suggestion to proceed to the dining room. *No sense putting this off. If the General has taught me anything, it is to confront the bad news first...*

"Mrs. Latoure, I have some critical information for all of you. That's why I asked for and received General Scott's permission to come here today. I believe it better if we discuss it before dinner and I think it necessary that we discuss it in an exterior setting that affords total privacy." With a nod of his head he indicated the gardens evident through the tall glass doors leading from the formal dining room. "I suggest we step out there."

"Certainly, Lieutenant," said Mrs. Latoure, smiling through the surprise written on her face. "Though I can't image the need for such secrecy. It does seem rather exciting, however, doesn't it, dears?" The expressions on each of the younger women had changed: Jaine's eyes had narrowed as she stared questioningly at Tom, while Lucille's furious glare had faded to a somewhat sullen look of puzzlement.

Thomas escorted the eldest Latoure lady to the far end of the garden, this afternoon bathed in a warm spring sunlight, before deciding that here their conversation would not be inadvertently overheard by the household staff. *Well, hopefully this will last a bit longer than this morning's disaster at Arlington...*He looked directly at Mrs. Latoure:

"Ladies, I am about to tell you something which will shock you. It concerns the Duke of Wellington's speech tomorrow..."

"I worked hard to obtain tickets for tomorrow, Lieutenant," interrupted Lucille in an icy tone, "as a birthday surprise for my mother. I'm sure we can all wait to hear the Duke's address from his own lips."

"...which I understand you will attend as guests of General Scott."

Never taking his eyes from the mistress of Cranford, he delivered the news in a monotone he hoped was both straightforward and

THE DOMINION'S DILEMMA: THE UNITED STATES OF BRITISH AMERICA

neutral, continuing through a series of gasps that gradually turned from disbelief to anger. None of those gasps, however, had slipped from the lips of the plantation's mistress.

Her unblinking stare, however, reminded him of the legendary hardfaces both Scott and Wellington were capable of flashing at will. *Damn, no wonder this whole operation runs so well. She can radiate an air of command with the best of them.*

"We appreciate the courtesy exhibited by General Scott in allowing you to come here today, Lieutenant. I have some questions, if you don't mind."

Well, at least she didn't turn and walk away. "Yes, Madame, I'll answer to the best of my knowledge."

"It is my understanding the Duke arrived here before the special session ever started. Has General Jackson known of this emancipation plan since then? When was he told? Who else knows? And when did you and General Scott find out?"

"I believe the G-G is being informed of London's plans as we speak, Mrs. Latoure. It is my understanding that you are among the very first British Americans, certainly among the first dozen, to know. As for General Scott, I have no idea. I myself was informed a few days ago.

"Why are you telling us this Lieutenant?" Jaine's voice, though tense, was an imitation of her mother's; any coquettishness had been discarded in light of the seriousness of the subject matter.

He was blunt: "So that you'll have time to prepare, Miss Jaine."

"Prepare? Prepare for what, Lieutenant? To plant and harvest our own crops?" Lucille's scorn cracked whip-like through the air. "Or does General Scott plan to send a regiment under your command to do that for us?"

Tom turned slowly to look at her, hoping to project his own imitation of General Scott's drill-stare.

"To prepare for any eventuality of a security nature which may arise once word of the Duke's speech reaches Alexandria, probably late Sunday or Monday."

Lucille's anger was replaced by a look of bafflement. "Security? Whatever do you mean?"

Mrs. Latoure turned to her eldest. "He means, my dear, any eventuality once our people get wind of London's plans."

She and Tom exchanged looks of mutual understanding.

Tom might have felt he had taken all necessary precautions before briefing the Latoure ladies on the Duke's upcoming speech. But Sebastian ferreted the secret out anyway---and in record time.

The heads-up butler knew something of the highest importance to Cranford was to be discussed the moment the white folk adjourned to the garden. He couldn't interrupt, of course; nor could he send a child of the plantation to spy from a nearby tree.

The cagey Sebastian simply kept his ears open during the ensuing meal. While he couldn't piece all the puzzle's parts together, he came away with the definite impression that the Latoure girls had been stunned into virtual silence by Lieutenant Tom's news.

And that the Lieutenant's table conversation with the Mistress of Cranford centered on three things: someone named Wellington; a speech to Congress next week and emancipation. Sebastian had no real idea who this 'Wellington' fellow was, but he knew 'emancipation' was a fancy word for 'freedom.' And that this 'Wellington' planned to preach emancipation to the white folks' 'Congress.' And while he couldn't follow all the details, one phrase kept reverberating through his increasingly excited mind: "seven years."

The question was how to quickly get this news to Moses. Even a trusted house servant couldn't simply leave a plantation, even one as benevolent as Cranford. Even if he could come-and-go (which he most definitely could not), there were papers to be readied and signed by the Mistress authorizing the trip. Papers which would undoubtedly be closely scrutinized by hard-eyed, armed whites more than once between Cranford and Georgetown. Virginia had not forgotten Nat Turner...

Sebastian had about quit racking his brain in frustration when the solution presented itself. Mammy Anna, Mrs. Latoure's personal maid and the acknowledged head female slave---some said the acknowledged head slave, period, Sebastian thought wryly---came to the Mistress as the white women were bidding adieu to Lieutenant Tom on the mansion's steps.

"Miz Angeline, we need da papiz for us to get on over to Arlington 'morrow for da weddin'."

Sebastian's head jerked and he stared at Mammy. Of course! The wedding of Mammy's niece, Clerisa, one of the Lees' house servants, to Smithy, who ran Arlington House's stables and blacksmith shop! In all the excitement, he'd completely forgot! Why he, Sebastian, had been invited himself! He wouldn't even have to attract attention by asking for a last minute pass…

And once the service was over and the barbeque begun, he'd have time for a very private conversation with the presiding minister…The Rev. Jugurtha Numidia himself.

CHAPTER TWENTY-SEVEN

British Liaison Office
Georgetown, D.C.
March 1, 1833, 1 p.m.

Sir Arthur was waiting for the Governor-General at the top of the steps. They greeted each other formally before turning to enter the building, Frank Blair and Burrell falling in behind them.

The Duke was still congratulating Jackson on the sharp appearance of his honor guard when they stepped into the big corner office Sir John had vacated upon Wellington's arrival some 30 days before. A servant poured three teas and a coffee for Jackson as the small talk continued rather uneasily; the British were tense knowing what was coming, while the uncertainty made the two Americans uncomfortable.

The Duke sipped his tea as he waited for the door to close behind the servant. Jackson, unaccustomed to the subordinate role and eager to be done with this, decided to begin by briefing Wellington on arrangements for the next day's Capitol Hill ceremonies. The Duke curtly cut him off.

"I'm sure your protocol people have everything under control, Governor-General. They seem satisfactory with the pomp and circumstance, judging from the welcoming ceremony last month. However, that's not what I called you here today to discuss.

"By now you and Mr. Blair have certainly realized there may be more to my visit here than a simple private tour. The Government has dispatched me here, Governor-General, at the King's direction, to inform you and the Dominion's citizens of legislation to be introduced in Parliament this month which will have a major impact here."

He paused and sipped his tea, eyeing the two Americans. Jackson's guard was up, as expected. The shrewd narrowing of Blair's eyes indicated that the 'closest advisor' was running the possibilities through his mind.

"Governor-General, (the emphasis on and reiteration of Jackson's official title was deliberate, as all present by now realized) a bill supported by both the Whig government and my own opposition Tories---and co-sponsored by at least one member of the Dominion delegation---is being introduced which calls for a seven-year phased-in and compensated abolition of slavery throughout the Empire. This emancipation program will begin on January 1st of next year, if passed and signed into law, which it undoubtedly will be."

He again paused, not to sip more tea, but to stare directly at the now scarlet-faced G-G.

"I am somewhat incomplete in describing my task here, Governor-General Jackson. I am also to ascertain that the Dominion government is fully cognizant of its responsibilities under terms of the Colonial Compact to accept and enforce the legislation as written. In its entirety."

The ticking of the huge grandfather's clock was the only sound in the room for several minutes after Wellington finished. To Burrell, though, the thought occurred that the sound very possibly instead might be the throbbing of Jackson's pulse.

Sir John was not the only one holding his breath concerning the G-G's reaction: Blair was congratulating himself on having had the foresight to have taken Andy's ever-present cane and placed it out-of-reach on the back of an empty chair. Wellington, meanwhile, was speculating that he might not have to invoke the Compact clause on dismissal of a seating G-G. *If Jackson keels over---as he very well may--- Colonel Burr's son could be sleeping in The Residency tonight...*

Jackson was indeed struggling to retain control of his emotions. His brain as yet refused to accept the enormous implications of Wellington's words. Instead, it concentrated on more picayune matters:

These 'tours' Sir Arthur has taken...with my full encouragement! Has the Duke let the Virginians and the others in on the secret? Before telling me, the chief elected official of the Dominion? Damn it! And so much for my carefully crafted inaugural address! If Wellington announces emancipation tomorrow, issues like the Bank and western expansion will be the farthest thing from anyone's mind! What am I supposed to say on Monday? By the Eternal!

The others continued to watch as the G-G's facial expressions changed as rapidly as his color. Blair was considering suggesting an unorthodox but seemingly appropriate strengthening of their beverages when Jackson finally spoke:

"You have achieved surprise, Your Grace. You've caught me with my pickets in. While my advisors and I have questioned whether you were, indeed, here simply to sightsee, we did not foresee this attempt at mandated redeployment of our Southern workforce coming. In truth, we thought more on the lines of possible Crown revenue enhancement...

"I now see why you, ah, *requested* that I clear my schedule for the entire afternoon. Also why you *suggested* that Frank here accompany me rather than Donelson." He paused briefly, staring directly at his former commander. "One of the keys to your success on the Peninsula, Sir Arthur, in my view was your willingness to share the estimate of the situation with your subordinates.

"I would like to hear something along those lines at this time. First, however, I believe I am entitled, as the duly elected leader of the Dominion, a bit of background on this amazing news you've finally chosen to share: Just how long has this been considered in London? And how much study has there been on the possible consequences here in America? What encouragement, if any, did the designers of this legislation receive from members of the Dominion's delegation to Parliament? What opposition? If any USBA MPs participated in drafting this bill, I should like to know which ones. I need all this information to help formulate my response."

The relaxation of tension on the three other men's faces was evident: the G-G had his emotions at least temporarily under control. The trigger mechanism on the fearsome Jacksonian temper was in the 'lock' position.

Wellington nodded. "Certainly, Andrew. As Governor-General, you are of course entitled to a full briefing on the bill's particulars. Sir John will do those honors. You and Mr. Blair are welcome to interrupt with questions at any time. I will then brief you on the bill's development before sketching the 'estimate of the situation', as you so accurately phrase it, from London's perspective."

For the next two hours, the two Americans received an education on London's philosophical/political conception of the Empire, and the USBA's place in it, as well as the Government's view of the internal Dominion political situation.

By the time Wellington had finished an 'estimate of the situation' that left little doubt that Jackson's second term hinged upon his willingness to enforce the emancipation process, Blair knew that it was time for a brief pause: the G-G was showing all the signs of an imminent eruption. At his suggestion, the Americans repaired to a small room off the Duke's office. Wellington, meanwhile, signaled his own aide to the corner window.

"We've come to the first crucial hurdle, Burrell. Jackson is ready to rebel. Not yet at the concept of emancipation, but at the very idea that we are, in his view, forcing this down his throat. Which, of course, we are. That's the initial hurdle: to make the Americans--- from Jackson down to the most illiterate of his fellow-citizens--- realize that the Colonial Compact allows, in fact was designed, with this sort of crisis legislation in mind.

"Deep down, Andy is aware of that. For all his gruff demeanor, for all his propensity to play the 'frontiersman' role, he is an educated gentleman who has studied the law and the Compact. In the next room, he is not even thinking as yet about emancipation as anything other than an abstract issue affecting the relationship between Georgetown and London.

"Let us hope and pray that he accepts the Government's constitutional right to impose emancipation. If he does, he'll come around on it as a practical matter, perhaps not today, but eventually, sooner rather than later. But if he can not clear this initial hurdle I may be forced to take action, unpopular as it may be. God help us if it comes to that."

Jackson stood aganst a wall of the small room, sucking in the cool late afternoon spring air from the window Blair had just now opened, and tried to breathe naturally despite the anvil that was apparently pushing against his chest. As in a dream, he accepted the flask that had magically emerged from Frank's jacket pocket and took a long swig of Tennessee whisky. He momentarily closed his eyes, feeling the warm liquor burn down his throat before relaxing the tightness in his chest. Reopening his eyes, he stared at the flask as if seeing it for the first time. He handed it back to Frank and walked to the window, leaning down and staring at his honor guard, which still surrounded his carriage in the driveway.

"God damn them," he said finally, turning to look at his confidant. "God damn them all! They treat us like unruly children---to be humored and patronized---until something important comes up! Then, we're expected to meekly accept and obey, as if Parliament issued its edict from the very heights of Mount Sinai, with Wellington as Moses and we of the USBA the undisciplined, uneducated, unreliable children of Israel!

"I was elected and reelected because the citizens of the USBA agreed with my positions on the issues which affect their daily lives. Am I now to relinquish that mandate in order to placate the guilt-plagued consciences of the British ruling class---nobles, merchants, mine and manufactory owners, landlords---who hold the majority of their own people in conditions far worse than that of the most ill-treated slave in the South?

"By the Eternal, I think not!"

Blair looked sadly at his old friend. "Actually, Andrew, according to the terms of the Colonial Compact, that is exactly what you must do. Either that, or resign…"

The veins on the G-G's again-scarlet forehead bulged as he glared at his friend and advisor. Foam literally formed at the corners of his mouth as his lips opened, though no coherent words escaped. He pivoted and again stormed over to the window, grabbing the sill with both hands and rocking back-and-forth.

Blair felt entitled to a taste of the Tennessee mash himself. He let it roll around in his mouth as he waited for this latest eruption to die down. *Get it out of your system now, Andy, so we can come up with a response for these two Brits waiting in the next room. Vent your anger here, and then let's get down to some serious deliberations…*

The rocking of Jackson's body gradually slowed before ceasing entirely. The sound of his breathing also slowed, till it was overwhelmed by the street noise. Four-to-five minutes had passed since Blair had bluntly advised the G-G of his limited options. More than a quarter hour had passed since they had left Wellington.

Jackson finally turned and looked Blair in the eye. "Is that your only advice? Kiss Wellington's ring...or resign? Surely you have more to add?"

Blair was now pacing the room, as was his habit while considering knotty issues. *There is nothing to be gained by reconvening this meeting today. The Brits have announced their intentions; now it is our responsibility to soberly consider before responding. Wellington knows better than to expect an immediate answer. Let's get back to The Residency and gather the kitchen cabinet. We've got at least 48 hours to respond privately...and another 18 or so before the inaugural. It's obvious the Duke and his people put a great deal of thought and preparation into their presentation today. We need to do likewise!*

"General, you heard Wellington say this thing has been 24 or more months in the works. Well, we deserve 24 hours, at least, to formulate our response. I suggest we move back inside and request an adjournment until we have thoroughly studied the matter, with all its implications. It would be unreasonable for them to demand acquiescence immediately. Wellington knows that.

"If you call your advisors in tonight, we can begin to plan a public response for Monday. Meanwhile, we have all weekend to confer with the Congressional leadership--from both parties. And all sections."

Jackson nodded in grim satisfaction. "That's more to my liking, Mr. Blair. A plan of action, not surrender. Let's inform these Limeys that we're done here for the day."

Blair cracked his first smile in hours. "Now, Andrew. Let's politely *request* an adjournment; not storm back in to announce we're leaving and then slam the door in their English faces!

"Remember our sense of *simple American* protocol?"

CHAPTER TWENTY-EIGHT

Alexandria Highway
March 1, 1833, 6:45 p.m.:

Tom had briefly considered stopping off at Arlington House on the way back to Georgetown but wearily rejected the idea. There was no telling when Robert Lee would arrive...and he was fairly sure Mary would leave him cooling his heels on the veranda if her husband was still enroute. So he rode slowly down the road towards the Long Bridge, barely glancing up at the imposing mansion on its hill facing the capitol.

His mission to Cranford Plantation had been as professionally satisfactory as it had been emotionally disappointing: Cranford would be quietly secured tomorrow by trusted employees of Alexandria Import-Export Co., judiciously selected in equal parts for their brawn, familiarity with light arms and levelheadedness. Mrs. Latoure didn't think her 'people' were apt to erupt in violence, but agreed with Tom that a precautionary show of force would put the damper on spontaneous outbursts by any potential hotheads.

Lucille's unremitting coldness hadn't been melted by his gesture of concern, however. While she agreed that protective steps needed to be taken, she didn't seem the least bit grateful. In fact, once they had agreed to his suggestion that Company workers be brought to Cranford as security guards, her major concern seemed to be social: whether the speech's content would affect the status of the Congressional reception slated to follow, as well as the dinner party she had planned to attend tomorrow evening at the incoming Vice G-G's residence.

The Lieutenant had forgotten about the reception and had been unaware of the dinner party. In fact, he wondered whether she could possibly be so shallow as to be more concerned about her social life than her safety. Or had she mentioned her weekend plans simply to let him know she would be moving in a social circle he had little hope of penetrating?

Frankly, he was too damn tired, physically as well as emotionally, to worry about it. A few beers and some supper in the Indian Queen taproom---dinner at Cranford had been limited to some cold meats during the security discussions---and he would be hitting his pillow.

He had a feeling The Residency would be boiling tomorrow morning: Jackson won't take the emancipation news quietly. And General Scott had ordered him to report to his home for a 7 a.m. briefing on today's meetings. So Saturday would be busy...

And that would be even before the Duke of Wellington lights the match that will blow up the world as we have known it...

Van Buren's Residence
Georgetown, D.C., 7 p.m.

Aaron Burr had been holed-up in his son's house since arriving before dawn yesterday. Matty Van had been alerted by Sir John Burrell Wednesday evening that "Colonel Burr" had been clandestinely summoned by the Duke. Since they were "fellow New Yorkers and, we understand, acquainted," would it be too much for the new Vice G-G to quietly put the old man up during his stay in town? The Duke would consider it a personal favor, etc...

Though astonished, Matty Van had been amused and impressed. Even more so when his father, after scampering into the townhouse from the unmarked Liaison carriage, had related the story of Captain Bratton's appearance at his Reade Street office. After a leisurely breakfast---the Vice G-G had cancelled his morning appointments---Van Buren had gone about his business. Burr had rested; the two had then had a late supper and spent the evening discussing the possible reasons for both the summons and the secrecy surrounding it. A mystery which intensified when Major Layne had appeared at their door after dark with a note from the Duke inviting himself over for supper this evening...

Wellington looked none the worse for wear---he bore no outer marks of his bruising afternoon session with Jackson---when he alighted from the same unmarked Liaison carriage and bounded up the steps to Van Buren's front door, followed by Captain Bratton.

The Vice G-G (though not officially until Monday noon) had the door open and welcomed in his supper guests. His own houseguest, face ruddy and eyes alight with humor and a hint of mischief, waited in the parlor. The two Britons were immediately struck, though they tried to downplay it, by the obvious generational similarities: as Wilder and Scott had once discussed (though not in the Brits' presence), the two diminutive New Yorkers were unquestionably related.

"Well, Your Grace, it is an honor to finally meet you after all these years," Colonel Burr began with a merry twinkle in his eye. "I never had the pleasure during my sojourn in London…"

The Duke was taken back: "I was unaware, Sir, that you had graced England with your presence…"

"I did Sir Arthur. As an isle of refuge from an illegal murder charge, I can recommend no place more highly."

The others laughed nervously, Matty Van shaking his head at the Duke in a gesture of fond helpless filial exasperation. Port and Claret were being offered by an Irish butler. His father, however, was far from done:

"It strikes me, however, Your Grace, that perhaps it would have been better for your purposes tonight if my friend Hamilton had exhibited the steadier hand that morning on the Weehawk Heights. That is, if it is the Bank you are here tonight to discuss. Certainly, neither Matty Van nor I have ever claimed to be the financial genius that we both acknowledge Alex to have been." He sipped his Port and looked expectantly at the Duke, who found, to his astonishment, that the tiny, elegant old man had somehow gained the immediate, if temporary, upper hand.

"Actually, Sirs, the Bank is not the subject of the evening." Wellington paused, sipping his own Claret, and continued, looking from one American to the other: *Yes, no doubt about it: father and son.*

"We have much to discuss, so we had better get right at it. Mr. Vice Governor, I am aware that you are a proponent of relocating the USBA slave population back to Africa or to Central America, though you have, on occasion, maintained a personal 'servant' of your own. Your record in the Senate and as a member of Jackson's first administration demonstrates, however, that you are not prepared to lead the abolitionist movement at this time."

He turned to the older American. "Colonel Burr, are you, too, equivocal on this sensitive issue?"

A look of dawning understanding was spreading over the Colonel's face. "Well Your Grace, if you are asking if I have abolitionist sympathies, I do. But formulated only as a matter of common sense. Unlike the hypocritical Jefferson, who wrote that 'all men are created equal' when in fact he meant 'all white, Protestant, agriculturally-minded men of independent means,' I do not profess to believe in the equality of the races.

"No, Sir Arthur; however, slavery is a cancer spreading perhaps irrevocably through the body of the USBA. It affects the natural growth and development of the Dominion in ways subtle and obvious; it begins to affect our relationship within the Empire in terms of foreign policy and it poses a grave long-term internal security dilemma…"

The Duke interrupted. "In what way, Colonel?"

"The mechanical age is well upon us, Your Grace. More efficient ways to plant and harvest the South's major monetary crops---tobacco and cotton---will be available within a few generations. What then will we do with a suddenly obsolete, uneducated and unwanted workforce who could total four millions or more within 30 years? One which the planters will, believe me, disown the moment slavery becomes economically unfeasible?"

Burr gave the two visitors a hard look. "Will they become a permanent underclass, seething in poverty and crime-prone, like the Irish in New York City? Or turn into actual banditti? Or will our successors have to carve out a Haiti-style enclave and allow them to misrule themselves?

"Not good options, gentlemen. So you see why I believe this cancer must be cut from our Dominion's body as soon as possible!"

Van Buren had been studying the Duke's face as his father explained his position. *Strange that he should be smiling, when the Old Gentleman is being brutally frank. And the Captain is maintaining the quintessential British stiff upper lip. I wonder, is mastering that a requirement for graduating their top schools? At any rate, what's going on here? Was Scott right: have they sent Wellington here to announce a slavery tax of some sort? Is that what tonight is all about?*

He looked to the inconspicuously waiting butler, who nodded. The meal was ready to be served. "Well gentlemen, shall we move into the dining room? We can continue our discussion over our food."

The first course had not been served before Van Buren was dissuaded of the validity of the slave tax theory. Wellington's first comment after sitting down addressed that speculation; his later comments left no room for further speculation at all.

"My meeting this afternoon with General Jackson was adjourned somewhat, ah, prematurely, Mr. Van Buren. The Governor-General was not at all surprised to be informed that my visit here is actually an official one. Mr. Jackson was surprised, however, to learn that I am not here to announce some sort of tax on slaves, as Georgetown rumor apparently has it."

The Duke gazed from son to father and back before continuing. Van Buren, staring directly at him, looked like any British politician hungry for secret information, resembling nothing so much as a starving dog ready to pounce on a choice, unexpected morsel. The Colonel, however, had a glint in his eye that told Wellington the shrewd old fellow might already have figured this out.

"Gentlemen, as the official representative of the Government, at the direction of His Majesty, I today informed our Governor-General that a seven-year, phased-in bill to emancipate all slaves in the Empire, with due monetary compensation to their owners, will be introduced into Parliament this month. I emphasized to him that there is no doubt the final Parliamentary-approved legislation will bear the King's signature by summer's end."

There was neither rush of blood, nor straining of veins, on the faces and foreheads of his hosts, Wellington observed. Neither were there any involuntary gasps of disbelief or anger. Instead, a serene silence reigned for over a minute, until broken by a chuckle from the Colonel.

"Well Your Grace, I see you English have not lost your sense of drama. Shakespeare himself could not have done better. But tell me, how did Andy take this news? Not well, I'd wager."

Turning to the Vice G-G, he added: "Now we know the reason for tonight's summons to The Residency…"

"Ah, so the Governor-General is already meeting with his advisors," smiled the Duke. "I had little doubt that was the plan he and Frank Blair had concocted when they asked for an adjournment this afternoon. I'm sorry to divert you away, Mr. Van Buren, but it is essential we discuss this privately at this time, as you may play more than an advisory role as this crisis progresses."

Wellington's smile faded as he sipped more Claret. "This is excellent wine, Vice-Governor. No Colonel, one can not say our G-G was pleased to hear of the emancipation bill. His initial reaction, however, tended, as I had expected, toward the issue of London-Georgetown relations: that the situation is being presented here as practically a 'fait accompli.'

"And that is a good thing. When---if---Andy accepts the Government's right under the Colonial Compact to order the abolition of slavery here in British America, he will then address the situation in both domestic political and personal terms. And I believe he will then come around on those issues as well."

Watching closely, Burr saw Wellington's face harden into a commanding stare as he looked toward the Vice G-G. "If he can not accept that right, Mr. Van Buren, I have been authorized to take action also spelled out in the Compact. That's why I am here tonight."

It was close to midnight before a tired but satisfied Wellington reboarded his coach, assisted by a Captain Bratton who had absorbed invaluable lessons in both politics and leadership tonight.

Over the course of dinner and further discussions over brandy and cigars before a cozy fire, Wellington had extracted much from Van Buren: an acknowledgement that the Government indeed had the right under the Compact to unilaterally abolish slavery in the USBA (especially under terms of Empire-wide legislation); a commitment from the Vice G-G to work privately to rally Northern and Western support (it was agreed that publicly, as an Administration member, he should take no stand that might seem to challenge The Residency) and a private commitment to, in the last eventuality, enforce emancipation if circumstances forced Jackson's removal from office.

"So the eel has some backbone after all," the Duke said as the carriage rolled toward The Residency. "Perhaps it was the father's influence, but my level of confidence in Van Buren's ability to lead the Dominion in a crisis, if necessary, is increasing. Hopefully, we can still avoid that painful possibility, but it is reassuring…"

With Bratton listening and saying little, the Duke and the two Americans had decided that Daniel Webster should be asked to

THE DOMINION'S DILEMMA: THE UNITED STATES OF BRITISH AMERICA

assume the main Northern role; the Vice G-G would sound out Henry Clay concerning the West. "Fortuitously, both will be present here tomorrow night for a post-speech dinner-party," Van Buren had said. "I'll have a private word with Harry then. As for Webster, he'll probably be informing *me* that he'll be speaking out..."

"As students of human nature," Sir Arthur had at one point remarked, "we all know it is inevitable that you, Vice Governor, will be gradually eased out of Andy's inner circle, at least till this crisis passes. No matter how close you have been in the past, you pose a threat---how ever passive---to the G-G's tenure in office. That, Colonel, is why I've asked you down here."

Burr was puffing contentedly on a cigar, *as if he had been briefed on this in advance,* thought Wellington. *I'm damned if he doesn't already know what I'm about to propose. It's uncanny...*

"Colonel, you've known General Jackson longer than virtually anyone. I believe this is not the first storm you two will be weathering. You do know what is expected of you, I assume?"

The old man's eyes were bright with relish and mischievous, mocking humor: "By the Eternal, I do Sir! You want me to help keep the lid on Andy's famous temper; don't allow his emotions to run roughshod over the facts. And to assure him that no one, particularly Matty here, is planning some sort of 'coup.'

"Now then, Sir Arthur, if I'm not mistaken, my job begins tomorrow. While you're causing an uproar on Capitol Hill, I'll be at the other end of Pennsylvania Avenue. I'm to slip into The Residency while no one's looking and privately talk some political horse sense to the G-G."

To Bratton, it seemed as if the devil's own horns had suddenly sprouted from the old man's bald palate. Burr grinned again.

"Well Your Grace. At least I'll get the first words in. It takes quite a bit to shock Andy into silence, but *me* walking into his Residency office unannounced should do the trick."

CHAPTER TWENTY-NINE

General Scott's Townhouse
Georgetown, D.C.
March 2, 1833, 7:45 a.m.:

A shaken Lieutenant Wilder was coming down the steps after his briefing of General Scott when he heard himself hailed. The Lieutenant's meeting with a still night-clothed USBAA commander had just delivered him a body blow (despite the diminished look that posing in such attire most often gives older men, Scott still looked ridiculously impressive, he had thought, if a bit impressively ridiculous).

Scott had grunted his approval of the security plans for Cranford and had grimaced at Tom's description of his disastrous interview with Mary Lee. He had then turned to glance at his wife as she descended the stairs. "As we expected, my dear, Mary Lee did not take the news well. In fact, she all but bodily tossed the Lieutenant here down Arlington hill."

"And Robert? What did he say?" Maria looked anxiously at Tom.

"Hadn't arrived from Fortress Monroe when I left for Alexandria, Mrs. Scott, and I did not think it appropriate to stop again at Arlington on the way back. I thought there might be a chance I'd meet up with Robert on the road, but that didn't happen, either."

"All right, Lieutenant. You did your best." The General was brisk. "Now then. Report back to the War Department as per usual for a Saturday, after checking in at The Residency. Things are liable to be tense over there, but that shouldn't involve you. In case I'm in conference or have already left for the Capitol, your orders are to order up a Department carriage and proceed to Mr. Van Buren's house, timed for a 1 p.m. arrival. An elderly gentleman will be waiting. You're to take him to The Residency, escort him to the G-G's office, then wait outside to return him to the Vice G-G's. With the least attention possible, understood?"

The General turned to go back up the stairs and then pivoted again. "By the way, Lieutenant: I've read the draft of your officer-availability report. It needs more work on the junior officer segment. Make that Monday's priority."

Tom was halfway down the steps before the full implication of Scott's words hit him.

———

It was, surprisingly, Dave Harper who hailed him. Despite the relatively early hour, Harps looked chipper, though Tom had come to recognize enviously that his friend did not seemingly require sleep.

"Well Lieutenant, a high level meeting with the boss so early? Seems like the whole town's astir this morning. Even I climbed out of the sack at the crack of dawn."

Tom snorted. "Your own, or someone else's?"

"Why Lieutenant, by my very attire you can see that I spent the night in my room at The Deerhead. I've an important breakfast meeting of my own this day."

"Is borsch on the menu, or is Joanne fixing you steak and eggs?"

Harps feigned a look of outraged superiority. "Neither, Lieutenant. As it happens, I'm on my way to the Liaison Office. Captain Bratton sent me a note late yesterday inviting me to breakfast to discuss, and I quote, 'a matter of some potential importance.' Any idea what it could be about?"

Tom shook his head. "No idea, Dave." *Bratton's a professional,* he thought to himself. *He's not calling Harps in to discuss their mutual paramour. Got to have something to do with emancipation, but God knows what.*

They parted at Pennsylvania Avenue. "Let me know how it goes, Harps. Maybe we can have a few beers this evening, if you're not already booked…"

"Sounds good, Lieutenant. By the way: what exactly *are* kippers?"

———

The Residency
Georgetown, D.C.
8 a.m.

Secretary Cass' official War Department carriage was among a handful already parked in the circular driveway fronting the Main Portico when Tom walked up the grounds. Congressman Polk was arriving on horseback and the Lieutenant could see Mr. Blair making his way across Pennsylvania Avenue from his townhouse.

Looks like the kitchen cabinet is about to convene. I wonder if they met last night or if Jackson's going to drop Wellington's bombshell on them now...

One look at the grim demeanor on the faces of the advisors already gathered inside awaiting Jackson's descent from the second floor private quarters and Tom knew the answer: the G-G's men were aware of the impending crisis.

He made his way quickly across and down the hall to his own cubbyhole office and closed the door. *Let them go into their meeting; then I'll find out what I can. The tension in here is thick enough to cut with a bayonet...*

After a briefing from Jackson and Blair that had been met with initial disbelief, last night's marathon meeting had gotten down to hard cases. The kitchen cabinet, minus the flagrantly missing incoming Vice G-G, had broken down the issue into five debatable sections: constitutionality; Administration response; enforceability; immediate impact on the Dominion and long-term impact. Each section, of course, was inevitably and automatically debated in the tint of Democratic Party politics...

The meeting had finally broken up around midnight--it had started a few minutes after 6 p.m.---and the advisors were off the grounds by the time the Duke's carriage rolled in. The plan had been for each advisor to study one or two sections he was most familiar with and come up with options this morning. The meeting was scheduled to break around 11:30 a.m., leaving all but the G-G--- whom protocol discouraged from attending---time to get up to the Hill for Wellington's 1 p.m. address.

Since Andy Donelson was taking notes of this morning's session---as he had last night---Tom was unable to determine exactly what was being discussed inside the G-G's office. All the few other professional aides in the building knew was that the G-G had returned from the Liaison Office in the worst mood exhibited since the height of the nullification crisis. Servants were immediately sent to fetch Cass, Polk and the others. Coffee, tea and a light supper had given way by 9 p.m. to Tennessee mash and other spirits.

The head usher had told Tom flatly that the mood had remained sober, however, despite the large quantities of liquor dispatched. "Whatever the Governor-General brought them in for was a shock to their systems," he said. "I'd say the liquor was more medicinal than anything…"

Per General Scott's orders, Tom left the Residency around 10:15 a.m. There was nothing more to be learned on this side of Pennsylvania Avenue and he had to arrange for that Department carriage. Anyway, he'd have plenty of time to pick up the details later, while he waited for the "elderly gentleman" to finish his interview with the G-G. The General hadn't identified the dignitary, but Tom had an idea who he might be. He thought the odds were good he'd last seen him on the Broad Way…

War Department
Georgetown, D.C.
March 2, 1833, 10:30 a.m.

The General was in conference when Tom walked into the building. A nod of the Lieutenant's head had brought a whispered comment from the ranking non-commissioned officer on duty that the General had arrived some 40 minutes ago. "And ran right into a stone-faced lieutenant named Lee, Sir. They went inside and have been closeted ever since."

So Robert knows what's up; and he isn't happy about it. Well, what do you expect? He's sworn an oath to uphold a flag and government that now seeks to devalue his family's wealth by at least a third… If the government tried to nationalize---imperialize---Shamrock Shipbuilding, I might have second thoughts about my oath myself! Well, better see about that carriage. If the General wants me, he'll know how to find me!

Tom returned through a rear door from the adjacent stables a quarter hour later to see Scott's bulk literally barricading the main doorway. The look of sadness on the General's face when he pivoted to return to his office imparted on Thomas a sense of inevitable, uncontrollable catastrophe he would remember all his days.

The Capitol
12:50 p.m.

The few stony-faced members of Jackson's kitchen cabinet were swallowed up in the overflow crowd of Congressmen, Court, diplomatic corps, other high-ranking dignitaries both civil and military, as well as civilians lucky enough to have bagged tickets for the Duke's speech.

The crowd was in a holiday mood as they moved across the grounds and into the Capitol itself; a major speech of any sort made interesting any given day in dreary Georgetown. Today's speech by the highest-ranking Empire statesman to ever appear at the unfinished brownish structure---though not expected to be particularly newsworthy---was excuse enough to schedule parties and receptions. The major topic among the ladies, in fact, was which and how many appearances the Duke would make this afternoon and evening; a tweaking or even reordering of the social strata might even occur, depending on the Duke's visitation whims...

So the sight of the Duke's carriage and his honor guard---an uneasily-mixed detachment of Royal and USBA Marines---brought cheers from the privileged as well as Georgetown's ordinary citizens. The throngs lined Pennsylvania Avenue as the procession came out The Residency's gates and moved towards the Hill.

Inside, Wellington's air of supreme confidence was not matched by the tenseness emanating from his three aides. Major Layne was chiefly concerned with the Duke's safety; not so much now, but what about after the conclusion of the speech? He had been in Georgetown last year when some Western Congressman had pulled a pistol on one of Jackson's protégées; fortunately for both, the gun had misfired. *What--who--could stop some enraged Southerner from whipping out a handgun and taking a shot at the Duke?*

As the Liaison's top political hand, Sir John Burrell was more concerned with The Residency's reaction, not to the speech itself---Jackson already knew what would be said---but to its mandate. There had not been a word from the Governor-General since leaving yesterday's Liaison Office meeting.

Harry Bratton, too, was concerned about the upcoming response by the G-G. But he was more concerned by Congress' reaction to the emancipation news. Nothing he had seen nor heard since arriving on *Irresistible* had changed the opinion he had offered Palmerston's committee back home: in the end, Jackson and the Southerners would fight to the last man to save their cherished way-of-life.

As the carriage halted at the foot of the Capitol, Burrell was identifying for the Duke members of the joint Congressional leadership chosen to escort His Grace into the building and to the podium. Bratton looked at his pocket watch and back at the smiling Duke. It was 1:20 p.m.

———————

Aaron Burr did not recognize Tom, but the accent and name rang bells. "You wouldn't be related to old Jack Wilder, now would you, Lieutenant?" The elegant little man glanced over as they walked to the carriage. At Tom's affirmative reply, the Colonel's eyes twinkled: "George or young Jack's boy? George's, eh! So, yours is the branch with the priest in the family…"

Burr reminisced for most of the trip, as if he had no cares in the world, Tom observed. Though he did ask several shrewd questions concerning Tom's duties in Georgetown, particularly as an aide to General Scott. "Then we'll be seeing you tonight, Lieutenant?" he said as the carriage pulled onto The Residency grounds. "I'm dining later at the General's, along with the Duke. Not sure who else will be there…" It was news to Tom, whose orders apparently ended with the delivery of the old man back to the Van Buren house.

Burr stepped down from the carriage with the grace of an athlete, and then bounded up the steps ahead of the Lieutenant. There was no one to meet them at the door, so Tom ushered the Colonel in and down the hall toward the G-G's office.

"By the Eternal!"

The oath shattered the cathedral-like silence engulfing the seemingly empty building. "Damn it all, it is *you*, Colonel Burr! I'd recognize that damn strut of yours even in hell…which is where I had expected to encounter you next!" Jackson, just outside his office, stared in amazement. "And escorted by one of my own aides! What the devil is going on here, eh? Answer me Lieutenant!"

Jackson's original astonishment was fast being replaced by a fit of temper, but Burr simply grinned and stuck out his hand. "It is a pleasure to see you again, too, Andrew." He glanced mischievously at the paintings of Jefferson, other former G-Gs and Royal dignitaries hanging from the walls. "There seems to have been some improvements in the décor since my time. Well, if this is hell, I'll anticipate with relish our mutual return…"

The G-G shook his head and laughed reflexively, his spat of anger overcome by the words and actions of the incorrigible New Yorker. "All right, Lieutenant. I'm sure the Colonel somehow maneuvered you into this. Go about your business." He pivoted with the help of his cane and slapped Burr's back. "Now see here Colonel," he said as he escorted him into the office and shut the door. "Your showing up like this is no coincidence. How did that damn Wellington get you down here?"

The Capitol
2:40 p.m.

Burrell and Bratton stood off to the far left of the Speaker's rostrum in the House of Representatives' chamber. Both houses of Congress were crowded into the rows of desks and on the aisles. Marshall and the Court, as well as the joint leadership, were spread out behind the Speaker's platform. The diplomatic corps, government and military leaders and other guests overflowed the visitors' gallery. Layne, whose first impulse had been to throw a ring of Royal Marines around the rostrum, had gone off to confer with the commander of the USBA Marines: the small Capitol Building police force was widely known to be little more than glorified ushers.

The tumultuous cheers that had greeted Wellington's march down the aisle had barely subsided when Speaker Stevenson of Virginia brought on a second standing ovation with his flowery introduction of the Duke. By the time an equally flowery return round of acknowledgements of Congressional and Court leaders by Wellington was concluded the time had been approximately 1:40 p.m.

Now, even those so inclined to cheer were in too deep a shock to do so.

The Residency
2:30 p.m.

Burr had anticipated the diatribe against London that Jackson launched immediately upon pouring them both Tennessee mash, neat. He waited patiently for the Jacksonian eruption to run its course before getting down to the serious business at hand.

The Colonel was relieved that Andrew angrily conceded that London probably had the legal authority to order emancipation, under existing terms of both the Colonial Compact and the USBA Constitution, "damn those idiots from Franklin to Madison who threw away our rights."

Burr, however, was aghast when Jackson began to apply a disguised version of the nullification principle. "Constitutions, compacts are living things, Colonel Burr. They must have room to breathe, to grow. They must adapt to the times, the conditions prevalent in the countries or dominions to which they are applied. Otherwise, they will die and cease to be any more than antiquated scraps of paper."

The G-G peered over his glass as he waited to see how the other trained lawyer would react.

"Bullshit, Andrew...Mr. Governor-General...

"In your own Tennessee parlance, that dog won't hunt...and we both know it."

The blood raced to the G-G's face and Burr settled back to enjoy another eruption. But Jackson, staring directly into his old friend's face, suddenly burst out in a bitter laugh.

"Of course *we* do, Colonel. But what about the rest of the South? What about Andrew Jackson, private citizen, who worked his way up from a dirt-floored cabin on a played-out North Carolina hillside to own The Hermitage? How is he, how are they, supposed to react to the high-and-mighty 3000-miles away Parliament and fat, dumpy little King, who if not for the luck of birth might be eating pork and cabbage in a German tavern, deciding to strip us of our hard-earned property?

"And, Colonel, spare me the righteous compensation argument. I've been through that with His Grace, the Duke." Jackson spit out the title with a sneer. "We're talking pennies on the dollar..."

"And all this time, Andrew, I thought it was we Yankees who worshipped the 'Almighty dollar...'" Burr sipped his whisky and grinned impishly at the fired-up G-G.

Jackson's fist came crashing down on his desk, spilling his own glass and shaking every other item on it.

"Careful, Andrew. That desktop looks firm...and your hands may be a bit more brittle than you care to admit."

A smile broke reluctantly out on the G-G's face. "Damn you, Aaron. You always knew where and when to insert the knife. My Rachel always said: 'Don't ever get into a debate with Colonel Burr, General. He's the one man you can't intimidate...'"

Burr reached across the desk to the still rattling whisky bottle and poured them each another glass. "Well Andrew, isn't it time we talked turkey?"

The Deerhead Inn
3:10 p.m.

Dave Harper snapped awake from a short nap brought on by fully 90 minutes of as intense physical exertion as he could recall. He could hear the low, even breathing of his partner as he reached to run his hand across her smooth, olive-skinned back.

The wife of the French Counsel-General opened her eyes and stretched leisurely as she gazed at her new lover. "What time is it? I see the sunlight, so it can't be too late."

Harps pulled his watch from the pocket of the jacket unceremoniously discarded earlier on the floor. "A little after three. They'll be finishing up at the Capitol soon. When do you have to get back?"

Jacqueline Jean-Claude smiled archly: "Not quite yet, Cheri. Jacques will stay for the reception, especially since he was able to use my ticket to seat his crony, Count Karl." She moved into Harper's arms. "A puzzling situation, that. Do you remember the stranger with the eye patch at my supper Wednesday night? Somehow, he appropriated the Count's ticket..."

Political intrigue was normally the farthest thing from Harps' mind--especially when he held a beautiful, naked woman in his arms---but he had rendezvoused with Jacqueline soon after returning from the Liaison Office. To his amazement, practically the sole topic of his breakfast with Captain Bratton and, unexpectedly, Major Layne, had been the wiry, eye-patched Russian: what had Countess Caroline said about this 'Andre Karlhamanov'? He had been observed being introduced to the supposed 'exile' by the Countess at the French Consulate the other evening. And what, if anything, had Harper discussed with the man?

Almost nothing, really: Karlhamanov had been visibly unimpressed when he learned David worked for Interior. But yes, he had a date to go riding with the Countess tomorrow and, yes, he would attempt to casually sound her out. Right now, all he knew was that Caroline seemed uncomfortable with the fellow...

With an embarrassed look that had surprised both Layne and Harper, Bratton had then shifted the questioning: did David recognize the Russian from anywhere else? No, not that he could recall. (The carefree Harps, when getting the signal over repeated nights that Joanne was unavailable, had simply moved on (without inquiring as to the cause). There were simply too many fish in the sea---as today was proving--to worry about one who wished to swim away. Especially a piranha like Mrs. Casgrave!)

Harps now shared a long kiss with Madame Jean-Claude and then grinned: "How could I forget him? You pointed him out as we were making our, err, 'arrangement.'" The grin faded into a frown: "But I don't understand. I thought Count Renkowiitz was in charge over there? How did M. Eye Patch end up with his ticket?"

Jacqueline, however, had lost interest in the inner workings of the Russian Consulate. "Enough of that, Cheri. We have two more hours. Let's make use of them..."

Well, thought Harps, *even if the Countess clams up tomorrow, I've already got some juicy news for Captain Bratton. But that can wait...Vive La France!*

The Capitol
3:30 p.m.

One newspaper account of the scene highlighted the "funereal atmosphere descending on the Chamber." Another contrasted the 'solemn faces" of Justice Marshall and his associate jurists with the "dark fury evident on the features of the new Senator from South Carolina."

All written accounts of the Duke's historic speech, however, recorded the gradual transformation from celebration to shock in both the well of the House and in the galleries. Knowing what was coming and where to look, Burrell would remember amazement turning to glee on Webster's face, as well as the blank expression Van Buren, sitting with the Cabinet members, maintained throughout.

There were few avowed Abolitionists in Congress and even fewer among the spectators. Thus there were no outbreaks of sustained applause or celebration. The Southern delegation's reaction was twofold: stunned disbelief or incoherent fury. Most civilians in the galleries were Southern: they shared their leaders' reactions. The diplomatic corps sat in amazed fascination as the Empire's most famous man announced a self-manufactured crisis; even 'Andre Karlhamanov' found it hard---though gratifying---to realize that Wellington's blunt-though-understated words contained the seeds of a civil war. Among the military and government hierarchy, men looked at each other with thoughts of promotions, resignations, repudiations and fratricide in their eyes. Their wives looked at their husbands and each other with incredulity, with sadness, with horror.

Major Layne had found the USBA Marine detachment commander, a hard-boiled captain named Goodwin, and had convinced him with some difficulty to bring his men into the building's Rotunda. (The Royal Marines waited outside with The Residency's carriage.) Goodwin, on verbal orders from General Scott (Bratton had located and approached Scott to share Layne's growing concern), quietly provided security for the Duke as he left the rostrum, marched through the House well and up the same aisle he had come in. If any Southern hot heads entertained thoughts of assassination, they were either too paralyzed by shock or intimidated by the Marines to act on their inclinations.

Which is not to say that the Duke's journey back to the Rotunda was a victory march. The anger of the Southerners was blatantly evident; the astonishment of moderates like Kentucky's Henry Clay and Thomas Ewing of Ohio was obvious and the feelings of most New Englanders were subdued. Like Clay, Webster shook Wellington's hand as the former P.M. moved back up the stairs; unlike Clay's perfunctory grasp, there was a silent but solid commitment of solidarity in the Massachusetts senator's grip.

Wellington, of course, acted as if he was greeting the crowds in Trafalgar Square. He never winced, blanched or otherwise acted as if he had done more than deliver the King's best wishes to his loyal British American subjects. "They don't call him the 'Iron Duke' for nothing," an impressed Bratton whispered to Sir John as they finally cleared the House chamber.

"Today may not be the 'Ides of March,' but this walk will go down with Caesar's final stroll through the Forum," Burrell replied. "Let's just hope it doesn't end the same way."

The Duke waved to the crowd as if campaigning as they moved outside and prepared to reboard the carriage. He even chose to ignore the contingent of Royal Marines drawn up to reinforce Goodwin's detachment. "Well, gentlemen, I've a dinner engagement at General Scott's this evening. I believe a short recap and a nap are appropriate in the meantime. So let's proceed back to The Residency, shall we?"

The show of bravado lasted till the carriage was rolling back down Pennsylvania Avenue (under renewed cheers from a populace unaware of the sudden turn-of-events). Wellington sighed deeply and fell back in his seat. He looked at his two aides (Layne rode outside with the mixed Marines) and shook his head: "That, gentlemen, was worse than enduring Marshall Ney's cavalry charge at Waterloo. The hostility by the end was thick enough to cut with a knife.

Bratton was placating: "The problem, Your Grace, is the location. How the devil did the Northerners allow their capital to be located down here in the slaveocracy? The reaction, I'm quite sure, would have been much more positive if you had delivered your speech in Philadelphia or New York..."

Wellington shook his head. "No Captain. The problem is just as you analyzed it in London: Like you, the people in that ugly, pretentious capitol building of theirs see emancipation as the powder keg which will blow this whole Dominion apart, no matter their feelings on the subject. From a distance, the USBA appears a vibrant, thriving monolith. In fact, it is as fragile as a plate of china."

He looked at each aide in turn. "Thank God whatever happens can be contained internally. We are very fortunate that there are no other Powers in a position to intervene. If there were, I'm not sure we could hold this together...or put it back together...

"Whichever becomes necessary."

CHAPTER THIRTY

The Residency
Georgetown, D.C.
March 2, 1833, 4 p.m.:

Lieutenant Wilder had spent a boring 2 ½ hours in his tiny office and wandering the halls. He dared not leave; *who knew when the meeting in Jackson's office would break?*

Not surprisingly, he had found two communications in his office that needed immediate attention: General Scott's order that he deliver Colonel Burr to his home at 7 p.m. necessitated alerting the enlisted man driving the carriage that both their days would be a bit longer. The other note informed him that Candice was in residence at her townhouse and would expect him after 5 p.m.; fortunately, one of her 'people,' Stephon, had waited for a reply. Press-of-duty would delay him, Tom had written back. He'd be there sometime after 8...

Now he could hear the Duke's arrival back from Capitol Hill. Standing at attention in his cubbyhole's doorway, he could see the hook-nosed old man tiredly cross the Main Portico and head up to his suite of rooms, followed by the tense-faced Bratton and Burrell. Striding to the main doors, he could see the Marines depart in separate formations. *Should he,* the thought came too late to act on, *have informed the G-G Wellington was back? Perhaps not: Jackson would have ordered him to stand watch if he wanted to be on the steps to greet the Duke. And Wellington himself hadn't looked right or left to see if the G-G was coming. Significant...and not good.*

Major Layne was now taking the steps two at a time, his long legs propelling him quickly into the building and across the hall to the stairs. "Well Lieutenant. Been here all afternoon? Missed the fireworks, you did, up the road..." Tom merely nodded. *And you missed the fireworks here, Major. Though you may still be in time for an encore performance...*

With that, the door to Jackson's office opened and the G-G, his left arm around the smaller man's shoulders, emerged with Colonel

Burr. Jackson walked his guest over to Tom. "Your orders are to take good care of this old relic tonight, Lieutenant. Just have him back here tomorrow at 4 p.m. sharp." The two ancient adventurers looked each other in the eye and shook hands silently. Jackson was still watching from the Portico as Thomas helped the Colonel into the War Department carriage.

The driver had some difficulty working his way through crowds that were building up outside The Residency gates. Tom was baffled; he'd never seen a Georgetown crowd this big, this quiet and at this time on a Saturday afternoon.

"Well young Mr. Wilder. Not used to seeing a crowd transform into a mob?" Burr had put on a sad, wise face. "The Duke's message has gotten to the streets…and Georgetown's citizens don't seem to be taking it well. They'll disperse, though, once word filters down that Andy will answer the Duke on Monday."

"Answer him, Sir?"

"Certainly, young man. Whatever do you think we talked about in there for almost three hours? Come now, if you're an intelligence aide to General Scott, you already know the gist of Wellington's lecture, err, address to Congress. I was simply helping the Governor-General formulate his response. Of course, it's still an early draft. We'll have another session tomorrow afternoon, once he's spoken with the Congressional leadership."

For the first time, the old man looked grim. "And after I've spoken to the Duke. And General Scott…"

The Capitol
4:45 p.m.

If the House Chamber had looked *funereal*, then the reception room resembled a huge Irish wake. Groups of mostly four or less; some loud, some somber, all with glasses in their hands; all talking at once.

Lt. Robert E. Lee was standing with Angeline and Lucille Latoure when he saw the huge bulk of General Scott across the room studying him carefully. The General seemed to grimace slightly; then turned to face Senator Tyler, who had pushed his way through the guests. The Senator began talking rapidly, accentuating his emotions with thrusts of his hands and forearms. To his left, Lee could see Senator Troup of Georgia with his index finger in Henry Clay's chest. *A not-so-gentile riot could break out in here any minute*, Robert thought. *I hope the bartenders are watering down the liquor...*

Mrs. Latoure was addressing him over the ever-increasing noise: "So, Robert. We understand from Thomas that Mary did not take the news well. Had she adjusted any by the time you rode down this morning?"

"I'm afraid not, Mrs. Latoure. I tried to assure her that whatever London was proposing would not mean the end of Arlington House, but she is still extremely upset. How can anyone blame her? The plantation is not just her home, it is her life." He paused. "Am I right in assuming you ladies will be staying the night in Georgetown? If so, could I impose upon you to stop at Arlington tomorrow? I have to leave early in the morning to catch my boat back to Norfolk. Even though we'll have the evening, I know she'd appreciate having you to discuss this with tomorrow."

"Certainly, Robert. We're attending a dinner-party at Mr. Van Buren's house tonight, but we'll be on the road by late morning. We'll certainly stop."

The first real smile of the day broke out on Lieutenant Lee's face as he turned to the daughter: "The new Vice G-G's, eh? Make sure Tom's boots are buffed and buttons are shining, Lucille. We want him to make his best impression in front of his fellow New Yorker's other distinguished guests."

"Why Robert," she purred, "and what makes you think Lieutenant Wilder was invited? Or has he been demoted to social aide to the Vice G-G? Oh dear!"

She curtsied and moved away, leaving her mother to shake her head in dismay. The chagrined Lee watched her disappear into the crowd.

"And so Robert, what was *your* reaction to the Duke's announcement?"

The Southerners were drinking more heavily and talking more loudly. Daniel Webster pulled Ohio's Ewing aside: "I'll take care of my people if you see to yours, Senator. These damn Southerners get any more liquored up and a civil war could break out right here..."

"What we need, Daniel," said Ewing slowly, looking around at the red-faced and increasingly boisterous Dixie lawmakers and guests, "is a series of caucuses early tomorrow: Western; MidAtlantic and New England. Bipartisan. Then, we should meet later in the day and send a representative delegation to The Residency. Old Jack had to have some word this was coming…even if he received it in just the past few days.

"We need to isolate the Southerners for the moment; at least until we determine how the rest of us feel."

Webster looked warily at the Ohioan: "Feel about what, Senator?"

Ewing was direct: "About London suddenly charging in here and upsetting the apple cart, so to speak! Damn it, Daniel, I thought the unwritten article in the Compact which made all this work was the provision that London would allow us to iron out our own problems. Not just walk in and announce they're ramming this down our collective throats!"

The senior Senator from Massachusetts nodded in agreement: "It would seem, Senator, that London has forgotten that unwritten directive. Or has been suddenly endowed with such a sense of self-righteousness that it has overlooked our half-century of autonomous, democratic-style government."

He paused and smiled ironically: "Or still believes that we of the USBA are not qualified to discuss or decide the major issues facing us…"

Ewing nodded. "Agreed. However…"

His expression slowly changed as he coldly looked Webster in the eye: "…I do not think I will be alone, Senator, once today's remarkable address is reviewed overnight, in seeing the fine hand of Quincy Adams somewhat and somehow behind all this.

"I pray, Sir, for the sake of non-Southern Dominion unity that Mr. Adams has kept his own counsel in this. My Western associates would not be pleased to learn that New England had prior knowledge of the Duke's announcement and kept it from the rest of us."

The Ohioan broke eye contact and walked away.

This Irish wake, like any and all others of its kind, went on long after the scheduled 5 p.m. ending.

By then, the leading Southerners had adjourned to Troup's townhouse.

Georgetown
March 2-4, 1833

Jurgurtha Numidia had been stunned Saturday night as he rode back over Long Bridge from the Arlington House wedding. But his potential jubilation was muted by the thought that Sebastian, in his own excitement, might either have exaggerated the fragments of overheard conversation in his own mind or had misinterpreted what this Army officer had said.

While Jurgurtha knew a growing number of British Americans considered slavery to be either morally wrong or increasingly economically impractical---an "anachronism", he had heard it described as recently---he believed the struggle to be far from over. Now, if Sebastian was reporting correctly, the British Crown itself was stepping in to put an end to the abomination...

By the next afternoon, Jurgurtha had confirmed that Sebastian had gotten it right: emancipation was on the table!

The issue now was what to do concerning runaways already in the system and how to pass on the runaways most quickly to Boston and the New England Abolition Society. At this most sensitive time, Jurgurtha did not want a failed escape to lead to an expose of *Exodus*. Not only could such an expose fatally hurt the emancipation cause...but it would make he himself look bad... *For Jurgurtha, in addition to his commitment to abolition, knew how to look after his own best interests.* Quickly adapting to the startling new day would inevitably enhance his own standing with the Society...

This Sunday evening, religious services completed, Jurgurtha was back inside his quarters above the stable when Tousaint walked in, from appearances directly after a long sojourn at that old woman's saloon the boy and his friends frequented.

"Boy, the Sabbath is for celebrating and worshipping the Lord Our God Himself, not some false god of pleasure. Don't you spend enough time kneeling before the altar of Bacchus during the week that you can't give Our Lord Jesus Christ your Sunday?"

Jurgurtha glared at his son, who smirked and wiped his hand over his mouth. "Wasn't Bacchus I was worshipping tonight, old man. But

Bibesia sends you her warmest greetings…"

In spite of himself, the father grinned through his grumble: "Four years of ancient history at that log cabin college of yours and all you retained was an appreciation of the Roman wine goddess?"

"Maybe if you sent me to Harvard Yard, I'd have learned the name of the Greek wine goddess. Or the Babylonian. Or the Egyptian… At any rate, there are some very fine young waitresses and such at Monticello. You really ought to get out more yourself, Reverend. Unless that Melissa of yours is spending more of her time at the Samples townhouse…"

This time, Jurgurtha's grumble was real. But as he reached for the neck of the backstepping, grinning son, the solution to the *Exodus* problem flashed into his mind.

"Sit down boy. We got something more important than female pulchritude to discuss. Haven't you heard the news from Capitol Hill? Or have you been chasing skirts since yesterday morning?"

"Heard it all right, old man. Not worth celebrating, though. Some old Englishman says the King wants to free our people. In seven years or so! You really think all the massas from here to Mississippi are just going to sit back and let some fat little bastard 3000 miles away in London tell *them* what to do? I don't see it…"

Jurgurtha managed…barely…to keep the lid on his temper: "Boy, you may have a college education…but sometimes I doubt you have a shred of common sense. Forget the damn white men's politics. Just concentrate on how this will affect *Exodus*…and us."

Tousaint respected his father, even as he considered him too cautious. So he listened and accepted Jurgurtha's directive, even as he began to formulate plans that diverted from the older man's orders.

Before leaving the stables the next morning, he sent word via a young urchin who frequented the place that Marion Motley was to come to the Hill as soon as possible. When the big man arrived, nursing a sore head from his own Monticello Sabbath overindulgence and grumbling about being awaken on his day off, young Numidia was brisk: Get ahold of Doby and Donfield. They were all to meet at Monticello at 7 p.m.

"How's I supposed to get in da Spanish house? Gettin' Doby ain't goin' be no problem. But I ain't guarenteein' nothin' 'bout Crispus.."

"Do the best you can. Tell Ugene its important. I'll brief you all tonight." *If Crispus missed the planning session, it really wouldn't matter. He could bring Donfield up-to-date later…*

Tousaint, meanwhile, had already carried out his father's orders regarding *Exodus*...and Daniel Webster. The Senator arrived---spright and spiffy---at exactly 9 a.m., much to the surprise of his small staff, who never knew if-or-when the playboy orator would make his first post-weekend appearance. He listened carefully to Tousaint's relay of Jurgurtha's message: all *Exodus* operations would be frozen until Boston assessed the changing situation. Those runaways now in flight would be stopped and hidden along the route. *Exodus* would not be the cause of any backlash against the emancipation plan...

Webster nodded and issued his instructions: sit tight. Let the legislative process take its course.

———

Van Buren Home
March 2, 1833
7 p.m.

It was obvious to Tom that some of Van Buren's guests had come straight from the post-speech reception. Certainly Daniel Webster had; or else had continued to imbibe elsewhere. He was now eloquently if somewhat boisterously speaking with an enthralled circle about the need for "bipartisan cooperation in support of this just crusade."

Henry Clay, however, had apparently limited his legendary intake. He, too, was the center of a small circle of guests. And yet despite Tom's efforts to shield Burr from view, the Kentuckian spied the old man coming down the stairs. He quickly moved to intercept them by the front door. "By God Colonel Burr, it is you!" he said quietly. "Haven't seen you since the trial, but I'd know you anywhere. What the devil are you doing here?"

Burr flashed his mischievous grin but Clay wasn't ready for an answer as yet: "And with a uniformed officer as an escort, no less! So you're here officially...

"But not staying for the dinner-party, I see. So where are you off to? The Residency, by chance, under cover of darkness?"

The Colonel modestly shook his head: "Now Harry, why would I need cover of any kind? I'll wager there aren't five people in

Georgetown who remember, much less recognize, me. As for The Residency…"

The conspirator's grin broke out: "…Tennessee mash is not recommended for people my age after 5 p.m. A shot or two of good Irish whiskey, however, is another matter… Enjoy the evening, Harry. Matty Van sets the best table of anyone I know."

Clay's jaw dropped as Tom opened the door for the Colonel. When the Lieutenant looked back after assisting the old man into the War Department rig, he was still staring after them.

Burr was chuckling. "Well Mr. Wilder, I would rather have escaped unseen, but it was worth it to see Harry speechless. Poor Matty, though; Clay will pester him no end to find out why I'm here…and where I've gone." He laughed again. "Perhaps it is for the best. Matty promised the Duke last night he'd enlist Harry to rally the West. This will provide the perfect entrée to the conversation. Not that Matty needs help, but …"

But the Lieutenant was no longer listening. As he escorted the Colonel to the carriage, they had passed a trio of arriving guests. With Lucille and her mother was the bachelor political chief of the Liaison Office, Sir John Burrell.

Long Bridge over the Potomac
7 p.m.

Robert E. Lee dismounted near the Virginia side of the Bridge and looked up the hill to the lights of Arlington House. *Could it be just 24 hours ago that I rode up the long driveway so eagerly anticipating a joyous homecoming?*

One look at Mary's face in the vestibule and I knew something was gravely wrong. Thank God little Custis was there in her arms; otherwise I'd have thought him deathly ill. Instead, I found reports of a crisis of another, most unexpected kind….

And today it has been confirmed: Parliament apparently intends to abolish slavery throughout the Empire without so much as asking our opinion! They intend to uproot the entire economic and social fabric of the South starting next year…and we're to actually participate cheerfully in this cataclysm in exchange for what amounts to a small monetary bribe!

He shook his head in disbelief.

Anyone who has known me understands I am uncomfortable with our peculiar institution; in any case, the Lee family's slaves were long ago seized to pay my late father's debts. I did not mature in this culture... And my wife knows I have given much thought to freeing the slaves up on that hill when the time is right and I am available to oversee their orderly transition into free, hired workers.

But not now---and not on order of some faraway politicians---before either owners or slaves are ready...

Mary is sure the Yankees are behind this. I myself am not; their representatives seemed as shocked as our own during Wellington's address today. And General Scott looked as sorrowful as a man can be in our meeting this morning. But then the General, too, is a Virginian, as is his wife. Yet he made it clear that our duty under the oath we swore upon becoming officers requires us to support and enforce this intolerable act, if and when it becomes law.

But there is a higher loyalty: to Virginia. The General sees the possibility of organized resistance, particularly in the Deep South. He is already thinking in terms of smothering it. But what if Virginia becomes an integral part of that resistance?

That, sadly, is where General Scott and I differ. It is not up to the Dominion to decide this matter. That is the right and prerogative of the states. If Virginia decides to enforce emancipation, I will acquiesce. If Virginia determines that the Empire has overstepped the bounds; if London has violated the terms of the Colonial Compact and Georgetown the terms of the Constitution, I will have no choice but to cast my lot with my native soil.

But surely it will not come to that! Surely a compromise will be reached, just as in 1776. There must be a way to settle this issue without bloodshed, without the Empire physically imposing its will on the South. I pray to God there are men of good faith on both---all---sides willing and able to do so...

In as black a mood as he could ever recall, Robert E. Lee remounted his horse and rode slowly up the hill to Arlington House.

Scott Townhouse
8:00 p.m.

There was an unexpected guest already in the parlor having a quiet drink with General Scott and the Duke when Colonel Burr was ushered in. If Burr was surprised to see the Chief Justice, John Marshall was literally silenced by pure shock to realize who it was offering a small, callused hand.

295

"Well, Mr. Chief Justice. Don't recall seeing you since we all left Richmond...Yes, yes, it is I. The former Vice Governor-General turned traitor-indictee, who managed to escape Jefferson's gallows in large part due to your fearless management of the trial! What do you think Cousin Tom would say if he knew we were together again, eh?"

Still dumbfounded, Marshall automatically took the thrust-out hand, while Burr grinned passed him to the host and Wellington. "I'll wager you were unaware that the Chief Justice sat in judgment on me, Your Grace. The General can tell you; he was there. Yes, a fine comedy was played out that summer in Richmond, won't you agree, Mr. Marshall..."

"What I will agree with, Colonel," said the still dazed Chief Justice, "is that my late uncle neglected to present any evidence of an overt act which would have found you guilty, if any such evidence in fact existed."

Burr turned at the sound of Maria Scott returning from giving Captain Bratton a tour of her home. "One piece of evidence we can in fact agree exists, Mr. Chief Justice. That our host indeed married above and beyond himself..."

"I can see why Jeremy Benthem considered you 'perfectly civilized,' Colonel," Captain Bratton said, with a bow and to applause and laughter.

With a sweeping gesture of her own, Maria indicated the dining room to her guests "as we are all here now."

The Duke wasted no time once everyone, including Mrs. Scott, was seated.

"Mr. Chief Justice, Colonel Burr and I dined last evening at the home of the incoming Vice G-G. General Scott and I have had private talks since soon after my arrival. We are all in agreement that you, as the Dominion's leading legal scholar, should be asked to join our efforts to contain this crisis. So I ask you flat out: do you believe the Government has the right to impose Parliamentary-approved emancipation legislation under terms of the Compact? And are you also in agreement that, under the terms of the USBA Constitution, the Governor-General is required to enforce such legislation?"

Marshall had by now shook off any lingering symptoms of Burr-induced astonishment. It soon became obvious he had been ready to articulate his position prior to the Duke's question; perhaps even before entering the Scott home:

"Gentlemen, I have participated in more than 1000 decisions during my 31 years on the Court. In fact, I've authored more than 500 opinions myself. My record is quite clear: the supremacy of Dominion law over state law. It thus follows that I also support the supremacy of Parliamentary law as agreed upon in the Colonial Compact, particularly in cases, such as this, when that law is directed at the Empire as a whole."

He paused and his tired, severe face broke into the tiniest of smiles. "You of course, also wish to know, Your Grace, my stand on slavery as an institution. I am not of the planter class in that neither my late wife nor I have ever owned slaves. In fact, I have been active for many years, and have been president for a decade, of the Richmond branch of the American Colonization Society."

The relief on Wellington's face was plainly evident. He rose and, walking around the table, extended his right hand in the American manner as the Chief Justice rose to extend his own hand. "Welcome to the team, Justice Marshall. Your counsel will be most gratefully appreciated.

"Now then, Colonel Burr, a briefing on your afternoon at The Residency, if you please."

Marshall's head had spun around to stare at the Colonel as he retook his seat. The others were also looking at Burr; apparently, the old man had been dispatched to see the G-G while everyone else of note was at the Capitol.

Burr's report was alarming, if not surprising. Jackson was not yet willing to concede that the Compact gave the Crown the right to arbitrarily abolish slavery; thus whether he himself would recommend---much less enforce---such abolition among his fellow Southerners was still debatable.

Apparently, there had been much discussion of applying a version of the nullification principle on a grand scale---that governing agreements should always be subject to review--in the kitchen cabinet. "Fortunately, Andy---though he'll raise it---doesn't really believe in it. I gather Polk is its foremost proponent, while Blair is dead-set against it."

Instead, the G-G was basing his opposition on the grounds that slavery, having been accepted by the Crown as a de facto "condition of affairs" in America in 1776, was therefore "exempt" from Parliamentary interference now or in the future. Polk, Blair and the others were apparently united behind this position.

The G-G, he concluded somewhat anticlimactically, wanted him to return late tomorrow afternoon---going in through a back entrance from a private carriage---after the Congressional leadership had been consulted. "The advisors are back there now after having heard your speech, Duke. The Congressional leaders have been asked to be at The Residency at 12 noon."

Scott and Marshall were looking at each other glumly, but Wellington surprised them with a large smile.

"We are gaining ground, gentlemen. If the G-G concedes that the Government has the right to impose emancipation without consultation with the Congress, then he will ultimately agree that his duty, under the Constitution, is to enforce it. He has not yet ruled out so conceding, according to Colonel Burr. This 'exemption' argument has no legal standing. Even I recognize that. It's a tactical retreat to buy time and see what compromises can be worked out."

Wellington's enthusiasm was falling on deaf ears, however, Captain Bratton, sitting quietly at a corner of the table, observed. Sir Arthur's words had failed to lift the gloom emanating from the General and the Chief Justice. Burr, too, looked somewhat less than enthusiastic.

Scott answered for the trio, looking not at the Duke, but at his own tight-lipped wife:

"That the Governor-General has not denied the Crown's right to impose emancipation arbitrarily is significant, Your Grace, but not much of an advance of ground. And until the South is heard from, there is no cause for celebration.

"Unless I'm very wrong, Calhoun and the others are formulating their response even as we speak. Colonel Burr here got to General Jackson early. He appealed to his Dominionist side and received some acknowledgement of the strict constitutionalist interpretation we were seeking.

"When the Southerners are in with him tomorrow, however, the appeal will be somewhat different. They won't be appealing to Andrew Jackson, Governor-General of the Dominion. They'll be seeking to fire up Andy Jackson, Southerner and planter. When we have the G-G's response to *that*, we'll know how much ground we have yet to cover."

The Duke had sat---fallen---back in his chair during Scott's analysis. Marshall and Mrs. Scott stared into their wine glasses as though contemplating a Southern revolt. A deafening silence engulfed the table.

It was Burr, naturally, who broke it, after signally for another round of wine for all. "You are of course correct that the fire-eaters will be in to see the G-G, General, though I'll lay odds they'll be storming The Residency gates this night.

"So let me tell you what Andy's response will be. To the Southerners as well as the rest of the leadership tomorrow afternoon. So you don't think all I did over there was drink up his Tennessee mash..."

The Residency
11:30 p.m.

Troup and McDuffie, as the representatives of the fire-eaters chosen by Calhoun to sound out Jackson, stood on the steps of the Main Portico with Polk, who had escorted them outside to their carriage.

How much of their agitation was liquor-induced was hard for Polk to tell: both men were as riled now as when they had arrived, despite the fact that Jackson had ordered the servants to stop serving the moment they had been announced.

"It's a compact, not a commandment," McDuffie continued to sputter. "An agreement. Well, agreements sometimes need to be revisited; if necessary, renegotiated. Or terminated. That applies to the Constitution, too. The individual states entered into both pacts peacefully and of our own free will. If necessary, we will seek to withdraw in the same manner."

He looked at Polk. "That Jackson acknowledges the potential for such an extreme solution is one of only two rays of hope we can carry back to our caucus, Mr. Polk. That and the position that slavery is exempt from tampering as a condition of the Compact itself! I suggest he get word to the rest of the leadership tomorrow morning that the South expects their support when we jointly caucus in the afternoon. That is, if he and they care about maintaining the Dominion intact.

299

"A united front will send the Duke scurrying back to advise Parliament against ram-rodding this abomination down our throats." He nodded grimly. "It's the leverage we'll need to negotiate this, under Jackson's leadership.

"Make sure, Mr. Polk, that he and they understand that," McDuffie added as he and Troup climbed into their carriage.

It's a brilliant political ploy, thought Polk, *Calhoun has devised: having the South act as if we naturally expect the support of the rest of the Dominion. Because if that support fails to materialize, we have yet another grievance to place before our Southern people.*

And even though the legal grounds for the exemption are flimsy at best, that argument, too, will strike the average Southerner as a question of inherent rights threatened. What sane man would argue that Randolph and the other Southern delegates to the Continental Congress would have agreed to the Compact if they thought it could be turned into a weapon against our institutions?

The Governor-General will not be immune to the call of the South. In the end, he'll fight for the way of life he's known and loved. I see three options here: a complete Dominion exemption; break-up of the Dominion into slave and free provinces or complete independence. Jackson has the prestige to see any of the three enacted. With Calhoun and the others pressuring from the outside and myself secretly doing the same on the inside, the Old Man will come around...

Let Parliament debate emancipation in London. Here in Georgetown, we will debate the value and importance of the Compact itself.

CHAPTER THIRTY-ONE

The Residency
Georgetown, D.C.
March 3, 1833, 7 p.m.

Leaning on his cane, Jackson stood at the window of the second floor private dining room and watched the snow fall furiously. After a two-week warm spell that had appeared to signal the coming of spring, the weather had now turned mulishly, even vengefully, colder and nastier. *Well,* he thought with a grin, *whoever does turn out tomorrow for the Inaugural will be hoping for a short speech. Which is exactly what I plan to deliver...*

Burr had arrived, as requested, about two hours ago, through the Rear Portico, though the steadily falling snow had provided sufficient camouflage in and of itself. He was now charming Eliza Blair, who had apparently never heard of him, as they awaited the arrival of Sarah Polk for dinner.

Frank Blair had been astonished when the Colonel had been announced into the kitchen cabinet meeting, the G-G thought, still smiling. *I'll have to remind him that Burr's stay in town is not grist for that newspaper of his,* The Globe. *Though the paper will again be a vital Administration tool in this new crisis. Polk, who of course knows of the Tennessee legends concerning Burr and myself, did not seem totally surprised. Lewis Cass, however, was floored...*

Perhaps James' capacity for astonishment has already been exceeded by the weekend's events; he had sat back quietly to see what new surprises were in store after being introduced to Aaron. Cass, meanwhile, had stared at Burr as if the Colonel was Lazarus exiting the tomb...

Without disclosing the whereabouts of their meeting *(I must remember to question young Wilder tomorrow),* Burr had reported that Wellington approved of the plan to call the 23rd Congress into session in early June to deal with the crisis. *That will allow plenty of time for all factions in the new Congress to get a handle on the people's opinions before opening the debate here.* The Colonel had added, seemingly off-handedly, that Chief Justice Marshall was "confident" a majority of the Court would rule, if called upon, that Parliament was well within its rights under terms of the Compact to impose emancipation…and that the Constitution required the G-G to enforce it.

We were all caught by surprise at the mention of Marshall and the Court, though I should have anticipated it.

"His Grace has been thorough, Colonel Burr," Blair had said, "lining up the Court well in advance of any legal challenge. What other 'allies' has he lined up, may I ask?"

Polk had also moved quickly in: "Yes, especially what about Mr. Van Buren? He has been most conspicuously absent these past few days…"

Burr had smiled (*how the Colonel is enjoying this!*): "I have spoken with the incoming Vice G-G. He finds himself in an unusual and delicate position. He has been a key member of the Administration and expects to remain so throughout the second term. However, he fully supports the Compact…and the Constitution."

Everyone present had immediately grasped the old man's meaning. Cass, in particular, had seemed outraged, but I wasn't particularly upset…or surprised:

"I understand Matty Van's position, Colonel. In his shoes, I would probably feel and act likewise."

Wellington has sent multiple messages tonight: the Court will rule in London's favor, which will influence public opinion, especially in the MidAtlantic and Western states; my new Vice G-G also supports London and is thus both available and ready to replace me, unless I go along; and I have until Congress convenes to convince the South to accept emancipation.

Yes, my old commander, it looks like a rout at the moment. But you've had the benefit of surprise. Now it is up to me to turn that surprise to my advantage…

The G-G broke his reverie and turned around at the sound of Sarah Polk's arrival to face his guests. "Well ladies, I'm afraid we'll be breaking my usual rule about limiting political talk at Sunday evening supper. We spent so much time this afternoon listening to Colonel Burr here tell us about his discussions last evening that we never had time to tell him what went on with the Leadership earlier today.

"It was actually quite interesting, Colonel…"

The Capitol
Georgetown, D.C.
March 4, 1833, 12 p.m.:

The snow continued to fall sporadically and the heavy gray skies seemed matched by the mood of the small, tense crowd that was gathering on and in front of the steps leading to the Capitol's main entrance. A dais and temporary seating, now being dug out by teams of civilian and USBAA workers, had been constructed on the steps of the entrance, which, illogically, faced southeast…away from the city.

There had been talk about moving the ceremonies inside but Jackson had rejected it. So a crowd limited mainly to members of Congress, high Administration figures and heartier members of the diplomatic corps, as well as the press, were on hand as Jackson's carriage and Marine honor guard pulled up to the steps. (Wellington was seated in a place of honor among the dais' dignitaries, to the incoming Vice Governor-General's right.)

Assisted by the Marine officer, Goodwin, Jackson climbed carefully up to the dais, where Van Buren and Marshall greeted him. "Well Mr. Van Buren. So the rumors of your demise are unfounded. We have much to talk about. I'll expect you in my office 10 a.m. sharp tomorrow."

Matty Van flashed his trademark noncommittal smile and bowed his head quickly. "As you wish, Governor-General." Marshall, looking judicially formal in his long black robe, merely shook Jackson's hand and gestured him to his seat.

The ceremonies proceeded quickly: Marshall administered the oaths of office, first to Van Buren and then to Jackson, without placing special emphasis on any word or phrase in either oath. To the uninformed, it would have appeared an impressively solemn though less-than-dramatic performance.

That was how Count Renkowiitz, wrapped in a heavy fur great coat and standing in the crowd with Count Ignatieff, perceived the scene. Nicholas, however, studied the proceedings with a professional eye. As at the two previous Capitol Building speeches, the lack of armed soldiers surprised him. *If I had been in charge of security arrangements, Jackson would have come out from the Capitol Building to a dais built on the top landing. The crowd would have been kept considerably farther away. And the steps would have been filled with troops armed to the teeth…*

Now Jackson, who had stood facing the Chief Justice behind the dais' podium for the oath, turned and looked out at the politely cheering crowd. The snow had, at least momentarily, stopped but there were no breaks in the dismal overcast. The G-G opened the folder that had been previously placed on the podium and quickly ran through the customary dignitarial acknowledgements before pausing.

"Fellow Americans…" Jackson began, and a gasp raced through the crowd.

The Duke looked up in puzzlement as the buzzing continued. Van Buren understood, but dismissed the thought to explain that Inaugural Addresses traditionally began: "Fellow citizens of His Majesty's Dominion…"

By chance, Henry Clay stood no more than ten feet from the previous Vice G-G. The new Senator from South Carolina nodded shortly to Representative Polk, who had turned to him, as the G-G resumed his remarks.

"…my original intention was to share with you today plans for a revision in our banking system and to announce the comprehensive, systematic program for Western expansion which I will be sending to London shortly. Such issues are still of vital…"

The incoming Senator from New Jersey, Samuel Southard, nodded his own head and muttered to those around him: "Damn right the bank issue is vital. Unless the old fool wants to lead us into a crash…"

"…48 hours ago, an issue of such grave magnitude was announced to the Congress, after having been brought to my attention for the first time the previous afternoon, that all other issues must…"

Burr, standing in the rear of the crowd, turned to the attending Lieutenant Wilder. "Here it comes, with the vinegar still on, as they say out West…"

"…therefore, I will call the 23rd Congress into existence on June 3rd, 93 days from today, to deal with the emancipation issue. This timeframe will allow those members of Congress here today to travel back to their districts and consult with their constituents. It will as well allow new members to likewise consult, once the news reaches their respective districts. By the time Congress convenes, news of the progress of the legislation through Parliament…"

Along with a self-congratulatory epistle from the great Quincy himself, thought Webster.

Jackson had again paused, as the crowd's murmurs increased and visions of a historic Congressional debate formed in most minds.

"…As I wish the citizens to carefully consider the ramifications of this issue in every possible context, I will refrain at this time from delivering myself of an opinion concerning it…"

Good, thought Frank Blair, *that's placing yourself above the fray for the time being. Wellington certainly can't act to remove you, if you haven't announced a position, publicly or privately. Let's take the people's temperature first…*

"…Our Dominion, fellow Americans, was forged in the white-hot heat of 1776. The Compact written by Franklin and Burke has benefited those on both sides of the Atlantic. The Constitution our forefathers drew up has guided the Dominion to internal prosperity of a degree not conceivable 57 years ago.

"Yet these two beloved and prized documents skirt an issue that has lurked in the shadows for more than 150 years…"

Representative McDuffie looked over Floride Calhoun's head and at her husband. A single word formed on Calhoun's lips: "Exemption."

"…thus, for better or for worse, the issue is placed in front of us. Even if the heat rising from it becomes itself white-hot, we---the generations of British Americans active today---must confront it.

"That process will begin as the members of the 22nd Congress arrive back in their home states. In three months, the members of the 23rd Congress will convene in the building behind me to determine the will of the people.

"Meanwhile, we will continue here in Georgetown with the business of government. God Save the King! And God Bless America!"

The Residency
March 4, 1833, 8 p.m.:

This time the Tennesseans, who had mostly foregone the snow and cold of the Inaugural ceremonies for the warmth of the city's numerous taprooms, were limited in their admittance to the mansion.

Emily Donelson had been firm with her uncle: order and decorum would be maintained during the reception. She had even commandeered a squad of USBA Marines to regulate entry to The Residency. Lieutenant Wilder was on duty tonight in his social aide capacity but Arthur Goodwin, after placing his Marine honor guard in ceremonial positions along the walls, had also assumed responsibility for the entrances.

So it was that the social chaos of Jackson's first Inaugural was replaced by the quieter---though deadlier---chaos of high-stakes politics:

Despite their eagerness to depart for their various homes, most of the Congressional leadership passed through the mansion, worriedly conferring with other members of their own parties and sectional factions as well as members from other sections with whom they were personally friendly.

The Duke of Wellington, attended by Captain Bratton and Sir John Burrell, appeared cordial and remarkably serene to all factions: he chose to project an air of confident complacency that Parliament's intentions, once announced, would thus automatically be initiated. Only the two aides were aware how deeply troubled he was, not only by Jackson's maneuverings, but also by the overall reaction of the USBA political and economic governing classes to the emancipation concept.

Though gravely worried, General Scott utilized his tried-and-true public posture: the USBA military never commented on civilian legislative matters.

The diplomatic corps buzzed among itself. Jacques Jean-Claude expressed it best to a group including Prussia's Van Benes and the Mexican, Valenzuela: "It is like watching a Shakespearean drama unfold in place of the comedy previously promised."

Jackson himself was the picture of composure: he stood with his niece welcoming all his guests and accepting congratulations and good wishes, occasionally turning to whisper some comments to Blair or Cass. Only the kitchen cabinet was aware of the conflicting pressures tormenting the G-G.

The Vice G-G was also continuously circled by well-wishers; only those at the highest levels had yet thought through the crisis far enough to realize the inevitable deterioration of his relationship with Jackson.

Only Colonel Burr, standing quietly anonymous in the crowd, seemed to be truly enjoying the reception: the old adventurer was relishing his role as secret go-between and advisor. And now Lieutenant Wilder had just introduced him to a most remarkable creature: Candice Samples. *Andy had it right after all,* the Colonel thought with a chuckle: *God Bless America!*

Monticello Tavern
8pm:

Even Cris Donfield made it to Monticello by the appointed hour, to find Tousaint's group virtually the only customers in the dusky, dirty barroom. He moved toward the rear table they regularly occupied and ordered a beer.

He and the others---Ugene Doby and Marion Motley---were still stunned that a government plan to end slavery might be at hand. And they were even more stunned to find out how angrily Tousaint Numidia disapproved.

It was very simple, Tousaint explained as patiently as his fiery temper would allow: "The British Congress---what they call their Parliament and which has power over the Congress here in Georgetown---agrees that slavery is an abomination.

"But not so much of an abomination that they want to end it now. No, this Parliament wants to wait seven more years---seven more years during which our maumba will continue to suffer and die---before they do anything about it."

Tousaint looked at his followers: "What kind of uhura is that? If Parliament can abolish slavery in seven years, why wait? Why not now!"

There was silence around the table as Tousaint, in an imitation of his father which somehow lacked the same effect, slammed his fist on the rough wood surface, rattling his own glass of rum and the beers of the others.

Ugene, whose Interior clerkship gave him a somewhat more sophisticated view of the world than that available to a hotel porter or a consulate maintenance man, shook his head.

"I don't know, Simba. Don't seem there's much we can do about it. If the Brits are serious about emancipation, that's the best news I've heard in years. Even though it might be sometime down the road…"

Donfield was shaking his head in agreement: "That's right, Simba. Sure, we'd like emancipation right away, but at least we do know now when it's coming."

Tousaint was growing angrier by the second. "Don't you dumb bastards understand? Seven years from now is 1840. Lot could happen by then. Just suppose that King William over there dies? Who's to say this young girl who's next in line for the throne will go along? Who's to say she'll be allowed to go along? Who's to say she'll even be queen?

"And these damn planters! Give *them* seven years to organize and who knows what will happen. Moses says the Brits are prepared to back up emancipation by force…"

"Then whats you be worried 'bout Simba? Da Redcoats make 'em do it at da barrel of a rifle!" Motley spoke for the first time.

Numidia looked at Motley and smiled as if about to explain something fundamental to a child. "Because, Marion, there's no guarantee the Royal Army will be able to enforce emancipation…"

Doby laughed: "Shit, Simba, who's gonna stop them? Not those tin soldiers over at the War Department!"

Tousaint was grim: "Those tin soldiers threw the French out of the Louisiana Territory and helped the Brits defeat Napoleon, Ugene. Don't underestimate them. But I wasn't talking about the USBA fighting the Brits. Europe's gone 20 years now without a war. That's some kind of white man's record. By 1840, the Royal Army could be tied up anywhere from Greece to India…"

"You done lost me, Simba." Motley was laughing. "Only grease Ah knows be on a wagon wheel. As for Injuns, ain't that who da Dominian army be fightin' wit' now?"

Tousaint's frustration was obvious, so Ugene, the most educated of his followers, decided to call a halt. "Okay, Simba, you ain't happy with the wait. We get that. Is that why you wanted to meet here tonight…to let us know you're pissed…or do you have something else to add?"

Numidia grinned. Doby was a lot smarter than he looked…or let on. "Right Ugene. I got a plan. A plan that will force the damn Brits to declare uhura. Now!"

Donfield groaned. "I was afraid of this. Okay, Simba. What you got in mind...knowing that we ain't necessarily agreeing to follow through on whatever the hell it is..."

His leadership confirmed, Tousaint looked around the table in triumph. "What I have in mind, gentlemen, is to encourage Parliament to speed up the uhura process..."

Now it was Ugene's turn to roll his eyes and groan. "And exactly how..."

"By taking the Duke of Wellington prisoner and holding him for ransom."

"For ransom?" Donfield spit out the words along with a mouthful of beer. While the others sat looking at Tousaint in shock, he continued: "Why, so we can buy our maumba free ourselves?"

"Not for money. We ransom Wellington for a speed-up in uhura. A formal agreement to free all the slaves in the USBA within 12 months time."

"Dear Lordy." Donfield was pounding both his head and his fist against the table. "We're dealing with a madman. Lord help us..."

Doby, however, was assessing Numidia with a sober, somber look. "I know you've thought this out, Simba. So tell me: how is four niggas gonna blackmail the British Parliament? What makes you think the Brits---or the USBA authorities---will keep any bargains they make with us?

"Hell, the moment we give Wellington back...and that's saying we can snatch and hold him for as long as it takes...they'll hunt us down like Nat Turner..."

Tousaint silently played with his rum glass long enough to let Doby's question sink in. "I agree, no question they wouldn't honor any agreements with us, Ugene...

"But don't you think they would with the New England Abolitionist Society?"

CHAPTER THIRTY-TWO

Constantinople, Ottoman Empire
March 10, 1833, 7 a.m.:

Sir John Ponsonby, British Ambassador to the Porte, was a student of ancient history as well as an amateur archeologist. This Sunday morning, he was up early and had left the Embassy with an aide to explore some recently uncovered ruins just outside the city walls. Prior examination indicated the find might predate the Roman period.

So it was that he was among the first residents of Constantinople to witness the amazing sight: A rag-tag armada of warships was escorting a remarkably-diverse convoy of merchant vessels, fishing boats, pleasure craft and barges moving slowly and carefully through the Straights.

Sir John's puzzlement at the sight---the warships' designs were unlike any he had previously understood the Sultan's pitiful Navy to possess and yet looked remarkably outdated to even his nonprofessional glance---grew as guns began to boom on the city walls. It soon became clear, however, that the Turks were intent on greeting, not destroying, the fleet which now moved closer to Ponsonby's vantage point atop the shoreline ruins.

Alistair Tudsbury, the Embassy's talkative second secretary, stood at the Ambassador's side, his mouth open and gargling sounds alone escaping. Young Tudsbury had been as startled as Ponsonby himself when the ships had come into view and the artillery salute commenced. Now Tudsbury, who had served a four-year hitch as a junior officer in the Royal Navy and had the best eyesight at the Embassy, was pointing at the two ships-of-the-line, his hand visibly shaking.

"Sir John, do you see it? What the devil...? I say, this is most improbable!"

Ponsonby turned to his now red-faced aide: "What is it, Tudsbury? Damn it! What do you see? You know how nearsighted I am! This bloody flotilla is too far out in the Straights for me to make out anything definitive…"

The shaken Ambassador now looked up at the walls. A growing clamor rose from the throngs of merchants, workers and other city residents staring at the stunning scene. The uniformed Ottoman soldiers, however, were gazing out impassively, while the gun crews continued the salute now being answered by the ships in the Straights.

Tudsbury, having regained his self-control, spoke to his superior while looking out onto the Bosporus: "I count two 70-plus gun warships, Sir. Four frigates of roughly 40 guns apiece. A dozen or more gunboats. Haven't had time to count the transports, but they're clearly packed with men and horses. Can see some artillery, too, Sir John."

The former ensign, pausing, now turned and looked Ponsonby in the eye: "And they're all flying the white double eagle flag…

"That, Sir John, is a Czarist fleet coming through the Straights. With the permission, apparently, of the Porte. Headed out into the open waters of the Mediterranian…"

Rose Hill Plantation
Yancyville, N.C.
March 20, 1833:

Count Nicholas Ignatieff, aka Andre Karlhamanov, rode up the winding driveway that led to the home of North Carolina's senior USBA Senator, Bedford Brown. He carried with him an invitation that had arrived while he was visiting Virginia Senator Tyler's plantation in Charles City County.

Nicholas was thus far pleased with the results of his travels and meetings with the Southern leadership. Both Governor Floyd and Tyler had angrily denounced Parliament's unilateral move to abolish slavery. Floyd was also particularly incensed that Wellington had violated Virginia's hospitality by never mentioning the issue when previously visiting Richmond:

"The man comes down here virtually unannounced, holds talks with us on a number of Dominion issues and then returns to Georgetown accompanied by both Tyler and Rives. Yet he never mentions the real reason for his visit here! That verges on the duplicitous, Sir!

"God knows I'm on record as wanting a quick end to this impractical, obsolete system of labor. But it is an issue for each state to determine individually and in its own good time. Parliament has no right to arbitrarily abolish it by vote or Imperial decree!"

Keeping strictly to his role of visiting college professor and fascinated observer of the American Dominion, Nicholas had listened respectfully, nodding and asking appropriate questions, both at the Governor's residence and later, while visiting Tyler's Walnut Grove Plantation. He had been impressed with the beauty of the state while traveling south towards North Carolina, the prosperity of its (white) people and their fierce love of what they regarded as their true homeland.

He had in fact remarked to Senator Tyler---who was resting up during a break in a hastily arranged statewide speaking tour---on the ambiguity of the Virginians' feelings toward Dominion and Empire.

"We are not as extreme as the South Carolinians," Tyler had replied with a smile, "who resent any Dominion or Imperial 'intrusion,' so to speak, in their affairs. We are more practical: we understand that there is a give-and-take. The Dominion maintains order, provides a unified currency and allows for free trade. The Empire protects us internationally and provides markets for our crops, particularly cotton and tobacco. In return, we abide by decisions affecting all the states as determined in Georgetown and London.

"However, our peculiar institution is not a Dominion-wide issue. It is, by and large, confined to the South. Thus, its future must be determined by the South. When Franklin and Burke sat down to negotiate their famous Compact, they purposely refrained from mentioning slavery as it was not an issue causing conflict between the mother country and the colonies, nor among the colonies themselves. Since it was never considered, never debated and never voted upon in '76 by either the Continental Congress or the Parliament, it is not an issue that either of those august bodies can at this late date take it upon themselves to adjudicate!"

Secretly pleased with the apparent determination of the Virginians to oppose Imperially-imposed emancipation, Nicholas had put on a face of confusion: but how could they stop the procedure, short of armed resistance...unthinkable, correct?

312

Tyler had been grim: "Once the North and the West realize that this mandatory abolition is unacceptable, they will accede to our wishes. The Western economy, especially, is dependent upon our good will. They must have free access down the Mississippi River to deliver their goods to New Orleans for shipment. And Jackson is a Southerner, a planter himself! He will rally his supporters in the other sections and then, backed by a united Dominion, force Wellington to the bargaining table.

"Let the Empire impose its will elsewhere. We of the Dominion enjoy a special status. An exemption will be negotiated..."

Nicholas had looked at the fiery Virginian with a most earnest, solemn expression. "And if either the North or Parliament refuses...?"

Tyler was hard-faced: "In that extreme instance, which I pray and expect will never occur, the Dominion as a whole, and the South in particular, will consider its options..."

The Senator was on his way back from meetings in the state capitol and was expected later in the day, Mary Brown said in welcoming her visitor. The couple's bevy of rambunctious children raced from across the landscape with various playmates of darker shades, all eager to see the unexpected visitor.

Eye patch firmly in place, Nicholas/Andre was an object of intense fascination to the children, both white and black, as he relaxed and awaited his host, whom he barely remembered from Georgetown. (Nicholas actually had difficulty remembering one Southerner from another, with a single exception: John C. Calhoun. That object of his highest intentions had not yet issued an invitation to visit Fort Hill Plantation, but Nicholas hoped to prevail on his 'official' South Carolina host, Congressman McDuffie, to so arrange.)

Brown, who had entered politics at the ripe age of 19 with election to the state legislature, turned out to be an affable man of about 35. His views on emancipation---tempered by his ownership of some 200 slaves---were much the same as the Virginians: the call on abolition was the right of each state, not the Dominion or Imperial governments. Any phased-in emancipation plan was also out-of-the-question for a variety of practical reasons: impact on the Southern and Dominion economies; obvious inability of the 'servants' to fend for themselves; etc.

"I'm not a highly educated man, Mr. Karlhamanov," the Senator said as they sat on the mansion's veranda after dinner. "But I am a practical one. I see advances in science, mechanics, engineering which will someday transform the way we operate our plantation system. That transformation will be gradual. Concurrently, we will transform the blacks into a self-sustaining, productive and relatively unsupervised segment of the overall Southern society.

"It can not happen overnight, or over seven years or at Parliamentary whim, however, Sir!" Brown looked hard at Nicholas, as if seeing him clearly for the first time:

"Surely you don't advocate the immediate and unplanned emancipation of your country's serfs, Mr. Karlhamanov? I thought not. You, of all foreigners in the USBA, should understand the South's position.

"We will not have the fabric of our society torn apart at the whim of a deliberative body 3000 miles away which would be better off looking at the social injustices so famously prevalent on their own side of the Atlantic!"

Nicholas could not keep the smile from his face. "I realize more each day the commonality of our two societies, Senator, the Southern and the Russian. Though I am a mere subject of the Czar here unofficially and privately, I believe my government would not be unsympathetic to the South's plight if London attempts to forcibly impose emancipation. Nor do I believe my government would be upset to learn that such sentiments were, unofficially, expressed to key members of the Southern leadership, such as yourself.

"In fact, I would enjoy expressing that view to other key members…"

Highly educated perhaps he was not, but Senator Brown knew the universal language of politics.

Mr. Karlhamanov---if that is your real name---you are not here on an extended holiday. I'm not yet sure what game you are playing, but you may be useful in the high-stakes game we have been dealt into…

"Tell me, Mr. Karlhamanov, do your travel plans include South Carolina? There are several gentlemen down there who might enjoy speaking with you…"

Foreign Office
London, England
March 28, 1833:

The Ambassador had hired a fast sloop and dispatched Tudsbury towards Gibraltar before the Russian fleet had completed its progression through the Straights. The second secretary carried a hurried verbal message for the Foreign Office.

Now he was being ushered in to see Lord Palmerston himself. Although he had calmed the shaken Ponsonby somewhat---evaluating the dilapidated Russian fleet as unworthy of comparison with a British squadron---the Ambassador had insisted that an eyewitness report be made to London.

So Tudsbury had made the voyage, though he had no definitive information about where the Russki armada might be headed. He had, of course, reported in to Admiral Hotham at Gibraltar, so the Mediterranian fleet was already notified and on alert. Tudsbury had been mystified by the Admiral's reaction, however; the C-in-C, Med had been more interested in the transports than the warships...

Palmerston's reaction, after an initial outburst of indignant swearing, had also been surprising. "Yes, yes, Mr. Tudsbury, no doubt we could take the whole Russki fleet down before breakfast. But had Sir John no idea they were coming or where they were headed? Constantinople, I've always understood to be a veritable hot bed of espionage, with rumors flying in all directions. Additionally, a warning was dispatched from here last month..."

"Never received it, eh?" The Foreign Secretary sighed and continued:

"All right, Mr. Tudsbury. You'll await an F.O. pouch now being prepared for Sir John and then return to your duty post. Shouldn't be more than two-to-three days. But tell me, now: what is the official mood in the Porte over this Egyptian insurrection? It looks from here as though the Arabs might actually make a run on Anatolia itself! What have you heard?"

The Second Secretary was stunned and chagrined: *why hadn't we stopped to analyze the options?*

Lord Palmerston saw the dawning of understanding in the younger man's eyes. "Yes, Mr. Tudsbury, we've had some indication here for several weeks that the fool Sultan has asked Czar Nicholas for help against the forces of Mehmet Ali now besieging Acre. I'm disturbed that Sir John in Constantinople hadn't yet gotten word of that before the Russkis came sailing down from the Black Sea! They're headed to Syria, all right, with as many as 10,000 troops, to head the Arab army off.

"Nothing we can due officially at this point, of course. Not with the Russians formally invited to intervene. But Sir John must watch closely for any signs that this detente between St. Petersburg and Constantinople doesn't turn into an alliance. Our road to India must remain open. That's what's actually at risk here. It will all be covered in the instructions you'll carry back. But emphasize to Ponsonby my deep concern. Every effort short of war must be made to keep the Russians and the Ottomans from signing a pact!"

Palmerston shook his head, the unique beard that allowed for a clean-shaven chin but bushy outgrowths down both sides of his face now bristling. "Yet, if Ali is successful, I'm afraid his delusions of a pan-Arabic kingdom throughout the Near East could also threaten the India road."

The Foreign Secretary peered over his glasses at Tudsbury, who was nodding his head like the ensign he had once been.

"Quite a diplomatic tightrope you people are walking there in Constantinople, wouldn't you say?"

Palmerston pointed his head at the door in dismissal. "Good luck, Tudsbury. And find out what the devil happened to that pouch informing Sir John the Russians were coming!"

War Department
Georgetown, D.C.
March 29, 1833:

Winfield Scott put down the latest version of Lieutenant Wilder's report on USBAA officer strength, minus its Southern contingent. The report had been revised several times, the latest to reflect possible defections among British Army half-pay officers currently serving with the Dominion forces.

"This is more like it, Lieutenant," Scott said, the leonine head nodding approvingly. "Eighteen percent of our officer corps are half-pays. I agree that most half-pays won't cut their ties to the Mother Country, but about 10% is a conceivable figure. There undoubtedly are some, like this Lieutenant Bassett, who have put down roots in the South."

Half-pay officers, like Harry Bratton, were regular Royal Army officers demobilized but subject to sudden and immediate RA recall. They received half the salary due active officers of their rank as inducement to remain on-call, but were allowed to pursue other avenues of employment while deactivated. Some, like Bratton, opted for positions in the Government. Others joined, with RA approval, other active forces associated with the Royal Army: many served in "John Company's" Indian Army. Others were serving in the USBAA or in Australia or Cape Colony. Lt. Harry Bassett, the second son of a Sussex baronet (many half-pay officers were younger sons of minor nobles who stood little change of succeeding to the title), had recently married the daughter of the Governor of Mississippi.

"I believe we now have a more accurate evaluation of our potential officer strength minus all prospective defectors," Scott continued, "senior and junior officers, plus the half-pays." He paused and grimaced, then glared at Tom fiercely.

"Just because it's accurate doesn't make it promising, however, Lieutenant. Out of a total available active officer corps of 2,400 we figure to lose about 80% of the Southerners. That's about 960; a tremendous dent. Then add in a half dozen or so half-pays. That doesn't leave enough competent officers---in confidence, I judge roughly 10% of the entire pool incompetent under any circumstances---to maintain order on the frontiers, keep the Quebecois sullen but not mutinous, and put down any potential Southern rebellion."

His glare turned to a strange, mirthless smile. "Any ideas, Lieutenant?"

Tom, who was still shattered by the possibility, however miniscule, that close friends like Robert Lee and, yes, Joe Johnston, might soon be facing him across an open space---as well as respected senior officers like Zach Taylor or the legendary Albert Sidney Johnston---looked mournfully at his boss.

"Well, Sir. There are the state militias, especially the Western ones…"

"Yes there are. Some of those Ohio and Illinois boys fought well against Chief Black Hawk. I was particularly impressed with one Ohioan, Colonel Felton. But go on."

"There's certain to be foreign volunteers. I mean, Sir, real foreigners, like French or Prussians. As well as perhaps some more half-pays from England…"

Scott scowled: "Yes, no doubt we'd see some European adventurers. For what they'd be worth. As for half-pays, if they volunteer, fine. But we will not ask the War Office for help." His entire huge bulk shook forcefully. "There's another potential pool of experienced officers, Lieutenant. I'm surprised it hasn't come to mind. Especially with your education…"

Cheeks blazing red, Tom frantically concentrated on Scott's last words. Of course! The most obvious pool of all!

"Yes, Sir, there is another experienced pool. Unfortunately, any potential rebel force would also be drawing on it…"

"Nothing we can do about that, Lieutenant. If we can't stop active duty West Pointers from resigning their commissions to go South, we certainly can't stop former West Pointers who have already resigned. But we'd get our share. That's the main secondary pool I'm relying on."

"How do we go about identifying and contacting them, Sir?"

Scott smiled his first true smile of the meeting. "I have already initiated the project, Lieutenant. Before your friend Colonel Burr left town, I asked him to carry a verbal message to Colonel Thayer at the Point. While you've been honing your list, Colonel Thayer has been working on his. I've heard from him. We can expect projections by mid-April."

Tom was by now used to the back channels being utilized in this crisis, but sending Colonel Burr with a message to the Point Superintendent still stunned him. Apparently, it showed.

"You seem surprised, Lieutenant. Is it the message…or the messenger?"

"Well, General, I guess I am a little shocked. I've assumed Colonel Burr was some sort of go-between from Wellington to Jackson and back while he was down here. But I guess utilizing him on a strictly War Department matter does surprise me, Sir."

General Scott stared at his aide for a long minute, an eternity it seemed to Tom, before replying. "Lieutenant, this is the most serious crisis the Department---and the Dominion---has ever faced. But it is still under control. There haven't yet been the whispers of secession heard during the nullification crisis---as least not that we've heard here--nor have any shots been fired. So far...

"Those things could easily come to fruition, however, if word that we were preparing contingency plans to put down a rebellion got out. Yet, we'd be derelict if we didn't begin such planning. That's why your report has been kept under such tight wraps. Same thing with the ex-West Pointers. We need to see what we can expect from that talent pool. Yet I can't risk having a written order inadvertently---or advertently---uncovered that could be used to fan the flames.

"Colonel Burr has demonstrated a certain flair for this type of thing. And, he was heading back to New York in any case. As far as anyone who might ask knows, he simply took the Hudson steamer to the Point on his way to see a client in Orange County, Newburgh or thereabouts."

Tom nodded his head. "I see, Sir."

The General smiled: "Intelligence work is at least as complex as engineering, won't you agree, Lieutenant?"

"Yes Sir. And quite a bit more interesting." For the first time ever, his face didn't redden at a Scott jibe concerning his West Point record.

"Now then, Lieutenant: what's new on the frontiers? Has Zack Taylor ever located Sam Houston? What's your analysis of *that?*"

#10 Downing Street
London, England
March 29, 1833:

Armed with notes from his Tudsbury meeting and a draft of the instructions for Ponsonby, Palmerston was meeting with the P.M. and Lord Melbourne. The Government, he wryly observed, was faced with a series of interlocking dilemmas.

A dilapidated, tottering Ottoman Empire was more pliable than a vigorous new Arab Near East kingdom would be. Therefore, it benefited the Empire to see the Turks put down their rebellious vassal. Yet, calling in the Russians to do so, while it would most probably end the Egyptian threat, had the potential of bringing worse: the Russians, once ensconced, never withdrew from newly-occupied territory voluntarily…

So the threat to unrestricted overland access to India was potentially more alarming once the Bear chased the Gypos back across the Nile than even a successful Arab takeover of the Ottoman domains would be…

The tired-looking P.M., however, questioned the seriousness of the Egyptian threat: "This Ali Pasha. Does he pose a realistic danger? These desert chieftains are just glorified banditti, are they not? Like the Tripoli pirates we used the USBA Marines to clear out back during the Boney wars?"

Palmerton shook his head firmly. "No Prime Minister, I've concluded that they could pose a serious threat. In fact, I wrote Ponsonby a private note about Ali just this morning. Let me read from it to you:

"…Mehmet Ali's actual aim seems to be establishing an Arab kingdom embracing all the Arabic-tongue peoples. This project may contribute to dividing the Ottoman Empire, and there is no excuse for allowing an Arab king to supplant the Turks in controlling the road to India…"

Lord Melbourne shook his head in agreement. "I concur. It is in our interest to keep the Ottomans in power and the Arabs subjugated and divided. So we have to root for the Russians to put Ali in his place.

"But once done, how do we convince the Bear to leave Syria? That's the question, Henry."

Palmerston looked firmly at the others. "A delicate combination of diplomacy and saber-rattling, my Lords. For various reasons, their own security and otherwise, the other Powers do not wish to see a more powerful Romanov empire anymore than we do.

"We must raise a diplomatic coalition in opposition, while at the same time polishing our own bayonets a bit. The Mediterranean fleet must be reinforced and the Army put on alert. Also, Prince Leiven called in for a discreet discussion."

Melbourne again nodded his head in agreement. The Prime Minister, however, was gazing for some reason at the portrait of his discredited predecessor, Lord North, on the far wall.

"That's all well and good, Henry. And I approve and authorize the steps you propose. Now tell me, however: what affect do you see this crisis having on the Duke of Wellington's mission to the USBA?"

The two Cabinet ministers appeared stunned. They looked slowly at each other and then at the P.M. It was Melbourne who spoke first:

"By God, Prime Minister. In all the excitement over the Near East, I'm afraid we've overlooked America and the emancipation issue completely. This could indeed be a sticky wicket on that front..."

The Foreign Secretary had stood up and was now pacing the room. "Wellington must be informed immediately of the Ottoman developments, of course, Prime Minister. It is more essential than ever that he arrange peaceful acceptance of emancipation in British America. Certainly, we cannot afford trouble over there while we attempt to safeguard India and keep the balance of power in the Near East.

"That chap from the Colonial Office who briefed the committee and expressed the opinion that the South would resist. He went to Georgetown with Wellington, did he not? Well, we must reemphasize to the Duke that the man's prediction must simply, *by no means*, be allowed to come to fruition."

He turned to the others. "With your permission, Prime Minister, I'll write the Duke tonight and send it by special packet. He must be informed how the international situation has changed. And that he must, accordingly, adjust. The last thing we can afford is anarchy in America!"

CHAPTER THIRTY-THREE

Tuscaloosa, Alabama
April 2, 1833, 3:30 p.m.:

Despite the assistance of Senator Brown, Nicholas had never caught up to John C. Calhoun. Not, at least, until today.

The South Carolinian had apparently deposited his wife at Fort Hill Plantation and then embarked on a series of meetings and speeches throughout the South, angrily condemning Parliament for the effrontery of even introducing an emancipation bill. He was also demanding that Jackson a) denounce the "abominable concept" and b) force his Northern supporters to do likewise.

Calhoun had crisscrossed the deep South---Louisiana, Mississippi, Alabama, Georgia and Florida Territory---always several steps ahead of the "visiting Russian liberal professor." Ignatieff had engaged in healthy conversation with Georgia's Senator Troup when he encountered that worthy firing up a crowd in Savannah. Troup had also caught the inferences in Nicholas' respectful style that Brown had originally picked up. He had "wondered" aloud how the Czar's friendship could be significantly helpful to the South.

Troup directed Nicholas to this rough-and-ready village on the Black Warrior River that served as Alabama's capitol. Though the legislature was not in session, Calhoun was addressing a large outdoor gathering here most of this hot, sunny afternoon.

Perhaps because their planter society was so new---the last Indian tribes had barely been cleared from the state---and their lives resultantly so suddenly prosperous, the Alabamans had a more primeval reaction to the emancipation news than those in the older, more established states. They were angry and rebellious even before the great orator began his speech. By the time Calhoun reached his peak, the crowd was ready to burn any British flags---and Britons--- found in the town.

Ignatieff, who admired Calhoun's style even if he could not literally or philosophically follow some of the Senator's more

322

outlandish rhetorical tangents, waited patiently under a tree (and out of the sun) for the speech to conclude.

Although the Russian would not have understood the term, what he was hearing was an early version of the stump speech for which Calhoun would soon be even more (in)famous, one in which he asserted that slavery was a 'positive good.'

All societies, the Senator claimed, are ruled by an elite class that enjoys the fruits of the labors of the less-privileged. (Calhoun illustrated with examples ranging from the Spartans' domination of their Peloponnesian neighbors to the Empire's own exploitation of India). Unlike the laboring class in the Northern and European cities, cast aside by the owner-class to die in poverty when too old, sick or feeble to work, the Southern slave was cared for even when no longer productive.

Nicholas, who had never given the Russian serf system much thought---that the serfs allowed themselves to be bullied and terrorized by the local estate owner, backed by a handful of Cossacks, marked them as little more than two-legged work animals---saw no necessary reason for such a lofty offensive-defense. The system in place was benefiting those in the crowd; naturally they'd fight to maintain it. But he could see that it fired up the Alabamans.

Cries of "bravo," "damn straight," and even a few "down with the Crown" punctured the blistering, humid air. At the end, Calhoun was carried off on the shoulders of his jubilant supporters, leaving Ignatieff to follow in their wake, sputtering Russian oaths.

He didn't have far to go: the crowd headed immediately to Tuscaloosa's largest inn, The War Eagle, from whose veranda Calhoun again addressed the crowd. This time, the fire-eater confined his remarks to the inviolability of states rights, and complimented the citizenry on having the wisdom to elect such Southern-rights activists as the two men standing with him, Governor John Gayle and Congressman Clement C. Clay. The crowd then happily pushed on inside, occupying every inch of the bar and two dining rooms, spilling over into the dusty street. Beer and harder spirits suddenly, magically, appeared in every hand.

It therefore took Nicholas some time to work his way close to Calhoun and the other politicos, who were standing hard, surrounded by a semi-circle of admirers, against the center of the bar. They were drinking, he observed, as thirstily as any spectator. Troup had described the one aide Calhoun was traveling with: a tall, frail red-headed young man. Ignatieff finally managed to edge close enough to the aide to whisper in his ear and pass an envelope given him by the Georgia Senator. Glancing briefly at the note, the young man's eyebrows rose and he quickly moved in to get the fire-eater's attention. Calhoun briefly scanned the note and, after whispered instructions, sent him back to Nicholas.

"The Senator of course can not receive such a distinguished visitor in the midst of this mob," the aide shouted over the crowd's increasing roar. "However, he invites you to meet him here at the bar after supper." The young man studied Nicholas carefully. "Apparently, Senator Troup believes you are an interesting conversationalist…"

'Supper,' for Nicholas as well as Calhoun and the other politicos, consisted of partaking in the vast barbeque/bonfire set up in Tuscaloosa's main square. No gourmet---he ate mainly for fuel, not pleasure---Ignatieff found he enjoyed the Southern cooking as much as he disliked the egalitarian style in which the food was dispensed.

Now he leaned against the bar in the half-empty taproom and awaited the Senator's return. Calhoun, who had delivered yet another vitriolic attack on Parliament while the crowd partook of the barbeque, walked through the doors looking grim, even as his companions---Governor Gayle and the Congressman---looked alcoholically boisterous. (Nicholas, of course, didn't know the South Carolinian well enough to realize Calhoun *always* looked grim.)

The great man spotted Ignatieff immediately and strode towards him. "Were we not introduced, Sir, however briefly, at the French Consulate in Georgetown some weeks back?" he asked---demanded---in as imperious a tone as the Count had ever heard the Czar Alexander employ.

Ignatieff bowed formally. "Yes, Senator, we were. I am Andre Karlhamanov, late of the university in St. Petersburg. And I am honored that you'd remember, with all that has since occurred…"

"Sir," Calhoun growled, looking at the Alabama officials. "It is not every day that the French Counsel-General goes out of his way to introduce a Russian visitor, of all things, at a Georgetown party." He glared at Nicholas with a half menacing look (though he exhibited the

Southern courtliness not to reference Andre's most prominent physical characteristic, the eye patch).

"So sir, Senator Troup writes that you offered several, ah 'interesting observations' during a recent discussion in Savannah. What were you doing in Georgia, eh? And what brings you to Tuscaloosa? Come to think on it, sir, what are you doing in America?"

Nicholas had maintained a blank smile during the introduction and sudden barrage of questions. Now he bowed his head slightly and indicated a corner table. "Perhaps, Senator, if we could adjourn to a more private place, I could explain to you and your associates over a round of after-dinner drinks."

The foursome---Calhoun signaled his aide to remain at the bar---was soon seated in semi-privacy. After blandly offering his usual excuse for coming to the Dominion, Nicholas, still in his 'Andre' character, began to steer the conversation to the issues at hand:

"I must say, Sirs, I certainly seem to have chosen a most exciting time to make my tour. When I arrived in Georgetown neither my own Russian Counsel-General nor the British officer with whom I traveled much of the way from New York let on that such momentous events were about to unfold here. Apparently, I am observing an historic turning-point in the history of your, ah...land?" He smiled innocently and put on a surprised face when Clay sputtered indignantly.

"There, sir. You have hit the nail on the head." The Congressman turned to the others. "This foreign visitor has defined the problem concisely with one uncertain question.

"That's our problem: what is this 'land?' Are we a mere colony of the British, to be ordered about without regard for our own opinions? Are we a 'dominion'---whatever the hell that means---with certain rights of autonomy, at least in domestic issues? Or are we a number of geographically linked states united to provide for mutual defense and trade, yet free to establish and maintain domestic institutions of our own choosing? With tenuous ties to a Mother Country that provides a secondary system of defense and trade in exchange for a certain percentage of our prosperity? Geographically linked states which are free, individually or in number, to decline further participation with the other states and/or the Mother Country at a time of our own choosing?

"I say the third! And it is time the South made both the Yankees and the Empire so aware!"

The dark smile briefly illuminated Calhoun's features. "Well said, Clement." He turned to Nicholas. "Yes Sir. You do indeed seem to have arrived at a most portentous moment in history. This *Dominion* of ours is about to be defined."

Face once again turning grim, he motioned toward the Troup note in his jacket pocket. "My distinguished colleague from Georgia informs me that you sense, ah, 'similarities' between our Southern society and your own which could be mutually beneficial in the months and years to come. Perhaps you could amplify those sentiments for us...."

Tuscaloosa-Chattanooga Road
April 3, 1833:

The bonfire's embers were still glowing when Nicholas claimed his horse and began the ride northeast across the state towards Tennessee early the following morning. His meeting with Calhoun and the Alabamans had been even more revelatory and successful than he could have hoped: *these Southerners are not only willing to fight to save their 'peculiar institution,' they seem hell-bent on throwing the proverbial first punch...with or without aid from abroad.*

While Congressman Clay had abruptly passed out after his eruption, Calhoun and the Governor had kept their wits about them. Gayle despite the prodigious amount of whiskey he continued to consume. (Calhoun, while no teetotaler, seemed a moderate imbiber.) Ignatieff himself had stuck with beer...there'd be no 'accidents' similar to the unfortunate evening in London...

The message had been received clearly by the dour fire-eater, whose original quizzically-demanding expression had gradually turned speculative and thoughtful as Nicholas elaborated on his comments to the Senators Brown and Troup.

(Though the Russian was unaware of the fact, Calhoun had served two terms as Vice G-G---the first under Quincy Adams---and had also been Secretary of War for over six years. The positions had provided him an education on world affairs available to few British American statesmen. He had thus quickly dismissed Ignatieff's "visiting professor" persona as a ruse and saw him for what he was: an Imperial Russian agent of an as-yet-undetermined level.)

Calhoun has thought this through, Nicholas decided as he headed up the rutted dirt road (in actuality, just minimally more than a trial*), and is willing to consider any and all options to achieve his goals. My vague danglings of possible financial aid, recognition as an independent state and even military assistance may make secession from the Dominion look more enticing...as well as realistic. Realistic enough, at least, to help make it more plausible an option when their Congress goes back to Georgetown.*

How did Calhoun phrase it as the meeting was breaking up?

"The South needs and will welcome the friendship of any like-minded peoples, Sir. While we remain committed to the Dominion and its unique place in the British Empire---with the caveat that our domestic institutions be left sacrosanct---the knowledge that there are other peoples, other governments, other world leaders who believe in and maintain similar domestic institutions of their own will be a comfort to the Southern people in the trying times ahead."

Tuscaloosa-Huntsville Road
April 3, 1833:

Calhoun, his young aide and a very hung-over Congressman Clay were the sole passengers on a hot, dusty stage ride north to Clay's plantation. The great orator planned to rest at the Clay home---and give several speeches in Huntsville---before traveling on into Tennessee. As the carriage thundered north, the Senator was putting the pieces of last night's strange meeting together in his mind.

"Are you familiar, gentlemen, with the French term 'agent provocateur'?"

He shook his head as Clay winced at a sudden jolt as the stage hit a rut. The Alabaman looked ready to be sick. The aide, Jefferson Munroe, merely looked tired; the young man had escorted them all to various beds the previous night but obviously had delayed retiring himself.

"The term translates, quite simply, as an agent of 'provocation;' one who stirs up existing trouble or conjures up the same where none existed before. An interesting, though dangerous, occupation, would you not say?" He looked thoughtfully at his fellow passengers.

"Senator, there is a time and place," Congressman Clay groaned. "While I admit to deficiencies in my French language ability, this does not seem an appropriate time nor place."

"Ah, but it is, mine host-to-be."

Munroe saw the slightest of smiles break through the dour features before receding like a weak sun on an overcast day. "You see, we were entertained by a skilled practitioner of those arts just last evening…"

While Clay closed his eyes in agonized exasperation as the stage bounced merrily through and across a seemingly connected series of ruts, ridges and rocky patches, Munroe rubbed his eyes in an attempt to remain alert.

"That Russian professor Senator Troup endorsed, Sir? I was surprised at the amount of time you spent with him…"

"Very good, Jeff. Yes, that *professor* is without question an agent of the Czar. I recall McDuffie questioning his bona fides that night at the French Consulate. Thought the Russian C-G deferred a bit too much to a mere 'professor'…

"That's not the telling point, however. I've observed these foreigners in action over the years. Never once has a private visitor so bluntly raised the issues this Russian did last evening. More importantly, no private visitor---especially from an autocratic state--- would ever dare, on his own, initiate the possibility, however remote, of his country's intervening in the affairs of the Empire.

"No, gentlemen. That was an official contact last evening by a duly-appointed representative of Czar Nicholas."

Munroe shook his head in disbelief: "But what would the Russians have to gain by intervening in our domestic affair? Surely the Czar isn't so altruistic that he would risk London's wrath in a show of sympathy for our somewhat similar institutions of labor?"

Calhoun nodded his head, the long hair jostling his shoulders. "That, of course is the question, Jefferson. I understood this Russian to be on his way today to visit Congressman Polk in Columbia. Perhaps he will reveal more to James."

The Senator looked over at the now-gagging Congressman. "I see however, that conversation concerning such global diplomacy is inflicting considerable pain on my honorable colleague. We will leave the matter in abeyance for now."

He looked out the window at the planted roadside acres being tended by dark-skinned field hands. "I have arranged to meet with

328

this 'Andre' once back in Georgetown. Perhaps by then the Czar's motives will be more apparent."

The Senator turned and flashed his trademark dark smile at the aide. "Perhaps by then it will also be apparent if the British realize there is a Russian agent on the loose here in our midst."

CHAPTER THIRTY-FOUR

Cranford Plantation
Alexandria, Virginia
April 7, 1833:

Lucille Latoure wasn't formally educated in the sense that her sister, Jaine--who had attended a private institution of higher learning for young women called a 'female seminary'--was. She did, of course, hold advanced 'degrees' in the arts and sciences for which Southern belles were noted: coquettishness; insincere flattery; manipulation of the other sex, as well as dancing, side-saddle riding (though she actually could ride a horse in the regular manner as well as most men) and a more subtle projection of her sexuality than her 'rival', Candice Samples, preferred.

In the month since the tumultuous weekend in which *emancipation* had been transformed from an epithet to a very-real possibility, however, Lucille had sought and absorbed a multi-faceted education in politics, military science and sociology.

Despite her angry outburst at Lieutenant Wilder the day he had broken the news, Lucille hadn't really comprehended the crisis he had come to warn of: the retort had been personal in view of his 'misconduct' viz-a-vie broken dinner-engagements; that bitch Mrs. Samples; and his general 'inattentiveness.' It was actually the casual off-hand comments of Sir John Burrell the next evening during the party at the Vice G-G's that had radicalized her.

Sir John---who danced superbly (Tom exhibited the grace of a Cranford plow horse on the dance floor); projected what she imagined a sophisticated European air, complete with a darling thin, drooping mustache (the Lieutenant's proverbial "map of Ireland" face came complete with freckles); and was, after all, the King's top resident political representative in the Dominion (not some sort of military messenger boy)---had been among her Georgetown beaus since arriving in the capitol two years before.

Though he was a bit old---closer to 40 than 30, she'd guess---with Joe Johnston gone off God-knows-where with a 'real' Army unit, he had begun to look more appealing. He had offered tickets to the Duke's speech; learning that she was already in possession of some but free that evening, he had offered to escort the Latoures to Van Buren's dinner party.

In conversation over cocktails with a group that included Senator Clay and the new Interior Secretary, Mr. MacLane, Sir John had expressed the opinion that the seven-year phase-in plan was "extremely liberal, wouldn't you say?" The "Government," he continued---with an emphasis that left no doubt that he was referring to London---had obviously drawn up a "careful, meticulous and generous" plan that looked out for the interests of all concerned: planters and their soon-to-be-former slaves alike.

The Liaison officer's attitude, to a thunder-struck Lucille, breached her defenses as she later imagined a backhanded slap across the face might: condescending, parental and infuriating. *Do they actually consider us the equivalent of misbehaving children who can be bribed to end their embarrassing conduct much as a parent would promise candy to a group of unruly off-spring?*

Her cherished way-of-life! Subject to the whims of some faceless clerks 3000 miles away? *Perhaps that is what has Mary Lee so fired up!*

She had listened quietly---and for the first time ever with full attention---to the political conversation for the remainder of the evening. The education---the radicalization---of the belle began that night and continued thereafter.

Lucille had come back to the capitol two days later for Jackson's inaugural address and, escorted by Senator Webster, had attended several parties (though they had not gone to The Residency, believing the Tennesseans would be reenacting their rampage of '28). Since then she had remained for much of the time in Georgetown, quietly observing and absorbing as the Administration tried to maintain a semblance of normality. At affairs such as Maria Scott's monthly ladies-only luncheon, she listened carefully, not for social gossip but for any political news or opinions that might be related. She took no one into her confidence except Mary Lee.

On Easter Sunday, she had returned to Cranford. On the way, she had stopped at Arlington House to see Mary and Robert, who had wrangled leave for the holiday. She would be returning to the capital in a day or so, however, she privately informed Mary. Word that she was staying regularly in the townhouse was beginning to lead to invitations from varied social-and-political circles in Georgetown.

Both young women hoped---prayed---that a compromise would be worked out. As reports began to trickle in concerning the response in various sections of the country, however, the two had begun to fear for the worst. And to consider how they could be of service...

Latakia, Syria
April 7, 1833:

General Boris Mikailov, after more than a month cramped up aboard the dilapidated flagship of the Imperial Black Sea Fleet, was happy to set foot on solid ground, even if he wasn't quite sure where he and his disembarking command were.

According to Admiral Valeri Kharlamov, commander of the Black Sea Fleet, this sleepy port was well north of Tripoli. Advanced elements of the Egyptian army, according to questionable intelligence reports by the Ottomans, had occupied that fabulous old city in late February. The main body, however, was apparently still camped in and around Acre, even farther south along the coast.

Mikailov's orders, which seemed even more dubious now then when he had received them two months ago, were to locate the Arabs, head off their apparent march into the Anatolian heartland of the Turks, and by a show of force, convince this Pasha Ali to turn back. If possible, this show of force was to be accomplished without firing a shot... Though how in the name of Ivan the Terrible he was supposed to pull that miracle off, he had no idea!

He and Kharlamov had picked Latakia for its spacious harbor and gentle rise to the main Syrian plain. Marines landed several days ago had reported that the Army could comfortably camp outside the town while keeping in close touch with the fleet, in case a sudden reembarkment became necessary. Water and provisions were also readily available for seizing in the surrounding area.

The cavalry would begin probing southward tomorrow, while Admiral Kharlamov had already sent his most powerful (*most seaworthy*, the General thought with a snort of disgust) frigate down the coast to ascertain the situation at Tripoli.

Mikailov shook his head: some assignment! *I've fought the French, the wild hordes in Central Asia and even the Mongolians. Each time, it was to defend or extend the motherland. What possessed St. Petersburg to land us in the middle of a Moslem civil war is beyond me! Let's just hope that the Arabs will be as terrified of us as the Turks seemed to be…otherwise, we'll need more reinforcements than St. Petersburg has the ability to transport to us…*

Albany, New York
April 17, 1833:

Aaron Burr had received a rude shock when he arrived here two days ago via Hudson River steamboat to organize the Albany Regency's meetings with Wellington: William L. Marcy, Matty Van's hand-picked new governor, was at best non-committal on the emancipation issue. There were, in fact, indications that Marcy was actually sympathetic to the slave power!

The Regency itself was Van Buren's creation (with the Colonel's sage backstage help) and had ruled the state for over a decade through strict adherence to a mutually agreeable and beneficial agenda. While neither the Vice G-G nor any of the other power brokers could be called outright abolitionists, no one had suspected that Marcy harbored Southern sympathies!

It will hurt Matty in the long run---to say nothing of the personal embarrassment to me---if Wellington sees we can not control our own state, the Colonel thought with dismay as he prepared to dine with several Regency stalwarts at the Quackenbush House, reputedly the city's oldest building.

Albany, New York
April 19, 1833:

The Colonel had worked feverishly to convince Marcy to see the light, cashing in many of the Vice G-G's political chips in the process. The canny old political boss had even promised the Governor a leading place in any Van Buren cabinet once Matty Van took possession of The Residency.

Well, Matty can deal with the outrage later, if he is ever forced to deliver on the promise: four years is a long time in politics. Who can say what the situation will be then? Or who will be around to say it?

The meetings with the Duke should now go well, the Colonel thought with satisfaction as he left a tense meeting in the Governor's mansion on Eagle Street. *As long as that fool Marcy keeps his mouth shut... How can a politician from Troy, New York, support the continuance of slavery? And what was Matty Van thinking to put such an idiot in the Governor's chair?*

Burr would keep a low profile during the official events of Wellington's visit, especially the reception tonight co-hosted by Marcy and Mayor Corning at the Schuyler Mansion, of course. While the Regency crowd was well aware of his influence, to most New Yorkers---as well as the rest of British America---he was virtually forgotten; recalled if at all as an unwholesome relic of a bygone era. When he occasionally made news---in his recent unfortunate divorce, his wife, the former Eliza Bowen, was represented by Alexander Hamilton, Jr.---it was as a curiosity.

Albany-Hartford Road
April 22, 1833:

The Duke of Wellington was in a jubilant mood as he rode toward what he had been informed would be an enthusiastic reception in the abolitionist-stronghold Connecticut capitol. The key Northern states were falling in line to support, if not emancipation, the Colonial Compact with a quiet determination he had, at first glance, doubted they possessed.

"The Compact, as we had always hoped, is the key," he told Captain Bratton as they headed southeast through western Massachusetts on a lovely spring morning. "There's no great love for the blacks in either the West or these last two states we've visited. And no great guilt over slavery, either. They'd allow the institution to whither on the vine, given their druthers, if that was all that is at stake.

"But the Dominion, now, that's an entirely different cup of tea. They're damned if they'll allow the Southerners to destroy it…over slavery or anything else."

Bratton was troubled, however. "This *exemption*, Sir Arthur. We keep hearing reports that Calhoun is making it the centerpiece of his resistance. And you'll recall this chap Wolf broached it back in Harrisburg…"

The Duke shook his head forcefully. "There will be no exemption, Captain Bratton. London sent us here to announce emancipation, not compromise with the slaveholders. Wolf was just-- how do the Americans say it--*testing the waters*. Why, it never came up in Albany at all."

For the Duke, who loved new gadgets and inventions, the highlight of the visit had actually been the exciting round trip on the new Mohawk & Hudson Railroad to the nearby town of Schenectady. Albany's mayor, an industrialist named Erastus Corning, was the driving force behind the road. "Our state will soon be entirely linked by track as well as these new canals to Lake Erie and Lake Champlain," he predicted as they rode at the breathtaking speed of just under 15 miles per hour. "Together, they will make our boast of being the 'Empire State' an uncontestable fact."

The Mayor had turned sober as he continued. "Those damn planters down South! They're stuck in the 18th, if not 17th, century, progress-wise. Machinery is the key to the 19th century…not human bondage!"

Wellington chuckled now, thinking back on his visit. "I say: that Colonel Burr of yours is first rate. Had that Regency crowd all lined up before we ever arrived. Why, their Governor even took me aside to privately reassure me of their support, politically and otherwise."

———

Russian Consulate
Georgetown, D.C.
April 26, 1833:

Dispatches from St. Petersburg indicating that the Syrian expedition had been ordered forward had been waiting when Count

Ignatieff returned from the west. *So, the great game in Asia has begun. Perhaps I should have gone there from St. Petersburg. And sent someone else to deal with these damn colonials...*

His stay with Congressman Polk had not been as successful as the previous stops in the deeper south: the man had not risen to the bait even after hearing of Nicholas' conversations in Tuscaloosa.

At first, the Count was inclined to write off the incident to a naiveté or slowness on Polk's part. After traveling with the Congressman to several speaking engagements in the eastern half of Tennessee, though, Ignatieff had realized that he was dealing with a crafty, slippery political operator who simply refused to acknowledge that anything was afoot.

Compared, however, to his reception in Kentucky, the Polk visit had been wildly successful. Slavery was obviously a fact-of-life in Kentucky; black faces seemed almost as common as white. The gentry, however, appeared more resigned to emancipation. It had taken a chance conversation in a Louisville saloon for Ignatieff to begin to realize the reason.

A well-built smallish young man, clearly of the upper class, named Harold Reese explained: "Cotton is not king here, sir. We've a varied economy and more small farmers than planters. Horses, sir; that is what we grow in the bluegrass! The darkies are already a hindrance to some of our quality people. Could manumit the lot, but where would they go, what would they do? Can't sell them south, either. No sir, after so many years that would be heartless. This plan of Wellington's now; as some of us understand it, will be a godsend. Take 'em off our hands, yet get something for them! Still, some folks don't see it that way. They're mighty comfortable bein' waited on, hand and foot, by their 'people.' Some may side with the fire-eaters. Don't think Kentucky as a whole will, though."

He grinned at the Count, who was trying grimly to maintain a carefully neutral look. "It was only 40 years ago, you know, that this land was settled. Why, there's many a man alive right here in Louisville who knew Daniel Boone personally. People like that who fought so hard to get into the Dominion---the Frenchies were very active here, you know---well, those people have passed on a love for the USBA to their children. London freeing the darkies---even though it does seem right high-handed---doesn't strike me as enough of an issue to go over to Calhoun and his hotheads."

Riding back through Virginia had cheered Ignatieff up somewhat. Word of the emancipation had been slow in reaching into the Blue Ridge but the people---planters and small farmers alike--- were outraged. *Well, perhaps Calhoun changed some minds in Kentucky. He was scheduled there late last week. Meanwhile, there is work to be done here in Georgetown...*

Drago, the Consulate security chief, had not been the only unenthusiastic face when Nicholas had ridden up to the compound gates after some six weeks on the road. Count Renkowiitz's easy hand was again evident throughout the Consulate as Nicholas strode imperiously into the building. An atmosphere that quickly changed once word of his unexpected arrival filtered throughout the compound.

An afternoon meeting with Renkowiitz and his daughter--- brought in at Ignatieff's express command---revealed that Georgetown was tense but quiet, as if awaiting the onslaught of a thunderstorm already visible on the horizon.

"And you, Count? Was your trip all you expected?" Renkowiitz was nervously cheerful.

"It had its moments." Ignatieff was dry and brief. "Is the Congress still expected to meet the first Tuesday of June? And what word of Wellington? Is he still touring the North?"

Despite his best effort to conceal it, Renkowiitz's renewed surprise at the unwanted St. Petersburg visitor's interest in Dominion politics was clearly evident.

(Putting two and two together and coming up with five, Count Karl had decided that Ignatieff was in British America on some secret mission of assassination or abduction. Assassination or abduction of a British official, though visions of Fernando Valenzuela lying in his Consulate's garden, or some back alley, with his throat cut had also appeared in his mind's eye. After all, hadn't Ignatieff mentioned Ft. Ross and the Imperial settlements flourishing in what was supposed to be Mexican California?

(Renkowiitz had been more inclined, however, to wonder if the Czar wanted Wellington to have an 'accident' while in America. When Ignatieff had vanished the Wednesday after Jackson's inauguration, the C-G had presumed and planned for the worst.

Amidst public fanfare, Wellington himself had embarked on his tour of the Western and Northeastern states a few days later. Karl had worried for several weeks, until word filtered back that Ignatieff was indeed in the South. The C-G had finally shrugged his shoulders. *Whatever the security operative was up to, it apparently was of such an obscure nature that the Motherland's relations with the Dominion would not be affected.)*

"The new Congress will indeed gather on June 4th, as called by Jackson last month, my dear Count. And the Duke has been busy twisting arms and influencing both legislators and citizenry from Illinois to New England, by all accounts. *Campaigning*, I believe both the British and the Americans call it."

He paused and smiled. "One of the few instances in which their use of the language is consistent. Normally, their usages are much in common as Chinese and Arabic..."

Countess Caroline, who had been quietly studying Ignatieff's demeanor since being summoned---she had her own opinions on the purposes of his visit---laughed softly. "Why Papa, you know what Sir John Burrell told us." She looked over at the Count. "According to Sir John, 'It is a fallacy to think the English language is one of the pillars of our Empire. In India they don't understand it; the Irish and the Scotch can't pronounce it and the Americans won't use it.'"

Ignatieff nodded in amused appreciation. *Clearly, she cannot be this fool's natural daughter.* "So Countess, what has happened in the past six weeks in this great metropolis which might interest His Majesty the Czar, were he here today?"

Caroline, who had shared several interesting conversations with her admirer Harper that had included references by one or both to Ignatieff, smiled demurely. "Actually, Count Nicholas, there is little to relate. With the Congress gone home, Georgetown is an even smaller village than usual. The Governor-General has been holed up in The Residency; some say he is ill, but according to others, he is planning for the upcoming crisis. The government, such as it is, seems to be holding its collective breath..."

Drago, later in the day, had provided Count Ignatieff with an update on his original sketchy report about Captain Bratton. The man was held in high regard as a quiet, efficient problem solver by both the Liaison Office and Scott's War Department, apparently. He had left town with the Duke and thus wasn't expected back in Georgetown until early May. The Consulate security specialist had little else to offer, other than a more-than-adequate surveillance report on The Golden Eagle:

"Business is down, as it is all over Georgetown at this time of year, Sir. However, the establishment seems to be flourishing. As for the proprietress, Mrs. Casgrave seems to have held up under the strain of your absence…"

Ignatieff jerked his head and looked, possibly for the first time ever, into the gargantuan guard's eyes. *So, this big, dumb animal has also fallen under the seductive Joanne's spell. Well, she couldn't be expected to remain celibate while I was gone…*

"Captain Drago, you will have one of your aides send my greetings to Mrs. Casgrave and announce my attention to have a late, private dinner with her this evening.

"Commencing immediately, you and your aides will devote your full attention to determining when this Captain Bratton will return to Georgetown. Your future in the Czar's service…will depend upon your success in keeping this British agent in hand until I am ready to deal with him. Do you understand?"

Drago, who considered himself fortunate to have risen from the Ukrainian wheat fields but hated the Muscovy nobility nonetheless, acknowledged Ignatieff's authority, however grudgingly, with a subservient nod of his head.

His thoughts, however, were more rebellious: *If the chance arises, my dear Count, you may depend on me… To put a bullet or a blade deep into your aristocratic chest…*

––––––––––

Ignatieff's interest in visiting Joanne his first evening back in Georgetown was not completely carnal in nature: during the long, boring hours of travel he had formulated a contingency plan which called for the utilization of both the tavern/brothel-keeper and her dim-witted bartender.

He did not fully understand the hold Joanne exercised over the strange fellow, any more than he completely understood the rationale by which she ruled the Eagle's other employees (both on the ground floor and in the bedroom complex above) with her tiny iron fists. Nicholas now intended to craft the bartender into a *nyjj ruchnojj…*a "special tool"…that he could wield if necessary at the appropriate time to cause maximum havoc. Whether that time would ever arise---or what havoc he would choose to unleash---the Count would leave to the future to determine.

For now, he would simply reassert his will---physically and emotionally---over the whorehouse madam. Through her he would turn the unstable Lawrence into his creature…

CHAPTER THIRTY-FIVE

USBA Military Academy
West Point, New York
May 1, 1833:

Lieutenant Wilder had stepped onto the grounds of the Point for the first time since graduation yesterday afternoon, after an almost two-day voyage by Coastal Guard packet with General Scott from Georgetown.

They had been met at the Academy's Hudson River landing by Superintendent Thayer, a committee of senior faculty and a cadet honor guard. The hosts escorted the General up the Palisades to The Plain. There the Corps had passed in review in the sort of elaborate pomp-and-circumstance ceremony that Scott loved (and had helped earn him his not-always-fondly attributed moniker).

Taking it all in with a lower lip tightly bitten to harness the grin that threatened to break out at any moment, the Lieutenant had two immediate happy thoughts: how much better it was to be observing, not marching; and how many recognizable faces were glancing his way in astonishment as identification of the Commanding General's aide rippled through the assembled faculty.

The General, of course, had then inspected both the Corps and the Academy itself before addressing the Cadets at the evening meal. His remarks were strictly limited to their situation and responsibilities as members of the Corps as well as to the future of the Army in the Dominion's movement westward. The burgeoning crisis, what little news of it had penetrated the Point's gates, was not so much ignored as rendered moot.

The failure to address the issue was, naturally, a coldly calculated omission by the General, designed more with Georgetown audiences in mind than that of the young men and their officer-professors in the Cadet mess at Washington Hall. The announced purpose of the visit was Scott's annual conference to discuss assignments for the graduating seniors. Routine, the General was signaling, both to the War Department staff (including the Southern-born officers who dominated it and had participated in the speech's development) and to any other interested parties.

The assignment review was a valid cover for coming to the Point. Scott had earlier secretly informed Thayer that he would in all likelihood concur with the overwhelming majority of the Superintendent's recommended branch postings this year.

Both senior officers knew that the assignments stood a good chance of being short-term, at best.

For the real reason Winfield Scott had forsaken the Potomac for the Hudson was to incorporate Thayer's report on Dominion officer potential among ex-West Pointers currently enjoying civilian life into his plans for an expanded USBA Army. An Army that he prayed would be capable of putting down any emancipation-sparked Southern rebellion.

Col. William Worth, who headed the Northeastern command (with particular responsibility for keeping an eye on the French Quebecois), had arrived from his headquarters in upstate Plattsburgh. That had been a tightly-held secret. Worth, with a single aide, had disembarked from the Albany steamer last evening at the town of Hudson. After spending the night at his family's farm, he had ridden unceremoniously onto the Point in mid-morning while classes were in session. He had joined in the assignment discussions and was a full participant in the more important meeting, which had begun immediately thereafter.

"Well gentlemen, let us review," the General said as the bugle call to the evening meal sounded through the partially-open windows of the commandant's quarters.

"If, or when, the necessity arises, the new Army will assemble at Carlisle Barracks in Pennsylvania for organization and training. Colonel Wool will be in temporary command, while Colonel Worth, having turned over his Northeastern command to his deputy, will organize the defenses around Georgetown." He turned to the tall, spar Worth: "You will utilize approximately 20% of the available regulars; the Corps of Cadets and the battle-tested Illinois and Ohio volunteers I hope to have mobilized." Worth broke off a crisp "Yes, Sir."

"When the Georgetown defenses are completed, you, Colonel, will proceed to Carlisle, where you will assume command of II Corps.

Colonel Wool will command I Corps." Scott paused and said, formally: "Both you and Colonel Wool will assume the temporary ranks of brigadier general upon initiation of the operation."

Other than acknowledging his orders, Worth remained stone-faced through the recital. His disapproval of John Wool was well-known to Scott and Thayer. The commanding general, however, having few enough senior officers to choose from---he refused to plan any significant role for his deputy commander, Gaines (if the Virginian elected to remain loyal)---felt compelled to rely on both men.

"I myself will of course be in overall command of the Capitol's defenses, even before you leave for Carlisle and until such time as the bulk of the Army is ready to march. I have yet to determine who will then have tactical command at Georgetown.

"The Carlisle Army will consist of the remaining available Regulars and volunteer units from the other Northern states. The Army will be augmented by Regulars returning from Southern posts we must assume will have been occupied by rebel forces." Scott stared grimly at his subordinates. "If the situation deteriorates to that level, I do not want soldiers loyal to the Dominion making heroic-but-foredoomed isolated stands. I need live fighters, not maimed or dead heroes. As for the forts and posts, well, that's what we're organizing to take back."

The others nodded in agreement with the General's hard-boiled, pragmatic view as he continued: "The officer corps will include both Regulars and ex-West Pointers, as well as volunteer unit-elected officers, most of whom will be those very same ex-West Pointers."

Scott's ham-sized face rearranged its features into a half-smile/half grimace. "At least, that is my hope...

"Colonel Thayer, having led the Corps of Cadets to the District of Columbia, will become my chief-of-staff, with the rank of brigadier general, and will assume command of logistics, supply, armament production and transportation."

Thayer nodded his head in acceptance; though he craved action, he understood that his best contribution in the crisis would be his organizational abilities.

Despite the fact that Mrs. Thayer's sudden appearance in the study of the Commandant's Quarters indicated that dinner was about ready, Colonel Worth felt compelled to bring up the subject of frontier security: "General Scott, it does not appear your plans leave us with adequate forces to patrol and control the frontier from Minnesota to Arkansas. Or, for that matter, in my own present command. Left to their own devices, the Quebecois can be relied upon to cause trouble…"

Scott's huge head shook in agreement. "You're right, Colonel. Pulling the regulars off the frontier will be tricky. A certain number will probably have to be left, augmented by volunteers from the territories. However, hopefully this business, if it comes to fruition, will be over before the Indians become aware of the situation."

The lines around his mouth settled into a frown: "Quebec poses a different problem. We will indeed be forced to maintain a strong Northeast command…though as yet I'm not sure who will lead it. That means some of the New York and New England volunteers will never set foot south of Plattsburgh.

"That is also the one area where we will request Imperial assistance. Elsewhere, I'm determined to put down any rebellion with Dominion forces alone. Quebec is unique, however. The Royal Navy will have to establish a presence---perhaps a temporary station---on the St. Lawrence River. We'll also set up a camp midway on the border with Ontario and stock it with that state's militia and volunteers."

The hedge-like eyebrows went up and the nod was emphatic: "That should be enough saber-rattling to keep the Quebecois cowered for as long as the fighting in the South lasts…"

Lieutenant Wilder had taken notes for Scott throughout the day. (Colonel Thayer's secretary, a gangly non-commissioned officer from Vermont, was taking the official meeting minutes. Tom had decided that the sergeant must have invented some sort of code in order to keep up with the quickly moving review. How he kept writing hour-after-hour without his hand cramping was as totally mystifying as it was awe-inspiring.)

Though the Lieutenant had put together most of the raw numbers, he was fascinated as he watched those numbers (and names) magically transform into regiments, divisions and corps. Equally fascinating was how Scott selected the various commands--- including cavalry and artillery---from the rapidly shrinking list of potential commanders.

Tom now had let his mind drift to the make-up of the Georgetown force---and his individual role---and thus was surprised when the senior officers suddenly stood to break for dinner. He scrambled to rise and, in doing so, knocked over the chair and writing table Colonel Worth's aide had been utilizing. Glancing his way, Colonel Thayer seemed to suddenly realize his identity.

"So, Mr. Wilder. Do you plan to visit with your favorite engineering and mathematics professors while you're here at the Point? I daresay none of them have forgotten you..." Sylvanias Thayer's eyes twinkled in a manner Tom would previously have thought impossible.

General Scott's bark of a laugh eliminated any need for Thomas to reply.

"The Department is expansive enough to have need of even the Lieutenant's rather eclectic skills, Colonel. Why, if this catastrophe we are planning for but praying against does, God forbid, occur---and he survives---he may even make First Lieutenant..." The Commanding General signaled the coming heavy punch line with a rising of his bushy eyebrows. "...in 10 or 12 years..."

Even the Vermont sergeant---to Tom's mortification---joined in the laughter.

Georgetown, D.C.
May 2, 1833:

A weary Duke of Wellington and his equally weary aide, Captain Bratton, arrived back in Georgetown this afternoon at the conclusion of their historic tour of the non-Southern portions of the Dominion.

Sir Arthur was as elated as he was tired; the tour had been remarkably successful: only New Jersey and New York City had pledged less than complete support to the emancipation legislation. Even those two holdouts were in philosophical agreement with both the principle of emancipation and the Government's right to enforce it.

Colonel Burr, however, was at work in the City and was reasonably certain his political organization---this Tammany Hall---would win over the New York merchants in the end. "Their reaction is simply 'knee-jerk,'" he had told the Britons over dinner last Saturday evening at a small, side street French restaurant, Madeline's Petite Paris.

The old man grinned as he continued his lecture: "The merchants and traders haven't thought yet past the potential loss of their Southern markets. They've yet to grasp the nature and resiliency of our Dominion economy and the new transportation realities: as quickly as the Southern markets, however temporarily, dry up, others will open from the West. If the Mississippi is closed, why, that simply means more goods shipped across the Great Lakes and through the Erie Canal."

Burr had then shot Wellington that now-familiar mischievous grin: "To say nothing of the certain increased demands of the War Department...

"Don't worry, Sir Arthur, New York City will not announce its own secession, despite what that damned *New York Post* threatens." The Colonel grinned again: "After all, how can any newspaper founded by Alexander Hamilton be taken seriously?"

British Liaison Office
Georgetown, D.C.
May 3, 1833
8:30 a.m.

The Duke and Captain Bratton had been separately jolted by 'eyes-only' dispatches waiting for them this morning at the Liaison Office.

Wellington, who had made it a habit when in the capitol to forego the 'pleasure' of an early morning Residency meal in favor of the traditional English breakfast prepared specially for him at the Office, had almost choked on his marmalade-and-toast upon reading the news from Palmerston: the Russians had landed---at Constantinople's invitation---somewhere on the Syrian coast!

His aide had been equally speechless---though sputtering--to learn that Scotland Yard, in conjunction with the Foreign Office, had ascertained that the Russian agent previously rumored to have passed through London in January (though the details were still unclear) had been reliably identified as the legendary Count Nicholas Ignatieff!

While the Duke could only ponder the long-term implications of the Russian strategic initiative---and digest the Foreign Secretary's warning that any unrest resulting from emancipation would have to be quelled internally---Captain Bratton had gone immediately to work. After sharing with Major Layne the report from London, the two were now reviewing the Liaison agents' reports from Charleston and New Orleans received since the 'dissident's' tour of the South had commenced some days after Jackson's inaugural.

"We must arrange for that damn eye patch to be *accidentally* dislodged," Bratton had mused after reading Layne a description of the Russian Count that highlighted the blue/brown eye. "Then we can confirm whether 'Karlhamanov' has been playing us for fools all these months…

There was little in the reports; the Russki had kept a low profile while traveling. Nor was there much concerning the week since Karlhamanov had been spotted back in the capitol. Apparently, he had resumed splitting his time between the Russian Consulate and The Golden Eagle…with the Eagle holding a considerable advantage, time-wise. "And, he has made no attempt to disguise his activities," Layne observed. "He's been openly moving around Georgetown, as if daring us to track him."

Bratton, having dismissed, at least consciously, romantic thoughts about the Eagle's proprietress, concentrated on Karlhamanov/Ignatieff's possible reasons for being in the USBA. His mind went back to the tip---received last month from young Harper---that the 'professor' had usurped Count Renkowiitz's ticket to the Duke's Congressional address.

At the time, it had made no sense; and anyway, departing with Wellington on a God-only-knew-how-long tour of the north and west USBA, Bratton had shelved, if not discounted, it. It made perfect sense now, however, assuming that Karlhamanov was simply Ignatieff's latest alias: the Russian agent would far outrank a mere C-G and would, as a matter of course, preempt the Wellington speech ticket…

Knowing what he now did--or surmised---the British agent realized he had made a serious error: Karlhamanov should have been tailed to wherever and whomever he had traveled last month! That he was back in Georgetown could mean any of a thousand things…and none of them were good!

"I wish this situation met the extremity stipulations," he told the Major, who looked less-than-shocked at the inference. "Unfortunately, we have no firm substantive evidence of anything…not even that the fellow is Ignatieff! We need more before we even consider going to the Duke for permission to 'go under the rose.'"

(The elimination of a foreign agent could be carried out, under the Government's 'extremity stipulations,' only if specific criteria were met. The French agent Bratton had eliminated 'under the rose' in New Orleans back in '28, for instance, had been demonstratably organizing a plot to assassinate the French-speaking governors of both Louisiana and Quebec as part of an elaborate plan to spark simultaneous revolts.)

"Yet, I feel quite certain that Ignatieff---disguised most probably still as Karlhamanov---has somehow ingratiated himself with emancipation's most emphatic---and dangerous--opponents."

Layne puckered his lips in frustration at the dilemma: "Clearly, the fellow is an 'agent provocateur.' It is no coincidence that he arrives here just as this crisis erupts…"

"…but how do we eliminate him from the scene," Bratton picked up the thought, "without causing an international incident? He has, as well as can be determined thus far, done nothing that could justify such a step."

The two stared at each other in frustration before a slight smile broke out on the Captain's face. "Do you remember, Major, that Interior Department chap we breakfasted with the day of the Duke's address? The fellow seemed to be developing some interesting back-channel contacts within the diplomatic corps. I believe it is time we chatted with him again."

Layne smiled. "I'll make the necessary arrangements…"

"Yes," Bratton repeated, "it is time we sat young Mr. Harper down again." He glanced at the wall clock. "It is also time I informed His Grace that my earlier suspicions, unfortunately since we have not acted on them, appear to have some validity. And God alone knows how the Old Man will react to that!"

The Duke's immediate reaction was that they were stretched too thin. Bratton had been asked to do the impossible: keep track of a possible foreign agent 'touring' the Dominion's Southern states while simultaneously accompanying him around the rest of the USBA.

No sense worrying about past omissions and errors; however, the job now is to ascertain who this Russki really is and why he is really here! And how precisely his presence ties into either or both the emancipation crisis and/or this incredible Syrian situation!

That it must, Wellington had no doubt: *one of the Czar's most-feared and reliable agents does not turn up by accident in the middle of a British Empire internal crisis. Nor is he lightly sent 4000 miles away on holiday while St. Petersburg embarks on a foreign adventure that has the potential to change the entire European balance-of-power.*

The Duke rose from the desk he had appropriated from Sir John and walked to the window, with its view of both The Residency and the Potomac. *Quite a beautiful place this time of year,* he thought idly, *though they tell me it will be India-like in a month…*

He turned to Bratton, who had remained seated in front of the desk and was now sipping from a rapidly cooling cup of tea. "Captain, despite some misgivings, I am afraid we will have to rely more heavily on Major Layne and his people this time around vis-a-vie this Russki character. I want fulltime surveillance placed on him, both here in Georgetown and wherever he might wander off to next. You will receive twice-daily reports while we're here; direct supervision will have to fall to Sir John later this month when we go south."

Wellington was thinking rapidly: "Round up Sir John and Layne and get them in here for a briefing in one hour. A dispatch has come in from the Foreign Office that casts this situation in a new light. The three of you must be aware of it. Meanwhile, I need some time to turn all this over in my own mind."

He returned to the desk and settled into the chair with a sigh, then looked at Bratton, who had risen and was preparing to leave. Wellington smiled: "This is becoming quite the sticky wicket, eh Captain? I daresay, there's quite a bit more to this than informing some colonial cotton growers they'll have to pay their help from now on, wouldn't you agree?"

The Residency
Georgetown, D.C.
May 4, 1833, 9 a.m.:

Andrew Jackson was this morning reviewing the latest crisis reports from around the country.

While the Duke of Wellington's 'tour' of the North and West had been conspicuously private---Sir Arthur had not made a single speech---the G-G's allies were reporting that Wellington had secured the backing of most major leaders of both parties.

That New England would enthusiastically support emancipation Jackson had never doubted. That the West was lining up was a bit of a surprise: the G-G had never known the Westerners to give much thought to any developments in the states they had left behind.

It was the reports from the MidAtlantic States that had at first shocked him. He had been surprised that George Wolf up in Harrisburg was apparently in favor; then Frank Blair had reminded him that Wolf had a large constituency of small farmers and immigrants. "Philadelphia does not speak for Pennsylvania any more," Frank had said. "The commercial interests there are all-powerful in the city, but have lost much of their clout in Harrisburg."

That damn Aaron's hand is clearly visible in New York: the Vice G-G's political organization controls Albany, but any doubts that Burr still possesses, in Frank's word, 'clout' in the City has vanished. The old fellow has Tammany Hall lined up, apparently, and is working on the merchant classes.

Jackson shook his head at the *New York Post's* mutterings about secession and becoming a *city-state.* "As if London would sit still while they turned the Mayor into a--what was it they used to call the ruler of Venice---Deluge?" he observed disgustedly to Lewis Cass as they perused the reports over breakfast. Cass smiled: "I believe the term was 'Doge,' Mr. Governor."

Jackson grunted. "Perhaps I should recall the Creek and send *them* up there. Those damn New Yorkers are always bragging about how they bought their island from the Indians for $24.00. Well, maybe we should inform the city fathers that we're sending them their $24.00 back and that the Creek *and* the Cherokee are on the way, too. That's one bill that ought to sail through Congress without much opposition!"

Jackson's sarcastic musings, as well as breakfast, were interrupted by the sudden appearance of a visibly excited Frank Blair, who had apparently crossed Pennsylvania Avenue from his own home in something of a run. A flapping packet of papers, apparently letters, was clutched firmly in his left fist.

"Mr. Governor-General," Blair---who never addressed Jackson formally--blurted out as he quickly crossed the room. "Reports from Kentucky..." he stopped suddenly to catch his breath.

"Well, Frank, now that you've joined us, take a seat and calm down. Whatever's come out of Kentucky can wait. Mr. Cass and I have solved the Georgia Indian problem." The G-G glanced across the table at his Secretary of War and then raised his eyebrows as a new thought entered his head. "Or perhaps, we've solved the emancipation issue."

Blair dropped into a chair and let a servant pour him coffee as the grinning Jackson continued:

"At first, we thought we'd offer any of those damn Indians who don't like it out West the option of picking up stakes again and moving to Manhattan Island. But now, Mr. Cass, I have an even better idea." He looked at the Michigan politician and winked before turning back to the incredulous Blair. "Perhaps we'll instead send the darkies up there. That'll give the New Yorkers seven years to get ready...or evacuate the place..."

Blair was now arranging his features into a more dignified, statesman-like face, having completed the arrangement of the papers he had carried into a semblance of order. He sipped the coffee and allowed the G-G and Cass to finishing chuckling.

"Andrew, we've read the reports from the North, both the people's reaction to emancipation and on Wellington's secret meetings. We also know what the reaction has been in the deep South. We've been waiting to hear from the border states. Well, the news is starting to come in. There's been a public meeting in Louisville. Both Clay and Calhoun spoke..."

The G-G's favorite oath split the air. Then: "One thing I'm determined to do before I leave office is shoot Henry Clay and hang John C. Calhoun..."

Blair put down his coffee and leaned across the table. "Well Andrew, depending how you eventually come down on this emancipation business, you may have the chance to do one or the other. Not, apparently, both…"

Cass now interrupted: "Well now, Frank. Why don't you take it from the top and tell us exactly what's happened out there in Louisville?"

The editor/advisor nodded. "We've known, of course, that Calhoun has been speaking all over the deep South, demanding the support of the other sections in the special session coming up. He's hinted pretty strongly that the South won't accept emancipation, whether rubber-stamped by Congress or not. An *exemption*, he's been talking about."

Blair paused and put on a pair of reading glasses before picking up the top sheet in his paper stack. "He's gone further out on the limb than ever before with his remarks in Louisville. Listen to this: for the South, '…freedom is not possible without slavery…' And if emancipation goes through, '…we have two choices: to be slaves in the Dominion or freemen out of it…'"

Jackson's fist slammed down on the table; the remnants of breakfast, both solid and liquid, were immediately airborne. "The damn fool! This isn't the time to be making threats. I've called Congress into session in part to demonstrate to Wellington and London that we're capable of serious, judicious debate; of consideration of all options; of coming forth with a realistic alternative proposal.

"Did Calhoun learn nothing from the tariff business? Demanding special privileges in public forums will not lead to an exemption! Reasonable men, elected representatives of the people, rationally discussing the issues might."

He glared at the others: "Don't think that means I've made up my mind, either. I haven't. There's a part of me that understands--- and agrees---with Calhoun's position. But there's another part of me that loves and cherishes this Dominion we've built above all else.

"But even the part of me that understands Calhoun's position knows this isn't the time to articulate it!"

The G-G rose and, reaching for his cane, turned his back on his advisors and hobbled toward the window. He stood, basking in the sunshine, before suddenly pivoting.

His voice dripping sarcasm, he growled: "So what pearls of wisdom did 'Harry of the West' have to add to the proceedings?"

"Actually, Andrew," Blair looked up from his papers and smiled, "Mr. Clay's words seem remarkably similar to your own of this morning: conciliatory, hopeful and statesman-like. He too seems not yet to have formulated a final position..."

Latoure Townhouse
Georgetown, D.C.
May 3, 1833, 1 p.m.:

Lucille Latoure couldn't wait for Tom to return from wherever he had vanished to; vanished, in fact, without even telling her he was leaving!

Under normal circumstance, that kind of incivility would have been enough to set her off on another extended period of icy retaliatory snubbing. The stakes now were different, however: Lucille had realized that the Lieutenant's position gave him access to the kind and level of information she now craved. So she had put aside her---rightful, as she saw it---anger at his previous *mis*behavior and had again allowed him to pursue her.

It wasn't that Thomas was spilling---*as yet*---any War Department secrets. He was simply so pathetically happy that she was displaying interest in him and his work that he was unintentionally serving as a sort of political science professor.

Lucille had manipulated their relationship for so long that she automatically assumed she was extracting everything he knew about the deteriorating situation. If she had dared share her new-founded information with Mrs. Scott---or Mrs. Blair; or even Candice Samples, for that matter---she would have been stunned to discover that Tom, while overjoyed to talk with her on any subject, was delivering edited, abbreviated lectures.

Lucille at this point in her political evolution did not consciously intend to betray the Lieutenant's trust; he was still high on her short list of prospective matrimonial candidates. Her fury at the reaction of the Yankees and the British---Sir John Burrell was off (if he had ever been truly on) the short list--to this threat to the South's (and her own family's) way-of-life had, however, indeed changed her.

Yet she was intelligent enough to realize that she needed an education in the ways-and-means of Georgetown if she was to be of any benefit to her beloved South. So, believing Tom was so enamored that he would tell her everything, she would not have accepted that her admirer had a conflicting, overriding, allegiance.

In any case, Mrs. Scott had let drop that Tom was off with the General on a short, mid-week trip. She intended that her *education* would continue the moment he arrived back in town!

The Golden Eagle Tavern
Georgetown, D.C.
May 8, 1833:

The big world-weary waitress, Kathy, shook her dirty-blond head one more time this afternoon in amazement: *the black-haired little bitch is acting like a schoolgirl caught up in her first romance.*

The arrival of this Russian had changed everything, Kathy observed, shaking her head once again. 'Andre Unpronounceable' had moved into the little bitch's bed the first night he had walked through the door. Sure, there had been others, of course, while he was away these past six or seven weeks, but Joanne had turned school-girlish again the moment he had made his reappearance. They had been inseparable since.

Well, she and the other 'downstairs' staff couldn't complain; the more time the little bitch spent mooning over her lover, the less time she had to criticize and order them around. (What went on upstairs, Kathy---whose looks and figure had vanished into a gin bottle during the last decade---didn't want to know.)

Andre not only had the proprietress wrapped around his finger, but he also seemed to be gaining the allegiance of the strange man behind the bar. Since his return, the Russian had shared several meals---and bottles---with Lawrence. Andre actually seemed willing and able to tolerate the fellow's company for extended periods: why, just Sunday, they had gone riding. This Saturday afternoon, according to Lawrence, they were going into Maryland to try out a new rifle Andre had apparently purchased. "And he's promised to show me how to shoot targets with a pistol," Richard had bragged a little while ago.

USBAA Southern Command HQ
New Orleans, Louisiana
May 11, 1833:

Colonel Zachary Taylor was enraged: personally, professionally and personally-professionally.

And when Colonel Taylor, a hardnosed, no-nonsense type---he had risen to fame by successfully defending a miserable Indiana outpost, Fort Harrison, against an overwhelming attack by French-armed Indians under the great Tecumseh himself back in the '10s---was enraged, both his family and staff knew enough to scatter. That's why he was alone in his office his afternoon.

The Colonel had plenty of cause, in his view, to be damned enraged.

He had just received a report from the Nacogdoches country that Sam Houston was definitely in Mexican Texas and had allied himself with that pompous young fool, William Travis, to talk insurrection against the Mexican authorities. Now he would have to write Winfield Scott that Houston had slipped through his hands. If Houston, Travis and the others got Stephen F. Austin to join them, there'd be hell to pay. New Orleans---all Louisiana---would demand he go to their aid if Santa Anna marched north! He wouldn't be able to lift a finger, of course, unless-and-until Georgetown gave the okay, which would make life in the Bayou rather uncomfortable for him and his command...

That was professional. Personally, Zach, though Virginian-born, had been in the Army all his life; hell, he'd never been in one place long enough to qualify to vote in a gubernatorial-general plebiscite, including the last one! Sure, he owned a few house servants: with five kids and him gone so much, Mary deserved a household staff! *But this emancipation thing, now....*

He was no politician---leave that to old Scott---and he hadn't much of a formal education. But he could read. And the G-G's speech up in Mississippi last year (which he had read only after getting back from the Black Hawk War in October) made it perfectly clear what Jackson wanted: Texas and the rest of the Mexican West taken in to form more slave states. He wasn't sure that was a good thing; he'd been up North enough to sense a vigor and vitality in the free states that wasn't present in the South. Now Calhoun was practically blackmailing Georgetown: get the South an exemption from this Empire-wide abolition…or the South goes its own way!

This Dominion deal has worked pretty well since old Franklin and the boys cooked it up. I'm not at all ready to leave. But I'm a Southerner. How the hell I go against my own people?

Speaking of 'own' just got him madder. He'd thought dragging that damn hot-headed young fool Davis with him up to Illinois would be enough to cool off the Lieutenant's romance with Sarah Knox… But Mary was warning him that the young people had not only corresponded during the fighting, but had resumed their courtship right here under his nose since he and the staff had returned! He should have ordered Davis to take leave when they sailed down the Mississippi; he understood Davis' brother owned a big plantation near Natchez. It wasn't that 1st Lt. Jefferson Davis was a coward; far from it! The boy was a natural-born soldier. He'd eventually lead troops out West.

That's one problem: I'll be damned if any daughter of mine is going to marry into this man's Army! Mary's a saint to have put up with the separations. I don't want that for Knox or any of the other girls! Little Dick is only six; if he wants to go to the Point and make the Army a career, that's his prerogative…

The other problem is that I just don't like Jeff Davis! Syl Thayer warned me about him years ago: thickheaded; self-righteous, one of these 'cavaliers' who wants to duel if you look at him the wrong way…not what I want for Knox.

Well, I can order him, as Knox's father, to stay away. Can't court-martial him if he doesn't, though. Maybe I ought to send him *to Texas. Him and Travis would make a fine pair! Two hotheads with pistols at 50 paces. Hopefully with Sam Houston in the middle! Hum…that'd solve two problems…*

Taylor grinned to himself momentarily.

But what about emancipation, Colonel? What if Calhoun and his fire-eaters do talk the South into secession? Which side you going to choose then, eh, Zachary?

God, I hope it doesn't come to that…I kind of like it here in New Orleans. Would hate to see a couple British warships starting bombarding the place.

State Capitol Construction Site
Raleigh, North Carolina

May 16, 1833, 1 p.m.:

The Duke had been told that North Carolina, the "Old North State," was actually the most conservative of Southern states. That's why he had chosen this special occasion for his own single major address before the new Congress organized in less than three weeks.

The ostensive reason for the Duke's journey was to lay the cornerstone for the new State Capitol Building. The Old Capitol had burnt down in '31 and the Carolinians had spent two years arguing over designs and financing for a brilliant new Greek Revivalist structure. Once word reached Raleigh that Sir Arthur was in the Dominion for an extended visit, the state fathers pushed to have the Hero of Waterloo perform the honors.

As the official party proceeded through the city's main square to the construction site on East Edenton Street, passing through cheering crowds, the Duke was aware that the arrival last night of an unexpected guest had altered the atmosphere in which the address was to be given.

Wellington and Captain Bratton had traveled by Royal Navy sloop to coastal Wilmington and then had ridden west to this splendid little city, not yet 50 years old but founded specifically to be the state capitol. They had arrived early yesterday afternoon after a leisurely three-day journey. "Well Captain, at least the planners of *this* capital picked a decent location." Sir Arthur looked around as they rode in. Bratton grinned: "Indeed, Your Grace. Not a swamp in sight..."

North Carolina's youthful new governor, David Lowery Swain, had thrown a private dinner party hours after their arrival at the impressive brick Governor's Mansion on the south end of Fayetteville Street. 'The Judge,' as Swain, 31, was known---he had resigned from the State Supreme Court in January to accept the General Assembly's election---was a Dominion-Republican. "Refreshing in itself," Wellington told the Captain. "Thought they only elected fire-eating Democrats down here. Apparently, this state truly is rather conservative..."

Senators Brown and Magnum, though Democrats, had also been on hand. One look at the trio and Wellington could feel his age: *by God, not one of them is 35!*

"I say, Governor: does your state constitution bar mature men from office, or did a particularly virulent plague strike the previous generation?" Wellington used his wine glass to indicate the two Senators.

Swain looked momentarily abashed, but then laughed. "Certainly not, Your Grace. Mature North Carolina gentlemen simply consider politics childish. We eventually outgrow it and graduate to other pursuits…"

Wellington smiled and nodded in agreement. "A sensible attitude. One I may soon adopt myself…"

Any retort from the Governor died on his lips as he saw an aide frantically signaling from across the room. He excused himself and hurried over as Wellington was engaged in conversation by a member of the state's Congressional delegation.

Standing nearby, Captain Bratton could see Swain, after a quick word from the aide that appeared to surprise him, begin to recross the room, only to pause to whisper in Brown's ear. The Senator looked startled and reflexively turned to stare at Wellington. The two Carolinians put their heads together, and after a brief, animated conversation, marched in step back to the Duke.

Having conversed briefly with the Congressman, Wellington had moved away and was now talking with the state's beautiful new First Lady, whom, he judged, to be not more than 25. He smiled as Swain and Brown approached.

"Governor. If sharing the company of this magnificent lady is part-and-parcel of the job, I may disregard your older generation's example and run in the next election myself…"

"Thank you, Your Grace." The Governor bowed formally and then turned to smile affectionately at his wife. "However, Mrs. Swain accompanied me to Raleigh…and has agreed to depart whenever the General Assembly tires of my attempts to bring some modernity to our beautiful but backward land…"

Amidst laughter and applause, Senator Magnum, just joining the group, said: "The Judge is an advocate of 'internal improvements,' Sir Arthur, at a speed somewhat faster than our poor state is accustomed. I'm afraid he's been corresponding with Governor Floyd up in Richmond again…"

Another round of easy laughter rippled through the room. (*These Carolinians don't take their politics or themselves overly-serious, I'm relieved to see,* Wellington thought.) But Swain then put on a grave face and the laughter quickly died away.

"It seems, Your Grace, that an unexpected visitor of some distinction has just arrived in Raleigh to hear your address. While I do not expect him to appear here this evening, I anticipate that he will attend tomorrow night's celebration, as well as the formal ceremonies."

The Governor paused and glanced briefly at Bedford Brown, whose own face was arranged in a frown of embarrassment. Wellington caught the glance and motioned for Swain to continue, as Willie Person Magnum's eyebrows shot up in puzzlement.

"North Carolina's hospitality comes without strings, Your Grace, and I am in no way indicating or suggesting that John C. Calhoun will conduct himself as anything other than the gentleman that he is. However, as the Senator's recent speeches have espoused a position somewhat different than the one you enunciated in your address to the Congress, I wanted to inform you immediately upon learning that the Senator is here in Raleigh."

Wellington's chuckle broke the silence before it could become embarrassing: "I look forward to conversing with Senator Calhoun, if the opportunity arises. I also trust he will listen tomorrow with an open mind, as I know all North Carolinians will. I say, however: is the man's horse named Pegasus? He seems to turn up all over the South. Man's perpetually in motion…"

This time, the Carolinians' laughter seemed twinged with unease. Fortunately, the butler indicated that dinner was about to be served.

Wellington's speech was met with polite applause at times. And polite silence when the emancipation issue was raised. The majority of the Raleigh gentry apparently opposed the freeing of their 'people,' but out of respect to the Duke---and in honor of the occasion of which they were duly proud---they did not express that opposition.

Wellington, for his part, employed a conciliatory approach: the Crown was offering compensation as well as a seven-year period in which to accomplish the task. Surely at the conclusion of that period the former owners would see financially induced increased productivity from their servants-turned-workers! After all, the workers would be inspired by the knowledge that not only their survival but a better life was entirely up to themselves. The former owners would be relieved of the odorous---and expensive--obligation of lifelong care… Employers would be free to dismiss any non-productive workers with no governmental interference!

And, of course, he gently but firmly reminded them, under terms of both the Colonial Compact and the USBA Constitution---both voluntarily signed by representatives of their state and approved by their own Legislature---the Government, with the King's approval, was legally entitled to issue an emancipation degree…

That portion of the address brought the only serious mutterings from portions of the crowd, but also, Captain Bratton could see, nods of approval and acknowledgement from others.

The Colonial Office man had made it his business to study Calhoun's reactions: Bratton had been surprised when the fire-eater had simply smiled rather, he thought, smugly during the Old Man's prophecy of increased prosperity-through-abolition.

The dark features had become taut, however, during the enunciation of the legal justification. Calhoun's eyes seemed to burn like two coals as the Duke, in his own way, repudiated any and all nullification arguments.

There'll be no compromising with this one, Bratton thought sourly. *This is a fanatic; he seems bound-and-determined to take this to---and beyond---the limits.*

If his is the majority Southern opinion, then my prediction back in London (my God, was that just 4 ½ months ago?) will have been correct. Even if the old man in The Residency decides to support emancipation…these people will not give up their 'peculiar institution' without a fight!

Governor's Mansion
Raleigh, North Carolina
May 16, 1833, 7 p.m.:

The astonishing letter John C. Calhoun carried in his breast pocket had been hand-delivered to Fort Hill Plantation. Floride, after scanning it quickly, had summoned a trusted young neighbor who, riding hard for long hours, had caught up to the Senator's small traveling party south of Raleigh.

Now Calhoun carried the amazing correspondence as he entered the ballroom of the beautiful, multi-storied brick building with the '1814' logo above the front doors, though he had not disclosed its contents to anyone, including his young aide, Munroe.

Although they had been formally introduced in Georgetown, Senator Calhoun and the Duke of Wellington---whom the South Carolinian had come to regard as his *real* opponent in this crisis (Jackson being old and on-the-fence)---had never actually discussed or debated the merits of the issue.

What Calhoun held in his pocket, however, he now considered the trump card: not to be fully disclosed---though hinted strongly at---until the moment when its enormous significance would virtually ensure the exemption he demanded...

For his part, the Duke looked forward to a face-to-face with the fire-eater; it reminded him of when his pickets had first clashed with Bonaparte's scouts south of the Waterloo battlefield. *We've got to get a taste of the man's mettle. Let's determine whether he has the intestinal fortitude to play this game to its potential finale...*

The original purpose of the formal, state-sponsored celebration had been to commemorate the laying of the cornerstone. That had now been eclipsed by the collision of the two giants: the states-rights apostle, John C. Calhoun; and the guardian of the Empire, Arthur Wellesley, Duke of Wellington.

Raleigh had never seen the like...and held its collective breath.

As Governor Swain had predicted, Calhoun behaved as the Southern gentleman he was. The Senator waited his turn to be introduced to the guest of honor and congratulated Wellington on his health before proposing that, "if Your Grace can find the time before the evening is complete, perhaps we could talk privately."

The Duke was immediately agreeable: "Certainly Senator...and if such an opportunity does not materialize, without question before we both depart this lovely city." Studying his face once again, Wellington was reminded of Scott's original description of the South Carolinian: '...burning with the fanaticism of an Old Testament prophet...' *Well, Winfield, you certainly had this one pegged correctly. My God, the man reeks of self-righteousness...*

Calhoun passed through the receiving line to quickly become the center of a large circle of admirers. Though the noise emanating from the circle grew ever louder, Harry Bratton, standing alone near a well-stocked (and well-frequented) bar, could see that the fire-eater himself rarely said more than a few words at a time. Wellington, for his part, played the role of honored guest, flirting with the ladies and conversing in generalities. Repeatedly, he countered questions and opinions from well-wishers with a broad smile: "Tonight is a celebration of your city and state. We shall leave the politics at the construction site..."

It was past 9 p.m. as Calhoun made his way through the ballroom once again, escorted by Bedford Brown into the Governor's study. The dallying guests then being ushered out by Mrs. Swain and the mansion's servants last saw the Duke in earnest conversation with the city's beloved Intendant of Police, Joseph Gales, Sr.

"'Intendant of Police,' Mr. Gales? I say: and what precisely does the 'Intendant' do?"

"It's a term the founders of our city apparently borrowed from the French, Your Grace. For all intents and purposes, I'm the mayor...and have been since 1819."

Policeman or politician, Gales was not, however, asked into the study moments later when Governor Swain came over to escort the Duke. In fact, only Calhoun, standing by the unlit fireplace, and the two seated Senators awaited Wellington as Swain closed the door behind them. The Governor quickly offered Sir Arthur use of his desk, but Wellington preferred to remain standing.

"Well Senator Calhoun, I am glad to see that your state has not followed North Carolina's example and ruled mature men ineligible for high political office."

The fire-eater looked nonplused as the three young North State officials joined in a nervous laughter somewhat heartier than the mild joke occasioned. It was Governor Swain who explained: "Upon his observations last evening on our relative youth" (with a broad wave he indicated the two Senators and himself), "I informed His Grace that, as gentlemen of North Carolina reach a certain age, they abandon this childish game in favor of more intellectual, adult pursuits..."

Not even the outline of a smile managed to crack Calhoun's stone-cold features. Instead, the South Carolinian was typically grim, blunt and straightforward: "On the contrary, Sir, I believe the elections of you three splendid young men demonstrate the faith the older generation has in you all to maintain and promulgate the policies, traditions and institutions so vital to the South's well-being."

The clearly enunciated phrase 'policies, traditions and institutions' crackled across the room with an intensity that left Wellington with the clear mental image of Calhoun wielding a whip snatched from the hand of his own plantation's overseer. He recalled Captain Bratton's prediction of the previous evening: *"No compromising...a fanatic...beyond the limits."*

Calhoun's impatience at small talk was obvious, as was his purposeful single-mindedness:

"The hour is late so I suggest we dispense with further jovial frivolities and get to the point." The fire-eater's eyes blazed as he glared directly at the Duke. "The message of your speech today, Sir, is unacceptable to the South. Slavery was a long-established institution in the South, a bulwark of our prosperity, long before the Colonial Compact or the Dominion Constitution.

"We reject the hypothesis that the Crown or any of its governmental units---either in Georgetown or London---can legally force us to give up our institution. Nor will we be bribed into doing so...at any price!"

The silence in the study at the conclusion of Calhoun's outburst was so total that Swain, for one, could hear the carriage wheels creaking down the circular driveway on the opposite side of the house, as well as the incessant chirp of the ever-present crickets.

If Wellington---after all the conqueror of Bonaparte as well as a former British Prime Minister---was offended by Calhoun's tirade, thought Senator Person---*and how could he not be*---the Duke was giving no such indication. His color remained the sun-burned red he had arrived with but had not deepened to a blood rush-induced scarlet. His hands, stuck in his pockets since entering the room, did not seem to be trembling. Except for a slight, almost unnoticeable pursing of the lips, even his facial features had not changed.

The silence threatened to extend into minutes when at last Wellington opened his mouth:

"Our's is an empire of laws, Senator. Some formulated and approved in Parliament; some likewise passed by the Congress of which you and your esteemed colleagues are members. These laws may be tested, as it were, by challenge and appeal to the appropriate courts-of-law.

"I submit that the bill to emancipate the Empire's slave population will without question be approved by both houses of Parliament before summer's end. You are welcome, indeed encouraged, to challenge the bill, either through your elected members of that august body, or in the Empire's highest courts. But you will not win.

"Further, you will have the opportunity for debate in your own legislative arenas in Georgetown. Based on my extensive conversations in other sections of the Dominion, I am comfortable in stating my confidence that you will lose there, also. Once again, you may challenge in your Supreme Court. Justice Marshall, however, has been quite explicit in stating that your Court will also rule in the Crown's favor."

Swain and Brown exchanged worried glances as the Duke paused briefly. *My God*, thought the Governor, *Calhoun looks ready to take the fireplace utensils to Wellington! And the Duke seems intent on enticing him to try!*

Wellington continued: "As for your position of prior existence, I'm told by Justice Marshall that this has no legal merit on either side of the Atlantic.

"Finally, Senator, I do not believe that you---and you alone---speak for the South. Views more moderate than your own may yet be expressed by Southern voices, including possibly some present here tonight."

The lumps of burning coal masquerading as Calhoun's eyes seemed to blaze even brighter. "I would not be so presumptuous, Sir Arthur, in counting Southern votes---or determining who speaks for the South---on this issue." He turned and glanced meaningfully at the other two Senators before pausing.

A strange smile, to the on-lookers' amazement, seemed then to break out on Calhoun's face though it by no means reached his still-blazing eyes.

"Even if all you claim is true, Sir Arthur, and I am in no way acknowledging that it is, the South will in the end proceed unabated with our 'peculiar institution.' And with your blessing and that of your Government, I might add." The South Carolinian's smile had evolved into a near-smirk visible to all.

"For what Congress will vote on next month will not pertain to the abolition of slavery. Instead, it will vote---and approve---an exemption to Parliament's measure. An exemption that you, Sir, will work out with the Governor-General and which he will then submit. Once passed, you will return to London to shepard it through

Parliament. I have no doubt that you will be successful in this endeavor."

The three North Carolina officials' mouths were now all ajar, while Wellington, while maintaining his stiff upper lip, had in fact blinked rapidly and repeatedly.

Regaining the small measure of self-control he had momentarily let slip, the Duke quietly asked: "Is that so, my dear chap. And what on earth could lead you to that remarkable conclusion?"

Calhoun, his long hair providing a frame for the gaunt face now completely dominated by the fiery eyes, raised his right arm and pointed the extended index finger at Wellington.

Even the crickets seemed to have ceased their repetative chirping in order to listen in:

"Because, Sir, the Empire can not afford a crisis here in the USBA. Not when you are facing such a serious one in Europe…"

He paused and looked at the younger men. "…or, to be more precise, in Asia Minor."

The fire-eater looked back in triumph at the Duke, who was now conducting a protracted interior battle to maintain his composure:

"After all, Sir, as righteous as your Parliament may consider emancipation of *our* slaves, it considers the security of *your* own British India to be just as righteous. So that John Company can continue its own righteous work of merrily looting that fabled subcontinent...to the benefit, of course, of King, Country and Empire."

Calhoun moved past Wellington and across to grasp the study's door handle before pivoting. "Think on it, Sir Arthur. The Empire does not need a truly unnecessary and avoidable crisis on one side of the world while you have to deal with a very necessary and unavoidable one on the other. And the only price to make your American crisis disappear is one small exemption."

The other four men were still staring as Calhoun's face relaxed into its first complete smile of the evening.

"Until June 4th, gentlemen, in Georgetown. Good evening."

The door closed gently behind him.

CHAPTER THIRTY-SIX

Liaison Office
Georgetown, D.C.
May 23, 1833, 10 a.m.:

The Duke had returned to the capitol on Monday, just in time to experience the lovely Georgetown spring turn equatorial overnight. He had hastened his return to determine if anyone in Georgetown was aware of the Russian incursion into Syria...and to determine how Calhoun had discovered it!

Captain Bratton immediately, of course, had jumped to the conclusion that this Russki secret chap---whatever his name really was---had informed the fire-eater. "Not only is this the sole plausible way Calhoun could have gotten the information, Your Grace, but it confirms that Karlhamanov actually is Count Ignatieff!" Thus Bratton's argument on the ride back to Wilmington after being briefed on the private meeting in the Governor's study.

Wellington had not discounted the validity of Harry's theory, but wondered aloud how, if the Russian had been in the USBA since February, he could know much about the Syrian crisis. "And how, and how much, information could have been conveyed to Calhoun?"

The Duke had paced worriedly throughout much of the pleasant voyage back to Georgetown. He braced himself for the worst: had *The Times* published stories about the Syrian crisis in issues one or more of which might have survived an Atlantic crossing? And had knowledge of the incursion already been absorbed and factored into the emancipation business over here? What did Jackson know? And how, if he did, is he reacting?

Now that he was back in the capital, Wellington assessed the situation and found it less volatile than feared: while the upcoming special session---with all its increasingly-frightening implications---was on everyone's minds, there was no mention of the Syrian affair, either among their American contacts or in diplomatic circles.

Nor did the G-G appear to have any knowledge when they breakfasted yesterday. (Jackson had apparently been enjoying an extended weekend at Frank Blair's Silver Spring country mansion when the Duke and Bratton arrived back early Monday afternoon.) The talk, of course, had been dominated by emancipation...and by Jackson's adamant refusal to reveal his position: "I stand by my Inaugural speech: I am waiting to hear the people's voice as conveyed by their elected representatives. I'll make my decision then and only then..."

*Jackson could be sly and tricky---as a hapless French army at New Orleans once discovered---*Wellington thought, *but he is not devious. The G-G,* the Duke determined with relief, *is unaware of the Syrian complication.*

General Scott, after being appraised of the situation over dinner at his home Monday evening, had been adamant: the European crisis was not yet known to official Georgetown. "I'll grill Lieutenant Wilder tomorrow morning, Sir Arthur. But I've no doubt The Residency is unaware of this. The Lieutenant would have observed any increase in excitement or intensity and reported it, even if he did not have the details."

(Winfield had sent Wilder to the Office yesterday: to the best of the Lieutenant's knowledge and observation, no information of a foreign nature was being assessed at The Residency. Based on his faith in Scott's evaluation of talent, the Duke accepted Tom's assessment as accurate.)

All was also quiet at the neglected State Department, which was the Administration's principal, though mostly ignored, liaison with the consulates. So Burrell, whose job included monitoring bureaucratic Georgetown, reported.

Now the Duke was convening a meeting with Bratton, Sir John and Major Layne to consider the situation--and their options:

Do we abduct this Russian and grill him here in the Office basement? At what point do the Extremity Provisions---Harry, trust him, had brought them up on the voyage from Wilmington---come into play?

If-and-when is the Jackson Administration entitled to a briefing on Syria?

Most importantly, if-and-when do we inform our political allies in the North---from the Vice G-G on down---of the Syrian problem? And its potential impact on the emancipation question?

Wellington shook his head wryly. *Who would have thought the advance of some upstart Gypo Pasha into Palestine could affect the freedom of some 2,000,000 Godforsaken darkies in America?*

Asheville, North Carolina
May 23, 1833:

Despite his farewell at the Governor's Mansion, John C. Calhoun did not leave Raleigh until three days after the cornerstone-laying ceremony, long after the Duke himself had ridden east.

He in fact met with Senators Magnum and Brown the following day; as a Dominion-Republican (and thus considered 'soft' on slavery), Governor Swain was pointedly not invited. The fire-eater put off their questions concerning his, as Brown called it, 'Asia Minor riddle': "In due course, gentlemen. First, let's observe its effect on the great man. All will become clear once the Congress convenes."

And that was all Calhoun would say on the subject. The two young North Carolinians were too much in awe to press him further, despite their curiosity. "That damn old man acts as if he's operating on a higher plane than the rest of us," Magnum fumed privately later. "He expects us to toe the line…but won't say where the line leads."

"Obviously, to a confrontation with Wellington and perhaps Jackson in Georgetown," Brown replied. "One in which he believes he holds all the aces. I'm not happy either, but for the sake of the South, we must go along for now. If he's overplayed his hand, there'll be time for compromise up there. At least, I pray to God there will be…"

Senator Calhoun had delayed leaving Raleigh ostensibly because he received several invitations to speak over the weekend at various Democratic rallies in the capitol city. More importantly, having digested the contents of the amazing letter while still on the road, he had sent word to Congressman Polk to meet him in this small Blue Ridge town almost equidistant from Raleigh and Polk's east Tennessee plantation.

The Senator had checked into the Wolfpack Inn late Monday but Polk, along with his young law partner, Gideon Pillow, had not shown up until the following evening. Calhoun wasted no time once young Pillow was banished to the bar to join his own aide, Munroe, in briefing Polk on the letter at a back table.

The Tennessean was astonished, as Calhoun knew he would be; and also immediately grasped the implication; which is why he had been shown the letter. "Speak of this to no one, James," Calhoun directed, staring at Polk's still-dropped jaw. "Digest it, and we'll speak on it again in the morning. You can see now why I had you come to Asheville. This is much too valuable to chance having fall into the wrong hands."

Calhoun's coal-black eyes began to blaze anew. "Before I tell you of my meeting with Wellington, and hear your news from Tennessee, let's be clear why I've shared this with you: You are our best conduit for information in and out of The Residency. You're the only member of our inner group who's also an advisor to Jackson. We need you back in Georgetown post-haste. So you must head back to your plantation immediately after our talk tomorrow morning, collect Sarah and start out for the capital.

"I am headed directly back to Fort Hill. There I will pick up Floride and McDuffie and sail for Georgetown myself. We must organize for the special session as soon as possible, counting on whatever information you obtain concerning Jackson's leanings or decision."

Though stunned by the contents of the letter, the Congressman was marveling at its potential power: "I understand completely, Senator. The information contained," he tapped at the letter before handing it back to Calhoun, "if true, puts the entire situation in a new perspective."

He paused and shook his head while fingering the half-empty whiskey glass in front of him. "Obviously you believe this Russian's news..."

Calhoun nodded affirmatively.

"...I tend to concur. Why would he---or anyone else---make up such an astounding story? This letter may give us the upper hand in this crisis...and checkmate the damn abolitionists once and for all."

Calhoun smiled his dark smile. "My thoughts exactly, Congressman. Now let me relate my 'interview' with His Grace, the great man himself..."

Early this morning when the two met again privately, their two baffled aides at a separate table, Calhoun returned to the letter over their bacon and eggs:

"At some point Wellington will have to brief Jackson on the Syrian adventure. That's why I showed you the letter, so you'd know in advance of walking up The Residency's steps. This may be the weight that tips the G-G's scale in our favor. That damn old man has enormous prestige in the North and West. If we can fix things behind-the-scene so that it appears that *he* has arranged the exemption as a compromise---without anyone knowing what *really* caused Wellington to cave in---the other sections will, reluctantly, go along.

"Otherwise, I fear Wellington's visit and news of Parliament's emancipation debate may give the abolitionists too much momentum, especially in the North." Calhoun paused to take a small bite of his rapidly-cooling eggs and looked over at his colleague.

Polk was nodding his head in agreement as Calhoun summed the situation up:

"Without the exemption, the South has but one option, as acceptance is intolerable."

This time it was the Tennessean's eyes that glowed: "Senator, I have always anticipated and feared a political compromise would be ultimately unfavorable to the South. Yet our chances for independence-by-arms or -threat have likewise seemed improbable at best.

"If I have correctly grasped the overall implications of this remarkable Syrian news, the Empire will have its hands full in the eastern Mediterranean for quite some time. An armed insurrection over here---even if eventually quelled---would be an unacceptable drain, both in money and manpower."

The South Carolinian's fork paused halfway toward his mouth and he silently nodded affirmatively.

"Now then," Polk continued, "I believe the Russians have fortuitously made our threat viable. The game is still a series of inter-locking gambles, but now the odds have lessened: London is more likely to give in here than risk an insurrection; and, if it does, the North is equally unlikely to press for emancipation without London's backing. As those Yankees might say, 'it simply isn't good business.'"

The Congressman motioned toward their empty coffee cups. As Calhoun nodded, the dark smile breaking out around his taut mouth, Polk called to the waiter for more. Once delivered, he proposed a toast:

"To our Russian ally, whatever his real name and title. No matter his motives, the South owes him an enormous debt of gratitude."

Calhoun softly tapped his cup against Polk's in smug satisfaction: "To our Russian ally."

———————

Russian Consulate
Georgetown, D.C.
May 25, 1833, 11:00 a.m.:

Countess Caroline Renkowiitz was out-of-sorts.

The Countess' weekly Sunday afternoon ride with David Harper (which now began in mid-morning and extended, with the help of a picnic basket, through late afternoon) was scheduled for tomorrow.

Caroline had come to value these outings, both because of her growing affection for the witty and handsome young American and because they provided an escape from the increasing tension inside the Consulate. But she was dreading tomorrow.

Count Ignatieff's on-going presence, though no one at the Consulate ever knew when he might suddenly appear, had everyone on edge. But Caroline carried a special burden: only she was aware of the amazing news from St. Petersburg concerning the Ottomans.

Ignatieff had confided in her for a basic yet astute reason: while he himself was fluent in English, his ability was verbal. The Count knew he could not afford to make the slightest error or misrepresentation in his letter apprising Calhoun of the Syrian situation. So he had been forced to bring Caroline in, knowing of her impressive fluency in the language. And, he had said, he was "impressed with your splendid grasp of the USBA domestic political scene."

So Caroline, soon after the Count's return from the South, had been told of the departure of the Imperial Black Sea Fleet---and a 10,000 man army---for Syria. Together, they had drafted the letter that Captain Drago had then been entrusted to hand-deliver to Calhoun in South Carolina.

Caroline had since become increasing uncomfortable in talking about the crisis with David. This after all being Georgetown, politics invariably wound its way into every conversation (as her thus-far platonic admirer's very secret and very carnal relationship with the beautiful Madame Jean-Claude could have demonstrated). She had turned the conversation to other things the last few Sundays, out of a vague sense of guilt.

Now, however, she knew that a second letter with updated information had been written. General Mikailov had landed on the Syrian coast and was planning an advance into Lebanon or Palestine (depending on where exactly he located the Pasha's army). It had once again been dispatched, utilizing Drago, to South Carolina.

What could---should---she say when David inevitably turned the conversation to the crisis? She felt ashamed to mislead him, but...

It was not just her growing attachment to the Interior Department official that had the Countess feeling confused.

Caroline had come of age in stuffy, rigid Russian consulates in such autocratic strongholds as Belgrade, Prague and Buenos Aires. She had never before been exposed to the heady air of freedom one breathed so effortlessly in Georgetown. She liked British America. Somehow, she had become party to a plot to destroy it...

Brown's Indian Queen Hotel Taproom
Georgetown, D.C.
May 25, 1833, 2:30 p.m.:

Tom Wilder was both furious and determined as he sipped a much-anticipated cold beer: he had learned during the General's usual late Saturday morning stop-bye at the Department that the Scotts were scheduled to attend a dinner party for the Duke this evening at Justice Marshall's home with a guest list that included Miss Latoure.

The General had actually seemed taken back---his massive forehead had reddened---when Tom had informed him that: "I'm sorry, Sir, but I have no invitation to dine this evening with Miss Latoure. At Justice Marshall's or elsewhere...I will be on call, however, if my presence is required..."

While the General simply shook his leonine head and retreated to his own office, his aide made a quick decision: calling one of the few enlisted men present on this balmy Saturday, he entrusted him with a short answering note informing Candice that he would indeed be available after approximately 5 p.m.

Let Lucille talk politics---or flirt---with Sir John, Joe Johnston or whoever else appears at the damn dinner party! He'd be ensconced between the biggest pair of lungs in British America...

Chief Justice Marshall's Home
Georgetown, D.C.
May 25, 1833, 7:15 p.m.

Maria Scott had straitened her husband out on the carriage ride over from their townhouse: Lucille Latoure was not playing Tom for the fool once again! The invitation to dine had actually been extended to Mrs. Latoure, an old friend of the Marshalls. Lucille was in fact escorting her mother...

That minor annoyance cleared up, the General was now concentrating on the important issue. Wellington had sent a brief note to the townhouse late this afternoon alerting Scott that 'news from abroad' had arrived at the Liaison Office this morning. They would need to excuse themselves for a few minutes tonight and speak privately.

"Whatever the 'news' is, it can't be positive," the General told his wife, "or Wellington wouldn't have referred to it in such a stealth manner." He sighed as Maria glanced at him worriedly.

"I had hopes that the Russkiis would turn tail and sail back through the Straits once the Royal Navy showed the flag. Well, either the Navy is late in getting to the Syrian coast or the damn Russians have put their army ashore anyway..."

Much of the capitol's entrenched, full-time elite was gathering when the Scotts were announced. The Vice G-G, as elegant and formal as ever, greeted them in the parlor. The new Interior Secretary, Louis MacLane, was also on hand, as were the Blairs and several other Supreme Court justices, including Smith Thompson of New York and Massachusetts' Joseph Story.

Justice Story was holding forth as the Scotts entered: "…simply no constitutional grounds. Nor covered in the Compact, either. Why, it's plainly nullification with new wrapping and a bow…"

Van Buren smiled and, as he took Mrs. Scott's hand (while warily avoiding the General's ponderous paw), said softly: "Apparently, the Court is considering Mr. Calhoun's latest legal invention already. I have labored under the impression that briefs are normally first filed…" His eyes twinkling, he shook his head in mock sadness and moved away to engage his fellow New Yorker, Thompson, in quiet tones.

Wellington was speaking with the host as General Scott deposited Maria in a group that included the Latoure ladies, Eliza Blair and Mrs. Story. Captain Bratton, he could see, was eyeing Lucille Latoure appreciatively while posed at the Duke's side.

"Ah, General Scott. Our host has pointed out the remarkable number of native Virginians regularly in top positions in your Army: Gaines, Taylor, yourself. This chap Harrison who defeated Tecumseh. How is that, eh? Are you Virginians particularly warlike? After all, Washington was one of you also, I daresay…"

Eyes brightening, Scott smiled as he glanced from Marshall to the Duke: "Well Sir, Virginia produces leaders of all varieties. Our host is of course the Dominion's leading jurist. And certainly no one would have described Jefferson or Madison as warriors…"

Both Marshall and Wellington laughed as Scott continued: "…however, the Dominion does produce fighting men from all the states. Two of my leading commanders now are from New York, Colonels Worth and Wool." He paused and grinned again: "As of course is your new friend, Colonel Burr…"

The Duke's laugh could be heard throughout the room; those glancing over saw the Chief Justice shaking his head rather ruefully…

"Well, on that note, Mr. Marshall," Wellington said, "I need a few moments privately with the General. If we could borrow your study…"

Moments later the two were sequestered behind closed doors, Captain Bratton standing guard while attempting to make eye contact with Miss Latoure.

Wellington was immediately to the point: "A dispatch this morning from Lord Palmerston. That Russki fleet has landed their army on the Syrian coast. Elements of our Mediterranean fleet arrived while they were still disembarking. Our flotilla is shadowing the landing site but hadn't made contact, on Downing Street's orders. Seems the Cabinet feels there's no grounds. To complicate matters further, Admiral Hotham in Crete has taken ill and resigned. A new commander, one..." Wellington reached into his coat pocket for a paper, "...Pulteney Malcolm has been sent out to relieve him."

The General remained impassive during the report. Wellington now put the dispatch back in his pocket and stared up into Scott's face. "You do realize the implication for this domestic problem of yours, Winfield? The Russkiis' Syrian adventure has plunged Europe into a diplomatic crisis to rival the Greek rebellion some years back.

"The Foreign Secretary, in his capacity as head of the emancipation committee, writes that, and I quote...Wellington pulled the dispatch out again, "'...I trust you are realizing success in securing the Americans' agreement to abide by the emancipation bill...'---which, apparently, is sailing smoothly through Parliament--- '...as the Government will have its hands full in the Near East for some time to come. I pray Quincy Adams' fears of armed resistance are as overblown as is much other of his rhetoric.'"

Wellington made a show of folding the dispatch and again replacing it in his coat pocket before staring back up at Scott.

"In other words, Winfield, this crisis will have to be addressed solely with the resources already on hand here in British America. What spare forces the Empire can muster are already, I suspect, alerted for possible Near East duty."

As radicalized as Lucille Latoure may have become, a belle she remained. Though balding men physically repulsed---and Brits in general infuriated---her, this tall balding Brit officer who kept looking her way was, after all, the aide to the Duke of Wellington. There might be some interesting information to learn by some harmless flirting...

And so Lucille allowed the Coldstream Guardsman to escort her into dinner after General Scott and the Duke emerged from their private meeting. After all, no one said learning couldn't be fun...

Rock Creek Trail
Georgetown, D.C.
May 26, 1833, 1 p.m.:

As a native Northern European, Countess Caroline Renkowiitz, even in her second summer in Georgetown, could not handle long exposure to the tropical weather that had suddenly descended on the capitol. Nor could the Cossack escort that trailed, by now at a more comfortable distance, during her weekly rides with Dave Harper.

So by mutual, unspoken agreement, today's ride had mercifully been halted after an hour or so in favor of a tree-shaded picnic. That was fine with Harps, of course, especially as the Cossacks maintained their distance while setting up their own meal.

(Harps actually tended to forget the guards were around: several times he had come perilously close to making a potentially mortal error, he had admitted to a chortling Tom Wilder. "This is crazy, Tom: instead of 'hear no evil, see no evil,' this is 'hear no evil, 'see everything as evil.'"

(Tom had put on a formal face: "I'm sorry, Mr. Harper, but I can offer no advice. I, you see, have no experience with nobly-born ladies…"

("No, Lieutenant. Only nobly-built ones…")

The picnic should make it easier to raise a delicate point than an extended ride would have, Harps thought with some relief.

Captain Bratton, whom he had not spoken to in more than two months---since passing along the news that Karlhamanov had apparently pulled rank concerning the Inaugural ticket---had asked him to a Thursday noon-time meal at the Liaison Office. The purpose was simple: to have him quietly sound Caroline out about this Karlhamanov.

(Harps was not surprised that the Brits knew he was still seeing the Countess; he and Caroline had crossed paths with Major Layne last Sunday while riding in this same area.)

"I need not point out, Mr. Harper, that our interest in this Russian is strictly professional," Bratton had said, though the thought of Joanne's deliciously lithe body was instantaneously in the mind's eye of both as Karlhamanov's name was mentioned.

Harps had tried to hide a smile as the Captain, after a quick glance at a Major Layne busily staring at the King's wall portrait, hurried on:

"We have reason to believe this Russian has purposefully misrepresented himself here in the USBA." He paused and looked again at Layne, who was now staring hard at Harps. "That, of course, is privileged information, Mr. Harper. I trust you are aware of the significance and will act accordingly.

"Now then, when will you ride next with the delightful Countess? This Sunday? I say: that's terrific. Now what we need to know is this…"

Harps, his amorous instincts for once secondary to the task at hand, now wondered whether to allow the conversation to proceed naturally, or to bring Karlhamanov's name up himself.

Though political conversation was as natural and addictive as breathing in Georgetown, and had been a staple of their earliest rides, he could see that Caroline, for some reason, was seemingly avoiding the subject today.

So, after a second bottle of chilled Crimean white wine had been opened under a copse of shade trees and cheese, bread, fruit and cold chicken partaken, Dave plunged in:

"As you know, Caroline, I often meet Lieutenant Wilder for an after-work beer and some supper. Among the inns we frequent is one called The Golden Eagle, just a few blocks from the War and Interior Building.

"One of your countrymen is again many times there after a disappearance of some months. I believe he goes by the name of 'Andre.' Are you aware of him?"

From the suddenly reddened checks and troubled look in her bright blue eyes, he realized he had hit a nerve.

Caroline sighed and turned to gaze over to where the two Cossacks were enjoying their own Sunday feast. "An expatriate professor of that first name has been in and out of the Consulate in recent months, yes. Apparently, he comes from a rich St. Petersburg merchant family but was exiled for teachings deemed dangerous to the regime…"

David studied her face closely. *She is beautiful... and also uncomfortable talking--lying--of this. Maybe Bratton and Layne are on to something... But she'll offer no more without further prodding.*

"I only ask, Caroline, because he seems to have won the favor of the owner, one Mrs. Casgrave. Their relationship is the talk of the inn..."

Caroline's face, surprisingly, did not again redden. Instead, it indicated only surprise. "I was...unaware of Andre's..."---she now blushed profusely---"...social life." She paused and composed herself before continuing. "Well, that is no concern of mine. Nor the Consulate's, as I do not believe it violates the terms of his exile. At least, I have never heard it mentioned." She paused once more. *I'm not very good at dissembling, am I? Especially to dear David, who, for all his charm, is so naïve about these matters of state.*

"As for his 'disappearance': I have no idea or interest in his travel...or his acquaintances, either here or elsewhere in your country. Actually, I have no interest in the Co...M. Karlhamanov at all... It begins to become chilly here, Mr. Harper. Perhaps we should resume our ride..."

War Department
Georgetown, D.C.
May 27, 1833, 10 a.m.:

The Deputy Commanding General of the USBA Army could barely see The Residency from the window of his tiny office. *That,* Edmund P. Gaines thought, *pretty much sums up my job: just close enough to see power, but too far removed to exercise any...*

All that might just be about to change, however, Gaines thought. Lt. Lucius Beaufort had come to him earlier in the month, while Scott was away at The Point playing God, with a startling set of papers. The Commanding General's secretary had discovered notes---a draft plan, actually---in Lieutenant Wilder's desk that seemed to discuss a major Army expansion. Other papers reviewed the officer corps...with all Southern-born officers set apart.

Beaufort had, of course, come to his house at night with the papers; Gaines seldom set foot in the Department. *(I'm only here today because Scott's off attending to some damn problem at Fort McHenry.)* First off,

Scott refused to delegate any responsibilities to him; secondly, it wasn't good for staff morale to see the tension between them. Gaines had known Scott harbored a dislike for him stemming from the old days in the Upper Louisiana campaign. But it wasn't until he arrived in Georgetown that he realized that Scott had only grudgingly accepted his appointment, one forcibly insisted upon by Jackson. Anyway, the dynamite contained in the papers wasn't something to be openly discussed at the War Department, in any case.

Luke Beaufort might be Scott's secretary but the young man hailed from one of Mississippi's leading planter families. Gaines knew he resented the relationship young Wilder---*a typically arrogant New Yorker*---had established with Scott. But as Beaufort laid out the papers on Gaines' own dining room table, he quickly saw that the issue far exceeded personal jealousy.

"It would appear, Lieutenant, that Mr. Wilder has been working on contingency plans for an all-Northern Army.

"Now what would possess the Commanding General to order up such a study?" The sarcasm dripped from Gaines' voice as he and Beaufort stared at one another. "Unless of course he fears the South will stand up for its rights and refuse to be bullied into relinquishing its property without a fight?"

He had ordered Lieutenant Beaufort to copy the papers and return the originals to Wilder's desk before Scott and his fair-haired boy returned to Georgetown. Luke had done so and presented him with the copies. They had then turned to the task of preparing a draft report of their own: a capsulated description of the Wilder papers plus a draft plan for a Southern Army, built around the excluded officer corps and utilizing the militia regiments of the Southern states.

That now-completed secret report rested with the copied papers in a locked safe at home. Also resting in the safe were copies of letters and original communications with such leading Southern officers as David Twiggs and Zach Taylor...though Gaines wondered whether old Zach was smart enough to read between the lines!

The next step, he reminded himself as he continued to stare out the window, *is to meet privately with Calhoun and make a presentation of the facts. That'll stroke the Senator! Even if Calhoun and Jackson work out a compromise to get the exemption and keep us happy in the Dominion, they'll never forgive Scott for even thinking about contingency plans for fighting the South...*

And if they can't get that exemption, well...one way or the other, we'll see who's commanding what Army...and who's retired in disgrace!

Liaison Office
Georgetown, D.C.
May 27, 1833, 3 p.m.:

Captain Bratton and Major Layne were waiting with Sir John Burrell when David Harper was ushered into a spacious conference room decorated with a massive British flag and equally large portraits of the King, his father George III
and the Prime Minister.

Harps had sent the Captain a short note early this morning and the Colonial Office man had requested his appearance at this hour "if your schedule at the Department permits. Otherwise, please specify a time." Three o'clock was fine with David: it should leave him free before Interior closed at 5 p.m.. The new Secretary was making a show, he thought with a grumble, of keeping the Department fully manned until that hour, work, or lack of same, notwithstanding.

The amenities quickly disposed of, the Captain plunged directly ahead: "Well now Mr. Harper. I assume your afternoon with the Countess went well? Good; now what have you got for us?"

Harper hoped the three Brits would not be upset with the brevity of his report; not much had happened, but he felt it his duty to bring Bratton up-to-date anyhow. He hadn't expected the entire Liaison upper echelon to be present, however...

"The Countess is sticking with the official word that Karlhamanov is some sort of renegade son of a rich and influential St. Petersburg merchant family. But it's easy to see that's just the cover story..."

Burrell's delicate eyebrows went up: "Easy to see...how's that? What makes you so sure?"

Harper flashed the grin that had disarmed---and disrobed---so many females before continuing: "I've been seeing Caroline...the Countess...almost every Sunday for more than three months now.

She's doesn't seem to be a very good liar; I doubt she's had much practice…

"She turned away before answering my question about Karlhamanov, which was simply if she was aware of a fellow Russian who seems to split his time when in town between the Consulate and the Golden Eagle. Couldn't look me in the eye. And that's the first time in our, err, 'friendship,' that I've gotten such a reaction…"

The three Englishmen suddenly jumped to their feet as a hook-nosed old gentleman opened the conference room door and quietly walked in. *Oh my God, it's Wellington!* Harper thought, looking over his left shoulder before scrambling to rise himself.

"At ease, gentlemen." The Duke eyeballed Harper as he had a thousand young subalterns. "Young Mr. Harper of the Interior Department. I'm told you're our ticket inside the Russian Consulate…"

Harry Bratton, busy pulling out a conference table chair for Sir Arthur, quickly recapped: "Mr. Harper doesn't believe our friend 'Andre' is quite the 'Russian dissident' he has claimed to be. Says the Countess was…unconvincing…in so describing him."

The Duke returned his icy gaze to David: "Is that so. Hmm. Was she…unconvincing…in anything else she said?"

"Yes Your Grace," David's head was now bobbing up and down like a bouncing ball: "Carol…the Countess…also claimed she had no idea where he might have gone or who he might have seen during his time away from Georgetown. 'No interest' was the way she put it. She seemed rather upset…and insisted we end our picnic and resume riding…

"I think I know her well enough to detect when she's not herself. And my questions definitely flustered her. So, I have to think she knows quite a bit about his travels and, as she put it, 'his American acquaintances…'"

With an embarrassed look at the Duke---*I thought he'd have more than this*---Bratton quickly, almost pleadingly, asked: "Anything else, Mr. Harper? Surely more talk than that on a long Sunday afternoon together?"

Awed by Wellington's presence, Harps took a minute to reply. "Well Captain, she was definitely surprised to know of the man's relationship with Mrs. Casgrave…"

Bratton's forehead and cheeks suddenly matched the red of the Imperial flag displayed across the room. A sudden spasm of coughing simultaneously erupted from the Major, while Sir John's lips puckered in a strange way. Even the Duke took a moment to clear his throat.

"...but overall, it was her nervousness in even talking about him--and the Cossacks were far enough away that our conversation was strictly private---that most impressed me. Why, she even became confused..."

"To what extent, Mr. Harper?" Bratton's tone was interrogational, almost desperate.

"At one point, while we were discussing his absence from Georgetown, she even began to mix him up with her father."

"What? With her father...?" Sir John looked skeptically at the young American. "I say, in what earthly way?"

"She started to refer to him as 'the Count.' Only, she caught herself about halfway through. Then called him 'M. Karlhamanov.'"

Three heads stared momentarily at Harper before reflexively turning to look at their chief. The Duke of Wellington reached across the table and offered David his hand. "Thank you, Mr. Harper, you've been very helpful. I will send an appropriate note to Mr. MacLane for your permanent file. Major, if you will show Mr. Harper out..." Harry and Sir John were talking at once almost before the door closed behind the stunned Harper. "'By George, we've pegged him at last, Sir!" mixed with "We've got him this time. That's confirmation!"

The Duke, however, quickly held up his hand for silence. He waited till Robert Layne returned to the table before speaking in a quiet but forceful tone.

"'Pegged him,' Harry? Perhaps. 'Confirmation' though? Not yet. All we have is an apparent slip of the tongue by a Russian noblewoman speaking in a language not native to her."

He smiled softly as Bratton and Burrell fell back in their chairs, their excitement visibly fading. "Now gentlemen, no long faces. I daresay, I haven't said I disagree with your conclusion. It's simply a rather long leap of faith on very little tangible evidence." He turned to look at the now-seated Layne. "Major, what is your opinion?"

Layne licked his lower lip and paused for a long second: "Your Grace, I agree that the evidence at face value is flimsy. Until you recall something Mr. Harper told us the last time he was here." He paused again and looked at Bratton.

"You will recall, won't you, Harry, that young Mr. Harper told us over lunch that day that the Countess was so proficient in the English language that she was conducting classes at the Consulate several days a week?"

Encouraged by a nod from Wellington, as well as quick agreement from the Captain, Layne plunged ahead: "So this is more likely a slip of the tongue than a confusion of language." He stopped again before picking up a report that had been in a stack in front of him:

"After our initial, ah, 'mishap' concerning this Russki's whereabouts, I had a tail placed on 'Andre' until he left town; then resumed it when he reappeared. But I also have had the Consulate under 24-hour surveillance since March. Twice in the last," he looked down at the report, "30 days, one Captain Drago---whom we have long-since identified as the, shall we say, 'man of action' over there---has left town. As of this morning, he had not returned from the second jaunt."

Sir John shrugged his skinny shoulders in puzzlement. "So these Russkiis like to ride through Virginia...I fail to see what that..."

Layne paid his civilian counterpart no apparent mind: "I submit, Your Grace, that the two situations tie together: Captain Drago is being utilized by Count Ignatieff---as I believe the Countess inadvertently but correctly identified him---as the postman to deliver news to this Mr. Calhoun. News contained in letters or reports that the Countess has had a hand in preparing, under Ignatieff's direction."

Bratton and Burrell were silenced by pure shock, but Wellington smiled and nodded his head at the Major. "Well Major Layne, indeed. There may be a future for you after all, above and beyond this...hamlet. Good work."

He turned to the others: "However, gentlemen, even if accepting the Major's deductive reasoning as correct, we still do not have the grounds, the proof actually, to move in on our friend. And certainly not to invoke the Extremity Provisions...

"At this juncture, all we can do is continue to keep a close watch on the Consulate...and all its inhabitants."

He nodded grimly: "It may also be time to bring certain of our American political allies up-to-date on the Syrian adventure. And how Calhoun may be about to use it to his diabolical political advantage when their Congress meets."

CHAPTER THIRTY-SEVEN

Charleston, South Carolina, Harbor
May 28, 1833, 7:00 a.m.:

John C. Calhoun had been firm with the sloop's captain. If Congressman McDuffie wasn't aboard by this hour, the anchor was to be pulled anyway.

"Mac will just have to catch the next available boat," the Senator told Floride. "It's essential that I get to Georgetown as soon as practically possible. I'll not wait for McDuffie nor anyone else..."

To Floride's relief, and Calhoun's pleasure, as he often used the Congressman as a personal sounding board, McDuffie's hired hack came racing up to the dock before the gangplank was raised. "Better late than never," Calhoun grumbled as his House of Representatives' point man dashed on board. "Congressman McDuffie, Sir. This is no time to initiate a habit of tardiness..."

The winded McDuffie shook his head in disgust. "Damn hotel clerk forgot to waken me as ordered. I'd have skinned his hide, if there were time. Shows what happens when these transplanted Yankees are put in positions of responsibility. A proper darkie clerk would have had me up with time to spare..."

Laughing, the trio went below to breakfast privately in the Calhouns' stateroom. Once the fresh fruit was served and they were momentarily alone, Calhoun began to brief McDuffie on the Syrian situation, including the newest information delivered by Captain Drago: the Russians were landed and in search of the Arab army.

It took till the ruins of breakfast had been collected and carried away before the Congressman fully grasped the implications.

"If I understand you correctly, John, you intend to utilize the specter of insurrection here in the South as the weapon of choice to force the exemption concession from Wellington, based on the assumption that the Empire can not risk major conflicts in two places. But how can you be so sure the British are responding to the Syrian adventure? Seems to me, you have only the information this

385

'correspondent' of yours---who obviously is this Russian professor, or whatever his rank really is---has supplied you."

Calhoun's smile bordered on the patronizing: "Not quite, George. I've yet to tell you of my encounter with His Grace, the Duke of Wellington himself, earlier this month in Raleigh..."

The surprised expression on the Congressman's face at this news gradually turned to comprehension as he listened to Calhoun's version of the private session in the North Carolina governor's mansion.

"Well, John, sounds as if you bested the self-righteous old Limey bastard. Knew exactly what you were referring to, eh! And realized you hold all the aces... Bet that sent him galloping back to Georgetown in a hurry. Why, I wouldn't be surprised if he's worked out a compromise with Jackson already..."

Calhoun smiled at his wife while holding up a hand. "Congressman, please! I'm afraid it won't be quite this easy!"

He paused to sip some newly poured coffee before continuing: "Wellington is as astute as they come. He's certainly had someone--- probably Van Buren---counting heads. He knows it's going to be tight in the Congress and that Jackson is key, if it gets that far.

"I agree he probably *galloped* back to Georgetown, but I think it was to see any late-arriving dispatches. It's questionable as to whether Jackson---or anyone else up there outside the Liaison Office---even knows about this Russian complication." The Senator looked fondly at his wife. "In fact, outside of this room, only Jim Polk is aware of it."

"Polk?" McDuffie was confused. "How..."

"Met with him in Asheville last Wednesday. He should be on his way to Georgetown now. So, within 24 hours of our arrival, we should know what The Residency knows; and how the knowledge, or lack of it, is affecting Jackson's position on emancipation itself."

McDuffie raised his own coffee cup in salute. "Now I see why you are in such a damn hurry to get up to that god-forsaken swamp..."

Calhoun's dark smile flashed briefly. "For this and other reasons we'll discuss before we dock, George. This crisis is like a spilt inkwell: running in several directions at once. We're not going up there to clean up the spill. Just to channel it in one direction: permanent exemption from emancipation for the South...and the Southwest we'll soon be acquiring..."

———————

Van Buren Home
Georgetown, D.C.
May 28, 1833, 6:30 p.m.:

The "certain American allies" the Duke intended to update were now gathering for dinner: in addition to the Vice G-G, Chief Justice Marshall was on hand. General Scott, who had arrived back in town after the unpleasant duty of relieving a valued comrade-in-arms of the command of Fort McHenry due to chronic alcoholism, was also present.

"Well gentlemen, and ladies," the Duke bowed formally to Maria Scott and Mrs. Marshall, "there is much to discuss this evening…and none of it is particularly pleasant. So, once we are served yet another of the Vice Governor-General's most delectable meals, I suggest we wade into the subject…"

Two hours later, the table was ominously silent.

Each of the Americans was consumed with his or her own thoughts on the burgeoning crisis. Wellington himself, despite the stimulus of a steak dinner with roasted potatoes and several bottles of an excellent Bordeaux, was also deeply depressed.

It was the elderly Chief Justice who initially broke through the gloom that had permeated the main courses: "As I understand the situation, my dear Duke," (Marshall was another who despised utilizing the formal English address) "it appears that Senator Calhoun believes the Crown can not afford war on two fronts. Is his estimate correct?"

Wellington reluctantly nodded.

"So I must ask Winfield," Marshall continued, "would our own British American forces be so decimated by a Southern, I can think of no other word…desertion…that we would be unable to put down an…insurrection…without the Empire's help?"

Scott was vigorously shaking his massive head even before the old Virginian completed his question. "On paper, very definitely not, Mr. Chief Justice. Even under the worst scenario---the mass resignation of Southern-born officers to form the basis of a rebel officer corps---we would still have any rebel forces out-manned, and, of course, out-gunned. The South is simply not equipped to wage war; they don't have the artillery, or capability of manufacturing the artillery, for one thing, or the capability to manufacture the other items of war: ammunition, muskets and side-arms and so forth."

The leonine head stilled as a quite different tone entered the General's voice: "However, it remains to be seen if the other sections believe emancipation is worth fighting for. Just because we *theoretically* would have an insurrection out-manned and out-gunned doesn't mean we *actually* would, if it comes to that. On paper, the Dominion forces would simply grind any rebel armies down. But wars aren't fought on paper. The will to fight can not be overestimated. The South, from all reports, claims to have that will. Do the other sections?"

It was Van Buren who broke the depressing silence that followed Scott's rhetorical question. "That, ladies and gentlemen, aptly demonstrates the political acumen of the Governor-General. Mr. Jackson, from the moment the Duke initially briefed him, saw emancipation as a test of sectional wills; the final struggle over the issue of states rights…"

"And what is the G-G's current position?" The Chief Justice, normally the most decorous of men, broke in anxiously.

"He hasn't revealed it, of course," Van Buren admitted with a frown before brightening: "However, based on his record, my belief is that, after much soul-searching, he will adhere to his Dominionist principles."

The eyebrows went up and the Vice G-G flashed a smile that could have been interpreted as shy…or sly. "I seem to have broken my own first rule: never make predictions…"

The Duke raised his glass as most other guests clapped in appreciation: "Bravo, Mr. Van Buren. I salute you. Especially as your opinion concurs with my own."

The General, however, remained grave. "The issue here isn't the Governor-General's principles…whatever they may turn out to be. What matters most is the will in the North and West to fight for those, as you say, *Dominionist principles*. Can anyone here say with any certainty that they will?"

Wellington again raised his glass, this time to Scott. "Winfield, you always were, even on the Peninsula, the supreme realist. I salute you…"

The Duke looked around the table. "I, also, have an opinion on that subject. Based on my talks and travels, I believe the North and West will rally to the Colonial Compact, if necessary. And, if called upon, Winfield, under your banner…"

The Golden Eagle Inn
Georgetown, D.C.
May 28, 1833, 9 p.m.:

Joanne Casgrave was oblivious to the gathering political storm. The fact was that she simply did not give a damn about emancipation, exemption, nullification, the Colonial Compact or politics in general. Joanne was in the midst of the most intense relationship of her extraordinarily active sexual life. She had enjoyed dozens of lovers, as well as countless clients, since fleeing her family's small Long Island farm years before. Unlike most newcomers to Georgetown, it was lust, not politics, which had brought her here: she had come as the pampered concubine of an Army captain transferred from Fort Hamilton. One who had demonstrated the bad taste to die within months of their arrival, leaving her temporarily destitute. That's when she had begun the climb to her present station in life: a prosperous, if disreputable, business owner with a mysterious Russian for a lover.

Bored, sullen and rebellious---yes, and of course sexually hungry, too---while he had vanished on his Southern 'tour,' she had taken on a hulking officer from the Russian Consulate one night. In part, it had been an experiment: were these Russians better lovers or was Andre simply in a class by himself? The Russian officer, she had forgotten his name, if not his disappointing brutishness, had drunkenly identified Andre as "Count Nicholas" at one point between their couplings. She had been stunned and wondered if it could be true. Confirmation of which came the following morning when she confronted the love-struck barbarian who, horrified at his blunder, had begged her to never repeat the name. Which of course she agreed to…once the brute came clean with the entire story. The Russian officer had then fled, to her relief, and had not appeared at The Eagle again. It had taken her several baths to feel clean…

So it was simply a matter of time before Andre 'fessed up; after all, he had, since returning, finally admitted his feelings for her…

And now he was actually taking an interest in the operation of The Eagle…on both floors. He had advised the replacement of some waitresses and 'upstairs girls,' including fat-and-drunken Kathy, with younger, more attractive and easier-to-manage newcomers to the city. And he had taken supervision of Richard off her hands. That was a relief; while the strange man had always done whatever she had ordered, he still made her uneasy. But Andre seemed to have him completely under control…

The Residency
Georgetown, D.C.
May 31, 1833, 9 a.m.:

James Polk hurried across the grounds, anxious to discover the G-G's current position on the crisis. He had arrived back in town late yesterday afternoon, only to discover that Calhoun was still en route. Senator Tyler was already back, so he and Sarah had accepted an invitation to the Tylers' for supper. John, however, knew less---much less---Polk now thought with a smile, than he did.

Polk was shocked at Jackson's appearance when Donelson escorted him into the G-G's office minutes later: Andy looked five years older than he had in early March. As he rose in greeting, he seemed to rely on the cane more now for support than as a prop. A quick glance at the secretary confirmed that Donelson, too, was concerned about the G-G's health.

"James, it is good to see you. Now, first I'll want a report on the sentiment in Tennessee. Then we can discuss the whole picture…"

Two hours later, Polk had the information he needed: the G-G was still uncommitted and would remain so until he got a sense of the people through reports from the returning Congress. And, significantly, he knew nothing of the European situation…or its potential to tilt the emancipation issue.

It's just like these arrogant Limeys to withhold such crucial information, the Congressman thought. *The bastards believe the assignment of foreign affairs in the Colonial Compact to London is all encompassing…even when it directly impacts domestic affairs here in America. Well, this is one time when their high-*

and-mighty attitude is going to come back to haunt them: once Wellington realizes we know the Empire is eye-to-eye with the Russians---or maybe past that---he'll cave on the exemption. And Jackson will be so mad he wasn't let in on the secret that he'll join in pushing for the exemption to cover any future Southwestern expansion. Expansion he has Sam Houston working on in Texas right now!

―――――――――

Calhoun Residence
Georgetown, D.C.
June 2, 1833:

The Southern inner circle, for the most part (Senator Troup had not yet arrived), had caucused hours earlier and now, at 5 p.m., was winding up its meeting.

"Well, gentlemen, we all are now up to date." Calhoun looked at the group with tired satisfaction. "You all can now see how this fortuitous Russian adventure has given us the leverage to force Wellington to compromise. And while the old man in The Residency is still trying to make up his mind, we're about to make it up for him. Now, I again caution you: no word of the Syrian situation is to be spoken when we meet with our colleagues from the other sections tomorrow.

"Debate, as I understand it, is scheduled to begin Tuesday. We'll make our valid constitutional arguments for our institution and hope the soundness of our position convinces those from outside the South. Meanwhile, we bide our time and wait for the opportune moment to utilize the Russian weapon. From James' report, I would expect Jackson to address Congress late in the week, or perhaps a week from tomorrow. We'll hold back until after he announces his position."

He paused and nodded his head vigorously, his long hair flying. "Then will be the time to officially inquire how things are going in Asia Minor."

It took a moment before the others recognized the biting sarcasm reflected their leader's complete confidence in his plan.

―――――――――

As the meeting broke up in laughter, a servant entered to announce the arrival of General Gaines. Despite the quizzical looks from Brown and Tyler, among others, Calhoun ushered his guests out with the bland explanation that the General's wife and Floride were old and dear friends; the Gaines were honoring a long-scheduled invitation to dinner. That Gaines was alone in the parlor was, if not commented upon, noted by many...

After closing the front door behind the last of his followers, Calhoun returned to the parlor and noticed for the first time the satchel at the General's feet.

"Well General. Business...on a Sabbath evening? I thought only disreputable sorts like politicians so flaunted the Good Book..."

Edmund P. Gaines was the antithesis of Winfield Scott: short, spare and gaunt-faced. And despite Scott's dismissal of his fellow-Virginian as a "paper-pusher," Gaines had heard and seen his share of lead---and arrows---in large and small fights with the French and with Indian tribes from Michigan to Florida. Now, ironically, it was that very skill at pushing paper that was to impress the Senator from South Carolina.

The General got right to the point, picking up his satchel and giving Calhoun a hard look: "Senator, I have documents in this pouch which could easily get me cashiered, if not shot for treason. I suggest we go behind locked doors"---he indicated the dining room in which the previous caucus had met---"and examine them privately."

This time, Calhoun's smile was not sarcastic, but quizzical: "Certainly, General, if you think necessary. Though your concerns do seem, shall we say, perhaps 'overly-dramatic'...?"

"I doubt you'll feel that way, Senator, after you study the first set."

Once settled at the table, Gaines opened the pouch and retrieved the papers detailing the reorganization of the USBAA, including the list of potential Southern officer resignations. He gravely handed the papers to Calhoun and sat back.

The Senator's quizzical expression darkened as he studied the plans, occasionally pausing to stare at Gaines. More than 40 minutes passed before he threw down the final pages, though he continued to stare down at them. Finally, he looked up and nodded at the General.

"General Gaines, if those plans are authentic, it is not you who should be shot for treason. Now tell me how you obtained them…and how it is there has been no scandal over their disappearance."

Gaines sketched the process by which he had come into possession of the papers. The tale began with Lieutenant Beaufort's discovery while searching for a listing of Consulate military attaches the Liaison Office had requested while Lieutenant Wilder was off with General Scott on an inspection trip to West Point.

"There's no doubt whatsoever this document came from the locked desk of Scott's own intelligence aide, General?" Calhoun wanted the Vice-Commander's strongest assurance that the plans were real.

"None whatsoever, Senator. Lieutenant Beaufort says that, in retrospect, it is now apparent this plan is what Scott and Wilder have been working so diligently on behind closed doors for weeks. At the time, Luke, Lieutenant Beaufort, paid little heed. It seems Wilder is Scott's fair-haired boy. Says Scott is always calling him in privately and sending him on special missions."

Calhoun's mouth twitched in such a way that Gaines had little doubt he was trying to smother a smile: "This Lieutenant Beaufort, now, he wouldn't be…perhaps a tad…jealous… of his fellow junior officer?"

Gaines straightened up in his seat: "Senator, Luke Beaufort is the first graduate of the Academy to hail from Mississippi. He came to me as a Southern patriot."

Calhoun nodded his head vigorously in acceptance. "Now then, General: what do you suppose we should in response to all this…treason?"

Gaines stared at the Senator for a moment, then lowered his head and dug the second set of documents out of his pouch. He handed them over wordlessly.

Calhoun accepted the papers with another, just barely, quizzical smile and reviewed them quickly. His eyebrows rose on occasion and he glanced up at Gaines with a newfound respect at several intervals.

"It seems you, too, have been hard at work building a paper army, General. My congratulations. However, a question: these state units you list. Are they ready to fight?"

Gaines was hard-faced: "No unit can be accurately termed 'ready' until it demonstrates how it performs under fire, Senator. But our Southern militia are just-as, if not more-so, than the Yankees. Our boys meet and drill regularly. I doubt if 10% of the militia units in Scott's proposal, outside of the Illinois and Ohio boys who fought against Black Hawk, have drilled for anything other than Compact Day parades…"

Calhoun nodded and a thoughtful, faraway look came into in his eyes. "Do you agree with Scott's assessment that---what is the prediction, 85%?---of the Southern officers in the present USBAA will resign their commissions if it comes to a fight?"

Gaines grunted affirmatively: "I do. You see, Senator, Scott and I know most, if not all, of these officers personally. There's no need tonight, but we could go through that list and I could give you a performance evaluation on each man…as well as a personal history."

Calhoun puckered his lips and nodded in satisfaction. "All right, General. Now, dinner is getting cold and I heard your dear wife announced sometime ago. We can resume our discussion later.

"However, concerning these documents: I trust you've been housing them in a safe place? In a locked safe at your home? Good; return them to it tonight. For now, I want you to refine these organizational plans…but I don't want anyone else to know about them. I assume Lieutenant Beaufort assisted you? And no one else knows?"

The Senator smiled his dark smile. "Well, if we can keep the secret to one Senator, one General and one junior officer unless and until necessary, that will be excellent…

"My thanks to you and the Lieutenant. If the South is left no alternative but force to demonstrate our unwillingness to accept this emancipation abomination, your planning will have given us a vital headstart. Either way, you and Lieutenant Beaufort will be rewarded for your outstanding initiative, I promise you."

The Senator leaned across the table and shook Gaines' hand. The General grasped it firmly. "Senator, do you really believe it will come to that?"

Calhoun frowned: "General, we are hurtling towards a collision I believed was a decade or more away. Only the exemption can now stop it from occurring in a matter of months, I begin to be afraid."

Once again, the dark smile broke out. "However, I have reason to believe the exemption may be looking more attractive to our visitor from London. And may be the lifeline our Governor-General will use to pull the Dominion through this crisis."

His face turned darker and the frown returned: "If it is rejected, General, your next title will have the 'Vice' removed from the front of it..."

CHAPTER THIRTY-EIGHT

USBA Capitol Building
Georgetown, D.C.
June 5, 1833:

John C. Calhoun was wasting no more time. He intended to begin---and, thus, end---the debate by going immediately on the offensive.

There would be no excuses offered for slavery as a "necessary evil," or "vital to the economic prosperity of the South." Instead, he would build on the theme of his stump speech that had rallied support across the South: slavery is a "positive good," based on the equally rock-solid pillars of white supremacy and paternalism. As he had told cheering crowds from Norfolk to Tuscaloosa: "all societies, since time immemorial, have been ruled by an elite class which directs and then enjoys the fruits of the labor of the less-privileged." Today, he would expose the hypocrisy of the Northern---and English---ruling classes by comparing their attitude toward their own lower classes to the paternalism demonstrated by the planters of the South!

Van Buren, in his role as President of the Senate, was in the chair as Calhoun rose to ask permission to speak. The Southern caucus had spread word yesterday that the fireworks would begin the moment Matty Van gaveled the Senate into session; the galleries were now crammed with Congressmen, diplomats and anyone else who could force entry:

Sir John Burrell, representing the Duke, saw a black-haired, eye-patched man of wiry yet powerful build squeeze in between Count Renkowiitz and M. Jean-Claude. One look at Captain Bratton's grim face provided confirmation: so this is Ignatieff/Karlhamanov! Bratton's concentration on the Russian was broken when he glanced past to an upper row: that fabulous auburn-haired Lucille Latoure was moving to a seat, accompanied by Mrs. Scott. Frank Blair, after depositing Eliza in the gallery next to Sarah Polk, had now sighted

General Scott, off to the left and back of the podium. Scott, who had made arrangements to hear the debate with Blair, now grunted in acknowledgement of the sudden appearance at his side of an elf-like, elegant old man with a mischievous grin. He had wondered how long till Aaron Burr would be back in town…

After an awkward, self-depreciating attempt at humor concerning Van Buren's assumption in the new 23rd Congress of his own role in the previous one---"let us pray the quality of the oratory you will hear will be superior to that which helped drive me from your chair"---Calhoun moved immediately into the twin-pillar foundation of his speech.

He then fired his first salvos at the North and England: Southern slaves, unlike Northern or European laboring classes, were not cast aside to die in poverty when they became too old or ill to be of use to the governing classes:

"I may say with truth, that in few countries so much is left to the share of the laborer, and so little exacted from him, or where there is more kind attention paid him in sickness or infirmities of age. Compare his condition with the tenants of the poor houses in the more civilized portions of Europe (and the North)…look at the sick and the old and infirm slave, on one hand, in the midst of his family and friends, under the kind superintending care of his master and mistress, and compare it with the forlorn and wretched condition of the pauper in the poorhouse!"

The Senate erupted in cheers, jeers and outright groans and gasps of disbelief at this righteous depiction of Southern benevolence. Scott could see Webster on his feet, demanding to be heard as Van Buren hammered the gavel down repeatedly with a surprising strength. "Poor Matty will have finger calluses and shoulder strain before this day is through," Burr whispered in his ear. Elsewhere, Henry Clay could be seen shaking his head sadly, while Troup led the wild Southern applause.

Perhaps, Calhoun was now saying, the peculiar institution might not be the negros' permanent destiny.

"If at some point, it will be deemed wise and practical to emancipate the slaves," that point would come several generations from now when the blacks have been made "unfit for slavery and made fit for freedom by equally generous doses of education and discipline administered by the individual masters and mistresses of that time at the direction and close supervision of the respective state governments...not through arbitrary decisions made in either London or Georgetown!"

This was not a new, or even Southern, position, he added.

"During the great debates by the founding fathers at the Constitutional Convention, the following statement was recorded by the Convention's Secretary: 'The morality or wisdom of slavery are considerations that belong to the states themselves.'"

The dark smile flashed as he paused to await the abatement of the obligatory groans and catcalls. Then he pounced:

"James Madison, Secretary of the Convention, attributed that assertion to one Oliver Ellsworth." He paused again. "The delegate from Connecticut."

The South, the Senator now proclaimed, "comes here today with the expectation, yea, the assumption," that the other sections join in demanding that Parliament and Lord Grey's Government uphold the maxim enunciated by Ellsworth and abide by the articles of the Colonial Compact and the USBA Constitution concerning property rights: "a right no less sacred, no less inviolate that that of freedom of speech, assembly and the holding and bearing of firearms."

The previous gasps and groans could not match the uproar that followed Calhoun's final remarks. Ignoring the evidence of his previous stump speeches, he categorically denied that the South "seeks an 'exemption' from Parliamentary legislation. We seek to have the Compact and the Constitution revalidated; to have confirmation from London, based on the united stance of the peoples of this Dominion, these concurrent majorities, that our rights will be respected; our property conceded as our own and our tranquility guaranteed!"

———————

The Residency
June 5, 1833, 6 p.m.:

"Concurrent majorities!" Frank Blair shook his head disgustedly at the Governor-General. "That same damn theory Calhoun first floated back in '31! That no government can long operate without a general concurrence of its systems. And, if any one of the social or community systems of a government feel its survival threatened, it automatically will resist by all means possible; a war for survival is thus inevitable!"

"Unless, of course, the other systems give in…." Jackson was brief and dry.

The closest advisor nodded in agreement as he sipped the decanter of Tennessee whisky Jackson had handed him upon his immediate return from the other end of Pennsylvania Avenue.

"Calhoun has degenerated most dangerously," Blair said, "into a sophistical rhetorician inebriated with the exuberance of his own verbosity."

Jackson was now looking out the window toward the picturesque Potomac and the stately mansion on the hill. *Washington's adopted son, Custis, lives there. I wonder, old George, what you would say---or do--if you were in my boots? You held slaves, plenty of them, and never manumitted a one…until you were comfortably dead and buried. Yet, you had as much, if not more, to do with putting this system of government together---and making it work---than anyone!*

He turned to Blair, who was now pacing the room and had apparently asked a question. "I'm sorry, Frank, my mind was elsewhere. You said…?"

"I asked, Andrew, whether you think Calhoun could be so drunk on his own rhetoric that he actually believes the South can bully the rest of the Dominion---and London---with the mere threat of secession.

"Surely, he doesn't believe the Dominion---or the Empire---will just permit the South to secede, rather than risk a sectional insurrection? Or that the South can whip the Dominion's forces, especially with the British military ready to step in as needed, if it should come to a fight? Or that the rest of the Dominion will join in resuming the unpleasantness of 1775 out of some sense of continental loyalty?"

Jackson had poured himself a healthy refill and stood leaning against the window sill, Arlington House towering above him in the distance. He sipped and pondered for so long Blair was half-convinced he had no answer. A first time instance, if so!

The G-G finally spoke: "No, Frank, John C. Calhoun is playing the highest-stakes poker game this town has ever seen. He's flushing the other sections out; after today, they've no choice but to put their cards on the table. If he's right and the West and the Middle States--- New York, Pennsylvania---don't see emancipation as something worth fighting for, then he's won: Wellington will have to compromise…or risk reigniting that 'unpleasantness!'

"If the West and the damn Yankees up above us do come down in support of London's interpretation of the Compact and our Constitution, then he's demonstrated to the South he's been right all this time and that it might be better off going its own way."

Jackson had been fingering his cane with his right hand while sipping from the decanter in his left. Now he put the drink on the sill and began to tap the cane thoughtfully against the carpet before looking up at Blair.

"He knows that's impossible---the South going its own way--- without a fight, though. One even he isn't fool enough to think it could win single-handedly. So that means he's got an ace up his sleeve. Or two or three!"

The tapping became more forceful and the forehead began to darken through the range of reds. Blair recognized the telltale signs and knew a volcanic explosion was shortly due.

"By the Eternal! What does he know that I don't? What ace-in-the-hole is he relying on? Why does he believe I'll tilt toward his position when I haven't yet made my own mind up? Even though I do like your idea of a defined, short-term exemption? And what makes him so certain that Wellington will throw in his cards?"

The cane was now rapidly bouncing up-and-down on the carpet. "Frank, something's happening here that we aren't aware of; something that's key to this whole game. And I can't figure out what it is! Damn it, how can I address Congress---and the people---until I do?"

Monticello Tavern
June 5, 1833
7 pm:

Tousaint Numidia was, of course, too smart to think the New England Abolition Society would outright sanction the armed capture and holding of any white man, much less the world-famous Duke of Wellington.

The role he actually had in mind for the Society was that of a post-snatch intermediary, a negotiator of sorts between his band and the authorities. Intent on the particulars of Wellington's capture and secreting away, he had developed only vague plans for notifying the Society, through Moses, that it was being called in as a go-between to whom the prisoner would be turned over after London's acceptance of the terms Tousaint demanded and the Society would arrange.

The capture itself didn't appear to be particularly difficult. Wellington, like all influential men in Georgetown's power elite, moved around the city and surrounding countryside in a remarkably laisse-faire manner. Like Jackson, the Duke seemed to utilize bodyguards, in his case the Royal Marines, primarily on ceremonial occasions. The great majority of the time, he traveled by coach, with only a driver up front and a few Liaison aides possibly inside; or on horseback with one or two other Brits. Tousaint himself had seen Wellington emerge from The Residency and simply stroll over to the Liaison Office or elsewhere in the immediate vicinity.

"The key's to grab him and be gone before anyone realizes it, much less can respond," he told his band of followers on this night. Even Donfield, who had remained skeptical that emancipation was to be announced at all, had reconsidered after hearing the details of Wellington's speech as it was discussed and debated throughout Georgetown. But the Spanish Consulate maintenance man still hadn't committed to the capture.

"Okay, Simba. You were right about Wellington and this Parliament's plan. And I agree he moves around the city pretty much unprotected. So maybe we could snatch him. And maybe we could get the authorities---I'm not sure who, the Brits or the old man in The Residency---word of our demands. But where's safe to hold him? And how do we get word to the Society that we expect them to make the deal?

"We can't tell them before we grab the old Brit! If I'm in this, I want a sportin' chance to get out alive. And that don't mean telling no white folk ahead of time what we're planning... So where we gonna hold him? And for how long? And who's gonna guard him while we be working? And how we get the Society involved after the snatch?"

Tousaint grinned as Doby and Motley nodded their heads in Donfield's support. "All good points and questions, Crispus. But I'm miles ahead of you. I've got it all worked out..."

Donfield rolled his eyes. "O Lordy, didn't I know you would... Okay, Simba. Let's hear how we gonna grab this Duke and hold him till all our maumba be freed."

Streets of Georgetown
June 5, 1833
11 pm:

Lawrence Eugene Doby was indeed the best-educated of Tousaint Numidia's band. And Ugene knew a good thing when he had it: a clerkship at the Interior Department, which promised lifelong employment and a pension to keep him going in his declining years.

So Doby, though he like to flirt with the concept of uhura, wasn't at all sure he wanted to risk everything on Simba's daydream...especially when full and complete emancipation was apparently less than a decade away. *I have my uhura now,* he thought, *and the maumba will have theirs by '41.* Did it make sense to get involved in a conspiracy in which the personal risk so outsized the personal reward?

Doby had considered this point from all angles in the days before and after after Tousaint laid out his plans. The snatch itself was relatively easy, they had all agreed: grab the old man somewhere outside Georgetown when he was un- or under-guarded. But stashing, guarding and feeding him during the talks? *Tousaint says he's confident...but some might call that confidence arrogance...*

Simba's plan was to stick Wellington under the white folks' noses in Fairfax County, since that was where the snatch-and-grab would take place. Numidia had chosen the location for the hideaway: Huntley, a half-built secondary residence of Thomson F. Mason, Alexandria's mayor. It was located a few miles due south of the town, down the Gravel Road, and a part of Hunting Creek Farm. The farm was actually a plantation adjacent to the Potomac where Mason experimented by utilizing both slave and black tenant labor.

Since the plantation was not Mason's primary residence--- Colross, a huge mansion in Alexandria was---there was actually less white oversight than even at Cranford. Mason rode down most days and the overseer was strict but fair, as overseers went, the word from

402

the maumba was. As well as overworked himself. But with the free tenant labor, comings and goings were more relaxed. Once they got Wellington to Huntley, the prospects were fair that he could be successfully hidden. But for how long? Overworked or not, chances were the overseer would stumble on the hiding spot at some point. And Mason could always decide to check on Huntley's cellar if-and-when he decided to resume construction.

Simba had chosen Huntley primarily because Marion Motley's family was among the tenant laborers. He had eyeballed the place only from the Gravel Road and that just once. And he chose Fairfax simply on the general knowledge that Wellington liked to ride there. *I'm not sure I want to risk my neck on that kind of inspection. And the fact that Motley is in charge of making the arrangements over there doesn't exactly give me confidence.*

Doby knew it was time to fish or cut bait. Simba had announced that the snatch would go off Friday night. Wellington apparently was having dinner at Cranford with the Governor of Virginia in an attempt to line up his support for emancipation. Or so the Cranford butler, according to Simba, had informed Moses. *Numidia wants to grab him on the way back to Georgetown and have the old man in Huntley by midnight. Well Ugene, whats you gonna do?*

The Golden Eagle
June 5, 1833, 10 p.m.:

Count Nicholas was angry as he walked the distance from the French Consulate to the Inn. The consensus among the diplomatic corps gathered around the Jean-Claudes' dinner table was that the brilliant Russian initiative in Asia Minor---for word of the Black Sea Fleet's passing of Constantinople to the salute and cheers of the Ottomans and their subjects had filtered first to the various capitols and now, some three months later, to Georgetown---had tied the Lion's paws. From Prussia's Von Benes to Portugal's DeGama, the European C-Gs were unanimous in believing that the planting of the Double Eagle in Syria---which they anticipated to have automatically followed---had accidentally and coincidentally won the Dominion chess game for the South.

(The C-Gs, of course, had buzzed on this amongst themselves since word had begun to come in late the previous month. Closemouthed and condescending to their host government, they had kept the secret at their level. Today's entertaining tirade by the wild orator from South Carolina had thus been viewed from a different prospective in the diplomatic seats.)

Ignatieff's anger arose from this consensus: *Czarist interests would not be served if Wellington caved in to Calhoun's threats!*

He had told the damned Southerner about the Syrian operation to build up his confidence for a rebellion…not for a legislative victory! And what of this damnable Jackson? After four months in this wilderness, he had to admit that he still didn't fully comprehend how this damn government of theirs works…*who is in charge here, anyway? Wellington, Jackson, Calhoun…or nobody?*

He pushed open the tavern door and caught his first glimpse of the fool Lawrence behind the bar: *I've got to disrupt this compromise, if that's what is coming. Create enough havoc to get the Southerners boiling mad…and the others equally mad at them!*

He was reminded of Frederick the Great's dictum: *"ein Kreig beginnt mit enem einzigen Schuss"*: *"a war begins with a single shot." I require that single shot to be fired. So, by God, it will be…*

He crossed to the bar and into the arms of the coarse slut whose bed he was tiring of sharing. "Andre darling! And where have you been? I've missed you so all day…and evening…"

Indian Queen Hotel
Dining Room
June 5, 1833, 7 p.m.:

Housing in Georgetown was limited and expensive. Those members of Congress who, for whatever reasons, left their families home, scrambled to find lodgings wherever available. Thus, Army lieutenants stationed full-time in the capitol were apt to bump into famous Congressmen and Senators in the hallways and bars of what passed for "respectable" hotels.

If Tom Wilder had been in the Indian Queen's dining room tonight (he was instead ecstatically having supper at the Latoure townhouse on Tenth Street), he would have recognized "Harry of the

West," the famous Henry Clay, entering from the upper hallway to sit at a quiet corner table occupied by the Ohio Senator, Thomas Ewing, and a third man.

"So Samuel, is New Jersey ready to rally to the support of one of the other "peoples" of this proud but constitutionally 'concurrent' Dominion in its hour of need?" Though Clay had come from his room, it was obvious he had stopped off at this or another tavern on his way from the Capitol.

Samuel Southard scowled. "No, Senator. What New Jersey is ready to rally to is the status quo: business-as-usual. We've as little time, or interest, for constitutional engineering as we do for social engineering. Damn Calhoun for all this pompous political theorizing! And damn Parliament for seeking to interfere in our economy! And where the hell is Jackson on this, anyway? He's always been out front, leading the charge. Instead, he's bunkered down in The Residency!"

Thomas Ewing was philosophical: "Well, one thing that'll come out of this. We've got to stop making Parliamentary service a final reward for broken-down old American politicians who can't get reelected to Congress. All three of our states should be ashamed of the non-entities we've got over there. You get one man still in his prime---with an agenda---like the redoubtable Quincy, and this is what happens…"

"Yes, Parliamentary reform---American-style---should be forthcoming, Thomas." Clay sipped the Claret his presence at table had automatically caused to be placed in front of him. "Once this little issue is resolved."

He turned back to Southard: "Samuel, New Jersey has quite often voted with the Southern block. As has my own state on occasion. Despite John C's…careening…rhetoric this afternoon, its obvious we will soon be voting on an exemption resolution. How will your delegation vote?"

Southard's scowl had not left his face. "Depends on what the Southerners introduce. And where Jackson comes down: Damn it, what about our famous leader?"

Ewing sipped his own glass of wine as he called for the waiter so that supper might be ordered. "General Jackson, according to Frank Blair---strictly off-the-record, now, gentlemen---is in something of a quandary. As a strict constitutionalist, he's naturally opposed to this Calhoun mumble-jumbo, which of course is reheated nullificationizing.

405

"But as a planter, he's plenty steamed at Wellington, Adams and Parliament. Though it doesn't take emancipation talk to set him off on old Quincy, any more than he needs inspiration to go off about our friend Harry, here. By the Eternal!" Ewing, too, was obviously no teetotaler.

"Blair, I believe honestly, insists that the G-G wants to absorb the debate on the Hill before coming up to announce his own position. Frank thinks he'll come down for emancipation, because he recognizes its legality. But if he sees strong Congressional opposition, reflecting the feelings in most of the various sections, he may seek some sort of compromise."

Clay was direct: "Support of the exemption?"

Ewing drained his glass and signaled the waiter for another round: "Well, with Calhoun stating the position that the slaves are so much property of their owners and thus already accounted for in the Compact, the Constitution and all the way back to English common law, the exemption does begin to look like a compromise, yes. Especially if a timeframe for later emancipation---like 50 years or so---is tacked on." He grinned at the others: "Frank's idea, not mine."

Southard picked up the previously ignored menu and visibly relaxed. "Now, that's something New Jersey can accept. Glad someone's doing some clear thinking over at the other end of Pennsylvania Avenue..."

War Department
June 7, 1833
8:15 am:

General Scott was looking at Tom Wilder with a face the Lieutenant had never seen him put on before. "Are you serious, Lieutenant? You want me to believe a gang of darkies plans to seize the former Prime Minister of the British Empire and hold him for ransom in exchange for the freedom of two million slaves? That they've come up with this plan since his speech to Congress? And that *you've* uncovered their diabolical design?"

In truth, Scott was employing the sarcasm to buy a minute while he considered the possibility that his aide could be correct. *It's ridiculous, but let's not jump to the conclusion that the boy has jumped to conclusions...*

The General's gigantic right paw surrounded his cup of coffee, his first of the day and one hardly touched before Wilder had entered the office with his preposterous report. He took a sip and continued: "Okay, Lieutenant, let's take this again, and slower, and from the top... Give me the full 'who, what, when, where, why and how' of this thing in the manner I have been teaching you. And which you have hopefully absorbed..."

Carefully, Tom reorganized the story he had gotten from Dave Harper over supper at the Wagon Wheel late last night in the format Scott wanted. Scott's drill-like glare was still grinding through him when he finished, though the look of incredulousness had faded to a more frigid calculating expression.

"Hmm. Well you've certainly covered the intelligence basics, Lieutenant. My congratulations. A fine report. Except you left one thing out: What makes your friend Harper so sure his information is accurate? Why would a member of this gang get cold feet at the last minute? You say these other darkies practically worship this Numbia fellow..."

"Excuse me for interrupting, General. 'Numidia. Tousaint L'Overture Numidia', to be precise."

"Yes, well. A rather unusual name, to say the least. So, why would one of this Tousaint L'Overture Numidia's followers betray him at the last minute?"

"Dave, er Mr. Harper, says this Doby doesn't think they can pull it off, Sir. Says Doby thinks seizing the Duke will be easy enough, but he doesn't know if they can hide him for as long as this would take."

Tom paused. "Doby never said this, General, but David has the impression Doby also doesn't believe the Abolition Society will go along. That somewhere along the line, they'll be betrayed."

"What, that the Society will let us know where Wellington is stashed? Doesn't appear this Numidia plans to let them in on that all-important little fact..."

"Excuse my saying so, General. But Harps feels it's more along the lines that Doby thinks the Society will renounce any emancipation deal that might be cut the moment Wellington is back in Georgetown. Fear of white treachery and solidarity, you might say...

"And General, this Doby is rather bright..."

"You mean he's a mulatto; has a foot in both camps?"

"No Sir. This Doby---you've seen him in the halls, General; he's the only black in this building day-in and day-out---is darker than your coffee, if I may make the comparison.

"It's that Harper says Doby knows he has a good thing at Interior: a regular position and salary. And doesn't want to risk his own comfort since he'd never get his job back, whether this succeeds or not."

Scott rose from behind his desk and stretched, rolling his cannon ball-sized head and twisting his tree-trunk neck. Though the purpose of the exercise seemed self-evident, the Lieutenant knew Scott often practiced this routine while considering a newly-presented report.

Scott sat down again and a quill pen disappeared into his paw. After scratching out a few words on a sheet of paper, he folded and sealed the document and handed it to Wilder. "Get this up to Secretary MacLane post-haste. Then bring young Mr. Harper down here on the double."

"Yes Sir!" The relief in Tom's voice was obvious. *Thank God he thinks there could be some validity to this crazy story. As I told Harps last night, I wasn't looking forward to the General throwing me out his office window. Guess Arkansas will still have to deal with the Comanche without any more help from me...*

The Capitol Building
June 6, 1833, 11 a.m.:

While Calhoun had forcibly spoken for the single-minded Southern caucus on Tuesday (the few moderates like Georgia's Forsyth having been cast out like Biblical lepers), Webster had spoken not for, but among, the enraged abolitionists of New England yesterday.

A weary Van Buren had announced at the conclusion of the long, humid session---a cloud of pipe and cigar smoke had hovered over the chamber, its smell mixing with the hot air and sweating bodies to produce a truly uncomfortable atmosphere---that he would hope the remaining sections--the West, the so-called Border States and the MidAtlantic States--would follow the Southern example and choose a single spokesman.

Now Ewing signaled for recognition. Previously informed, the Vice G-G happily called him to the podium. The still-arriving crowd---which had drifted off yesterday, repetitiously bored---began to hum in anticipation: the West, even the diplomatic newcomers (Count Ignatieff among them) realized, would be key in determining Congressional reaction.

The continuing heat wave announcing the arrival of the equatorial Georgetown summer was joined in progress this morning by a crashing thunderstorm. The rain continued to beat its audible tattoo on the big brown Capitol dome as the Ohioan commenced his address in a tone appropriate for the dark, dreary but electric-laced weather.

The West, Ewing began---and he identified his constituency in this case as Ohio, Indiana, Illinois, Ontario and Michigan Territory---contained but 791 slaves overall, all but 44 of them held in southern Illinois, according to the 1830 census.

"Slavery, as a factor or condition in the daily lives of our constituents, is obviously negligible."

Internal improvements, including a better transportation system to get their products to the big Eastern markets, was the West's major concern, along with pacification of the Indians; he noted the raids the previous Fall by the Sioux into the western portions of the Michigan Territory and other Indian attacks in the unorganized but growing lands west of Ontario.

"We in the West do have a collective conscience, however," he declared, his tone becoming stronger and more forceful, "and a collective commitment.

"We believe literally in that portion of the preamble to the USBA Constitution that states 'all men are created equal,' and we are committed to that portion of the preamble, as well as the entire Constitution itself."

The crowd, which had continued to fill the galleries as the storm-aided congestion in front of the building gradually eased, had fallen silent when Ewing opened his remarks. Now, an audible gasp rippled through the galleries as the little-known Ohioan flung his verbal gauntlet at the stone-faced Calhoun. For the first time in some days, Count Ignatieff, once again sitting cramped shoulder-to-shoulder with Renkowiitz and the French C-G, began to relax. *This has possibilities,* he thought. *It appears Calhoun has underestimated the opposition…*

"Although our states were not party to the original Compact---indeed, a goodly portion of the West does not appear on any maps of the early USBA---we gave our solemn vow to abide by, participate in and cherish the Compact when we individually applied for statehood."

The galleries' rumblings grew louder and Van Buren was forced to utilize the gavel once again. Standing beside Frank Blair (General Scott was absent this day on War Department business), Aaron Burr whistled softly.

"One Dominion: once in, never out. So much for 'concurrent majorities' and our grandfathers' property rights.'" Blair gave the Colonel a ruefully-impressed look. As usual, the old man had summed up the issue with brevity and clarity. *He's still sharp as a tack. What a pair he and Andy must have made in the old days…and how the hell did Jefferson ever out-maneuver him?*

"We have heard, earlier in this debate, the claim by my distinguished colleague from South Carolina that the form of 'benevolent paternalism' he proclaims to be practiced by the planter class compares most favorably to the plight of the working classes in Europe and the large Northern cities.

"Having never been to Europe and having only a fleeting observation of living conditions among the workers of the great Northern cities, I will not debate that the slaves of the average planter may in fact be better cared for in their dotage than the city workers."

Gasps of delighted disbelief (from the Southerner delegation and their gallery partisans) and groans of dismayed shock (from other Senators and the remainder of the galleries) broke loose as Ewing paused.

"Except that no such *benevolence* justifies the forcible denial of personal liberty! The city worker is not forcibly sent to his manufactory, dock or stable; he is free to quit his position and leave! To leave Europe for America; to leave the North for the West! The North, in turn, welcomes the European worker and offers him wages for specified work. The West offers the migrating Northern worker the same, if and when he chooses to leave that manufactory position. *At his own determination and without opposition!*" Ewing's voice boomed across the chamber before he again paused.

"That, of course, is the difference," he began again in a softer tone that forced many in the galleries to lean forward to hear as the angry jeers of the Southerners rose in earnest.

"'All men are created equal.' Having ratified the Constitution, all the states are recorded as agreeing to that proposition. Having agreed that 'all men are created equal,' no rational man, nor group of men standing as representatives for all other citizens of their state, can then claim another equally-created man as his property. And, therefore, the ancient, revered and guaranteed right to hold property is, in this case, a specious argument.

"My southern collegues, you have already agreed that all men are created equal. *Thus, none can be considered property!*"

The entire Senate was on its feet; fights were breaking out throughout the galleries (some involving parasol-wielding ladies). Van Buren gaveled in vain and even Colonel Burr looked alarmed, while Blair quickly scanned the chamber in hopes that military uniforms might somehow appear.

Gradually, the dim quieted as peacemakers prevailed, both in the Senate well and in the galleries. (The Vice G-G was later to attribute much of the gallery policing to diplomatic volunteers.)

When peace, if not harmony, was eventually restored, the Ohio perpetrator of the explosion stood his ground behind the podium.

"These many individual states having agreed to the proposition that 'all men are created equal' when separately ratifying our Constitution; having so ratified in order to become part of a greater coalition; have thus subordinated their rights to act independently of the dictates of the greater coalition; just as they agreed to subordinate their rights to individual action independent of the dictates of the Empire when accepting the Colonial Compact, cannot now claim special regional rights."

The well and galleries were now apparently too spent to register their collective feelings on this blunt negative assessment of the celebrated states rights theory. An eerie silence engulfed the chamber as Ewing concluded his remarks:

"The West sympathizes with the South's predicament and will support any measures to make the legally-justified transition more palpable. But we will oppose, with all the strength we can muster, any attempts to ignore, nullify or forcibly restrain the implementation of this legislation where applicable any- and everywhere in our beloved Dominion."

411

The interior thunderstorm having abated, the exhausted Senators and visitors filed out of the chamber and into the Rotunda to discover that the exterior thunderstorm, too, was over. As they walked down and around Capitol Hill, to their carriages or towards their destinations afoot, they found the outside temperature equal to that of the crisis within.

Marine Hospital
June 7, 1833
9 p.m.:

This thing, thought Lawrence Eugene Doby, *has gotten completely out of hand.*

Never thought the white higher-ups, like this man Scott, would take a nigga like me seriously. Thought they scoff and snicker. That way, I could take part in the snatch, then, after they posted a reward, Ol' Ugene be first in line to claim it, since I done told them where the Duke be hidden even before the snatch. And even if they caught Simba and the others beforehand, that'd leave the way open for me to stay at Interior, maybe with a promotion...

He was still going to take part in the snatch as it now stood, but under the watchful eye of, as far he could knew, the entire USBA Army, or at least that part of it in-and-around Georgetown.

Eugene didn't know the details, but he was aware that the woods on either side of the road from Long Bridge past Cranford would be teeming with white soldiers long before the Duke ever left The Residency. But they wouldn't make a move until the gang actually accosted Wellington.

Doby hadn't understood that; had been educated only by his talk earlier this evening with Harper. He had been dragged down to Scott's office, put before the General and gradually realized that even though the whites were taking this seriously, Simba and the others would not be arrested immediately.

It had been Harper, to whom he had gone just two days ago with his story---the Northerner always treated him with more respect that the other, mostly Southern, Interior Department workers---who had explained:

"There is no legal ground yet to arrest anybody, Eugene. They haven't done anything and there's no proof they intend to. Just your word. Not enough, especially if all three of the others deny it.

"No, they have to be caught in the act. That's why this has to go down as planned---including you riding with them..."

"But what'll keep the soliders from shooting all of us once they do pounce?"

Harper was silent for a moment. He had been wondering the same thing himself. "Well, Eugene. You said Tousaint wanted to keep this non-violent. If your friends don't shoot first, the Army is under orders not to fire." *Which doesn't mean they haven't been authorized to use swords...*

Doby was dubious: "I don't know. Them soldiers see us pointing pistols at Wellington, they're liable to get the wrong idea..."

Pistols that you're not supposed to have access to, in any case. "Eugene, normally I'd agree. But the General has issued strict orders. He realizes Tousaint doesn't intend to harm The Duke. What would be the sense of that? Can't ransom too many slaves for a corpse... Besides, I understand you've given physical descriptions of your friends. The commander will have those, as well as your's...and he's under orders to make sure nothing happens to you, no matter what."

Doby shook his head as he remembered the conversation. *Yeah, this thing has gotten completely out of hand.*

So he thought, as he sat, under guard, in the barracks at the Marine Hospital complex at the intersection of Massachusetts and Georgia Avenues in far southeast Georgetown and waited for the dawn.

The Residency
June 7, 1833, 6 p.m.:

The Kitchen Cabinet meeting to discuss Jackson's scheduled Monday speech was reviewing the final day of opening sectional debate when Andrew Donelson broke in to deliver a note from Wellington.

Jackson and his key advisors---Blair, Cass and Polk---had been encouraged by the lack of fireworks today: Speaking surprisingly briefly apiece, border state representatives Thomas Hart Benton and Henry Clay had both pledged support for the Compact and

Constitution, but had urged the South to offer a compromise proposal.

"Defiance is self-defeating," Benton had warned. "Missouri did not come into the Dominion because slavery was tolerated; and it will not leave if it is banned."

Kentucky reported 165,000 slaves in the last census, Clay said. "More than Tennessee, Alabama or Louisiana apiece and more than Maryland, Mississippi and the Arkansas and Florida territories combined. But our state has three times as many free people who have enjoyed the peace and prosperity of the Dominion and the Empire. We will not sacrifice the latter to maintain the former; we do, however, share the concerns of our Southern neighbors as to the fairness of the Parliamentary legislation. At the conclusion of this debate, Kentucky will offer resolutions designed to alleviate those unfairnesses."

The MidAtlantic block had been blunt and business-like. "Free trade between the states and sections, as well as with the other portions of the Empire, has and will continue to propel economic growth," said New Jersey's Theodore Frelinghuysen, a staunch Dominion-Republican. "Nothing must be allowed to interfere. We will support compromise legislation and we will consider any resolutions, from Kentucky or elsewhere, which alleviate economic hardship on the South. However, the MidAtlantic States remain completely committed to both the Colonial Compact and the Constitution, both of which clearly allow King and Parliament to order the enforcement of Imperial law throughout the Dominion."

"The question now," Blair was saying, "is whether you, Andrew, should beat Clay to the punch by offering a compromise that…"

"Hold on Frank!" Polk interrupted with an anger that surprised the others. "Our position has not been determined, the last I checked. Yet you're for offering compromises…which translate into acceptance by the Administration of Parliament's right to shove this down our collective throats."

Cass began to open his mouth, then shrewdly closed it again in recognition of the sudden narrowing of the G-G's eyes.

"It would appear, James, that you have staked your position," Jackson said in a low voice that to the startled Blair sounded suspiciously like a rattlesnake's hiss. "Are we to understand that you have thrown in your lot with that of Cal…"

414

"Pardon me, Mr. Governor, but a note from the Duke." Donelson's eyes were wide and popping as he crossed the room and handed Jackson a folded slip of paper. "He's standing just outside there waiting for the answer."

The G-G opened the sheet and looked thoughtfully impressed. "It appears, gentlemen, that Wellington wishes to intervene in our little conference. Apparently wishes to brief us on a, ahem, 'matter of the gravest urgency.'" Rising from his chair with the help of the cane, he flashed his advisors a grim face: "Perhaps that vermin Calhoun has beaten us all to the punch: a compromise or ultimatum of his own."

———————

The others had risen as Jackson teetered his way to the door, exchanging baffled, dumbfounded looks. Polk, who had never before experienced Jackson's wrath, was both relieved and confused: he hadn't meant to show his hand concerning emancipation and he couldn't believe Calhoun would act without informing him...

"Well, Sir, come in. And Sir John also." Jackson was gracious but his surprise at seeing Burrell was evident. "You needn't an invitation to sit in on any meeting in this house, Sir Arthur." He paused again, his lips puckering: "A night off from the rigors of Georgetown's social circuit? Or simply killing time before a late supper elsewhere?"

The others laughed nervously as Wellington motioned them back into their seats. He indicated the whisky jug on a side table. Burrell then proceeded to pour two glasses as the Duke began to speak.

"Mr. Governor-General, gentlemen, I am here tonight on official Government business. That is why Sir John has accompanied me. A volatile situation has developed in Europe which unfortunately may have---may already be having---ramifications here in British America. You should be aware of them, Mr. Governor, before preparing your address..."

As Sir John's briefing progressed, Jackson's face reddened dangerously. Blair and Polk exchanged worried looks and even Wellington seemed aware that the G-G was waging an internal battle for self-control.

That goddamned Calhoun: cavorting with a Russian spy! No wonder the bastard seems so cocky. He thinks he's playing with a stacked deck... The G-G's anger finally burst and he slammed his cane down on the floor.

"You mean there's been a Russian agent floating free around this city---and elsewhere in the Dominion---for months and you people at the Liaison Office haven't done anything about it? And you haven't informed me or anyone else in this Administration!"

Wellington, who was prepared to flatly lie if pressed on whether "anyone...in this Administration" knew of the Calhoun-Russian connection, instead jumped on the Liaison Office's failure to act.

"Gentlemen, our hands have been and continue to be tied. Clearly, Calhoun knows about Syria and has deduced the strain a two-front war would put on the Exchequer's resources, especially with so much already committed to emancipation relief in this and other parts of the Empire. The man, after all, has been a senior member of your government for many years and is something of an intellectual. If a misguided one...

"We surmise that this Russian is a Czarist agent and has been in communication with Calhoun over a period of some months. But that is not illegal. We cannot arrest this Count, or whatever he is, for passing along news from St. Petersburg, much as we would like to. I admit, the reconnaissance we have had on him has been spotty at best and failed miserably when he slipped out of town. But there are no grounds to hold him, any more than there are grounds to arrest Calhoun on suspicion of meeting with him."

There was a short silence, broken by the pragmatic Blair: "Is this Russian still in Georgetown?"

Burrell was eager to furnish some positive news. "Yes. He's attended each day's debates and was seen at a function Tuesday evening at the French Consulate." His face blushing slightly, he continued: "He has been spending a great deal of time also at a local tavern. 'The Golden Eagle,' I believe it is called. You may be familiar...?

"At any rate, he apparently has developed a liaison of his own with the proprietress, one Mrs. Casgrave."

Wellington stood up. "As you see, gentlemen, we now have our friend in our sights. But his well-being is not why I briefed you. You, Mr. Governor-General, were entitled to know about this Syrian adventure, both as a senior officer of His Majesty's Government and because of it's, as I say, 'ramifications' for your internal debate. Having told you as much as we know, Sir John and I will withdraw."

Wellington and Jackson bowed stiffly and formally to each other and Sir John nodded respectfully to the others before leading

Wellington to the door. Wellington was halfway through the doorway when he paused and turned:

"The debate in your Senate, you know, has been most impressive; the arguments most cogent. I look forward to your decision, Mr. Governor-General, now that you have received that 'sense of the people' you so aptly sought."

The door closed; fortunately before Jackson could offer a retort...

Georgetown, DC
June 8, 1833
Dawn:

There were all kinds of consternation being expressed in Georgetown as dawn broke:

Tousaint D'Overture Numidia was muttering to himself over Ugene's failure to appear at Monticello last night. While Cris Donfield had passed off the no-show with the observation that Doby might have gotten lucky with some young lovely, Tousaint was more concerned that the Interior Department man had gotten cold feet and fled. *Well, won't take four to capture this old man and his big aide. And Motley's the key, anyway, since it's his people who will be hiding Wellington at Huntley. Still, it isn't like Ugene to get scared...*

Finally informed of the plot and its particulars, Capt. Harry Bratton was livid. Livid that these colonials had withheld information concerning the Duke's safety until last night's midnight summons to Scott's townhouse. Equally, if not more livid, that the colonials' plan---which there was no longer time to alter---put the Duke, *his responsibility*, at risk. And livid most of all that the damn Old Man had agreed to play the bait in this scheme, which seemed bloody unnecessary and designed only to conform to the rules of their damnable constitution! *Why, at home, we'd simply pick the buggers up right now and let them rot in the Tower---or someplace worse---until they confessed! I'm 100 percent for habeas corpus...but not when it interferes with national security and keeping Old Hook Nose alive and well. Especially on my watch!*

There was consternation and anger at The Residency, too. The G-G was livid…but not because of the uncovered plot. Jackson, as a planter, had lived with real and perceived slave plots all his life. He thought Scott's report last night had been plausible and his proposed response correct. No, what had the G-G enraged was the thought of another meeting between Wellington and Governor Floyd.

"By the Eternal," he thundered at Frank Blair, whom he had summoned for an early morning breakfast conference. "His Grace," Jackson made the title a sneer, "is supposed to be a messenger. He tells us what London is doing and waits for our response. Damn it all, he shouldn't be sticking his big, crooked nose in our internal political processes!"

"Now, Andrew." Blair was smooth and soothing as he broke open a hot roll and sipped coffee. "I think it takes an extraordinary amount of courage for Wellington to agree to risk his life in order to foil this insane plot. As for the meeting with Floyd, well, if the Governor can get His Grace to consider changing the emancipation bill's terms to get the blacks out of the Dominion and back to Africa or Central America or such, why not?"

Recently, there had been increasing sentiment for shipping all the blacks in the USBA to the newly-founded West African country of Liberia. Or, to sending them to some closer Central American jungle like Honduras or Nicaragua. Floyd was reportedly in favor of this approach, which also counted Henry Clay and Chief Justice Marshall among its adherents.

"Hmm. Can think of more than a few white men I'd like to ship to Liberia. Starting with Clay and Calhoun…"

Blair simply grinned and dug into his ham and eggs.

Tom Wilder wasn't happy, either. Since he had been the one to uncover the plot---in actuality, Harper had before simply dumping the report in Tom's lap---the Lieutenant thought he was entitled to command, or at least assist, the rescue party. But the General had assigned the duty to the Marines. Captain Goodwin would command.

Teacher's pets. Damn pretty boys. Always strutting around in their fancy uniforms. Look like heroes for taking down three or four damn darkies… Like to see them *chasing around Arkansas Territory after the Comanche...*

And so the hours passed till Wellington emerged from the Residency and, with Captain Bratton his only apparent guard, mounted up and headed for the Long Bridge and Cranford.

While Moses, who could and would have put an end to the whole grotesque scenario with one loud curse and a clenched fist, was left in the dark, greeting customers and shoeing and renting out horses in his stables next to The Church of Jesus Christ, Liberator.

Calhoun Residence
Georgetown, D.C.
June 8, 1833, 9 a.m.:

"I questioned how long it would be before our 'English overseer' decided to bring Jackson up-to-date on world affairs." Calhoun was his usual sarcastic self, even over the bacon-and-eggs.

"You say Jackson's response was muted, eh? Once he got over the initial insult, you mean!"

Polk and the Kitchen Cabinet had spent the remainder of last evening debating the position the G-G should take, in view of Wellington's bombshell report, in his upcoming speech. A speech, the Kitchen Cabinet had finally decided, that should be postponed some days.

This morning's breakfast had been previously scheduled and North Carolina's Brown, Troup, McDuffie and several other fire-eaters were also in attendance as Polk made his report.

Calhoun smiled his dark smile as he looked around the table while his negro butler oversaw the removal of dishes and the arrival of the next course.

"Wellington has not only brought Jackson up-to-date, but has sent him a multi-faceted message: The crisis in Asia Minor has precedence because of the over-riding importance of ensuring both the safety of India and the trade routes to-and-from. Therefore, the Jackson Administration must defuse the emancipation crisis here, with a military solution out-of-the-question.

"'And the only way to accomplish that task is by means of an exemption. But Jackson must arrange it himself; for while he, Wellington, will accept it, he must appear to have no prior knowledge of, or participation in, its development.'"

Smiles of impending triumph broke out across the table. Only Troup seemed concerned: "James, is that the rationale for the delay in Jackson's address? So he can 'arrange things himself?'

"Well, Senator," Polk paused and looked thoughtful, "I'm not completely convinced that the G-G has fully, err, 'digested'"--the others laughed in appreciation of the pun--"the Duke's message in the totality John has analyzed it.

"Once we got past Andy's predictable outburst over Wellington's high-handedness in withholding the news until this late date, discussion centered on the remarkable solidarity of the other sections in supporting London's subversion of the Compact and the Constitution. Actually, I think the G-G, though he'll never admit it, especially to himself, wants to see what Clay will offer on Monday."

Brown broke in anxiously: "Surely Frelinghuysen's speech made it clear that New York, New Jersey and Pennsylvania will support virtually any compromise..."

It was Calhoun who answered: "Yes, those damn Yankees will go to any lengths to preserve business-as-usual. And despite Benton and Clay's stand for the Dominion, there's 200,000 slaves in those two states alone. Neither state, Kentucky in particular, can simply adjust its way-of-life to the prospect of having all those darkies wandering around free and undirected...

"That's why I expect to hear from 'Harry of the West' in the next day or so. He'll work out an exemption that satisfies this man Ewing and his Westerners. Then, knowing the Yankees will go along with just about anything, he'll come to us. There may be strings attached that I'll have to cut off---perhaps accept a few to save several faces---but eventually, he'll present it to Jackson."

Nodding his head, the long hair bouncing off his shoulders, Calhoun looked pleased. "Probably through you, James, or perhaps Frank Blair. At any rate, by the time Jackson comes to the Hill next week, we'll have our exemption in the bag."

McDuffie looked at his chief. "And Wellington will go along?"

"Yes. In view of the Syrian situation, he'll have to. And once he puts his prestige behind it, Parliament will accept an exemption---

though perhaps not an all-inclusive one---despite Quincy Adams' predictable howling.

"After all, the 'Hero of Waterloo' will have saved the Empire once again by securing peace in America. And, therefore, in India, too."

The Deerhead Inn
June 8, 1833, 11 a.m.:

With a brood of over a dozen children to support back in Ohio, Thomas Ewing was resigned to the confines of a hotel room while in Georgetown. Shabby as it might be, the Deerhead was as good as any. Now, on Saturday morning, he was sitting at a back table in the dining room, grudgingly accepting a compromise proposal worked out by Clay, Benton and Frelinghuysen over the course of the two previous days. The trio had arranged in a late night message to meet him for a 9 a.m. breakfast.

"Then you're agreed, Senator, that we should now proceed en mass to The Residency to offer the G-G this compromise? Even before we propose it to either the abolitionists or the Southern radicals?"

Clay was sizing Ewing up shrewdly. He had paid scant attention to the Ohioan in the previous Congress, though Dan Webster had labeled him a 'comer' in their late afternoon drinking sessions in Clay's office. Knowing that his own very appearance might be enough to set Jackson off, Clay intended to remain in the background during the scheduled negotiations at The Residency this afternoon. Since Benton, too, had clashed personally with the G-G (an infamous Nashville bar brawl that had led to the young Benton's evacuation to Missouri over 20 years prior), someone else was required to take the lead. The patrician Frelinghuysen would, in his own way, also be oil to Jackson's water...

The Ohioan thought the proposal overly generous to the South---from the abolitionist point of view, to say nothing of London's---yet probably not generous enough for Calhoun's faction. The Southern fire-eaters smelled blood, in his opinion, and would not accept any limitations on slavery or its expansion westward.

Clay's compromise called for a 25-year exemption from the Parliamentary bill, on the grounds that, while eliminating bondage elsewhere would simply allow the slaves freedom in societies they would invariably come to dominate, the blacks here would be entering a predominately white, educated society. The 25-year exemption would be utilized in part to bring rudimentary education---financed by the Empire and overseen by the Dominion---to the slaves so that, at the end of the period, they would have a better chance for survival. While minimally affecting the Southern culture and economy.

To sweeten the deal further, the Administration, backed by Congressional resolution, would urge and work for Empire absorption of Texas, by whatever means necessary.

"Well, Senators," Ewing sighed and looked at the trio, "if we go to The Residency as a centrist block and can get Old Jack to sign on, it at least provides a starting point from which to negotiate. And might ratchet down the rhetoric among the wild men on both sides."

He frowned suddenly: "But what will Wellington say? He came here to enforce the existing emancipation bill. We're watering that down, from his original perspective, considerably."

"Well, Tom," Hart Benton said with a grin, "one duck at a time. Let's concentrate on getting a Dominion response."

John Tyler's Townhouse
Georgetown, D.C.
June 8, 1833, 7:00 p.m.:

The Southern inner-circle---the Calhouns, Troups, McDuffie---had all gathered for a previously arranged dinner-party at the Tylers when James and Sarah Polk arrived shortly before 7 p.m.

Polk, whose wife had become resigned to his prolonged absences, had spent a fascinating afternoon at The Residency after leaving Calhoun's breakfast meeting. Now he reported to an enthralled audience:

A group composed of Clay, Benton, Ewing and Frelinghuysen---calling themselves the 'Centrist Committee'---had appeared at The Residency around 1 p.m., expecting a sit-down with the Governor-General. Jackson, however, was closeted with General Scott and the

Secretary of War all afternoon. The G-G had come out briefly to authorize him and Blair to meet with the committee and to brief them on the Syrian situation, including its implications for the emancipation debate. The G-G's secretary, Donelson, had shuttled between the two meetings, updating Jackson...but never explaining exactly what was happening in the Old Man's private office.

Polk then explained, to much initial glee (though Calhoun's dark smile barely registered), Clay's proposal. "Now then, there are three additional steps ascertained: The Committee, or at least Clay and possibly Benton, will seek a meeting with you, John, for tomorrow. A message may be waiting at your townhouse. Another meeting, of course, will be arranged to brief Webster and the lesser of his fanatics.

"Finally, a meeting of the Kitchen Cabinet will begin at The Residency at 1 p.m. tomorrow to discuss the proposal. Hopefully, we'll find out what all this War Department business is about."

Calhoun waited till the comments had died off before speaking.

"I'll receive Harry and whoever else shows up. We can entertain any and all proposals without committing to any...until we see what Jackson officially has to say later in the week.

"As for this 'War Department business,' well, I have a good sense of what that's all about...and why the meeting went on so long.

"James, you'll of course let me know the outcome immediately post tomorrow's meeting. Pay particular attention to Cass' reaction to all this. I believe he and Jackson received quite a shock today in their meeting with Scott. See what you can find out...

"Meanwhile, ladies and gentlemen, while there are many long and excruciating turns yet to navigate, I believe our cause grows ever closer to reality. I believe a toast is in order." He smiled, tiredly but fully, for the first time all evening as the others applauded loudly.

Even though none, save Floride, were completely sure what *cause* it was...

Arlington-Georgetown Road
June 8, 1833
8 pm:

Since Tousaint and Ugene both worked for the Dominion

423

government, and had the necessary identification to prove it to any snickering guards, they had little trouble getting across the Long Bridge and into Virginia. Motley, with identification that demonstrated that his family were tenant farmers at Hunting Creek Farm, had come across the previous night and had remained south of Cranford. Only Crispus had significant explaining to do. Which he accomplished by flashing his Spanish Consulate ID and mumbling about delivering papers to the Spanish commercial agent in Richmond.

What none---except Ugene---suspected was that the guards had been instructed to let them pass with no more than cursory harassment. The guards, Marines dressed in civilian attire, had of course been furnished their descriptions and checked each off the list as they came across.

There was enough traffic on the Georgetown-Alexandria road that none of the gang wondered about the lack of enforcement between the Bridge and Cranford. Motley and Donfield were simply happy to disappear into the traffic, while Tousaint, with that cockiness that Ugene correctly identified as arrogance, thought that four young blacks, riding separately over two days, was too sophisticated a plan for any dumb white soldiers or marshals to decipher.

The operation was to commence when Wellington, alone or with his aide, was sighted riding back from Cranford. While the other three were still at work, Motley, with a day off from the Indian Queen, had been hiding in the woods about halfway from Cranford to the Bridge since noon. He spotted the Duke---by this time everyone in Georgetown, white or black, could identify him--- accompanied by one solidly built aide, ride by about going south two hours later. Crispus, who had made friends with the white American in charge of the Consulate's physical plant and could get off an occasional hour or two early, rode in two hours later.

From Tousaint's perspective, getting Doby and himself to the rendezvous location on time was the trickiest part of the operation. But Ugene had been waiting when he rode past the War-Interior building around 5:30 on his favorite mount from the family stables. Tousaint grinned at Doby's problems with the horse Jurgurtha had rent him at noon time but made little conversation as the two passed through the apparently flimsy security and clattered out onto the Bridge. *Unless Wellington has indigestion or something and leaves early, we'll be there with time to spare.*

General Scott had set up his operational headquarters at Arlington House and, with a good view of the road, had been waiting since leaving the Residency. Still smarting from the General's decision to place the operation in the hands of Captain Goodwin and the Marines, Lieutenant Wilder was with him, though Tom was sent by back roads to secure the proposed southern escape route to Hunting Farm once Tousaint and Doby were identified as coming down the road. A strong Army guard also set up a roadblock just above Arlington to seal off the northeastern route back into Georgetown. Both Tom's command and the soldiers north of Arlington had fanned off the road under Scott's design to close off the woods as if by swinging doors inward should the gang attempt to escape by scattering. A third USBAA contingent from the 4th Artillery had already secured Hunting Creek Farm itself once Motley had been spotted heading northeast.

A sudden shrill whistle, a bird call they had used while hunting ducks in Foggy Bottom, alerted Tousaint that he and Ugene had arrived at the rendezvous. Motley and Donfield emerged out of the growing dusk. Instantly taking command, Numidia quieted the mutual greetings and sent Motley and Doby back to the east side of the road. Donfield, who had the best eyes of the foursome, was ordered up a tree to keep watch on the road north from Cranford. It was 6:35 p.m. by the Williams College class watch Tousaint glanced at before replacing in his vest pocket. He pulled his horse off the road, dismounted and sat leaning against a tree to wait.

And wait. The time dragged on so slowly, but surely, that Numidia began to consider the chances that the Cranford conference had dissolved into a liquor-soaked supper that would keep the participants at the plantation overnight. (The possibility that he had misinterpreted Sebastian's report to Moses of course never occurred to Tousaint.)

Just as he had begun to consider that the snatch might have to be called off for the night, Donfield was suddenly back.

"Two riders coming up the road. One's big enough to be that Brit aide of Wellington's…"

And the other?"

"Hard to tell. But they're both ridin' real easy."

Tousaint cursed. "Can't spring a trap on *that*. Is it Wellington or not?"

Donfield spit. "See for yourself. They'll be along any minute…"

———

Arthur Goodwin closed his telescope and turned to his second-in-command. "Damn good thing there's a full moon tonight. Makes things easier when you can see your prey…"

"How about the bait?"

"Can't see anyone coming up that road, but our friends down there are getting into the saddle. *They* must think its Wellington…"

Goodwin and his troop had worked their way to a hill northwest of the rendezvous point after tracking Numidia and Doby from the Long Bridge. Rather than risk detection by dividing his command and sending half east of the road, Goodwin was counting on split-second timing and surprise to overwhelm the blacks before they realized a trap had been sprung. The Captain knew an Army unit under Wilder was following Wellington up the road. That cut off the escape route south. But he had no intention of requiring the Army's assistance. The Marines would take care of this little chore themselves. Piece of cake…

———

An avid fox hunter, His Grace Sir Arthur Wellesley, Duke of Wellington, now found that he rather enjoyed the role of the fox. Of course, knowing half the colonials under official arms in the District of Columbia, directed by his trusted old comrade Winfield Scott, were lurking in the area made playing the role somewhat less tense. Even though he could hear Harry's muttering that they would have been better off with a full contingent of Royal Marines surrounding them…

Despite Bratton's being an accomplished 'diplomatic,' Wellington knew Harry considered himself above all a bodyguard. So even though the Captain, on an intellectual level, knew security in this case must be left to the USBA authorities, it was only human of him to want the best security available. And, as an Englishman, that meant the Royal Marines.

But the Duke had ruled that all out. He had had no choice, really, once Scott had proposed and outlined the plan, but to let the Americans handle things their way. Even though he had a sneaky feeling Scott had enjoyed turning the hunter into the hunted...

Well, one trap or more to be sprung, it wouldn't be much longer.

Law-abiding young men that they had always been, neither Tousaint nor his followers had ever been in a confrontation like this, much alone a potential firefight. He had instructed Doby and Motley to simply ride up out of the east woods, while he and Donfield came in from the northwest. Neglecting even to disguise themselves with handkerchiefs over their faces, the foursome suddenly materialized around Wellington.

Bratton's roar of rage was real, giving Tousaint an undeserved sense of security---the man was obviously shocked---even as the roar seemed to unnerve Doby's horse. The animal reared and whined, giving Ugene the opportunity he was seeking to drop out of the fight. He slipped off the horse, and pretended that the fall had knocked him unconscious.

Numidia, meanwhile, had grabbed the reins of Wellington's horse and began to turn the animal around. That's when he disbelievingly began to discern shapes emerging from the darkness onto the road. As he looked back, he saw Donfield, who had never fired a pistol--- neither had Motley---nonetheless aiming one at Bratton, who had pulled out his own gun.

Tousaint, who had planned for Motley to dispose of the aide by knocking him out and tying him to a tree, now saw the big man reach over and pull Bratton from his saddle. As he did, the Brit's pistol went off and they both fell to the ground: Bratton with the wind knocked out from the force of Motley's initial yank; Motley from the bullet that blasted into his stomach.

Another shot rang out virtually simultaneously. Donfield had fired his weapon into the space Bratton had occupied just seconds before. But now a terrible cry of pain rang out as, from the darkness of the woods suddenly, three, four, five shapes materialized from the same spot and, waving their swords, hacked at Crispus and pulled the reins of his horse. Blood flew into Tousaint's astonished face as an object, later identified as Crispus' right ear, went sailing by.

Numidia never knew what that object was. A shocking, searing pain exploded on his left side and he crumbled from his horse. Dead before he hit the ground, nor did he ever know that a Marine's bayonet had penetrated below his third rib and traveled up to the heart. It was a classic Roman legionary thrust. This night, it claimed another Numidian...

Regaining control of his horse, Wellington, the lifelong soldier, still looked around at the carnage in amazement. No more than 60 seconds had passed since he and Bratton had been surrounded. Now two blacks lay prone with multiple Marine bayonets pressed to their throats and chests, one bleeding and moaning profusely, the other strangely shouting out a name he claimed as his own. Another, huge, black had regressed to a fetal position, holding his belly and groaning softly. The final conspirator, the one who had grabbed Wellington's own horse, was also lying on the ground, silent, but with still more Marine swords and bayonets hovering above his still, bleeding body.

A dirty-faced Marine with captain's bars finished touring the scene, walked up to Wellington and saluted.

"Good evening, Your Grace. I trust you are unhurt? The USBA Marines have the situation under control, Sir!"

Wellington shook his head dazedly and smiled. "Indeed it would seem so, Captain...?"

"Arthur Goodwin, Your Grace. Georgetown Ceremonial Detachment, USBA Marines."

"Ceremonial, ay?" Wellington grunted and stroked his famous nose as he watched the road suddenly flood with armed men in USBA military uniforms. "If you chaps are the ceremonial detachment, I bloody well wouldn't want to face the fighting men..."

CHAPTER THIRTY-NINE

Georgetown, D.C.
June 9, 1833:

It rained heavily all that Sunday but few of the participants in the crisis used the weather as an excuse for a day of rest.

The Kitchen Cabinet met to debate the Clay compromise; state-sponsored education of the slaves was the major point of contention. In the end, the G-G decided to reserve judgment until later in the week. After all, his speech was now rescheduled for Wednesday, the 12th.

Calhoun and Webster received, separately, the Centrist Committee. Calhoun demanded two additional concessions: the 25-year 'cap' on the exemption must be extended and the Texas commitment must be changed to include "the entire Southwest." (Exactly how "the entire Southwest" was to be defined was not made clear.) While Calhoun remarked while showing his guests the door that he was "off to a diplomatic function, something at the Prussian Consulate," he did not tell them of another conference planned for that evening, one arranged in the morning with a civilian representative of the Russian government...

The foiled Wellington snatch was still a closely guarded secret, known to only a few at The Residency, the War Department and the Liaison Office.

Webster and two of his fellow New Englanders, the veteran Rhode Island Dominion-Republican Nehemiah R. Knight and New Hampshire's first-term Democrat, Isaac Hill, reacted in a predictably enraged fashion to the very idea of an exemption, to say nothing of the expansion commitments. The patrician Frelinghuysen alone saw through Daniel's act: Webster, to maintain his prestige among the abolitionists, had to initially howl. By not rejecting the compromise outright, however, he was signaling his willingness to work behind-the-scenes, however, to support a compromise of some kind...

429

It was not the rain that had forced cancellation of Dave Harper's weekly riding date with Countess Caroline. The Countess had reluctantly been forced to call off their date in order to prepare for the late afternoon reception at the Prussian Consulate honoring some half-forgotten Napoleonic Wars general who had just arrived for a tour of America. Apparently, he and the Duke of Wellington were old comrades; Wellington had agreed to attend. As for the current men-of-the-hour in Georgetown, Von Benes had also invited Calhoun, Ewing and Benton. So she was now discussing the protocol with her father...and Count Nicholas.

Harper's gloom over the cancelled riding date was short-lived: the spectacular Madame Jean-Claude, who had rented a summer cottage on the Latoure plantation as a get-away, summoned him for a 2 p.m. rendezvous. Jacques, if all went as planned, might even cross paths with David on the Long Bridge...

Count Ignatieff was intent on discovering Calhoun's estimate of the situation: did the Southern leader expect this Jackson to side with the South? Were the other sections indeed ready to enforce the emancipation bill? Ignatieff felt it imperative to gauge Calhoun's true feelings...and to remind him that Russia stood by its commitment to aid an independent South.

Aaron Burr was scheduled to dine privately with Jackson tonight. It would be their first meeting since that memorable one in March. Georgetown's cooler senior heads---Marshall, Scott and the Duke--- were anxious to know where Jackson currently stood. Especially since Ewing had announced last evening the Centrist proposal at a Van Buren-hosted dinner...

Numidia Stables/War Department
June 9, 1833
10 a.m.:

Jurgurtha Numidia was lifting a horse's right rear leg when a shadow appeared in the stable stall. Without looking up, the massive blacksmith/preacher ordered: "Get out of my light, you damn fool. Can't you see I'm trying to shoe this animal? Don't need him getting skittish and kicking me in the chin..."

Lt. Tom Wilder automatically moved to one side and then stared as Jurgurtha finished hammering the shoe in, dropped the horse's leg and unfolded to reveal his full height. *Jaysus, Mary and Joseph, this one's bigger than the General... I didn't think that was possible...*

The huge black man took in the stubby young Army officer at a glance and, showing no sign of deference to race or rank, growled. "So? State your business. Got a lot to do this day. With summer coming, the white folk all be hiring horses and carriages for their picnics in the countryside, once this storm blows out."

Tom took a deep breath. *Damn, sometimes I wish I was back chasing Comanche...* "Jurgurtha Numidia, if, as I have been informed, you are he, by order of the Governor-General, I am to escort you to the War Department... Immediately."

A laugh that began deep in his huge chest rumbled up through the black man's throat. "You are, huh? By order of Andy Jackson himself? What's the matter, General Scott quit? 'Old Hickory' need an experienced officer to take his place?" The big man's laugh caromed off the stall walls.

Tom found he was coming to full attention. "I am not at liberty to say, Mr. Numidia. My orders are simply to escort you to the War Department, post-haste. Now, if you would, please..." The Lieutenant motioned toward the stable door, where Jurgurtha, looking out for the first time, could now see a squad of mounted, armed and drenching wet USBA Marines.

"Well, son, seeing as I can't hardly turn down a personally-delivered request from the Governor-General of the United States of British America---out of curiosity, if no other reason---let's go."

The man had a sense of dignity about him that made Tom want to blurt out a warning of what awaited him in the War Department's cellar. Instead, he simply marched back outside and remounted, then waited for the blacksmith to bring out his own horse.

There was no talk as the squad rode through Georgetown's muddy streets, though there were stares from the few Sunday morning passers-by at the sight of a huge black man being escorted by a contingent of armed Marines. Occasionally glancing back, Tom was struck by the black man's calm demeanor. *He's either the coolest character I've ever seen, or he actually doesn't have a clue about what happened to his son and his gang last night. I've got a hunch it's the latter...*

Leaving their mounts in the custody of the Marines, Tom and Jurgurtha walked up the building's steps and down the hall toward the War Department. An enlisted man standing between two big, hard-eyed guards at the Department door quickly vanished back inside before returning with the General's secretary. Lt. Luke Beaufort's eyes widened slightly as he took in Jurgurtha before nodding slightly to Tom and stepping back inside, presumably to inform General Scott.

Wilder took a deep breath and motioned for the big black man to continue down the hall to a door which led to downward stairs. Jurgurtha had to lower his head as they descended, which meant an instant's delay before he could take in the tableaux before him: two black bodies lying on parallel tables, sheets covering them from forehead to knees.

A grim USBAA officer and several enlisted men hovered over the bodies, while the room was ringed with armed soldiers. As Numidia stepped deeper into the room, into space vacated by Wilder, the grim officer---Jurgurtha had no way of knowing he was a doctor---pulled the sheet down from one man's forehead to his chest.

A wail of anguish that the Lieutenant never forgot erupted as Jurgurtha recognized the form and features of his son.

"Dear Lordy; oh, dear Lord, oh dear Lord Jesus Christ no!" The *no* vibrated through the cellar as Jurgurtha collapsed onto Tousaint's inert form and began pounding his ham-like fists against the side of the table.

None of the white men moved as Jurgurtha rocked back and forth, intoning the Lord's name as well as that of his son. Finally, the big man rose as in a trance and stepped around and in between the tables, where he removed the covering from the other body.

"Marion, you damn fool," he whispered, "how did you and my boy end up like this? How, Marion?"

There was a significant silence in the room before a deep voice answered. "We are hoping you can help us answer that, Mr. Numidia..."

Winfield Scott stood---or rather, filled---the stairway.

Jurgurtha never turned to respond. Instead, he gently pulled the sheet away from Motley's body, revealing the insultingly-large hole the point-blank shot from Captain Bratton's pistol had blown in Marion's stomach, the blood still encrusting the circumference of the wound.

432

Shaking his head sadly, Moses replaced the sheet as high as Motley's throat before slowly turning around. As he did, Jurgurtha came into almost level eye contact with the uniformed and bemedalled Scott. The two stared at each other before Jurgurtha ripped off the sheet covering Tousaint.

Searching for evidence of gunshot wounds, Numidia at first was puzzled by the lack of evidence of what had caused his boy's death. Looking up inquiringly, he seemed poised to ask the obvious question when the doctor lifted Tousaint's left arm and exposed the bayonet cut beneath the third rib.

Letting out a moan, he turned and moved back toward Scott: "Why? What could they have done to deserve this? These boys ain't never been in trouble. My boy is a college graduate. Why did you people butcher them?"

Two soldiers leapt in between the ebony-and-ivory giants but Scott motioned them back.

"I'm truly sorry they could not be taken alive, Mr. Numidia. My men had orders not to shoot unless fired upon…and to use their swords only for protective purposes. But this man Motley was shot while attempting to dismount a Royal Army officer. And your son was stabbed while attempting to flee with a prisoner…after a third member of his…party…one Crispus Atticks Donfield, opened fire on USBA Marines who had intervened."

Numidia's bitterness showed through his grief. "*Intervened?* Intervened in what? What could three young black men who have never, ever flaunted the law do to have half the USBA Army and Marines come down on them? *Waving swords and bayonets and with pistols cocked to fire?*"

Numidia stepped forward. He and Scott were now chin to chin. "Tell me damn it, Massa General Winfield Scott, Sir: what could three young black men who have never owned a gun between them have done to rate this… *this ambush? This massacre? Tell me!*"

Scott never twitched a facial muscle and his right hand was steady as he again waved away the advancing guards.

"Mr. Numidia, your boy and *three* others attempted to seize His Grace Sir Arthur Wellesley, Duke of Wellington and former prime minister of the British Empire, for ransom…"

"*What?*"

"…The ransom being the immediate emancipation of every slave held in the United States of British America."

Numidia's look of outrage slowly turned to one of sorrow as he felt the full brunt of Scott's famous blue-eyed stare and realized in his bones that the big white man spoke the truth.

Slowly blinking his eyes, he turned again to gaze at his son before releasing a terrible moan as he collapsed once more against the table. "Oh, your damn hotheaded young fools! Seven years! Just seven years and the Day of Salvation will be here! You just couldn't wait, could you? You damn young hotheads! What could you have been *thinking*?"

Scott waited till he was certain the last burst of immediate emotion had dissipated itself before speaking.

"That, Mr. Numidia, is something to be discussed privately in my office."

The General turned to Lieutenant Wilder: "Give Mr. Numidia appropriate time to grieve, Lieutenant. Then escort him, under guard, to my office. Thirty minutes from now." Scott turned and began climbing back up the stairs, followed by the doctor and all but four of the soldiers.

By the time Lieutenant Wilder led Jurgurtha Numidia into the General's office at approximately 11:30 a.m., a small group of influential Administration figures had gathered, along with Sir John Burrell.

The group---Attorney General Roger B. Taney; Interior Secretary MacLane; Vice G-G Van Buren and Frank Blair---studied Jurgurtha closely for signs of telltale nervousness and/or bluster. But the big black man had regained his composure before leaving the cellar and seemingly had also overcome his shock.

"Well Mr. Numidia, can you tell us how your son and his gang knew about emancipation so early? We have discovered that this plot had its origins in February. Yet the Duke did not announce Parliament's intentions until March 2." General Scott was direct and to the point; there would be no expressions of apology for the successful, if bloody, rescue of the Duke.

Jurgurtha stared at Scott, whom he had already sized up as the key interrogator. "Damned if I know."

"Well then, Mr. Numidia, would you mind telling us how *you* knew?"

For the first time, a look of confusion flashed briefly crossed the blacksmith's face, as he rapidly thought back to the scene in the cellar. *Had he burted anything about Exodus?* His features hardened and he resumed his staring contest with Scott. "No idea. No idea at all." He shifted to slaves' slang: "Ain't got no idea what Massa and de uder white bosses talkin' 'bout."

Blair guffawed and sent a strong, straight flow of tobacco into the General's spittoon. "Spare us the linguistic disguise, Mr. Numidia. We may not as yet know as much about you as we soon will, but one thing we do know: you're an educated man who, in your role as a minister, preaches regularly to your flock about the need to assimilate into society in order to prosper, beginning with speaking the King's English...

"Yes, we know about the 'Church of Jesus Christ, Liberator.' A congregation which seems to flourish without any evident resources. And we know your late son"---Jurgurtha winced---"is a graduate of Williams College in Massachusetts.

"Quite a financial load for a blacksmith to carry, won't you agree?"

"I'm the best damn blacksmith this Godforsaken swamp village has ever had..."

A lanky, cadaverous man with prematurely white hair shifted in his seat. "Yes, Mr. Numidia. And it would be a real shame if the city lost the services of its 'best damn blacksmith' if I'm forced to lock you away for an indefinite period due to your unfortunate lack of cooperation."

General Scott broke the ensuing silence. "Mr. Numidia, I should have introduced you to these gentlemen earlier." Nodding at the cadaverous man, he said: "This is the Attorney General, Mr. Taney. The first gentleman to address you was Francis P. Blair. I trust you read his newspaper daily? Secretary MacLane of Interior..."---an obviously Scotch-Irish face nodded grudgingly---"...and the Vice Governor-General round out our group. My aide, Lieutenant Wilder, you have already become acquainted with. And Sir John Burrell of the Liaison Office.

"Now then. We already know that your son worked in the office of Sen. Daniel Webster of Massachusetts. We also have the occupations of the other conspirators. None of the others, even Doby in Mr. MacLane's department, were in any position to discover the most closely-guarded secret in this town's history until after the

Duke's speech.

"So, Mr Numidia: did Tousaint let you in on this secret...or did you tell him?"

Jurgurtha, feeling Scott's drill-like stare, attempted to retaliate with a glare of his own.

"Come, Mr. Numidia. No one is accusing you of masterminding this insane, amateurish plot. Your heartfelt reaction downstairs has convinced me, at least, of your innocence in that regard. But we want to know how the secret came to be in your family's possession. Now, Senator Webster has been called for and should arrive shortly. His responses should narrow the options even further. So, tell us: how did the Numidia family learn about emancipation?"

Jurgurtha felt trapped inside a redhot griddle. *Exodus* was at stake: on one side the escape system itself; on the other, the funding and influence of the Society.

He turned from Scott and gazed out the window to the hills of Arlington House. "Ain't got no idea what Massa an' youse uder bosses be talkin' 'bout."

After Lieutenant Wilder escorted Jurgurtha--under guard---to a cell attached to the building's stable, the group considered its next steps. It was agreed that Webster was to be informed only that his employee had died in a shocking attempt to capture the Duke.

"Daniel's too smart to be directly involved in anything like this," said Blair. "He won't tell us anything we don't already know. Even if he does know something."

The conversation then turned to the living conspirators. It had already been decided that a public trial was out of the question. "It would make the Administration look weak at a time, with this emancipation issue heating up, when that can not be borne." Blair was direct. "Just think what Calhoun and his damnable firebrands could make of this: 'Jackson has lost control of the nigras. See what happens when any of them are let loose without strict supervision?'"

Crispus Donfield was instead to be exiled to Liberia, leaving on the first available Royal Navy vessel out of RNS Baltimore. Lawrence Eugene Doby was a harder decision: the man had, after all, reported the conspiracy in the first place. A reward was justified, but allowing him to stay in Georgetown was out-of-the-question. So Doby would be shipped to the USBA Consulate in Paris, with a clerk's position comparable to his old job at Interior.

It was about then that Senator Webster was announced. An hour later, convinced of the orator's lack of knowledge of the incident, the meeting broke up, though Blair remained behind when the others exited.

"He's hiding something, you know. Damn it all, how could a poor black smithy learn a secret as closely guarded as any in this town's history? Why, until March 2, probably no more than 10 people in Georgetown were aware of it!" Blair kicked at the rug in frustration. "Is there some sort of wide-ranging abolitionist conspiracy operating under our noses here? An organized movement toward a coordinated slave uprising? Dear God, isn't dealing with Calhoun's firebrands enough? Could we have two volcanoes heating up under our feet? How could these freemen know so much, so early?

"And how could they put a plot like this into operation? It wasn't that *insane* or *amatuerish*, you know. If not for one of the gang getting cold feet, they might well have pulled it off: the snatch, at least!"

Scott reached across his credenza to refill a coffee cup that had long turned cold from a freshly-brewed pot just brought in by Lieutenant Beaufort. "Not from any official sources, that's for sure. But the distinguished Senator didn't know anything about this particular plot. Just as the Attorney General or MacLane, until March 2, didn't know about the Parliamentary bill."

"Did you see the look on Taney's face? He's apoplectic. Not just about the plot. About this whole emancipation business in general. You'd think he would approve, him having freed his own slaves some years back...."

"That's Roger. Personally hates slavery...but doesn't think the Constitution gives government the right to interfere." Scott was matter-of-fact.

"Pretty narrow interpretation."

Blair was now smoking a large cigar. Blowing out the smoke in blue circular clouds, he moved back to the main topic. "All right General. What do we do with this blacksmith-preacher? What do we recommend to Andy, that is?"

Scott took his time answering, marching over to his window

with its view of the Potomac while he considered. "I believe there's more to this man than meets the eye, Frank. This smithy-preacher business; I suspect it's just a charade. A camouflage, if you will. There's more to this Jurgurtha than that. You can see it in his eyes: he's always wary, always thinking... But since the Attorney General sees no grounds to hold him..."

"Taney didn't say that!"

"Hell, Frank, if Roger thought he had evidence the fellow broke the law, he would have arrested him on the spot..."

"So?"

"So we recommend that Andy release him...and then get a good watch on his activities indefinitely. Infiltrate that funeral, for example."

"Think there'll be one?"

"Hmmn. Just the biggest black one in the city's history..."

"Andy won't like that..."

"Nothing he can do. Jurgurtha's got a right to bury his son. And that other boy. But..."

Blair smiled. "But..."

"But not until I get another chance to talk with him. Privately."

Blair stuck out his hand reflexively, realizing too late the crushing pain he was about to absorb. "I look forward to hearing the details, General." The closest advisor grimaced and extracted his reddened digits and palm gingerly.

Prussian Consulate
June 9, 1833, 5 p.m.:

Because of Von Benes' serendipitous decision to invite the Senator to the reception, Calhoun and Count Nicholas were able to forego their planned 9 p.m. meeting. However, Harry Bratton, in attendance as usual with the Duke, was able only to later report that the duo talked briefly but animatedly during the height of the evening's pre-supper reception.

Calhoun, to Harry's surprise, seemingly had no qualms concerning a public conversation with the eye-patched Russian; in fact had introduced him to his wife. The Count, in turn, introduced the Calhouns to a visibly nervous Countess Renkowiitz.

"Recognition of the South's position has become a topic at the Imperial Court," Ignatieff--tonight again masquerading as Karlhamanov--said, staring Calhoun in the eye. "Support for your position is strong. The Czar himself has expressed his interest." Nicholas paused to determine that the message had been received.

Calhoun was equally brisk in sending his coded reply: "That the plight of the South has aroused the sympathies of so great a world figure as Nicholas of Russia means much to our people. We will count on his friendship."

Seeing Von Benes himself looking over and knowing his time with Calhoun was thus limited, Ignatieff pressed a blunt question: "Will that support be necessary at the conclusion of this special session?" Caroline looked shocked, but the Senator smiled his dark smile. "Just knowing of that support is beneficial to the South at this time, Sir."

Calhoun nodded and, taking Floride's arm, moved into the crowd.

———

Standing in a group that included DeGama and Valenzuela, Count Renkowiitz had eyed the encounter as anxiously as Captain Bratton. Count Karl waited an appropriate time before joining Ignatieff, who was standing alone near where what was optimistically labeled in Georgetown as an 'orchestra' had set up. (Countess Caroline had been taken up by their Prussian host to meet the Duke and his crony, old General Von Below, who had apparently survived several disastrous engagements with Bonaparte to emerge as some sort of Teutonic hero.)

The conversation was brief. "Calhoun apparently believes this crisis will be settled peacefully, Renkowiitz. Which would ill serve our cause. And would not please the Czar. I doubt you have picked up any encouraging news?"

Renkowiitz shook his head. "The consensus among our fellow diplomats is that Jackson will propose a compromise. Whether Wellington will then agree or not, it will postpone the crisis, as the counter-proposal will have to be sent back to London."

The wolf's stare, as always, startled Renkowiitz. "That is unacceptable. Our goal is to tie the British up by means of an insurrection here so that they cannot oppose our march to India.

Increasingly I see a covert intervention here may be our only chance to attain that goal."

The wolf's stare faded. "Well, my dear Count. You and your lovely daughter should stay here and pick up any information you can. I will soon depart in order to think on our options for such intervention." The stare returned. "We will discuss this at precisely 11 a.m. tomorrow." Ignatieff turned on his heel and moved toward the bar, leaving the nominal head of the Russian Consulate pale and aghast.

The Residency
June 9, 1833, 10 p.m.:

Aaron Burr had arrived depressed. He was departing in a somewhat different state of mind. He had always considered Andrew Jackson a man of action, one who whose legendary hair-trigger temper was matched by an equally lightening-fast decision-making ability. The G-G's apparent foot-dragging was becoming dangerous: all sides were taking it as a sign of weakness

Now, as the Vice G-G's carriage carried him back to Matty Van's house, he shook his head in admiration at Jackson's audacity…and wondered if the ploy could succeed.

"By the Eternal, Colonel!" the G-G had bellowed in frustration as Burr had prodded for a public indication of his leanings. They had just spent 3 ½ hours discussing the issue in minute detail over a simple but excellent roast beef dinner. "Not you, too! I simply am not yet prepared to intervene in the Congressional debate. Let those people up on the Hill reach some sort of accord! Or come here to tell me they're hopelessly deadlocked. Then I'll propose my solution. That's why I've pushed my speech back. And why I'll reschedule it again, if necessary!"

Jackson drained a glass of after-dinner Tennessee whisky and poured a refill from the jug that had replaced the wine bottles on the table. His tone became more reasonable:

"Aaron, my feelings about this damn bill have not changed since His Grace, the Duke," he snorted the title sarcastically, "dropped this on us three months ago. I didn't like the idea of these Parliamentary

Limeys---and that sanctimonious Puritan bastard Adams---interfering then...and I don't like it now..."

He paused and grinned ruefully at Burr. "But as I do recognize their right---watch it, Colonel or, by the Eternal, I'll wipe that smirk right off your face---I intend to exercise our right to come to a final decision here.

"That's why I'm withholding my position, if you must know. There'll be no 'compromise proposal' sent back to London with Wellington, accompanied by a Congressional committee, hats in hand!"

He stared at Burr over the top of his whisky glass. "I'll go to the Hill in a few days, after the boys have talked themselves hoarse. I'll announce my decision, based on their debate. The country will fall in behind it, as it appears it will be the majority opinion...Then we'll pack His Grace off to 'jolly ol' England' with the response of a united Dominion."

The Colonel had paused, sipping from his own glass---this one containing Claret---and weighing the odds.

"Are you telling me, Andrew, that you---of all people---have suddenly become pragmatic?"

"What I am telling you, Colonel Burr---and this is not for anyone else's ears until further notice---is that the Governor-General intends to defuse this crisis by rallying our people around the flag." He paused and stared hard at Burr. "The Stars and Stripes, *not* the Union Jack...

"Slavery is on its way out; even the most diehard planters know it can't last more than another few generations. But we can deflect the sectional bitterness by informing His Majesty's Government that 'we in the Dominion will see to our own business, thank ye very much...'"

Jackson paused to take another long swallow of his favorite mash. "Focus 'em on solving our problem internally..." He paused and nodded vigorously. "That'll do the trick...Get 'em so mad at London that they'll do anything to show the Limey bastards up...

"...too mad to try to show each other up." Jackson paused again. His next remarks came out, to even the secular Burr's ears, as a sort of prayer:

"I only hope to the Eternal that it'll work... Otherwise..."

As he rode back to his son's house, Burr, an agnostic whose grandfather had been the redoubtable fire-and-brimstone preacher Jonathon Edwards, hoped--prayed?--that Andy's strategy *would* work.

Capitol Hill,
June 10, 1833, 12:00 noon:

James K. Polk encountered Calhoun and Congressman McDuffie at the foot of the Hill.

It did not take him long to relay the results of yesterday's Kitchen Cabinet meeting as they began their climb: Jackson had postponed his speech until Wednesday in order to obtain a sense of how the 'Kentucky resolutions'---"Andy will not acknowledge them as Clay's, of course," he noted with a grin---played out. "Then, he will announce his position."

Calhoun grunted. "Still won't get off the fence, eh? Can't see that the issue has been decided? Well, once we receive confirmation that we've isolated those damn abolitionists with our amended Cla... *'Kentucky'*...resolutions, his opinion will simply be a rubber stamp."

McDuffie seldom contradicted Calhoun, but he did so now. "Rubber stamp as far as Congress is concerned, quite possibly, John. But in the eyes of the British: an imprimatur. It's obvious now that Wellington came here with the authority, under that damn Compact, to relieve Jackson, if necessary."

"He'll think twice about that, however, once he sees that the Congress---and the various sections other than New England---are lined up in step with that old man."

Calhoun paused midway up the Capitol Building's steps and smiled his dark smile at the panting McDuffie. "You must get more physical exercise, Mac. The South can't afford to lose the brand of political acumen you occasionally dispense..." His smile broadened slightly to soften the sarcasm.

"I agree, Jackson is key in dealing with London..."

"But all in good time, gentlemen. For now, let's concentrate on getting the exemption---sunsetted, not capped---through both Houses. Then, we'll deal with the Duke.

"By the way, have there been any late dispatches from London? Or Syria…?"

His co-conspirators laughed as they parted in the Rotunda and Calhoun made his way to the Senate portion of the Building.

The Golden Eagle Tavern
June 10, 1833, 4 p.m.:

Count Ignatieff had not revealed the details of his "covert intervention" to the nominal Russian C-G at their brief 11 a.m. meeting (to which Caroline, to her relief, was not summoned).

Ignatieff had instead simply informed Renkowiitz that he had determined on a possible course of action, based on the outcome of the Congressional debate; meanwhile, the C-G was to make arrangements for 'Karlhamanov's' sudden---if necessary---disappearance. After some brainstorming---mostly on Nicholas' part---it was decided to utilize the services of the New York-based merchant, Tretiak.

Nicholas vaguely recalled the merchant bragging about his wide-ranging enterprises (all Imperial-backed) in such cities as Boston, Baltimore and Charleston. After a quick check, they determined that Tretiak also maintained an office and warehouses in Richmond, 90 miles to the southwest. If his cover was blown and the British began a search for him, they agreed, that search would most likely center on Baltimore as the nearest port of embarkation to Europe. The small Tretiak operation in Richmond would not attract attention, yet was both far enough away to hide him and close enough to allow him to slip back into Georgetown, if the need arose.

Ignatieff gave the order to inform Richmond to be alert. He then departed for Capitol Hill, where Senator Clay was scheduled to present his compromise resolutions at 1 p.m.

Now, alarmed by the conciliatory tenor of the proceedings (even the Southern hotheads had seemingly received the Clay proposals calmly, if not enthusiastically), Nicholas had decided on his course of *covert intervention.*

"Ah, 'King Richard,'" he greeted the morose bartender, who was just beginning his daily shift. "It's a shame we couldn't practice because of the rain yesterday. Were you able to fire off a few rounds in my absence today?"

Lawrence nodded his head, a bleak smile breaking out at the sight of the one person to befriend him in this city of strangers. "Yes, Andre, I went across Rock Creek and practiced with all the weapons: pistol, derringer and musket. Just as you have taught me."

"And you were not disturbed?" Ignatieff's only concern when suggesting the previous evening that Richard practice today was that he would be observed and reported to the authorities (whoever they might be in this disorganized hamlet!).

Lawrence was shaking his peculiar long, lean, angular face: "There was no one in the woods. And, I took care to keep the weapons out-of-sight in their canvas bag."

The sound of footsteps clearly identified the approach of the proprietress. "Andre, darling, back from the Capitol, so soon? I didn't expect you for another hour or more." She lowered her eyes in that false modest look that had bedazzled so many customers (and clients): "Perhaps we have time for ourselves, after all…"

Ignatieff shook his head. "Later, my sweet. Just now, I believe we should have a conference…just the three of us." He looked at the bartender. "Why not pour us all a drink, Richard, yourself included."

Joanne's eyes narrowed at this break in strict Eagle procedure, but Andre's glance---as always---melted her annoyance. "Yes, Richard, why not join us in a drink." She turned to Ignatieff. "But what, darling, is the occasion?"

Ignatieff waited till the round---beer for himself; Madeira for the others---had been set on the bar. "Simply to announce, my darling, I have become convinced that Richard has been correct in his complaint." He stared up and into the bartender's dull grey eyes.

"After much study, it is obvious to me that this Andy Jackson *is* the culprit: he is the impediment to Richard rising to his rightful place as King of England." He raised his glass in salute before quickly downing half the mug. At his direct glance, a baffled Joanne---who was too astonished to laugh---likewise raised her glass, though she simply sipped her wine.

Lawrence was staring back at the Russian, immediate shock turning to glee: his claims were not so far-fetched, it seemed! Andre, his friend, now accepted them. He raised his own glass and finished off the Madeira in one long gulp, wiping his mouth with the back of his hand as he finished.

Ignatieff indicated for another round, smiling archly at the still-stunned but now-frowning Joanne. After Lawrence put the Madeira bottle, now almost empty, back behind the bar, he finally spoke:

"The question now, Your Majesty, is how we remove this impediment to allow you to assume your rightful place?"

———————

The Residency
June 11, 1833, 6 p.m.:

The depleted Kitchen Cabinet was at this hour deep in session with Jackson to polish his speech.

Van Buren's absence was no longer noted by Blair and Cass: Matty Van's singular situation eliminated him as an advisor; at least until this crisis passed, if not forever...

Cass had remarked, as the meeting was starting, on Polk's non-appearance; Jackson had looked grim. Later, when the G-G hobbled out to briefly meet with Donelson and Wilder concerning the ceremonial aspects of tomorrow's trip up Pennsylvania Avenue, Blair filled him in:

"Andy is suspicious of James' true loyalties in this. He's become concerned Congressman Polk has become a mole of sorts, relaying what goes on here to the fire-eaters."

Cass was startled: "Does he have evidence, or is this just one of Andy's 'gut feelings?'"

"Well, that outburst the other night when I brought up beating Clay to the punch with a compromise sort of confirmed some earlier suspicions in Andy's mind. Seems he's also gotten word from Tennessee that Calhoun was at Polk's plantation last month..."

Blair looked hard at the Secretary of War: "Think back to Wellington's little bombshell the other evening, Lewis. Took you by surprise, didn't it? Shocked the hell out of me...and the G-G. But James never blinked an eye. Like it was old news or something..."

———————

The Golden Eagle Tavern
June 11, 1833, 11 p.m.:

Joanne Casgrave was furious.

After the tavern closed last night at 2 a.m. (the brothel business, as per a Monday, had died off around 11 p.m.), Andre had plied the idiot bartender with still more drinks, while continuing this ridiculous "King Richard" talk. Joanne didn't know whether to be more professionally or personally offended: A drunken Lawrence might fly off the handle in any direction; while she, herself, required Andre's consummate attentions...

When Andre had finally put the drunken Richard to bed on his basement cot and entered her 'boudoir,' he had been curt---and, she reflected ruefully, unnecessarily rough---before falling quickly asleep.

This morning, she had awoken to find Andre already gone; only when she descended for breakfast did she discover that Lawrence was also out of the building. The bartender had returned in early afternoon, carrying that ominous sack which she knew contained weapons; Andre had not appeared unto early evening.

She intended to have it out with her lover tonight: exactly what was going on? She saw no reason to get Lawrence all excited; the key to keeping him under control was to dampen his spirits. And, if truth be told---though Joanne was constitutionally incapable of telling the truth, even to herself---she was becoming alarmed at Andre's increasing aloofness. She longed for the early days of their relationship, before he had traveled...wherever. The Russian simply fulfilled her as no other man---Casgrave, Bratton, even young Harper or any of dozens of others---ever had. And she was sure he loved her...hadn't he admitted as much on his return? So why was he ignoring her...and spending so much time with this village idiot?

The Residency
June 11, 1833, 12:00 midnight:

The speech was now in the hands of Donelson, who would have to stay up much of the night recopying and rearranging the various fragments into a coherent, flowing address.

Stunningly, they had been joined in early evening by Aaron Burr.

That the Colonel had dined alone with Jackson two nights previously had been known to Blair. But he had not expected Burr to help put together the most important speech of Jackson's

446

career...yea, arguably the most important in the history of the Dominion.

Apparently, the two ancient adventurers had Sunday night concocted the unorthodox arguments Jackson would lay before Congress and the people tomorrow:

*Under the Compact and the Constitution, Parliament does have the right to mandate emancipation; however

*The Administration and Congress, as the elected representatives of the British American people, also have the right to reject financial incentives---and a fixed timeframe---in overseeing such emancipation; so long as

*A workable, functioning emancipation policy agreeable to the people of the USBA is passed into Dominion law and is implemented in a reasonable timeframe.

"In other words," Cass had said after digesting the gist of the G-G's plan, "you in London have the right to order us to abolish slavery; but don't force your ideas on how to do it down our throats..."

The G-G laughed openly: "Well said Mr. Secretary. That about hits the nail on the head."

Cass was looking doubtful. "Putting aside for the moment, General, the compensation issue, it seems to me London---Parliament or whomever---is focused on the seven-year transition period, beginning next January 1st. How can you be certain they'll accept any delay, especially as they'll naturally tend to believe we are simply obstuficating?"

Frank, meanwhile, was shaking his head in wry amusement: "Would you two first care to let us in on how you arrived at this position?"

Burr was also smiling, though a harder look was evident in his eyes. "As we discussed this over a particularly fine roast two nights ago, it suddenly became obvious that London's plan is financially---not sociologically---based. We then proceeded down the logical path from there."

The War Secretary looked confused: "I beg your pardon?"

Burr shot him a patronizing look. *Scott is right: A politician...not a political scientist. Can't imagine what Andy sees in him...*

"Mr. Secretary, how do you think London arrived at the seven-year transition limitation? Or, more properly, which do you think was arrived at first, the compensation...or the transition period?"

There was a brief silence as Blair and Cass exchanged glances before Frank spoke for them both:

"Are you two implying that the transition period was determined by fiscal constraints? That London decided how much to pay...and then how much of the overall amount they could afford annually?"

Burr grinned impishly as Jackson banged his cane down on the desk.

"Frank, we're not *implying* anything. It's obvious to us---and should be to you---that London came up with a figure they could afford..."

Burr interrupted: "...were willing to cough up..."

"...at any rate, added up the cost of emancipation throughout the Empire and then determined how much they could afford..."

"...were willing..." The impish grin once more.

"...to pay annually and divided that into the overall total. That, gentlemen, is how our English masters arrived at a seven-year transition...and why it is not written in stone."

Cass returned to the compensation issue: "Compensation as called for in the Parliamentary bill is miserly enough, I admit. But it is something. What makes you think the South will go along with your call to reject it entirely?"

Jackson and Burr exchanged looks.

"Mr. Cass, I am not *rejecting* compensation. Only Parliament's conception and payment of compensation. The Congress will determine the compensation due the planters. And, working with the Administration and private interests, how best to raise and distribute it."

That perspective once agreed to, construction of the speech, though slow, was not particularly difficult.

Calhoun Residence
June 11-12, 1833, 1 a.m.:

Sleep would not come tonight.

As Calhoun gazed out his bedroom window, he attempted to weigh the options:

The 25-year exemption---only, of course, with a sunset provision, not a cap---was the safest route. He'd presumably be in his grave by renewal time, but he owed it to the others, and the children, to fight at least for that...

No one knows, apparently, exactly what that old man in The Residency will propose tomorrow. It might be worth considering; then again, perhaps not. Jackson is, after all, a planter, but he is also, unfortunately, deep down a Dominionist...

The other option is more exciting...if also more dangerous: independence from the Dominion! A whole new Southern Dominion (including Cuba, Texas and the Mexican Southwest). With ties to London, probably---but not automatically---but free from the inexorable advance of Yankee political power fueled by immigration. And with a commitment from London of domestic freedom in the new Southern confederacy...including the right to hold slaves, for as long as it remains fiscally prudent to do so.

A third option---total independence---is the most desirable, of course; the South free of *both* the damn Yankees *and* the damn British...free to chart its own course!

Well, he thought with a yawn, *tomorrow will not be just another day; it promises to be the biggest day. At least, the biggest this town has ever seen...*

The Golden Eagle Tavern
June 11-12, 1833,
2:30 a.m.:

"Even Joanne will be impressed, Richard. You do want that, don't you? Most of all, in fact, as you, above all, know how hard it is to impress her."

The standard dull, empty look in the bartender's eyes was gradually replaced by a sparkle of childish excitement and desire. *Did his friend Andre mean what he thought he meant?*

"Of course, when I'm King, I kin have any wench I want." Richard licked his lips greedily. "That's part of bein' King, ain't it? Still, Joanne..."

Count Ignatieff exhibited the monumental self-control necessary to continue in a seemingly serious vein: he literally bit his tongue to keep from laughing in the fool's face. Too much was now riding on this to act as if the premise was anything but obviously plausible:

"Once you arrive in England to be crowned, of course all Europe's women of noble birth will be throwing themselves at your feet. But until proper accommodations can be arranged aboard the fastest Royal Navy vessel available, you'll have time here to enjoy your new position. Joanne will have to fight the other women away..."

Richard grinned hungrily and reached for the wine bottle sitting between them. But the Count was quicker (and more sober). He grabbed the neck and poured them each a short one.

"Enough for tonight, my friend. You have much to accomplish in the day. Tomorrow night the world's supply of vodka; of rum; yes, even of gin..." He paused as another fire lit the benighted bartender's eyes. "...will be yours for the taking. Best now get some sleep, however. I'll be down to wake you at the proper time...."

Ignatieff had risen as he was finishing speaking. He now got the cadaverous drunk to his feet and pointed him toward the cellar. "Pleasant dreams, Your Majesty..."

Lawrence grunted and staggered to the door. As he turned back, Ignatieff was pointing sternly. "Tomorrow, Richard. The start of your reign!"

As the door closed behind him, Ignatieff became aware of the familiar scent. He pivoted to see his lover step out of the darkness of the back dining room.

"All right, Andre. I think its time you told me what's going on here." Though she attempted the stone-cold look and hiss that, for whatever reason terrified her employees, Joanne's demand actually came out as more of a desperate plea.

Nicholas/Andre stared back at her for an instant before smiling graciously and extending his hand. "Yes, my darling, I believe it is time we discussed 'what is going on here.' He led her back to the bar and poured them both drinks from fresh glasses. Downing fully half his drink, he lowered it onto the bar and, in the same motion, pulled her into a tight embrace, kissing her passionately. As always, she melted into his arms, her show of anger unmasked as the fraud it was.

"I assume you heard enough to know Lawrence thinks he will soon have the power to make you a queen, my sweet. That, of course, is as insane as he himself obviously is. I however, have the power to make you a countess..."

Her eyes widened from their glow of animal contentment as the words registered slowly in her brain. "Andre...."

He cut her off with another, almost savage kiss. "I understand you have had reason to question my authenticity, my darling. And you are right: 'Andre Karlhamanov' is an alias I assumed upon arrival in New York last winter. My real name is Count Nicholas Ignatieff, of His Imperial Majesty, Nicholas, Czar of All the Russias, personal staff. I am here at the direction of Czar Nicholas himself..."

He paused and looked into her loving eyes. *This will be even easier than I anticipated*, he thought. *She has no conception of the consequences of what I have just told her...*

"With your assistance, my beloved Joanne, tomorrow I intend to use that fool Lawrence to advance the banner of my country by igniting a full-blown crisis here in America."

They shared another long kiss before he picked her up and carried her to the stairs. "Andre---Nicholas---I want no one but you, no matter who you really are. I'll...I'll do anything you ask..."

He smiled down at her. "And you will *have* no one, my darling, once you do as I ask: help me dispatch 'King Richard' to his destiny tomorrow." They laughed into each other's shoulders as they climbed towards her bedroom.

CHAPTER FORTY

Georgetown, D.C.
June 12, 1833, 9:30 a.m.:

Missing today was the festive atmosphere that normally marked the day of a major speech. In part, it reflected the unbearably hot and humid weather that signaled the imminent arrival of another electrical storm. But the mood was somber as the crowds piled into the streets, hotels and taverns. Grim-faced politicians and military figures making their way to Capitol Hill brushed shoulders with bemused members of the diplomatic corps. Captain Goodwin led the official Marine Guard honor detachment down Pennsylvania Avenue to The Residency. All were collectively gasping, for the air, even at this relatively early hour, seemed squeezed and wrung of all freshness...

The Residency
10:00 a.m.:

For the Governor-General, a decision once arrived at, a policy once determined, a position once adopted, were singular and irrevocable. His demeanor today betrayed his single-minded determination to set the plan he and Colonel Burr had devised---without *compromise*---in motion for the good of the Dominion. Sectional interests be damned, by the Eternal!

Jackson came down the stairs with a vigor and determination that Lieutenant Wilder, standing in the doorway of his cubbyhole office, had seldom witnessed. Andy Donelson was waiting at the bottom of the stairs with a cream-colored folder; the Private Secretary had completed the final, clean copy only 45 minutes ago. Now he handed it over as the G-G, followed by Blair and Cass, passed him. Outside, Arthur Goodwin could be heard calling his Marines to attention.

452

Jackson went out onto the Portico without a glance at the staff and servants lining the vestibule walls. He grunted as the ugly weather hit him a body blow on exiting the building, but he continued down the Portico steps and toward his official carriage. Jackson eyeballed the Marines professionally and nodded curtly at their commander before being assisted into the vehicle. The two advisors climbed in after him. At Goodwin's direction, the procession was immediately off down the driveway. It was 10:07 a.m.

———————

The Golden Eagle Tavern
10:15 a.m.:

Her lover had never performed better, she thought drowsily. Their couplings had been frenzied and seemingly continuous. After all this time, after all her experience with countless men, she had thought nothing could any longer shock her. But Andre's vitality was amazing...more than six hours...with remarkably few breaks!

She felt her eyes closing again now. Andre had gone downstairs to wake Lawrence; he had promised to return immediately upon dispatching the fool on his 'errand.' And she wanted---needed---her strength for his return.

She had heard their voices some time ago in the alley below her window. Surely he'll return momentarily... She rolled contentedly over onto her side and slid into a deep sleep.

Now boots sounded lightly in the hallway. The door creaked open. Count Nicholas Ignatieff stared with contempt.

You aging slut! You are definitely not at your best in the morning, even on this appropriately dark one! God, how have I been able to get it up for you these past few months? I deserve a principality at the very least for this, Nicky, my Czar and friend!

He quietly closed and locked the door before walking toward the bed.

———————

The Capitol Building
10:30 a.m.:

The Vice Governor-General, in his role as President of the Senate, waited on the Capitol steps with the Speaker, Mr. Stevenson of Virginia, and the honorary 'welcoming' Tennessee delegation.

Van Buren was glancing with amusement at Rep. David Crockett. The legendary frontiersman's presence would certainly not be welcoming to the G-G; they loathed each other. The Vice G-G was also looking forward to the reaction of Jackson to Congressman Polk; Colonel Burr had related the G-G's suspicions that his protégé was secretly a fire-eater…

The Vice G-G and the others could see Jackson's carriage and honor guard making its way through the ominously quiet crowds on Pennsylvania Avenue. People had been pouring into the city for days as word spread that Jackson would finally speak directly about the crisis. Now the Marines gently but firmly moved the citizenry out of the way so that the G-G's carriage could complete its journey. Van Buren looked skyward: the dark sky seemed ready to explode with lightening, to say nothing of thunder. The air itself was crackling with electricity.

Inside the building, the usual array of privileged---diplomats, military, Congressional wives and local planter aristocracy---were already crowded into the galleries. Lucille Latoure, by now expert at obtaining entrance, had today produced tickets for herself and mother issued originally to the Vice G-G and presented to her by that dear old gentleman, Colonel Burr.

("Now there's a woman worth fighting a revolution for," Burr had told General Scott. He had shaken his head admiringly but sadly: "And to think she has only these barbaric young Georgetown bucks to choose from. If only I was 20 years…" Scott had cut him off: "Colonel, if you were 20 years younger, you'd be a prime candidate for her mother's hand." Burr had given a good impression of bristling as he drew himself up to his full 5-foot-5: "And who, my dear General, can say that I am not still…" Scott simply shook his head. *Incorrigible…but, apparently…useful.*)

As the Senate had once again come over to the House chamber for the joint address, Calhoun, Troup and the other Southern Senators had settled in with their home states' House delegations. The buzzing in the House well was approaching a roar as the scheduled 11 a.m. starting time drew near.

Speaker Stevenson had ordered the House clerks to examine the entrance badges at the various doors to the Chamber. While it was a more efficient system for inspection---fewer doors meant fewer uninvited guests---the decision had left the Capitol's outer doors unpoliced.

Captain Bratton had noticed that when he had arrived with Sir John Burrell. "Any riffraff in the city can walk right up to the chamber itself," he had observed. Burrell's response was typically patronizing: "No worse, perhaps better, than the riffraff within, my dear Captain. Have you ever gotten within feet of this man Crockett?" Bratton had grinned. "Well Sir John, perhaps we can serve His Grace best if we separate for the moment. You handle the riffraff within; I'll stay out here till Jackson arrives. Save me a place…"

Richard Lawrence, in a newly-purchased set of second hand clothes (funded, though he did not realize it, by Czarist gold), would have been entirely unrecognizable in what was, admittedly, if not a mob then a rowdy crowd, except for his peculiar tall, gaunt frame. Still, he had left early enough to have secured a spot in the Rotunda next to a column near the main entrance to the House chamber. "Just lean back against the column and wait," Andre had told him on their repeated visits to the building. "When the time arrives, step forward." As he looked around, he could see that, as usual, no one was paying him any attention…

Capitol Building Driveway
10:35 a.m.:

The Marine out-riders, still horsed, were at attention before the Gubernatorial carriage rolled to a stop. The other Marines were quickly down and forming a ceremonial corridor leading up to the official hosts. Captain Goodwin and his final two honor guards walked Jackson, who refused help descending from the carriage, to the Vice G-G and the Congressional leadership.

Van Buren put out his hand. The G-G's still-hard grip brought the slightest color to Matty Van's face. "Welcome, Mr. Governor-General. All is in readiness for your address." The two men exchanged quick glances of solidarity: Colonel Burr had obviously briefed the Vice G-G on what was planned. It was a different story with the next dignitary in line: though Speaker Stevenson was an old friend and ally, his support could not be assumed on this issue. The Virginian's handshake was firm but his eyes were troubled. Neither man was sure their alliance could survive...

The Vice G-G was observing this encounter with interest when he felt a strong grip on his arm. A grinning Blair was indicating ahead to the waiting Tennessee delegation. No words were necessary as they watched Jackson approach the world-famous frontiersman.

"Congressman Crockett." The G-G was cordially formal. "And how are things back in our beloved Tennessee?"

"Fair to middl'in, Gin'ral. Betcha wished they'd a sent a Frenchie this time, rather than me agin, huh?" Crockett grinned before rattling a nearby spittoon with a remarkably accurate stream of tobacco juice.

The major blood vein snaking down Jackson's forehead was suddenly quite visible. That, however, was his only response. Instead, he moved on to the next Congressman in line: "Mr. Polk. I trust you'll provide me with your reaction and counsel at the conclusion of my address? Perhaps this afternoon or evening?"

"My pleasure, Mr. Governor. As my input in preparing the address was so minimal, perhaps my analysis will thus be that much more appreciated."

Jackson's eyes narrowed and flickered dangerously, but he simply nodded and moved on. Van Buren and Blair looked quickly at each other. Both had noted the sudden paleness undercutting the deep tan of Polk's face.

The Golden Eagle Tavern
11:00 a.m.:

Nicholas wiped the razor clean. The bowl in front of him was filled with clomps of his rich black hair. He toweled his now shining skull and took the bowl to the dressing room window, where he emptied it carefully and fully. With any luck, the coming storm would scatter the shavings in its fury...

He debated whether to take the eye patch with him for disposal elsewhere; in the end he decided to leave it hanging from the bed-frame. The implicit taunt amused him: yes, you colonials---and you too, Captain Bratton---Andre Karlhamanov was certainly here. But where has he gone? Or, more precisely, where has Nicholas Ignatieff gone?

The Count returned to the bedroom. At first, perfunctory glance, Joanne Casgrave seemed soundly asleep: her face buried in the pillows. Only the angle of her slender neck seemed slightly ajar. That, of course, would lead to a closer inspection, involving turning her over in any futile attempt to wake her.

Perhaps the purple coloring on the face and forehead will have receded by early afternoon. Though the bulging eyes will most definitely remain at their sockets' edge... The marks on her throat where her lower larynx has caved in will naturally reveal the cause of the collapse. Other distasteful signs of her demise will have dried but still be visible on the beddings...

Nicholas pulled on his coat and adjusted the two guns enclosed in his vest. He reached for the black hat he had had her purchase for him last week. It now came lower on his head, concealing from a distance the identifying colorings of his right eye.

He strode to the door and glanced back for one last look. *You stupid colonial bitch! I'll admit, you helped pass the time...and served my purposes well. But Nicholas Ignatieff---Count Nicholas Ignatieff---Любви вам? Я даже не как вы. (Love you? I never even liked you...)*

The Golden Eagle Tavern
11:15 a.m.:

The stranger in the wide-brimmed black planter's hat descending the Golden Eagle's back stairs looked---to the earliest rising of the Eagle's newly-recruited (at 'Andre's' direction) 'girls'---to be simply another overnight client. No one: *miserable, pampered cooks included,* he thought with disdain, was yet functioning. He crossed from the bar through the kitchen and exited a back door. The horse 'King Richard' had obligingly had saddled and readied for him was tied to a nearby post. He mounted and headed for the Long Bridge.

The news from the other end of Pennsylvania Avenue was yet to filter down Capitol Hill. No one thought to stop or question him as he rode off the Bridge minutes later and pointed his horse toward Richmond.

The Capitol Building
11:02 a.m.:

The Gubernatorial-General party paused at the top of the steps. Somehow, Jackson---probably at the sight of Crockett and/or Polk---had left his speech on the carriage seat!

Captain Goodwin hurried down to the driveway and returned with the cream-colored folder as the G-G and his aides enjoyed a rueful laugh. The party proceeded into the Capitol, the Marine guard opening the path through the crowded Rotunda: Jackson now tightly clutching the folder, Van Buren and Stevenson following him, the Kitchen Cabinet and the Tennessee delegation bringing up the rear.

No one was paying much attention to the tall, cadaverous fellow in the clean but threadworm suit, other than to envy him the height that allowed a commanding view of the area. Apparently, no one standing nearby could hear his heart beating and the blood pounding against his temples. As the G-G's party pushed through, Jackson stopping frequently to shake an outstretched hand, the gaunt observer drew his hands inside his waistcoat.

The Marine trio, Goodwin in the lead, was suddenly past. The G-G himself was now within five feet of the man standing at the base of the column, stopping again to shake yet another hand while balancing himself on his ever-present cane.

The rumbling that had filled the soon-to-be-King's ears like so many horses charging trackside suddenly cleared.

Richard Lawrence could hear his friend Andre's command: *"Fire now!"*

He stepped through the crowd and, pointing the two new Patterson pistols slightly down, pulled both triggers...

Astonishingly---since they had been well tested and cared for---one of the pistols misfired; more precisely, failed to ignite at all. The other, however, worked perfectly: a ball exploded into the G-G's chest under the left side of the breastbone. The force, combined with the three-foot proximity, sent the ball crashing out Jackson's lower back. Incredibly, the velocity was such that it lodged in the right knee of Secretary Cass, who stumbled forward into the G-G, who was now collapsing backward.

No one present would ever forget the sudden complete silence. Nor the bedlam that then followed.

Goodwin and the Marines had turned at the sound of the gunfire. The Captain was the first to react, pushing past the two enlisted men and jumping at the tall man who still held both pistols as he studied with seemingly detached curiosity the havoc he had just rendered. Later, men would remember Goodwin attempting to draw his sword as he pushed toward Lawrence. The assassin, seeing him coming, reached back before slamming the barrel of the pistol in his left hand into the Marine's head. Snarling incoherently with rage, Goodwin seemed oblivious to the blow but then the force of the companion pistol's barrel on his forehead pole-axed him. He collapsed in a heap at Lawrence's feet.

The bartender had reacted instinctively; now his addled brain was confused: *Why are they charging me? They should be cheering! Andre said they would...*

Now Lawrence could feel other arms grabbing him from the sides. And, suddenly, an enormous black-winged creature came flying over the Marines' shoulders and landed on him. The force of the collision sent everyone crashing to the floor, though Richard's head cracked back against the column, opening a gaping hole on the back of his skull and sending blood and brain matter flying. So he never saw the huge fist that splintered his face from nose to chin.

It may have been that either of those two successive head blows would have done him in. Various neck bones were broken and certainly, the chunks of teeth and gum---to say nothing of the blood---that exploded back into his throat might have choked him, taken in conjunction with the fact that the openings to his nasal passages had been destroyed. Twentieth century forensic examination would have revealed that the blow to the face had driven the bones constituting the bridge of the nose into the brain, however.

Certainly, despite the blood, it was not the ugly gash near his third rib where Goodwin's sword had embedded itself. (No one later was quite sure who administered that blow...or how.) Nor was it the ball from his own previously malfunctioning weapon, which perversely chose to send a round into his left hip during the floor scrimmaging.

When order was finally restored---General Scott had personally flung spectators aside to reach first the G-G/Cass heap and, after a grunt, the assassin's entanglement---it was apparent that the carnage had been fatal to both major players.

Jackson was most probably dead before he even toppled backward into his Secretary of War; the ball passed directly through the heart at a 90-degree angle before exiting the lower back with the spent force that would deposit it in Cass' leg.

The cataclysmic explosions to Lawrence's head and face---evident when Davy Crockett and the two Marines were pulled off and the one bystander, a local Maryland planter who had held firmly to the assassin's left arm, was freed from under him---left no doubt that he, too, had departed the planet.

In the finest tradition of the Imperial Russian secret services, a textbook operation of flawless planning and execution; and of chaotic result.

The Capitol Building
12:00 noon:

The United States Capitol Police, formed just five years earlier, were nominally in charge of 'security' on the grounds. As on every other major occasion since 1828, 'security' in this case had been defined as 'crowd control.' With just 18 members and a chief, that function itself had exhausted the force in the 10 days since the special session had convened; still, all but the four who had served the overnight shift were on hand.

They were hardly augmented by the District's token force: Georgetown employed a force of 24 'watchmen' headed by their own chief, to keep order. That had been defined, for the most part, as keeping an eye on the taverns, back allys and places of lesser repute. Just six were arrayed around the city this day.

The remaining members of the Marine ceremonial detachment--- the ones originally posted outside with the carriage---actually kept things under control, once Scott had ordered them up the steps. The General had also dispatched a bystander back to the War Department. Lieutenant Wilder and most of the staff were now also on the grounds.

Not that there was any rioting; everyone---from the Congress through the citizenry at large---was in a state of shock. Mostly, the uniformed men slowly and sadly moved the crowds out of the Building and off the Hill. The Congress adjourned to its cloakrooms; the diplomatic corps to the French Consulate and the guests to various townhouses and hotel lobbies. The threatened thunderstorm materialized, aiding in forcing everyone else in off Pennsylvania Avenue.

While doctors were summoned to assist the wounded---Captain Goodwin had suffered a concussion and Cass' knee required attention, while the others had minor bruises---the G-G's body had been temporarily removed to Van Buren's office. Two of the Marines stood guard over the covered remains of the assassin, who still lay beneath the Rotunda column.

If not peace and tranquility, at least a sorrowful silence descended on dark Georgetown, only to be shattered by the increasingly powerful thunder that shook down from the sky, punctuated by violent bolts of lightening.

By early afternoon, however, the tragedy's impact began to ripple across the city like a series of waves. If the tsunami concept had then been understood, perhaps Georgetown would have been better prepared for what was to come...

CHAPTER FORTY-ONE

Capitol Building Rotunda
Capitol Hill
12:30 p.m.:

Captain Bratton had positioned himself near the main entrance to the House Chamber and so had heard, not seen, the assassination.

Harry immediately recognized that his role must be strictly that of an observer; this was an American crisis, for better or worse. So he had thought until he managed a look at the assassin's dead body. Despite the massacre to the face, he recognized the prone figure as The Golden Eagle's bartender. Instantly he realized the implication: *My God, what will the Duke say? Now we know why Ignatieff is here!*

Sir John was suddenly at his elbow. "I say old chap. This is shaping up badly! Without Jackson, all hell could burst loose!"

Burrell glanced quickly at the assassin's crushed face with distaste. "Didn't get far, did he? Can't think he expected to escape..." He was now looking at Bratton with a dawning sense of astonished horror. "Good God, man, you...know this chap...don't you? To identify, at least..."

Harry took his colleague by the arm and walked to a deserted spot. "Without going into the details, Sir John, this has Ignatieff's signature all over it. No, no, don't ask me how. Just be assured it does. You've got to get back to the Liaison Office and brief the Duke. I'll be along shortly, once I pass on a few details to General Scott."

Burrell's eyes were still wide: "What will you tell him...them...the American authorities?"

Bratton smiled though his eyes were grim. "Simply that this man has served me at a local tavern and that they perhaps should send someone over there... Not that they'll find what *we're* looking for, however..."

Sir John was now thoroughly confused. "And what does that mean...?"

462

"Simply, Sir John, that the instigator of this hellacious crime, I imagine, is no longer within the Georgetown city limits…"

Senate President's Office
Capitol Building
12:50 p.m.:

The hushed crowd---Harry recognized several Senators and Congressmen---was out the office door and spilled into the hallway. He could see General Scott's head towering above the tightly-packed bodies in the office, though little else.

"Marshall's administering the Oath of Office," Senator Webster whispered upon recognizing the Brit at his side. "With Jackson's body cooling on the couch next to him, if you can believe it…"

Bratton was appalled: "So soon? Some decorum…"

"No, its right in our Constitution. Already been researched. Immediate transfer of power. So there's no question and no confusion." Webster looked quizzically at the Liaison Officer. "What's the Duke's reaction? Beyond damning us for being so barbaric?"

Bratton smiled shortly: "Doesn't know yet. Burrell is on his way back to inform him…I have information that someone in authority really must hear. Can we get in?"

After a few minutes of shoving and elbowing, the duo found themselves at the room's crowded center. The new G-G, a somewhat glazed look in his eyes, was gravely shaking hands with a seemingly endless line of self-important Congressmen and Senators. Frank Blair stood guard over the covered remains of the assassinated former G-G, his anguish plainly visible. In a corner, Scott now towered over Aaron Burr, whose habitually impish grin had been replaced by a face of sorrow.

Senator Webster quickly got the General's attention: "Captain Bratton here says he has information for the authorities, General. As I assume martial law will be declared---if it hasn't already---that looks to be you."

Bratton was brief: "The assassin, despite the head and face wounds, is identifiable as the bartender at The Golden Eagle Tavern, an establishment some blocks from The Residency. At least, he was the bartender some months back."

Scott directed his drill stare: "I'm familiar with the place. At least its location. You're sure? Any idea of his name? There were no papers found on the body."

"As I recall, he was referred to intermittently as 'Richard' or 'Lawrence.' No clue as to which was his surname…or even if they were truly his." Bratton paused. "Forgive me, General, but might it not be wise to send some men over there?"

"A good suggestion, Captain." He looked around and found the eye of one of the Marines now closely guarding the new G-G. "Lieutenant Wilder's somewhere on the grounds. Find him and get him in here. While you're at it, do you know Lieutenant Beaufort? Good, get him in here, too."

His gaze returned to Bratton, who had been exchanging sympathy looks with Blair. "Would this have anything to do with your Russki agent, Captain? Do I correctly recall from your briefing that he, err, frequented the place himself?"

Bratton returned the steely look: "Possibly, General. We'll know more after we get to The Eagle, I daresay…"

"'We,' Captain?"

"Yes Sir. I respectfully request permission to accompany Lieutenant Wilder. Or whomever you're sending over there."

Scott nodded: "Permission granted. And it will be Wilder. Along with a couple Marines. I believe it will be prudent to place The Golden Eagle off-limits, at least until we get to the bottom of this. If word gets out their bartender did it, a crowd might be inclined to torch the place anyway, so…

"By the way, Captain, the new G-G will be leaving for The Residency fairly soon. Can't run the government from this broom closet. The Duke should be made aware."

Bratton nodded. "Sir John should be at the Liaison Office now. I suspect His Grace will be waiting when the new G-G returns to The Residency." He glanced at Jackson's body, which workmen were now lifting into a casket. "And for the return of his old comrade from the Peninsula days…"

The Golden Eagle Tavern

1:30 p.m.:

Tom, Harry and the two Marines who had piled onto the assassin tied up their horses outside The Eagle. Now that the storm had abated, the crowds had again surged into the streets, making their progress slow enough for Tom to review the rapidly-occurring events:

Luke Beaufort had been placed in temporary command of the War Department staff Tom had led up to the Capitol. Grudgingly, General Gaines had been assigned overall command of the cherry-picked "security forces" Scott could cobble together; the commanding general really had no other option. A rider had been dispatched to Carlisle Barracks some time after the shooting; Col. Edwin Sumner would have his Heavy Dragoons in the Capital by late tomorrow. "I don't expect trouble," Scott had growled to the new G-G and Interior Secretary MacLane, "but the forces we'll have out all this night will need a break by then. Bull's people also look the part: no rioters or insurrectionists will want any part of them."

The remaining Marine guard, sans their beat-up commander, would momentarily escort, under Scott's personal direction, the new G-G down Pennsylvania Avenue. The official carriage would follow the hearse carrying Jackson's remains. A grief-stricken Donelson had already been sent down to make The Residency arrangements.

All were orderly and logical developments, if anything could be considered 'orderly and logical' at such a time, Tom thought. What baffled him was Frank Blair's reaction to the discovery that Jackson's speech was missing. Surely Andy Donelson had another copy? But Blair, the new G-G and the rest had been horrified. Even old Colonel Burr's eyes had narrowed as he exchanged a seemingly-significant look with the General. *Damn it, what am I missing?*

Once inside The Eagle, the subject quickly slipped his mind.

The Residency
5:15 p.m.:

They sent General Scott the word after discovering the body in the second floor back bedroom of The Eagle, but it had taken almost three hours to handle the situation.

It had quickly become clear that an entirely new staff had replaced the familiar faces on the tavern floor; neither Tom nor Bratton could have recognized any of the 'upstairs' girls in any case. While plainly shocked, no one had anything helpful. Andre and Lawrence had been drinking in the bar at the close of business, as usual. Joanne had retired to her room in an obvious bad mood. But none of the 'girls' had seen nor heard anything unusual, either during the night nor in the morning, other than the stranger in the big black hat who had hurried away towards the kitchen...

The kitchen and wait staffs were sent home and the 'upstairs girls' allowed to return to their rooms. The Marines were instructed to guard the place until some Georgetown watchmen could be detailed.

The Eagle was closed, indefinitely...

Now they were waiting to report to the General, who was coming out of a conference in the G-G's office. It was a shock to Tom, in many ways confirmation of the passing of the guard, when he caught a glimpse of little Matty Van seated behind Jackson's desk. Despite the bodies on the Rotunda floor and in the Eagle bedroom, the whole thing had seemed something of a dream.

But the stone-cold blue-eyed stare of Winfield Scott was certainly real enough: "Well gentlemen, apparently the carnage wasn't limited to the Capitol. So this Casgrave woman was murdered too, eh?"

Tom delivered his report at attention: "Yes, General. Apparently, sometime after dawn, according to the coroner. No forced entry...the door was locked from the outside. And no sign of a struggle. The coroner thinks she may have been asleep."

Bratton cleared his throat loudly. "Excuse me for interrupting, General, but in answer to your earlier question at the Capitol, no one saw our 'friend' leave this morning, though one of the, um, 'ladies,'..."

"Whores, you mean, don't you, Captain?"

"Ah, yes, General. One of the early-rising, um, 'whores' did see a man wearing an oversized black planter's hat and of the approximate size descending to the first floor around 11 a.m."

Tom was confused: "However, the assassin---the name, at least at The Eagle, was 'Richard Lawrence'---was already at the Capitol by then..."

His commander and the British agent shared a look. "So he was, Lieutenant. While Lawrence may in fact be the real name of the assassin, it is clearly not the name of the dead woman's murderer." He paused. "Is it, Captain Bratton?"

"Sir, unfortunately, I believe the murderer is one Count Nicholas Ignatieff, a high officer in the Czar's secret intelligence service. He is undoubtedly also the instigator of the plot that resulted in the death of your Governor-General."

The Lieutenant looked from Bratton to Scott and back in open-mouthed amazement.

Scott was blunt: "Sent this fool Lawrence to kill Jackson and then disposed of the only one who might be able to tie him and Russia to the crime, eh? Where do you suppose he's headed?"

Bratton had not expected to go into this much detail with Scott before briefing the Duke. Wellington, however, had joined the group. Apparently he had read Lieutenant Wilder's note, which confirmed much of what Bratton had relayed via Sir John. The Duke indicated for Harry to continue.

"Well, if he believes he's caused the maximum havoc he can, then he'd head for a port. Not necessarily directly to Europe; he's too smart for that. Cuba, perhaps, or a Dutch or French island in the Caribbean. That way he could monitor the situation and slip back in, if needed. Mexico, even."

Scott nodded: "I've already sent word to Fort McHenry and Fortress Monroe." He paused. "Would he try to elude us by going overland first...Philadelphia or Charleston, say... Embark from there?"

Bratton was dubious: "Well, Sirs. He did come in through New York." He grimaced. "That's how I met him, actually, damn it all! But I don't think he'd head north. Too far and too much chance of detection, even if he has altered his appearance again. My guess is a local port. Or he'll simply lose himself somewhere in the South."

The Lieutenant was having a hard time following these exchanges, but knew enough to keep quiet. Obviously, the General had a better grip on the situation. As he demonstrated momentarily:

Looking at Wellington, who had remained silent throughout, he asked Bratton bluntly: "Do you people think he's caused *maximum havoc...*?"

Harry frowned and looked at his own chief. Wellington's nod was barely perceptible.

467

"That would depend, General, wouldn't it? On your people's reaction: both to Mr. Jackson's demise; and the speech he was stopped from giving…"

Wellington and Scott exchanged significant looks.

The General sighed: "All right, gentlemen, good work. Lieutenant, you need to get with Andy Donelson about the funeral arrangements. Looks like poor Jackson's going to be laid out in the Rotunda before he's shipped back to Tennessee. See to it." Tom saluted and walked toward the secretary's office. He could hear Scott ask Captain Bratton one last question:

"You're absolutely sure this Russki is behind this whole thing?"

Tom slowed his way to catch Bratton's answer: "General Scott, we have been consistently wrong, or rather, late, concerning Count Ignatieff since he arrived. However, in his arrogance, he left us his calling card, so to speak…"

As the Lieutenant turned, Captain Bratton was withdrawing a black eye patch from his coat pocket. "This was hanging from the bed post above Mrs. Casgrave's body…"

Calhoun Residence
8:45 p.m.:

James Polk had been at The Residency most of the late afternoon and early evening. After some time, however, it became clear that, while he may have been on suspension from Jackson's Kitchen Cabinet, he was not a member of any status in Van Buren's band of intimate advisors.

So he had finally acknowledged the obvious and ridden over here, where the Southern inner-circle had gathered after leaving the Capitol. *I might not have much news from The Residency, but the papers I retrieved from the Rotunda floor are powerful enough intelligence for one day's work…*

Polk had briefly scanned the contents of the cream-colored folder himself, then wordlessly handed them to Calhoun before heading to the other end of Pennsylvania Avenue. By now, he surmised, the entire Southern leadership would know that Jackson had been about to betray them in the name of Dominion unity.

He shook his head as he tied up his own horse; none of the servants were visible.

That damn old man knew the Syrian thing gives the South the leverage to extract a 25-year emancipation 'sunset' provision…and to grab Texas and the whole Southwest before Mexico City can react. Yet Jackson intended to squander that once-in-a-century opportunity in favor of a Dominion convention to settle the slavery issue once-and-for-all. Basically, he was for trading the South's constitutionally-guarenteed property rights for some vague domestic autonomy status in the Empire…

Polk stood on the porch and shook his head. Andrew had been a mentor to him, yes, and he felt his death greatly. A terrible shock, especially coming in the manner it did.

But for the good of the South, perhaps---no, definitely---it is better he is gone, if that speech is any indication…

Alabama's Clay had the floor, a stone mug of whisky in his hand. In fact, it appeared to Polk that virtually every member of the inner-circle had his own supply…though some supplies were more dented than others.

"…complete sellout of the South," Clay was sputtering. "Can't believe a planter could come up with such foul treason. I see Frank Blair's hand in this. That damn newspaper editor…"

Calhoun, his dark smile in place, was evidently allowing the boys to blow off steam. He sipped from a small glass and look expectantly at the newcomer. "Well, James, back from The Residency. So what is the mood over there on Pennsylvania Avenue?"

Polk looked around the room. "Shock, depression, confusion. What you would expect. Some barely-concealed glee, too, in my opinion, from some of those damn Yankees, Webster and the lot…"

North Carolina's Brown stood. "What news? When's the funeral? When will Van Buren address the Congress? Have they discovered this fiend's identity yet? Or his motive?"

Polk raised his hand. "Slow down, Bedford, all in good time." The others chuckled and someone handed Polk his own mug. He sipped shortly and began again:

"The funeral is foremost on their minds, along with securing the city's stability. Though, if this had been a coordinated insurrection of sorts, any hell would already have broken loose. Looks like this may have been a single madman, who, by the way, apparently butchered his landlady before going to the Hill..."

He cut off the instant buzz. "Later. More importantly, Van Buren doesn't seem to have focused on the crisis yet. I'd say emancipation's off the table for a few weeks." *No reason to confess just yet that I've been cut off from power over there,* he thought. *Who knows what tomorrow may bring...*

"Now, I'm anxious to hear this group's thinking regarding this damnable speech the Old Man was about to make..."

The Residency
11:45 p.m.:

The crowd had dwindled to the five of them now: the new G-G, Scott, Wellington, Blair and Colonel Burr.

Men and women had continued to come and go throughout the evening:

General Gaines reporting that, in part thanks to the arrival of elements of the 4th Artillery from their post outside the city, Georgetown was quiet; the 10 p.m. curfew was being observed. A delegation of New England Congressmen to urge the new G-G to announce his unequivocal support for emancipation as early as tomorrow. Ewing, Benton and some other Westerners to offer support and urge caution. Candice Samples, among other women, to console Emily Donelson. Finally, some 45 minutes ago, Donelson and Wilder with detailed plans for the funeral.

Now, formal attire loosened or shed---including a decoration-littered commanding general's tunic---the group was scattered around the room, sipping their own beverages of choice as they planned a course of action.

"Put off your speech until next week, three or four days after the funeral," Blair advised. "Let things calm down a bit before the people have to look emancipation in the eye again. A brief respite will do us all good..."

Burr poured himself a cup of tea; despite the mugginess of the night, he apparently felt his habitual chill. "I believe Frank's correct, Matty. Let the people concentrate on their grief; if nothing else, it unites them. There's plenty of time to return to this Parliamentary hot potato." He grinned: "Serve Congress right if you keep 'em here all summer…"

Blair again: "What worries me is the disappearance of that folder. Mark my words, Calhoun has already read it. And begun making his plans…"

Wellington cleared his throat. "Since this is late at night and off-the-record, Mr. Governor, I must say I share Mr. Blair's concern. That folder did not simply blow away in the storm. Someone snatched it; someone with impressive presence of mind, considering the circumstances."

The discussion continued nearly till dawn. Among other things, the new G-G was astonished to learn contingency plans had been drafted to field a Southern-less army…

Indian Queen Hotel Taproom
June 18, 1833, 7:00 p.m.:

In the blur of events since the previous Wednesday, Tom Wilder was sure he had spent at least a few minutes with his friend Dave Harper. He just couldn't remember when; or where.

Possibly it had been after the joint War-Interior Department briefing last Thursday when the Liaison Office spelled out its theory on the assassination. Or, more accurately, its theories considering the escape and/or hiding plans of this Russian agent, Ignatieff.

Or, it could have been during or after the Saturday funeral procession to the Capitol, where Andrew Jackson had been laid in state in the Rotunda, at the exact spot of the assassination. Estimates were that more than 50,000 had passed through in the next 24 hours, though General Scott had scoffed. "Use your head, Lieutenant. There aren't half that many people within 100 miles of Georgetown. Where did they all come from?"

Wilder hadn't really given it much thought: he had been too tied up with the ceremonial details. Scott himself had overseen the security preparations. Tom grinned to himself; maybe that 50,000 included all the troops. The General certainly packed Georgetown with the two services!

Some of those troops---including Bull Sumner's dragoons---had left town Sunday afternoon, escorting the G-G's body back to

Nashville. That had meant more planning, so it was doubtful he had seen Dave over the weekend.

He had, of course seen Candice---*if* seeing *is the correct word for it,* he thought, grinning---late on several evenings. Her grief at her old friend's demise was very real. *But, she hadn't allowed it to adversely affect her appetites.*

With all preparations, security and otherwise, completed for Van Buren's address to the Congress tomorrow---like everyone else, Tom was still having trouble thinking of Matty Van as 'the G-G'--- the Lieutenant had found he did have some free time tonight.

As Candice had decided to retreat to Twin Peaks on Monday, he had no other commitments; Lucille, he thought with a frown, had gone home to Cranford last weekend, though she was due back for the speech. He hadn't seen her since Mrs. Latoure invited him to a small dinner-party two nights after the assassination. With the Tylers, Joe Johnston and Mary Lee also in attendance, it hadn't been much fun…the others' grief over Jackson's death was more than tempered by their anger over emancipation.

Thus, with no duties or other commitments, he was free to meet Harps for a few beers. Fortunately, Dave had agreed to come over from The Deerhead, though both taprooms were now habitually extra-crowded, with The Golden Eagle still shuttered…

Harper was standing at the bar with a strange look on his face when the Lieutenant came down the stairs from his room, the mug of beer in front of him already half consumed.

"What's the matter, Harps? Not some late-blooming grief for the unfortunate Joanne?"

"Of course not, Lieutenant. Any mourning I conducted for her---and believe me, it was strictly of a carnal nature---was over months ago. Ghastly thing, but…funny you should bring her up, though…"

"Why's that? Nothing funny I can see about getting strangled, asleep or not…"

Harps downed the rest of his beer and whipped his mouth with the back of his hand. He looked around the bar suspiciously before lowering his head and voice:

"I've just come from the Liaison Office again, Tom. Bratton and his boys want me in touch with Caroline. Find out what she knows about Ignatieff."

Wilder stared at his friend. "They think she was in on the plot? That's ridiculous...."

"No, no, of course not. And, they don't think he's hiding out at the Consulate.

"They do think Count Renkowiitz---or someone over there---does know where he went. Or headed, at any rate."

"So you're to pry this international secret out of Caroline? Come on..."

Harper pulled himself into a comically erect posture. "I have been provided choice seats in the visitors' gallery. Two of them. I am picking up the Countess at 9:45 with an Interior Department carriage. After the speech, we will proceed to visit the various receptions. At some point, hopefully she'll let something slip. At least, that's the idea."

"Jaysus, Mary and Joseph..."

"Don't worry Thomas. If-and-when we see the 'redoubtable Miss Latoure,' I'm sure Caroline will be happy to pass along your greetings."

Calhoun's Residence
June 19, 1833, 8:00 p.m.:

The fire-eaters had departed the Capitol livid. Except for Calhoun. As far as the head fire-eater was concerned, things were moving along nicely.

That didn't mean he hadn't been shocked and shaken by the events of the previous Wednesday. Calhoun had detested Jackson and most everything he had stood for. Everything, damn it, now that the old man was on record as betraying his own planter class!

Though he certainly did not condone assassination as a political instrument, Jackson's forcible removal from the scene, however, was a positive step toward that goal he had set, though never publicly enunciated: separation of the Dominion into free- and slave-holding entities. A Southern confederacy that might---or might not---choose to remain in the British Empire!

So Van Buren's speech today, infuriating the fire-eaters by revealing and endorsing the old man's ridiculous plan to call a special Dominion convention to deal with the emancipation issue, didn't bother him. A reaction that startled and baffled his associates until he carefully explained his reasoning.

"By all accounts, the entire Dominion is shocked by the assassination. There is an excess of emotion: grief, outrage and yes, a feeling, somehow, of guilt, on the part of the people. Understandable, actually. The people are, in the end, simply a mob. Their reaction is thus predictable to anyone who has dealt with mobs.

"Van Buren wants to harness that grief and guilt to ram emancipation through. A monument to the slain hero, so to speak, completed while the guilt is still strong."

He looked at the others, whose facial expressions now ranged from outright confusion to sly understanding.

"We must divert that grief and guilt. How? By denying, plausibly and continually, that the emancipation convention was Jackson's answer to the crisis. By charging that the whole thing is a fraud…an abolitionist plot; a scurrilous attempt by unscrupulous men to transform a tragedy into a travesty."

He smiled his dark smile: "After all, Andrew Jackson, the master of The Hermitage, suddenly calling for abolition? How ludicrous the very idea; how bizarre the concept! How dare they think the British American electorate could be so naive?"

Chuckles of understanding and admiration rippled through the room. George Troup raised his whisky glass and called for a toast. Others followed until Calhoun smilingly cut them off.

"Gentlemen, please. We've much planning yet this night. A coordinated effort will be required, starting with the opening gavels tomorrow."

Senator Tyler had occasionally quietly sipped his own glass of Claret while refraining from commenting throughout the evening. Now he rose and addressed Calhoun:

"What, sir, do you propose if the Yankees do manage to call this damnable extra-constitutional convention, eh? Suppose, despite our best efforts to discredit this, the Westerners, the Border State people and the others go along with Van Buren. Agree to a convention. What do you propose then?"

The dark smile had vanished, the face now dominated by a sudden glowing of the eyes. The confident politician replaced by the Old Testament prophet:

"In that case, John, I believe we'll have grounds to call a convention of our own. A Southern convention. To discuss not just our peculiar institution, but the future of the South itself.

"Frankly, I believe we'd be left no alternative…"

The Residency
June 21, 1833, 5 p.m.:

"There's no hope then? No chance that they'll compromise? Even with a Supreme Court ruling in our favor?"

The G-G looked at his Congressional visitors sadly. "Calhoun is that sure of his position? That we'll back down rather than risk a secession crisis?" Van Buren got up from behind the desk and, shaking his head, walked over to the window with its view of the Potomac and the Virginia hills.

Ewing was the first to break the silence: "Calhoun is so far along in this I'm not sure he'll even accept a damn exemption. The man's got most of the Southern delegation believing these scurrilous claims that you replaced Jackson's speech with one Webster wrote up for you…"

Colonel Burr, sitting on a couch off to the side, chuckled. "Only half? You listen to reports in your Capitol Hill cloakrooms and you get the distinct impression the South is already solidly arming to the proverbial teeth. With the Québécois clamoring for ammunition to join them…"

Henry Clay was in no mood for levity: "This is serious, Colonel. Have you heard about McDuffie's speech today? Wants an investigation of the assassination by a Congressional committee. 'The Executive Branch can not be expected to investigate itself.' Says such an investigation must be completed before any consideration of Matty's emancipation convention proposal can even begin."

The G-G turned and stared at Frank Blair, who was sitting with the Colonel. "We'll put a stop to that. For a variety of reasons, gentlemen, including embarrassment to the Crown itself, there'll be no formal investigation of any kind, though I'd certainly like to know how Calhoun got his hands on Jackson's speech…"

The G-G's attempt to divert attention to the theft of the folder was only partially successful. Benton and Ewing picked up on the reference to the British immediately, though the ploy apparently got the Kentuckian's mind centered.

"We could bring Andy Donelson up to the Hill and question him under oath, I suppose. At least that might put a stop to these outrageous fraud claims…"

Benton shook his head violently: "No Senator. That's playing into John C.'s hands. This session was called specifically to deal with the emancipation issue. Nothing else matters. Start investigating the disappearance of the folder and you've opened Pandora's Box: Did this Lawrence character actually act alone? What possible motive could he have had? Did someone in high places put him up to it? If so, why? Did he also kill that woman, or was that strictly coincidental, as unlikely as that might seem…"

The Missourian looked around. "Personally, I've got some questions myself. Don't think you fellows have shared everything about this business with us up on the Hill." He paused and shrugged. "Well, maybe you have your reasons, Mr. Governor. They'd better be good ones, 'cause this *will* come out, in the end. But for now, with all due respect to poor Andy, we've got bigger fish to fry."

Ewing let the silence in the room linger for 30 long seconds before getting back to the proposal the Senators had come to The Residency to discuss. "Mr. Governor, we've spoken with members from both parties and all sections. Even these New England radicals are willing to have your right to call a special convention placed before the Court. We think the Attorney-General should proceed, forthwith."

Frank Blair was on his feet: "But wouldn't that play into Calhoun's hand, in terms of dragging this out? As it is, Wellington still expects the Parliamentary legislation to pass by August. That's getting closer by the day."

Clay had apparently refocused on the main issue. "We've spoken with Marshall, as I'm sure you have. He's agreeable to hear arguments next Monday, as the entire Court is in town. Apparently, he foresaw there might be Constitutional questions during this special session and arranged the circuit schedules accordingly. Says the actual arguments won't take long, no matter whom Calhoun sends over to make them. Can render a decision by the 28th."

Blair was counting heads and thinking fast. "As you are no doubt aware, old Johnson is the only diehard Southerner on the Court. Even if Gabriel Duval from Maryland joins him, we should have a majority decision of no less than 5-2. Assuming Marshall himself votes affirmatively, of course…"

The Colonel also stood up, though, to Benton's thinking, there was little change in height. *First time I've ever seen him and Matty Van together. So the rumors really are true…*

Burr was reassuring. "I believe my old friend Justice Marshall will join the majority opinion, if not write it himself. As a matter of fact, I would not be surprised if he's drafted a tentative opinion already."

Van Buren had returned to his seat behind the desk. "Well, gentlemen, let's get the Attorney-General in here and proceed."

Calhoun Residence
June 22, 1833, 7 p.m.:

The Calhouns were dining with John Tyler and his wife when Congressmen Polk and McDuffie arrived from the Hill after a bumpy carriage ride over Georgetown's rutted roads.

"So, gentlemen, the Administration has in fact gone ahead and submitted the convention proposal to the Court, I take it?" Calhoun was serene in the face of his two associates' breathless announcement.

"Well then. We shall see them in court on Monday. However…" He turned and looked pointedly at Tyler. "I see no reason to postpone or cancel our plans for a Southern caucus in Richmond next month. As Senator Tyler and I were discussing, July 8th looks a good date for the South to begin discussing this among ourselves. I understand Governor Floyd has already begun making the physical preparations…"

War Department
July 3, 1833, 8:30 a.m.:

Lieutenant Wilder kept looking up from the copy of the *Charleston Mercury* on his desk to the grim faces of Lieutenant Beaufort and David Harper.

It had been Harper who had rushed into the Department from Interior's adjoining space in the building, clutching the newspaper in his hand. Coming out of General Gaines' office---the USBAA vice-commander had begun appearing more regularly since Jackson's assassination---seconds later, Luke Beaufort had paused at Tom's desk for a look.

Dated June 27th---the same day the Supreme Court had ruled against the South on the emancipation convention issue---a huge eight-column headline screamed out from the *Mercury's* black-bordered front page:

"OLD HICKORY: A MARTYR TO STATES RIGHTS"

A crude five-column illustration of the assassination depicted Richard Lawrence in a whaler's hat and overcoat. Smaller headlines on either side bellowed:

"Abolitionists Cheer V-B's Speech Fraud"

"Why Congress Won't Investigate"

"Jackson's Anger at London Ultimatum"

"Secretary McLane is reading Monday's *Richmond Examiner,*" Harps said. "The headlines may be a little different, but the message seems about the same: 'The abolitionists had Jackson killed to stop him from denouncing the emancipation bill. Then Matty Van substituted a pro-emancipation speech and tried to pass it off as Jackson's original.'"

Tom shook his head in disbelief. "But this is all ridiculous. You and I met Lawrence enough times to know the man couldn't spell emancipation. He had more than one screw loose; the damn fool thought he was entitled to be King of England..."

"That's apparently beside the point, Lieutenant..."

"No sirs, it is the whole point." Beaufort interrupted in a hard, low tone. "As you say, this fellow was some sort of cretin; incapable of planning, let alone carrying out, the assassination of the Governor-General of the United States of British America."

A small crowd of enlisted Department clerks had begun gathering around Wilder's desk. They were listening intently as Beaufort continued: "Cast Lawrence's delusions aside momentarily. The cretin was merely the instrument utilized by a group of well-organized fanatics to subvert the Administration's to-be-announced response to Parliament's illegal attempt to override our property rights."

Beaufort looked around at the clerks, a few of whom were beginning to nod their heads in agreement. Others were tight-lipped, some staring at Lieutenant Wilder as if expecting him to rebut.

"The G-G was returned to office last fall in a landside; he carried all sections of the Dominion. He would have rallied opposition everywhere. So, he had to be eliminated. Enter this bartender with his delusions of glory. A handy weapon to replace a defiant leader with a puppet Wellington and the abolitionists could control..."

The ensuing silence was broken by a deep growl from the rear of the circle: "Quite a theory, Lieutenant. Based on what evidence..."

"*Atten-hut.*" Wilder, rising to his feet, joined the others in coming to attention. Even Harper stiffened as the commanding general moved through the parting ranks and glanced down at the *Mercury*. Still reading, he barked: "I believe you men have duties to perform this morning..." The crowd of clerks evaporated.

Picking up the paper he seemed to notice Harper for the first time. "Am I to understand that this newspaper is the property of the Interior Department? Then tell Mr. McLane I shall return it to him shortly."

Harps nodded and quickly turned and left as Scott ordered the two aides into his office, handing the *Mercury* to Beaufort as they crossed the threshold.

Closing the door behind him, Scott moved towards the coffee pot on the credenza before turning to address the two Lieutenants now standing at attention in front of his desk.

"I'll take that paper, Lieutenant." Scott sat and, sipping his coffee, read for several minutes; the aides still at attention before him. He finally looked up.

"Gentlemen, I swore an oath to defend the Constitution and the flag of this Dominion almost 30 years ago. The day you two entered West Point, you did the same. For as long as you wear that uniform, I'll expect you to uphold that oath. The moment you no longer feel you can, I'll expect your resignation." He paused.

"A crisis of unparalleled magnitude is evidently approaching. The Dominion needs both you men; we shall need every man."

He paused and stared from one to the other, from Mississippi to New York. "I'll require you both to refrain from further political discussion in the Department proper; and to see that the men go about their normal business."

My secretary's already made up his mind, Scott thought. *Wouldn't be surprised if he's composed his resignation letter, at least in his mind.* He opened the newspaper to an inner page. *More of the same!*

Dear God, is it starting already?

"Dismissed!"

Latoure Townhouse
July 5, 1833:

Robert Lee had wrangled leave and was home for 10 days, so Lucille had thought to throw a small dinner party in his honor. Despite the brutal Georgetown weather---high heat, unbearable humidity and scalding rain during the daily thunderstorms---no one of importance had left the capital. No one, that is, as of yet: the Southern Congressional delegation was scheduled to leave en mass for Richmond tomorrow to prepare for the "caucus" scheduled to open on Monday.

Despite her newly minted political awareness, Lucille retained her social and entertaining skills: the food excellent, the service impeccable and the wines outstanding. A cross-section of Georgetown's young elite, in terms of status, profession, nationality and gender, had been invited. Stimulating conversation would be a given…

Yet the dinner party was an unmitigated disaster.

Senator Brown was tight-lipped; his wife's gaiety forced. Mary Lee pointedly refused to speak to Tom or any of the other "damn Yankees," who included, apparently, Countess Caroline Renkowiitz, as she had come with Dave Harper. Robert had been embarrassed; both at his wife's blatant hostility and his own unexpected awkwardness with his old classmate Tom. Judith Walker Rives, the vibrant young wife of Virginia's junior Senator, had become a mentor of sorts to Lucille. Yet, neither she nor her intellectual husband---at 39 the oldest in the group---could rally the conversation. Even Jaine Latoure, accompanied by her longtime beau, Lt. Luke Beaufort, seemed to find the landscape studded by crisis landmines.

"I'm afraid it is hopeless," Jaine confessed to Major Layne, who had come with a daughter of Senator Frelinghuysen, an old classmate of Jaine's from the 'Female Seminary.'

"This crisis is like an earthquake. It has opened a gulf between the South and the other sections. Neither side trusts the other to be truthful or honorable any more. It's like we've already divided into two separate peoples…"

Layne, not used to playing the diplomat---and equally unfamiliar with Southern belles of Jaine's obvious breeding---tried the gallant approach: "Gulfs can be bridged. Surely the chasm can not have become so wide due to the one issue alone that it will affect all other relationships?"

Jaine smiled sadly at the Major and Abigail Frelinghuysen. *Perhaps my sister is right; perhaps these English do consider us unruly children.* "I grow afraid, Major, that all the bridges have been burned. And that the assassination was the torch…"

Numidia Stables
July 6, 1833
9 am:

General Scott's one-on-one interview with Jurgurtha Numidia had, at the direction of the G-G on the advice of his Attorney General, been postponed.

Free blacks, Taney determined, had the same rights per habeas corpus as white citizens. And since there was no evidence Jurgurtha had been involved in the botched Wellington seizure, the man must be allowed to go free.

Which was just as well, Scott thought in retrospect. *With everything else going on around here, I might not have gotten around to him for days. And the man was entitled to the opportunity to bury his only son…*

The Tousaint funeral took place two days after the G-G's aborted speech to Congress. And in the uproar that had followed Jackson's assssination, little, if any, attention had been paid it outside of black Georgetown. Except by Scott, who had a report from his own butler, Ronaldo, who had attended. *And according to him, the service, while boisterous and grief-stricken, had been uneventful…*

Now, with the capitol pausing to catch its breath after the reaction to the G-G's death, and before the Southern "caucus" began, Scott himself stood in the double doorway that opened Numidia's stable to the street.

The blacksmith was pulling a carriage from the rear of the building when he caught sight of the General. Jurgurtha merely grunted and continued through the stable until Scott realized he had no choice but to step aside or be run down.

Smiling inwardly at Jurgurtha's opening gambit, the General turned and followed a short distance into the driveway, where Numidia had been forced to stop, due to the phalanx of Scott's horsed bodyguard.

"All right, General Scott. Can see I won't get any work done till your visit is over. So what is it this time?" Jurgurtha shook his head in apparent resigned disgust.

Scott motioned to the tiny stable office and the two went in and closed the door, leaving the Army guard to dismount and rest their animals.

As usual, Scott was direct, launching his steely-eyed drill-glare at the blacksmith: "The fact that the whole town---Dominion---now knows about emancipation doesn't mean the government has any less interest in finding out how your son knew, Mr. Numidia. And, whether you cooperate or not, I will find that out, eventually. But I didn't come down here to reiterate that.

"You're an interesting character, Mr. Numidia. Nice little business. Acknowledged leader of the town's free blacks. Advisor and confessor, or so I hear, to the local slave population. Preacher capable of fiery, thunderbolt-hurling yet eloquent sermons. But something is missing, isn't it, Mr. Numidia?" The drill was at full speed.

"Like Ah say dat last time, Ah ain't got no idea what Massa talkin' 'bout…"

Scott laughed harshly. "Knock it off, Jurgurtha. You're an educated man. Self-educated, mostly, I'd guess, but still educated. Don't hide behind that stupid lingo."

"Like you hide behind them stars?"

Scott laughed again. 'Don't think you're going to bait me, Jurgurtha. I don't *hide* behind these stars, I earned them and utilize them for the good of the USBA."

Jurgurtha spat. "'The good of the USBA', huh? What's dat got da do with me, Massa? Me and ma people?"

"You're here aren't you?" Scott spoke quietly. "Making a living. Preaching to your flock. Sent a boy to college. I'd say this dominion has been pretty good to you these last...what? Fifteen years or so, by our calculations?"

Numidia shook his huge cannonball head. "My boy's in the ground. The Army camp out on my driveway much longer, I won't have any customers left. And my...*parishioners*...don't want any trouble with the authorities. So, most will stay away from the 'Church of Jesus Christ, Liberator.'"

It was Scott's turn to shake his head in disgust. "Come on, Numidia. Both your customers and your...*parishioners*...are more loyal than that. You command respect..."

The General paused for effect. "...which isn't the only thing you've ever commanded, is it, Jurgurtha?"

It was hard to tell, but Scott thought he had finally made Numidia blink.

"Now who's baiting whom, General?"

Scott gave Jurgurtha an exaggerated full length inspection. "You carry yourself with a military carriage, Numidia. And you're comfortable and self-assured in issuing orders. I've been at this business a long time, Jurgurtha. Over 30 years. And at one time I believe this was your business, too, wasn't it?

"I'd guess Haiti, based on your late son's name. But it could have been with Bolivar in South America. Or somewhere in between. But you've faced fire...and you've led troops. Haven't you?"

"Like Ahs keep sayin', Massa, Ah ain't got no idea what you be talkin' 'bout."

Scott sighed and walked to the door. He opened it, glanced at his escort, and turned to face the blacksmith again.

"Mr. Numidia, you're a smart man. Smart enough to know that emancipation may blow the top right off this dominion of ours. On the one hand, we've got the Southern extremists, men like Calhoun and Troup, who will oppose emancipation to the last breath of the last man. On the other, we've got hotheads like your son---or Nat Turner---who think seven years is a century away. Your own brand of fireaters wants two million uneducated slaves turned loose immediately despite having no way to feed, cloth or house themselves or their families…in the midst of some 12 million whites who want nothing to do with them.

"This is a perfect powderkeg, Mr. Numidia. One that could blow at any time. And might be about to do so."

Jurgurtha was staring at Scott incredulously: "Are you recruiting me, General? To fight for the government that just killed my boy?"

"The government didn't kill Tousaint, Jurgurtha. His own recklessness caused his death. That and his naiveté…"

"Be that as it may. You expect me to help a government that holds two million of my people in chains?"

"No, Jurgurtha. I'm just suggesting that you, as an educated man, must see that Parliament's proposal will at least offer your people some help in assimilating into our society, our Dominion… Unless you're in favor of all two million pulling up stakes and moving to Liberia, or Central America, or wherever…"

Jurgurtha spat again. "Hell, no. Black blood's at least as deep in this land as white blood. We're not going anywhere."

"Then I suggest you give some thought as to how you and your people might help the government of this Dominion…if worse comes to worse."

Now it was Numidia's turn to pace the office. Scott waited patently, studying his subject thoroughly. *Yes, a leader, all right. And a professional. Wonder whether he fought the Frogs or the Dons? Maybe both…*

Jurgurtha finally stopped and stared at Scott. "You really think this could come to civil war? Why, the Crown will send in the Redcoats to crush it…"

"The Crown has responsibilities and commitments around the world, Jurgurtha. My feeling is, any problems over here will have to be dealt with by the available resources over here."

He gave the big black man a hard stare. "Think about it. Maybe that's all it will be: thought. But also think what's in it for your people. Have you read the details of Parliament's bill? No? Do so. Seven years isn't really that long, when you look at it from Parliament's perspective. Keep that in mind. Maybe we'll talk again."

Scott turned without offering a hand, opened the door and strode out of the stable as his escort sprang to attention.

———

The Residency
July 13, 1833, 3 p.m.:

"A committee carrying credentials from the Southern caucus currently in session in Richmond requests an audience, Mr. Governor-General."

Andrew Donelson's flat and formal tones did not betray the excitement that was clearly evident in his eyes.

The G-G, in conference with the recuperating Secretary of War, Mr. MacLane of Interior and Frank Blair, was equally formal: "Show the gentlemen in, Mr. Donelson."

Senator Brown came in, flanked by Congressmen Polk and McDuffie. The dust clinging to their riding clothes indicated the trio had not stopped since crossing the North Anna River hours before. Brown retrieved an envelope from his jacket pocket and placed it on the G-G's desk.

"Mr. Governor-General, the document enclosed in this envelope represents the determination of the caucus of the South's Congressional and other elected officials which has met in Richmond since Monday last. I will summarize in the interests of time:

"The series of events and actions emanating from the announcement of Parliamentary legislation to abolish slavery throughout the British Empire has convinced the elected representatives of the various states now comprising the portion of the present United States of British America in which the institution is maintained that continued participation in the Dominion is no longer viable nor desirable.

"This series of events and actions includes but is not limited, to:

*Acceptance of Parliamentary authority to impose such legislation in clear violation of the Colonial Compact's commitment to freedom of property rights;

*Malicious misinterpretation of the USBA Constitution concerning the inherent powers of the Imperial, Dominion and State governments, as well as property rights; and the

*Abuse of Executive Branch powers by illegal interference in the organization and operation of the Legislative Branch.

"Specific crimes include the substitution of a Gubernatorial-General address to Congress by a fictitious replacement; opposition to a Legislative investigation of the assassination of the previous Governor-General; unconstitutional removal of a Cabinet officer and replacement of same without Congressional approval; and the calling of an extra-constitutional convention without Congressional approval."

(Attorney General Roger B. Taney, having refused to argue the Administration's case for an emancipation convention at the Supreme Court, had been summarily fired on June 21. The G-G replaced him with New York State lawyer and legislator, Benjamin F. Butler.)

Pale and sweating under his deep tan, Senator Brown paused and looked to his companions for support. After an emphatic nod from the smirking Congressman McDuffie, he continued:

"In light of these crimes and illegalities, the Southern states listed below, as determined by their duly elected representatives, inform the Governor-General of the United States of British America that the common bonds that have tied the South to the other sections of the Dominion have been severed.

"The South wishes only to reside in peace and harmony with its neighbors to the North. However, it is determined to conduct its affairs in a manner that the South…and the South alone…determines acceptable and reasonable."

The silence grew from seconds to minutes as the G-G daintily opened the envelope and scanned the complete document. Finally, he returned the document to its packet and placed it on the corner of his desk. Looking up at the Southerners, he said in his Dutch-tinged whispery voice:

"Thank you gentlemen. You seem to have ridden hard to deliver this document. I'm sure you are as tired as you are dusty. Good day." He nodded to Donelson to see them out.

CHAPTER FORTY-TWO

The Residency
July 14, 1833
12:00 noon:

Wellington had been enjoying supper at the French Consulate when the Southern commissioners dropped their explosive news on the G-G. As Van Buren and the Duke were working in much closer concert than Jackson had preferred, Wellington's whereabouts were no mystery. A messenger had been sent and a late night meeting arranged.

The Southern commissioners' meeting with Wellington and his aides, Bratton and Sir John, this morning had therefore been somewhat prima forma: the Duke received the delegation stony-faced and expressed real emotion---anger---only at the Southerners' sneering dismissal of Parliament's authority to arbitrarily enact Empire-wide legislation.

The Duke and Sir John were now in the G-G's office with Van Buren's version of a kitchen cabinet: Blair, Cass, new A-G Butler, and Colonel Burr. General Scott, though not officially a member, was also in attendance, due to the military ramifications.

Wellington was blunt in his direction: Van Buren was to take whatever steps were necessary, including the use of force, to maintain control. He was authorized to call for volunteers, as London would be unable to provide military help in the foreseeable future. However, the Government still held out hope of a negotiated settlement.

"You gentlemen should be aware that the Syrian crisis has entered a new and more delicate phase," he added. "Word was received from London some time ago that the Egyptians have retreated. Apparently, this Pasha Ali, once the Russians finally located him, took one look at General Mikailov's artillery and decided he didn't really need to worship at the Mosque of St. Sophia after all...

"The situation now is the one that fool of a Sultan should have thought of before he asked the Russkis in: how does he now get them out? It may be summer, but if I know the Bear, he's hibernating already…"

Wellington looked at the grimly chuckling group. "However, that is not our problem. The mask is now off: the real question is before us. This is, no more or no less, a struggle for political power. Are you gentlemen convinced the Southerners will see this through? Or, as Sir John here feels, is this a desperate ploy now that they've realized the other sections are in favor of emancipation in some form or other?"

The new G-G was nodding his head vigorously and affirmatively. "They mean to see this through, Sir. They've gone too far with this declaration to back down now. Their antique code of honor will not allow them to capitulate, though it would allow them to graciously accept *our* capitulation…"

Blair now stood and addressed Wellington. "I'm afraid the G-G is right. You yourself hit the nail on the head, Your Grace. This is a struggle for political power. If the South capitulates without a fight, they lose more than their slaves. They lose any hope of maintaining or reviving their dwindling power here in Georgetown by bringing Texas and the rest of the Mexican Southwest into the Dominion as states bonded to them. After all, just as slavery is the common bond tying the Border States to the South, so it would be with the Southwest. Take slavery out of the equation and what would those wild, untamed lands stretching from the Red River to the Pacific have in common with South Carolina?"

Colonel Burr was chuckling, which seemed somehow to annoy Blair: "You disagree, Colonel?"

"Certainly not, Frank. It simply strikes me as the ultimate irony in this catastrophe: the South threatening to secede in part because of its intention to extend slavery to the Southwest."

He flashed his now-familiar mischievous grin: "Doesn't it strike you gentlemen as ironic that they seem determined to fight the rest of the Dominion over land that we do not rule in order to plant their peculiar institution where it may well be economically-impracticable? Who's to say if the soil out there is suitable for raising cotton and tobacco?

"If their damned," he nodded at the G-G, "antique code of honor hadn't gotten, as usual, in the way, they've have stood a good chance of squeezing a long-term exemption from Andy's emancipation convention. And based on the Duke's word from Syria, London would have been forced to go along."

He grinned again, this time at Wellington. "After all, that 23-million pounds Exchequer wouldn't have had to send over here could instead have very nicely financed whatever action may have to be taken against the Russians. Come to think on it, it seems in any case that it will..."

The Duke cleared his throat loudly. "Yes, Colonel, an interesting perspective..." He cleared his throat again.

"However, I'm more interested at this moment in hearing the plans for putting an end to this so-called secession business. Mr. Governor-General..."

Van Buren was cautiously firm: "Actually, Your Grace, there is little in the way of immediate action that we can do. We certainly cannot override their right to free assembly, so they can meet unimpeded. And their right of free speech allows them to label such meetings anything they wish, including a 'constitutional convention' or whatever they will now term their infamous caucus. We can, you realize, move against them only if or when they attempt to interfere with such Dominion business as tariff collection or the postal service..."

"Or when they attempt to seize Dominion property such as arsenals or coastal forts." Scott had been silent throughout the meeting. "Reinforcing such facilities of military significance is something we can do immediately, Sir."

Now Cass, despite his bad leg, was ponderously getting to his feet. "I'm not sure if that's such a good idea, Mr. Governor. Might be seen as a provocation, actually goad them into doing something calamitous..."

The damn fool, Scott thought. *Damn politicians. The hell with it...*

"*Calamitous*, Mr. Secretary? They've already announced they've seceded. Do you think they're going to wait for us to hand over the keys to Fortress Monroe or the Harper's Ferry arsenal? If we don't reinforce our military installations throughout the upper South right now, you'll see some damn banner floating over them by fall in place of the Stars and Stripes. And then we'll have to go back down and retake them..."

Cass fired back, glaring at his old rival. "You're insubordinate, General. It's not your place to argue policy. You've overstepped your bounds..."

"Then what the hell am I doing here, Mr. Secretary?"

489

"That will be enough, gentlemen." Matty Van's voice was low but surprisingly commanding. Scott, who had seemed poised---*at least in the Colonel's approving view*---to throw Cass out the open window and onto The Residency lawn, stepped back. The icy blue eyes, however, continued to drill into the Secretary's face.

The G-G looked from one combatant to the other: "Your points are both well-taken. However, you'll recall the Duke's opening remarks, which I choose to take as London's explicit direction: maintain control."

He now expanded his gaze to include the others in the room. "I believe reinforcing the garrisons falls under that directive. General Scott will proceed to reinforce in an orderly and understated manner. No provocative show of force; just beef up their defenses.

"Meanwhile, we will continue to negotiate but will refrain from calling for volunteers unless or until this Southern caucus, or whatever they will be branding themselves, makes a belligerent gesture." He could see Wellington precipitously nod his head, the eyes glowing.

Ben Butler, the new Attorney General, however, wasn't satisfied: "I beg your pardon, Mr. Governor, but could you, ah, define 'negotiate'?"

Van Buren smiled for the first time: "Perhaps that is too definitive a word, Benjamin. *Continue to talk* might better express my intention…"

"Are you quite sure about that, Matty?"

Every head, including Wellington's, turned to look at Burr. While he had regularly contributed his views, till now he had never questioned Van Buren---or Jackson---directly. "Why just *continue to talk*? Why not continue with the emancipation convention preparations as if this Southern manifesto had never been delivered?"

Butler began to smile as the logic of Burr's proposal dawned. "Yes, Colonel, I believe I see your point. By continuing with the convention preparations while 'continuing to talk,' we demonstrate to the people their government's continued willingness and commitment to compromise. We cast the Southerners as aggressors while we simultaneously carry out London's direction to negotiate."

"A fine idea, Colonel, I endorse it."

Wellington rose, a small smile on his face. "I asked for this meeting, gentlemen, to ascertain your response to this crisis. I shall write London that the authorities in Georgetown are committed to a peaceful solution, but are taking prudent steps to cover any eventuality. Now, I am due at the Liaison Office. I'm told there was another ship due at RNS Baltimore late yesterday with further word from Syria. It also, apparently, is carrying a report on this Russian agent. Seems the chap caused a small commotion in London on his way here..."

After the G-G walked the Duke into the hallway, he returned to address the group: "All right, gentlemen. I'm happy Wellington got a taste of the American method of decision-making. Rather more *democratic* than he is accustomed to, I daresay..."

The reactions of the others ranged from Scott's grunt to the Colonel's outright laugh.

"Well now: Benjamin, your department should proceed with the convention preparations...

"I trust you and General Scott, Lewis, can proceed to reinforce the garrisons without 'goading' those temperamental Southerners unnecessarily...

"It will fall to you, Frank, to keep tabs on this caucus of theirs. We need to know if they're turning it into a provisional rebel *government* of sorts."

The G-G's face was hard in a way only his fellow New Yorkers had seen it before. "That will be the signal, you realize. Once they create positions and name men to them: that will be the crossing of the Rubicon. We must pray they remain perched on the far bank..."

State Capitol Building
Richmond, Virginia
July 17, 1833:

General Gaines had met privately with the Southern commissioners last Saturday, shortly after their unpleasant Wellington meeting. That same day, he had accompanied them back to Richmond, leaving word of his whereabouts only with Lieutenant Beaufort.

At the start of today's military organizational meeting, he had reassured the other members of the 'War Department' committee Calhoun---in his capacity as provisional leader of the temporary Southern government---had appointed, that his absence from

Georgetown would probably not be noted for some days. "Scott won't miss me, that's for certain," he said bitterly. "That damn traitor hasn't given me anything meaningful to do since I reported in from Florida two years ago."

"Are we certain that Scott is not with us?" asked Senator Rives, who was chairing the committee (and knew full well the answer).

Jaws dropped across the table as Gaines briefly outlined the USBA War Department working papers he had obtained through Lieutenant Beaufort. "So, gentlemen, you can trust me that Scott has as little sympathy for the South as Daniel Webster..."

The meeting proceeded to the question of coalescing the seceding states' individual militias and volunteers into one or more unified armies.

Across Richmond, similar committees were working on, among other things, a constitution; procurement of a treasury; a structure of operational government; naval development and diplomatic policy for the newly declared entity calling itself the "Confederate States of America."

A final committee was preparing options concerning relations with the British Government.

Liaison Office
Georgetown, D.C.
July 23, 1833, 12:30 p.m.:

A large map of the eastern portion of North America, with key USBA military installations carefully identified, had been placed on an easel in Wellington's office. The Duke and Captain Bratton were discussing the question of USBA Army defense of those in the Upper South when Sir John appeared at the door.

"A delegation, Your Grace, identifying itself as the 'Confederate States Imperial Relations Commission' seeks a meeting. There are three, ah, gentlemen in all, headed by John Tyler..."

Wellington's mouth curved downward and his eyes narrowed. He took a deep breath as he shook his head from side-to-side angrily, glaring at Burrell. "I'll not recognize any such 'Commission.' Great God! The impudence of these fellows!"

He walked to the window and stared out, while Bratton made a silent motion for Burrell to remain. The Duke turned the matter over in his mind for several minutes before pivoting.

"Tell Mr. Tyler and these other chaps, Sir John, that as His Majesty's Government does not recognize any such entity so identified, there can be no formal meeting.

"However, as the Liaison Office is in business to coordinate the relationship between the Government and its North American subjects, I will be pleased to meet informally. If they wish to accede to those conditions, you may show them in..." He paused and nodded affirmatively, the beak nose bobbing up and down.

"At 1:30 p.m."

The Liaison's political chief exchanged tart smiles with Bratton and bowed. "Certainly, Your Grace. If those conditions are acceptable, I will usher them in after they've...what's the American colloquial? 'Cooled their heels,' I believe...for 55 minutes."

Considering the sweltering Georgetown weather that heated up the Liaison Office to near combustible temperature, the meeting was, as Burrell later remarked to his crony Senator Webster, "singularly cold."

The Confederate commissioners---though Wellington repeatedly refused to recognize them as such---offered what amounted to a take it-or-leave it proposition:

"The states of Virginia, Kentucky, Tennessee, North and South Carolina, Georgia, Alabama, Mississippi and Louisiana, as well as the territories of Arkansas and Florida, have formally severed their voluntary relationship with the USBA, Sir," spokesman Tyler announced. "Whether the fore-mentioned states, which have formed a new government we have tentatively named the Confederate States of America, remain a part of the British Empire as an autonomous dominion or become an independent nation is contingent upon a single, non-negotiable issue: property rights as they have been traditionally defined."

The gaunt, goateed Virginian paused as if expecting a response. Seeing Wellington simply staring inscrutably at him, Tyler hurried on:

"The CSA requires a total exemption, in perpetuity, from the legislation now before Parliament requiring the mandatory emancipation of all slaves in the Empire." He paused again momentarily before adding:

"This exemption once agreed to, will allow for the discussion and resolution of other issues of concern to the CSA: chief among them the question of foreign policy initiatives directly affecting our citizens."

Indian Queen Hotel
July 23, 1833, 6:00 p.m.

"When Tyler finished, the silence in the room was…" Burrell reported to Webster that evening in the Indian Queen's taproom, "…profound.

"Not a muscle moved in His Grace's face for what seemed a bloody eternity. The, ah, commissioners began to fidget. One of the others---can't recall the chap's name---opened his mouth at one point as if to speak, but apparently thought the better of it.

"The Duke finally rose from his chair and walked to the window. He remained looking out towards The Residency for some further time. Finally, he turned and, with his hands folded behind him---no doubt so the Southerners couldn't see his clenched fists---spoke in a tone best described as 'uncompromising':

He had met earlier in the month with another *informal* delegation. Perhaps he had not cogently expressed the position of His Majesty's Government: strict adherence to the Colonial Compact. Under its terms, the government now permanently established in Georgetown is recognized as the sole representative governing body of the British American people, both domestically and imperially. *In perpetuity.*

"When it became obvious that the Duke was finished; had no intention of considering, let alone discussing, their 'non-negotiable' demands, Tyler gathered up his papers and rose from his seat."

"After his fellow commissioners followed his example, he addressed the Duke in formal tones:

There would be no further attempt by the CSA to reach a settlement. The terms of the Colonial Compact having been violated by both London and Georgetown, it was now declared by the South to be null-and-void. His people wished only to be left in peace to conduct their own affairs in their own way. However, any attempt by either London or Georgetown to subjugate the South would be resisted, by means of armed force if necessary.

"Without another word, the Southerners turned and marched out of the building."

Webster shook his head. "They've lost touch with reality. Calhoun's mesmerized them all. The damn fools…"

Burrell smiled. "The Duke's thoughts, exactly. In fact, he paraphrased something General Scott apparently told him some time ago. It seems you have a saying, some of you: 'South Carolina: too small to be a nation; too large to be an insane asylum.' His Grace now thinks the asylum needs to be expanded…"

The Massachusetts Senator downed his drink and called for another.

"Well, Sir John. They're still too small to be a nation… Unfortunately, it looks likely it will take quite a large quantity of blood to demonstrate their insanity…"

War Department
Georgetown, D.C.
August 8, 1833:

The abrupt, though anticipated, resignation of Luke Beaufort on August 1st had strained the Department's already taunt workforce, especially as two non-commissioned officers (one unexpectedly) had also gone South.

Lieutenant Wilder was thus pulling double-duty, though General Scott had gradually removed Beaufort from access to sensitive material over the course of the last six weeks. It was Tom's unpleasant duty, therefore, to present the General with another in the growing number of officer resignation letters. This one cut more deeply: "First Lieutenant Joseph Johnston of the 4th Artillery regrets that events of recent days have made it impossible…"

After laying the letter in front of The Old Man, Tom tried to beat a hasty but quiet retreat. He hadn't gotten more than halfway to the door when Scott growled: "Come back here, Lieutenant."

THE DOMINION'S DILEMMA: THE UNITED STATES OF BRITISH AMERICA

Tom sheepishly returned to the front of the big desk and was indicated into a seat. The General read the short letter again before staring past Tom's right shoulder to the window with its view of the Potomac. Minutes passed in silence. Finally: "Get a messenger to Fortress Monroe. I want Lieutenant Lee here as soon as possible." Thomas nodded and jumped to his feet. As he turned to leave, Scott beckoned him again. "Lieutenant..." Their eye contact made words superfluous. "No, that will be all."

As Tom exited the General's office, the thought occurred: *he might well be the only junior officer to have ever seen Winfield Scott's eyes redden...*

War Department
August 9, 1833
11 a.m.:

General Scott looked up from a desk covered with maps of northern Virginia upon hearing the crisp knock on his door. "Come in Lieutenant. This had better be either important or interesting..."

Stepping through the doorway and securing the entrance behind him, Tom Wilder came to full attention, but with a faint outline of a grin at the corners of his mouth. "Sir. Do you recall meeting, some weeks ago, with a man of color, head like a cannonball, arms like tree trunks, fingers the size of pistol barrels..."

"Jurgurtha Numidia."

"He's standing in the outer office, General, and requests a private interview."

Scott's own mouth twitched. "Well, Lieutenant. Maybe not important, in view of everything else going on. But definitely interesting. Show the man in."

As Jurgurtha stooped to keep from hitting his head on the doorsill, the Lieutenant closed the door from the outside and stuck his right hand in the face of the non-commissioned-officer-in-charge. They had bet months before on whether anyone other than the General would be forced to incline his head to gain entrance. Having seen Numidia at close range, Tom had gambled that the gigantic blacksmith would one day, for whatever reason, appear at the War Department

Scott had remained standing next to his desk. "Mr. Numidia."

"General Scott." Jurgurtha was equally formal without any sense of either subservience or bitterness.

The General nodded to the tall, sweating pitcher and accompanying glasses. "Water?"

"Thank you, General. Hot as hell out there. As usual…" Jurgurtha moved towards the credenza, reaching it in two huge, easy strides.

"That's Georgetown, Mr. Numidia. But I don't have the time or inclination to discuss this swamp's wretched weather…and I don't believe that's what brought *you* here, either…"

"Sure 'nough not, Gen'l…"

The two men stared at each other, Jurgurtha with a tight smile and Scott with a look of exaggerated disgust.

"Hmmm. Well, then, Mr. Numidia, state your business."

Jurgurtha slowly sipped his water and continued to stare at Scott for perhaps 30 seconds before answering. "General, when last we met, you may recall suggesting that I give thought to, as I remember it, 'how my people and I could help…if worse comes to worse.'

"Well, General Scott, that having become the case, at least from your perspective if not from mine, I'm here to see what can be worked out."

Scott grunted and marched over to the credenza himself, coffee cup/water mug in his right paw. He poured and took a long swallow before answering. "Is *Exodus* offering to secretly lead a portion of my army behind enemy lines so that we can attack from both sides? A Cannae, if you will?"

Jurgurtha raised his glass in salute. "My compliments, General. If and when time allows, I'd be interested to hear how you discovered our little operation…and why you haven't closed us down…"

"Why close you down now…*Moses*? You're providing a service to the Dominion. Anything that hurts the so-called Confederacy, even in a small way, benefits what will soon be the USBA war effort. Up to now, it's been the occasional escaped slave coming this direction. In the near future, it could be messages, or more, going South…

"As for discovery, well, Doby knew just enough to get us started…"

"Doby? That black bastard…I knew it was him. Only one not

hurt or killed. Well, we'll deal with him our ownselves..."

"I doubt it." Scott was dry. "Doby's a long way from Georgetown. And if he's smart, he won't ever come back. Not that we've abandoned him. Let's just say his opportunities look more promising where he is now... By the way, Donfield's also gone. Too much trouble to put him on trial. Politics, you know... No, Mr. Crispus Attucks Donfield is now enjoying life in Monrovia, Liberia. Perhaps the Spanish he picked up working at the Consulate will benefit him there...if he can hear with only one ear."

Jurgurtha was shaking his head. "So Doby was in it alone, eh? Spilled the beans beforehand. How many pieces of silver?"

Scott shook his own head. "Didn't ask for anything. Just wanted to keep his job at Interior. Which, of course, would have been like handing him his death sentence once word leaked out, as it always does.

"As for *Exodus,* Doby didn't know much at all. We just picked up the threads from the other end. Your son's job with Senator Webster. That led us to the New England Abolition Society...and back to you and *Exodus.* Full circle."

The *Exodus* station chief shook his head in reluctant admiration. "Damn... Pretty thorough. Or lucky..."

"Now then, Mr. Numidia, as I said at the onset: state your business."

———————

Scott leaned back against his desk, pushing the coordinated maps into a shambles, and heard Jurgurtha's proposal to raise a force of free blacks to serve with the USBA forces without changing facial expression.

"And just who would command such a force, Mr. Numidia...just supposing all the other obstacles were overcome and we decided to field this force? My loyal officers are fighting for a principle, all right. But it's the concept of the Dominion and its relationship to the Empire. Not emancipation. And, being human, they're interested in promotion. Don't know any offhand who would be happy leading a battalion or regiment of blacks. Doubt even my own aide out there, Lieutenant Wilder, who is hunkering for a command---which he won't get---would be interested in commanding such a force. I'm afraid most of my officers would look at it as a demotion."

Scott stared at Jurgurtha, his eyes suddenly bright and his mouth twitching as if to keep from smiling. The black man smiled back.

"Perhaps, in your surprise at the proposal itself, you didn't hear me completely, General. I said I'd raise the force. That means I'd command it, too."

Scott appeared to be giving consideration to the declaration, though his lips were fighting off a pucker.

"I see. So, in essence, you expect me to inform the G-G and Secretary Cass, as well as the Duke, that I intend to raise a force of free Georgetown blacks, up to regiment-strength and including black seamen and perhaps a few escaped slaves, train them over the next few weeks, arm them and send them into my lines under the command of a man of God?

"And, by the way, how do you think that will play in Missouri, Kentucky and Maryland, which Mr. Van Buren is trying desperately to hold on to for the Dominion?"

Numidia had returned to the credenza for a refill, but now he angrily slammed down his glass. "So what were you talking about that day in my stable, General Scott, *Sir*? Maybe utilize my people to hold the white boys' horses, build their campfires and cook for them? You know, like that Southern army is undoubtedly utilizing *their* blacks?"

Scott grinned. "Well Jurgurtha, that's what I originally had in mind. But ideas evolve. Especially when more information is made available; information that can tip the scale in one direction or another.

"Like the information in the New England Abolition Society files on one Jurgurtha Numidia. Col. Jurgurtha Numidia, that is, retired from the Haitian Army and veteran of the wars of liberation against Napoleon...

"So, Colonel Numidia: how many men do you think you could raise and how long before you could put them in the field?

"Bearing in mind, of course, that this is all very theoretical? And that Matty Van and Wellington may have me retired and shipped to Bedlam for even bringing the subject up?"

Harper's Ferry, Virginia
August 18, 1833, 4:20 a.m.:

If the crickets are chirping this early, it's going to be another hot one, Maj. Luke Beaufort, 1st Cavalry, Army of Virginia, thought as he placed both hands on his saddle horn and looked down on the quiet village.

The 1st had risen at 2:30 a.m., ridden quietly---the horses' hooves wrapped in burlap---and come up onto the Bolivar Heights from the southwest, having crossed the Shenandoah River miles downstream yesterday afternoon. Now they were northwest of the village; 'behind it', so to speak, as Harper's Ferry opened west-northwest from the triangle formed by the confluence of the Shenandoah and the Potomac River. The arsenal, armory buildings and other War Department buildings seemed scattered haphazardly throughout the triangle, though Luke knew that in actuality it was the shops, inns and houses that had sprung up haphazardly around the government buildings.

Harper's Ferry had been producing and storing USBAA weapons since 1799. It was a treasure chest that General Gaines, now commanding Virginia's forces---the CSA hadn't yet formalized its army structure---had targeted as absolutely necessary.

"There aren't three ironworks in the entire South capable of producing muskets, side arms and ammunition, let alone artillery," he had told Calhoun and Governor Floyd. "Even if there were, we don't have the luxury of waiting for production to commence. Once Scott's trained those two corps they'll be organizing at Carlisle Barracks, he'll come at us. We've got to supply our boys with modern weapons or he'll roll right over us. And the only way to obtain those weapons is to seize them from the Dominion forts and arsenals."

Although Scott had reinforced the meager security garrison at the Ferry---Major Beaufort knew there were some 200 Dominion troops guarding the place---few were on duty this time of morning. Spies--- locals loyal to Virginia---had reported that the Ferry's USBAA commander had divided his men into three shifts, with the 'graveyard' detail composed of deadbeats and anyone working off punishments for drunkenness or fighting. With the number of taverns at the Ferry, and with the opportunities for fights and other trouble with both the locals and the construction gangs in town digging the new canal, there was always more than enough to fill the midnight-to-8 a.m. shift. Those on duty at this hour would be worn out from dealing with the usual agenda of Saturday night drunkenness, fighting and petty thievery.

THE DOMINION'S DILEMMA: THE UNITED STATES OF BRITISH AMERICA

That meant less than 70 armed soldiers scattered around a five-mile perimeter, with more than half stationed along the rivers and cliffs. Luke had 300 well-armed horsemen on Bolivar Heights who would hit the town from its lightly-guarded rear just before dawn. Half would overrun the USBAA temporary camp located southeast of Washington Street, near the Shenandoah cliffs. The rest would charge through the town, driving the guards back to the Potomac. Once secured, the arsenal would be emptied and the artillery confiscated. (Luke had little concern about the construction crews; they were disarmed and camped for the most part across the Potomac on Maryland Heights.) The entire operation shouldn't take more than an hour; they'd be loading their haul by 7 a.m.

Nor was Beaufort worried about retaliation. His was the only mobile force in northwestern Virginia. *Anyway*, he thought, *it'll be early Monday before word gets down to Georgetown. By that time, we'll be back in the Blue Ridge.* He chuckled. *Like to see the look on Scott's face when Tommy Wilder gives him the news... Like to see the look on Wilder's face when he finds out, too...*

He turned to his right. He could begin to make out the grizzled features of Sgt. Isaac Smith in the pre-dawn light. Smith had been top sergeant in Troop B of the Dragoons when Beaufort had joined them in '27. Luke had been overjoyed to discover Smith, who had retired in '31 and come home to Virginia, among the first volunteers when the 1st Virginia Cavalry formed less than two weeks ago.

"Soon as I heard about this 'mancipation nonsense, I knew it'd come to this," Smith had said. "Damn Yankees can't leave well enough alone. Limeys, too. Well, was bored anyway. Not much to do down in Charlottesville, 'sides pour beer and clean up after the pretty boys at the university." He had grinned and spit. "'Spect I'll be seeing some of them, sooner or later. Kind of looking forward to that... Shoe'll be on the other foot...boot, actually." Smith had grinned and spit again.

Major Beaufort took a deep breath and checked his watch: 4:57. "Well, Sergeant, let's proceed down this hill and obtain General Gaines his ordinance..." He shifted left in his saddle to his second-in-command. Capt. Lewis Washington, a great-nephew of the second G-G, as a resident-planter in the Ferry area had done much of the initial planning for the raid. "Captain, if you're also ready..." The planter, waving a sword he claimed to be one the original

Washington had used at Boston, nodded. "Let's give those Yankees a little bit of hell…"

———————

As expected, it was over within an hour. Though to the raw Virginians, it had seemed the longest hour of their lives.

The astonished perimeter pickets at the foot of Bolivar Heights, looking up into the still-dark western sky, heard the Virginians before they saw them. Beaufort and his men smashed through the perimeter, a small force of pre-designated troopers stopping to round up the pickets.

Washington peeled off with his select force and thundered down on the USBAA encampment. A few of the Dominion soldiers--- mainly those who had stayed near their tents the previous evening--- got off shots. Two Virginians were wounded, one seriously, and one killed, though it was determined he had broken his neck in a fall from his horse. The Dominion casualties were also light; most of the hung-over men surrendered without picking up a musket. The same, unfortunately, couldn't be said for their unlucky commander. Maj. Stephen Daley fell mortally wounded, bullet holes in his stomach and shoulder and a sword incision deep in his chest. The encampment was secured by 5:45 a.m.

Major Beaufort and the remainder of the 1st raced through the Ferry itself, detachments surrounding and securing the government buildings. The pickets made an initial stand at the intersection of High and Gillmore Streets but fell further back into the sack. They made a last stand on a line anchored by the Wager House Hotel and Galt's Saloon near the confluence of the two rivers. Here Major Beaufort dismounted his remaining men---somewhere over 100, by later estimate---and formed a line.

"How many you think they've got?" he yelled to Sergeant Smith, who had stayed close since the charge began. They were standing at the corner of one in a series of unconnected buildings, which apparently were shops. The men had formed between and on either side of the row.

"Not more than 20, but they're well armed and we've lost the advantage of coming out of the dark." It was now 5:30 and becoming brighter by the minute.

The Dominion men had put together a piecemeal barricade of overturned wagons, carriages and furniture hastily dragged from the two buildings. USBAA sharpshooters were in the process of picking off foolhardy upright Virginians whose wild charge had left them with an undue sense of invulnerability.

Smith saw that first and motioned the boys to the ground. "We've got to drop back some, Major. Pull back to this line of shops; that'll give us some protection."

Beaufort looked around and nodded. "You're right. Even lying flat, out front here we're sitting ducks. Those Yankees can keep picking us off one by one as long as their ammunition holds out. Let's get them back…" He waved his sword in a backward motion and several non-commissioned officers began pushing the troopers backwards.

At least a half-dozen more Virginians went down in the retreat, but the Dominion fire suddenly stopped. When Beaufort realized it, he ordered his own cease-fire.

"What do you think, Isaac? Think they've had enough?"

"In a way, Major. I think they're out of bullets. Don't see any white flag yet, though." He turned and looked back through the town. "Horseman coming in from the west, too, Sir."

Beaufort looked that way as the rider drew close enough to expose the grey distinguishing cloths tied around both arms and on his hat. "Appears to be a messenger from Captain Washington. Sounds like the gunfire out that way has died off, too."

After receiving the messenger's report of the encampment's surrender, Luke had a white flag of his own raised. Despite Smith's grumblings that he was taking an unnecessary chance, the Mississippian marched under it and across the street, pausing midway.

"Identify yourself." The shout came from behind the barricade.

"I'm Major Beaufort, commanding 1st Virginia Cavalry. Who's in command back there?"

"Hell, ain't nobody in command. And ain't nobody ever heard of the 1st Virginia Cavalry, neither." The laughter was loud and bitter.

"But, since you got us cornered and we're out of ammunition, looks like we'll be surrendering to you anyways…"

A different voice: "Unless that white flag means you come to surrender *to us*…"

CHAPTER FORTY-THREE

The Residency
Georgetown, D.C.
August 19, 1833, 4:15 p.m.:

"Major Daley will be mourned throughout the North as the first fallen hero of the struggle."

Scott snorted. "That may be, Sir. But if he had lived, I'd have cashiered the damn fool. Three shifts instead of two…and a majority of the guards, apparently, along the riverbanks! What the hell was he thinking? That they'd sail up the Shenandoah and try an amphibious landing?"

The report had come in around noon from an exhausted USBAA messenger dispatched after the rebel cavalry vacated the Ferry late yesterday afternoon. The arsenal and its artillery park had been striped clean. Moments after the firing ended, wagons had appeared from Bolivar Heights. The Virginians had piled in muskets, side arms and boxes of ammunition and had seized enough Dominion wagons and carriages to carry the overflow. Casualties had been relatively light: 19 USBAA, including six dead; the raiders had 14 dead, mostly in front of the Wager House, and carried away several wounded.

Scott glanced at the report. "Our wounded are being cared for at the Dispensary and in several of the local churches…"

Burr looked over gravely: "Their wounded won't get far…"

"They won't have to. I'm betting they've already been left with local farmers along the way back."

The G-G was shaking his head. "I actually didn't believe, deep down, that this day would come." He sighed and pulled out a paper that had been locked in a desk drawer.

"I had Mr. Donelson prepare this proclamation some days ago, after your initial report on officer resignations, General. It authorizes and calls for the 30,000 volunteers projected in your contingency plan.

"I will issue it tomorrow morning. I'm also ordering you to activate the remainder of the contingency plan. Including putting a garrison around this city…"

"I'm putting together a makeshift garrison now, Mr. Governor. We'll utilize the 4th Artillery, the other Army troops in and around Georgetown and the ceremonial Marine detachment. Additionally, I've sent a rider to Fort McHenry. By tomorrow afternoon, Major Judge and most of his command will be on the march here."

A-G Butler's eyebrows rose questioningly.

"The Royal Navy at RNS Baltimore will augment the skeleton force Judge is leaving behind. I don't expect any trouble there…"

"But you are worried about Georgetown, General." Colonel Burr's tone indicated a statement of fact rather than a formal question.

Scott's face was hard. "Until Colonel Thayer gets here with the Corps of Cadets---whom I've already ordered down---and we receive those battle-hardened Illinois and Ohio volunteers the plan calls for, yes."

Van Buren turned to look out the window toward the Potomac as if he expected to see rebel forces poised on Arlington Hill. "What's the likelihood of a rebel attack in the next week or so, General?"

"This morning I'd have said negligible, Mr. Governor. But that was before this came in." He indicated the Harper's Ferry report he still clutched in his huge paw. "I must admit they've surprised me: that raid seems to have been professionally organized and commanded. Didn't think Gaines was capable…"

Cass was startled: "Gaines? You think Gaines is commanding the rebels?"

"Not enough time for any of the other possibilities like Zach Taylor or Davy Twiggs to have gotten up to Richmond yet. Twiggs, to the best of my knowledge, is still at Fortress Monroe, wearing a blue uniform. No, it's Gaines." He paused. "And, Mr. Secretary, this raid was commanded by someone you may also recall, if vaguely."

He looked down at the report once more. "Their commander identified himself as 'Major Beaufort.' You may remember my secretary, Lt. Luke Beaufort of Mississippi. Resigned August 1st. When I called him to Georgetown, he was serving in Bull Sumner's Dragoons. Seems his new command is something called the 1st Virginia Cavalry."

The G-G was grave: "How many more of these, shall we say, 'instantaneous' regiments can they field, General?"

The leonine head shook and the blue eyes seemed to frost. "None, I pray, Mr. Governor. At least till Brian Judge gets here. Even then, it will be dangerous for some weeks."

The General paused and glanced toward the Potomac himself. Speaking softly, almost as if to himself, he continued: "I expect they're slapping other units together now, but my belief is it will take several weeks to put together enough to threaten us. My guess is this 1st Virginia Cavalry raid was a one-shot deal: the best riders and marksmen available, under crack professional officers. It will take time to duplicate. Also, to form up and train infantry.

"Any attack would be little more than a nuisance raid; conducted for its shock value..."

Van Buren had sat back behind his desk. Now he jumped to his feet again. "Militarily perhaps simply a 'nuisance,' General. Politically, a disaster of the gravest consequences. If nothing else, think of the ramifications. Think of London's view. We must demonstrate to the British our ability to put down this apparently all-too-real revolt. Harper's Ferry can be explained away: a surprise attack, etc. Losing the capital, now..." He looked around the room. "Gentlemen, we simply can not allow it. Georgetown must be held...at all costs!"

War Department
August 22nd, 1833, 2 p.m:

General Scott had been clear: there were to be no interruptions during his conference with the Duke. But the sudden appearance of a grim-faced Lt. Robert E. Lee was enough for Tom to risk the General's wrath. He knocked on the closed door and awaited the expected explosion:

"This had better be damn impor..." General Scott stopped, his mouth open, and stared out the office door and over Tom's shoulder to Lee. He automatically grasped the seriousness of the situation, whatever it was. "Come in Lieutenant Lee." The door closed behind them, leaving Tom to turn and shrug wordlessly at the unspoken questions on the faces of the Department clerks.

Inside, Scott quickly identified Lee to Wellington. Then: "Your report Lieutenant."

Robert had been labeled the "Marble Monument" by his West Point classmates for many reasons besides his unfathomable, awe-inspiring perfect conduct record. Among them were his emotional self-control and military bearing. He needed both to deliver the shocking news.

"Sir, I have come from Hampton Roads by Coastal Guard sloop to deliver this pouch to you." Still at attention, he handed Scott a slim leather packet and continued: "Sir, it is my duty to inform you that yesterday morning at 6 a.m. Colonel Twiggs turned over Fortress Monroe and the Norfolk CG yard to General Gaines. The General informed the assembled garrisons that he was assuming command in his capacity as chief-of-staff of the Confederate States Army."

Scott, who had begun opening the pouch's ties, quietly placed the packet on his desk and glanced at Wellington. A quick pursing of the lips was Wellington's only immediate response though the eyes seemed to brighten considerably. *The old warhorse has caught the scent of battle,* Scott thought. *He's ready to pick up a sword right now...*

Scott looked back at the ramrod-straight Lee: "Take it from the beginning, Lieutenant. Exclude nothing..."

It was not a particularly long report: General Gaines, in civilian clothes, had arrived two evenings ago with a small party of similarly clad aides. He had immediately gone into the Colonel's quarters; the Lieutenant had been about his own business and had not known of the conference until the next day. Yesterday at morning reveille, Gaines, now in a grey uniform of sorts, had addressed the troops. Fortress Monroe, due to its very location on Virginia soil, obviously was the property of Virginia. As commander of Virginia's army, now a part of the new CSA army, he had requested Colonel Twiggs to cede possession. The Colonel had agreed and CSA guards were now patrolling the walls. On behalf of Governor Floyd and acting head-of-state Calhoun, he assured the USBAA garrison of safe passage 'back' to the Dominion; however, all troops are encouraged to resign and join the CSA.

"I was then sent for. With Colonel Twiggs, who was dressed in a grey military jacket somewhat the color of General Gaines', and with Gaines himself was Captain Savage, CO of the infantry at the Fortress. Captain Savage, now the ranking USBAA officer at Monroe, ordered me to deliver the pouch. CGS Albany, Sir, was the only Coastal Guard vessel at the base when I arrived. I am told that when word reached the anchorage that…" Lee paused, obviously embarrassed, "…a 'force' had occupied the base, the other ships pulled anchor and sailed for Baltimore. Albany was apparently dockside and unable to flee in time."

Scott stared hard. "That all, Lieutenant?"

"Yes Sir."

"Your uniform is a bit muddy Lieutenant. I assume you were rowed in from the Potomac?"

"Yes Sir, forgive me, but the marshes…I felt it my duty to deliver this pouch and my report immediately…"

"Then I can also assume that you are reporting as an active officer in the USBAA? That you have not, as they are calling it, 'gone south?'"

If it is possible for a monument to stiffen, Lee appeared to do so. "At this moment, Sir, I am reporting as a Lieutenant in the USBAA."

Scott and Wellington exchanged looks. "Do you have any questions of this officer, Your Grace?"

"Just one, if I may. Lieutenant, ah, Lee, how many officers and men took the rebel Gaines up on his, ah, 'suggestion' that they, in General Scott's apropos term, 'go South'?"

"Captain Savage told me privately, Your Grace, that he expected to march about 90% of the men and…" he paused, again of apparent embarrassment, "…approximately half the officers North. He said to tell you, General, that he expected to move out this morning. My apologies for neglecting to include that information earlier."

Scott nodded. "You are dismissed, Lieutenant. Report back here at 0800 tomorrow."

Scott was rising from his desk even before the door closed behind Lee. He indicated the pitcher of icy water on the credenza and poured tall glasses for both the Duke and himself. Wellington accepted wordlessly and watched Scott walk slowly across the room to the big window. The General turned and sipped his water.

"This has been in the works for sometime, I believe. They waited to see if the Harper's Ferry raid would be successful, then struck. I imagine Sumter in Charleston, Mobile, all the Southern forts will fall like dominos."

"Its my fault. I believed Twiggs was honorable; would do the honorable thing and resign. It never occurred to me that his particular brand of treason would extend beyond his own person. To arrange the surrender of his entire command…unprecedented perfidy!"

He turned back to the window and spoke over his shoulder to the still-sitting Duke. "Lee didn't mention it, but they must have overpowered the guards; Twiggs couldn't have managed to have them all pulled. Must have been some casualties. Must have been some subterfuge, too, getting the rebels inside in enough force to take even a skeleton guard detachment."

"Your security directive was disobeyed, General Scott. That's obvious. This man Twiggs brazenly cooked this up. Well, let's turn to the estimate of the situation: what does this mean in a military sense? Is Fortress Monroe vital to your plans?"

"Not in an immediate tactical sense, Your Grace. Only if we were scheduled to land an army on the Tidewater Peninsula, which we have no plans to do. No, the immediate value to the rebels is in terms of artillery. When completed, the Fortress is designed to boast 300 guns of up to 32-pounds. About two-thirds are already in place. The rebels took Monroe for two reasons: because their sense of honor demanded it; and because of those guns."

Scott grimaced: "That's a lot of artillery our boys will be running into when we move to take Virginia back…"

The White House
Richmond, Virginia
August 30, 1833:

"Sir, there is a gentleman here asking to see you." Jefferson Munroe was hesitant as he stood in the doorway of John C. Calhoun's makeshift office in the mansion vacated by the president of the Bank of Virginia. It was locally referred to as 'The White House.'

The newly installed president of the Confederate States of America looked up from the piles of paper littering his desk. "General or cabinet officer?" The sarcasm was heavy but on-target:

the President's secretary spent much of his time shooing away office-and commission-seekers.

Munroe smiled. "Not this time, Sir. This one is a bit different. He announces himself as the official representative of His Imperial Majesty, Nicholas I, Czar of All the Russias..."

The President's eyes began to shine.

"...Says his name is Count Nicholas Ignatieff. However..."

Calhoun sat staring. "Go on, Jefferson, you have more..."

"Yes, Sir. I...I believe we met him in Alabama some months ago. Under a different name. His appearance is also somewhat altered."

"Well, by all means, Jefferson. Bring in the 'official representative of the Czar of All the Russias.'"

Ignatieff strode confidently into the room and bowed his head formally. "Excellency, it is good of you to see me on such short notice. I am aware how busy you must be."

Now on his feet, the President briefly flashed his dark smile: "'Mr. President' will suffice, sir." He rocked back gently on his heels and studied his guest intently. "Count..." He looked over at Munroe.

"Ignatieff, Sir."

"Thank you. Yes, Count Ignatieff. Welcome to Richmond, sir. I understand you claim to be the 'official representative' of your Czar? In that case, sir, I assume you have papers to that effect so identifying you? If that is the case, you may present them now..."

Ignatieff 's smile did not reach his eyes, which remained locked with Calhoun's. If the President was surprised by the oddity of the right eye's dual colors, he did not betray it, surprising the Count. Well, Nicholas thought, *if he demands we play this diplomatic farce, I shall acquiesce...*

"Obviously I carry no papers from the Foreign Ministry in St. Petersburg---or from the Czar himself---addressed to the 'Government of the Confederate States of America.' However, I do possess credentials. Unfortunately, they are written in Russian. While I would be happy to have them examined by anyone you should so designate, I give you my word of honor as a gentleman that they do in fact instruct me to make contact with the leader of the Southern people."

Calhoun leaned back against the front of his desk and glanced briefly at Munroe, who was staring at the Russian dubiously.

"You will understand, Count Ignatieff, my aide's skeptical attitude, in that you have previously presented yourself, apparently fraudulently, as Mr...Karlhamanov...I believe it was? If your previous persona was indeed a charade, what evidence other than an apparent document, as yet unpresented, in a language few here in Richmond could decipher, would lead us to accept your bonafides as the Czar's man and not an imposter of acknowledged skill and daring?"

Ignatieff again smiled, though with a lack of humor obvious to the Southerners. "When you have my direction from the Czar..." he tapped his jacket pocket in apparent indication of the paper's location, "...'deciphered'...you will see that my orders are also to ascertain the strength of the Southern independence cause and to assist it in the event such a cause is viable.

"Certainly you can see that the initial phase of my mission could be carried out more effectively in the guise of a common, though prominent, 'exile' than as a ranking member of His Imperial Majesty's service. In that persona, I analyzed your chances for success...and assisted you with certain information. Information that I assume helped you arrive at the momentous decision that has led us both to Richmond.

"Here in your new capital, such secrecy and deception is unnecessary."

Calhoun's dark face was now hard and his words direct: "And how do you propose to assist us now, if we choose to accept you in your latest persona?"

"Initially, your acceptance of my presented credentials amounts to my country's formal recognition of the Confederacy as an independent country. A major diplomatic coup that opens many possibilities throughout Europe. My instructions are also to investigate the possibility of direct financial and military aid. In other words, an alliance of our two beloved countries. If such an alliance, Mr. President, would be helpful to you..."

The Deerhead Inn
Georgetown, D.C.
August 30, 1833, 8 p.m.:

Capt. William Savage was not surprised by his promotion to lieutenant colonel of volunteers. Like all USBAA regulars, he had known the huge expansion of the Dominion's forces in light of the South's secession would mean early jumps in rank and responsibilities.

"Didn't expect it just now, that's all," he said over a celebratory beer in the taproom with Lt. Col. Brian Judge. Judge, too, had received word of his promotion directly from General Scott upon arriving with his Fort McHenry garrison. "Considering I was caught flatfooted when the damn rebels took over Fortress Monroe and all..."

"Hell, Billy, you weren't caught flat-footed. The rebels caught you sound asleep..."

"Thanks a lot, *Colonel* Judge..." The two old friends---they had served together in the Southwest and in Quebec---grinned at each other.

"Actually, Colonel Savage, the Old Man couldn't hardly hold it against you personally. I mean, I hear tell he would have court marshaled that poor bastard Daley, had he lived. But you weren't in command down there. They say Twiggs turned traitor overnight, though Lieutenant, err, Captain Wilder says the General believes Twiggs and Gaines started cooking that up last month..."

"No doubt about that. It was too slick for a spur-of-the-moment thing. The two sons-of-bitches... Even some of the Southerners were embarrassed. Lieutenant Lee..."

"Heard he's gone south now, too."

"Well he's resigned his commission, that's fact. Damn near broke the General's heart, according to Wilder. Says the Old Man pleaded with him. Told him he was making the mistake of his life. Wilder was pretty broke up, too. They were roommates at The Point, apparently. Tommy says Lee looked him in the eye and told him he'd never take up his sword again, except in defense of Virginia."

"What a load of crap. Where the hell does he think this big fight that's coming is gonna take place? Texas?"

The two friends grinned again. Then the bulky Savage, whose men always said he'd been assigned to the infantry in consideration of the Army's horses, grew more serious. "Actually, Brian, Wilder knows Lee fairly well, if anyone can say they know him. Strange young man. Most serious junior officer I've ever met. Yet to hear him crack a joke, even in the officer's mess at the Fortress. Anyway, Tom thinks that was Lee's way of saying he won't condone or participate in any hit-and-run raids on Georgetown."

Judge was unimpressed. "That's damn Christian of him. Seeing how he ain't cavalry. Damn prudent, too, seeing how he knows we've got enough regulars here now to handle any attack short of brigade-strength..."

Savage drained his beer and signaled for two more. "Brigade-strength; still sounds strange hearing that. I mean, we've studied brigade and division organization, dreamed about leading corps. After all these years in our miniature little army, just never expected to be discussing it so casually, so matter-of-fact..."

Judge took a deep pull from his own beer. "We'll be doing more than discussing them. Organizing and training are to officially begin at Carlisle Barracks September 15th, though I hear old Wool's on his way there now. Apparently, the Pennsylvania troops are already shaping up there." He sighed. "I'd wondered if the people up North would even respond to our call for volunteers..."

"Oh, they're responding, Colonel Judge. Haven't you read the Boston and Philadelphia papers? "It's "On to Richmond!'"

"'On to Richmond?' By God, Billy, they have to give us a chance to whip an army together! We can't possibly be ready to fight before late fall. Otherwise, we'd just be leading an armed mob..."

Savage's look was half-grin, half-grimace. "Don't believe we'll have that long, Colonel. Wilder tells me the South has a slogan, too. It's 'On to Georgetown!' Apparently, it offends their Southern sense of honor that *our* capital is situated in *their* country..."

"What?"

Savage laughed as his friend choked on his beer. "Didn't you know? They're claiming all the land south of the Mason-Dixon line."

Colonel Judge shook his head. "The bastards *are* crazy. I hear they claimed Kentucky and Missouri were in this *confederacy* of theirs, even though Clay and Benton and most of the rest of the Congressional delegations have remained loyal. Same with Maryland."

"That may be true, Brian, but the Southerners haven't let facts get in the way since this whole thing commenced. They get one soldier, one Congressman and they claim the state. Hear they've invited Quebec to join them, too."

"Now that *is* insane." Judge shook his head again as a grin broke out. "Come to think on it, they're welcome to those damn Frogs. God knows, they're more trouble than they're worth..."

"That they are, Colonel. Apparently, General Scott thinks so, too. Rumor is, his contingency plan calls for the British to keep Quebec quiet."

Judge looked thoughtful. "Is that a fact? Well, good thing. We're gonna need every last one of Matty Van's 30,000 volunteers down here. The Southerners may be insane, but they can fight. Harper's Ferry proved that."

Savage took a deep chug on his newly arrived brew. "I think we already knew they possessed the ability, Colonel Judge. What the Ferry proved was the will."

The White House
Richmond, Virginia
September 1, 1833
10 a.m.:

John C. Calhoun's leadership style, his enemies in the North would say, inaccurately, was autocratic. In this, as in so much else about the man, their estimate was slightly off kilter. And in many ways, it was this misconception that had led to the present situation.

For although Calhoun's leadership style was forceful---he simply believed he instinctively knew what was best for his beloved South--- he recognized and practiced the key leadership principle of delegation. While it was from his fertile brain that much of the concepts of states rights and nullification had first sprung, he had delegated responsibility for espousing much of those doctrines to others. It was Senator Troup who was known as the "Hercules of States Rights", after all, while Representative McDuffie had drafted the address to the Dominion from the South Carolina Nullification Convention back in '31.

Calhoun practiced the art of delegation in putting together the CSA government. Nowhere was this more evident than in his startling selection of a Secretary of War. While the usual suspects--- Mangum, Edward Hayne---were bandied about, Calhoun reached into the ranks of the old USBAA and plucked the obscure former Chief Engineer, Charles Gratiot of Missouri, to head the Department. The President wanted a War Secretary who would build the Confederacy its armies, but not interfere once the men were in the field. Who better than this very early West Point graduate who had built his career exclusively in the Corps of Engineers, administering the USBAA's massive program of river, harbor, road and fortification construction?

Now Calhoun and Secretary Gratiot were debating the selection of the commanding officer for the force Gratiot was constructing to meet Scott's anticipated drive on Richmond.

Edmund Gaines was certainly a candidate. The acting chief-of-staff had demonstrated organizational and tactical skill---and surprising daring---in putting together the Harper's Ferry and Fortress Monroe operations. But, at age 55, he was somewhat old to lead men into the fight. Better that he remain in Richmond as the CSA's chief war planner.

David Twiggs, 43, was obviously a prime candidate. He had volunteered during the Louisiana campaign and had served ever since, including action against the Seminoles in Florida and other tribes in the West. Calhoun and Gratiot were grateful that he had turned over Monroe with a minimum of bloodshed; yet, there was something somehow distasteful and dishonorable about his 'midnight' action. No, Twiggs would receive his general's commission and a command, but it would be a subordinate one...

Rumor had it that Zach Taylor was on his way from New Orleans. If it were true---and Calhoun had sent messengers south in several directions to find him---*there* was the commander they were seeking! Taylor might be somewhat unorthodox---there might be 'spit' but there was clearly no 'polish' to him---but he was a magnificent soldier who had been leading men into combat since his days fighting Techumseh.

Yes, they agreed, Taylor would be offered the top command, with Twiggs under him. They had some time yet; their already active spy network in Georgetown reliably told them that the target date for organizing the enemy force up in Pennsylvania was still two weeks away. That should be enough time to ascertain if Taylor was with them. If not, they'd revisit the issue. Meanwhile, Gratiot and Gaines would go about building up the CSA's own forces.

The chief emerging issue was the shortage of other identifiable qualified senior officers. The younger officer recruits were magnificent. This Albert Sidney Johnston had already proved himself in combat, while Gratiot himself had been talking up Robert Lee for weeks. Major Beaufort appeared to have the makings of a cavalry commander, while Joseph Johnston seemed to know his way around artillery. All, of course, were West Pointers; there'd be more, Calhoun and his War Secretary agreed. Still, they could use some slightly more mature professional officers. The word was that British half-pay officers were applying for posts in the USBAA. That's a resource the Confederacy wouldn't be able to mine, they agreed. Thus far, only this Capt. Harry Bassett had resigned his commission and offered his services. That was to be expected, of course; after all, the man was married to the daughter of the Governor of Mississippi!

Well, there were bound to be some adequate officers among the state regiments. But it would take a fight to highlight them.

And, if there's one thing both sides agreed on, it was that one big fight is all it will take to decide this issue…

CHAPTER FORTY-FOUR

Latoure Townhouse
Georgetown, D.C.
September 13, 1833
10 a.m.:

Lucille had watched them march in over the past month with a growing sense of rage.

First, the regulars from Ft. McHenry under an impossibly tall and lanky officer that Thomas had innocently later identified as a Major Judge. Then, the young cadets from West Point led by their commandant and another officer. Tom had remarked that the commandant, Colonel Thayer, was to be Scott's chief-of-staff. The second officer apparently was the grim William Worth, who she had informed Richmond---via a surprisingly easy secret correspondence---was currently the 'tactical' commander---whatever that meant---of the Georgetown defenses.

The regulars she could tolerate; even the cadets, since she had been informed that scores of Southern-born West Pointers had resigned and were pouring into Richmond.

But now these tough-looking men! The 1st and 2nd Ohio were marching down Pennsylvania Avenue, led by a tall, solidly built, terrifying-looking officer. Rumors in the city had another Ohio regiment, one from Indiana and some Illinois volunteers not far behind!

These were the Black Hawk War veterans, Tom had helpfully explained the previous evening, battle-hardened troops who would go right into the defenses as their combat experience negated any need for the training camps now opening at Carlisle Barracks.

"We can all rest easier now," he said. "The Reb threat to Georgetown, if they were planning anything anyway, is over for now. In fact, we'll be sending reconnaissance parties into Virginia any day now."

'Reconnaissance parties', he carefully explained, were well-armed scouting patrols looking for any signs of Rebel activity.

Lucille was now including that in her latest report to Richmond, along with the information that the vaunted and long-expected western volunteers had begun to arrive. The report would go to Jaine at Alexandria, carried by one of their Cranford 'people' along with other mail, newspapers and supplies. Jaine would then forward it to Richmond, using middle-aged married men from Alexandria Importing-Exporting who were not as yet needed by the Confederate Army. Even though Alexandria was technically in 'enemy territory,' a strange twilight attitude had been adopted by both sides: mail was exchanged and travel was unimpeded in the area between Georgetown's Potomac-side defenses and the as-yet-undetermined (at least by the USBAA) Rebel picket line somewhere outside Richmond.

Lucille and her cohorts, Jaine and Mary Lee, were taking full advantage of the situation to send a flood of raw information, rumor and gossip to the Confederate leadership. The pipeline had been brought to the CSA War Department's attention by Major Beaufort, who had explained the allegiance of the Latoures (Mary Lee's support was of course naturally assumed) to General Gaines. The General had been pleased and, secretly, amused to discover that among the pipeline's unsuspecting sources was Scott's own intelligence aide.

Captain Wilder was sophisticated enough not to drop serious military secrets, even to Lucille. The identification of the various regiments and commanders pouring into Georgetown could not be kept under wraps for long in any case. But in inadvertently putting the pieces of the puzzle together for Lucille, he was speeding up the identification process that she was then hurrying down to Richmond.

Tom was for the most part too busy and preoccupied with military matters to give much attention to his checkered romantic life. In any case, Candice was at Twin Peaks, supervising negotiations with the army for her prized horse herds. Lucille, whose interest in the crisis he found encouraging, had become more cordial as things worsened. He had begun dropping by the townhouse most evenings for a quick drink or supper. Naturally, or so he thought, their talk centered on the war...

Lucille was folding her report to give to Sebastian when she remembered a last detail. The commander of the Ohio troops, that big, scary-looking officer, was one Col. Dennis Felton.

———————

Governor-General's Office
The Residency
September 14, 1833, 12 p.m.:

With the Georgetown defenses now overflowing---most of the troops had been placed north of the city, as Scott assumed any Rebel movement would come out of the Blue Ridge and down across Maryland---General Worth had departed for Carlisle, where Northern volunteer regiments continued to come in. Meanwhile, elements of the Regular Army were also converging on the Barracks, some from half-denuded Western posts. Others would eventually arrive from the South, where most coastal forts had been abandoned on Scott's orders. As he had explained to the G-G and Wellington, "we can't supply the coastal installations indefinitely. Not with half the Royal Navy's Atlantic Squadron ordered to the Mediterranean. And I can use the troops up here, where the main fighting will be. We'll stay at Key West and Mobile Harbor for now as they are in more isolated locations where CG brigs can reach them without being subject to fire. Anyway, I expect this to be over before any evacuation order could even reach them, much less be implemented."

Troop E in Arkansas were also a special case. "The Troop is essentially the only organized military unit in the territory. But they can't hold on forever without resupply. So I've ordered them to march northwest toward Missouri, where they'll be nearer supplies. I'd like to have them for the fight that's coming, but they're simply too far away to be counted on. If this thing is extended, we can build a western force around them later."

Seated behind Jackson's old desk, Van Buren's face paled: "Extended, General? You've led me to believe a single battle, our own Armageddon, will settle this."

The two warriors looked over the tiny G-G's head at each other before Scott spoke. "Well, Mr. Governor, a decisive battle is certainly what we're pointing for. However, there is always the possibility that the fight will be less than conclusive..."

"I agree, General Scott." The Duke was brisk but reassuring. "You see, Mr. Governor-General," he said, turning to Van Buren, "one must always have a contingency plan to fall back on. General Scott is being prudent in planting the core of a western force near Missouri against the unlikely chance extended fighting might call for a contested march back into central Arkansas or Mississippi."

"...Additionally," Scott resumed, "it will have a positive effect on keeping Missouri in the Dominion."

Wellington turned back to Scott: "That too, I can see. However, General, the main theater of course will be in northern Virginia. How soon will you be ready?"

The General began to pace the room, his long legs eating up the distance in four or five steps. He paused before the open window with its view of Arlington House in the distance.

"I would prefer to march approximately November 1st. That would allow us a month of relatively decent weather. Enough time to meet a Rebel force in the field or to invest Richmond, in the unlikely case they choose not to come out and fight. However..."

He held up a huge paw as Matty Van began to voice his strenuous objection. "...I am aware, Mr. Governor, of the pressure you are under in the northern press and from London..." He glanced ruefully at Wellington, shifting his legs in his chair---the politico and the soldier doing internal battle---before continuing.

"...So I have ordered Worth and Wool to be ready to move out October 15th. General Thayer informs me he can have the Carlisle army fully equipped and supplied well before that."

"A reasonable compromise, General." Wellington looked over at Van Buren. "I concur. October 15th is the optimum date: it allows enough time for training while also allowing enough time for a fall campaign."

The G-G nodded. "All right, gentlemen. I will accede to your decision. October 15th it is."

As Scott and Wellington walked down The Residency steps, the General turned to his old chief: "Optimum time, Sir ? You know as well as I that 30 days is foolhardy and dangerous. Damn it, Sir! We shouldn't move out until spring..."

Wellington mounted his horse before looking down at the glowering Scott and replying: "You are militarily correct, of course. In an ideal world, yes. But under the present conditions, intolerable delay...

"Consider these facts, General: the Rebels will have had as little chance as your forces to train and coalesce. And, General, we hold the ace:

"You."

Wellington pulled on his reins and trotted down the driveway. Scott, meanwhile, let loose with a series of quiet oaths that would have made the lamented Jackson blush...

Camp Washington
(outside Richmond)
September 16, 1833:

General Twiggs was pleased. The Camp was filling rapidly with regiments from across the Upper South, with the exception, of course, of Tennessee. *Even the Kentuckians---who are calling themselves "The Orphans" because that damn Clay convinced the state legislature to remain in the Dominion---are already here in regimental strength.*

He had five regiments of Virginians thus far and an almost equal number from North Carolina. There was even a regiment from Maryland, even though that state had also failed to secede. *All told, I have about 12,000 infantry in a dozen regiments and another 1700 in cavalry, along with six batteries of artillery.*

Of course, that is on paper. These men might be formed into regiments, but they are scarcely trained as yet. Sidney Johnston's seeing to that, however. The West Pointers, both those come directly from the Old Army, and others who have come from their homes leading their local regiments, are shaping these boys up. And young Joe Johnston is proving a godsend in drilling the artillery.

The thought of the big guns made Twiggs smile, then frown. *Those damn Yankees have to be kicking themselves at the thought that we're getting ready to hit them with their own artillery.* But the whispers that his action in turning over Fortress Monroe to Gaines was, somehow, tainted burned. *Tainted! By God, I've delivered the "Gibraltar of the Chesapeake" to the CSA without the loss of a single Confederate soldier and that, damn it, is less than honorable?* He knew what it was all about: *that damn little Gratiot!* They had rubbed each other wrong as far back as their mutual posting in the Michigan Territory 25 years ago. And they had clashed about Monroe's design every time Gratiot had come down to Hampton Roads. *Now, incredibly, the bastard is Secretary of War and even*

Gaines reports to him. The other day, ol' Ted all but admitted Gratiot intends for Taylor to command the field army, if Zach gets up here in time!

Well, we'll see about that. Scott isn't going to wait to see if Zach's in Virginia before coming after us! He'll come when he's ready…which could be as early as next month. If Taylor has arrived and Calhoun puts him in overall command, so be it. I'll be the good soldier and follow orders.

Because, unlike most everyone else in Richmond, I don't believe this will be over in one day or one fight! We can't quit, not now. And we'd have to just about annihilate the Yankees---another Cannae even---before Winfield Scott quits. Well, let old Scott march into Virginia in a few weeks. Whether Zach's here or not, I'll be waiting for him. Maybe conduct a Cannae of my own…

Albert Sidney Johnston was a big man who in a short time had carved a big reputation. Maj. Robert E. Lee had graduated from The Point only three years after Colonel Johnston but looked at him with a certain degree of awe. That was because the Kentuckian had rocketed through the USBAA ranks, serving as a captain and chief-of-staff in the Black Hawk War just six years after his 1826 graduation. Even General Scott had considered Johnston an officer apart, entrusting him with responsibilities far beyond his years and experience.

Johnston was a natural leader of men and the obvious choice to oversee the CSA Army's training. He had a hand in assigning the resigned Old Army officers and had concurred with Lee's appointment to command the 1st Virginia Infantry. There were other officers commanding regiments who Johnston had his eye on; if he couldn't have them replaced---for political reasons---he had already decided to influence the design of the order of battle to keep them under his thumb as much as possible.

It was Johnston who, in traveling east from Missouri, had brought the first word that Tennessee had exploded in its own mini-civil war. He had thought about staying on to fight Colonel Crockett and his Dominionists. But the issue would be decided in Virginia and so he had hurried on to Richmond. Calhoun and Gratiot had welcomed him with open arms and General Gaines had quickly arranged for him to assume direct responsibility for preparing the Army for battle. It was going to be strange, going up against the blue uniform…

But the South's destiny was south and southwest: Mexican Texas and beyond, Cuba, even California. He was a soldier and he was a Southerner. The choice had not been difficult...

Carlisle Barracks, Pennsylvania
September 28, 1833:

Sylvanus Thayer was worried. Not about the build-up of the Army; the volunteers were arriving in surprising numbers. Even Ontario had sent a regiment after successfully appealing to Van Buren about Scott's decision to restrict its participation to what amounted to occupation duty in Quebec.

Regulars were also coming in from the Northern and Western posts. The Chief-of-Staff agreed with Scott's plan to build the Carlisle army around this tough core; only enough officers and non-coms to establish order in the most out-of-control volunteer regiments were to be detached. *Though that might be more difficult that Scott expects, Thayer thought.*

That's why Brian Judge had been transferred from his Fort McHenry command to take over the 1st New Jersey. The Dutch farmers from Bergen and Passaic counties were not mixing well with the Irish-born volunteers from Newark and Jersey City. *Well, Judge is a Jersey native; they'll respond to his brand of discipline.*

Lt. Col. Savage was that rare officer who had risen from the ranks. Thayer didn't know where he had been born. But John Wool had taken one look at the 1st New York and removed its elected commander. *Damn it, these volunteers have to be taught that command isn't a popularity contest.* Thayer himself had suggested Savage when Wool's request had reached the War Department. Scott had grumbled a bit---"at this rate, my orderly'll be the ranking Regular in the defenses"---but had ordered Savage to Pennsylvania himself.

No, what worried Thayer was the weakness he had spotted that gorgeous day last May when Scott had unveiled his plans in the Commandant's Quarters at The Point: Wool and Worth were oil and water.

Wool was a crusty old veteran who guarded his prerogatives jealously. He had done a fine job of establishing the training facility here. Everything had run surprisingly smoothly, in fact, until Worth arrived to begin building II Corps. Worth had naturally begun issuing orders, diverting men and supplies. The key argument was over the Regulars, naturally. Wool had enjoyed first crack as the closest ones came in from Plattsburg, Fort Hamilton and other posts of the East. Now Worth was claiming the companies arriving from the Western outposts, men fresh from combat conditions and presumably tougher than troops "softened" by "easy" garrison duty back East.

That's why Thayer had traveled up from Georgetown; the first full-dress parade of the Carlisle army was good for morale, of course. But this situation had to be ironed out. The answer might be to reorganize the Regulars into two regiments...and assign one to each Corps.

And there was the nagging question of how heavily to rely on the half-pays. Thayer understood the concept but also wondered if he had detected the fatal defect: exactly why were they on *half-pay* anyway? Individually, that is? Why had London singled *them* out? For the overwhelming part, they had proven good peacetime officers. But how good were they at leading men when the lead was flying? If there were character flaws that had led London to place them on half-pay status, the heat of battle would expose them. Only then, it would be too late...

The Old Man thinks I worry too much. Maybe he's right; after all, he did serve with the British army in Spain and I did not. But worrying is what this damn chief-of-staff job is all about.

That and coaxing certain one-stars to act like field commanders, not children...

Richmond, Virginia
September 29, 1833,
1 p.m.:

One of the advantages of delegating authority, thought President Calhoun, *is that it frees up time to think and plan long-range.*

Calhoun utilized his freed-up time to take a daily ride. Out of the stuffy White House office and in the clear air, he could think and consider his options on any number of issues. Usually, that is.

Today Count Ignatieff was riding with him. The President didn't personally care for the Count---the man radiated danger---but as the official representative of the Confederacy's only ally, he had to be tolerated. That Ignatieff was indeed the Czar's representative was no longer in doubt; enough official paperwork had secretly arrived in Richmond from the Georgetown Consulate to verify his bona fides.

The two men rode within a protective cohort of CSA cavalry. Calhoun uncomfortably accepted, in light of Jackson's demise, his advisors' insistence that he be provided round-the-clock protection.

The irony was not lost on his companion…

"Well, Mr. President, rumor has it that General Scott is expected to begin his advance as early as next week. May I ask if your intelligence service has confirmed that as fact?"

Calhoun smiled his dark smile: "Rumor also has Wellington awaiting the arrival of a British army of immense size and power, my dear Count. Yet we have not confirmed that report, either…"

Ignatieff laughed as he tugged at his horse's reins. They were now moving out of the city and toward Camp Washington on its eastern outskirts. "I believe we are both comfortable with the fact that no British army is within 3000 miles of northern Virginia, Mr. President.

"In fact, one of my reasons for intruding on your ride was to report that the British are finding it exceeding difficult, apparently, to raise a coalition to force us out of Syria. As expected, Prussia has publicly declared its disinterest in the crisis; Asia Minor and the Balkans have no charm for Berlin. Louis Philippe likes being King of France; he intends no serious foreign entanglements. Only the Hapsburgs, apparently, can see further than the length of their very prominent noses. Vienna has joined with the Lion to seek our withdrawal…"

"Can you blame them? They've been waiting to grab the Balkans from the Ottomans themselves. And if you get long-term right-of-way through the Bosporus…"

The Count pulled off his hat and, bowing, swung it cavalier-fashion. "I salute you, Mr. President. Your grasp of European geopolitics, at this critical time…"

Calhoun was grim. "European geopolitics formed a part of the equation which resulted in our declaring our independence at this time, Count Nicholas. All such factors demand my grasp…" He pulled up slowly and leaned forward to pat his horse gently. "Much farther and we'd be at the Camp, sir. My presence causes too much of a fuss. I suggest we proceed northward instead." He indicated this to the escort commander.

Ignatieff nodded and pulled his own animal around. "Certainly, Mr. President. And if I may be so bold…will your army also be proceeding north…in force?"

Calhoun was silent for sometime. Finally, turning to the Russian, he grimaced: "Unfortunately, I'm told that will be the case sometime next month. All indications are that Scott is training a massive force to lead against us before winter sets in. The Northern press is screaming for a march on Richmond. The pressure on Van Buren must be enormous. And I'm sure Wellington is adding to it."

He looked over at Ignatieff and flashed his trademark dark smile: "The Great Man's reputation is at stake, you understand. Lord Grey sent him here confident his prestige alone would be enough to see emancipation through. It's all blown up in front of his hook nose. Now he needs a quick and thorough Dominion victory. Otherwise, he'll be looked upon as having thoroughly botched his assignment. On top of his rather ill-regarded term as Prime Minister, it would negate Waterloo and those other military campaigns he came so agonizingly close to also botching."

Ignatieff pulled up and looked Calhoun in the eye. "Can you defeat the Dominion army, Mr. President? And is there anything I can do to help?"

Calhoun shook his head. "Unless you can speed us those military supplies you've promised---and get them through the blockade that's reported to be forming off the coast---I fear not, Count Nicholas.

"As for our chances for success? Well, I am relieved that General Taylor has arrived to take active command. It has boosted morale among our professional officers. And I am told our professionals---officers and non-commissioned officers alike---are pleased with what they've seen of our troops. However, the Yankees do have one major advantage, as my Secretary of War keeps reminding me.

"*They* have General Scott."

CHAPTER FORTY-FIVE

War Department
Georgetown, D.C.
October 1, 1833, 12:30 p.m.:

An exhausted Capt. Thomas Wilder rode a tired Bay Ridge, as hot, dusty and thirsty as he was, up to the War Department and gratefully handed him over to a private who volunteered to take the magnificent animal to the rear stables.

Looking up the steps, he discovered Generals Scott and Thayer coming down, apparently heading for dinner.

"Well Captain. Looks like you've been doing some hard riding. Anything new for General Thayer and me to chew over, or can we enjoy our noon meal for once?" The two generals paused at the bottom of the steps and casually returned Tom's hasty salute.

"I don't wish to spoil the generals' appetites, Sir, but the Rebs have advanced as far as Fairfax Court House. I ran into their pickets about dawn."

The two senior officers stared at each other. "Fairfax Court House! Why that's only 12 or 13 miles from here. In what strength?" Even startled, Scott got immediately to the core of the issue.

"Closer to 15 miles, sir. Right behind the Court House itself, on Old River Turnpike. It was cavalry, about 30 men, but they camped there last night. It wasn't a scouting patrol, General. More like an advance party. Had to get out of there after a couple of their pickets spotted me... but they didn't follow. Looks like they are setting up their line right there."

Thayer licked his lower lip and looked at Scott. "So they're over Bull Run, eh? Looks like they want to make the fight as close to Georgetown as possible..."

Scott indicated at Tom's holstered pistol. "Use that thing?"

Tom nodded. "Yes Sir. I was a little north of the Court House, off the connecting road. I think they call it Ox Trail or Ox Road, I'm not certain. Was trying to work my way down to get a closer look at the camp when they changed guards around 8 a.m. The fresh Reb saw me and they both got off a shot. Didn't come close, though. I don't think either one was very familiar with their muskets. In any case, I fired back and they both hit the ground. Gave me enough time to get back to Bay Ridge, who was tied up about a quarter mile back in the woods. They never chased me."

"Did you hit either one?"

"May have winged one of them, Sir. Hard to tell, they both hit the ground almost simultaneously. Someone got off a couple more shots, but I'm pretty sure it was from a hand gun. As I reported, there was no pursuit."

Thayer nodded. "Sounds like they're setting up a defensive line, all right. Orders likely are to protect the perimeter, but don't advance any further. Cavalry, you said. Were they this 1st Virginia we've heard so much about?"

"I don't think so, Sir. I got close enough to make out their flag. The reports from Harper's Ferry and Fortress Monroe mention blue flags. This outfit was flying a red flag with a white star in the middle."

Scott wiped his brow. The equatorial summer heat showed no signs of abating; in fact, the humidity today was July-like. "Maybe they've adopted a common banner. Or maybe they were from another state. That could account for the non-pursuit: they aren't that familiar with the area and are proceeding cautiously. In any case, they're bound to have more than one mounted unit by now…

"Very well, Captain. I'll expect a full report when we return. Then get some rest. I want you back across the river by 3 a.m. With a full patrol. This solitary scouting is very romantic and has been somewhat fruitful. But if the rebel army is moving up in force, I'll want reports sent back from the field. Be prepared to stay out 72 hours. Get up and down their line. How long is it…are they anchored or in the air…and in what force?"

The two generals began to head down the street before Tom could get off a salute. But Scott quickly turned.

"You omitted something of critical importance, Captain. How were these rebels uniformed?"

Tom reddened. Damn, how could he? "In blue, Sir. Not exactly our blue, a bit lighter. But blue."

"Keep that in mind when you get back across the Potomac, Captain. Your's won't be the only Dominion patrol over there. But just because you or your men see blue, it won't necessarily mean they're friendlies."

———————

Camp Washington
October 1, 1833, 3 p.m.:

Twiggs was seated on the hard chair his orderly had brought from Monroe, bent over a portable desk the sergeant had somehow acquired for him. *All this damn paperwork,* he thought, the sweat dripping from his forehead onto the official report he was preparing for Gaines. *We picked some year to secede... This isn't even Indian summer! Just a continuation of the real thing. If this weather doesn't break, Scott'll have a nice long campaign season. Till Christmas, maybe...*

There was a commotion outside his tent but he ignored it. *Sergeant Reynolds would pop his head in if it's something I need to attend to.*

The grizzled old sergeant, his black beard now half-gray, did open the tent but came to full attention once inside. "Sir, Colonel Johnston is here to see you. Should I bring him in?"

"No, Sergeant, too damn close in here for one man, let alone two. Tell the Colonel I'll be right out."

When Twiggs emerged, blinking in adjustment to the brilliant sunshine, Sidney Johnston saluted, a strange look on his aristocratic face.

"Pardon the intrusion, General, but a new unit has arrived. I thought you would want to greet them personally."

Twiggs squinted, his face quizzical. "Colonel Johnston, I thought we had agreed that all incoming regiments would be mentioned singularly after the Saturday morning parades..."

"I realize that, General. But this case is somewhat, ah, unique."

Twiggs could see that Johnston was trying to contain a smile. "Unique...Colonel Johnston?"

"Yes Sir. A truly unique opportunity, General. To welcome a new regiment...

"In French..."

Johnston pointed into a nearby field to a force of about 500 men in shiny new uniforms of dark blue coats and red trousers, the majority at attention with their muskets sparkling in the sun. Their apparent officers were also drawn up at attention, their swords extended upward at arm's length. Facing the formation was a single burly individual holding a stanchion harnessed to a belt around his waist. A royal blue banner divided into quarters by a thick white cross hung straight down from the pole's far end. Each blue quarter was centered by a single white fleurs-de-lis.

Twiggs stared and looked questioningly at Johnston. The Colonel could no longer suppress the grin.

"General, I have the honor to announce the arrival of the 1st Quebec Volunteer Infantry. Or, to be more precise, the 'Premiere Infantere Volontaires de Quebec.'"

The Residency
October 3, 1833, 5 p.m.:

They were all standing around Van Buren's big desk, staring down at the printed map of Northern Virginia that Scott was in the process of marking up. The G-G was as fascinated as he was appalled. He had never before attended a military briefing so the General's translation of a series of brief pencil-scratched messages from the field into an all-encompassing picture---however harrowing---was gripping.

"The rebels are maintaining an outpost at Fairfax Court House, nothing more," Scott was saying, pointer in paw. "At first we thought they might advance in force, but indications now are that it's a screen designed to mask their real build-up behind Bull Run. And, its there to alert them if we come straight on instead of moving toward either flank. They have similar detachments both northwest and south." He ran the pointer across the map in a semi-circle.

"Captain Wilder penetrated as far as Centerville here," he moved the pointer west several miles. "You can see this town's importance as a junction of several major roads, including the Warrentown Pike.

"Wilder says the rebels are not yet there in enough force to stop a determined push, but it is conceivable they'd make a stand there because of the juncture. And because these heights just west of the town are an ideal defensive position."

The G-G looked around the desk. Colonel Burr looked grave, pursing his lips…always a sign of his concern. Secretary Cass was scowling; whether at Scott's analysis or the rebels' audacity, Van

Buren couldn't tell. *At least Lewis seems to get on with General Thayer.* The new Chief-of-Staff was standing deferentially to the side and a step behind Scott. The G-G wondered with an inner chuckle how much he could see with the mountainous Winfield hovered over the map. Wellington and his aide, Captain Bratton, completed the group. The Duke studied the map carefully before pointing his right index finger well west of Centerville.

"It would seem more likely, however, might you not say General Scott, that the rebel army will make its stand here at the stream?"

"Yes Your Grace. If it is a defensive battle they want, that's where I'd make the stand. No matter which route we take---east, central or west---we'll have to cross Bull Run at one or more of these fords." He indicated a half-dozen or more from Sudley Springs Ford in the northwest to an unnamed ford close to the village of Manassas Junction in the south.

"But Zach Taylor's taken command now. At least, according to the Richmond papers, which exhibit as little regard for secrecy, apparently, as do our own."

He glared around the table, as if expecting to find a reporter hiding behind one of the others.

"Zach's unorthodox, to say the least. Audacious, is probably a better description. If he feels confident enough to go on the offensive, he could march his men up the Shenandoah and into Maryland. Plenty of open space there to maneuver. Could be looking to hit us as the main body is marching down from Carlisle."

Surprise and/or dismay were evident on all the faces around the table save General Thayer. Scott swung his pointer angrily.

"Their intelligence about our readiness and intentions is good. Too damn good, if you'll excuse my profanity. Why, their papers have even printed the make-up of our Georgetown defense force…and my appointment of Colonel Felton to command it. While we aren't even sure where this Camp Washington of theirs is located!"

Wellington broke the embarrassed silence that followed Scott's outburst by clearing his throat. "Yes, General, it does seem a bit odd that they have deduced the name of this militia leader, as well as the composition of this rather remarkably diverse force you've slapped together in the defenses. Yes…however, what is your estimate of the situation? Will they come at you and, if so, where?"

Point made and emphasized, Scott returned to the main issue. "As of now, gentlemen, we don't believe, based on our reconnaissance, that Taylor is moving out of this Camp Washington---wherever it is---yet in force. So the odds of a battle in Maryland are low. Yet, if he has our timetable, or gets wind of it before the week is out, it remains a possibility."

He looked around the table again at men now as grim-faced as he himself. "The odds are greater that we'll run into him somewhere due west of Georgetown. As far east as Centerville or as far west as Groveton. Depending on his inclination to take the offensive."

"And what is your *inclination* General Scott?" The G-G.

"Mr. Governor-General, *we* are going to Richmond."

War Department
Georgetown, D.C.
October 4, 1833, 10 a.m.:

"Bull, its 80 miles from Carlisle to Chain Bridge, give or take a few. The rebels don't appear to be bringing their main body up to contest the Carlisle army's march to Alexandria. But their cavalry can break the army's spirit before it ever gets to Virginia with hit-and-run, guerilla-style raids."

General Scott's blue-eyed drill-stare was focused on Col. Edwin Sumner, formerly commanding officer of the USBAA Dragoons, now commanding the USBAA Regular Cavalry.

"You will screen the army's route east of the Blue Ridge, moving out Sunday morning. It is essential our army arrive at the Alexandria encampment site intact. Seal off the countryside, west-to-east, from the Maryland-Pennsylvania line down. I'll be splitting the army at Gettysburg. Wool with I Corps will have the right or western flank, coming down the Emmittsburg Road. That's the one that concerns me. Worth will proceed on the Tanneytown Road. I don't see how he'll be harassed, if you work your screen movements efficiently and keep sweeping the country west of Wool's advance. The artillery will go with II Corps. They'll also have a cavalry screen, though smaller."

Sumner looked up from the map that Scott had been referencing. "Yes Sir. I hear N.B. Buford is back from Harvard Law School. Have you placed him in command of the artillery?"

Scott nodded affirmatively. "For the present."

"How many men will I have, General?"

"I've scraped together about 600. That's every Regular we've got here who's seen any mounted time. The ones previously assembling at Carlisle are now here in Georgetown. You'll have them all. The secondary force will have to be from the volunteer regiments. Gilbert Hodges will be in command, temporarily detached from I Corps."

Sumner's head jerked up. "The Englishman? A half-pay officer..."

The drill bore in: "Hodges has proven himself. And he was stationed at Carlisle. Sent him down to Harper's Ferry after the raid. So he's familiar with the line of march. He's a fine officer."

"No question, General. But commanding volunteers..."

"As far as they're concerned, he's USBAA.

"Now then, see to your command."

———————————

Cranford Plantation
October 10, 1833:

Lucille Latoure knew she should be infuriated. The Yankees at Cranford! Instead, she was gleeful.

When General Thayer had arrived, unannounced, at Cranford late last month to negotiate with her mother and sister to rent the western portion of the plantation as part of a staging camp, she had been in Georgetown, energetically seeking information to pass on to Richmond.

Jaine's hastily scribbled note blandly announcing the deal had sent her scurrying back to Alexandria. The two sisters enjoyed a hysterical private laugh when Lucille walked into the mansion: here she had been in the capitol, her ear to the ground seeking any bits of gossip, rumor or hard fact to pass on to the CSA! And now the Chief-of-Staff of the USBAA was handing them the biggest intelligence coup of all: access to the Yankee army. They'd be able to inform Richmond of the exact date the Yankees were marching! And, possibly, even the route!

———————————

Camp Washington
October 11, 1833:

Maj. Jefferson Davis was incensed. His personal code of pride, honor, duty and courage had all been compromised.

Major Davis had accepted his assignment as temporary aide de camp to the commanding general of the Confederate Army with the understanding that once they'd reached Virginia, he would be transferred to the line. Now the first regiment of Mississippi troops had arrived and this Englishman, this Major Bassett, refused to relinquish command to him! And General Taylor refused to remove him!

Bassett wasn't a Mississippian, even if he did manage to marry the Governor's daughter. He, Jefferson Davis, should be leading them!

Everywhere Major Davis looked in this Army men he had attended West Point with, less-qualified men, without doubt, had commands: Robert Lee was here, commanding a regiment of Virginians; Luke Beaufort was off in Maryland with his cavalry! His old friend and mentor from The Point, Sidney Johnston, had tried to calm him down, saying it was only his professionalism that kept Taylor's eccentricities from turning the entire command structure into chaos. *True enough, but...*

If truth be told, though Davis would never admit the obvious, it was the idea that Joe Johnston had tacit command of the artillery that drove him over the edge. Old Prior of South Carolina---a relic of 'Mad Anthony' Wayne's days as Army commander, for God's sake--- had official command. But Johnston would lead the guns.

Davis had never forgotten or forgiven that night in Highland Falls when he and Johnston had stepped out the backdoor of Benny Havens' tavern and taken off their jackets. Johnston had dropped him with a hard combination to the jaw after lowering his guard with a shocking right upper cut to the stomach that left him gasping for air. The bastard had then gone back inside and claimed Dora, Benny's beautiful waitress daughter, as his prize.

That he himself was now officially engaged to Sara Knox Taylor changed nothing, in Davis' view.

And he was entitled to the command! It was inconceivable that he'd be pushing paper while some half-pay Englishman led real Mississippians into the fight...

———————

Liaison Office
I Street
October 13, 1833, 5 p.m.:

Dave Harper paced the conference room floor nervously. He had ridden here directly after saying his farewells to Caroline at the Consulate's F Street gates. He had urgent information for Captain Bratton.

The Captain was not in the building but Major Layne had sent a messenger after listening to Dave's news. Sir John Burrell had also been summoned and was speaking quietly with Layne as they all waited for Bratton, who they could now see riding briskly up Pennsylvania Avenue from The Residency.

Layne wasted no time once the Captain was in the room and had safely shut the door. "Well then Mr. Harper. From the top and include every detail."

Harps quickly painted the picture: as his 'friendship' with the Countess had progressed over the summer, and especially since the disappearance of Ignatieff at the same time as the Jackson assassination, he had gradually gained more access to both the Countess and the Consulate. In fact, he had even been invited for dinner on occasion. Today, however, he had been barred entry. Even at the gates he could sense a renewed level of tension. And when Caroline did appear for their customary Sunday ride some 40 minutes later, the Cossacks were back at her side.

Their day had been a failure. Caroline had been morose, agitated and nervous; not at all the Countess he had come to know. While they picnicked, the Cossacks just out of listening range eating their own meal, she had explained: sometime in the darkness of early yesterday morning, Count Ignatieff had returned. She had been astonished; her father had inferred that Ignatieff would be in St. Petersburg or perhaps Syria by now. They had not mentioned him all summer!

Ignatieff's presence had everyone at the Consulate on edge. He had spent Saturday exercising and conferring with Count Renkowiitz and the security chief, Captain Drago. Her father had been pale and worried last evening; he had cancelled his usual dinner arrangements with M. Jean-Claude and remained at the Consulate. Ignatieff himself had disappeared late in the afternoon but was back in the compound when David had arrived. Whether Ignatieff was still holed up there now was anyone's guess; Caroline had no idea what his immediate plans were.

Layne and Bratton exchanged several stares during Harper's recital. When he concluded, Burrell was pacing the room, while Bratton seemed to study the ceiling. It was Burrell who spoke first:

"A good report, Mr. Harper. I'm sure the Duke will add another letter to your growing file. But the report is incomplete. We must know the reason for this jackal's return...and know it forthwith."

"Actually, Sir John, I think we already know the reason. It is the subject that Countess Caroline must provide." Bratton stared once again at David. "We can assume our Russian fiend has returned to further destabilize the situation. Some act of sabotage that would add significantly to the turmoil."

Dave's baffled look gave testimony to his confusion. "I don't understand. I mean, I assumed...hasn't he been stalking the Duke all this time? With the Empire and Russia at each other's throats in the Middle East..."

The three Brits looked at each other. The secrets of Jackson's assassination were plainly not common knowledge, even in their government. It was Bratton who spoke: "I commend Lieutenant Wilder's professionalism. No, Mr. Harper, His Grace was not the original target. Though he may now very well be...

"In any case, you must convince the Countess to help us. She must ascertain and relay Ignatieff's plans. What do you say? Can you get word to her?"

"I can try. We were planning to go to dinner tomorrow evening. The Golden Eagle has reopened you know, as a restaurant; it's called 'Grant Street Cafe' now..."

"We'll expect a report then, first thing Tuesday morning. We're counting on you, Mr. Harper. I can assure you both the Duke and the Governor-General will anxiously await your report. But take care, sir. This Ignatieff is a very dangerous sort. Both you and the Countess must utilize every precaution."

The two officers had their heads together even as Sir John escorted Harper to the door. As he turned to rejoin them he smirked at Bratton. "Dangerous sort, eh? I'll say. His dozier lists eight confirmed professional killings. To say nothing of masterminding Jackson's murder..."

"And the woman." Major Layne.

"Actually Robert, the unfortunate Joanne was his second female. Seems he got the habit while in London. Scotland Yard has confirmed that, while in an apparent drunken rage, he caused the death of an Embassy maid..."

"Ghastly." Sir John shuddered. Then: "Do you think young Harper could be right? That it's the Duke he's after this time?"

Bratton rubbed his chin as he considered the possibilities. "Well, if we proceed from the assumption that his mission all along has been to cause trouble enough over here to divert or weaken us in Asia Minor, would killing the Duke move that mission?"

"Do you mean that the commotion it would raise at home---if attributed to the rebels---would force Downing Street to send an army over here to help put down the rebellion?" Major Layne was dubious.

"Yes, it does seem a stretch..." Sir John nodded and looked at Bratton. "But I suppose we have to consider it..."

The Captain was hard-faced. "No possibility can be discarded. Even if-and-when we hear back from young Harper and his charming friend. For now, we assign round-the-clock Royal Marine protection to the Duke. And immediately resume the same sort of surveillance at the Russian Consulate. We sight him, we grab him."

Harry rose and headed for the door. "I'll brief His Grace on the situation. And appeal for imposition of the Extremity Rules..."

There were no objections from the table.

CHAPTER FORTY-SIX

Catoctin Mountain, Maryland
October 17, 1833, 11:15 a.m.:

The sweat poured down the Sergeant's face in multiple steady streams. He wiped the back of his hand on his brow for the umpteenth time this morning and looked over at the big blond kid wearing the expensive gray jacket with the new gold lieutenant's bars on the collar. The Sergeant, whose lean weather-beaten face led many to mistakenly believe him a decade older than his 32 years, didn't begrudge the planter's son his commission. After all, the kid had been awarded it for gallantry at The Ferry.

It was more that the boy, who this time last year was attending the university at Charlottesville, was too reckless, at least according to Ike Smith. The Sergeant, a hunter out of the Shenandoah Valley who had never been in an army before either, had gotten to know and respect First Sergeant Smith over the past few months. "Courage is fine but impulsiveness is stupid," Ike had said when the battlefield commission had been announced after they had returned to Camp Washington. "Deadly, too. For him and his command..."

Ike had known the boy in the college town, apparently. He'd liked and helped him as the 1st Virginia was forming. But he had warned the Sergeant---like he'd warned all the non-coms---about the university boys. "Arrogant. Reckless."

Now the kid---the Lieutenant---was in command of this patrol on the northeast slope of the Mountain, a few miles southwest of Emmitsburg. And neither Smith nor the Major were here to rein the boy in. *How the hell did we end up this far north? Damn near in Pennsylvania. And all alone...*

"That's interesting." The Lieutenant handed the Sergeant his field glasses. The Sergeant still wasn't used to them and took some time to adjust the sightings. What came into view finally stunned him: a long blue snake withering all the way back to Emmitsburg and headed southwest, probably towards Frederick.

539

There were some murmuring and low whistles among the boys, at least the ones with good eyes, as the blue snake slithered closer. When the Lieutenant continued to stare, as if transfixed, on the snake, the Sergeant put up his own hand to quiet them.

"What do you make of it, Sergeant?"

"I reckon it's what they sent us to find, Sir."

"Agreed, Sergeant. But we need to get closer. Can't tell from this distance how many there are."

The Sergeant shook his head in disagreement. *This is what ol' Ike meant. Impulsive. Reckless of his command.* "No need, Lieutenant. We stay put here a few hours, out of sight, we'll see the whole parade come by. Close enough to make a fine report."

"Hell no, Sergeant. We stay here and the head of the column'll be five miles down the road in a few hours. Some other patrol will run into them and get their report in first. No. We saw 'em, we count 'em and we get back to Turner's Gap. I'm filing the first sighting of the damn Yankees. After all, we're the ones who penetrated damn near into Pennsylvania."

A more experienced sergeant would know how to talk this boy around, the Sergeant thought. *My inclination is to cold-cock him with my Kentuck rifle butt. That won't do, though...* "Well Lieutenant, maybe if we proceed kind of along side them a ways, we can get the information we need." *Without getting our asses shot off moving down into open country...*

"Parallel 'em, you mean? Not a bad idea, Sergeant. We can get a better idea of their strength and destination and then head back over the Mountain to Headquarters at the Gap."

They moved out in single file, heading south along the road, a path, actually, that ran the length of Catoctin. An experienced commander---or an experienced sergeant---would have put someone "riding point"---out front a hundred yards---to scout the terrain immediately ahead for sign of the enemy. The Lieutenant, however, was engrossed in estimating the size and composition of the blue snake that moved slowly but relentlessly down the road. The Sergeant had dropped back to make sure the boys---there were 12 riders in all---didn't straggle or make themselves visible to the blue infantry.

The Lieutenant, virtually born in the saddle, was casually riding first, the reins in his left hand and his right holding the saddle horn lightly, body shifted at a 45-degree angle to the left as he studied the column coming down the Emmitsburg Road. The first shot blew him into the tall grass lining the path, the bullet penetrating the breastbone to the right of the neck and exiting from under the left shoulder blade.

The fire of the USBAA Regulars converged on the patrol from the woods on the flank and rear. Two more troopers dropped immediately, while a third was thrown clear of his terrified, bucking horse. The Sergeant's own horse reared, but he regained control while simultaneously drawing his pistol, the rifle dropped when the animal jerked his front legs skyward. It was that bucking and lurching that saved him and kept him in action momentarily. He fired wildly into the brush, all the while knowing the futility of the effort.

Damn, so soon?

The shot that knocked him off the horse got him on the right shoulder. His pistol went flying into the air as he tumbled backward. It was the rock that did the most damage. His head caught it squarely and blood and brains emptied out backward to form a dark, spreading pool. He never knew the Lieutenant had somehow staggered up, impossibly reaching for his own pistol, when a Dominion corporal old enough to be his father, coming up from behind, terminated with a close-range pistol shot through the throat.

After the initial blast from their muskets, the dismounted Regulars, who had been tracking this particular CSA patrol since late yesterday afternoon, finished off the firefight with their pistols. Then they grabbed the fallen muskets, equipped with ugly-looking bayonets that made them resemble short lances, and charged. The few Confederates on their feet---the entire patrol had dismounted, some more voluntarily than others---threw up their arms and begged to surrender.

It was over in less than a minute. The Regulars unveiled the Stars and Stripes and waved the flag toward the column now halted in the road. The distant cheers and huzzahs were dimly audible...

Camp Washington
October 18, 1833:

"Thanks to the transfer of Fortress Monroe, I believe we can safely rule out an invasion from the Peninsula. And assume that the Dominion invasion will come somewhere along this route." Zach Taylor traced a route due west from Georgetown.

President Calhoun stared down at the map but made no comment. It was Secretary Gratiot who posed the question. "Will you utilize the natural defenses of Bull Run, or do you want to take them on in the open?" He was careful to avoid indicating his own preference, which, as an engineer, was to take advantage of the natural defenses afforded by the long, winding stream.

Taylor grinned. "What do you think? Charlie… of course I'll make use of the Run. Be a damn fool if I didn't. The question is whether Scott'll come west," he pointed to Sudley Spring, "or down here by Blackburn's Ford and this unnamed one."

The President was confused. "You mean he won't just come straight on? Scott is a battering ram. I'd have expected him to come right down the Warrentown Pike."

The Secretary and the two generals---Twiggs was also hovered over the map in Taylor's quarters---exchanged smiles. "That's a given, Mr. President. If there's anyone who'll try to ram his way through, it'll be Winfield Scott. But he's sophisticated, too.

"He'll attempt to stretch us thin by dividing his force. Thing is, he won't have enough troops to come from both flanks and the center. It'll be the Warrentown Pike plus one of the others. I'm betting he'll go east." Taylor's finger moved from Blackburn. "Two short, powerful drives. Easier to hook back up once across, too. That's from his perspective, of course. Getting across, I mean…"

The others laughed, somewhat nervously in at least one case.

"Une Maison Sans Danger"
6th & G Streets
Georgetown, D.C.
October 18, 1833, 9 p.m.:

Dave Harper was unaware of the phrase "safe house." Nevertheless, tonight he was being introduced to the concept, though his French lover referred to it as a "une maison sans danger."

Discreet residence it apparently was; Jacqueline Jean-Claude seemed supremely unconcerned that the Counsel-General would burst through the door at an inopportune time. (This being their first rendezvous since the Army set up camp at Cranford, turning the guest cottage into a temporary headquarters building.)

"No Cheri, Jacques is out of the city...if such a term can be applied to this miserable little village." Her smooth ageless naked olive-skinned body glowing as always after their initial mutual assault, she seemed to glide across the room, carrying a tray with a bottle of Bordeaux and two glasses. "He'll be gone at least overnight."

Harps quickly rose from a prone position to balance on his left elbow. "Left the city? This is a strange time for traveling..." The crisis had raised even David's previously dormant intelligence instincts: *was it possible the French C-G was secretly in cahoots with the Rebels?*

"Ah Cheri." Jacqueline fondly rubbed the back of one hand on Dave's check while handing him a glass, which she promptly filled. "Like us, the Russians maintain une maison, as, I suspect, all the consulates do. Being Russian, of course, they probably have more than one... At any rate, Jacques and Count Karl rode out this afternoon to inspect one of their's somewhere north of the city. The Count wants to see if perhaps it would be feasible in case of a siege."

Harps found himself personally offended: "Do they think so little of our Army that they expect a mob of motley Rebels to come charging across Chain Bridge and overrun our own capital?"

Jacqueline sighed a smile and kissed her younger lover lightly on the lips. So unsophisticated. Except in l'amour...how exciting...how lucky...to have been the teacher of such an apt student...

"We are Europeans, my darling David. We have seen all too much of war. Bonaparte burned Moscow; the Terror in Paris... These are simply precautions. And besides, the more une maison sans dangers the Russians have to inspect, the more time we have to enjoy this one... Ah, I see you're becoming ready. So soon and so well..."

Liaison Office
Pennsylvania Avenue & 21st Street
October 19, 1833, 8:30 a.m.:

"So you think Ignatieff may be hiding out at this 'discreet residence' somewhere north of the city, eh?"

Harper was sitting at the big conference table, sipping tea and reporting his suspicions to Major Layne, the only one of his British contacts up-and-about yet this Saturday morning.

He had left a purring Madame Jean-Claude at the side street maison and come directly here. Jacqueline said she expected the two C-Gs back in early afternoon, but would get word to The Deerhead if there was a change of plans that would leave her free again this evening...

He had performed to her satisfaction---her own responses had made that clear---after their interesting interlude conversation, but his mind was elsewhere during those periods when she drifted off to sleep (or, perhaps, passed out).

Caroline had told him during a second dinner at the new Grant's Street Cafe---which featured Italian food, a first for Georgetown---that Count Ignatieff had disappeared again. Her father had confessed, however, that the Count was still in the Georgetown area. His demeanor had been plain: whatever Count Nicholas was planning shocked and appalled him.

All in all, it had been a bad few days for Count Karl, his daughter sadly reported. Harper now began to tell Layne and the just-arrived Captain Bratton her indignant tale.

According to Caroline, Renkowiitz, as the British officials undoubtedly already knew, had been called to both The Residency and the Liaison Office. He had returned from the former even paler than from the latter.

Her father had endured a fierce harangue, he had told her more in dismay than anger, from the Governor-General. Van Buren read verbatim from the Richmond newspaper reports hinting at recognition and an alliance between the Double Eagle and the Rebels. A formally correct Duke of Wellington had later icily reminded the Count that as the King's official representative in British America---and therefore responsible for foreign policy---he could justifiably ask for Renkowiitz's credentials in light of these Richmond reports, coupled with the burgeoning Syrian crisis.

"Perhaps even worse," Caroline had said in a shocked whisper, "was an incident after my father left the Governor-General's office. Before he could leave The Residency, he was accosted by Mr. Frank Blair and a tiny, aged man he described as uncannily resembling the G-G. They took him into a small office---just a closet, apparently, near the Portico---and threatened him!"

David, who had listened to her tale in somber silence, weighing the possibilities, couldn't resist a smile. "Dear Caroline," he jumped at the opportunity to reach across the table and take her hand, "perhaps being somewhat upset, he misconstrued the conversation, overreacted to their words…"

Caroline's eyes blazed in a way that surprised and fascinated him. "No David, Papa *misconstrued* nothing. This old man---Papa said he was virtually identical to Mr. Van Buren though obviously older---reached up on his toes and roughly jabbed Papa in the chest with his walking stick. Accused my father of complicity in the murder of Mr. Jackson, which they claimed Count Ignatieff arranged! As well as another American, a woman." Tears began to surface in her eyes.

Though he had never witnessed this brand of emotion from her before, David was sure the tears were legitimate. He now pressed her hand between both of his while thinking rapidly. *Of course! Lawrence didn't necessarily strangle Joanne! Maybe Ignatieff put him up to it before he dispatched him to Capitol Hill. Or, maybe, sent the idiot bartender on his way, then killed her, himself, so there'd be no trail leading back to him, Count Ignatieff! And Bratton warned me he was* dangerous! *Sometimes these damn Limeys carry this understated business too far…*

"I'm sure Mr. Blair and this old man didn't speak for the G-G, dear Caroline…"

"Oh David, I'm so worried. Wasn't all. The room was very small, you see. That horrid old man kept forcing my father back until he fell against a desk. Then he grabbed my father by the lapels of his coat. Said he and Mr. Blair had been close friends of Jackson and took his death personally. Said they intend to track down Count Ignatieff, whom they had been informed is back in Georgetown. Said my father would never see Baltimore, much less the Baltic Sea, unless he told them where Nicholas is."

"And…"

"My father claimed diplomatic immunity and threatened to file a formal complaint with the Liaison Office. That damnable old creature told him to 'stick his diplo…' well, sneered at him, so to say. Reminded him they were private citizens. That his diplomatic immunity didn't impress them."

Despite the gravity of the situation---and Caroline's emotional condition---Harper had all he could do to keep a solemn face. "And…"

545

"Mr. Blair removed that awful old man's grip on my father's coat and escorted Papa to the door. Told my poor father that he'd be under *American* surveillance---not British---from now on. That he better deliver Nicholas to them, dead or alive."

The Captain and Major Layne kept exchanging glances as the report poured out. Harry reached across and shook Harper's hand. "I congratulate you, Mr. Harper. Your brand of espionage is somewhat unique, but nevertheless productive. It may explain why our vigorous searches of Georgetown's back alleys and places of lesser repute have failed to turn up evidence of this fiend...

"So the Russians maintain at least one secret location here. Interesting. Apparently, Count Karl is using M. Jean-Claude as a sort of 'cover.' And now we know where the French residence of discretion is...

"Well, please continue your unique work. While we continue to seek out this Russki." Bratton glanced back at Major Layne as the trio rose from the table and walked toward the door.

"Though I wouldn't care to wager against Colonel Burr getting to him first. All in all, the fiend might well consider surrendering to His Majesty's Government. His fate might be a bit more...*civilized*. Don't you agree, hum?"

Samples Townhouse
Connecticut Avenue
October 19, 1833, 10:45 p.m.:

"So you passed the head of Worth's Corps this afternoon?" Candice and Thomas sat at a small table in her boudoir, drinking red wine and polishing off a cold buffet served earlier by grinning servants.

Thomas' dusty, sweaty uniform and muddied boots had disappeared for cleaning and he was now clad in a dressing robe after having enjoyed a warm bath. The Captain had arrived directly after reporting in at the War Department from another reconnaissance near Centerville some three hours earlier.

Candice, meanwhile, was now dressed in a ridiculously revealing black lace nightgown. The equally ridiculously revealing dress she had momentarily worn to greet him had also vanished.

"Yes darling, the column appeared on the Taneytown Road in front of Twin Peaks Thursday morning. I set out in my carriage early this morning and cleared it finally north of Rockville. Precious, where are they headed? Surely they're not going to camp them here in the city?"

Thomas smiled. Word of the Alexandria encampment was by now prevalent in Georgetown, but Candice had been at Twin Peaks for most of the past month. *Which still can't account for the ferocity of her hunger.* As dirty, unshaven and, yes, *rank* as he had been, she had launched herself on him the moment he stepped through the door. *Got to find a new description: 'insatiable' just doesn't do her justice...*

"They're headed for Alexandria, Candice, via Chain Bridge. The whole army's forming there. Some of the Georgetown defense force is already there and Wool's Corps is coming down from the northwest. I understand the engineers are almost done with a new bridge at Edward's Ferry."

"Then the fight can't be long off." The seriousness of her tone made Tom look up from the cold chicken he was devouring; it was his first meal in two days. The frowning look on her face was also more concerned than he could ever remember, her green eyes glistening in a most unusual way.

"Well, General Scott is transferring headquarters to Alexandria on Monday. He'll be coming back most nights, but I don't know how much of Georgetown I'll be seeing from then on. But, yes, the battle isn't far off. A few weeks, at most."

She stared at him intently as he resumed his assault on the buffet. Then:

"Eat hearty, darling. You're going to need your strength." The emerald eyes now began to glow as the frown dissolved in a smirk that emphasized the double entendre.

Still smirking, she rose and pranced over to the bed, before reclining onto it in a pose her beloved romance novels would inevitably have described as 'lascivious.'

Tom regarded her over a sip of wine. *We ought to send her to Richmond. She could wear out a division...if not the whole damn Reb army!*

Russian Une Maison Sans Danger
Maryland Countryside

October 20, 1833, 5:30 a.m.:

Capt. Arthur Goodwin glanced at the slowly brightening sky. He had arranged his platoon of 20 Marines in a circle covering the inconspicuous old farmhouse from every angle. If, as General Scott had informed him, the 'mastermind' of the Jackson assassination plot was indeed inside, the bastard had two choices: surrender or die…

He consulted his watch and looked over at the Dominion marshal who had apparently been out here yesterday.

On the ride up---they had left the War Department before midnight---Marshal Stubas had briefed him. Stubas had been assigned to track the Russian Consul-General's movements anytime he left the Consulate. Friday afternoon, Count Renkowiitz had ridden over to the French Consulate. A few minutes later, he and a dapper-looking middle-aged man Stubas' partner had identified as M. Jean-Claude, the French C-G, had emerged on horseback and ridden out of the city. Stubas and his partner had trailed them to this farm, where the C-Gs had tied up their horses and gone in. Yesterday, mid-morning, they had emerged with a third man, a wiry, black-haired man with a long, drooping mustache. Meanwhile, several farm workers and a stout woman of middle age had been in-and-out. After a set of formal European-style bows, the two C-Gs had remounted and set off back to Georgetown. The black-haired man had stood on the farmhouse porch watching until they were some distance down the road before going back inside.

What made Scott believe the 'mastermind'---until then Captain Goodwin, like most everyone else in Georgetown, had thought the crazy bartender had acted alone---and the black-haired man were one and the same, the General had not said. Goodwin's orders were simple: take the black-haired man, alive if possible. But take him…

"Well," Goodwin said, as much to himself as to Stubas, "there's no time like the present. Shall we proceed…?" Stubas nodded as Goodwin barked the order. The ring of Marines tightened its circle around the old house, sharpshooters utilizing trees and rocks where possible. Where not, the Marines went to the ground, piling stones in front to afford some semblance of protection.

"In the house. This is the USBA Marine Corps. We have you surrounded. Come out with your hands raised high." A rooster crowed in the barnyard.

Nothing…

Goodwin waited 60 seconds by his hand-held pocket watch. "I say again. This is the USBA Marine Corps. Surrender or we will commence firing."

Shutters opened on several second floor windows. Arms were outstretched and voices in an incoherent babble---at least to the Marines' Anglicized-ears---shouted down.

A white pillow or sheet fluttered from the cautiously opening front door. A stout woman emerged, followed by two men. Others came out seconds later.

No one resembled the black-haired man Marshal Stubas had seen talking with the C-Gs less than 18 hours previously. Nor did a careful, thorough search of the barn and out-buildings discover any cowering men.

Neither the woman nor any of the others claimed to speak or understand English. Though someone had obviously heard and understood the order to surrender...

Nicholas Ignatieff was a superb secret agent well versed in the nuisances of his craft. As soon as Count Renkowiitz told him of the disastrous series of interviews with Wellington, Van Buren and the civilian pair, he had realized it was time to move on. He waited until after dark, in case the two C-Gs had been followed. Then he rode several miles away and slept in a field under the stars.

The Count had slipped through the Americans' hands before the Marines were even enroute.

The White House
Richmond
October 20, 1833, 1 p.m.:

President and Mrs. Calhoun walked leisurely back from 11 a.m. services at Monumental Church on Shockhoe Hill. The assistant pastor, Reverend Norwood, had delivered a satisfying sermon favorably comparing the Confederate troops still arriving at Camp Washington with the Archangel Michael's fighting legions.

Generals Taylor and Twiggs were waiting in the parlor with the latest reports from the front.

"The column that the 1st Virginia sighted moving toward Frederick will cross at a bridge they're constructing at Edward's Ferry, probably starting tomorrow, Mr. President. Our sources in Georgetown say another column is coming down further east and will cross at Chain Bridge in the next day or so. They're both heading for this staging ground." General Taylor pointed to Alexandria. "Scott has set up a camp just west of the town, taking over land belonging to several plantations."

Calhoun studied the map. "That's less than 10 miles from our forward line at Fairfax Court House. We won't get much advance word when they march…"

"On the contrary, Mr. President, we think we'll know right down to the day. Mary Lee and her friends have been accurate thus far." General Twiggs smiled confidently.

"These young women…we rely on the reports of…*belles*?"

The two generals smiled. "Well, Mr. President, Scott's headquarters is apparently a converted guest cottage at Cranford Plantation, the Latoure family estate.

"These…belles…have, ah, front row seats. We expect to know almost immediately when the Yankees have completed their movements to the camp. After that, it's just a matter of time. Between our pickets, our other 'friends' in Georgetown and the Lee ladies, we'll know the date before Winfield finishes designing his line of march."

The Residency
Governor-General's Office
October 21, 1833, 9 a.m.:

"So your raid missed him by a few hours, eh? Slipped through your hands…too bad. This Russki is as sharp as Satan, apparently. Sounds like he never sleeps in the same place twice."

Colonel Burr looked at Wellington. "Well, damn it. He's got at least one less place to sleep, now. *If* he's aware we've hit this hideout."

The G-G had his elbows up on the desk, his tiny fingers forming a miniature tent. "This young fellow Harper. I recall him from my days at Interior. He's been useful, you say. I think he can safely be detached from his, err, 'official' duties and assigned to this manhunt full-time."

550

The Colonel chuckled. "The magnificent Jacqueline *and* the delectable young Countess. The boy's official duties obviously are not overtaxing him...yes, I agree, Matty, let's utilize him where he'll do the most good..."

The others smiled and the G-G turned to Wellington. "No sense having overlapping searches, Sir Arthur. I suggest we consolidate our efforts, as this is something of an emergency situation. I should think Captain Bratton to be charge, with young Harper and our Justice Department marshals under him. The Marines will also be available."

The Duke nodded affirmatively. "Agreed, Mr. Governor. We have to take this diabolical Russian off the board before he can create further chaos. Let's bring Harry in now and give him his marching orders. Also, it might be advantageous if you summon this young Lothario so we can hear firsthand what if anything he picked up on his, ahem, Sunday picnic."

The Colonel coughed discreetly. "If you gentlemen don't mind, I will join the search ...in an 'unofficial' capacity, of course..."

The old man's eyes narrowed and the familiar twinkle was gone, icicles now seeming to protrude from the sockets. In the Duke's mind's eye flashed a scene on a cliffside ledge overlooking the water, a hot morning sun breaking through the lingering fog, two hushed groups of men standing apart under trees while two small figures in shirtsleeves and vests stood facing in a clearing, pistols in their right hands pointing upward, awaiting the command to fire...

"...as I should very much like to meet this Russian myself."

Bethesda Meeting House
Rockville Pike, North of Georgetown
October 22, 1833
2:15 p.m.:

The wiry, clean-shaven bald man sat erectly on his horse in the shadow of the Presbyterian church. Even in the shade, the heat was intense and he took off his hat to wipe his brow, the head glistening.

At their meeting Saturday, M. Jean-Claude had volunteered to relay messages to and from him, so as to mislead the British, who undoubtedly had the Russian Consulate under constant watch. The Frenchman's help was especially appreciated now that Nicholas had confirmed that the Americans were also on his trail. He had watched the comedy at the farmhouse from a safe distance. The Marine contingent had awakened him as they rode by less than a quarter mile from his makeshift camp. He had followed, guessing immediately where they were headed.

Now he could see a single rider coming up the Pike. Surprisingly, it was Jean-Claude himself; Nicholas had expected to rendezvous with the Consulate's security chief. He waited as the Frenchman paused and looked around, then eased his horse slowly onto the meeting house grounds. The C-G's animal joined Nicholas' mount in nibbling on the plush grass.

"I appreciate the effort, Consul-General, even as I question the judgment; this is a risky business for the chief representative of a supposed neutral…"

"Nonsense, my dear Count. I am a familiar figure, riding in and around Georgetown on an almost daily basis. Nothing could be more routine…and my country has its own interest in seeing the Lion tied up in knots here in North America…"

"As you wish, Consul-General. However, you and Count Karl were almost certainly followed; the Americans launched a raid on the farmhouse before dawn Sunday."

"Sacre bleu!"

"Fortunately, I had taken the precaution to camp in the open fields. They found no trace of me. However, tell Renkowiitz to find another une maison sans danger. That one's usefulness is at an end. Now, what have you for me?"

Jean-Claude was visibly shaken by Ignatieff's news and glanced around nervously, to Nicholas' disgust. "Come Monsieur, quickly: what news?"

The C-G forced himself to concentrate on his verbal report. "They opened their Alexandria camp this morning. By tomorrow, their entire army will be across the Potomac. Word in the capitol is that Scott will march by week's end; certainly by this time next week." He wiped sweat from his eyes; Ignatieff grinned his wolf's grin and wondered how much was due to the heat and how much to his reaction to the news of the American raid.

"Is that all?"

Jean-Claude was continuing to shift nervously in his saddle. "My dear Count. Before I entered the diplomatic service, I served in the

Grand Armee. If I knew an enemy agent was lurking out here, I would send cavalry to sweep the area…"

Ignatieff nodded and grinned again. "So would I. And so have they. I have been dodging their patrols all morning. I found a quiet inn to pass last night, but it appears I must again take to the fields this night."

The C-G was shocked: "What, why I saw nothing coming up here!"

"Probably because they have swept the area and moved further north." Ignatieff was dry. "So you had best depart. However, did that fool Renkowiitz find out when Scott leaves for Alexandria?"

"I saw the General and a group of riders heading toward the Long Bridge early this morning…"

"Merde alors!"

"However, that does not mean he will stay in Virginia."

"What do you mean?"

"I do not think he intends to remain on his horse until the last of the Carlisle regiments has arrived. He may well be back at the War Department as we speak, after officially welcoming the first troops to Alexandria."

Ignatieff nodded. "Tell Renkowiitz to find out for certain. There is a small French café, the Ille de France, on 14th Street. Are you familiar with it? Good. Arrange with Renkowiitz to have a professional--someone cool and competent who can avoid being followed---meet me there in two nights: Wednesday evening, after 9 p.m."

Jean-Claude stared into the strange eyes. "You will risk coming into the city?"

Nicholas snorted. "Why else would I have come back? What I must do is better done on this side of the Potomac."

Jean-Claude was halfway back to Georgetown when, suddenly, he knew what the Russian intended to try.

Sacre bleu!

The Residency
October 24, 1833, 4 p.m.:

The Ignatieff group had taken over Tom Wilder's cubbyhole (it was, in fact, where Colonel Burr's memorable interview with Renkowiitz had taken place). As the Colonel observed: "There'll be no party planning at The Residency for quite some time…"

The group had decided, at its first meeting Monday, to place a watch on the French Consulate. The surveillance, however, hadn't been operational until Tuesday. By then, Jean-Claude had passed Ignatieff's message on to the Russian C-G. The surveillance had been fruitful, however: the steady stream of messengers and visits exchanged between the two consulates confirmed that, in all probability, they were working together.

But now a Russian messenger was on the Portico, having walked over, apparently, from the Interior Department. The Colonel's eyes twinkled wickedly as a doorman announced a message for Harper. "Well Mr. Harper, shall we see what this is all about? Perhaps the Countess needs some attention?"

David, reddening, rose and, walking into the hallway, accepted a small envelope from a heavy-set woman---he recognized her as Caroline's maid---who gave no indication of any sign of leaving. "Expecting a reply, Mr. Harper. Must be important…and immediate." The Colonel was now openly grinning as he watched from the cubbyhole's doorway.

The message was short and, on the surface, correct: "Finding my schedule for this evening unexpectedly cancelled, I am now free to accept your supper invitation at The Hungry Peddler, 7 p.m. Caroline."

Harps quickly scribbled his confirmation and handed it to the Russian woman, whose bright blue eyes betrayed an intelligence not otherwise apparent on her round peasant face. She turned without a word and shuffled toward the doors.

David watched her disappear across the Portico before turning to Burr with a strange smile on his face. "Countess Caroline has reconsidered, apparently, and accepted my invitation to dinner this evening. We're to meet at 7 p.m. at a local tavern."

The Colonel grimaced. "My congratulations, but I had hoped for something more…appropriate…to the present situation than a social engagement."

"But Colonel: I issued no such invitation."

Burr stared. "Captain Bratton and I will await your return. No matter what the hour."

Grant Street Cafe (The Golden Eagle)
Grant & 18th Streets
October 25, 1833, 1:30 a.m.:

Nicholas had not been happy when informed that The Eagle had reopened. But the report he had received from Captain Drago, via the French agent who had also delivered a well-stocked carpetbag, was that the upper floors were unoccupied. Apparently, the new management lived elsewhere...

He slipped out of his back room at the Ille de France at 14th & I Streets after midnight and walked head down, the brim of his wide hat pulled low, unchallenged and virtually unnoticed the mile or so towards the alley behind the Eagle. Those he did come across included the usual assortment of drunks, thieves and honest workers coming or going about their own business. With the Army now settled at the Alexandria encampment and the remainder of the defense force stationed northwest of the capitol, there were few soldiers in Georgetown. The police presence, of course, was virtually negligible. Lightly carrying the carpetbag in one hand, his other resting on a pocket-held pistol, he arrived without incident.

He extracted a tool from the bag and easily picked the newly changed lock on the kitchen door. He pushed open the door gently and stepped inside. No sign of life. *Drago is right: no one stays here overnight.* He grinned in the darkness: *fear of ghosts, perhaps?* He walked through the bar---nothing had apparently been changed---and dragged tables to the front doors. He piled them up to the top of the doorway and then pushed a second set against the first. Anyone attempting to break down the door would have a struggle. Quickly and quietly he made his way back to the staircase leading to the second floor. At the top he did not even pause to glance at the back boudoir where he had lived with---and murdered---Joanne. Instead, he turned toward the front of the building, to the small corner bedroom that one of the whores---he couldn't remember her name, only her wild blond hair---had used.

The door creaked but was unlocked. He strode toward the window overlooking the street. He opened it slightly; the air in the room was stifling. Going to his knees, he pulled out the prototype

French rifle the Consulate had provided him; it was capable of firing three shots before reloading. *Our army must get its hands on these,* he thought, idly; *if they can be practically produced en mass, they would change the entire equation of infantry battle tactics.*

After pushing the weapon's barrel through the window and experimenting with several potential angles, he finally was satisfied and pulled the rifle back down. He turned his back to the wall; he had several hours before his prey would most probably be riding by. Incredibly---a compliment to his iron nerves---he closed his eyes and napped.

Streets of Georgetown
October 25, 1833, 3 a.m.:

In light of the emergency, Captain Bratton and Colonel Burr had tossed protocol---and the constitution---aside. All fighting men must be utilized on this deadly manhunt...and that included the Liaison Office's contingent of Royal Marines.

His Majesty's forces were now surrounding both the Russian and French consulates, making no effort to keep their presence a secret. Major Layne himself was in command, with orders to arrest anyone who interfered...and to shoot to kill, if fired upon.

Captain Goodwin personally led the squad of USBA Marines who had broken down the front door of the Ille de France an hour ago and thoroughly searched the building. The angry French-born owner was roughly shoved aside as the Marines tore the place apart. Other Marines were busy taking up guard around The Residency and patrolling the streets.

Larry Stubas had mobilized his USBA marshals and they were questioning---none too politely---the various denizens of the night unfortunate enough to be prowling the streets.

This explosion of activity, like lava out of a suddenly erupting volcano, had resulted from the quiet words of Countess Caroline over barely-eaten meals at The Hungry Peddler.

Harper had found her waiting in her carriage, the usual Cossacks shockingly absent, when he arrived at 6:45 p.m. "We must act gay, as if nothing is amiss, even though what I will tell you is very shocking,"

Caroline whispered as they made their way to the dining room. The Residency had quietly secured for them an isolated back booth.

As Harps had been dimly aware, he had had a rival all these months since they had first met at The Residency Christmas party. As infatuated as Caroline was with him, she had also developed strong feelings elsewhere: for the USBA itself.

"I have grown to love this place, this Dominion of your's," she said in starting the conversation. "I cannot, somehow, see myself going back to Russia or following my father to another post in some petty dictatorship or fossilized autocracy."

She took his hand across the table gently, though her eyes were blazing: "Whether or not our relationship succeeds, dear David, I will not leave America! That is why I am now betraying Russia with the information I give you."

It took almost two hours for the story to play out, for she began with the sudden apparition of Ignatieff the previous winter. When she finally revealed her secret information, David was aghast that so much time had been wasted. He hurried her outside and packed her back in her carriage. Climbing in next to her, he yelled down at the outraged tavern owner, Steve, to send the bill---"with a big tip"---to The Residency. The carriage spun away, adding dusty insult to the man's injury.

Two minutes after jumping off at The Residency gates, he was relaying the news to Bratton and Burr...

———————

By 5 a.m. it was obvious that Ignatieff had eluded them yet again.

"So where will he make the attempt? Where can he hide until daybreak?" Colonel Burr banged his walking stick in the dust in front of the Ille. "Damn it, he's a foreigner. How many hiding spots in Georgetown can he have?"

Harry, David and the Colonel looked at each other in growing frustration.

"Chap's been here a considerable while, you'll agree. Appears he made use of his time..."

"Damn it, Captain Bratton. This is no time to get philosophical." Colonel Burr was as close to losing his composure as he himself could recall. "What time is the escort forming up?"

"There's no chance of dissuading him?"

"Captain Bratton, he just hit me with that stare." Burr shook his head. "Felt like a drill going through me. 'I'm due in Alexandria for reveille,' he says. As if the army will oversleep unless he's there to wake them up!"

Harps was silent. Some things the others had said were bouncing around in his brain. 'How many hiding places...' 'He's been here a considerable...'

"My God, I think I know!"

Bratton and Burr spun to look at him.

"If the escort proceeds normally, it'll pass by the War Department on the way to the Long Bridge..."

Bratton smile of condescension was barely visible in the predawn. "Come, my dear fellow. The fiend isn't likely to gain access to your own building..."

"Of course not, but what's just a block away? Right on the way, with second floor windows opening onto the street..."

"The Eagle! Of course! And God knows, he's familiar with its every nook-and-cranny." Bratton was calling for his horse. "The escort in all likelihood is already in motion. There's no time to spare. Tell Captain Goodwin to gather his men and meet me there!"

Before Burr and Harper could react, Harry was mounted and halfway down the street.

His eyes had always been very sensitive to light. Whether there was any correlation to the telltale two-color oddity, he didn't know nor care.

In any event, Nicholas snapped awake as the first dim glimmerings appeared in the dark sky. He remained motionless for a moment; although confident he would have heard anyone entering or moving around in the building, his training had taught him to be cautious. Convinced he was safely alone, Nicholas rechecked his weapons: the French rifle, his pistol and the dagger he always carried in his boot. The trusty two-shot derringer remained in the coat he had carefully placed next to him, along with his hat.

Ignatieff was counting on the inevitable commotion---shock, disorientation, aid to the victim---to ease his getaway from the building. Once in the street he would easily blend into the crowd. Just another Georgetown resident on his way to work...and yes, what *was* that noise over on Grant Street anyway? The Americans would soon blanket the area with troops but he was betting they'd concentrate their search in a northerly direction into Maryland (after having closed the Potomac bridges to all traffic, of course). To go south of the city would apparently trap him in a dead end peninsula...

With luck, though, he could make his way southwest of The Residency through Foggy Bottom to the banks of the Potomac. The same French security man who had met him at the Ille had been instructed to wait there with a small boat. He'd land somewhere south of Alexandria and make his way back to the Confederate lines and safety...

The sky was brightening. Did he chance opening the window and looking up the street? No need: from the sound of the hoofs, a considerable party of horsemen was approaching from the northeast.

Bratton started quickly but almost immediately became ensnared by the very troops he had ordered onto the streets. He was reduced to a slow trot even before he reached New York Avenue and continually forced to identify himself as he pushed on in the direction of The Eagle. He quickly considered and discarded the idea of abandoning the horse and continuing on foot; riding gave him stature, he looked more authoritative on the horse.

Maybe the bloody Russki's given up; maybe this show of force will convince him he can't get away with this...

No, if there's one thing I've learned about Ignatieff is that he'll allow nothing to stop him. Ruthless bastard! But good, very good! He's weighed the odds and thinks he can pull this off. Just didn't count on the Countess's conscience. He'll try it! Must get there in time...

Ignatieff saw the escort come down Grant Street, the point rider carrying the stanchion with the flag fluttering in the wind. Two riders in file on each side of the target, one bringing up the rear. Perfect! The Frenchman had informed him this was the formation they had utilized all week and he had made his plans accordingly. The rifle slid under the window that he now adjusted to allow enough room to maneuver without banging the barrel. His only concern was the recoil; he regretted he'd not had time to test-fire the weapon. But he'd been firing muskets and rifles all his life; he was used to having a weapon's butt crash back against his shoulder. He'd make the necessary allowances…

The target grew ridiculously big as the escort came into focus; the man was the size of a Siberian bear! His finger tightened around the trigger…

The first shot caused much of the havoc that followed: purposefully, Nicholas took out the horse of the lead rider nearest him. The animal collapsed in a heap, pinning the trooper under it as it trashed about. The second horse whined and reared, instinctively attempting to sidestep the tangle, its rider desperately struggling to maintain control. The primary target, visible momentary confusion turning almost instantly to outrage, now was in unobstructed view.

The shot should have knocked the General completely off his horse. But the massive Scott grabbed on to the saddle horn with his huge left paw and instead slid slowly off the right side of the saddle as the horse pulled up, incredibly without rearing up on its back legs.

Ignatieff wasn't watching; he turned slightly to get off a final shot at the back point rider, who was beginning to look up in his general direction. But by now the adrenalin was pumping too fast, even for Nicholas. Though he aimed for the chest, the shot went high. It blew a chunk of the regular's skull and brain all the way onto the wooden sidewalk. The trooper spun out of the saddle and collapsed into the street, rolling over onto his back close to the spot where his brains had landed.

Nicholas didn't wait to assess the damages. He pulled the rifle back in and dropped it on the floor, grabbing his coat and hat in the same motion. He strode quickly toward the hallway, pulling both on as he moved.

Harry heard three incredibly quick successive bangs before he rounded the corner from 17th Street onto Grant. *Three shots that close together? By God, has he recruited a bloody team of assassins?* He spurred toward the chaos. The carnage was evident: one soldier lying outstretched on his back; horses shying and shoving. Two troopers covering Scott, who leaned unsteadily against his horse; at least he was still standing. A horse down and another trooper attempting to drag a body from underneath it. Yet another soldier, this one holding a flag-attached stanchion, pointing to The Eagle and shouting for assistance.

Harry jumped off his horse and ran toward the side alley adjacent to the Eagle.

The Count raced through the hallway and down the stairs. No one was even banging at the front doors yet; with luck he'd be out the kitchen door and down the back alley before they even broke in. He sprinted through the kitchen, knocking over china and pots as he slid on floor grease and grabbed a carving table to catch himself. *Damn, could have turned an ankle! ебать этих поваров! (Fucking cooks!) Joanne at least always insisted the kitchen be spotless before they left for the night...*

Now he unlocked the door and took two steps down into the alley. Less than a hundred feet to the right a connecting side alley would lead him out to 18th Street. He sprinted toward it.

Captain Bratton pulled his pistol from his waistband as he ran up the side alley. He heard a door slam even as he skidded to a stop at the corner of the building and peered cautiously around. A man in a wide brim hat and coat was running toward the far end of the back alley, no more than 60 feet away. *It has to be Ignatieff or one of his team of assassins!* He stepped out, knelt and fired, using his left hand to steady the right.

The man glanced back over his shoulder and stumbled but regained his balance. He was closing in on the corner... *Bloody hell,* Harry swore, reaching into the waistband for his second pistol. *The bastard's going to make it!* He fired anyway...and the figure crumpled to the ground, rolling over into the connecting alley.

Both shots had missed but the Count had instantly realized at the sound of the first shot that he could not expect to lose himself on 18th Street if someone was chasing him.

He resolved to play possum---though he had never heard the maneuver so termed, of course---if his pursuer got off another shot. Otherwise, he'd wait for him at the corner of the two alleys. At the second shot he dived onto his left shoulder and rolled into the shadows extending from the back of the building facing 18th. And waited...

———————————

Harry reloaded as he walked cautiously up the alley. He doubted he could have more than winged the assassin at such a distance. He looked quickly up at The Eagle's kitchen door; suppose someone was hiding there in ambush? He jumped the steps and crashed through the door: no one in the kitchen. Quickly he turned and raced back outside. *Maybe the lost time would aid the wounded assassin; no matter, he'd have gone free anyway if someone was waiting there to blow my head off as I passed by!*

He continued up the alley at a steady pace. Now he was approaching the corner. The west side of the alley was still shaded. *Did the bastard get around the corner while I checked out the kitchen?*

———————————

Ignatieff watched him come on. *So, Captain Harry Bratton it is! We meet again...*

Nicholas stepped back and around the corner and aimed from the shadows. Bratton's reflexes were such that he was moving at the sound of boot on gravel. But his own boot turned over a small stone and he momentarily stumbled, still peering into the darkness. In that instant, Harry Bratton knew he was a dead man.

The Count fired, the weapon's spark giving away his position. But it didn't matter; what Count Ignatieff aimed for he invariably hit and he had aimed for the left side of Harry's chest.

The bullet pierced the heart and the big Brit tumbled backward, dropping his own reloaded pistols. One went off harmlessly, the bullet ricocheting off the walls. The other simply bounced toward Nicholas, who fielded it and stuffed it in his own waistband. He turned and ran around the corner toward 18th Street.

Pausing at the alley's entrance, he adjusted his hat and smoothed out his coat, vest and waistband. He walked purposefully but unhurriedly down 18th and across E and C Streets towards Foggy Bottom.

By the time a sorrowful Colonel Burr---his walking stick poking Harry's body---stood shaking his head over the corpse, Nicholas was crossing the Foggy Bottom marshes. The French agent was waiting on the Potomac bank as planned. They pushed the small boat into the River and rowed southwest towards Virginia.

CHAPTER FORTY-SEVEN

The Residency
October 25, 1833,
12:30 p.m.:

"Well, Mr. Governor. It looks like he'll make it, but he'll be out of action for some time."

The Secretary of War stepped into Van Buren's office direct from a visit to General Scott's bedside at The Infirmary on M Street. He was sweating profusely and not simply because of exertion, shock and fat; the incredible heat wave showed no signs of abating even as November approached.

Van Buren was in conference with Colonel Burr and a somber Duke of Wellington. Captain Bratton's shocking death was almost as catastrophic as the attempted assassination of Scott. Van Buren had just expressed the feeling that "the veneer of civilization seems to have shattered; have there been this many successive assassination attempts in one Western city since the fall of the Roman Republic?"

The Colonel, who had broken the difficult news of Harry's death to the Duke himself, looked up at Cass. "How long is 'some time,' Mr. Secretary? When will he be able to take the field?"

Cass hesitated. It was a delicate situation, with Wellington so obviously affected by the loss of the Captain. "Perhaps later, Colonel. The Duke..."

Wellington shook his head, the hook nose slicing the air. "No Mr. Cass, the Colonel is right. We must put aside our grief and look to the emergency at hand."

"Well, he's lost a lot of blood. Collapsed while they were awaiting the ambulance wagon, you know. Fortunately, the bullet struck him at the confluence of the chest and shoulder. But he lost more blood while they were carving it out. There's a serious risk of infection, from what I understand. As to your specific question, he'll not be fit for field command on the schedule as it now stands..."

The Attorney-General came into the room as the options hung in the air unsaid: wait for Scott; postpone the campaign until spring (no one could envision a winter campaign); or place one of the corps commanders---or someone else---in field command for the duration. Unattractive options, all in all...

"Well Mr. Butler, have we apprehended that *bastard?*" The G-G's vehement---and virtually unprecedented---use of the profanity shocked even his alleged father.

"Unfortunately, Mr. Governor, there is no sign of the...*bastard*. He seems to have vanished into thin air."

The G-G scowled and banged his tiny fist on the hard desktop. "How does he do it? How can a foreigner simply move among us so effortlessly and inconspicuously, commit his mayhem and just disappear? Does he have some sort of supernatural power?"

"For one thing, with the help of half the diplomatic corps, it would seem." Colonel Burr growled. "I'll wager Jean-Claude has a hand in this. We've had the Russian consulate under constant surveillance. There's no way they could have assisted him. Either the French are hiding him...or they've already helped him escape."

Wellington was as downcast as anyone had ever seen him. "I suspect the latter, gentlemen." He turned to Van Buren. "You may as well reopen the Potomac bridges, Mr. Governor. If he chose that route, he's long gone. And your cavalry sweeps north and south of the city, in my estimation, will also prove fruitless. As for the chances of him hiding out in Georgetown, well, I ordered the Royal Marines to a certain 'house of discretion' we have discovered the French maintain near 7th and M. If he was hiding there, we'd know by now...

"No, in my judgment, Count Ignatieff is back across the river in Virginia, well on his way to Richmond."

The Colonel was grave. "The Duke may well be correct, Mr. Governor. However, this Russki has outmaneuvered us at every turn. Better maintain close watch at the bridges. He may have gone underground here in Georgetown and plans to wait for the heat to die down, if you'll excuse my choice of words. Especially since the Russians may be maintaining 'une maison sans danger' here in the city in addition to that damn farmhouse our people raided last weekend.

"Now, as painful as it may be, I suggest we concentrate on who should lead the upcoming campaign. Or if we should have one at all..."

The others deferred to the Duke, the acknowledged military man among them. "I believe, gentlemen, that the campaign must proceed as planned. Both the Compact and the Constitution require it…"

Well now, thought the Colonel, *he's had another letter from Palmerston. The Russkiis must be setting up permanent shop in Syria…*

"The question then becomes: who shall be placed in command? That, gentlemen, I must leave to your judgment. Frankly, I have considered Winfield both invaluable and indestructible. I've not studied the list of possible replacements from within your ranks.

"In any case, that is a decision for you to make. Meanwhile, I've duty, unpleasant as it is, at the Liaison Office. The staff will be assembling for a private memorial service. I'm overdue."

The others rose and, with grave faces and formal nods, again offered their sympathies. After the Duke, who seemed to have aged a decade in a day, was shown out by the A-G, they all began to talk at once:

"Can't we wait for Scott? This damn heat wave may well extend into mid-November…"

"Maybe Thayer should take active command…"

"Who's senior, Wool or Worth?"

The G-G signaled for silence. "Gentlemen, one issue at a time. And one opinion as well."

Frank Blair, who had crossed paths with the Duke in the corridor, now entered the room and the conversation. "I've come from The Infirmary. Winfield has been given a sedative. The doctors are alarmed at the loss of blood. He'll be invalided for at least a month."

"Well, gentlemen, that answers the secondary question." The G-G was grim. "If we proceed with the campaign, we need a new commander. So, let us begin with the primary question: should we proceed?"

The A-G was first to break the silence that followed: "With all due respect to the Duke, the Compact and Constitution clearly do not set any timetables for a governmental response to an insurrection." The others chuckled knowingly as he continued: "However, politically, Mr. Governor, I don't believe you have any choice. The country won't stand for a postponement of operations until spring."

"To say nothing of the benefits in morale and preparation such a postponement would afford the Rebels." Colonel Burr was blunt.

Blair was nodding his head in agreement. "I concur, Mr. Governor. Politically, we've no choice. Not only would you almost certainly face resolutions of impeachment in the House---those abolitionists have the reins in their teeth now---but from what I can gather from Mr. Butler's comments concerning the Duke, the pressure from Downing Street to remove you would force Wellington's hand. No, postponement is not a viable option."

The G-G turned to his Secretary of War: "Well Lewis, you have your order. The campaign is to proceed as soon as possible, given the change in command. What recommendations have you on that decision?"

The beefy red face now drained of color despite the equatorial conditions in the G-G's office; without a hint of breeze, it was at least an oppressive 90 degrees. Only the Marylander, Blair, did not appear to be suffering.

"Mr. Governor, while my opinion of General Scott's abilities is not quite as...effusive...as that expressed by Wellington, I must confess that I too have not considered the possibility of this campaign proceeding without him. Forgive me, but I must consider those possibilities before offering my recommendation."

Colonel Burr made no effort to conceal his impatience. "Come, come, Mr. Cass. Matty isn't seeking an ironclad final recommendation. What are your options?"

The Secretary grimaced. *This damnable ancient hardass! Just because he's no turf to protect...*

"Well, technically, the Chief-of-Staff, I suppose, is first-in-line..."

"But Thayer has virtually no experience under fire." Colonel Burr.

"Yes, that is correct. General Thayer is an engineer by training and an administrator by experience. The only troops he's ever led are the Corps of Cadets. Anyway, he's vital in his present position..."

The G-G nodded firmly. "I agree. No sense upsetting the logistical applecart too."

"So, Mr. Governor, I suppose it is between Wool and Worth..."

This time, Blair broke into Cass' labored brainstorming. "Isn't there anyone we can reach down and pluck from the ranks? The Army must have produced some capable professionals below field rank?"

Cass smiled tartly. "Certainly, Frank. General Scott was nurturing an outstanding cadre of mid-level professional officers. Unfortunately, most of them went south…"

With malicious understated glee, the Secretary now extracted the proverbial knife he had just inserted in the General's broad back. "However, there may be some. Bull Sumner is an excellent officer. Our best horse soldier. But can he handle an army of two corps? The same question would apply concerning any others we might, as you say, 'pluck' from the ranks.

"No Mr. Governor, gentlemen. It's John Wool or Bill Worth. Or some combination of the two, along with Syl Thayer."

The ensuing silence, A-G Butler thought, was as loud as a groan. *No one is particularly happy with this…*

The G-G's sigh seemed to underscore Butler's opinion. "Well gentlemen, we don't have to decide this today. The main point is, we're agreed that the campaign must move forward.

"Now, I believe it behooves me to visit General Scott's bedside, whether he's conscious or not. And then I'll pay my respects at the Liaison Office." He paused.

"Captain Bratton might not have been the easiest man to like…that air of English superiority…but he was a damn fine professional.

"This devil Ignatieff," he shook his head, "to have bested a man like that…"

USBAA Encampment
Cranford Plantation
Alexandria, Virginia
October 26, 1833, 4 p.m.:

"It is the Governor-General's desire, gentlemen, that I assume temporary command but conduct this campaign at present from this encampment. You will remain in command of your corps in the field."

Brig. Gen. Sylvanus Thayer placed his orders on the command table and looked hard at Wool and Worth. "Now then, do we have General Scott's plan of attack? I have not seen the latest drafts."

General Worth spoke first, after an aide had unfurled a large, detailed map of the area from Georgetown west and south to the upper reaches of the Rappahannock River at the foot of the Blue Ridge near Front Royal. "I believe it is General Scott's intention to move due west, pushing aside the enemy forward lines at Fairfax Court House and Centerville," he traced the route with his right index finger, "and proceed along the Warrentown Turnpike to Bull Run, where the Rebels are known to be massing in force.

"Once in position, he intended to rely on the reports of our scouts as where to ford the stream, depending on the exact location of the Rebs."

"That is not my understanding, General Thayer." General Wool's voice was icy. "Once at Bull Run, we will cross in three columns, up at Sudley Springs," he ran his own right index finger up and around a series of hills until coming to rest north and west of the supposed Confederate concentration, "south of the Pike to one or more of the several available fords, while making the final thrust here where the Pike crosses the Run at the stone bridge."

"That's preposterous, General Wool!" Worth was aghast. "Divide two corps into three columns? General Sco…"

"A corps on each flank and the Georgetown defense force in the center…General."

Worth looked at Thayer with disbelief. "The Georgetown defense force? Why, all that's left of that are untrained volunteer regiments from the West. The Regular infantry has been broken up to form the core of the Army. The Regular cavalry is scattered all over Maryland looking for this assassin. Even when they return and are rested, you'd use them as dismounted troops? We need them to screen the advance…"

"Screen the advance…" Wool was dismissive.

"That's enough, gentlemen." Thayer's order came out more like a plea. *Dear God, how do I coordinate a campaign with these two hotheads? Scott has the personality for this. Me? I'm just a school master…Well, here goes…*

"I suggest our final plan will be predicated on the disposition of their army. I'm sure each of you has been privy to various options the General was considering, based on the location of the Rebel positions. Once we clear Centerville and are able to scout the enemy dispositions, we'll be in a position to ascertain which option to implement."

Wool scowled. "And when might that be, General? Obviously the original plan to move out tomorrow is now moot..."

Thayer nodded. "Correct, General. As were you, General Worth, in noting the absence of the Cavalry.

"The search for the would-be assassin, whom, you gentlemen may be surprised to know, is thought to be a Russian agent who apparently also masterminded the murder of General Jackson, was called off earlier this afternoon. The troops are to be rested and refitted." He nodded to Worth.

"It is the G-G's order that the campaign commence no later than Wednesday. You shall therefore prepare your commands to move at first light that morning, October 30. With the grace of God, we will find and crush the Rebels and put an effective end to this obscenity by Election Day, Tuesday, November 5."

The White House
Richmond, Virginia
October 27, 1833,
11:00 a.m.:

Jefferson Munroe stuck his head into Calhoun's office. "Excuse me, Mr. President, but Colonel Johnston is here with the latest reports from Georgetown." The private secretary paused. "I know you're due at Monumental Church soon, but there seems to have been some rather momentous developments..."

A minute later Albert Sidney Johnston, the 'beau ideal' of the Confederate forces, was briefing Calhoun. "Mr. President: shocking news via our 'belle express.' Two days ago there was an assassination attempt on the life of General Scott..."

"Dear God!"

"Apparently the General survived, but is badly wounded. The talk in Georgetown is that he'll be laid up for months and that the invasion may be called off until spring."

Calhoun's glasses had slid off his nose and he looked at Johnston in amazement. "This has been verified? Our sources...these young ladies...they are certain? I must confess, Colonel, I am not quite at ease with the idea of relying on...belles..."

"Well, Mr. President, the attempt took place in broad daylight, on that extension of New York Avenue west of The Residency that everyone still calls Grant Street. Scott was down in the street, so that part is verified.

"Miss Latoure is also a friend of Mrs. Scott and presumably had spoken with her before getting off this report. And, Sir, the young lady has other, err, 'sources' in Georgetown…"

"Yes, yes, she is---or was---a leader of society among the younger set…"

Colonel Johnston was smiling. "And, Mr. President, Major Beaufort informs me that her primary beau, whom everyone expected her to catch after he had chased her long enough, is Scott's pet aide, Lieutenant Wilder."

Calhoun stared at Johnston, unsuccessfully attempting to stifle the smile breaking out at the corners of his mouth. "By any chance has this lovesick young officer divulged the name of Scott's replacement? I assume one must have been chosen, given his supposed wounds?"

"Not as yet, it appears. But the note is dated Friday noon, just a few hours after the ambush. Perhaps another report is already making its way here…"

"I also confess I still find it difficult to believe their security is as loose as their lips appear to be, Colonel. Everything these…belles…have sent us thus far has checked out…"

"Indeed it has been most useful, Mr. President."

"…but could that be the plan: to feed us accurate information until we become accustomed to relying on it? And then to spring the trap of misinformation at the crucial moment?"

Johnston nodded grimly. "That of course is an option which must not be ignored, Mr. President, though I tend to believe the…belles…are not…puppets…of a sinister Dominion spymaster.

"The moment of truth, Sir, will come soon enough: if-and-when the 'belle express' announces the date and direction of the invasion. Or its postponement."

Cranford Plantation, Virginia
October 27, 1833, 9 p.m.:

Lucille wasn't the only Latoure becoming comfortable in the espionage game. Jaine, though inwardly raging at the Army's high-handed occupation of so much of Cranford, had made herself such a familiar figure riding and flirting with the officers as to become taken for granted. And thus able to ferret out choice morsels of military intelligence.

When Lucille had sent her word yesterday morning that the troika of Thayer, Wool and Worth would temporarily replace Scott (Lucille had overheard Frank Blair discussing the news with Maria Scott at The Infirmary), Jaine had not been in a position to immediately send it on. Thus, Thayer's appearance riding across the Plantation to the headquarters building later in the day had been confirmation. The news had been dispatched after dark.

This evening, Jaine was working on a choice new morsel. Among the USBAA officers who had fallen under her spell---for, though Tom Wilder would have angrily disparaged the very idea, many men considered her the fairer of the two fabulous sisters---was a slim, olive-skinned, remarkably handsome young Regular with jet black hair and eyes and a charming accent who answered to the name of Capt. Joseph Francis. This was an Anglized adaptation of his Fernandes surname, for his family was minor Kingdom of the Two Sicilies nobility. A youthful indiscretion with an older, married and resultantly-pregnant higher-ranking noblewoman had led to Giuseppe's hastily arranged appointment to West Point. An uncle in the Naples foreign ministry had friends in the British Foreign Office.

Now Captain Francis---'Crickett' to his men for his constant chirping while on the march from Carlisle---was among Jaine's most ardent admirers. While walking the Cranford gardens earlier this evening---at about the same spot where Lieutenant Wilder had broken the emancipation news months before---Crickett had chirped once more: the Army would be moving out Wednesday morning...he had grown so fond of her in so short a time...

Jaine, who carried an enclosed miniature of Luke Beaufort---though never in that young cavalier's presence---on a thin gold chain around her neck, had played the comedy through. Now she was composing an urgent coded message for Richmond. It would go before midnight...

Centerville, Virginia
October 31, 1833, 3 p.m.:

"Looks like they aim to put up a fight, Captain."

"Perhaps, Sergeant Major. Or maybe they're holding on to make sure the main body's really coming this way."

Tom Wilder was commanding an elite squad of Regular Army scouts. They had moved off the Warrentown Pike to the north to see if they could flank the Rebel line in front of the town. The mission was to seek any sign that the Southerners were moving up in strength. In past sorties, the Captain and his men had determined that the CSA line here was limited to less than a thousand men. Now, of course, the line had been reinforced by Rebs who had retreated from Fairfax Court House the moment it became obvious the Dominion army was advancing in force. That probably added another 500 or so.

The question: is Zach Taylor bringing up his main body to make a fight out in the open, or is this simply a glorified picket line shielding the Rebel army somewhere to the south? That's what Headquarters back on Cranford wanted to know.

Headquarters back on Cranford! Captain Wilder shared the sentiment of the professional officer corps---he didn't know it, but the experienced volunteers officers felt the same way---that having Thayer in nominal charge back there---and no one in direct command at the head of the advance---was just one more recipe for disaster. *An army advancing without a field commander! An army? More like an armed mob,* as his Sergeant Major had so eloquently put it earlier today.

Tom shook his head in disgust, remembering the scene back at Fairfax this morning. They had probed at first light but the Rebs were gone, abandoning the breastworks they had constructed behind the Court House, pretty much in the same place he had almost gotten himself captured---or worse---a few weeks ago.

The raw volunteers---that they were still very, very raw was obvious even to young, relatively untested professionals like Tom---had acted as if they had won a major victory. It had taken all the bawling and cursing of the Regular non-coms now dispersed in the volunteer regiments to regain order. He had looked at the Sergeant Major, an oldtimer named DeGraw, and muttered: "they're too damn green. Even I know that." DeGraw snorted and spit a stream of tobacco an amazing distance. "Well, Captain, I figure the Rebs is green, too. Both too green for this."

Now the detachment, with outriders of their own on the lookout for Rebel cavalry, moved slowly uphill northwest of the Confederate line. A private rode back from the point. "A party of mounted Rebs coming up the Pike, Sir. About 20 riders. At least three flags…"

Before Tom could finish ordering the men to dismount, DeGraw had them down in the high grass, two privates bundling the reins and leading the horses farther back over the crest of the hill. The CSA party was raising clouds of dust as they came on, riding easily, casually, as if to a dance. The Sergeant Major, a veteran of the Louisiana campaigns, crawled up next to Tom and let loose with another remarkable expectoration of tobacco juice.

"Arrogant bastards they is, Captain. Nobody ridin' point. Look at 'em come prancing up. Like they own the road…"

Tom smiled but his eyes were hard. "Well, this is Virginia, Sergeant. But we'll teach them some humility. Right now, though, recognize anyone?"

DeGraw squinted. "The big top in the gray coat and the blue army pants. That's Sidney Johnston, I'm thinkin'. Served with him last year in Illinois." He turned to Wilder, who had his glasses fixed on the group. Tom gave a grunt of surprise.

"Johnston, huh? Damn, you're right… That droopy mustache threw me off. Haven't seen him since I was a plebe. And looky who's with him…" Tom pointed towards a tall, slender rider whose blond hair was evident below his hat. "…Haven't seen *him* since The Point, either. Jeff Davis! Haven't missed him, either. Figures he'd find his way next to Johnston. They were real tight at The Point…

Tom rubbed the back of his right hand across his dusty, dry lips.

"Question is: what are they up to here? Is Johnston taking command? If so, that's a good indication they're planning to fight right here. Tell the men to lay low, Sergeant. This hill is as good an observation post as any. We may be here awhile."

By now Johnston's party was riding into the lines, which were flying the same red flags Tom had noticed in his original reconnoiter at Fairfax Court House. He now knew they signified North Carolina. Johnston's party, however, rode under a new banner: two thick red bars sandwiching an equally thick white one. In the upper corner nearest the stanchion, a blue field with what appeared to be white stars.

574

DeGraw nudged Tom and motioned toward the incoming riders. "Not a lotta imagination, huh Captain? Might get confusing in a fight…" Tom quickly nodded. *Damn thing does look like our flag. Until they got close, I thought it was…*

Johnston and his party were now halted and conferring with what evidently was the Centerville commander. Now some horsemen came down the Pike from the direction of Fairfax. *Damn, how'd we miss each other? That could have been nasty…*

Johnston was now standing in his stirrups, peering north through his field glasses. The sun was now starting down and the shadows were darkening the road. He climbed down and walked through the line, then paced up and down, his arms behind his back. He turned and said something to Davis, who was vigorously shaking his head. Then Johnston turned, looking up the Pike as more pickets on foot poured in. He walked briskly back behind the defenses and remounted, then appeared to give the North Carolinians' commander his orders. Then Johnston and his party pulled around and rode hard back toward Bull Run. Within minutes, the entire Reb force was falling back.

"Well, Sergeant Major, I think we've got our report. The Rebs are abandoning Centerville. Looks like the fight'll be at Bull Run…"

DeGraw spit another remarkable stream another remarkable distance. They had scouted all the way to the Run together last week. Now they glanced at each other with puckered mouths.

"Yes Sir, Captain. Just what our mob needs: to ford that damn stream in the middle of those damn woods. Under fire, no doubt." He grinned humorlessly. "Just like a march across The Plain, eh Captain?" The ensuing length of his inevitable expectoration defied all logic.

Carefully, they withdrew to the horses and made their way around the retreating Rebels and back to the lead elements of their own Army. Despite the darkness---or perhaps because of it---they ran right into the Dominion troops.

The tobacco juice absolutely sizzled as it hit the still-hot sun-baked rocks…

———————

THE BATTLEFIELD AT BULL RUN

While the Dominion forces were making their long trek south from Carlisle to Alexandria, the Confederate army, constantly reinforced by regiments arriving from all across the South, had moved out of Camp Washington and come north. Zach Taylor, in field command, established his headquarters near the crossroads hamlet of New Market. There, the east-west Manassas-Sudley Road intersected with several other roads and trails, opening potential avenues for quick reinforcement at virtually any crossing along the meandering Bull Run stream.

As General Taylor and his key commanders---David Twiggs and Sidney Johnston---studied hastily drawn maps of the area on the night of October 31, a picture of a potential battlefield resembling, in the later words of one eminent historian of the Rebellion, "a spraddled X," emerged.

"Bull Run flowed from the northwest to the southeast to form one cross-member..." wrote the revered historian Shelby Foote. "...Warrenton Turnpike ran arrow straight, southwest-northeast, to form the other."

Bull Run, though not particularly deep, was "steep-banked, dominated by high ground and difficult to cross except at fords above and below a stone bridge spanning the Run where the Turnpike intersected it."

The CSA commanders agreed that if Winfield Scott was commanding the Dominion advance, the main thrust would come with a battering ram attack across Stone Bridge and two fords just below it, Lewis and Ball's, reachable from a useable road sprouting off the Warrenton Pike less than two miles east of the Bridge.

But Scott was laid up in the Infirmary in Georgetown. Had he previously prepared a plan of attack that the two field commanders, Wool and Worth, would follow? Or would the two bickering Dominion officers---their mutual dislike had been legendary in the Old Army---improvise? (The Confederate high command, while respecting Thayer's performance at The Point in turning out high caliber young officers, scoffed at his tactical talents.) And would Wool and Worth---Taylor still had difficulty believing the Yankees had taken the field without an overall commander---coordinate their improvisations, if indeed they were free to design their own plans of attack?

With answers to these questions still be to determined, Taylor waited at New Market, ready to make his dispositions once the Yankees moved down the Warrenton Pike from Centreville. Meanwhile, the 1ˢᵗ Virginia Cavalry and other mounted CSA troops were positioned in the hills and woods on either side of the Pike north of Bull Run, watching, ready to send New Market word when the Yankee advance developed.

In his latest message to General Gaines and President Calhoun, waiting with growing trepidation back in Richmond, Taylor had written:

"I have pulled the advance elements out of Centreville with the intention of making use of the favorable terrain in and around Bull Run, west of Manassas Junction. As it has taken the Dominion army two full days to advance the 15 miles from Alexandria without opposition, I do not expect the enemy to reach the Run until mid-day, November 3. The battle, I expect, will commence sometime the next day, though whether north or south of the Pike we do not yet hazard a guess. In any case, we are favorably placed to meet them wherever they cross."

CHAPTER FORTY-EIGHT

Centreville, Virginia
November 1, 1833, 9 a.m.:

Tom and his scouts had grabbed some hot food and a little sleep before going back down the Pike shortly after midnight. They returned by dawn to report that except for a few scouting patrols, the Rebels were back south of the Run. The generals and their two staffs, however, had apparently taken until now to agree on a site and time for a joint planning meeting. So the foot soldiers, as their predecessors of more than four millennia had so often done, waited. In the growing heat of what promised to be another broiling day. At least, pointed out their veteran non-coms, the dust was down. In the army, these volunteers were finding, you learned to appreciate such nuances...

9:30 a.m.:

The two generals hadn't really taken three hours to agree on a place to meet. Both Wool and Worth had studied Tom's latest report, along with those of other scouts sent out overnight, and utilized the early morning to developed proposed plans of attack. The plans, of course, were entirely dissimilar, as Captain Wilder, among others, was soon to discover.

Wool's plan was a slightly modified version of the one he had floated a week before in the meeting with Thayer: he would move west off the Pike at a crossing approximately 1 ¼ miles east of the Stone Bridge and lead I Corps up and around the Run, finally crossing at the Sudley Springs fords. This would presumably place him southwest of the Confederate lines hugging the stream and in position to sweep their flank, if not rear. Tacitly acknowledging the dissolution of the Georgetown Defense Force, his plan now called for Worth's II Corps to demonstrate at the Stone Bridge in order to draw the Rebels to the area in force, but to make its major crossing at Ball's Ford, about ¾-mile southeast. The attacks would be coordinated to distract the Rebels from Wool's own advance down from Sudley.

Worth, on the other hand, wanted I Corps to push across at the Bridge, while he took his Corps across at nearby Lewis and Ball's fords. "This is the style of attack General Scott would favor. I see no reason to abandon his style in order to attempt a dangerous division of the army with complicated coordinated attacks from positions miles apart."

The two staffs were finally gathered in the Rocky Run Episcopal Chapel on the Pike at Braddock Road. The chapel's front door had been taken off its hinges and placed across several pews to form a table now littered with maps.

Wool was contemptuous of the II Corps plan: "Nonsense, General. I will not tie my entire Corps up trying to take one narrow bridge when I can move up and around the enemy and enter the field from the rear. We can forge a true Cannae by rolling them up between our two pincers. Crush them, Sir, and end this so-called rebellion in one day!"

Worth was shaking his head angrily. "Roll them up? We aren't even sure what their dispositions are! All we know for certain is that they're somewhere back behind this stream. That's why we must stay consolidated until we've crossed and reformed!"

"On the contrary, General. Their dispositions would be formed for them: your plan forces us through a narrow crossing, like meat through a grinder. They'll be firing from both sides, grinding us into so much sausage as we feed our troops in piecemeal. No, we need to spread out and take them from both flanks. Catch them in between us and crack them. Like walnuts in a giant nutcracker!"

Wool banged his hand now on the table before pointing to the Pike junction north of the Bridge. "The army will camp here tonight. I Corps will move west well before dawn. The exact hour will be determined and reported to you. I anticipate forcing the Sudley fords at first light. That will give you more than enough time to move your Corps into position in front of the Bridge and the two other fords." His finger moved casually to indicate Lewis and Ball's.

Worth was now griping his side of the door-table with both hands, battling to control his temper in front of the staffs. Wool smiled coldly. "I see you continue to disagree, Sir. Therefore I suggest a compromise. We remain here today and send for General Thayer. Let him choose the plan of operation. Meanwhile, our troops can be rested and our scouts can determine exactly what Zachary Taylor's famous 'dispositions' are. Do you agree?"

Bill Worth rapidly ran the consequences through his mind. *This heat wave isn't showing signs of breaking, so one more day won't matter. The troops don't need rest, but they do need cohesion; the formations have been coming apart on the march. And I* would *like a better idea of just where Taylor has placed his army…and how many men he's got.*

"All right, General Wool. Let's get General Thayer's opinion to settle this thing. Meanwhile, let's get the scouts back out and over the Run."

As the two commanders departed the chapel by the different entrances from which they had arrived, Captain Wilder, who had presumably be invited because of his constant reconnoitering of the area in question but had never been called on, looked around at the two staffs. Some were shaking their heads in disbelief, others simply staring at each other, the maps or into space.

That Syl Thayer's an administrative genius is widely accepted. That he's never demonstrated any tactical skills is just as widely known. And now the college dean will choose between the plans, as if marking final exams…

CSA Field Headquarters
New Market
November 1, 1833, 12 p.m.:

"You mean they're just sittin' there? No sign of preparations to advance?" Zach Taylor was incredulous. "Just sittin' in the hot sun?"

Major Beaufort was grinning. "That's it precisely, Sir. Their whole army is camped on the south side of Centerville, on both sides of the Pike just below the heights. There's no indication of imminent movement. The cavalry screen is up close to the Stone Bridge," he pointed to the map in front of Taylor, "but behind it, there's no one on the Pike at all. And the artillery is parked east of the village."

Davy Twiggs was scratching his beard and pondering the map when Sidney Johnston broke into the conversation. "Pardon me, General, but it occurs that the answer may be rather simple…"

Taylor looked over and smiled. "Your opinion is always valued, Colonel..."

"Well, General, I propose that the reason they've stopped is because they don't know---or can't agree---on how to proceed. They were hoping to catch us out in the open north of Bull Run. Since we didn't oblige them, they may just not know what to do next. Or else, they're sitting there arguing."

He looked around the table and grinned. "The belle express reported that Wool and Worth were in joint command. I believe that joint has already cracked..."

Zach Taylor broke out laughing. "You do have a way with words, Colonel. And in this case, they're, if you'll pardon my French, 'apropos.'"

He looked at Twiggs, Davis and the others. "That means I concur. They simply can't agree what to do next...which gives us time to ponder their options...and plan our responses.

"If-and-when they do make up their minds..."

Off the Warrenton Pike
Two miles east of Bull Run
November 3, 1833, 5 a.m.:

I Corps had been roused at 2 a.m. and on the road 30 minutes later, trudging up the hilly terrain west of the Pike, as historian Foote would write, "stumbling over logs and roots...stabbed by branches in the woods, clanking as they ran to catch up or...stock still in the thick dust..." Behind them came horse-pulled---and man-pushed--- caissons of smooth bore cannon, wheels creaking and sometimes breaking as they, too, ran up against the logs and were caught by the thick roots. Along with wagons carrying ammunition and other supplies. Five batteries worth that the veterans were already betting would never see Sudley Springs intact.

In a second conference yesterday morning, with General Thayer present, Captain Wilder had warned that there was no realistic road off the Pike and up to Sudley. "The maps may indicate a road, but it's a simple, single-file trail," Tom had explained. "It's mostly uphill through overgrown fields and woods. Same thing once you turn south again to Sudley."

But General Wool had smiled his superior smile and brushed off the report. "I've had the route scouted independently and am told it is of moderate difficulty. That's one reason I have chosen it: if, like Captain Wilder, the Rebels think the march is impractical, they will not be expecting us to come down behind them." He looked around as if lecturing at The Point. "The element of surprise, gentlemen. Never underestimate its value..."

Tom's eye caught that of Colonel Felton, the Ohioan. *Yeah*, the big man seemed to be thinking, *never underestimate the value of surprise...especially on* you.

———————

Dawn was now breaking, but I Corps was still making its way up hill, far from the left turn that would lead it to the fords at Sudley. Colonel Felton had had a gut feeling ever since yesterday's conference that Wool was overly optimistic. *That young Regular's been over the ground. The boy knows his business better than this pompous blowhard...who apparently thinks he's about to recreate some famous battle from antiquity.* Felton didn't know much about antiquity, but he had been fighting Indians for over 20 years. And there had never been a battle--a firefight---that hadn't surprised *him...*

Between the uphill march over, around and through the natural impediments, and with the ungodly heat---even in the darkness the temperature was in the 80s--men were sweating, huffing and coughing already. They had long since shed all 'unnecessary' paraphernalia: blankets, jackets and cooking equipment. Their arms, ammunition belts and canteens were all that was left. Still, men dropped back or out. Felton gave orders to hurry the stragglers along. *If we don't get to these damn fords pretty soon, these men are gonna be too exhausted to fight.* The Colonel leaned into his saddle horn as he sat horsed to watch the line go by. *I don't like this, not one damn bit...*

———————

"Colonel Buford, I want your artillery across that damn bridge the moment it's secured. The Regulars, followed by the 1st New York, will fan out once they're across to screen you. They'll give you enough space on the east side of the Pike to temporarily park your guns. Don't know yet where you'll be headed, but we'll play it by ear."

It was 6 a.m. and General Worth stood with his artillery chief just yards from the north end of Stone Bridge. He paced, waiting impatiently for any indication from the west that I Corps had reached and crossed the fords at Sudley Spring. Bill Worth still thought the plan to divide the army and attempt to coordinate attacks on an enemy whose exact location had yet to be positively determined was folly.

But when Thayer's eyes had lit up at the complexity of Wool's plan, he knew he was outvoted.

Damn engineers. Designing a battle plan isn't like designing a bridge. Simplicity. Simplicity plus power. Coordination requires communication. Better communications than we can hope for in this wilderness. Should just blast through. Blast through, reform, find 'em and hit 'em with all we got. One big Sunday punch. Not some plan based on a battle 2000 years ago. Maybe I should have reminded them: Hannibal won that battle, but the Romans won the damn war... Now where the hell is Wool? It's nearly 6:30...

New Market
6:30 a.m.:

Colonel Johnston glanced at the message from the CSA scouts on Matthews Hill. The dominant ground on that part of the field, it centered a rounded-corners rectangle formed by the meandering Run on its north and west sides and the junction of the Pike and the Manassas-Sudley Road on its south and east. Extended out to the stony Sudley Mountain, it highlighted the northwest portion of the "spraddled X" and offered an unobstructed view of the terrain to the west. Terrain that the Dominion's I Corps was laboring to clear...

He hurried over to General Taylor, who, in an open-necked shirt and planter's hat, was standing at a makeshift map table with Twiggs and some junior commanders. Including, he noticed, Lt. Col. R.E. Lee. "General, we've got confirmation now. Our scouts have picked up Yankees north of the bend of the Run, just northwest of Sudley Springs. They're spread out all the way around the bend. Must have jumped off the Pike a couple miles north of the Stone Bridge. Could be as much as a whole corps, plus some artillery."

Taylor glanced at the map and pointed to the Bridge. "And what of the main body, Sir? The force poised just north of here? What is its disposition?"

Major Davis spoke up. "General, our men along the south bank report the Yankees appear ready to cross, both at the Bridge and at the two immediate lower fords, Lewis and Ball's. They came up before dawn and we thought they'd move at first light, but they're still on the north bank."

Twiggs: "General, the Yankees' lower force---the one at the Bridge and the fords---is obviously waiting a signal to coordinate the attacks. If we reinforce at the Bridge and those two fords, pulling out every unit we've got guarding the lower fords and sending them into the fight, we can hold them long enough for my troops further west to deal with whatever's coming down from Sudley. If we can prevent a hook-up, we can beat them in detail!"

Taylor turned to Sidney Johnston. "Colonel, you are quite sure there is no enemy in strength, east of Ball's Ford? Or back on the Manassas-Centreville Road?" He ran his finger up a long, winding road that crossed the Run at Mitchell's Ford. "Quite sure?

"All right then, gentlemen. The battle will be here." He ran his finger in a circle around the Pike from Matthews Hill south to Ball's Ford. "Bring everyone up from the eastern fords. Colonel Lee, that means your Virginians. See to it. Colonel Johnston, I want the artillery here." He pointed to a rise listed as Henry Hill. "Have them placed north and west in a semi-circle. That way they can face both fronts. General Twiggs, I thank you urging yesterday that your command be placed on the Manassas-Sudley Road. You may have an opportunity for a flank attack when that force from the northwest crosses Sudley Springs and heads down Matthews Hill. See to it, but keep me in constant touch."

Twiggs nodded, put on his hat and turned to leave. Then: "Will Headquarters remain here, General?"

"No, I believe I will join the artillery on Henry Hill." Taylor looked at Sidney Johnston. "Colonel, join your command on the northern front. Keep those Yankees bottled up until General Twiggs has dealt with the ones coming down from the west. Good luck."

Johnston came to attention and saluted. "Advantageous terrain and short interior lines, General. We couldn't have asked for anything more..." He strode to the orderly holding the reins of his horse and pulled himself into the saddle. "...Didn't those Yankees learn anything at The Point?"

THE ARMIES OF BULL RUN

Historians of the Rebellion would note the similarities as well as the differences in the two armies that met at Bull Run, though Sergeant DeGraw is readily conceded as most accurate in describing them as 'armed mobs.' The Dominion Army continued its tradition of utilizing a numbering system to differentiate its units: The I Corps, the 3rd Illinois, etc. While the Confederacy officially adopted this system, in practice their units were more commonly known by the names of the commanders. Thus, the 1st Virginia Cavalry was usually referred to as "Beaufort's Cavalry"; the 1st Corps as "Twiggs' Corps."

As another noted student of the Rebellion, Noah Andre Trudeau, has written, the two most important unit formations were the column and the line:

"A column was a marching formation; with three or four men abreast, it packed a regiment into as compact a space as practical for rapid movement along a road or across open ground." This was the formation the Dominion's I Corps had departed the Warrenton Pike in to begin its long, hot trek up to Sudley Springs. Due to both field conditions---the "single file trail and open fields" reported by Captain Wilder but scoffed at by General Wool at the previous day's conference-- and the lack of training and conditioning of the troops, the line had lengthened dramatically and unsatisfactorily long before Sudley was sighted.

"Once engaged in (or for) combat," continued Trudeau, "columns transformed into lines of battle---usually at least two and sometimes three, with the third standing by as a reserve. These lines, each containing perhaps three hundred men or more, were jointed by companies, allowing one section of the line to face one way while another portion faced in a different direction. The ends of the line were its flanks; the process of bending back a segment of the line so that the men stood at an angle to their original orientation was referred to as 'refusing the flank.'" When General Twiggs left New Market to rejoin his Corps, which had marched by column up the Manassas-Sudley Road the previous day and now rested in the woods adjacent to the descending southern slope of Matthews Hill, it was to form them into lines of battle. This, too, is what General Wool intended to do when his column finally concentrated at the Springs.

The lines of battle relied on, as taught by Bonaparte, a massing of muskets and cannon and the resultant firepower for its effectiveness. "Often positioned in advance...and more dispersed were irregular detachments known as skirmish

585

lines. Their purpose was to harry the enemy, break up advancing formations and provide the main body with ample warning when trouble was coming. Skirmish lines could take many forms, from small cells of three and four men to widely strong lines consisting of individual soldiers posted several yards apart." As Trudeau indicates, these skirmish lines were effective when in advance *of an enemy. They were not, however, particularly effective if the main body was attacked on the flanks…*

The Dominion Army slightly outnumbered its Grey enemy, with over 29,000 men to the CSA force of about 27,000. As the two armies were designed by the two top commanders of the "Old Army," their organizational charts were relatively identical. Both armies were composed of two corps of two divisions each, with two brigades of five regiments in each division. The average regiment in each army consisted of approximately 600 troops and 25 officers. This allowed for brigades of 3000; divisions of 6000 and corps of 12,000 enlisted, led by approximately 1200 officers. (In the event, however, A.S. Johnston's (2nd) Corps entered the battle with approximately 9600 enlisted men as three Virginia regiments had been detached to operate as a small autonomous brigade guarding the eastern fords.) Each corps in each army was assigned five batteries of artillery. The major difference between the armies was their application of cavalry. While USBAA Regular Cavalry (Dragoons) had screened the Dominion advance from Carlisle, acting independently, General Thayer had divided the regiment and assigned three troops to each Corps. These were supplemented by the 1st Pennsylvania Cavalry and 1st New York (I Corps) and the 1st Indiana and 1st Illinois (II Corps). Thayer supported the traditional view of the mounted arm as the eyes and ears of the infantry and thus best suited to perform scouting assignments for the Corps commanders. Zach Taylor, however, concentrated his five cavalry regiments as an independent fighting force under his direct control. Thus, in any mounted clash, the Rebels would have a distinct manpower advantage of as much as 2-to-1, being capable of fielding up to 2500 mounted men to no more than 1250 for the Dominion.

Sudley Springs
8:15 a.m.:

Captain Wilder was waiting with his elite scouts when I Corps' lead columns reached the Springs. Colonel Felton, commanding the Corps' 1st Division, 1st Brigade, was to the fore, riding his big grey, as he led the lead 1st Ohio Infantry to the edge of the ford. The

Ohioans, veterans of the Black Hawk wars, immediately and unceremoniously plopped down to rest and eat.

"What have we got here, Captain? Any sign of the Rebs?" Felton remained in the saddle, leaning forward as he petted his horse's mane and squinted eastward.

"They're set up behind the Run as far as a half-mile or so east of the Stone Bridge, just like yesterday, Colonel. But some of the scouts report signs of major concentrations in the woods to the right of Matthews Hill, across that road down there." Tom pointed to the Manassas-Sudley Road visible some distance away.

"Does General Wool know about this?"

"I sent word about an hour ago, Colonel. But neither my messenger nor a response has come back."

Felton grunted and twisted around in the saddle as another 1st Brigade regiment began arriving at the ford. While more fashionably dressed than the Ohioans---whose 'uniforms' demonstrated a lived-in, comfortable look---these troops too exhibited an independent-minded spirit. They paid little mind to protocol---and even less to their officers---plopping themselves down even more unceremoniously. The newcomers, too, began to dig into their rations. The Colonel shook his head at the new arrivals.

"I thought I knew all the states in the Dominion; territories, too." He gestured toward the new arrivals' flag. The image of a red-haired woman in a flowing blue robe, carrying what appeared to be axes, was displayed on an otherwise all-white banner. The motto "Een Draght Mackt Maght" was printed in bold letters under the figure. Above it, in even bolder letters: "1st Brooklyn."

Felton grinned. "Look at that gibberish. What is it, German? Listen to 'em. Whatever they're speakin' don't sound like English to me. When I first saw them, I thought: 'has Matty Van gone and hired us some mercenaries?'"

Tom stared at the flag before shifting his gaze to the now-reclining troops. "Colonel," he said with a grin, "these troops speak the King's English in its truest form. Even if that motto is in Dutch. Means 'In Unity There Is Strength,' the official motto of the great independent City of Brooklyn, N.Y which, by the way, is my home town…" He turned as he heard his name called out.

"Tommy, am I glad to see you! Wait till Father George finds out…"

The Captain looked over at the grinning young lieutenant now on his feet and coming toward them. "Joe, what are you doing here? I didn't know you'd joined up!" He jumped down from his horse and looked at Felton. "Excuse me a moment, Colonel. That's my little brother." Felton smiled and nodded as the brothers embraced. "Make it quick Captain, I believe General Wool has finally appeared." He pointed to a party of approaching riders from the northwest.

"Joe, get back to your men. But first, what's this about George?"

"Our revered older brother's here, Tom. Came down with us. The regimental chaplain, they call him. Should be up any minute."

The arrival of the General's party ended the reunion and Tom came to attention, though Colonel Felton continued to lounge comfortably on his horse.

Wool looked sourly at the Captain and then turned his attention to the east. "Well Captain, your report?"

"That's Matthews Hill in front of us, Sir. Unoccupied. They've fortified behind the south bank of the Run about a half-mile east of the Stone Bridge as I reported."

"So we've gotten behind them as I planned, correct Captain?"

"Behind their troops at the Run, yes Sir. But we continue to observe movement in those woods to the south, General. Across that road." Tom once again pointed in the direction of the Manassas-Sudley Road.

Wool turned to an aide who Tom did not recognize. The aide shrugged. "Probably some cavalry, Sir. Most likely been tracking our advance and are waiting in the woods to observe our next movement."

Wool nodded. The 1st Division's commander, Col. Ethan Allen Hitchcock, shifted uncomfortably in his saddle, his lips puckered and his eyes blank.

"General, request permission to search those woods again. While the rest of the Corps comes up. Just to be safe, Sir." Tom looked past Wool to Felton, who was observing the exchange quizzically.

Wool shook his head negatively. "No need, Captain. They're obviously concentrated along the stream. Even if their cavalry has spotted our column, they haven't had time to move into those woods in force. No, we'll put out a skirmish line, but we won't engage until we reach the Pike."

I wouldn't be so sure, General. Tom saluted and backed away, then looked reflexively at Felton. Colonel Felton remained poker-faced but was pointedly looking off to the southwest. Hitchcock, whose grandfather's capture of Fort Ticonderoga could legitimately be said to have ignited the chain of events that had led to this day, turned again in the saddle, shaking his head.

Wool and his aides conferred privately with Hitchcock before calling Felton and the commander of the 1st Brooklyn, who had arrived during the discussion about the woods, to join them.

Tom, meanwhile, had glanced over at Sergeant DeGraw, who now enunciated his opinion with a record-breaking expectoration of tobacco juice. The Captain was making his way toward the Brooklyn soldiers when his younger brother reappeared with a gaunt figure in a blue uniform devoid of insignia. Tom grinned and embraced him.

"George, when did these cheeseheads get religion? Don't tell me you've been converting them?" He indicated the Brooklyn men, who were mainly---and plainly---of Dutch descent.

His brother smiled: "I'm working on them, Tom. But it's hard to reform the Reformed... Anyway, where have you been? We looked for you at Carlisle and Alexandria. Say, you've made quite the impression on Mrs. Latoure. She had us to dinner once I identified myself. Spoke most warmly of you."

Tom fought back the blush, wondering how he could actually feel embarrassment with the enemy right in front of them. "Was Lucille there? No, still in Georgetown, huh? Well, Cranford's some place, isn't it?" He heard his name called and turned to see one of Wool's aides beckoning him. "Take care of yourself, George. And take care of Joe. I believe we're about to run right into the whole damn Reb army... Begging your pardon, of course, Father..."

Warrenton Pike East
Of Stone Bridge
10:15 a.m.:

His Corps had been in place since dawn and now sat baking in the ungodly sun, whose rays sliced through the tree branches.

How the hell can it still be so damn hot? And where the hell is that damn Wool? No word, no sign, no noise!

589

General Worth paced back and forth on a small hill---little more than a long mound---that commanded views of both the Bridge and Lewis Ford. His men were concentrated from the Bridge approaches down to Ball's Ford. Colonel Buford had his artillery ready to blast across the Run at all the crossings to soften up the enemy before the advance.

The question is: how much longer do I wait? God damn that Wool!

"General, rider coming across the Pike." He spun around in time to recognize Captain Wilder making his way through the massed troops. *Now maybe we'll find out what Wool's up to...about damn time!*

Directed to the General, Tom quickly delivered Wool's message: I Corps had reached Sudley Springs unimpeded and clearly behind the enemy defenses. The 1st Division would commence its advance to and over Matthews Hill at 1030 hours. Unless unanticipated resistance is encountered, the Division will be positioned to attack the enemy rear south of Stone Bridge by 1130 hours. The 2nd Division will follow. It is highly desirable that II Corps be prepared to commence its attack no later than 1100.

The slapping of his gauntlets against his right thigh was the only outer indication Worth permitted of his inner rage. He turned slowly and gazed back across the Run before addressing an aide. "How about that, Major? Think we can 'be prepared to commence attacking by 1100?' After all, that allows us just 45 minutes to give the order to open fire..."

He turned back to Tom. "When did I Corps reach Sudley, Captain?"

Tom looked straight into Worth's coal-black eyes. "Lead elements---the 1st Division's 1st Ohio and 1st Brooklyn---reached the fords before 0900 hours, General. The 2nd Division was still coming up when I left to find you, Sir."

"Not quite the stroll in the woods General Wool was anticipating, was it Captain?" The disgust was evident in the shake of Worth's head. His next question was devoid of sarcasm, however. "Is the way clear all the way down to the Pike, Captain? Should resistance be...unanticipated?"

Tom looked south across the Run, where the Rebel forces were clearly visible. "General Wool is correct that Matthews Hill is unoccupied all the way down to the Pike, Sir. But..."

"But that's another long, hot march, isn't it Captain? Out in the open, under this damn sun. Is that what you're saying? That I Corps may arrive too exhausted to fight?"

"That's a...concern...General. But..."

"But what, Captain? You're the damn scout. Tell me what you've scouted!"

"General, there's thick woods adjacent to Matthews Hill on the south side. Separated by a road. Some of my scouts claim the Confederates are there in some force..."

"Didn't you probe the woods yourself?"

"My orders were to await the arrival of the Corps at the fords, Sir. When General Wool arrived and I reported the scouts' suspicions, he denied my request to reconnoiter the woods. Said the Rebels hadn't had time to move any significant force in there."

"...But you don't agree, do you Captain?"

"General, my men have been trading shots with Reb patrols for days. Even this morning. The Rebs know a large force has moved to the northwest. If that intelligence has gotten back to their high command, even this morning, they may well have had time to move into those woods..."

Worth was glaring at his staff. "Depending on whether they have a reserve to commit. And depending on just how deep they are over there." He indicated the Confederate positions to the south.

Worth's aide spoke up: "General, it's getting toward 1100 hours. Shall I send the order to open up as requested?"

Worth nodded. "Tell Colonel Buford to open up as planned at 1100. At 1115, the attack on the Bridge will commence. Simultaneously, assaults at both Lewis and Ball's fords will commence. Get word to all commanders."

He looked over at Tom. "No sense you heading back the way you came, Captain. Stay put. I'll make use of you shortly."

Confederate Position in the Woods
West of Manassas-Sudley Road
11:30 a.m.:

From the sound of it, all hell had broken out southeast of their position 15 or 20 minutes ago. Few of these troops had ever heard a cannonade erupt in anger and were naturally awed. Even General Twiggs himself was surprised by the sheer volume of the noise: *apparently Joe Johnston's artillery on Henry Hill is answering the Dominion cannonade. That probably signals the start of their advance across the Run. Now if Sidney Johnston can contain the main body, I can cut up this force coming down from Sudley.*

The pickets were coming in now from their positions on and around the crest of Matthews Hill. *That means the blue troops will be visible in no time…*

He turned to his aides. "Get the men up. We'll be moving across the road in a few minutes." He looked at Bedford Brown, resplendent in his fine grey jacket with the gold braid. "Well Colonel. Is North Carolina ready?"

Brown, the first---and one of the few---fire-eaters to put on a uniform, nodded nervously. "North Carolina is ready, General." *I just hope to God I am.*

Dominion flags were now popping up on the crest of Matthews Hill. Skirmishers were cautiously moving about. Riders followed slowly, as if on parade. Eyeballing them through his binoculars, Twiggs could see crusty old Wool among them. He identified several other officers, though not the tall powerful man on the grey horse now arriving at the head of infantry. *One of their militia leaders, no doubt. Well, welcome to a real fight, Mr. Militia. Commencing in about five minutes…*

The Dominion line of march offended Twiggs in every possible sense. Because the rag-tag advance was so unprofessional, it would be harder to attack: they were so spread out the key initial volley would lose much of its punch. An artillery-based ambush from the flank was supposed to turn an orderly advance into chaos. *This advance is already in chaos!*

The Dominion skirmishers were out in front again as they moved down the hill. They looked to be Regulars; but where were the outriders? There were none on either flank. *Wool must think we're all committed at the fords; he thinks he's behind us! Thinks he's going to come down this hill and get in our rear!*

The clamor from the woods to the southeast went on. *There must be a hell of a fight going on in there. I hope Sidney's holding…*

Twiggs could see that Wool and his staff remained on the crest of Matthews Hill, watching the ragged blue advance edge down. *Must say, that's a fine lead unit. Can't say the same for the rest of them, though… Almost a shame to hit the lead element. Ohio, the flag says…*

He lowered his binoculars and turned to an aide.
"Open fire!"

Stone Bridge
11:30 a.m.:

Lt. Colonel William Savage watched in admiration as Regulars from the 2nd Infantry fought their way across the Bridge in the face of steady artillery and sporadic musket fire. The Rebels gave ground grudgingly but orderly in a way that cheered his men but gave him qualms. *They're giving up too easily. I don't like this; it's like they're enticing us to come across...* Now the Regulars were on the ground at the Bridge's south end, signally its capture. Colonel Savage raised his sword and waved it over his head. *There's nothing for it now. Time to go...* "Second New York! Advance!"

He led his men across in a trot, then wheeled to direct them into position. "Fan out, both sides of the road!" The Grey troops had halted and reformed. The firing was now continuous up and down the line. Savage knew Dominion troops were also advancing across the Lewis Ford; as long as the fire came straight-on---wasn't flanking---it meant the advance was proceeding, they would be hooking up with Blue troops at the east end of the line.

Suddenly he was eating dirt; the crescendo of noise mercifully above him. One of his junior officers yelled and tugged at him. He held his breath and awaited the searing pain to inform him where he had been hit.

Nothing...

"Be careful, Colonel, that shell went off right in front of you!" *I'll be damned...still in one piece.* He pulled himself up on one knee and felt hands lifting him to his feet. A grinning private handed him his sword. "Hey Colonel. Hold on to that thing, will ya? Damn near beheaded me..."

The private put his head down and rejoined the advance. Colonel Savage lowered his bulky shoulders and followed. The 2nd New York was over the Bridge and across the Run. And the Rebs were backing up. Again.

Lewis Ford
11:40 a.m.:

The 1st New Jersey was now across Bull Run and forcing the Rebels back. Lt. Col. Brian Judge had led his men splashing and screaming into the water and up the south bank. Here too the Grey troops conducted an orderly, grim fighting retreat. Colonel Judge fanned his men out to the west, looking to make contact with the Dominion forces that had rushed the Stone Bridge. The 2nd Connecticut had crossed immediately after him and was now deploying to the east in order to hook up with the Blue soldiers scheduled to cross at Ball's Ford.

Judge knew his ridiculous height made him a prime target, so he ran hunched over before picking out a thick tree for protection. He stopped to survey the situation. *Can't see ten feet in any direction with all this smoke. The Reb artillery seems to be slacking off some. Maybe it'll clear enough to see how far these damn woods go before we hit open country. Right now, this is one screwed-up mess. One screwed-up uncoordinated mess!*

Field East of Henry Hill
Off Warrenton Pike
11:40 a.m.:

Albert Sidney Johnston was up in his stirrups, surveying the action up toward the Run through his binoculars. His men were conducting this ruse like veterans; all that training at Camp Washington was paying off!

The Confederate leadership had all agreed: a stalemate at the Run wasn't good enough. They wanted to get the Blue army out into the open where it could be defeated in a head-on battle, then pushed back into the Run in a rout. That the Yankees had made the task easier by dividing their army and marching one corps miles out of the way to Sudley Springs was an unexpected bonus. But it did not change the ultimate strategy: get the Yankees out in the open by sucking them across Bull Run. Then hit them hard with the reserve and see if they break. That was to be Twiggs' job, originally. Before the Yankees decided to split their army. Now the reserve would be the Virginians who had been guarding the eastern fords. Lee and his men. *Let's hope they arrive on the field in time!*

The Blue troops in his sector were visible in the woods. Soon they'd be in the open. He sat back down, shifted in the saddle and looked west through his binoculars. *Davy Twiggs has engaged on Matthews Hill. The rest of the Yankees are already in the open...*

Now let's hit them hard...all over this field. He raised himself back up in his stirrups and shook the binoculars over his head. The piercing, unearthly high-pitched growl that he had first heard from men cheering Beaufort's cavalry as they returned from Harper's Ferry now exploded from his own throat for the first time. What the Yankees would shudderingly come to call the "Rebel yell" now echoed across the field...

North of Bull Run,
   East of Stone Bridge
11:45 a.m.:

General Worth's "use" of Captain Wilder was an order to cross the Run and report on the situation in the field. "Two-thirds of the Corps is across and they've not come back, Captain, which may or may not be a good sign. Get across yourself and see what the hell is happening. I'm going to hold the remaining regiments in reserve until we have a better picture of the fight."

Tom pushed Bay Ridge across the stream and was up behind the Dominion lines in a few minutes. The Reb artillery had evidently found a more choice target---*Wool?*---because it had slackened off almost entirely in this sector, though he could hear the cannonading continuing further away. Since Buford's II Corps Artillery had also ceased in order to cross the Run---Tom could see one battery setting up in a field off the Pike at the southern end of the Bridge---the smoke had begun to drift away.

Binoculars to his eyes, Tom was scanning the field when he heard his name yelled out. Soot-faced or not, there were very few 6-foot-6 regimental commanders in the USBAA. He recognized Colonel Judge.

"Thought that was you, Lieutenant. Can't forget this horse. He's some animal. Who invited you to this party?"

"General Worth wants to know what's happening before he commits the remainder of the Corps, Colonel. Is it a good sign that there're no stragglers? Or are the Rebs just chewing you up?"

"Tell the General we've hooked up with the 2nd New York and the other units that crossed on the Bridge. We're pushing them back out of the woods but I expect a resumption of their artillery fire at any time. Tell him there's heavy fighting west of the Pike. They've apparently diverted the artillery fire in that direction, but for how long is anyone's guess.

"Our objective now is that big hill out there, see it? That's where their artillery is parked." Judge pointed due south to a wide hill with a small stone farmhouse perched on the crest. "That hill commands the field. Take it---and their artillery---and the rebellion's over by nightfall. Tell the General I strongly advise he commit the reserve. Now!"

Tom looked down at the sweating, dirty Judge and saluted. "Will do, Colonel." He stuck out his hand and shook Judge's before turning Bay Ridge around to gallop back down toward the stream. "Good luck."

Judge stood for a moment looking after him. *Luck, Captain, is the residue of design. Let's hope our design is better than the Rebels'...*

CHAPTER FORTY-NINE

Matthews Hill
11:50 a.m.:

"Jesus Christ! Where the fuck did they all come from?"

Lt. Joe Wilder was as amazed as the terrified private who was screaming in his ear. Ten minutes ago they were marching down the backside of still another hill after having sloshed across the stream. Then, moments ago, all hell broke loose: musket and cannon fire from the right flank, more cannon fire coming in from the front. Then a screeching, wailing sound---like all the world's nuns running their fingernails on all the world's blackboards---from the woods on the right. And out of those woods poured a host of men firing their muskets, then coming on as they reloaded, shining bayonets attached to the barrels.

Joe had looked for Colonel Van Dyke, but word quickly spread that the Colonel was down, shot in the first volley. Looking down the slope, Joe could see the Ohioans move smartly to their right and begin to return fire. He tried to think of the marching order for such a maneuver but couldn't; didn't matter, his regiment---what was left after absorbing the first volleys---was in shambles. Men were down: some bloody and moaning; some dirty and cursing from having crashed or tripped over the wounded as they tried to run back up the hill. A Vermont regiment had been right behind them in the line of march. Their discipline, too, had collapsed; some were running while others were simply hugging the ground. The ones running were now breaking up the cohesion of the battle line behind them. The formation of the Massachusetts and Connecticut regiments starting down from the crest was beginning to come apart as the fresh troops attempted to dodge both the Rebel fire and the terrified men running back up the hill.

And on the Rebels came.

"Lieutenant, form your men! Set up a line! Hook it up to Ohio!"

Joe looked up: Colonel Felton was desperately trying to improvise a counter-attack.

Another explosion from across the Pike: *how many cannon do the damn Rebs have?* The dirt and grass blew by in great chunks as the big man fought to retain control of his horse.

"Form a line, hook up with my boys!"

Joe looked over: damned if the Ohio troops weren't perfectly formed up and firing back! And hitting the damn Rebs! There were men in grey and butternut down over by the road! "Look boys! They ain't so great! Look at Ohio knock 'em down!"

But it was no good: the Brooklyn Dutchmen and the Vermont farmers had seen enough. Enough of their friends falling, crying out. Enough of those ugly bayonets glistening in the sun. Despite little clusters around screaming, pleading officers, the regiments melted away: some uphill and some simply turning and running north toward the Run. The panic now infiltrated the lines of the other two 1st Brigade regiments, the 1st Massachusetts and the 1st Connecticut. Ignoring the pleas of the Regular non-coms staffing their ranks, these two units began to melt away. Incredibly, General Wool had committed only the lead 2nd Brigade regiment, the 1st Maryland. Its battle lines now broken by the retreat, the Marylanders swung around to face the surging Confederates as best they could. But in the maelstrom, all order was gone...

———————

It was like watching dominoes fall. This hot, humid November day on Matthews Hill, it was not the lead domino that started the chain reaction. The battle-tested 1st Ohio firmly stood its ground in the chaos. But the rest of the half-trained, undisciplined volunteers of the 1st Brigade had never come under fire before. The dominos fell at the first push of Confederate lead and steel. By the time the rest of the 2nd Brigade crested the hill turn, the Rebs were already in command of the situation.

The Confederates would misconstrue the lesson of Matthews Hill: the South Carolinians, Georgians, Alabamans, Mississippians and, yes, the Premiere Infantere Volontaires de Quebec, were not braver than their Yankee foe. Nor were they that much better trained. But they were better led and thus got in the first punch. General Wool's arrogance and distain for the Rebels had led him into a trap of his own making. Davy Twiggs was simply smart enough to recognize its potential. And Wool's failure to bring his big guns up to the crest of the Hill---where they could have raked the advancing Confederates and broken up their charge---sealed the issue.

Instead, Wool sat horsed on the crest amid his standard-bearers watching the carnage below in stunned silence. Col. Gilbert Hodges, the big, ranking half-pay who was serving as 2nd Brigade commander, had already asked permission to lead the remaining four regiments in the 1st Division---for only six had crested the hill (including his lead regiment, the 1st Maryland) and been engaged---down the south side of Matthews to attack the Rebels from the road. Now Hodges tried again.

"General, if I lead a charge down the hill now, it's *their* flank that will be open! I can go through them like a bloody knife through hot butter! We must save the survivors of the 1st Brigade from being surrounded. Permission to charge, Sir!"

Wool shook his head. "No Colonel. I can't risk losing the entire division. The Rebels have won the field. Colonel Felton must cut his own way out."

The nonchalance that British officers strived to affect in crisis was apparently not in the big man's repertoire: he pulled off his hat and slammed it against his horse's neck. "Won the field? They bloody well haven't won any such thing! Look towards the Stone Bridge, General..." He pointed to the southeast, where the Stars and Stripes were visibly waving from numerous stanchions. "The II Corps is advancing! General Worth is pushing them back! We haven't even engaged our own 2nd Division! This field is still in play!"

Hodges looked around to Colonel Hitchcock, who was standing apart from Wool and his staff, watching the catastrophe unfold, his hat twisted roughly in his right hand. "Colonel Hitchcock, Sir! We must advance! It is your Division! Do you not agree?"

Hitchcock was silent, as if unhearing. It was the I Corps commander who spoke: "Colonel Hitchcock has been relieved of command, at his own request. You, Sir, are now in command of the Division." Hodges' jaw dropped and Wool continued:

"The II is advancing only because the Rebels are concentrating their artillery on this Corps. The day is lost, Colonel. We must retreat and then the Rebel artillery will cut the II to pieces." Taking off his hat, he paused and continued, as if lecturing himself: "I must keep the remainder of the Corps intact to defend against what will certainly now be a Rebel attack on Georgetown."

Hodges could barely contain his fury…or his contempt. He angrily reined his horse in a tight circle around Wool. "General, we have 14 fresh regiments and our own artillery. To retire now would be a disgrace; a bloody obscenity!"

Wool adjusted his hat. "You are relieved, Colonel."

West of Flat Run
Southeast of the Battlefield
11:30 a.m.:

Lt. Col. Robert E. Lee had pulled his 1st Virginia Infantry back from Blackburn's Ford to a dusty road that led to this offshoot of Bull Run. There they had met up, per his hasty written order, with the 2nd and 3rd Virginias, which had been posted at fords further east. Now he was hurrying the combined force across and up toward the sound of the fighting.

Robert was excited and surprised to be leading what amounted to a small brigade. His previous instructions were limited to coordination of the separate regiments' guard duty at the various fords until the direction of the Dominion advance became clearer. This morning, however, Sidney Johnston had made it official: he was to take command and hurry the regiments to the fight…as soon as the Cavalry definitively determined the Yankees were not forcing the southeastern crossings.

He had heard the opening guns of the battle almost three hours ago and had waited impatiently for the horsemen's report, having notified the commanders of the 2nd and 3rd of Johnston's order. The report had come in after 10:00 a.m.: there were no Yankees east of Island Ford. Now they were headed, a color-bearer with the new CSA colors in the lead, to the fight. Colonel Lee expected to join in once the brigade crested this big, wide hill looming just northwest of Flat Run. He'd sent messengers to report to Johnston and Taylor: the Virginia Brigade would be on the field by 12:30 p.m.

THE DOMINION'S DILEMMA: THE UNITED STATES OF BRITISH AMERICA

Confederate Field Headquarters
Henry Hill House
12:00 p.m.:

The battle was going better than he had any right to expect.

Still clad in his open neck formal ruffled shirt, USBAA enlisted men's pants and planter's hat, Zachary Taylor could see even without his binoculars that the Dominion advance down Matthews Hill had been broken up by Twiggs' attack. In fact, except for a vicious brawl wrapping around a meandering little stream about a quarter mile from the Pike, there was no longer any serious immediate opposition in that sector.

"Look here, General." Maj. Jefferson Davis offered his own glasses as he pointed up to the Matthews crest. "The Yankees appear to be abandoning the field entirely."

Peering through the glasses, Zach could see the color bearers beginning to move off the crest, disappearing to the west. *What the hell was that all about, anyway? They didn't have enough troops in that advance to do us any real harm, even if they had marched down and caught us in the rear. Why, there couldn't have been more than five or six regiments in that fight...*

He turned quickly to his aide: "Get word to Joe Johnston over there. I want all firing directed at the Yankees to our north. Cease firing to the west and direct all fire north!"

Even in the excitement of the fight, he could see Davis wince. His apparently-to-be son-in-law was furious that his old enemy from West Point now out-ranked him. And he could see that the boy was dying to get into the fight himself. *Well, there's still time. This battle isn't over yet...*

———————

Ball's Ford
12:10 p.m.:

The tall lanky captain was wryly thinking that he didn't know whether he should be happy or sad that the advance here was more than three hours late.

The march down from the Warrenton Pike had been a comedy of errors. They had taken a wrong turn and actually marched more than a mile northeast before someone realized the error as the head of the

601

column passed an unexpected junction. Instead of turning around, they simply reversed the line and headed due south for two or three more miles. That's why his 1st Illinois was now on the point. All in the hot sun, raising clouds of dust the captain was sure could be seen in Georgetown…if not Richmond. Now they had stumbled on the ford. Or so his commander thought that's where they were…

According to Major Parker, two companies of Regulars were supposed to be waiting here to lead the attack, following a softening-up cannonade. But neither the Artillery nor the Regulars had ever shown up.

Now Colonel Halas, commanding the brigade---the 2nd Pennsylvania, 1st Delaware, 1st Rhode Island and the 2nd New Jersey were the others---had apparently given up on the Regulars. His orders were to commence the advance at 12:15 p.m., with or without the Regulars.

The captain, who had managed to get through the Black Hawk War without hearing a shot fired in anger, was reminded of a story. He was just beginning it, to the bemused exasperation of his grizzled sergeant---who believed he'd already heard all the captain's stories at least a dozen times---when the Major shouted the order to ford the stream.

Matthews Hill, just
North of the Pike
12:15 p.m.:

This ain't a battle. It's a damn riot! Got to get what's left of my brigade out of here.

"Retreat! Head for the Pike! Disengage!" Colonel Felton frantically---angrily---waved his bloody sword. The remnants of the 1st Ohio (and a few companies of the 1st Brooklyn) had been holding off a Rebel attack---which had gradually lost its own cohesion once it started up the side of Matthews Hill---near a stream the maps called Young's Branch.

Now, as the deadly cannon fire from across the Pike suddenly slackened, Colonel Felton could see blue uniforms in control of the road in front of the Stone Bridge. *Don't know---don't care---who they are, just got to get my boys into their line.* Felton could see the young officer

602

from the 1st Brooklyn---hatless, bleeding from the forehead and arm, his right pant leg ripped open---urging the boys on. The lieutenant---young Wilder's little brother, he remembered idlely---was one of the few officers still visibly fighting. The others weren't all dead; *some of them,* he thought sourly, *outran their men back up the hill...*

Woods West of
Sudley Springs:
12:15 p.m.:

Colonel Phillippe Roberdeau had seen the opportunity some two hours ago. There were no Dominion scouts or pickets west of his line! After a quick exchanges of messages with General Twiggs, he had led his Brigade, stationed at the extreme left of the CSA line, further west through the woods. Now they were hidden in dense brush just south of the field leading to the rear of Mathews Hill.

That field was packed with lounging USBAA soldiers: some sitting, some leaning casually on their muskets. Their officers, apparently intent on escaping the blistering sun, had done a poor, almost non-existent job of posting sentries before heading for the shade of the nearest trees.

Their flank is in the air! We can roll them up and knock these Yankees all the way back to Georgetown!

The Colonel turned to Maj. Harry Bassett, commanding the 2nd Mississippi. Bassett had a funny accent, but the Colonel had come to respect his judgment on the journey up from the South. The English half-pay might have gotten his command because he was married to the Governor's daughter, but he knew his business. And, the Major had risked as much, if not more, than anyone else: if the British Army got their hands on him, they wouldn't go easy on one of their own who had thrown his lot in with the South!

"Major, you have the honor of leading the attack with your Mississippians. When you are ready, Sir..."

Capt. Joseph Francis was chirping. *Only this time*, thought his 1st sergeant, a schoolmaster from Stowe, Vt., *he's right: shouldn't we have some pickets out there in the woods?*

The initial volley caught half the 2nd Vermont: those leaning against their muskets. The dead, dying and wounded crashed down in heaps on their sleeping or daydreaming comrades. The 2nd Vermont disintegrated in 30 seconds; even those who chose to fight were bayoneted before they knew what had hit them.

Messengers from General Wool ordering a pullback of the 2nd Division had barely arrived at the Division commander's temporary headquarters when men began to stream by in a panic from the south. Roberdeau's Brigade was rolling up Wool's precious reserve Division as fast as the Rebels could fire; they had to reload while advancing and re-fire (a procedure that took approximately 45 seconds in practice but well over a minute under combat conditions).

When CSA troops returned to the area the next day to scavenger for weapons, ammunition, uniforms and anything else of value, they found, nearest the woods, the bloody body of a darkly handsome Dominion captain sprawled face-up near the bulleted-and-bayoneted corpse of a blond, intelligent-looking man in his 30s who sported the insignia of a 1st sergeant.

.

Edge of Field East of Henry Hill
12:30 p.m.:

"The attack's stalling. We've got to get these men moving again!"

Colonel Savage nodded his agreement but was at a loss as to how to proceed.

The right (Stone Bridge) and center (Lewis Ford) prongs of General Worth's attack had hooked up on the south side of the Run but now faced suddenly-renewed sustained artillery fire from the massed Confederate batteries on Henry Hill. Fortunately, the stalled Dominion line was shielded in part by a line of woods that stood approximately a quarter-mile south of the Run.

In front was an open pasture that offered defenders a clear field of fire against oncoming attackers. Even the Regulars who had led the assault over Stone Bridge had become bogged down by the combination of the artillery and stiff resistance by Sidney Johnston's

Corps, which included regiments from the Carolinas and Georgia. Now Colonel Savage was surveying his portion of the front with the captain who had led the Regulars' across.

"Fire's too heavy for a direct assault. No cover, either." He glanced west toward the Pike. "If we can get some more men on the other side of the road, we might be able to flank them, though..."

The captain, a tough young West Pointer named Reynolds, looked behind him. "There's still some regiments stacked up behind the Bridge. If you send word back to Division..." He turned back and grunted. "Damn, Colonel, look across the Pike!"

Savage, who had resumed studying the Rebel position in front of him, moved his binoculars to the right. Blue soldiers were flooding toward them from the slope of Matthews Hill. *So much for I Corps' pincer movement... If the Rebs chase I Corps completely off that hill, we'll be the ones getting flanked...*

"Captain, we've got to move men across the Pike and reinforce our line to cut off any enemy flanking movements." He turned to his aide, crouched down beside him. "Joe, get back to Division. Tell them I'm got a thin line of Regulars across the Pike. They must be reinforced as to prevent a flanking attack. Got that? Now go!"

"Captain Reynolds, take the rest of your men and form a line on an angle from the Pike back to the stream. Form a pocket to receive the survivors from that hill. Tell whoever is in command of the reinforcements what the orders are. Stop any attempts to flank and receive the survivors!"

Reynolds nodded grimly. Both men knew Savage was risking a pullout of his best troops in the face of a possible Rebel advance. Everything depended on how quickly the troops still east of the Bridge could reinforce the Regulars...once Reynolds got that pitifully thin line over there beefed up...

The 1st New Jersey and the other regiments of the center (Lewis Ford) prong of II Corps' advance were also pinned down by the heavy Rebel fire. Colonel Judge had led his men across with relatively low casualties but had run into stiff Southern resistance at the edge of the woods. Judge, without other direction from Corps, was still thinking offensively: Once his line hooked up with the advance from Ball's Ford, they should have enough strength to swing around the Reb position and take them in an arching movement from the southeast. As he had told Captain Wilder---who had reported the 1ˢᵗ Jersey's initial success at Lewis Ford back to General Worth's position east of Bull Run---the objective was still the artillery on Henry Hill.

Judge, whose long back ached from spending most of the last three hours hunched over, was now on his knees behind a big boulder. He took off his hat and brushed the sweat off his prominent brow. *Damn, I'm sweating like a dog. Those Rebs must be frying out there in the sun. How do the bastards take it?* A corporal he had sent south in the direction of Ball's Ford now slid in beside him.

"Well, any sign of them?'

"Yes, Sir. They's troops coming up a road behind that hill over there." The Corporal pointed to a rise on the south side of the small tributary stream that split the position at Lewis Ford.

Judge grunted. "About time. They wouldn't want to miss the party..."

"But Sir, that's not all. There's a bigger hill just past the road our boys are coming up..."

The Colonel glanced at his second-in-command.

"...and Sir. There's a whole lot of men coming down that hill. They'll be running into the boys on that road any minute!"

New Market-Warrenton Pike Road
West of Bull Run
12:45 p.m.:

The Captain was out in front of the 1ˢᵗ Illinois, marching alongside the 1ˢᵗ Sergeant. His major had just pulled off the road to await the arrival of Colonel Halas and the Brigade staff. The Captain could hear the battle on the other side of the hill to their right and wondered when the order would come to turn off the road and climb the hill. Unless it came soon, he reckoned, the Regiment looked to be marching *away* from the fight. Not that the prospect particularly bothered *him*, personally.

A muttering began to ripple across the column, from left to right rather than forward to back. The Captain looked over just as his Sergeant swore loudly: A large body of men, many in blue jackets, flying what appeared from this distance to be the Dominion colors, was advancing down the slope of the big, wide hill to the east. *Reinforcements*, the Captain guessed. *Those boys must have marched all night...*

Many of the men in the 1ˢᵗ Illinois were hardened veterans of the Indian wars. One of them was the 1ˢᵗ Sergeant. He had heard the orders this morning, overheard the discussion of the Major and his officers. They were marching point on the *left flank* of the Army. There weren't supposed to be any Dominion troops east of them!

"I don't like this, Captain. My gut tells me those are Rebels, sure enough!"

The Captain was perplexed: *the Ball's Ford crossing was supposed to be the far left movement. But they had crossed unopposed. What would a Rebel force be doing wandering around this far from the battle? And that does look like our own flags...*

On his own initiative, he nevertheless halted the column. "I believe they're our's, Sergeant. But let's wait for the Major..."

The force from the wide hill was within 100 yards now and the Captain could see a broad-shouldered officer on a fine grey horse among the cluster of officers congregating around the flags. The officer appeared to be issuing orders. The lead elements of the force coming down the hill now swung out into a battle line. They paused on command less than 75 yards away and raised their muskets...

"Get down! Prepare to return fire!" The 1ˢᵗ Sergeant wasn't waiting any longer for his story-telling Captain---or the Major---to come to a decision. *Blue jackets or not, that's the enemy up there... Rebs who showed up out of nowhere and right on our flank!*

The first volley tore holes in the 1ˢᵗ Illinois, but the 1ˢᵗ Sergeant's quick action probably saved the Regiment from the fate of so many other Dominion soldiers today. That, plus the fact that these veterans had sized up the advance from the hill individually and, like the 1ˢᵗ Sergeant, didn't care for what they were seeing...

The lanky Captain might have been one of those torn apart but for the reflex action of the Sergeant, who grabbed him and pulled him to his knees just as the men on the hill aimed their muskets.

"Still want to wait for the Major, Captain?"

The Captain, whose left pant had torn when he was dragged down, shook his head. "A little late for that, Sergeant. What do you suggest now?"

"That we pull the boys back off this road and up that hill behind us. That'll give the units behind us room to maneuver. We have to counter-attack or these Rebs'll push us right back across the Run."

The Captain began to nod in agreement as he looked back down the road. But what he saw was sickening:

While the 1st Illinois was a veteran unit, the next unit in line, the 2nd New Jersey, wasn't. The Jersey boys were making a stand, but out in the open road. Firing down on them as they advanced, the Virginia Brigade cut and diced them in a matter of minutes. Behind them, the 1st Delaware was stacked up on the road, with the rest of the Dominion force behind them. The Ball's Ford prong was gridlocked on the road running back to Bull Run…

––––––––––

Warrenton Pike just
West of Stone Bridge
12:55 p.m.:

Dennis Felton could hear the cheers of the Southerners---that infernal whoop---from the slope of Matthews Hill as he pushed the survivors of his Brigade toward the Blue lines near the Bridge.

He looked back to get his bearings. He was positioned now on a plateau of the Hill, about halfway between the point where Young's Branch stream curved south of the Dominion line. With him were a small core of officers and fighting men, including the still-bleeding lieutenant from the 1st Brooklyn.

"Keep them moving, the Rebs aren't advancing!"

Much to Colonel Felton's relieved surprise, the Southern advance had petered out after the initial attack had disintegrated his command. The Rebels were milling about above him, firing their weapons and cheering, but their own cohesion had dissolved despite the frantic, visible pleas of their officers.

"Come on, keep the men moving towards the Bridge! We can reform behind the II's line!" As he hurried the men along, the Colonel took time to glance back on the hill: no sign of Wool or his staff. *Damn, he didn't surrender, did he?* He could see nothing but cheering Rebels from the crest on down. *What the hell happened to the rest of the Corps?*

Western Rear Slope of
Mathews Hill
12:55 p.m.:

What the hell happened was that the orderly withdrawal of the remainder of the 2nd Division had been proceeding smoothly back to Sudley Springs when a mob of screaming men, some disarmed, some waving their muskets, had crashed into the lead ranks. Roberdeau's Brigade's surprise attack had rolled on after decimating the poor 2nd Vermont, pushing down other equally unprepared 2nd Division regiments.

When the wave hit the bewildered remaining 1st Division regiments--men who had watched as their comrades from the 1st and part of their own 2nd Brigades were mowed down by the main body of Twiggs' Corps---the orderly retreat became a panicked rout.

Men who had not yet fired their loaded muskets in anger abandoned formation and turned north in a sprint away from the crossings at Sudley. The scene grew more chaotic as the unit cohesion dissolved entirely. That one Southern brigade---its pursuit considerably slowed as its own semi-trained men paused to celebrate their initial success---could put some 14 Dominion regiments to flight was stark testimony to the unreadiness of the Dominion army for battle.

And where was General Wool? To his credit, the General valiantly tried to stem the rout his colossal collapse of nerve on the crest of Matthews Hill had sparked. After dismissing the fuming Colonel Hodges, General Wool had ordered the withdrawal of the remaining four regiments---the 5th New York, 1st Indiana, 1st Pennsylvania and 2nd Ohio---back down the rear slope and up towards the Springs. They were approaching the lead regiments of the 2nd Division when Roberdeau's attack came out of nowhere, much as the earlier assault by Twiggs' main body had caught the initial advance by surprise.

"Not more of them? Are the woods filled with Rebels?" Wool's adjutant looked to the southwest as the sounds of musket fire suddenly erupted. The General's party was still on the crest, at the moment turned due west to watch the retreat.

Wool took in the noise and seemed to calmly accept that he had been outflanked again. "Send word to the 2nd Ohio. They are to swing to the left and meet whatever advance comes across the field." He turned to another aide. "Who's behind Ohio? 1st Pennsylvania? Tell its commander to swing in behind. We must stop the Rebel advance and reestablish contact with the 2nd Division!"

Roberdeau's Brigade---mostly hard, first-generation Mississippians, Alabamans and tough natives of the Louisiana bayous---had marched to war bringing their trusty Kentucky Long Rifles. The Long Rifles were not favored by the 'Old Army' because of reliability issues with groove-clogging and weight of ammunition, but in the hands of men familiar with the weapon, they could be shockingly effective at longer distances than the standard smooth-bore, muzzle-loading USBAA musket. That's why the poor 2nd Vermont had been mowed down before it scarcely knew it was under attack.

Now these tough frontiersmen had moved past the groaning, bleeding wreckage of the 2nd Vermont. While the Alabamans on the west end of the line and most of Major Bassett's Mississippians unleashed their fire into the 2nd Division's stunned 1st Ontario, speeding up the collapse of that Division, the 2nd Louisiana sighted the Ohioans.

"General, we have to move back! Look…the main Rebel line has reformed and is moving this way!"

Wool turned slowly in the saddle and looked back. A Confederate force had coalesced out of the confusion on the forward slope and was now cresting the hill. In minutes, his command would be facing fire from two directions…

He looked at his remaining staff. "Let's get down this hill and back to the Springs. We've got to find General Kearny and the 2nd Division's staff." They swept right to pass the retreating 5th New York and rode down onto the field in time to be caught in the turmoil caused by the Louisianans' second volley.

If 1st Pennsylvania's commander ever got the word to reinforce the 2nd Ohio's defense, he either could not or would not comply: the Pennsylvanians, their eyes on the Run and apparent safety, brushed passed the Ohio line and headed west to the ford. The Ohio regiment, after absorbing the crippling Long Rifle fire, turned to discover blue uniforms racing, not to their aid, but past them. They joined the parade.

"Come on boys, do your duty, turn around and fight!" General Wool was frantically lashing out with his sword, screaming at running men who paid him no heed. His flag sergeant was down in the melee, though no one later could recall whether he had been hit or simply thrown from his terrified horse. At any rate, a staff lieutenant now grabbed the stanchion with one hand and pulled on Wool's horse's reins with his other.

"General, you have to get out of h…"

Wool was suddenly airborne, the blue sky raining black dirt and clumps of grass. He hit the ground with a hard thud and lay stunned. A black-beard was looking down on him with sad, sympathetic eyes. "Are ye all right, Gin'rl? That was some bounce ye took."

A second blast exploded near by and Black Beard fell protectively over him. "The damn Rebels seem to have got cannon to the crest… And I wonder what happened to our's?"

Wool rose to his knees and looked back at the crest. A new set of flags was visible, motionless in the sun, among the party of horsemen occupying the ground he had just abdicated. At least one full battery was now setting up to fire. He looked around: Shreds of his flag were visible on a blood stained body that no longer connected to a head. None of his staff were near. The grizzled black-bearded sergeant: "Aye, Gin'rl. That shot took your gang direct. I was watchin'. One moment yer ridin' glorious fast. Next moment, yer flyin' through the air…

"Ken ye walk, Gin'rl? Tis' a ways to the stream, but we've no choice. Can't stay here, and yer horse seems to have made his own arrangements…" Another blast from the crest and iron whistled overhead. Sgt. Black Beard pulled Wool to his feet. "Time to go, Gin'rl. While they're busy reloadin'."

They began to run, two more apparently anonymous men in dusty blue, desperately seeking the supposed safety of the Run. But both were over 40 and their days of sprinting were long past. Huffing, puffing, choking on dust and smoke from muskets, long rifles and cannon, they fell back before they were halfway to the stream. Dizzy, disoriented, they veered to their left…and right into the path of exuberant Rebs screaming their bloodcurdling yell.

"Give 'em the cold steel!"

Wool heard the shout in a daze. *I'm a dead man.*

"Don't stick'em, they're unarmed!" A long, lean man, sergeant's chevrons visible on his sleeve, pushed through the line of privates, some grinning, some snarling at their Yankee prisoners.

Wool felt himself shoved roughly to the ground, then felt Black Beard's considerable weight atop him again. The Sergeant boomed his brogue: "Aye, boys, ye've got us. We'll not be putting up a fight! We've had enough for one day…"

"That's right, boys. Let 'em be."

The weight was suddenly gone and Wool climbed to his knees. Dust and the beat of hoofs signaled the arrival of officers. Wool looked up to see a small party of riders under a thick red and white bar banner. An officer whose golden hair poured out of his grey hat grinned down at him from behind an equally golden mustache. His eyes widened as he took in the cut and design of the dirty blue uniform.

"Well, well. I say: what the bloody hell do we have here?" The officer---Wool could see that if the CSA had retained Dominion insignia he was a major---edged his horse up against him before pulling off the hat and sweeping it cavalier-style across his chest. He turned and waved the hat in a salute to his men. The English accent again incongruously issued from behind the droopy gold mustache:

"Well done, lads. It would appear the 2nd Mississippi has bagged ourselves a bloody general!"

New Market-Warrenton Road
1:30 p.m.:

The 1st Delaware was that rare Dominion unit today: a volunteer regiment that did not go to pieces under a surprise Rebel attack. The Delaware boys stepped in and around the dying 2nd New Jersey and hit back at the Virginia Brigade with an uncoordinated volley that held the Virginians on the east side of the road, even if it did little serious damage.

Their commander, a lawyer from Wilmington, urged his men back off the road and successfully hooked his lead company to the left flank of the 1st Illinois. Watching from the big hill across the road, Colonel Lee quietly acknowledged the feat with a slight nod of his head. *A fine piece of soldiering. That man knows his business.*

But Robert also knew his business. He could see that the Dominion advance across Ball's Ford had ceased. In fact he could see that part of the force was retreating back across the Ford. *Those people in front are now isolated on the slope of their hill…*

Robert had his buglers call out a cease-fire. He turned to an aide: "Pass the word: Reform the regiments. Restore the battle-line." He turned to another aide. "Lieutenant, kindly have the 2nd, when reformed, swing out to the left and ask Major Barksdale to swing the 3rd out on the right as well."

He sat on Marlborough looking through his field glasses before turning to his second-in-command: "Those are two wounded regiments over there. We will cross this road and if necessary squeeze them as if in a bear hug, until we are attacking from three sides."

Captain Applegate looked nervously towards the ford. "But if the enemy should re-cross the ford, Sir? They will hit our right flank..."

Lee glanced quickly to his right and shook his head. "There will be no further advance from Ball's Ford, Ross. They are confused and disorganized back there. No, sir. Our enemy is here, in front of us. We will hit him here."

The Captain of the 1st Illinois was sitting on the hill watching the Rebel maneuvers with interest when the Wilmington lawyer/commander turned up.

"Captain, see where the road curves out a ways back there? That sort of bend? Well, Captain...that's where I found Colonel Halas a few minutes ago. He's bleeding to death. And there was a major with him. One of the men said he's the commander of the 1st Illinois. Or, I should say, was. Got one in the side of the chin. Took most of his jaw away...

The Captain closed his eyes, his right hand reflexively reaching to rub his own long, lean jaw. It was the 1st Sergeant who spoke: "Well, Captain, 'pears you're in command now. Those Rebs are reforming. They'll be crossing the road and on us any time now...?"

The Captain sighed and looked at Delaware. "Major, you're the ranking officer. Your orders, Sir?"

The Major from Wilmington had his hat off and was running his hand through his thin brown hair: "Let's see what they try, Captain. But I don't see how our martyrdom would save the day for the Dominion, anyway. We'll defend this hill, but if they look to overrun us, we'll surrender." He turned to the Sergeant. "How many you guess are forming up over there?"

"About three regiments, give or take a few. Probably 16, 1700 men..."

"And we've about half that left."

Drum rolls from across the road caught their attention. The grey troops were up and moving in a thick wave. The lawyer from Wilmington and the two Illinois men could see the two flanks begin to curl around each side of their position as the Southern wave came up to the road. The Rebel line was now on the grass below them.

The Captain turned. "This is suicide, Major. Even if we cut down their first line, they'll be on us before we can reload..."

Nodding, the Major said simply: "I concur." He turned to the 1st Sergeant, while pulling a big white handkerchief from his back pocket. "Sergeant, if you will..." The Sergeant quickly speared it with the blade attached to his musket and waved it high in the air.

Watching from his hill, Robert saw the white flag he had prayed for go up. "Have the buglers sound halt!" Within seconds the grey wave came to a standstill. He spurred Marlborough and trotted down the hill, followed by Captain Applegate. They crossed through the ranks of the men and came up and over the road. Now he reined Marlborough to a halt in front of his line and waited.

From their position on the slope the Major from Delaware and the Illinois Captain had seen the Southern commander advance. "Well, Captain, ever surrender before? No, me neither. Guess we'll both find out how it feels..." With a gesture, the Major indicated for the Captain to accompany him. "Damn, look at him on that horse. Looks like a monument..."

The Southern commander saluted as the two Dominion officers reached him. "I am Lt. Col. Robert Lee, 1st Virginia Infantry. I also have with me today the 2nd and 3rd Virginias. Am I correct to assume your flag indicates the desire to capitulate?"

The Major nodded. "That's about right, Colonel. You outnumber us 2-to-1 and pretty much can flank us from both sides. Doesn't seem much reason to negotiate..."

Robert nodded. "Agreed. If you'll surrender your swords and side-arms, we can begin the process of disarming your men, Major..."

"Major Bayard, Colonel. James A. Bayard, Jr., 1st Delaware. And this is Captain, err..." He turned to the Captain from Illinois. "I'm sorry, Captain, but I don't believe we were ever properly introduced…"

"Lincoln. Abraham Lincoln, 1st Illinois. At your service, Major." He turned his lanky frame to the Southerner. "And at your's, Colonel Lee."

———————

Dominion Lines
Field East of Henry Hill
2:30 p.m.:

General Worth came out to look for himself. His men had barricaded behind rocks, boulders, fallen trees and anything else they could place in front of them when the drive had stalled in mid-morning.

It's actually a solid position, in and of itself, even in the face of all that damn artillery…

But Worth knew the strategic situation had rendered his tactically sound line vulnerable. The collapse of I Corps somewhere west of the Warrenton Pike---by now he knew that the Rebels not only held Matthews Hill but were apparently across Bull Run at Sudley Springs---and the non-appearance of his own left prong from Ball's Ford had isolated the remainder of his Corps. The II was in essence caught in a huge pocket; when the Rebels on Matthews Hill consolidated their position and moved up, they might actually trap him against the Run itself!

The General was proud of the performance of his Corps; at least, the portions of it north of Ball's. They had been giving as good as they had gotten from the Rebels in front of them---prisoners had identified the enemy as A.S. Johnston's Corps---but they couldn't make any headway in the face of the massed artillery on that damn Henry Hill…

He turned to his 1st Division commander, the Maryland Senator Ezekiel Chambers, a decorated veteran of Jackson's Lower Louisiana campaign. "Our own fight is a stalemate, General. They have too damn much artillery on that damn hill for us to advance, and we're too well protected and have too much artillery of our own for Johnston to successfully counter-attack." He paused as his other

Division commander, the tough Regular Edwin 'Bull' Sumner, came up.

"But the enemy is in control of Matthews Hill and, apparently, the area west of it. If they can get a force across the Run up there, they could close this pocket we're in… Colonel Sumner, what word from Ball's Ford?"

The big man with the close-cropped hair shook his sweaty head in disgust as he saluted. "My 2nd Brigade got thrown back, Sir. Most of it was already across and marching towards the fight when they were hit by a sizeable Rebel force, maybe a full brigade, that came out of nowhere from the southeast." He paused and kicked at the dirt in dismay and embarrassment.

"The 2nd Jersey took the brunt of it. They're finished. Along with Colonel Halas, the Brigade commander. He's dead, and so is the commander of the lead regiment, Major Parker of the 1st Illinois. The 2nd Pennsylvania and the 1st Rhode Island are safe back north of the Ford." He paused again. "But the Illinois boys and the 1st Delaware were cut off. Word is they surrendered to this Reb force."

"And where is this enemy brigade now?"

"I had Captain Wilder out looking for Halas' brigade, Sir. He reported back a few minutes ago that two or more regiments coming up from the southeast have hooked up with Johnston. And that a large group of prisoners is being herded back towards the Manassas-Sudley road…"

"Your missing Illinois and Delaware troops…"

"Looks that way, General." Sumner paused again. "One other thing, Sir. Wilder got a look at the Reb officer leading the hook-up with Johnston's men. Says it was Robert Lee…"

Worth shook his head in disgust but got immediately back to business: "Two, maybe three more regiments, maybe as much as a small brigade; Johnston'll wrap them around our left flank, reinforce what he's already got there. That side of the pocket's hemmed in.

"No gentlemen, we can't stay here. If the Rebels get across the Run west of us in force, they can march down and surround us." He slapped his left thigh with his gauntlets. "We have to disengage; pull back in the direction of the Pike and see if we can make a stand at Centerville. If we can beat the enemy to the Centerville heights, we'll be all right, at least for now."

He glanced toward the sky. Thick black clouds were rolling in from the west, blocking out the sun. "Looks like a storm's moving in." His smile was without mirth: "Trust the weather to break the day of the damn battle…"

Worth turned and summoned an aide. "Get Colonel Buford up here." He turned back to his deputies. "We'll disengage under cover of the guns. Buford should have enough ammunition left to keep up a steady fire and pin the Rebels down till we're back across."

He looked at the two division commanders. "Start pulling your brigades out once Buford opens up. But keep the lead elements of your advance this morning in place on the northern bank of the Run as long as possible, at least until the artillery can pull out." He looked hard at Chambers and Sumner, who were both nodding their understanding of the orders.

"This redeployment could easily turn into a rout. If it does, we stand the risk of losing the whole Army…and maybe Georgetown, too. Your lead regiments proved themselves this morning, but disengaging under fire is the toughest battle problem in the book. The future of the Dominion may depend on how well you execute it… Any questions?"

Chambers: "None, General. But let's not forget that the survivors from I Corps are already on the Pike, behind the line the Regulars threw up in front of the Bridge."

"Well, get them moving. Who's in charge up there?"

"The 1st Brigade commander is down. Colonel Savage of the 2nd New York is in command now."

"We need some cavalry up there and we'll need some below Lewis Ford, gentlemen. Can you see to it, Bull? Good. General Chambers, make sure Savage has the I Corps people moving. And let him know he'll have cavalry to screen his overall movement. He'll be alone on the Pike till we meet up at the original jumping off point." Worth shook his head. "Then it'll be a race back to the Centerville heights…"

CSA Headquarters
Henry Hill
4:20 p.m.:

With the renewed Dominion artillery barrage came the rain. Buckets of it fell in minutes, accompanied by a massive thunder-and-lightening storm. Zach Taylor wasn't sure what had his men more frightened---the cannon fire or the lightening---but he had an idea what the Dominions were up to:

"Colonel Johnston, the resumption of heavy cannonading means one of two things: either the enemy is preparing to advance; or is retreating. What, Sir, is your opinion?"

Albert Sidney Johnston, standing alongside the Commanding General under a makeshift shelter hastily erected when the storm first appeared in the distance, squinted northward. "It does not appear they are advancing, Sir."

Taylor, too, had discarded his field glasses in the downpour. "They're retreating, Colonel. Bill Worth is too smart to just sit there in that sack, thinking we're just going to hit him head-on. He knows what happened on Matthews Hill. He's pulling back before we can get behind him and pull the sack's string tight." He turned to Major Davis.

"What's the latest from General Twiggs? What is the condition and location of his command?"

"General Twiggs has pushed one of his brigades west of Sudley Springs, Sir. He reports they're bagging all kinds of prisoners. General Wool's entire corps has disintegrated, he reports. They've abandoned their weapons and are in full flight back to Centerville."

Taylor took off his planter's hat and shook it impatiently. "That's fine, Major. But what of Twiggs' main body? Can he take Stone Bridge and get behind Worth's command?"

Davis looked from one man to the other. "We have control of Matthews Hill, Sir. But the Dominions have a strong line on an angle from the Pike to the stream protecting the Bridge. Regular infantry, Sir…"

"They can't have much, Major. Our reports said the Regulars were pretty well dispersed among the volunteer regiments." Colonel Johnston.

"…but the big problem is that General Twiggs' whole command lost all unit cohesion during the fighting this morning. General Twiggs is having difficulty regaining control."

"Jesus, it's been three or four hours. What the hell's his problem?"

Davis' always-formal face was, if possible, even stiffer than usual. "General Twiggs is complaining of what he calls 'free-lancing,' General. Reports that some regiments have gone off on their own.

There's an unconfirmed report some of his units have trapped a Dominion force here, in this big bend where the stream turns south." Davis pointed on a side-table map to an area northwest of Matthews Hill. "There is another problem, General. A...err...lack of communication. The 1st Quebec and the 3rd Louisiana, Sir. In the heat of battle, they have apparently forgotten their English!"

"What!" Taylor swore and turned to look at Johnston, who was attempting to cough down a laugh.

"Yes Sir. General Twiggs says when the Quebecois get excited, they tend to think and hear only in French. And the 3rd Louisiana, well, they're all Cajuns from the bayous. English isn't their mother tongue, either."

"Damn! What do you say to that, hey Colonel?" Taylor looked at his Corps commander in disgust. "Did they teach you fellows how to command a bi-lingual army at The Point?"

Johnston tried rather unsuccessfully to keep a straight face: "Actually, General, I don't believe anyone in Paris would acknowledge what the Cajuns speak as French. Looks like we leading a tri-lingual army here..."

Taylor saw nothing funny in the situation. "Damn it! I've got a whole corps milling around up there on Matthews Hill while Bill Worth disengages under fire and pulls back out of our trap!

"Major Davis, get word to Twiggs. I want that damn bridge taken and our troops up the Warrenton Pike before Worth gets back to their starting point with his main body. Find him and get him organized!"

He turned to Johnston: "Colonel, you will advance across and around this pocket as soon as the enemy artillery withdraws. And utilize Colonel Lee's Virginians to push their left flank." He indicated Lee's position on the map.

"If we can catch up to Worth before he gets back to Centerville, this matter will be concluded tonight!"

Stone Bridge
6 p.m.:

"That's the last of my batteries, Colonel Savage. All my people are now across. Good luck with your own withdrawal."

619

Colonel Buford extended his right hand to the bulky Savage who, in three months, had gone from momentary Confederate prisoner to acting brigade commander. Savage stuck out a beefy hand that rivaled one of Scott's huge paws. "Thank God for this storm, Colonel. The way this lightening keeps crackling, those Rebels may think you're still firing…at least long enough for the Regulars to conduct an orderly pull-back."

He turned serious: "Colonel Buford, I've been promised cavalry support north of the Bridge to screen our movement. Now, it doesn't look like the Rebs have moved off that big damn hill over there, but I haven't seen or received any reports of Dominion cavalry. I'd appreciate a message if-and-when you sight some."

"Will do if possible, Colonel Savage. But between this storm and the demise of I Corps, things are in chaos. I suggest you expedite your own withdrawal. Let's get to Centerville and regroup. I'll see you there."

The 'chaos' Colonel Buford described extended to both sides: General Twiggs, despite Zach Taylor's angry order, failed to reestablish order in his Corps for a variety of reasons: inexperienced officers unsure how to assert battlefield control; undisciplined, exhilarated men prematurely celebrating what looked a knockout rout; the sudden storm and, mostly, the unfamiliar shock of battle on this major a scale. A.S. Johnston's Corps, meanwhile, had become bogged down in the slippery mud the rain had made of the field east of Henry Hill earlier churned up by the extended artillery exchanges. And in a thunder-and-lightening storm of truly biblical proportions, Johnston's regiments---like all soldiers not faced with a life-or-death situation---did the prudent thing: they waited out the weather.

The Dominion's II Corps was faced with that proverbial life-or-death situation and instinctively knew it, even if the rank-and-file had no idea of the strategic situation. The eight-hour test of fire had made veterans of the rawest of them and had brought the veteran realization that their attack had run its course. As veterans, they had no problem with the order to abandon a stalemated position, to withdraw from a position in which they were taking fire from three sides…

For the Dominions, the developing problem was the traffic piling up on the Pike. The debris of I Corps kept coming down from the southwest: not so dazed nor terrorized now that it was apparent, even to the most distraught, that they were not being aggressively pursued. But still confused and disorganized.

They were, however, adding to the clogging on the Pike as the lead elements of the II Corps brigade Savage had inherited tried to conduct a retreat in a semblance of order. This portion of Savage's brigade could also feel Buford's artillery pushing up behind them.

This mass of men, with some 2nd Brigade units---including Brian Judge's 1st New Jersey---adding to the congestion, was scheduled to run into the remainder of the II Corps about a mile further up the road at the junction that had marked the Army's original jumping off points early this morning. (Though it seemed days, if not weeks before.)

All this in the middle of the fierce storm that signaled, finally, the change of seasons in Northern Virginia. A storm that, even as the thunder and lightening died off, continued to drench both armies in an increasingly cold downpour.

Jump-off Junction
Warrenton Pike
8 p.m.:

General Worth had arrived here less than 15 minutes ago, after satisfying himself that the Confederates were not seriously pursuing. In fact, Captain Wilder, who had remained at Lewis Ford with some scouts, had just sent a message that the Rebels had paused at the Run and were making no apparent effort to mount a pursuit from any of the three crossings. Other cavalry patrols were also reporting in: the Rebels seemed content to claim the field west of the Pike. There were no signs of an advance from Twiggs' Corps in the area of the Run's bend, though the Confederates had crossed at Sudley Springs and were in considerable strength further west.

Though that *might be*, Worth thought with both pride and regret, *because of the fight put up by the 2nd USBAA Regulars on the other side of Matthews Hill.* Rumor had it that the Regulars, enraged by the collapse of I Corps, had made a stand up there somewhere and had fought at least one Rebel brigade to a standstill before running out of ammunition...

So the question was no longer who would win the race to Centerville; the question was how strongly---and quickly---he could establish a fortified line on the heights west of the town. *Taylor must be pissed as hell at Twiggs.* He grinned at the thought, his first real smile in days. *Here we are in a shambles, half our strength gone, and he can't consolidate and come after us. Ol' Zach must feel like a schoolboy with a big helping of ice cream in his hand on a hot day. It's melting through his fingers before he can finish it off...*

A dripping and shivering General Chambers rode up from the Lewis Ford road. "General, I ran into Bull Sumner back at the junction with the Ball's Ford road. He reports that his division has cleared that road and that he has cavalry vendettes posted to warn of any enemy advance. Same with the Lewis road; cleared and picketed."

"Well General Chambers, we're safe for the night. They're not coming, at least till dawn. Now, if we can clear this logjam here, we can bring the Corps back to Centerville in good order. I've sent the engineers on ahead. They'll have lines set up for the men to fall in to once they reach the heights."

Chambers looked around and bit his lip: "What about I Corps? They're sure to impede our progress..."

"Not as much as I feared, General." Worth could see the reflection of the torches and bonfires, which somehow burned despite the unceasing rain, in the Marylander's eyes. "There simply does not seem to be that many of them..."

Chambers gripped his saddle horn tightly and spoke in a tense low voice: "Is the whole Corps gone? Good God, what will the Governor-General say?"

Worth's smile was bitter. "As I understand it, Matty Van was in favor of this madness, sending half-trained amateurs out to assault fortified positions. Undoubtedly at the behest of His Grace, the Duke..."

He shook his head. "That's not important now. There'll be time enough for recriminations if we do succeed in saving Georgetown. But you misunderstand me, General: the reason there isn't as much impediment from the I Corps survivors as I had feared is explained in a message the engineers have sent back from Centerville. Apparently, as much as half the I Corps has already passed through the town. They'll be back in Alexandria by mid-morning."

He snorted in disgust. "Took four days to get to Bull Run. Take I Corps 12 hours to get back..."

Stone Bridge
9 p.m.:

"Sir, I believe General Twiggs is approaching."

Zach Taylor stood on the Bridge's southern end, the two Johnstons, A.S. and Joseph, among the circle of officers about him. It was Jeff Davis, however, who first spotted the First Corps commander.

"General Taylor, Sir." Davy Twiggs was apologetic. "I regret to inform you that my command was not in condition to pursue the Dominions. We became simply too…dispersed…Sir, to respond to your order to advance…"

Taylor looked at the crestfallen Twiggs. *This has got to be killing him…in front of all these others…*

"You won a victory today, General Twiggs. You essentially, from all reports I have received, destroyed an entire Dominion Corps. It could have been larger, yes. It could have been the battle of annihilation we discussed at Camp Washington. But it was a magnificent victory, General. You correctly saw that the Dominions would offer us their flank coming down Matthews Hill. You routed half their army. My congratulations.

"But now, Sir, we must look to the morning. What is the condition of your Corps now? Can you move on Centerville? Colonel Johnston," he indicated Albert Sidney, "suggests we probe with cavalry tomorrow while we reorganize and refit. But that will give Bill Worth time to firm up his defenses. Then, we'll be the ones attacking strong defensive positions…"

Twiggs looked around at the group. He shook his head, the water-soaked hat still dripping despite the rain's merciful let-up. "I agree with Colonel Johnston, General. My command is too disorganized to mount a successful pursuit. Will be for some time."

He paused and shook rainwater off his muddy uniform. "General, we did win a victory. But for some of my units, it was a costly one. Yes, some of the Dominion regiments ran like scared deer. But there was fierce fighting in at least two locations, at the little tributary near the Pike and up west where the Run turns. General, we trapped the

2nd Regular Infantry up there. The fighting was hand-to-hand after the ammunition ran out. It used up the equivalent of a brigade…

"And General, I must report that discipline is not what it should be, I had problems…"

Taylor nodded. "With 'free-lancing.' Yes, so I have heard. Something about communication, too, I understand…"

He turned to Johnston and the others. "Well gentlemen, it appears to be a consensus. We will limit our pursuit to cavalry; Colonel Mason and his men are already over the Run with orders to make the Yankees' retreat as uncomfortable as possible. Meanwhile, we will consolidate our position here, see to the wounded and refit as necessary."

He turned to Jefferson Davis. "Major, you will prepare a preliminary report for President Calhoun. Once I've approved it, you will hand-deliver it yourself." *And knowing Calhoun, he'll make a production out of promoting you on the spot…*

General Taylor looked back at his commanders. "I expect we'll see General Gaines and the Secretary of War in the morning. I half expected them by now…"

A.S. Johnston smiled. "Richmond must be full of rumors. I wonder how many of the good citizens have spotted Yankees coming up Shockoe Hill by now?"

Twiggs joined in the laughter: "They'll see plenty of Yankees in the next few days. We've bagged a lot of prisoners. I hope General Gaines is ready to put them up, show them some real Southern hospitality…" He slapped his hat against his leg and shook his head in embarrassment. "…Damnation, General Taylor! In the heat of the battle, it completely slipped my mind! Second Mississippi reports it took a significant prisoner. I ordered him delivered to your headquarters on Henry Hill, but you must have left before he arrived." He paused to draw out the surprise: "Apparently my Mississippians captured the Yankee Corps Commander himself, Brig. Gen. John Wool…"

Twiggs grinned as A.S. Johnston himself led a chorus of Rebel Yells.

Taylor, however, did not join in the merriment. "Indeed, General Twiggs. Let's hope the War Department has provided for these prisoners we've collected, including General Wool, if indeed we have him…

"And let's hope the Department has contingency plans for maintaining this army in the field. Because it is now certain we will be out here for some time. Perhaps until next spring..."

Hill Northwest of
Warrenton Pike near Centerville
November 4, 1833, 1:30 a.m.:

The deluge had slowed and steadied, a cold soaking rain that unequivocally proclaimed the changing of the seasons. Maj. Luke Beaufort, in a blue tarpaulin issued him years before by the USBAA, sat his horse on a wooded hill and watched the spectacle of the Dominion Army in retreat. He was still pondering the gruesome scene he had come across over two hours ago.

His orders from Colonel Mason, the Cavalry Corps commander, had been clear enough: harass the line of retreat; cut off small bodies of stragglers and capture any wagon trains or even single wagons. The CS Army, especially after this all-day battle, was dangerously short of military supplies, from arms and ammunition to medical to cooking utensils. His command had standing orders to 'appropriate' anything they could drag back...

That portion of Mason's orders was at root-cause of the calamity.

B Troop of his 1st Virginia had come across a small wagon train parked off the road leading west from the Pike. That had been around 8 p.m. There were no guards, so Lieutenant Wright ordered his men to take possession. As a detachment of dismounted troopers came up close, they were fired on from at least two of the four wagons. Infuriated on seeing their friends fall from ambush, the rest of the Troop charged. Within minutes all four wagons were overturned and ablaze, their occupants shot, slashed or run down.

"There was no stoppin' the boys, Sir," the Lieutenant had explained when Beaufort arrived on the scene. "Looked for all the world like an unarmed train, carryin' wounded and such, but then they opened up on us. Soon as the detachment went down, we charged..."

What made the damn fools think they could drive off a full troop of cavalry? Maybe in the rain and twilight, they mistook it for a small patrol. Or maybe they panicked…

At any rate, the train *had* been carrying wounded. Some of those lying now in the mud were obviously casualties of the day's fighting, the lost limbs testament to heavier fire than B Troop could muster. *The poor bastards who are still alive now probably won't be, come morning…*

Lieutenant Wright left the Major's side and walked among the dead and wounded Dominions, pointing out the unarmed and the patients the wagons had been transporting. He kicked at bodies clothed in bloodied white coats, doctors and nurses, of course. There were teamsters dead in the harnesses of their teams. Suddenly, the Lieutenant paused and knelt to pull some sort of chain from around the neck of a corpse whose blue uniform was devoid of insignia. The Lieutenant examined his find as he brought it to Luke.

"Look at this Major," he said quietly. "Know what that is?"

Luke turned it over in his hand, then fingered the carving hanging from the chain. He glanced down at Wright. After Harper's Ferry, he had attended a celebratory service at Monumental Church with the Lieutenant and knew him to be a fellow Episcopalian. He looked over at the body and then back down at Wright.

"A rosary. Last thing I expected to find on this field. A dead Roman priest…"

Colonel Mason's arrival caught Beaufort still in his reverie.

"Well Major. Looks like we've done all we can. That's regular infantry coming up the Pike now, the last of all of them. The whole Yankee army---or what's left of it---is back on those heights."

"Will we be assaulting them, Colonel? Looks like that could be a pretty formidable position…"

The Colonel, whose grandfather, George, had signed the Compact, shook his head. "Not any time soon, Major. We're pretty beat up, too." He turned his head and snorted.

"Don't expect to hear much of that '*one Southerner is worth 10 Yankees*' nonsense after this. We cut up their one corps pretty much, but the other one fought us to a standstill and then made a fighting retreat. And even on Matthews Hill there was some intense fighting."

"Then you don't believe the war is over, that we've gained our independence after all this carnage?"

"No, Major. This wasn't like Waterloo, or Bosworth Field, or any of those other one-day battles that decided a war." He paused and shook his head sadly.

"We won, but was it decisive? I doubt it...

"Maybe the politicians will think so. Maybe the Yankees will be so horrified at their losses that they'll let us go in peace. Or maybe the Crown will make them, on account of this Syrian business President Calhoun gets so excited about...

"Or, maybe, they'll lick their wounds and wait till spring, after they've raised a new army and Scott is recovered. And when, maybe, the British Navy will be available to lend a hand..."

Colonel Mason leaned down to pat his horse's mane. "It is quite possible, Major, that between the storm and the stand the Yankees made below Stone Bridge, we have lost our best chance for independence. Or, at least, without a lot more... *carnage.*"

CALHOUN'S CONFEDERACY

CHAPTER ONE

The Residency
Georgetown, D.C.
November 4, 1833,
3:00 a.m.:

Aaron Burr had intended to commandeer a squad of United States of British America Marines and ride out the Warrenton Pike yesterday afternoon. The Residency had received General Thayer's message in midmorning that the Army's movement across Bull Run had commenced, but nothing further. The squad was indeed sent but under the command of Captain Goodwin, the Governor-General expressly forbidding Colonel Burr to leave Georgetown. Grumbling, the ancient adventurer stomped off to the Samples' K Street townhouse. His intention: to resume his own campaign to advance his thus-far platonic relationship with its mistress to a more physical level.

He was now awakened, in his own bed at The Residency, by a servant. Captain Goodwin was back. The Colonel hurriedly dressed and made his way quietly downstairs to the G-G's office, where Martin Van Buren stood, short arms and tiny hands locked behind his back, staring out the window towards Arlington. Goodwin sat slumped, mud-covered and exhausted, in a chair.

One look at the tough Marine's tired face and angry eyes and Burr knew the battle had been lost. Goodwin nodded in recognition and acknowledgment but remained silent. Secretary of War Lewis Cass, whose wrinkled shirt and pants indicated he had been sleeping on the office couch, sat dejectedly, drinking a golden liquid from a crystal decanter embellished with the G-G's seal.

"We'll wait for Frank. I've sent word across the street. No need for the Captain to continually reiterate his report." The G-G remained staring out the window, the bitter words flowing softly over his left shoulder.

"The Duke...?"

"Whether His Grace hears the news now or in the morning will not significantly alter the situation."

Five minutes later, after the still-yawning Blair appeared, the Captain expanded his original brief report to the G-G. Soon, the others, too, were all sipping whiskey from the G-G's decanters...

Richmond, Virginia
November 4, 1833, 12:00 p.m.:

The city's church bells began to ring at precisely high noon, one after another, starting with the big cast iron bell atop Monumental Church on Shockoe Hill.

Rumors of all kinds had swept Richmond since messengers from Taylor's army brought word yesterday morning that fighting had begun along Bull Run:

"The Yankees are crossing the North Anna and will overrun the town by this afternoon!"

"No, our boys have the Yankees trapped at Manassas!"

"That's nonsense. Zach Taylor has Van Buren under guard at The Residency and is negotiating with Wellington...I have it straight from the War Department!"

"I tell you, Sir: Taylor's been killed. General Twiggs has retreated to Culpepper Court House!"

"You're all wrong. We've won a great victory but the Royal Navy has landed a British army at Yorktown! Taylor's turned our army around and is marching to meet them!"

Arguing, worrying, praying, the citizens of the capital now descended on the Confederate White House, where President John C. Calhoun had reportedly been observed receiving his grim-faced Secretary of War, Charles Gratiot, and General Gaines in the pre-dawn.

By 12:15, the streets surrounding the White House were filled. Men and women stood anxiously as far away as the Capitol Building itself, almost three blocks to the south. A cheer suddenly exploded from the front of the crowds as a broadly smiling President emerged out the front door and onto the landing atop the steps with a gaunt young officer whose tailored grey uniform was spattered with dried mud. Secretary Gratiot and the General followed, both also smiling, though not as broadly.

"My fellow Southerners! This outstanding young officer has heroically ridden directly from Manassas with a message from General Taylor." Calhoun paused theatrically as the crowd roared and Maj. Jefferson Davis looked sheepishly at his formerly black, now brown-spotted boots. The President put up his hands as if to call for silence, obviously relishing the moment.

"We have met the invader along the banks of Bull Run, northwest of Manassas around the Warrenton Pike..." He paused again as word rippled back through the crowd.

"The invader has been thrown back and was last evening in full retreat toward Georgeto..."

The crowds erupted with joy, planter's hats flying into the air, strangers hugging, Southern gentlemen sweeping staid---and flirtatious---women off their feet to hold them aloft by their waists. In the pandemonium, no one noticed the scattering of sad-eyed blank black faces in their midst.

Nor did anyone pay particular attention to the smiling, well-dressed, wiry gentleman with the planter's hat perched over his jet-black hair standing alone near the mansion's steps. If someone had, perhaps it would have been noted that his smile did not extend to his eyes. Even the curious half-blue, half-brown one...

Calhoun continued: "General Taylor reports that our army is in full control of the Bull Run fords and bridges and is across in strength. The pursuit of the retreating enemy is imminent."

As the wildly-cheering Richmonders surged forward to the bottom of the steps above which the Presidential party stood, Calhoun's arm now around Davis' shoulders, the quick, significant look that flashed from the War Secretary to General Gaines went unnoticed...

The rebellion that broke out in the southern portion of the British Empire's North American possessions in the second half of 1833 stunned much of the western world, though it was not a complete surprise to those who had kept tabs on the burgeoning, boisterous adolescent patchwork political entity established as a result of the Colonial Compact of 1776.

The Compact, a desperate, last-second attempt to foil off an armed secession of the original 13 American colonies from the Empire, had succeeded because the 'Continental Congress' accepted the compromise plan coauthored by Edmund Burke and Benjamin Franklin. This Compact converted the unamalgamated colonies into a united "dominion"---a new concept for the British Empire---labeled the 'United States of British America.'

The compromise essentially granted the new 'dominion' home rule in domestic matters (under London oversight) and representation in Parliament. London retained control of foreign policy. Its right to impose taxation was also accepted by the new entity. While the Crown continued to establish and operate military bases, primarily naval stations, in the USBA, the Dominion fielded (and funded) its own army and coastal guard to ensure domestic security. The Compact also incorporated the Empire's newly won Canadian territories, including the organized provinces of Quebec and Ontario, in the USBA.

The Compact clearly entitled the Crown's Government to intervene as a last resort in a Dominion domestic crisis, including the authority to remove from office democratically-elected officials, and equally clearly mandated that the USBA government implement Parliamentary-approved legislation of an Empire-wide scope. No such intervention nor implementation, however, occurred in the 57 years following the adoption of the Compact by both Parliament and the Continental Congress.

In early January 1833, however, the Duke of Wellington was dispatched to the USBA by Lord Grey's Government to inform the citizens of the Dominion, represented by their elected Congress and elected Governor-General Andrew Jackson, that such a piece of Empire-wide legislation, with anticipated overwhelming bipartisan support, would soon be introduced in Parliament: legislation that would abolish the institution of slavery throughout the Empire.

While Wellington's instructions called for him to utilize his enormous personal prestige to convince the USBA to accept Parliament's plan for a seven-year, phased-in emancipation with financial compensation for all slaveholders, he was authorized to take whatever steps, up-to-and-including the removal from office of the sitting G-G, he judged necessary to ensure compliance.

Wellington had hardly departed England by fast Royal Navy frigate when the Government found itself distracted by an unanticipated, perplexing and potentially catastrophic European crisis: the landing of a Russian army, at the request of the Sultan, in Ottoman Syria to confront the powerful forces of a rebellious Egyptian vassal. Czarist forces suddenly were in position to cut the Empire's vital land route to British India.

While London struggled to solve this crisis peacefully, the slavery powder keg exploded in Wellington's face in America. This disastrous explosion was caused in varying degrees by the incredulous fury of the Southern slavocracy, guided by Calhoun; the diabolical instigations of a ruthless Russian secret agent; the laissez-faire attitude of the non-slaveholding sections of the USBA towards the 'peculiar institution' and a sudden shocking leadership crisis in the Dominion capital, Georgetown, D.C.

These---and other---factors and events had led to a brutal confrontation between ill-prepared, and in some cases badly-led, forces of the USBA and the breakaway 'Confederate States of America' on the banks of a Virginia stream called Bull Run in early November, 1833.

———

The Residency
Georgetown, D.C.
November 4, 1833, 4 p.m.:

The Kitchen Cabinet had still been in session when the Duke of Wellington appeared about 7 a.m., although the G-G had given orders for a bath and bed for Captain Goodwin before 5. After a brief rest, the Captain had taken another Marine squad back across the Long Bridge shortly after 8 a.m.

Wellington had listened gravely to the second-hand account of Goodwin's report, shaking his head sadly at the news of I Corps' apparent collapse in the face of minimal enemy pressure. "It seems clear the Southerners were more prepared for battle. They apparently confounded your generals with their, shall we say, 'offensive-defensive strategy.' I say: how was such a state of affairs possible?"

Cass, who had been imbibing steadily since being awakened by Captain Goodwin's arrival, reddened even beyond the glow of the whiskey but remained silent. The others looked at the G-G, who simply shook his head in a show of mystification. The newspaperman, Blair, finally ventured an opinion.

"The Southerners have a martial tradition, Sir Arthur, which has been passed down the generations in the coastal states and of course among those who have recently settled in Alabama and Mississippi. On the other hand, it is a long time since anyone east of the Ohio has seen an Indian in war paint..."

"Yes, I can understand that. But the Devil I say, there simply must be more to the thing than that!"

As usual, it was Colonel Burr who cut to the chase. "Face it, gentlemen. They demonstrated better leadership. As Sir Arthur said, they confounded our apparent battle plan by enticing our generals to take the offensive, only to counter-attack when our advances reached open ground."

Now the group was gathered again, joined by Attorney-General Benjamin Butler. Maj. Robert Layne, R.A., the Liaison Office military chief who had barely succeeded this morning in convincing Wellington not to go to Centreville himself, waited outside, near The Residency Portico.

Some days later, after hearing the Army's ranking British half-pay officer's account of the Bull Run fiasco, the Duke privately expressed regret that he had not assumed command at the time of Gen. Winfield Scott's wounding. General Scott, the USBAA commanding officer, had barely survived an assassination attempt just days before he had planned to lead the Army against the Confederate position west of Manassas. In attempting to foil the assassination, a top British 'diplomatic,' Capt. Harry Bratton, had been murdered. The assassin, assumed to be a Russian count featuring a multi-colored right eye, was also believed to have orchestrated the earth-shaking assassination of then Governor-General Jackson in the Capitol Rotunda in June. As in that case, the Russian had seemingly vanished into thin air after wounding Scott and thereafter putting a pistol ball into Bratton's chest.

They were now anxiously awaiting the arrival of Captain Goodwin with an updated report. (Thayer had sent sketchy messages throughout the night that gave little real update. The lack of a reliable account of the current situation "was maddening and intolerable," according to the Duke.)

"Thank God we never announced publicly that the army was moving on Richmond," said Blair. "There have been a thousand rumors, but the lack of hard news has lulled the people to sleep. If in fact General Worth has established a defense at Centreville, we can reveal that in a quiet announcement tomorrow."

"Word is spreading quickly that Long Bridge is closed to all but military traffic. The people will be demanding the reason soon enough," said Cass, in a whisper, a cold towel lodged against his aching head.

"What's to keep Rebel cavalry from skirting around Worth's lines--assumi...Ah..." Colonel Burr, who had been standing guard at the office door, turned to the others. "Captain Goodwin is coming through the gates. Or so Major Layne appears to be signaling."

The Marine was in the office minutes later, dirty, his eyes blood-shot, though the Colonel could not tell if that was from fatigue or anger.

"Your Grace, Mr. Governor, gentlemen. General Thayer wishes to report that the... *redeployment*...to Centreville has been successful. Second Corps is in its lines on the heights to the south of the town. Cavalry patrols report the Rebels setting up their own lines about five miles south, at a junction less than two miles north of Bull Run."

"And I Corps?" Burr asked.

Goodwin ground the toe of his right boot into the carpet. "First Corps is strung out from Centreville to Alexandria. They've got the Turnpike so clogged I had to lead my squad off to the west just to get through." He paused and looked around the room. "Unarmed, mostly. Wagons spread out, too. That's the main source of the congestion." He paused and grimaced.

"Most of the transportation is breaking down, too. Looks like the teamsters just bolted at the first sound of the guns, drove hell-bent back towards Centreville. That may account for your question last night, Mr. Secretary, as to why I Corps never brought up its artillery." He paused again and shook his head in disgust before continuing:

"I ran into Captain Wilder at Thayer's headquarters. Said there's a trail of muskets, ammunition and other supplies clear along the route I Corps took to Sudley Springs. Said the Rebs are scooping it all up..."

"What is General Thayer's estimate of the situation? Will the Rebels attack and, if so, can he hold?" Wellington was brisk and professional.

"Both General Thayer and General Worth are confident II Corps can withstand any Rebel attack, Your Grace. But, General Thayer does not believe any Rebel movement towards Centreville is likely in the foreseeable future..."

"Did the Acting Commanding General offer a reason for his optimistic forecast?" Matty Van's voice was soft but icy.

"General Thayer is basing his...*optimism*...on the cavalry reports, Mr. Governor. It appears the Rebels are pretty banged up..."

"Stands to reason. It was their first battle, too, you know." Colonel Burr was nodding his head. "But General Thayer's report is incomplete, isn't it, Captain?

"What happened to I Corps' artillery? Is it, too, clogging the Warrenton Pike?" The old man shot Goodwin a shrewd look.

"No Sir. It is believed that the I Corps artillery has now been...*incorporated*...into the Confederate Artillery. The commander of II Corps' artillery was with General Worth when I spoke with him. A Colonel Buford, I think." The captain paused and shook his head.

"According to Colonel Buford, Zach Taylor presently has the USBAA outgunned significantly." The lines around Goodwin's mouth were taut.

"The Colonel says that if the Rebels can find enough ordinance---enough shells, cannon balls and the powder to set them off---Centreville may become untenable."

There was sudden commotion in the hallway. As the group turned its attention towards the open door, the entrance was suddenly blocked out. General Scott, in full dress uniform, right shoulder bandaged and arm tied tightly to his chest and bulging against the tunic, stepped into the room.

He crossed in three strides and, nodding "Your Grace" to Wellington, came to attention in front of Van Buren's desk. "Mr. Governor-General, I am reporting for duty. I regret the length of my convalescence, but I am now fit to resume command."

The first smile in three days broke across the G-G's small pale face, which began to glow from ear to ear. He came around the desk and took the enormous left paw in his own tiny hands. "Thank God, Winfie...General Scott. The situation is critical. Your return is not a moment too soon."

"And, if I may be so bold, Mr. Governor," Scott said, looking around at the others whose faces ranged from the Duke's sincere delight to Cass' pained expression (which may or may not have been attributable solely to his hangover), "what is the situation? The city is alive with rumors..."

Two hours later, having absorbed Goodwin's report and studied maps brought over from the War Department, he closed a lively, free wheeling discussion with Wellington and the Marine by addressing the G-G:

"With your permission, Mr. Governor, I will leave immediately for Centreville to inspect the defenses and assume tactical command.

I believe General Thayer is right: a battle of this scope and intensity must naturally exhaust both sides. The Rebels will need time to rest and refit.

"But I share Colonel Burr's concern about Rebel cavalry on our flanks. I believe it was a mistake to split our own cavalry. I intend to utilize it as a separate, independent force, operating as it did during the march down from Carlisle. It will guard the flanks, which I will gradually lengthen as various I Corps units are reorganized."

The relief of the men in the room was palatable, their relaxation visible. The Duke was nodding approvingly: *the warhorse is back...*

As Scott turned to leave, Colonel Burr stopped him: "One piece of encouraging news, General. In all the chaos and catastrophe, I nearly forgot..."

All eyes turned questioningly to the old man, who grinned his youthful, mischievous grin. "The weapon that fiend Ignatieff used to wound you. It's a fascinating piece of machinery, quite unlike any firearm seen on these shores before. French markings. A three-shot *'repeating'* rifle. I had it sent to Baltimore. The gunsmiths there, you know, are our finest. A young man named Colt, from Connecticut, the son of an old friend, has been working with them on something somewhat similar, a *'revolving'* multi-shot pistol.

"Young Mr. Colt has sent me encouraging reports. He believes we can replicate this three-shot weapon in volume. Says if he can obtain War Department backing, he can have the initial production ready in the early part of next year."

The Colonel's eyes were twinkling as he looked from Scott to Wellington and then, significantly, from the G-G to the suffering Cass. "In time for a spring offensive."

Scott's brilliant blue eyes began to glow in a way the observant newspaper editor, Blair, never forgot. He nodded, pivoted and strode from the room.

USBAA Lines
Centreville, Virginia
November 8, 1833:

The dramatic appearance of General Scott last Monday evening had boosted morale on the Centreville Heights. The mood of the II Corps and the survivors of I Corps' lead brigade---mainly Ohio and Brooklyn men---had turned sullen once they had filed into the lines and it became evident the Rebels were not pursuing.

What the hell happened? Why did we retreat this far? Why didn't we make our stand on the north bank? Having tasted Rebel lead and returned the compliment in kind, these men could not understand I Corps' collapse, either. *We gave the Southerners better than we got for almost eight hours, but most of I Corps ran away without ever engaging? Without ever firing a shot?*

Yes, they knew about the vicious fight put up by the Ohioans near the Pike. And, they were beginning to hear that the 2nd Regular Infantry had been virtually wiped out…but not before they had taken most of a Confederate division with them. *But the others turned tail at the first sight of the damn Rebs? And now they're back in camp in Alexandria, warm and comfortable with hot food and fires and tents on dry ground while we're out here shivering behind these makeshift barricades, without even any damn blankets?*

Scott's unanticipated arrival in full dress, riding the big white charger they had all admired when they first marched into camp, put an end to the mutinous mutters. As did the appearance the next morning of supply wagons bearing rations, ammunition, blankets and medical supplies. The rumor mill, however, was still cranked up:

"Did you hear? Wool's still missing… They say the Old Man's so mad, his orders are to shoot the bastard on sight!"

"Aw, Wool's dead or captured. Don't make much difference. Scott's reorganizing I Corps himself…"

"Yeah, well what do we do in the meantime? Damn Rebs may come up that road any damn minute!"

"Aw, the Rebs ain't comin'. The cavalry's out there. They'd pick 'em up!"

"Sure, like they did Sunday. The Ohio boys say the Rebs came out of nowhere to hit their flank. *Cavalry!*"

"Don't blame the cavalry. I hear ol' Wool was so sure he was behind the damn Rebs he wouldn't let the scouts out ahead in case they'd tip off the Rebs he was acomin'."

"Jes…is that what the fuck happened?"

Cranford Plantation
Alexandria, Virginia,
November 9, 1833,
11:50 p.m.:

Now, in the dark of night five full days after the battle, a played-out Capt. Thomas Wilder urged his tired horse the final mile of its journey from Bull Run.

As physically exhausted as he was mentally fatigued and saddled with a crushing emotional loss, Tom pointed Bay Ridge past the Army's staging encampment in the plantation's fields and toward the big house on the rise. The Captain, who could not remember the last time he had been off duty, had served in the dual capacities of intelligence aide to General Scott and social aide at The Residency before the South's secession. Since the winds of war had begun their relentless swirl, he had commanded a squad of elite scouts in the no man's land between the two armies.

In his pocket he carried two notes delivered some time this week---he could scarcely remember which day---by Sebastian, the Latoure family butler at Cranford.

"Thank the good Lord Ah's found you safe, Lieutenant Tom!" Sebastian was grinning as he handed over the notes in a tent just behind the front lines on the Centreville heights. "Miz Angeline, she'll be mighty relieved." He grinned again. "Miz Lucille, too, Ah'd wager."

Despite---perhaps because of---his exhaustion, and despite the crowd of officers and men around him, Tom had blurted it out: "Miss Lucille...is Miss Lucille up at Cranford?"

"Yes suh, Lieutenant Tom. Miz Lucille, she come home Monday. Been at Cranford all week..."

As Tom became embarrassingly aware of the cackling and snickering around him, Lt. Col. Brian Judge had looked up from the map table: "If you don't mind, Captain, we've got a war to fight..."

Red-faced, Tom had turned back to the dignified black man. "Thank you, Sebastian, Extend my thanks and compliments to the ladies. Tell them I'll be in touch."

Armed with Mrs. Latoure's warm invitation to visit *"at any time, day or night,"* and Lucille's curious note expressing *"my earnest prayers for your personal deliverance,"* Tom rode slowly up the driveway, tied his tired animal to a porch pillar and used the big decorative doorknocker. General Scott himself had ordered him to take leave. He was free until Monday…

As he waited, tottering with fatigue, the shock of what he had seen a few nights ago flashed back across his mind's eye. *Why the devil had his brother come? The 1st Brooklyn was basically cheeseheads; damn Dutch Reformed farmers and shopkeepers. Hell, there couldn't have been 50 Catholics in the whole damn regiment!*

Grasping a flaming candle by its tightly secured holder, Sebastian opened the door. "Come right on in, Lieutenant Tom. You come right in de parlor and I see to it Miz Angeline and Miz Lucille knows you here."

In Sebastian's eyes, apparently, Tom thought with his first small smile in days, *I'll always be a lieutenant…*

His sword left dangling from Bay Ridge's saddle, Tom collapsed into a high cushioned chair, leaning his head back and closing his eyes, only to see images of his dead brother's bloated and battered body immediately flash past. He could hear the sudden noise from the second floor and knew Sebastian had servants waking the household. The butler soon returned with a tray containing a bottle of Claret and a glass.

"Ah knows you don't drink hard spirits, Lieutenant Tom, but dis'll do you good…"

Tom gratefully took the liquor Sebastian poured and handed him. He was savoring the burning sensation in his throat as the mistress of Cranford came hurrying down the stairs.

"Thank the Lord you're all right, Thomas. No, no, stay seated, you look thoroughly exhausted… General Scott assured us you survived the battle… He stopped here with his staff to water the horses on his way to Centreville the other day… But he indicated you might have gone back out…"

There were more steps on the stairs. This time, Tom did struggle to his feet as Lucille came into the room. Dressed in a rich dark robe that set off her magnificent mane of auburn hair, she came up to him and in a glance detected that more than fatigue was lining his troubled face.

"Tom, I am so relieved to see you here. I was so worried…" She stopped. "I mean, we've been so concerned about you…and Luke, and Joe and Robert. Thank God this horror is at an end…"

She again paused momentarily as her younger, blond sister slipped into the room, Jaine looking intently at Tom as her own beau's name was mentioned.

"...and we'll soon have peace."

Mrs. Latoure, too, had been studying Tom closely: "What is it, Thomas? You've something terribly to relate..." She motioned for Sebastian to pour Tom another glass and sent into the kitchen for three more glasses.

Jaine's voice was firm though she had clutched her robe at the throat. "Tom, have you word of Luke?"

Tom managed a wan smile as he sipped the Claret. "'Major' Beaufort is fine, Jaine...at least, he was two days ago when I interrogated some of his troopers we captured trying to get a good look at our lines." He looked back at Lucille. *God, I want to put my arms around her...* "I got a glimpse of Robert during the battle. You can tell Mary we've no indication he's been hurt. As for Joe Johnston, well, he is supposed to have commanded the artillery on Henry Hill. That's about all I know."

"Then what is it, Thomas?" Mrs. Latoure was soft but insistent. "My God, not young Joe? The poor boy should never have been allowed to march out..."

Tom shook his head sadly, his eyes welling up with unshed tears. "No Ma'am. Joey's okay. A couple flesh wounds and some scratches, but he made it through. I saw him... Yesterday, I think..."

A sudden quiet, then:

"No Thomas, not Father George! Dear God in heaven!" Mrs. Latoure made a rapid Sign of the Cross and motioned to Sebastian, who helped Tom back into the chair.

His head slumped on his chest, Tom spilled out the story: The 1st Virginia Cavalry, Luke Beaufort's outfit, had sent a squad through the lines under a white flag with a wagon packed high with makeshift coffins they indicated contained noncombatants. Doctors and nurses killed during a firefight during mopping up operations after the battle. One body, however, carried no insignia. Just a rosary...

"Joe heard about it first, from Colonel Felton. He did the actual identification. They told me when I got back from a reconnaissance. The body was...disfigured...but he was so gaunt, it was still recognizable. It was him. My brother George. The Catholic chaplain of a regiment 90% Protestant..."

The Latoure ladies put him to bed soon after, but remained up talking for most of the night.

November 10, 1833,
9:20 a.m.:

Lucille was already up and in the mansion's garden when Tom emerged through the dining room's French doors. Her eyes widened as he strode purposefully toward her and gathered her in his arms, relishing the taste of the plush lips.

"I love you Lucille...I've always loved you..."

She smiled up at him. "I know, Thomas. I've known for some time."

"Will you wait for me? Until the war is over..."

She frowned. "But Thomas, the war *is* over. We...the peace. That's what we must wait for."

He kissed her again, more forcefully, before looking down at her. *For all her surface sophistication, she can be so naïve...*

"No...*darling*...the war is far from over. I'm afraid it has just begun. General Scot..."

"Damn Winfield Scott!" Her brown eyes suddenly blazed. "Your army's been whipped! The South has beaten back your invasion! In the end, General Scott must march your army---what's left of it---back across the Potomac. The South has won! All that's left is to decide if Georgetown will remain your capital. Or become ours!"

She had stepped back out of his arms as his look of astonishment turned to one of anguished comprehension. The words came out in a whisperish croak: "That's what you meant: *'my prayers for your personal safety...the horror is over...soon we'll have peace'...*"

He slowly repeated her last words as if refusing to accept them. "*'Your capital'...or 'ours.'*"

Suddenly, his brain was screaming an ugly thought. *No, it can't be!* He fought against the suggestion, even as he realized: *Yes, it could be!*

The weeks leading up to the fight...the sudden interest in the particulars of his job...the private, candlelight suppers at the townhouse...the questions about the deteriorating situation:

'These 'Black Hawk veterans?' They're from the Wes...Ohio and Illinois? The grim man with the one star? General Worth, you say? The 'tactical commander?' A temporary bridge? At Edwards Ferry? And: a 'reconnaissance?'"

He had been thrilled by her interest...pumped up:

Finally, she actually shows that she cares!

That singular smile! That once-in-a-lifetime look, hanging on his every word is if it were gospel... How he had craved it! How he had sought it...prayed for it! How he had vowed, when she had flashed it at Joe Johnston; at other, older and more prominent men: *Some day, she'll look at me like that!*

And how he had savored it these last few weeks when she finally began directing it at him!

Yeah, she had been interested! *'Pumped up' all right...pumped you up for information. And like a fool you gave it to her! Yeah, she gave you that smile; she looked at you like that! God knows what she did with that information... You damn, stupid...who looks naïve now, idiot?*

Jaysus, Mary and Joseph!

Well, it's too late to worry about that. And I'm not blaming her for poor George's death...

But she'll get nothing more out of me! Not now! And not later, damn it!

She had taken his hands in hers and was speaking quietly. "I am a Virginian, Thomas. Virginia has stood up for her rights. Your Congress in Georgetown...your Parliament in London...neither has the right to interfere in our way of life. We have now made that clear, though I am horrified and sickened by the fact that your poor brother had to die in the process."

She moved back and threw her arms around him. "We have a wonderful future to look forward to, darling. But we must wait. Until the peace is firmly established." She moved to pull his head down towards her, but he broke roughly away.

"No, Lucille. I'm afraid not. This war will go on. We're not retreating another inch. Nor are we about to negotiate anything.

"Perhaps we'll both...we'll all...survive this...rebellion. Perhaps, hopefully, Cranford will. But our relationship won't."

He turned to walk away, then turned back. "Our relationship is as much a victim of this war as my poor brother.

"And just as dead."

She stood dry-eyed, watching him as he reentered the house. *He'll come back outside in a few minutes. After reconsidering. We'll have breakfast, speak again. I know he loves me...* She strolled through the garden, past the dead and dying summer plants.

Minutes later, she heard a shout for his horse to be brought up. As she ran through the mansion and came out onto the veranda, he was leaning down from Bay Ridge, saying his goodbyes to her weeping mother.

As he reached the far end of the driveway, she was surprised to see him turn the big black stallion up the road towards Georgetown.

———————

Headquarters, USBAA
Centreville, Virginia
November 16th, 1833:

Two weeks after the battle, the Dominion army was regaining a smattering of its self-respect. There was none of the cockiness, the undeserved swagger, of the march down from Carlisle. These men, no matter how young chronologically, were veterans now; they had tasted lead and cold steel and now knew war to be a grim, serious...*killing*...business.

The mood, of course, differed in the two corps:

The II was proud of the performance it had turned in at Bull Run; even the collapse of the 2nd Division's 2nd Brigade was written off as bad luck. The Brigade had been surprised well east of the battlefield---where no Rebels had been reported---while still fording the Run. The Confederates' uniforms and flags had added to the confusion and camouflaged their intent. While three regiments had been lost---the only II Corps units to suffer excessive casualties---the remaining regiments, the 2nd Pennsylvania and 1st Rhode Island, had regrouped to secure the ford and seal the army's eastern flank.

General Scott generally agreed with this common analysis, though he was angered that no cavalry had been assigned to screen the 2nd Brigade. *No pickets or skirmishers either, apparently; it sounds like the 2nd proceeded like they were out for a training hike...*

No, II Corps could hold its head high now that it understood the rationale for the retreat all the way back to Centreville. And because it had begun to understand that its fighting withdrawal under fire from the Henry Hill pocket was apparently a textbook professional maneuver.

The broken I Corps was a different story: its self-respect would not, of course, be restored until it had successfully fought the enemy. The 1st was being reorganized ruthlessly from the company ranks up by the Commanding General himself.

Discipline was now hard-fisted, even brutal. Former officers were broken to the ranks, if not cashiered. Newly arriving Regulars from the West were inserted at every level in every regiment…and were drilling these men heartlessly.

Colonel Hitchcock had been promoted to Corps commander, while the hard-eyed half-pay, Colonel Hodges, had stepped up to head the 1st Division. Colonel Kearny was transferred to the II Corps to take Colonel Sumner's place when 'the Bull' was given command of the newly organized Cavalry Corps. Colonel Felton was promoted to command of Kearny's old 2nd Division, I Corps. These were all *organizational* promotions; everyone understood General Scott was in no mood to recommend increases in rank anytime soon.

Scott had authored this massive reorganization days of arriving at Centreville and interviewing the surviving commanders. He had also personally overseen the retraining and had signed off on the reassignment of each I Corps regiment from the Alexandria camp. Despite the threat, however diminishing each day, of a Confederate advance, they were released to the front only when he was convinced they were ready.

The lines had been gradually, gingerly, extended east and west, with the latest reorganized I Corps regiments sliding into the center. They were now to be joined by the first of seven new regiments coming down from Carlisle. These, too, would be slid into the line. But only after Scott was satisfied of their discipline and command structure. The cavalry, meanwhile, reorganized by Colonel Sumner into a separate arm, was patrolling each end of the line (which were refused to protect against the deadly CSA flank attack tactic), as well as in the no-man's land leading back to the Rebel lines near the juncture where Wool had departed for Sudley Springs.

Scott now nodded his approval as he studied an updated map at his headquarters in the old Rocky Run Episcopal Chapel, a map based on information from Sumner and Tom Wilder's elite scouts. He'd have plenty to tell Wellington and the G-G when they arrived this afternoon. Including the long-term strategy he had thought out during his convalescence. A strategy he had nicknamed *Anaconda*.

———————

Confederate White House
November 16, 1833, 11 a.m.:

"With Zach Taylor reporting the Dominions are going into winter camp, Mr. President, we can proceed with our plans for the West."

President Calhoun looked across his desk to Secretary of War Gratiot and General Gaines, the Confederate Army's chief of staff. They were presenting the latest report by the commander of the CSA force, now increasingly called the Army of Northern Virginia, facing the Dominion Army north of Bull Run. The report included an estimate that the USBA army would not venture beyond its Centreville lines until spring.

"General Taylor is apparently convinced Scott will not resume their invasion until late March or early April, despite the steady movement forward of new regiments," said Gaines.

"That estimate, of course, is predicated," Calhoun looked down at the report on his desk, "on the willingness to believe the reports that Scott has indeed resumed command."

"I think that can be safely assumed, Mr. President." General Gaines pulled a week-old Georgetown newspaper from his pouch. "The Yankees announced Scott's resumption of command the same day they reported this rather...*fanciful*...account of the battle. To sugarcoat the bitter pill, so to speak..."

The headlines in Blair's *Globe* called the fight a "reconnaissance in force" leading to a "redeployment" of the Dominion Army to Centreville. The article stressed that, in heavy fighting, the USBAA had moved some 15 miles deeper into Virginia and therefore closer to Richmond.

General Scott's return to active command all but assured final victory, the *Globe* insisted.

The following day's *Globe* had announced Van Buren's call for 30,000 more volunteers without commenting further on the situation at the front. Gaines now placed that issue on the President's desk.

Glancing at it briefly, his eyes narrowing, Calhoun returned to the subject of Scott and winter quarters. "This vaunted 'Belle Express' of yours, General. What has become of it? Has it, too, confirmed Scott's return?"

Organized by Mary Lee of Arlington House Plantation, wife of the CSA's youngest brigade commander, and her friends the Latoure sisters, Lucille and Jaine, of nearby Cranford Plantation, the 'Belle Express' had been passing unrefined pieces of military-related information through to the Confederacy for several months. Their biggest nugget was the date and direction of the USBAA advance from its Alexandria encampment down the Warrenton Pike towards the eventual Bull Run battlefield.

The War Secretary interrupted. "The 'Belle Express' has been slowed considerably, Mr. President, as would be expected with the entire Dominion Army between it and our lines. But the 'Belles' have confirmed that Scott is back in command. And that the lengthening of the USBA lines is a result of his reorganization of their defeated I Corps regiments, which he is gradually releasing to the front." He paused.

"The latest report from the 'Belles', which we received from Taylor yesterday, is that new regiments have also been arriving in Alexandria from their training base in Pennsylvania. I'm afraid that report was dated last Friday, however. We've received nothing since."

"And that is aside from Van Buren's call for 30,000 more?"

"Yes, Mr. President. These new regiments apparently were not ready when their main force marched south last month."

There was silence as the trio weighed the implications. It was Gaines who broke it:

"We have no choice, Mr. President. We cannot afford to let Scott build his army up to 60,000 or more this winter. We must force him to divide his command. And the only way to do *that* is to throw Crockett's army out of east Tennessee and then march on Louisville…"

"Or Missouri." Gratiot. "The target doesn't matter as much as the fact we're threatening to invade *them*…"

Calhoun was now massaging his temples with the fingers of both hands. "Gentlemen, you're urging an invasion of the Dominion, when we can't even clear that moronic Crockett's little posse out of our own territory! *How*, gentlemen?"

The two soldiers (Gratiot had resigned as the USBAA's chief engineer to enter the Confederate Cabinet) exchanged quick glances before Gratiot spoke.

"Mr. President we have received reports of volunteers forming and drilling all over the South. We propose to order the majority of these troops to a staging base, probably in northern Alabama, where they can be forged into an army. The rest will be ordered here to reinforce Taylor."

"And who will command this 'Army of the West'?"

Gratiot was crisp. "Albert Sidney Johnston, Sir. With the rank of major general. The same rank we propose for Zach Taylor."

"Johnston." The President mused. "A Kentucky man. Yes, and by all accounts shown to be a fierce fighter and inspirational leader.

"Yes, I begin to see the possibilities...despite his youthfulness ..."

He smiled his dark smile tartly over the desk. "I assume you two have committed your plans to paper?"

USBAA Field Headquarters
Centreville, Virginia
November 16, 1833, 1 p.m.:

General Scott paced in front of his headquarters at the Rocky Run Chapel watching the gubernatorial-general party, including Wellington, come down the Warrenton Turnpike with its no-longer-ceremonial Marine guard.

And with another force of newly-uniformed troops marching parade ground-perfect some 30 yards behind. Led by an enormous man, in a plain blue uniform with lieutentant colonel insignia, riding a coal black charger. But it wasn't their marching precision nor the size of their commander which had onlookers gaping, some with mouths open and other muttering oaths of amazement or disdain.

The 1st District of Columbia Colored Troops, Lt. Col. Jurgurtha Numidia commanding, had reached the front.

The bright blue sky, soft autumn sunshine and panorama of foliage all bespoke the gentle Indian summer which had descended on Northern Virginia once the powerful cold front that had put an end to the brutal and freakishly-extended tropical summer heat and humidity had passed a few days after the battle.

My favorite time of year: warm, golden days and crisp, star-bright nights. Just look at these gorgeous trees, all red and gold and brown and yellow! How is it possible that less than 10 miles down that road, the ground is blood-soaked, the leaves crunched and trampled and the trees mostly broken stumps...

Dear God, how did we ever reach this point? Where the Governor-General of the United States of British America and the former British Prime Minister can come no farther than Centreville? And then only with a bodyguard of field-equipped Marines! To inspect an army of 20,000 Americans who are recovering from a bloody brawl with 25,000 or more other Americans camped just five miles down the Pike! Having passed an encampment of 15,000 or so more Americans on the way! And with an authorized battalion of black men, armed, trained and now actually joining the Army's---my Army's---ranks!

As fond as Scott was of the pomp and circumstance that had led to his famous 'Old Fuss and Feathers' moniker, the General had not pulled his troops off the line for a dress parade and inspection. Though he doubted Zach Taylor and that damn Davy Twiggs had any notion the G-G and the Duke were nearing the front, he had purposefully ordered that only a single regiment be drawn up in front of the Chapel.

Just to let the politicos know there's a war on. In case they've forgotten...

He would have liked to have chosen the 1st Ohio for the honors. But that brave outfit was down to 40% strength. Normally, he would have been inclined to order it disbanded, its survivors assigned to the other Ohio regiments. Not this time, however.

The 1st Ohio is more than a shot-up regiment. It's a symbol. A symbol of how all Dominion volunteer regiments must fight... That's why the 1st is back at the encampment now, getting refitted. And re-manned.

When the 5th Ohio, one of the seven regiments left at Carlisle when the army originally marched south, had arrived at Alexandria, he had broken it up, the best companies reassigned to the 1st, the remainder split among the other Ohio regiments. The 1st, in fact, had already received its orders back to the front and would be marching down the Pike in four days.

Scott had considered pulling out the 1st Regular Infantry for the ceremony, as much in honor of its fallen comrades from the decimated 2nd as for its own conspicuous gallantry at the Run.

Not necessary. The 2nd is already a legend. What was it Colonel Felton said the other night? Oh, yes: "At Carlisle the regulars taught the volunteers how to be soldiers. At Bull Run, they taught them how to die." Hum...pretty good. Doubt I could have put it better myself...

He had heard good reports about the fighting qualities of two other regiments in particular, 2nd New York and 1st New Jersey. But their lack of military bearing during an inspection offended his sensibilities... In the end, he went for the symbolism: the 1st

Kentucky had been bloodied as part of 'Bull' Sumner's 2nd Division in II Corps.

There's a ton of slaves in Kentucky. And Rebs, starting with Sidney Johnston. It will impress ol' Hook Nose to see boys from there who have fought for the Stars and Stripes...

The G-G's party was now nearing the Chapel.

Good God, Matty Van looks ridiculous on that horse. Why didn't they take a carriage? Hope he doesn't get killed falling off or trying to get down!

Who the hell's next in the line of succession, anyway...?

---

4 p.m.:

"So that's the strategy, gentlemen. I intend to wrap our forces around the rebellious states with a blockade of the Atlantic and Gulf coasts, utilizing the services," Scott looked up from the large map spread out in what had been the sacristy of the old chapel, nodding at Wellington, "of the Royal Navy's North American squadron.

"Drive up and down the Mississippi from Cincinnati to New Orleans and squeeze the rebels as a large snake constricts and crushes its surrounded prey. At the same time we will use this weapon," he waved his right arm in the general direction of the front lines, "to push south to Richmond."

There was silence as the G-G's party, which included Secretary Cass, General Thayer and, inevitably, Colonel Burr, digested the plan.

"I see now why you called it the 'Anaconda Strategy' when you opened the briefing, General." Wellington sounded---for him---impressed. "I have read of this ferocious reptile, this so-called 'Anaconda' snake. South American, isn't it...

"Mmm, yes. I believe this strategy could do the trick..."

Wellington turned to the G-G and spoke formally: "I concur with General Scott's overall strategy, Mr. Governor-General. It is more than thorough. It is all-inclusive. Naturally, tactical mistakes and accidents will occur. Can't be helped. Wars aren't fought on map boards but out in conditions often primitive and subject, as we have seen, to the whims of Mother Nature.

"But it is my recommendation, Mr. Governor, that you order General Scott to proceed."

After a quick glance at Colonel Burr, who was smiling and also nodding affirmatively, the G-G looked to Scott.

"So, General, your plan is accepted and approved. Now then, how can we help you?"

Scott drew himself up to his full six-foot-seven and adjusted the ceremonial sword at his waist. He glanced from the Duke to the G-G, seemingly looking through the Secretary of War as if Cass was invisible.

"The first thing you can do, Mr. Governor, is build me an inland navy…"

TO BE CONTINUED

Watch for

"Calhoun's Confederacy: The United States of British America"

Between December '13 and March '14

AFTERWORD

Alternate history is, by definition, a novel and therefore fiction. None of the real-life characters portrayed were involved in all of the activities, nor necessarily said, what I have them doing and saying. But many were in positions akin to those I have placed them in…and some reacted in ways similar to how I have portrayed them.

Davy Twiggs, for instance, never turned Fortress Monroe over to the real life Confederacy in return for a general's commission. But he did surrender the Military District of Texas and, in return, was named a full CSA general. Winfield Scott was too old to put his Anaconda strategy into effect in 1861…but that strategy was the basis for U.S. Grant's 1864 coordinated multi-theater strategy.

From the conception, it was my intention to make this story as realistic as possible. Alternate history does not need time travel; alien invasions; vampires; climatological cataclysms and angry gods and spirits to be interesting to the non-history buff. It is my conceit that placing historical figures in settings to which the average reader can relate, utilizing their limited knowledge of actual history, makes the yarn both more plausible and more entertaining.

And why wouldn't Andrew Jackson, Martin Van Buren, John C. Calhoun and the rest have risen to prominence in an America recognizable to the reader…but with that point of diversion of 1776?

Students of American and British history will of course understand the "inside baseball" references and connections: Andrew Jackson did publicly proclaim his intention to "shoot Henry Clay and horsewhip John C. Calhoun before I leave office." Palmerston and the British cabinet did roundly curse "that fool of a Sultan." And Robert E. Lee famously wrestled with his conscience before resigning his commission, an act Scott did tell him was the "biggest mistake of your life." (Francis P. Blair, Sr. did not question Calhoun's verbal excesses with the attributed quote. The later British prime minister, Benjamin Disraeli, is credited with the remark, possibly regarding Lord Randolph Churchill. However, it was sitting there and seemed so very apropos…so.)

The mists of time have also obscured some characters I have utilized here: there was indeed a Princess von Lieven, who shook up the European diplomatic world from roughly 1810 to 1850. The real Richard Lawrence (a house painter, not a bartender) did in fact attempt to assassinate Jackson in the Capitol Rotunda; Davy Crockett in real life knocked his weapons away in time. The list, as sharp-eyed history buffs will attest, goes on.

Of the fictional characters, some are pure creation…and some are tributes to other, greater authors. Alistair Tudsbury in Constantinople is a tip of the hat to Herman Wouk's *War & Remembrance* books. The amoral Russian secret agent, Count Nicholas, is offered as the father of a major villain in George MacDonald Fraser's incredible *Flashman* series.

And yes, those minor character names that may have jumped out at sports fans are named after baseball, football, hockey and track stars.

A few of the major fictional characters are modeled on actual people of the period. Sally "Buck" Preston, a noted Southern belle who drove numerous Confederate officers, notably John Bell Hood, to distraction can be discerned in Lucille Latoure, as can the Confederate spy Rose O'Neal Greenhow. David Harper is loosely based on Lincoln's bachelor second secretary, John Hay.

Other names may jump out at certain readers: the mistress of Twin Peaks; a Tuscaloosa, Ala. inn. And, of course, those of a certain age who grew up in northeastern Bergen County, NJ may recognize a few other establishments and people.

Finally: Aaron Burr. Burr was a mere afterthought when this book was first imagined. But the Colonel soon became too fabulous a character to hold down. If any literary license is to be requested for what is, after all, a work of fiction, it is the liberal employment of Burr. Yet, it is not hard to imagine the Colonel right in the thick of things, pulling strings and offering counsel as depicted.

James F. Devine III
Dumont, NJ
12/24/2012

ABOUT THE AUTHOR

With the publication of his first novel, James F. Devine III closes the circle in a communications career begun as the sports editor of the *Mighty High Times* at Bergenfield, NJ High School. Mr. Devine has spent more than 35 years as a communication executive, primarily in the petroleum marketing industry, specializing in advertising and media and industry relations. A native of Brooklyn, NY, he served as a public information specialist in the USAF and has been a journalist, writing for both newspapers and trade publications, as well as a trade association executive. Mr. Devine, a graduate of Ramapo College of NJ, has resided for most of his life in and around the area of northeastern Bergen County, NJ once called Schraalenburgh.

ABOUT THE COVER

CathyAnn Fasano is a graphic designer /illustrator in Old Tappan, NJ. She can be reached at inspirationals11c@gmail.com.